Michael Price & Stuart Ya

Windows 8

special edition

In easy steps is an imprint of In Easy Steps Limited
4 Chapel Court · 42 Holly Walk · Leamington Spa
Warwickshire · United Kingdom · CV32 4YS
www.ineasysteps.com

Copyright © 2013 by In Easy Steps Limited. All rights reserved. No part of this book may be reproduced or transmitted in any form or by any means, electronic or mechanical, including photocopying, recording, or by any information storage or retrieval system, without prior written permission from the publisher.

Notice of Liability
Every effort has been made to ensure that this book contains accurate and current information. However, In Easy Steps Limited and the author shall not be liable for any loss or damage suffered by readers as a result of any information contained herein.

Trademarks
Microsoft® and Windows® are registered trademarks of Microsoft Corporation. All other trademarks are acknowledged as belonging to their respective companies.

In Easy Steps Limited supports The Forest Stewardship Council (FSC), the leading international forest certification organisation. All our titles that are printed on Greenpeace approved FSC certified paper carry the FSC logo.

Printed and bound in the United Kingdom

ISBN 978-1-84078-542-5

Contents

25 Windows performance 421

26 Windows Registry 441

27 Extending Windows 459

Index 471

1 Introducing Windows 8

This chapter introduces Microsoft's latest operating system, Windows 8. We see what editions are available, the new features and which features have been removed since the last edition. We also take a look at some free Microsoft software.

Windows releases

The original IBM PC was supported by PC-DOS and the more generic MS-DOS operating system, developed for IBM-compatible PCs.

There have been many versions of Microsoft Windows. The operating system was initially designed for IBM-compatible PCs, but was later extended to support larger computers such as servers and workstations. A derivative version, Windows CE, was also developed for smaller devices such as PDAs and cell phones.

The main versions of Windows that have been released include:

Date	Client PC	Server	Mobile
1985	Win 1.0		
1987	Win 2.0		
1990	Win 3.0		
1993		Win NT 3.1	
1995	Win 95		
1996		Win NT 4.0	Win CE 1.0
1998	Win 98		
2000	Win ME	Win 2000	Win CE 3.0, Pocket PC 2000
2001	Win XP		Pocket PC 2002
2003		Win Server 2003	Win Mobile 2003
2006	Win Vista		
2007		Win Home Server,	Win Mobile 6
2009	Win 7	Win Server 2008	
2010			Win Phone 7
2012	Win 8	Win Server 2012	Win Phone 8

There have also been many interim versions providing fixes and updates, as well as specialized versions such as Media Center editions.

The first three versions of Windows listed were designed for the 16-bit processor featured in the PCs of the day. Windows 95, 98 and ME added support for 32-bit processors. Windows NT was for 32-bit only while XP and 2000 added 64-bit support. Windows Vista, Windows 7 and Windows 8, and the newer server editions, provide support for both 32-bit or 64-bit processors.

Each version of Windows builds on the functions and features included in the previous versions, so that the knowledge and experience you have gained will still be valuable, even though the appearance and the specifics of the operations may have changed.

Windows 8

With Windows 8, Microsoft has taken its predecessor, Windows 7, and re-designed it to make it compatible with a range of devices including PCs, tablets and smartphones.

To make this possible, it comes with a new interface which, in this book, we will refer to as the new Windows 8 interface. This is a touchscreen interface of the type used in smartphones and tablets. Each installed program, or app as they are known, is displayed on the Start screen as a tile.

The apps themselves are more streamlined than traditional programs and, accordingly, offer much less in the way of configuration options. The whole setup is designed to be clean, straightforward and quick, and thus much less demanding of system resources. Much of the eye-candy seen in Windows 7, such as Aero and transparent window borders, has been removed.

This leads us to the rationale behind the new interface. As two of the primary requirements for mobile devices are power efficiency and touchscreen control, its introduction clearly indicates that Microsoft considers mobile devices to be where the future lies. While the traditional Windows (Desktop) is available in Windows 8, it can only be accessed via the Start screen. So, while many will want to, either because they don't like it or simply don't need it, it will be impossible to completely ignore it.

Compatibility is another factor. Windows 8 will share its styling and its kernel code with multiple platforms including smartphones, tablets, PCs and even the Xbox. This move toward cross-compatibility is one which is intended to establish Microsoft in the mobile market.

A key element in this is the SkyDrive app, which we'll look at later. SkyDrive enables users to store all their data and apps online and synchronize that data across all their devices. As a result, they will be able to log into SkyDrive on any Windows 8 device and immediately access their data, preference settings, etc. Whatever or whoever's device they are using, it will be as though they are using their own.

There is a lot more to Windows 8 than just the new interface though. An improved Desktop version is also available, which we will look at. However, we'll start by taking a look at the features the new Windows 8 interface has to offer.

Hot tip

Windows 8 comes in four editions:

1. Windows 8
2. Windows 8 Pro
3. Windows 8 Enterprise
4. Windows RT

Don't forget

In this book, the new Windows 8 interface is referred to as the new Windows 8 interface. The traditional Windows interface is referred to as the Desktop.

New features in Windows 8

Each new version of Windows adds new features and facilities. In Windows 8, these include:

- **Start screen** – a new interface that enables the operating system to be used on a range of devices. These include PCs, tablets and smartphones
- **Lock screen** – a customizable screen that prevents the user from making inadvertent inputs to a touchscreen device
- **Windows Store** – similar to Apple's App Store, Windows Store provides a convenient and secure location for the acquisition of apps designed for Windows 8
- **Touch gestures** – users who have a touchscreen can control their devices with gestures such as tapping and swiping
- **File Explorer** – an improved version of Windows Explorer that provides better access to common commands
- **Internet Explorer 10** – runs either as a Desktop program or a full-screen app optimized for use on touchscreens
- **Picture password** – a new security feature that enables a highly secure password to be set
- **Hardware support** – Windows 8 provides support for USB 3, enabling faster data transfer
- **Networking** – support for mobile broadband is improved, e.g. automatic configuration of connection settings, and the monitoring of mobile data usage
- **Refresh** – a system recovery utility that "refreshes" a Windows 8 installation by reverting it to an "as new" state without losing programs, data and settings
- **Reset** – this utility deletes all the user's data, settings and programs and then reinstalls a new copy of Windows 8. The procedure is the equivalent of a "clean installation" but is much easier and also quicker
- **Standard apps** – Windows 8 provides a number of pre-installed apps, such as Mail, Weather, News, and Photos

Hot tip 

The Start screen is the most noticeable new feature in Windows 8.

- **Startup** – Windows 8 provides a hybrid boot mode that hibernates the kernel. This enables the system to boot up faster on subsequent restarts
- **Microsoft account integration** – user accounts can be linked to a Microsoft account. This enables the integration and synchronization of data with other Microsoft services
- **File History** – this utility provides a type of "ongoing" backup that automatically makes a backup whenever changes are made to the system
- **ISO & VHD mounting** – enables ISO and VHD image files (commonly used in backup images) to be opened without the need for third-party software
- **Storage Spaces** – offers data protection by means of virtual hard drives (similar to RAID)
- **Encrypting File System (EFS) and BitLocker** – EFS enables individual files to be encrypted, while BitLocker enables entire drives to be encrypted
- **Sideload Windows Store apps** – this feature allows users to install apps without having to go through Microsoft's Windows Store and is mainly used by app developers
- **Boot from VHD** – this enables a PC to be booted directly from a virtual hard disk. Intended for use by system administrators
- **Hyper-V** – PC virtualization software that enables a fully functional virtual computer to be built and run within Windows 8
- **Windows To Go** – this feature allows Windows 8 to be booted, and run, from portable storage devices such as flash drives and external hard drives
- **UEFI Secure Boot** – a security mechanism based on the Unified Extensible Firmware Interface (UEFI) that prevents viruses infecting a system during the boot procedure

Hot tip 

Windows 8 includes true multi-touch technology, with gestures for zooming, rotating and selecting.

Hot tip 

One of the most improved features in Windows 8 is the Task Manager.

Editions of Windows 8

The table below shows the new features in Windows 8 and also some old features that have been revamped and improved. As you can see, some of the features are specific to certain editions.

Not all of Windows 8's features are available in all editions.

Features/Editions	RT	8	Pro	Ent
Picture Password	Y	Y	Y	Y
Start Screen	Y	Y	Y	Y
Touch Keyboard	Y	Y	Y	Y
File Explorer	Y	Y	Y	Y
Standard Apps	Y	Y	Y	Y
Refresh and Reset	Y	Y	Y	Y
Windows Defender	Y	Y	Y	Y
Improved Task Manager	Y	Y	Y	Y
ISO & VHD Mounting	Y	Y	Y	Y
Microsoft Account Integration	Y	Y	Y	Y
Internet Explorer 10	Y	Y	Y	Y
SmartScreen	Y	Y	Y	Y
Remote Desktop (* client only)	Y*	Y*	Y	Y
Windows Store	Y	Y	Y	Y
Storage Spaces	-	Y	Y	Y
Windows Media Player	-	Y	Y	Y
BitLocker and EFS	-	-	Y	Y
Sideload Windows Store Apps (^ Limited)	Y^	-	Y^	Y
Boot From VHD	-	-	Y	Y
Windows Domain Access	-	-	Y	Y
Group Policy	-	-	Y	Y
Hyper-V	-	-	Y	Y
AppLocker	-	-	-	Y
Windows To Go	-	-	-	Y
DirectAccess	-	-	-	Y
BranchCache	-	-	-	Y
RemoteFX Virtualization				Y
Network File System	-	-	-	Y
Microsoft Office Apps	Y	-	-	-

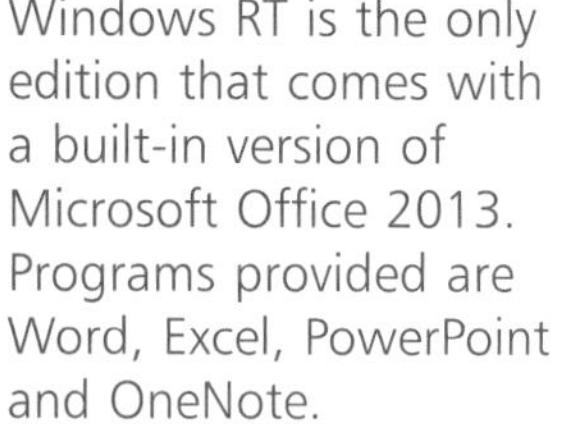

Windows RT is the only edition that comes with a built-in version of Microsoft Office 2013. Programs provided are Word, Excel, PowerPoint and OneNote.

Features removed

Windows 8 has been designed to run on a variety of platforms, a move that has necessitated radical changes to its underlying architecture.

As it is now intended to run as smoothly on a low-powered tablet as it does on a high-powered PC, the emphasis of the new design has been on the elimination of all unnecessary overheads. To this end, many of the features found in previous versions of Windows have been removed.

These include the following:

- Start button
- Start menu
- Aero Glass theme
- Windows Basic and Windows Classic themes
- Games
- Windows Media Center
- Windows DVD maker
- DVD playback
- Aero Flip 3D
- Desktop gadgets
- Windows CardSpace
- Windows XP Mode
- Default user account pictures
- File Explorer command bar
- "Windows updates are available" notifications
- The media guide in Windows Media Player
- Many of the sound files have been removed
- Many fonts have been removed

Hot tip

For users who cannot live without the Start button and Start menu, a free alternative is available at **http://classicshell.sourceforge.net**

Hot tip

Windows 8 does not provide Windows Media Center. However, WMC is available via the Add features option (see pages 18-19).

Windows Media Center

Of all the features removed in Windows 8, Windows Media Center (WMC) is the one we are going to highlight here. The reason is that while the others have all gone for good, WMC is still available.

You will, however, have to pay for it. If you are running Windows 8, you will need to install the Windows 8 Pro Pack – this includes WMC. The price for this at the time of printing is $99.99. If you are already running Windows 8 Pro, you must install the Windows 8 Media Center Pack – this costs $9.99.

Proceed as follows:

1. Open Search on the Charms bar
2. Enter add features in the search box and then click Settings
3. On the results pane, click Add features to Windows 8

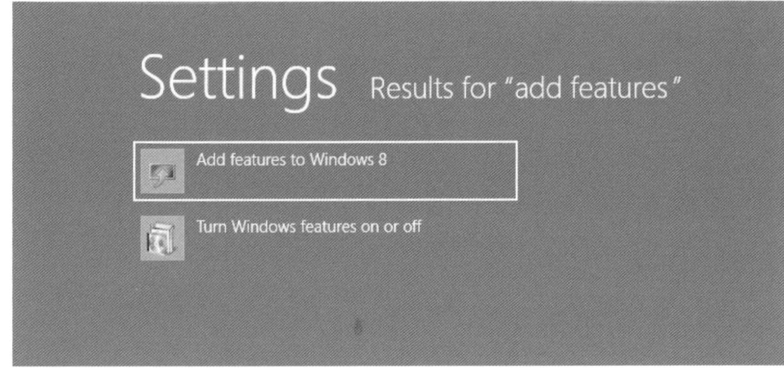

4. A new screen opens. If you need to purchase a product key, click I want to buy a product key online. Then follow the steps to purchase and enter a product key

   If you already have a product key, click I already have a product key
5. Enter your product key and click Next

Hot tip

Note that the Windows Media Center pack also provides support for DVD playback.

6 Read the license terms, select the check box to accept the license terms, and then click Add features

7 If you were running Windows 8, your PC will restart automatically, after which Windows 8 Pro with Windows Media Center will be available for use

8 If you were running Windows 8 Pro, your PC will restart automatically, after which Windows Media Center will be available for use

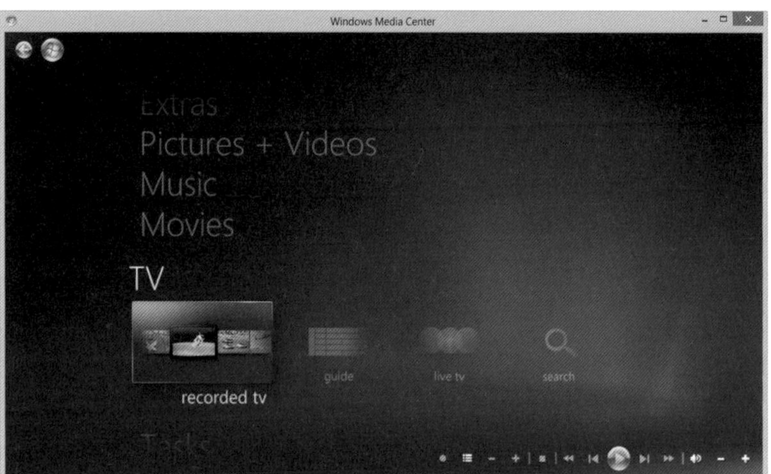

9 To access Windows Media Center, open the Start screen and scroll across to the right. At the end of the screen you will see the WMC tile

10 Alternatively, open the Search charm, type Windows Media Center and press Enter. WMC will open

Hot tip

The version of WMC supplied in the Windows Media Center pack is the same as in Windows 7.

Related operating systems

The Windows 8 operating system isn't used just in personal computers; related editions are found in tablets, smartphones, server systems, and in embedded systems. Getting a handle on what all these versions do, and what they do it on, can be confusing so we'll attempt to clarify things here.

Hot tip 

Windows Server 2012 and Windows 8 Embedded are not relevant for home users.

Windows Server 2012

Windows Server is designed for use with the server systems that provide corporate networking, Internet/intranet hosting, databases, enterprise-scale messaging, etc. It is a specialized operating system that provides functionality not required in home computing.

Windows 8 Embedded

Embedded systems are basically small computational and sensor-based electronic components that collect data and automate simple actions. These devices are widely embedded in many consumer and industrial applications such as vending machines, refrigerators, digital music players, automobiles and routine assembly line tasks.

Microsoft have focused on a section of this market called "intelligent systems", which combine processing power with networking and cloud computing to bring more computational prowess to devices. To this end, it produces a version of Windows known as Windows Embedded, the current version of which is 8.

Hot tip 

Windows 8 (8, Pro & Enterprise) is found predominantly on desktops and laptops. It does, however, have the potential to be used on all types of computers.

Windows Phone 8

Windows Phone 8 is intended for use with smartphones and nothing else. Just as with Apple's iOS and Google's Android, it provides typical smartphone functions, such as email, maps, internet browsing, contacts, etc. One notable difference is that the live tiles on a Windows Phone 8 smartphone provide more, and more current, information than the largely static icons found in iOS and Android.

Windows RT

Windows RT has been designed for use on tablet devices, such as Microsoft's Surface tablet. Essentially, it is a "stripped down" or "lite" version of Windows 8. Accordingly, it lacks several Windows 8 features – Windows Media Player for example. The main difference, however, is that RT will only run applications sourced from the Windows Store.

SkyDrive and Cloud

A very important function built-in to Windows 8 is its ability to utilize what is commonly known as the "Cloud". Essentially, cloud computing is a technology that uses the Internet and centralized remote servers to maintain data and applications. It allows consumers and businesses to use applications they don't own, and to access their personal files on any computer that has Internet access. The technology enables much more efficient computing by centralizing data storage, processing and bandwidth.

So how do you get into the cloud? There are actually several ways: One is to open an account with a dedicated service such as DropBox. You will be given a free amount of storage space, typically up to 18GB in which you can store virtually anything you choose to. If you need more, you will be charged a fee depending on the amount required.

A second way is to buy a product from a major software manufacturer. A typical example is True Image from Acronis – a data backup program. Buy this, and you will be given access to 250GB of online storage that enables you to create cloud-based backups.

A third way is courtesy of a Windows 8 app called SkyDrive, which can be accessed on the Start screen. SkyDrive is basically a portal that allows you to access 7GB of online storage that comes free with Windows 8.

To access your storage space, you will have to log in with a Microsoft account. Note that if you are already logged in to your Windows 8 device with a Microsoft account, you won't need to log in again to access SkyDrive.

Hot tip

You don't have to use the Skydrive app supplied with Windows 8. You can download a desktop version from **http://windows.microsoft.com/en-US/skydrive/download**
This runs on the Desktop and can be installed on On any PC (except those with Windows RT) – all you need is a Microsoft account.

Hot tip

You can log in to SkyDrive with any browser. Go to **https://skydrive.live.com**

...cont'd

Once logged in, you will see that SkyDrive has started you off with a number of pre-configured folders as shown below:

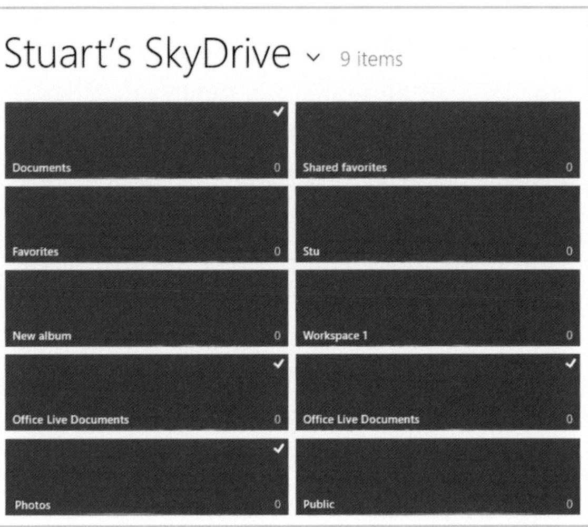

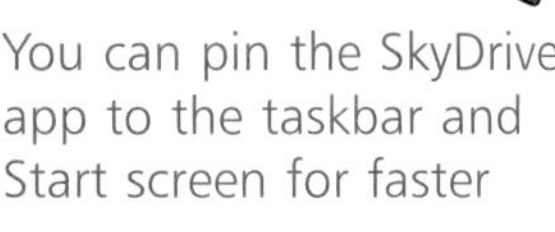

Hot tip

You can pin the SkyDrive app to the taskbar and Start screen for faster access.

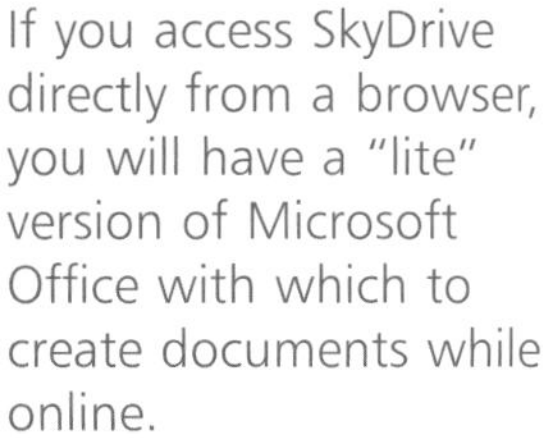

Don't forget

If you access SkyDrive directly from a browser, you will have a "lite" version of Microsoft Office with which to create documents while online.

You can delete these folders, rename them, create more folders, nest folders within folders, and upload/download files.

Once uploaded, your data can be accessed from any device, be it a smartphone, tablet, or PC, from anywhere in the world and at any time. You can also access, and upload, data from within programs in Microsoft's Essentials suite of applications, and Microsoft Office 2010 and 2013.

One of the coolest features of SkyDrive is that it enables online sharing and collaboration. On a personal level you can, for example, share your holiday snaps with friends and family regardless of where they are, while business applications include accessing documents while on the move or sharing documents between offices.

A key aspect of SkyDrive is that it enables data to be synchronized across a range of devices. For example, emails on your main PC can be automatically loaded on to your smartphone or tablet and vice versa. You can also synchronize various settings, such as personalization, e.g. desktop background, theme, colors, passwords, app settings and many more. This enables users to maintain the computing environment they are comfortable in across all their computing devices.

Microsoft Office 2013

Microsoft Office is a very important application for many people so we will take a brief look at it here and how it fits in with Windows 8.

The first thing to mention is that Office 2013 can only be installed on Windows 7, Windows Server 2008, or later. It is not compatible with Windows Vista or earlier versions of Windows.

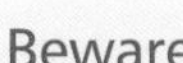

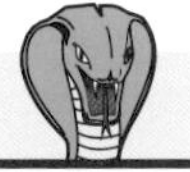

Office 2013 will not run on versions of Windows prior to Windows 7.

We don't have room here to discuss the ins and outs of Office 2013 but one new feature that's worth mentioning is its support for cloud computing. Users have an option in the "Save As" menu that allows them to save documents directly to their SkyDrive account. Also, it is possible to store office settings, documents, templates, dictionaries, and more on SkyDrive. This allows users to synchronize their office applications across all their devices for a consistent working environment.

Another important feature in Office 2013 is support for touchscreens. This makes it the first Microsoft Office suite that can be used with tablets and smartphones.

This leads us on to Office 2013 and Windows RT. Users of RT devices will find that a customized version of Office 2013 is pre-loaded, i.e. its free. However, they should be aware that the RT version does not have all the features of the full version. Amongst other things, for example, there is no support for macros, third-party add-ins and Visual Basic for Applications.

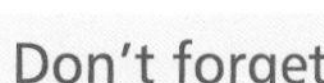

The version of Office 2013 bundled with Windows RT is not the full version

Nor does it offer all the applications in the suite – you just get Word, Excel, PowerPoint and OneNote.

Windows Essentials 2012

Hot tip

Windows Essentials 2012 can be downloaded from **http://windows.microsoft.com/en-US/windows-live/essentials-home**

Mention of free Microsoft applications brings us to the Windows Essentials 2012 suite. This is a collection of free Microsoft applications that offer email, instant messaging, photo-sharing, blog publishing, security services, and more.

Applications in the suite are designed to integrate with each other, with Microsoft Windows operating systems (Windows 8 in particular), and also with Microsoft web-based services such as SkyDrive and Outlook.com; with the intention of providing a seamless computing experience.

Windows Essentials 2012 includes the following applications:

- Mail
- Messenger
- SkyDrive
- Movie Maker
- Photo Gallery
- Writer

Beware

Windows Essentials 2012 will not run on Windows RT or versions prior to Windows 7.

For free downloads to customize, protect, and enhance your computer, go to **http://windows.microsoft.com/en-US/windows/downloads**

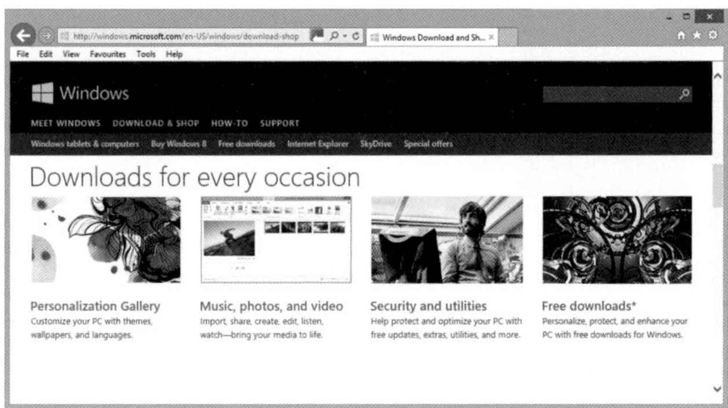

From here, you can get sets of pictures, window colors and sounds from the Personalization Gallery to personalize your computer. You can also download a free language pack to see Windows in the language of your choice.

2 Choosing your computer

In this chapter we examine the hardware requirements of both of Windows 8 and the computers on which it can be run. For example: CPUs, memory, touchscreens, sensors and much more.

Requirements for Windows 8

Traditionally, every edition of Windows has required more in the way of hardware resources than the editions that preceded it. This came to a stop with Windows 7, which ran quite satisfactorily on the same hardware that its predecessor, Windows Vista, did.

This has continued with Windows 8, so users upgrading from either Windows Vista or Windows 7 do not have to also upgrade their computer hardware.

The official system requirements of Windows 8 are as follows:

- **Processor** – 1GHz or faster
- **Memory (RAM)** – 1GB (32-bit) or 2GB (64-bit)
- **Disk space** – 16GB (32-bit) or 20GB (64-bit)
- **Graphics** – Microsoft DirectX 9 with WDDM driver

Please note that the above is the absolute minimum required. While Windows 8 will run on this hardware, it may not do so particularly well. To be more specific, it will probably be on the slow side, and if you run resource-intensive software such as 3D games, Photoshop, etc, it may struggle to cope.

If you wish to avoid this, our recommendation is to install twice the recommended amount of memory, i.e. 2GB on a 32-bit system and 4GB on a 64-bit system.

In addition, the following will be required to use some features:

- **Touch gestures** – a tablet/monitor that supports multi-touch
- **Snap app feature** – a screen resolution of at least 1366 x 768 pixels
- **Windows Store** – a Microsoft account and a screen resolution of at least 1024 x 768 pixels
- **SkyDrive** – a Microsoft account
- **DVD playback** – DVD playback software
- **BitLocker To Go** – a USB drive
- **Hyper-V** – a 64-bit system with second level address translation (SLAT) capabilities and an additional 2GB of memory

Don't forget

To get top performance from Windows 8, you need twice the recommended amount of memory.

Hot tip

Don't worry about the processor, disk space and video requirements. All modern computers and many older ones are more than adequate in these respects.

Processors

The Central Processing Unit (CPU), more than any other part, influences the speed at which the computer runs. It also determines how many things the PC can do concurrently before it starts to struggle, i.e multi-task.

With regard to speed, a CPU is rated by its clock speed, e.g. 3.4GHz. We saw on the previous page that Windows 8 requires a 1GHz or faster CPU. As the slowest CPU currently on the market is 2GHz (twice as fast), the issue of CPU speed is not something the typical home user needs to be too concerned about. It's only important to users who require more power, such as hardcore gamers.

The CPU's, and hence the PC's, multi-tasking capabilities may well be a different story though. Modern computers are frequently required to do a number of things at the same time. Each task requires a separate process or "thread" from the CPU, so anyone who is going to do a lot of multi-tasking will need a CPU that can handle numerous threads simultaneously.

This means buying a multi-core CPU. These devices are no faster than traditional single-core CPUs but because they have several cores, their multi-tasking capabilities are increased enormously. Currently, there are two-, four-, six- and even eight-core models on the market and, fairly obviously, the more your PC is going to have to do, the more cores you will need in your CPU.

There is also the issue of the CPU manufacturer. Currently, the majority of computing devices are laptops and desktop PCs. These both use CPUs from Intel and AMD exclusively. While Intel CPUs are considered to be better than AMD's offerings, there really isn't much in it. In other words, whichever of them you buy from, you won't go wrong.

For those of you looking to buy a smartphone or tablet, the issue of the CPU is more complicated. This is because the CPU in these devices is usually part of a combination chipset that also houses the system's graphics, memory, interface controllers, voltage regulators and more. This combination chip is referred to as a System-on-a-Chip (SoC) and its main benefit is that it reduces the space needed for these components. This, in turn, lowers power requirements and increases battery life.

Don't get fixated with CPU clock speed. You should also consider things like the number of cores and the size of the cache.

Hot tip

For most users, anything over two cores is overkill. Don't waste your dollars on performance you will never use.

Things are further confused by the fact that most SoC manufacturers including Apple, Samsung, Texas Instruments, and NVIDEA, use a CPU architecture called ARM that is produced and licenced by a company called ARM Holdings. Therefore, this part of a SoC will be identical regardless of the manufacturer; the rest of the SoC, however, will not be. This makes it very difficult to compare SoCs on a like-for-like basis.

Don't forget

When you see the term ARM used in reference to a CPU, remember that the CPU is not manufactured by ARM but rather by a company licensed by ARM Holdings to use its CPU architecture.

Virtually all smartphones use SoCs, as do some tablets. There are some though (usually the more capable ones) that use a specially designed low-power CPU of the same type found in desktop PCs. Intel's Atom CPU is a good example.

However, whatever the type of CPU, be it a full-size AMD FX, an Intel Atom, or an SoC, the basic premise of clock speed determining the speed of the CPU and the number of cores determining its multi-tasking capability, or power, is the same.

Hardware capabilities

If you are thinking about upgrading to Windows 8, there's a good chance you may also be considering upgrading your PC. If so, you need to give some thought to the hardware that will be in it. Alternatively, it may simply be time to give it a boost.

Whichever, to ensure your PC is capable of doing what you want it to, there are several components you need to consider. The CPU we've already looked at but there is also the memory, video system and disk drive to consider.

Hot tip

If you wish to upgrade the memory on a PC that's more than two or three years old, it will be almost certainly be using DDR2. You will not be able to replace it with the newer DDR3 – this requires a motherboard designed to use DDR3.

Random Access Memory (RAM)

As with the CPU, memory is a component that has a major impact on the performance of a computer. You can have the fastest CPU in the galaxy but without an adequate amount of memory, all that processing power will do you no good at all.

This is a more straightforward issue than CPUs. While there are many different types of memory, as far as desktop PCs and laptops are concerned, there is only really one choice – DDR3. This is currently the memory of choice and is installed on all new PCs. DDR2 will be found on many older PCs and is still a perfectly good type of memory.

The only issues for owners of modern PCs is how much memory do they need, and how much can they install? With regard to the former, this is a difficult question to answer – it depends mainly on what type of programs are going to be run on the PC. Applications that shift large amounts of data such as 3D games, video and sound editing, high-end desktop publishing, etc, will require a much larger amount of memory – typically 6GB or more. Less intensive applications such as web browsing, word-processing and Freecell will all run perfectly well on 2GB.

Don't forget

If you want to install more than 4GB of memory, you must be using a 64-bit PC.

The amount of memory that can be installed is determined by the motherboard. This is not going to be an issue for the average user as current motherboards can handle anything up to 64GB. However, the computer architecture being used may well be. 32-bit computers running a Windows operating system can utilize a maximum of 4GB of memory regardless of how much is installed. 64-bit PCs, on the other hand, can use an almost limitless amount.

Memory modules are rated in terms of speed, which is another consideration. Currently, speeds range from 1GHz to 2.6GHz. The faster the memory, the more expensive it will be.

Hot tip

Don't worry too much about memory speed. The real-world difference between the slowest and fastest modules is not significant. In any case, to get the best out of the high-speed modules, other parts such as the CPU also need to be top-end. Such a set up will be expensive.

Smartphones and tablets require much less memory than desktop PCs. High-end devices of these types currently come with about 1GHz of RAM. They also make more efficient use of the available memory by "suspending" apps that are not being used, thus releasing memory for other apps.

When considering a smartphone or tablet, it is also necessary to see what it has to offer in the way of in-built memory for storage purposes, and if it can be expanded by adding larger capacity memory cards.

You might think that devices such as smartphones, which do not generally come with much in the way of internal storage, would almost certainly offer a memory card slot. However, this is not always the case, as owners of iPhones will testify.

Video System

Video systems produce the pictures you see on the display. Two types are used in computers: integrated video that is built-in to the motherboard or CPU, and stand-alone video cards.

...cont'd

Don't forget

If you want the best quality video in your PC, you will need a video card rather than integrated video.

Of the two, video cards produce by far the best quality video – for hardcore gamers they are essential.

The problem with video cards is that they are not only expensive; they are also bulky, noisy, and power-hungry. Desktop computers and high-end laptops are large enough and powerful enough to accommodate these demands, but for smaller devices such as netbooks, tablets and smartphones, they are impractical.

Therefore, these all use an integrated video system. As we mentioned on page 28, in these devices the video will be just one part of a System-on-a Chip (SoC).

Solid State Drives (SSDs)

Disk drives, or hard drives as they are more commonly known, are the devices used to store a user's data. They are electromechanical devices that provide huge amounts of storage space at a low price.

Hot tip

If you have a need for speed, make sure your devices use SSDs.

A recent revolution in the hard drive market has seen the introduction of solid state drives (SSDs). These devices employ solid-state memory and contain no moving parts which, quite apart from anything else, makes them extremely reliable.

Other advantages include instant startup, extremely fast data access speeds, completely silent operation, a much smaller footprint, weight (they are much lighter than mechanical drives), and low power requirements.

These qualities all make SSDs ideal for use in low-power devices such as tablets and smartphones. Apple, for example, use them in their highly successful iPads, iPhones and iPods.

However, their use in desktop computers is somewhat limited by two factors: The first is the high cost of SSDs compared to mechanical drives. The second is that they provide much smaller storage capacities than mechanical drives. This has lead to low-capacity SSDs, typically around 60GB, being used for the boot drive (where the operating system is installed), with a high-capacity mechanical drive to provide data storage.

The result is a PC that typically boots up twice as quickly, is snappy and responsive to the user's commands, and also has loads of storage space.

Computer types

When it comes to buying a computer, buyers have quite a few different types to choose from, each having pros and cons that make them suitable for some purposes and less so for others.

Desktop PCs

Traditionally, the desktop PC comprising a system case that houses the hardware, plus a monitor, keyboard and mouse has been the most popular type of computer.

Their main advantage is that the addition of peripherals such as printers and scanners, turns them into work horses that enable almost any type of computational work to be done.

Other pluses are that they are cheap to buy, easy to upgrade and repair, and easy to expand. Disadvantages are size, noise, aesthetics, and lack of mobility.

Hot tip

A big advantage of desktop PCs is that they are easy to expand and to upgrade

All-In-Ones

Increasingly popular due to their small footprint, all-in-one PCs are manufactured by a number of companies, including Apple, Lenovo and Samsung. Pictured below is the Lenovo IdeaCentre.

Other advantages include being lightweight, a minimal amount of messy wiring, many come with touchscreens, and a definite element of style – many of these devices look rather cool and not at all out of place in the living room.

The downside is that they are very difficult to repair/upgrade due to lack of accessibility. All-in-ones are also prone to heat issues due to the lack of air space in the case – this makes them unsuitable for high-end applications. Also, if one part goes wrong the whole unit has to go back – it's all or nothing.

Hot tip

All-in-ones are produced by a limited number of manufacturers and tend to be expensive.

...cont'd

Hot tip

Hybrid PCs are ideal where mobility is an issue. Don't expect to do any serious work or gaming on them though.

Hybrid Computers

Continuing the all-in-one's theme of style and elegance, we have the hybrid computer. It is comprised of nothing more than a very small and usually stylish case that contains the hardware.

The user simply places it where it is to be used and connects a monitor, keyboard and mouse.

These devices have only one real advantage – they are extremely portable. They have the same disadvantages as all-in-one PCs and, as such, are only suitable for lightweight applications.

Laptops

A laptop is basically a desktop PC condensed into a small, flat, portable case. It has the same components as a desktop, albeit on a smaller scale, and is capable of everything the desktop is.

Hot tip

If you buy a laptop with a view to portable computing, check out the battery capacity. Some models have low-capacity batteries that don't last long before needing to be recharged.

Fairly obviously, their main advantage is portability – a laptop can be tucked under the arm and literally taken anywhere.

They also require little space and are easily secured, e.g. can be placed inside a safe.

As ever though, there are downsides: Probably the main one is cost – laptops are considerably more expensive than desktops of equivalent capability.

These devices are also more difficult to use due to smaller screens and the need for touchpads. There is a high risk of physical damage as they can be dropped, they are easily misplaced or lost, and are prone to theft.

Variations of the laptop theme include Ultrabooks and Netbooks. The former are an Intel invention and manufacturers of these devices must conform to standards set by Intel.

These state that Ultrabooks must use low-power Intel Core CPUs, solid-state drives and unibody chassis. This is to ensure that Ultrabooks are slim, high-end devices able to compete at the top-end of the laptop market where they will be up against the likes of Apple's MacBook Air.

Hot tip

Basically, Ultrabooks are aimed at the top-end of the laptop market, while Netbooks are aimed at the bottom-end.

A Netbook is simply a miniature laptop. They usually have 10-inch screens, scaled-down keyboards and touchpads to match, and are extremely small and lightweight. As a result, they are inexpensive and easily transportable. The downside is that they usually feature a resolution of 1024 x 600 and so are unable to run Windows apps. Their role is therefore being taken over by Tablet PCs and Convertible Computers.

Tablet Computers

Tablets are mobile computers that fit in between smartphones and Netbooks. The hardware is built-in to a touch screen and can be operated both by touch and by a keyboard (onscreen or attached).

Unlike smartphones, the displays offered by tablets are large enough to enable serious work to be done. For example, with a suitable app you can easily write a long, properly punctuated letter or email.

Hot tip

Tablets are a good option if you need ultra-portability as well as computational functionality.

You'll need to choose a Tablet PC that can run Windows. For Windows RT, it will have an ARM based processor. For Windows 8, it must have an Intel processor or equivalent.

Tablet PCs then offer the best of all worlds. The convenience and ultra-portability of smartphones, a camera, plus the ability to carry out serious computer work. Some even have a phone as well!

Convertible Computers

A convertible computer is essentially a tablet that can be quickly transformed into a small laptop or Netbook by opening an integrated keyboard. Typically, this achieved by means of a sliding or hinged mechanism. In all other respects they are just a tablet.

32-bit versus 64-bit

All modern CPUs support 64-bit architecture. But what is it and how does it benefit the user?

The term "64-bit" when used in reference to a CPU means that in one integer register the CPU can store 64 bits of data. Older CPUs, which could only support 32-bit architecture, could store only 32 bits of data in a register, i.e. half the amount. Therefore, 64-bit architecture provides better overall system performance as it can handle twice as much data in one clock cycle.

However, the main advantage provided by 64-bit architecture is the huge amount of memory it can support. CPUs operating on a 32-bit Windows system can utilize a maximum of 4GB, whereas on a 64-bit system they can utilize up to 192GB.

The caveat is that a 64-bit system requires all the software to be 64-bit compatible, i.e. it must be 64-bit software. This includes the operating system and device drivers (this is why more recent versions of Windows [XP, Vista, 7 and 8] are supplied in both 32-bit [x86] and 64-bit [x64] versions). Note that most 32-bit software will run on a 64-bit system but the advantages provided by 64-bit architecture won't be available.

So who will benefit from a 64-bit system and who won't? The simple answer is that every PC user will benefit as their system will be more efficient. Don't expect to see major speed gains over a 32-bit system when running day-to-day applications such as web browsers, word processing and 2D games, though; you probably won't notice any.

However, when running CPU-intensive applications that require large amounts of data to be handled, e.g. video editing, 3D games, CAD, etc, 64-bit systems will be faster. Also, if you need more memory than the current limit of 4GB possible with a 32-bit system, 64-bit architecture allows you to install as much as you want (up to the limitations of the motherboard).

Users running Windows 8 Pro have access to a virtualization utility called Hyper-V. One of the requirements for building virtual PCs with Hyper-V is that the computer must be running on 64-bit architecture.

To get a 64-bit system, simply buy a modern CPU and install a 64-bit version of Windows.

Don't forget

Modern CPUs automatically detect whether an application or operating system is 32-bit or 64-bit and operate accordingly.

Hot tip

If you opt for a 64-bit system, all your software, including device drivers, will have to be 64-bit compatible. Even though 64-bit systems are now common, there is still software on the market that that runs only on 32-bit systems.

Windows RT limitations

Buyers considering Windows RT need to be aware that this operating system has some serious limitations that may affect their intended use of the device.

The first is that it is not possible to upgrade an existing edition of Windows to Windows RT. It is only available pre-installed on a tablet – in other words you have to buy a new tablet to get the RT operating system.

The second is that there is no support for x86 software – the programs you run on your regular desktop PC. So if you have a Windows 8 desktop PC, which is able to run Photoshop for example, don't assume that it will also run on a Windows RT device – it won't.

Beware

Windows RT is not the same as Windows 8. The two operating systems have major differences.

This means that the only software available for devices running Windows RT is from the Windows Store. If the Windows Store doesn't offer the software you need, you have nowhere else to go.

The lack of legacy application support is exacerbated by the fact that Microsoft have not made it clear that RT is effectively a cut-down version of Windows 8. As it appears at first glance to be exactly the same as the full editions of Windows 8, many people are going to buy an RT equipped tablet thinking they are getting the full Windows 8 and then be extremely annoyed when they discover otherwise.

Another limitation is the lack of a built-in media player – something many users may take to be an attempt to force them to use Microsoft's Xbox Music service.

Business users should be aware that Windows RT cannot be used with a Windows Active Directory Domain.

Finally, many users will buy into Windows RT on the strength of the bundled Microsoft Office 2013 suite. However, this is not all they may assume it to be either. First, it is not the full suite – all that's offered is Word, Excel, PowerPoint and OneNote – no Outlook, note. Furthermore, some features and functions of the full suite are not available in the RT version. Nor can it be used for commercial purposes – you can use it at home but that's all.

Don't forget

The version of Office 2013 bundled with RT is not the full version. Also, it cannot be used on a commercial basis.

Multi-touch

An important feature of Windows 8 is its support for touchscreen control. If you are considering buying a touchscreen monitor in order to take advantage of this feature, you should be aware of the following issues:

Hot tip 

It's a requirement of Windows 8 certification that the bezel should be flush with the display or incorporate a 20 mm border between the edge of the display and the start of the bezel.

Bezel Design

Some of the touch gestures required to control Windows 8 – opening menus, for example – are done by swiping a finger inwards from one edge of the screen towards the center.

However, it is a fact that the vast majority of touchscreen monitors currently on the market have a raised bezel, which makes it more difficult than it need be to carry out this particular touch command. (*Correct at the time of printing.*) Our recommendation is that you choose a monitor in which the bezel is flush to the screen. Alternatively, look for a model that has at least a 20 mm border between the edge of the display and the start of the bezel.

Hot tip 

There are still touch screens on the market that only support two touch points – don't buy one of these.

Multi-Touch

Multi-touch refers to a touchscreen's ability to recognize the presence of two or more points of contact with the surface. This plural-point awareness is necessary to implement functionality such as pinch to zoom-out or the activation of predefined programs.

All modern touchscreens have this capability. However, to get the best out of Windows 8's touch feature, you need a touchscreen that supports at least five touch points – this allows you to use five fingers simultaneously.

Hot tip 

The down-side of capacitive touchscreens is that they cannot be operated with a gloved finger (not so clever on a freezing cold day perhaps!).

Screen Technology

There are various types of touchscreen technology; however, when it comes to computer monitors and mobile devices there are just two – resistive and capacitive. Resistive screens can be operated with any pointed object such as a stylus or a finger. Capacitive screens rely on the electrical properties of the human body and thus only react to human touch (or a capacitive pen).

Of the two the capacitive type is the one to go for – they are much more sensitive and accurate than resistive screens (these tend to be used more in business environments, e.g. shops and banks). Note that most current touchscreens are of the capacitive type but do check it out just in case.

Sensors

One of the main differences between static desktop PCs and mobile computing devices is the range of sensors employed by the latter. Some of these are important to the operation of these devices while others add functionality. Sensors that you should look for include:

Ambient Light Sensor (ALS)

This sensor enables screen brightness to be automatically adjusted in accordance with the ambient light level. If it gets darker then the screen brightness decreases; if it increases then the screen brightness increases. A useful side-effect of this is increased battery life.

Proximity Sensor

The purpose of this device is to prevent accidental inputs – something that's easily done on a touchscreen. The most common scenario is the ear touching the screen during a call and triggering an event or action.

The proximity sensor is located next to the speaker and thus can detect when the ear (or another object) is close by. Any actions generated are assumed to be accidental and thus ignored.

Accelerometer & Gyroscope

These two sensors are used to detect the orientation of a device so that the display can react accordingly. For example, if the device is moved from a vertical orientation to a horizontal one, the display will follow suit. Other uses include the camera – the sensors enable it to know if the picture is being taken in landscape or portrait mode.

Global Positioning System (GPS)

An embedded GPS sensor used in conjunction with a mapping service enables any mobile device to get real-time position tracking, text- and voice-guided directions, and points of interest.

Compass

Sensors that detect direction enable compass apps to be built. Sensors of this type do not sense magnet fields as do traditional compasses but rather the frequency and orientation of radio waves. In doing this, smartphone compass sensors are assisted by gyroscopes.

Hot tip 

Increasingly, data from the various sensors in a device is being combined to produce more elaborate applications.

Hot tip 

New types of sensor are being developed for mobile devices. Examples are altimeters (will detect which floor of a building you are on, for example), temperature & humidity sensors and heart rate monitors.

Other hardware features

Windows 8 includes several new hardware features not seen in Windows operating systems before. We'll take a brief look at two of them here:

Hot tip 

NFC is similar in concept to Bluetooth but is somewhat slower in operation. It does however, consume much less power.

Near Field Communication (NFC)

Near Field Communication (NFC) is a set of standards for mobile devices to establish radio communication with each other by touch or bringing them into close proximity – usually no more than a few centimeters. The technology is beginning to appear on mobile devices. Applications include:

Purchase Payment – used in conjunction with an electronic wallet, this effectively turns a smartphone into a credit card

Setting Up Connections – connections such as Bluetooth can be quickly and easily established

Smart Tagging – touching a smartphone to an NFC tag, e.g. tap-and-go at the gas pump

Hot tip 

Windows 8 also sees the introduction of support for USB 3.0.

Peer-to-Peer – sharing small snippets of information such as contacts, photos, and web pages is a typical use

Unified Extensible Firmware Interface (UEFI)

A computer needs an interface between its operating system and hardware to make sure they can work together. Traditionally, this role has been carried out by a chip called the BIOS (this produces the black boot screens you see when starting your PC).

UEFI is a replacement for the now archaic BIOS. Windows 8 takes advantage of a security feature in UEFI known as Pre-boot Authentication. This prevents any software that doesn't have a recognized and valid security certificate from running and, as a result, rootkits, viruses and malware are unable to load themselves into the system's memory during the boot procedure, i.e. before the operating system. (A virus that manages to do this could circumvent any antivirus measures on the PC).

Hot tip 

If your PC has UEFI, it can be accessed from Windows 8's boot options menu.

Another feature of UEFI is its graphical display that allows navigation with a mouse and keyboard. However, before you go looking for it, be aware that your computer's motherboard must provide UEFI support. Only computers built in the last year or so are likely to have UEFI.

3 Installing Windows 8

Upgrading options for Windows 8 can be a confusing issue – this chapter explains exactly which editions of Windows can be upgraded to Windows 8. We also look at the two types of installation – upgrading and clean installing, and the pros and cons of each.

Upgrade paths

When upgrading to Windows 8 or Windows 8 Pro, most users will be able to keep all their files, settings and desktop applications. However, there are exceptions to this as we see below:

Hot tip

Currently, Windows 8 Pro can be bought for $189.99. *(Correct at the time of printing.)*

The following operating systems can be upgraded to Windows 8 with the options of Keep Nothing or Keep Personal Files (only):

- Windows 7
- Windows Vista (Service Pack 1)
- Windows Vista
- Windows XP (Service Pack 3 or later)

The following operating systems can be upgraded with the above options plus Keep Windows settings, personal files, and applications:

- Windows 7

Additionally, Windows Vista with SP1 will have the following upgrade options:

- Keep Nothing
- Keep Personal Files (only)
- Keep Windows settings and personal files

Hot tip

When ordering Windows 8 Pro online, you can also request a backup DVD. This is priced at about $15.00. *(Correct at the time of printing.)*

The following operating systems are eligible for an upgrade to Windows 8 Pro:

- Windows XP
- Windows Vista
- All editions of Windows 7

However, only the following operating systems can be upgraded to Windows 8:

- Windows 7 Starter
- Windows 7 Home Basic
- Windows 7 Home Premium

Upgrade options

Upgrading an operating system can be done in three ways:

- An inplace upgrade
- A clean installation
- A migration

We'll start with the most common method:

Inplace Upgrade

With this method, the operating system is simply installed over the top of the old one. While this is the easiest way to do the job, it will produce the worst results. This is because any problems on the original setup (file corruption, malware, etc) will be carried over to the new installation. Issues of this type can also cause an upgrade to fail.

The only advantages of upgrading in this way is that the procedure is straightforward and that the user's data, files and programs are not affected – they will still be there at the end of it.

Clean Installation

With a clean installation, all potential problems are eliminated right at the start due to the format procedure, which wipes the drive clean of all data. Therefore, nothing is carried over to the new setup from the old one.

The drawback with this method is that the formatting procedure also removes all the user's data – settings, files and programs. So when the new operating system has been installed, it will then be necessary to redo all the settings, reinstall all the programs and restore the data. Another issue is the time it will take to do all this – the best part of a day in the author's experience.

Migration

This is not a true upgrade option but we include it here as the procedure does transfer files and settings from one installation to another. It does not transfer programs, though.

To do a migration, you need a suitable application such as the Windows Easy Transfer utility supplied with Windows. Basically, this copies the files and settings from the old setup to a medium such as a USB flash drive and then transfers them to the new setup.

Hot tip

Windows offers a "custom" upgrade option. Essentially, this carries out a clean installation as described on the left but without formatting the drive. The user's settings and programs are lost but personal files are kept. These will be found in a folder on the drive called windows.old.

Walkthrough clean install

Hot tip

It is possible to create an installation disk using a USB flash drive. First, you will need a program such as IsoBuster to extract the files from the image file. Then copy them to the USB drive and, finally, in the BIOS (see page 43) set the PC to boot from the USB drive.

Unlike an upgrade, which can be initiated from within Windows, a clean install has to be done from an installation disk. If your copy of Windows 8 has been supplied on a DVD then you're all set. If not, it will be in the form of an ISO image file. However, before you can use this it will have to be burned to a DVD, a procedure that will require a DVD burning program.

If you are upgrading from Windows 7, you have a DVD burner built in. Just pop an empty DVD in the DVD drive and follow the prompts from the AutoPlay window that will open shortly afterwards.

If you don't have a built-in burner, you can find a free one on the Internet. One that we recommend is ImgBurn (**www.imgburn.com**). Use it as described below:

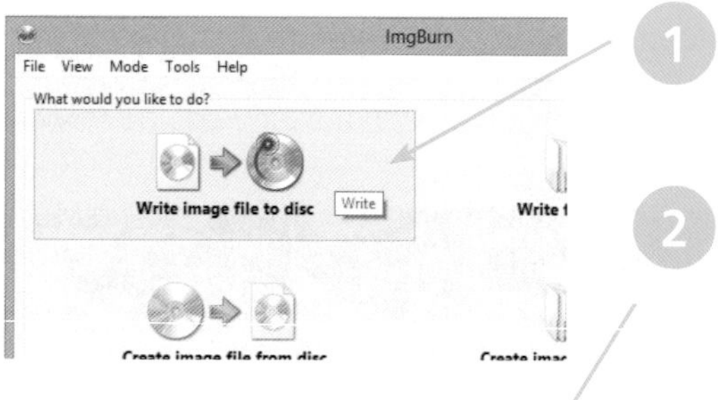

1. At the opening screen, click "Write image file to disc"
2. Under Source, click the browse link and select your ISO file

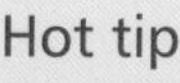

Imgburn is just one of many free disc burners available on the Internet.

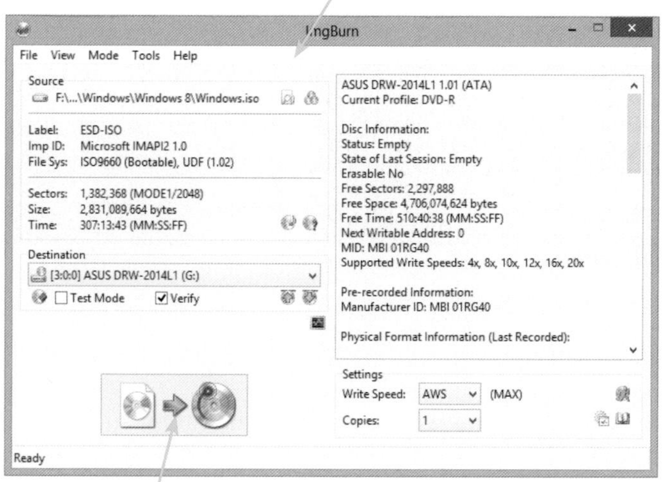

3. Click Write and wait while the DVD is burned

Set the boot drive

Having created your installation disc, you now need to configure your computer to boot from it. This is done as follows:

1. Start the PC and at the first boot screen, press the key required to open the BIOS. This is usually the Delete or F2 key (it is often specified at the bottom of the screen)

2. On the main BIOS page, scroll to Advanced BIOS Features and press Enter

3. On the next page, scroll down to First Boot Device. Using the Page Up/Page Down keys, cycle through the options and select the CD/DVD drive

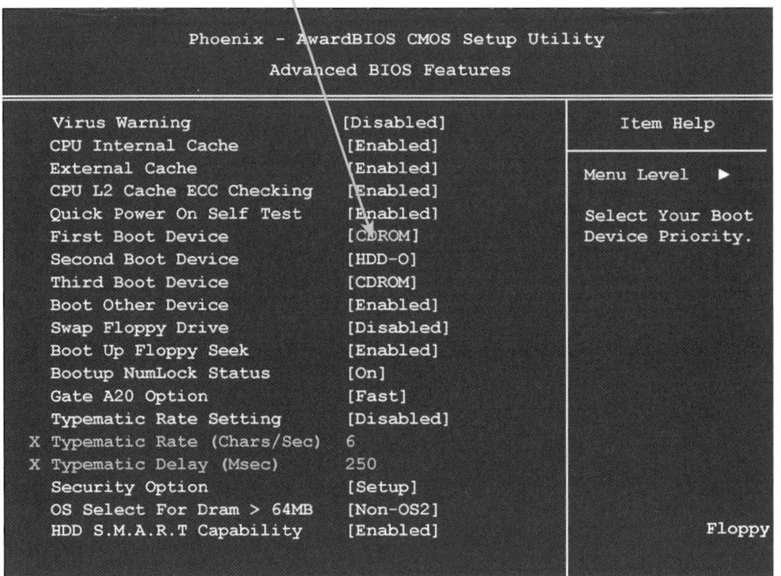

4. Press the Escape key to return to the main page

Note that you must save the change before exiting the BIOS, otherwise it will revert to the original setting. The option for this is on the main BIOS page at the right-hand side (Save & Exit Setup).

Hot tip

If you can't find the key to open the BIOS, check the motherboard manual.

Hot tip

The BIOS screens in your PC may differ from the example on the left – it depends on the age of your PC and the manufacturer of the BIOS.

Don't forget

All the tools needed to do a clean install of Windows 8 are on its installation disk. So, you must set the CD/DVD drive as the first boot device.

Windows setup

In the following pages, we are going to show you a step-by-step procedure for doing a clean installation of Windows 8.

Remember you have to configure the PC to boot from the CD/DVD drive.

1. Place the Windows 8 installation disk in the CD/DVD drive and start the PC. When you see a "Press any key to boot from CD..." message, do so. Windows will now begin loading its installation files to the disk drive

2. The first screen you will see is the language, time and currency format, and input method preferences. Make your selections and press Next

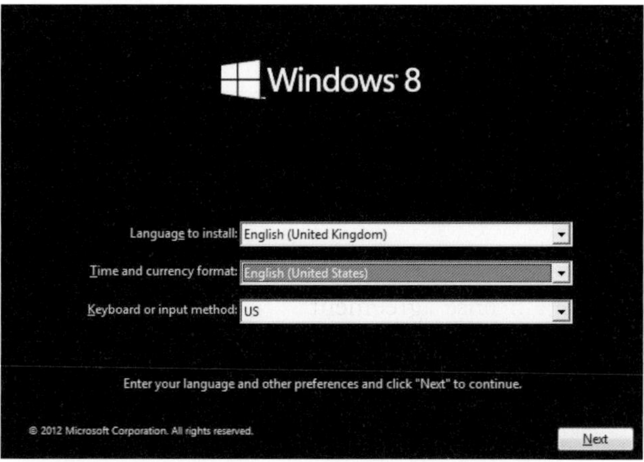

Before you start this procedure, make sure you have made a backup of any data that you want to keep.

3. When the second screen opens, click Install now

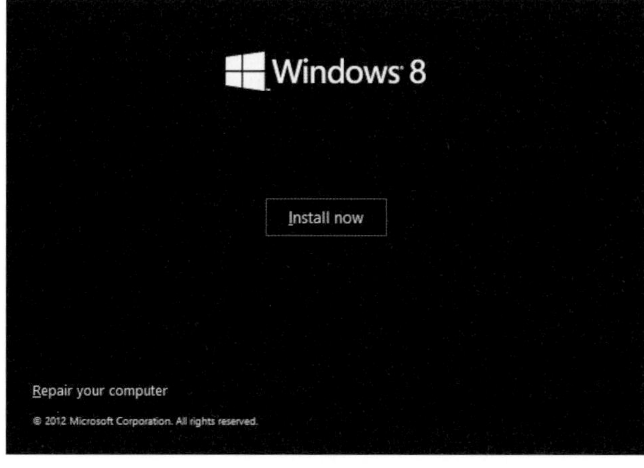

Enter product key

4 You will now be asked to enter your product key

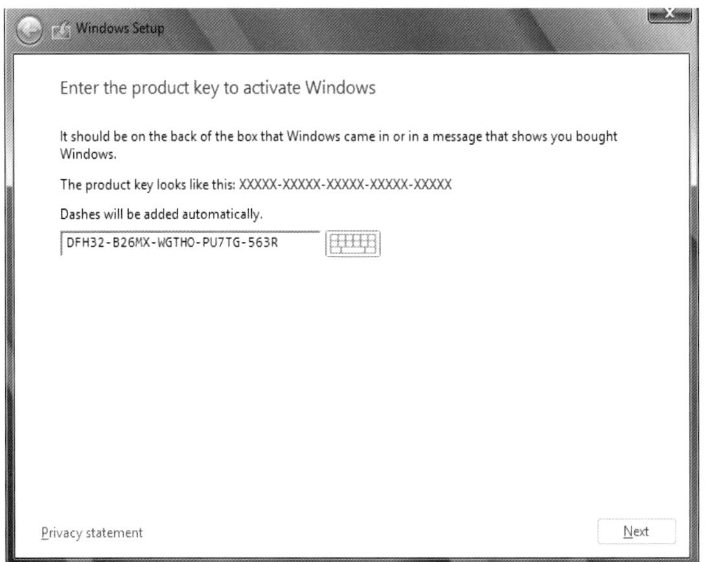

5 OK the license agreement

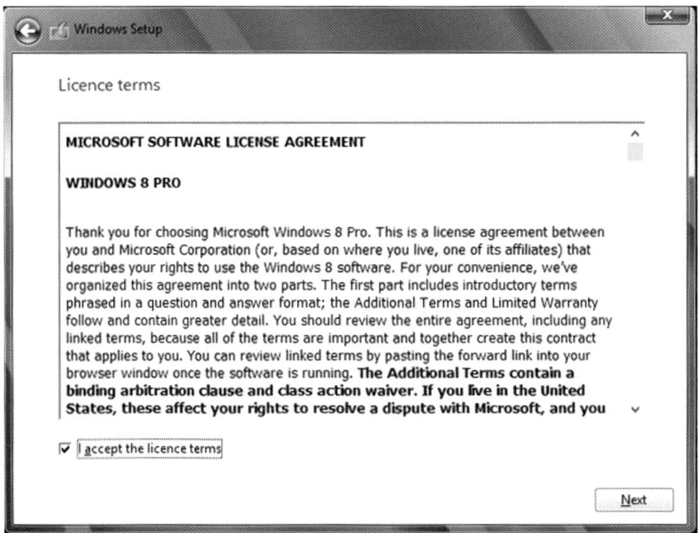

6 Click Next

Hot tip

The product key will be found somewhere on the DVD packaging. If bought online, it will be in the email confirming the sale.

Type of installation

7 At the Which type of installation do you want? screen, select Custom: Install Windows only (advanced)

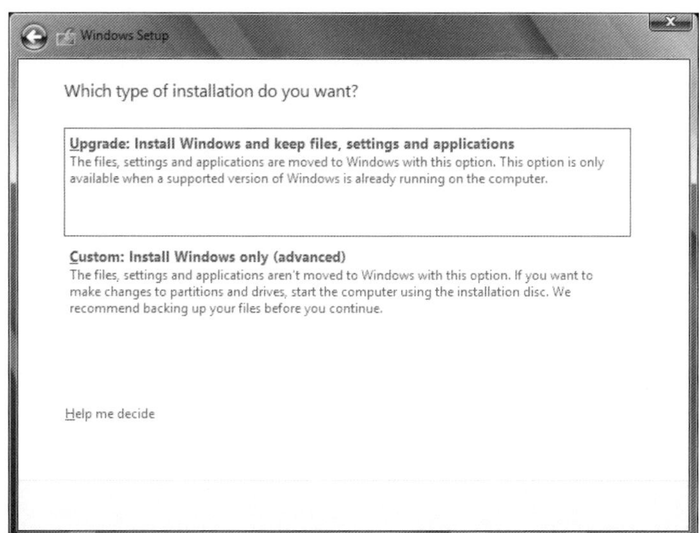

Drive options (advanced) enables the user to create and resize partitions.

8 In the Where do you want to install Windows? screen, select the required drive or partition. Then click Drive options (advanced)

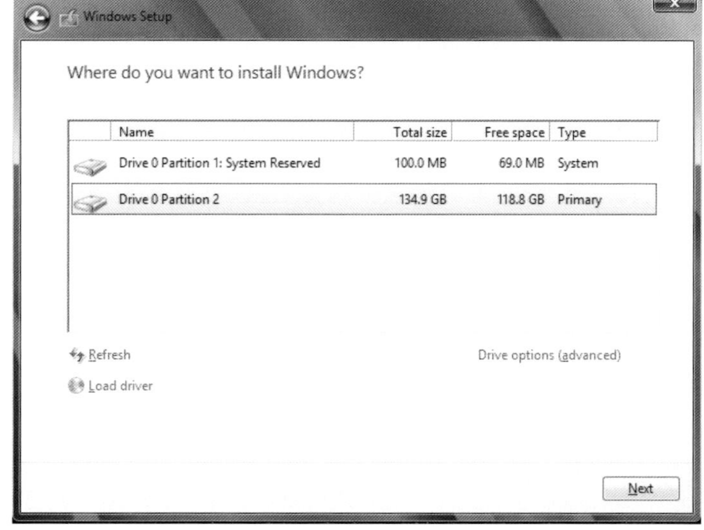

If your current operating system is Windows 7, you will see a "Drive 0 Partition 1;System Reserved" entry. This is not relevant to Windows 8 so you can either ignore it or you can delete it in the advanced drive options.

9 In the screen that opens, click Format. Note that this action will wipe your drive clean of all data

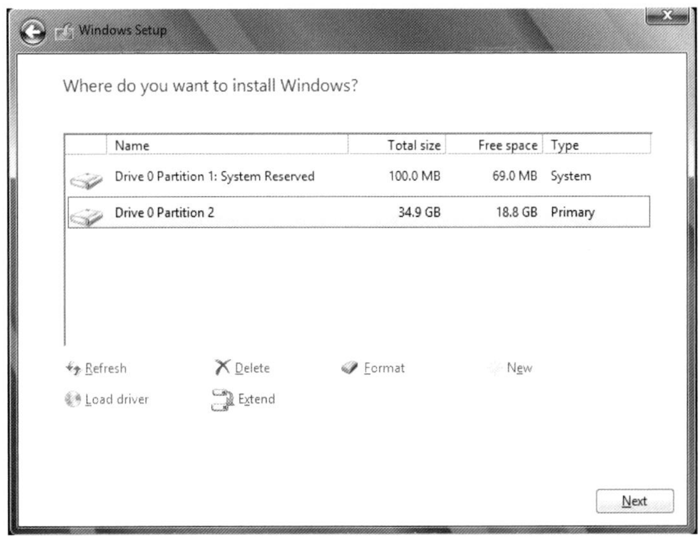

Hot tip

Your computer will reboot automatically several times during the installation procedure.

10 You will now see a message telling you that you will lose your data as a result of the formatting procedure. Ignore this by clicking OK. The installation routine will now begin – just sit back until you see the first setup screen

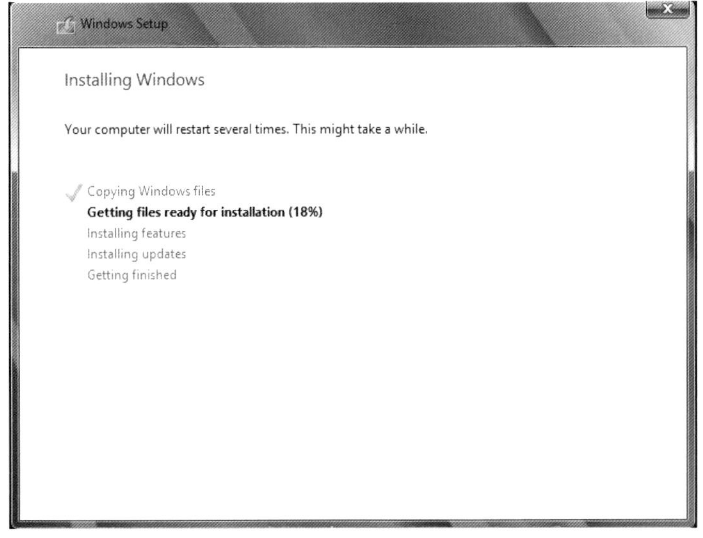

The end of the installation routine is signified by two screens – "Getting devices ready" and "Getting ready". The PC will then reboot into the new installation.

First start

When Windows 8 starts for the first time, the first thing you will see is a Personalization screen. This allows the background color to be chosen.

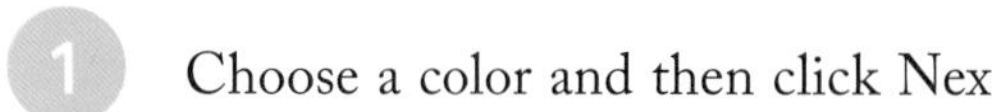

1 Choose a color and then click Next

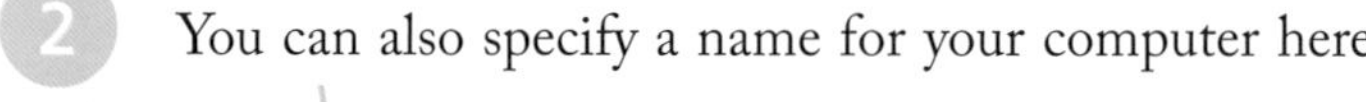

2 You can also specify a name for your computer here

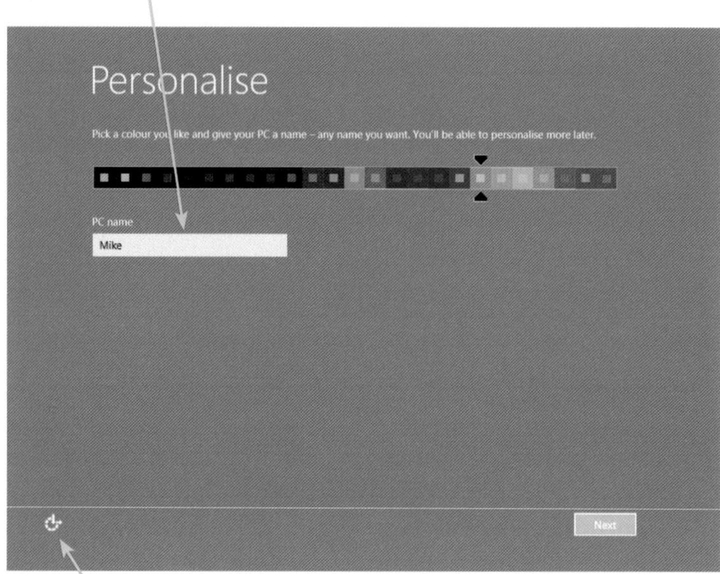

3 Click the Ease of Access icon to open the menu of related options shown below:

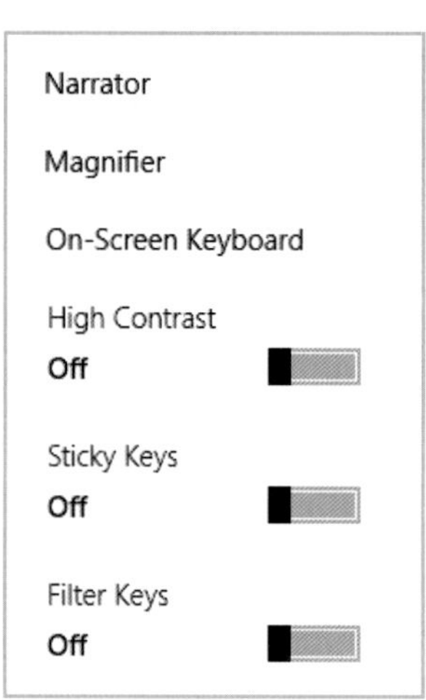

4 These provide a range of aids, such as Narrator and Magnifier for the short-sighted, an onscreen keyboard, Sticky keys and Filter keys

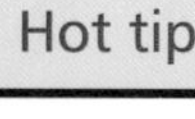

Hot tip

The color you choose can be changed later – you're not stuck with it.

Sign in to your PC

There now follows a series of screens that enable you to sign in to the PC for the first time. This can be done via a Microsoft account but if you don't have one, an option is presented for you to create one should you wish to do so.

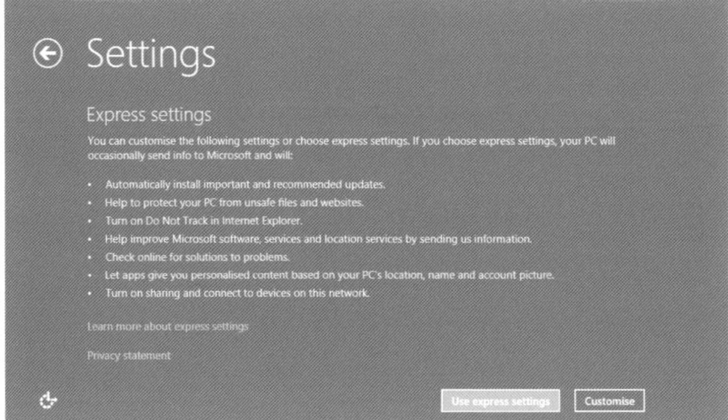

1. At the Settings screen, click Use express settings. This opens the Sign in to your PC screen

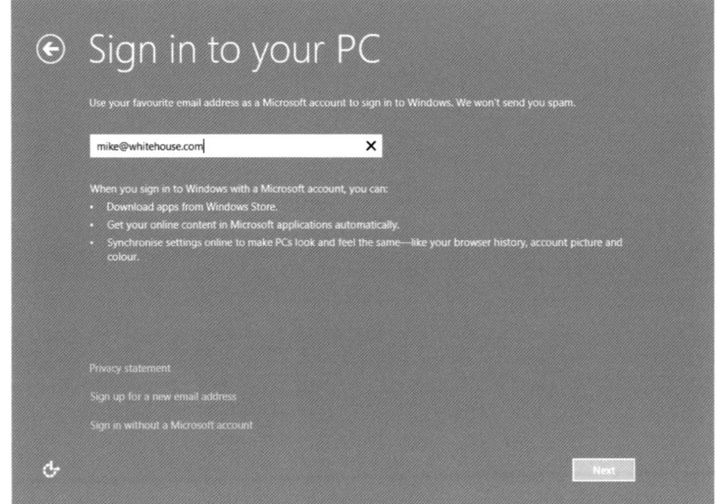

2. Enter your email address and click Next. If you don't have one but would like to, click Sign up for a new email address. If you don't want to bother with an account at all, click Sign in without a Microsoft account

Hot tip

The Settings screen Customize option allows you to turn on network sharing and device connection.

Hot tip

If you choose to sign in without a Microsoft account, certain Windows features will not be available to you.

3. The email address you entered will now be checked to see if belongs to a Microsoft account. If it does, you will be asked for the password

4. If the password checks out, you will be asked to provide some additional security information. Then click Next

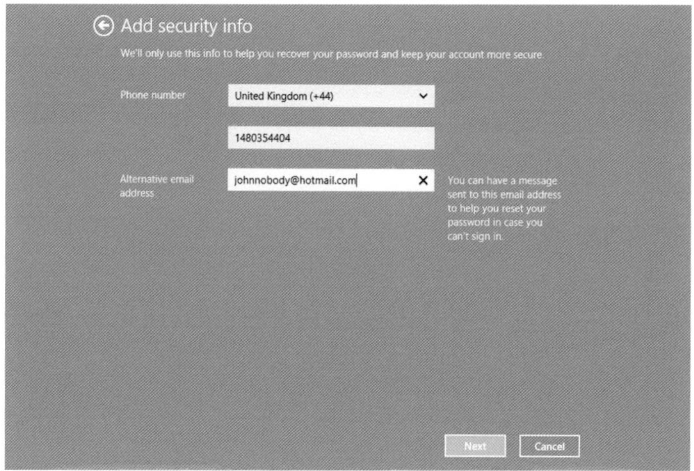

5. Your account will now be created. Unless you change the setup later, every time you log in to the PC you will need to enter the account password

It is not obligatory to provide additional security info if you don't wish to.

Finalizing settings

The two final stages of the Windows 8 setting up procedure are:

1. Getting the PC ready

We're getting your PC ready
This will take a few minutes

2. Installing the apps

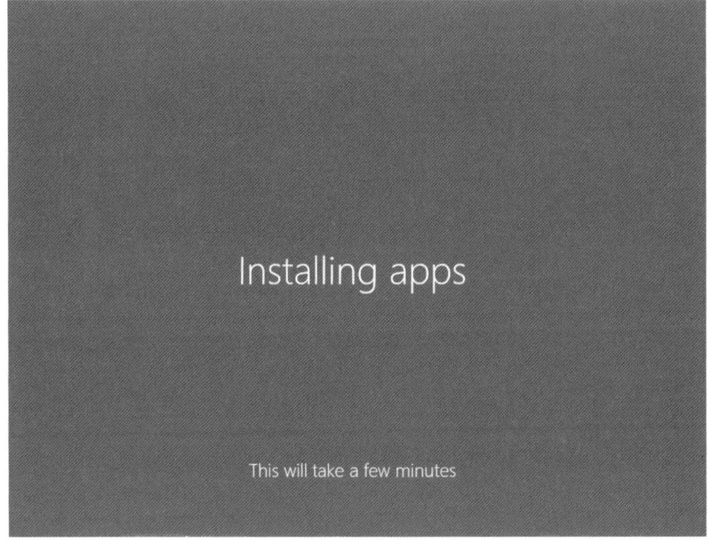

When these stages have been completed, your new Windows 8 installation is ready for use.

While the constant need to log in can be irritating, there are benefits to using a Microsoft account.

Hot tip

The final stage of setting up Windows is installing the apps. When this has been done, the PC is ready to go.

Restoring your data

Don't forget

You may need to install the drivers for your chipset and other hardware. If you don't have them, they can be downloaded from the motherboard manufacturer's website.

You now have a brand new operating system. However, apart from the apps bundled with Windows 8, that's all you have.

The first thing you have to do now is install essential system drivers. The most important of these are the chipset drivers and they will be found on the motherboard's installation disk. Pop this in the CD/DVD drive and wait for AutoPlay to open the disk's setup utility. Select the option that installs all the chipset drivers.

When the driver installation is complete, the PC will reboot. When back in Windows, the next step is to install the drivers for any hardware connected to the computer. Typically, these include video cards, sound cards, printers, scanners, routers, monitors, mice and keyboards.

Finally, install your programs and any data backed up from your previous installation.

Local accounts

As a final note, on page 49 step 2, we mentioned that it is not essential to have a Microsoft account to use Windows 8 and, indeed, it isn't. However, if you choose this option, you will find that some features of Windows 8 are denied to you.

Hot tip

If you opt for a local account, you will be asked to specify a password. However, if you don't specify one, you will be able to automatically log in to Windows 8 without having to enter a password.

The first is that you won't be able to synchronize your settings, email, passwords, etc across your various devices. This means that one of the big attractions of Windows 8 – the ability to create and maintain a consistent computing environment regardless of which device you are using – will not be available. While this probably won't be a big deal for most users, for some it most definitely will be.

Also, you won't be able to get apps from the Windows Store. It will still be possible to browse the store but you won't be allowed to download any.

Furthermore, some Windows 8 apps won't work unless the user is signed into a Microsoft account. Examples include the Mail, Calendar, People, Messaging, and SkyDrive apps.

4 The Windows 8 interface

In Chapter Four, we take an in-depth look at the new Windows 8 interface. This is a radical change from the traditional Desktop that people are used to. Navigating the Start screen is the first thing you have to learn and we show you how to do it with the aid of charms and hotspots. We also explain how to customize the Start screen.

Start Windows 8

When a Windows 8 PC is started, the first thing the user will see (once the boot screens have flashed past) is a black screen with the Windows 8 logo, as shown below:

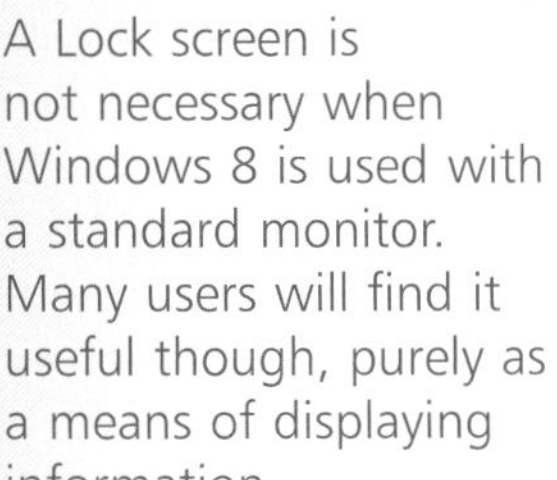

A Lock screen is not necessary when Windows 8 is used with a standard monitor. Many users will find it useful though, purely as a means of displaying information.

This is followed by the Lock screen. The basic purpose of this screen is to provide a protective barrier that prevents accidental inputs – this is necessary as Windows 8 is a touch-supportive operating system.

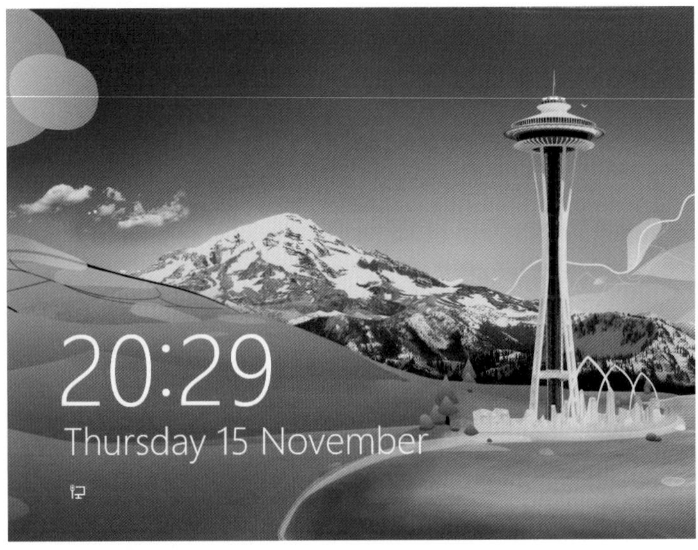

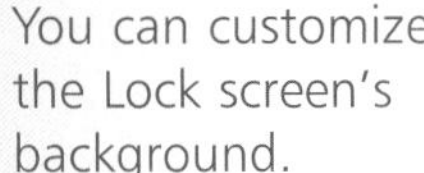

You can customize the Lock screen's background.

Microsoft have evolved this basic function by enabling users to customise the screen by changing its background, and by specifying various notifications to be displayed.

By default, the Lock screen shows the current date and time as in the image above.

Log on

Click or tap anywhere on the Lock screen and the log on screen will open. To the left of the log on box, you'll see the account picture. (This can be changed as described on page 64.)

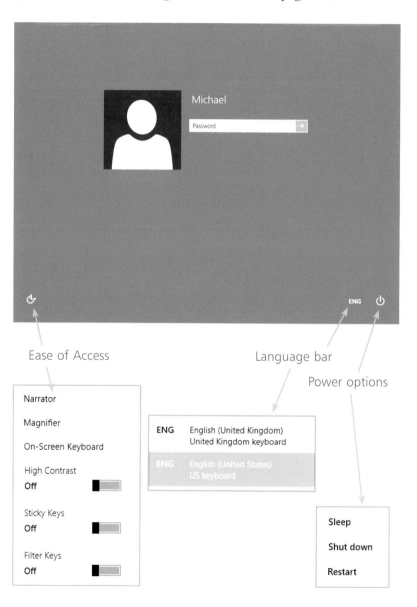

Michael

Password

ENG

Ease of Access

Language bar

Power options

Narrator

Magnifier

On-Screen Keyboard

High Contrast
Off

Sticky Keys
Off

Filter Keys
Off

ENG English (United Kingdom)
United Kingdom keyboard

ENG English (United States)
US keyboard

Sleep

Shut down

Restart

Hot tip

The menus on the log on screen are easy to miss as they are very small and placed right at the bottom of the screen.

At the bottom-left the Ease of access menu can be accessed, while the icon at the far bottom-right offers Sleep, Shut down and Restart options. Also at the bottom-right is the language bar.

Start screen

Hot tip

Although designed primarily for use with touchscreens, the new Windows 8 interface can also be operated with a mouse and keyboard.

When users log on to a Windows 8 computer, instead of going to the traditional Desktop, they are taken to the Start screen. This is a new interface and is just one of a number of significant changes in this edition of Windows. These changes are designed to improve the way the operating system is used with tablet computers and other touchscreen devices.

The Start screen is similar to the one found in Windows Phone 8, Microsoft's smartphone operating system. It displays a customizable array of tiles that are linked to various apps and desktop programs, some of which can display constantly-updated information and content.

Don't forget

Start screen tiles can be placed in groups of related apps.

These tiles can be resized, reordered, and organized into groups. They can also be pinned to the desktop taskbar, while live tiles can have their content switched off.

Tiles apart, however, at first glance the Start screen appears to be completely bereft of user options. There's no Start button, no taskbar and no Notification area. Right-click on it and there is not even a right-click menu.

However, as we'll see shortly, most of the traditional Windows options are still available, albeit in a different way. The new Windows 8 interface also introduces some new methods of accessing menus and options, such as hotspots and charms. We'll take a look at these next.

Hotspots and Charms

Access to the options available in the new Windows 8 interface is provided by what are known as hotspots and charms. On this page we'll see where to find the Windows 8 hotspots and what they do.

Hotspots are basically your way into the New Windows 8 interface. They are located in the four corners of the display and enable the user to access the App switcher and the Charms bar – see page 58.

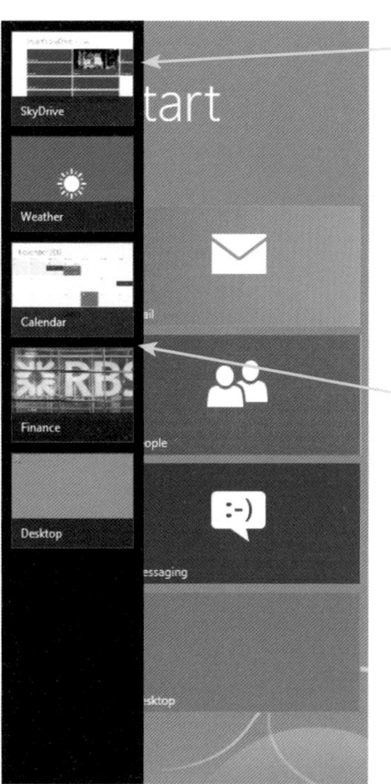

1. The left-hand corner hotspots reveal the App switcher. Initially, you just see the last opened app but the menu can be expanded to show all running apps

2. The App switcher enables individual apps to be selected and either brought to the foreground, or closed

3. The right-hand hotspots open the Charms bar

Don't forget

Use the left-hand hotspots to access running apps and the App switcher, and the right-hand ones to access the Charms bar.

Hot tip

The Charms bar can be accessed where ever you are in Windows 8.

The Charms bar is a universal toolbar that can be quickly accessed via the right-hand corner hotspots no matter where you are in Windows 8.

The following charms are available on the Charms bar:

Search Charm

This charm replaces the old search box on the Windows Start menu. It is a sophisticated search tool that enables the user to locate many different types of information. With it, you can search in Apps, Settings, Files, the Internet, and more. For example, you can search the Weather app to see the prevailing conditions in a specified location.

Share Charm

The Share charm makes it easy to share things such as photos, video, articles, etc, directly from the app currently in use. Just open the Share charm and a bar will appear on the right-hand side with the various sharing options available to you, e.g. Email, People. Initially, sharing options are limited but adding social media apps, such as Twitter and Facebook will quickly increase the usefulness of this feature

Devices Charm

The Devices charm gives you quick access to all the devices attached to your computer. This is the place to go when you need to configure the displays attached to your PC, use Play To for displaying PC- or device-based media on a compatible television or other device, and send files to portable devices using technologies such as NFC.

Start Charm

The Start charm does exactly the same thing as the Windows key on the keyboard or the Windows Key button on an ARM-based Windows RT device. It toggles between the Start Screen and the previously-viewed app.

Settings Charm

The Settings charm provides context-sensitive settings for the current app, the Desktop and the Start screen, as well as system-level settings such as Power, Sound and Notifications

Hot tip

You don't actually have to open the Search charm to do a search. Just start typing – the charm will open automatically.

Hot tip

Apps that show content have to be designated as able to share their content, and the apps that do the sharing need to be designated as able to share.

Navigate the Start screen

In its drive for Windows 8 to be all-encompassing, Microsoft has made it possible to manipulate the interface in three different ways: by touch, the mouse, and the keyboard.

Touch

Touch gestures include swiping, sliding, tapping and pinching. The best way to get to grips with these is to experiment. The following, however, will get you off to a good start:

Swipe from the right – moving a finger from the right-hand side of the screen to the left opens the Charms bar.

Swipe from the left – moving a finger from the left-hand side of the screen to the right opens the Application switch list, which shows all the open apps and enables the user to switch between them.

Swipe slowly from the left – by performing the above left-to-right action more slowly, it is possible to drag an app out of the Switch list and "snap it" to run side-by-side with the current app.

Swipe down from the top – moving a finger from the top of the screen to about halfway down will close the current app.

Swipe down – swiping down from the top of the screen brings up an option to view all the apps and programs installed on the PC, not just the Windows 8 apps. When performed in an open app, the same movement reveals related options. For example, in the Internet Explorer app, it opens a tab menu that shows a list of all open tabs, plus a new tab button.

Swipe down on a tile – this selects an app and at the same time opens the app bar at the bottom of the screen.

Pinching and stretching – pinching enables the user to zoom out of the Start screen or an open app. Stretching zooms in.

Slide left/right – sliding a finger to the right of the screen scrolls across the Start screen. Sliding it left scrolls back. The same movements in the Internet Explorer app opens the next and previous pages.

Tapping – this action is used to select an option or to open an app.

Hot tip 

The old Windows Task switcher (Alt + Tab) can also be used to show open apps.

Hot tip 

In many cases, the touch commands available are dependant on the application in use. For example, various rotational commands can be used to manipulate objects in drawing and layout applications such as Microsoft PowerPoint.

Hot tip

Spinning the mouse wheel while on the Lock screen will open the password box. When on the Start screen, it scrolls the screen sideways.

Don't forget

The Windows key is usually located at the bottom of the keyboard near to the space bar and often has an image of a flying window on it.

Hot tip

Two of the most useful keyboard shortcuts are Winkey + C to open the Charms bar, and Winkey + X to open the Power users menu.

Mouse

Using the mouse to get around in Windows 8 is no different to any other operating system. The trick is knowing where to position the mouse to reveal the menus and features provided by the new interface as covered in pages 54-57.

Keyboard

Those of you who use the new Windows 8 interface without the benefit of a touchscreen are well advised to get acquainted with the various keyboard commands relevant to it. In many cases, just as with keyboard commands and shortcuts in general, they are often quicker than using the mouse.

There is actually a whole bunch of these commands; the following being some of the more useful ones:

The key that will be used most is the Windows key (Winkey). Pressing this key toggles between the Start screen and the last viewed app. It can also be used in conjunction with other keys to perform other actions. For example, Winkey + X opens the Power user menu while Winkey + C opens the Charms bar.

The Home and End keys jump from one end of the Start screen to the other, while the arrow keys can be used to select a tile. The Enter key opens a selected app.

Tapping the space bar opens the app bar at the bottom of the screen. Winkey + Tab opens the Switch list that allows the user to switch to a different app. While the list is open, pressing the Delete key closes the apps in turn.

Alt + Tab opens a horizontal version of the Switch list. Note that you must have at least two apps running for Winkey + Tab and Alt + Tab to work.

Press Ctrl + Tab to open a list of all apps and programs installed on the computer and cycle through the list with the arrow keys.

A rarely-used key known as the Context Menu key (usually located close to the space bar) brings up an app bar, or menu, of related options when pressed in open apps.

PC settings – personalization

The new Windows 8 interface doesn't offer too much in the way of user personalization. Options are restricted to the Start screen, the Lock screen and account pictures.

To access the settings:

1. Open the Charms bar on the right of the screen and click Settings

2. At the bottom of the Settings pane, click Change PC settings

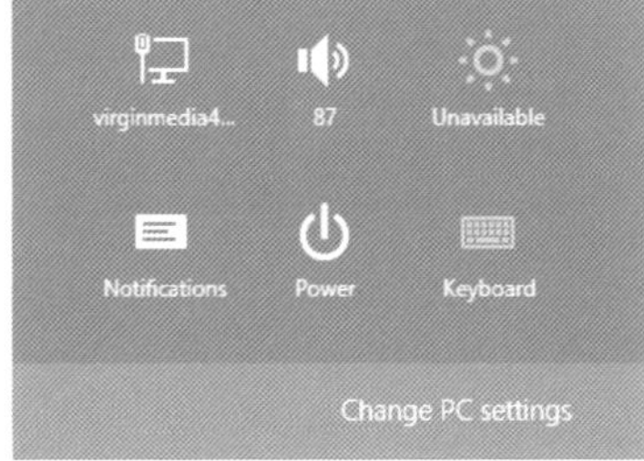

3. On the left-hand pane, click Personalize

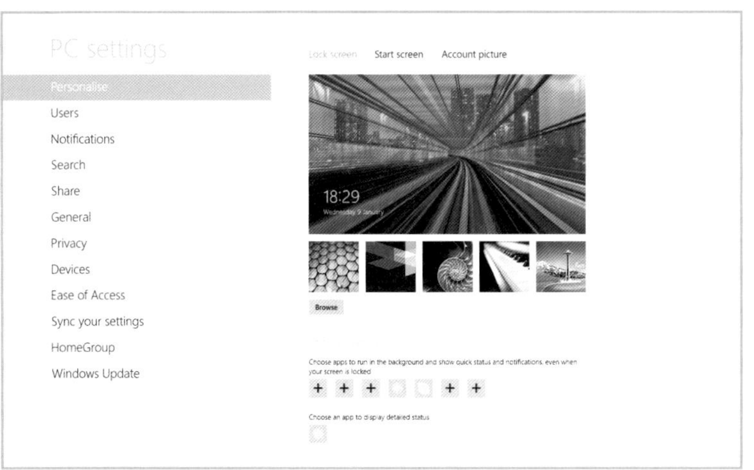

Hot tip

Don't expect the huge range of customization options offered by the Desktop interface. The Windows 8 interface is very restricted in this respect.

Don't forget

PC Settings personalization lets you customize the Start screen, the Lock screen and account pictures.

Lock screen

The Lock screen can be customized in two ways. Let's see how it's done:

Appearance

Probably the first thing most users will do is change the background image.

Don't forget

You are not restricted to the default lock screen images. Any images you place in your Pictures folder can be used.

1. Go the personalization settings as described on page 61
2. On the right, click Lock screen

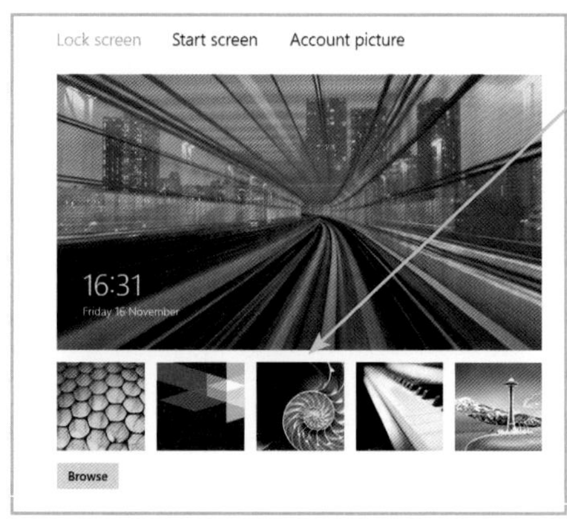

3. Choose from the available images
4. Alternatively, click Browse – this takes you to the Pictures folder

Notifications

If you look below the default background images, you will see options to change the notifications displayed on the lock screen.

Don't forget

You can use the Lock screen to display useful information. For example, unread emails.

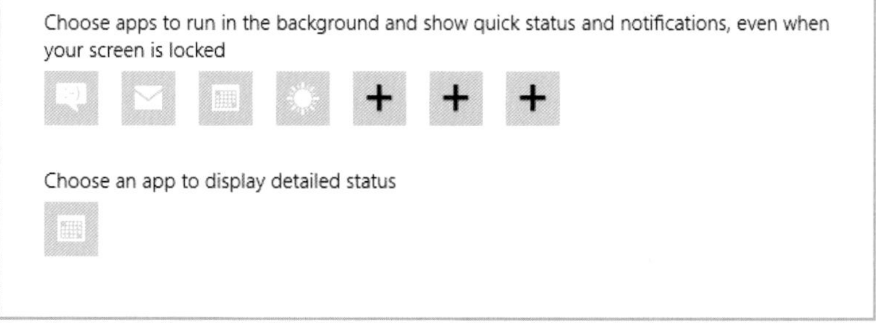

By default, the only app showing a notification on the Lock screen is the Calendar app. You can add more, simply by clicking one of the Add icons.

Start screen

The next aspect of the new Windows 8 interface that users will want to customize is the Start screen. The options for this are accessed in much the same way as described for the Lock screen.

1. Go the personalization settings

2. On the right, click Start screen

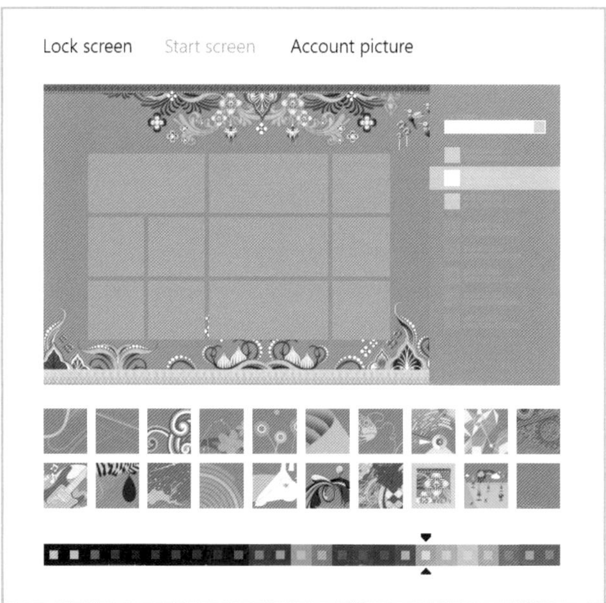

Customization options are limited to solid colors or colors overlaid with transparent patterned backgrounds. The latter can produce some striking effects as demonstrated below:

Hot tip

There is no option for choosing a background image from the Pictures folder as with the Lock screen. However, there are third party programs that offer this capability.

Hot tip

You cannot use screen savers on the Start screen.

Account picture

Access the account picture customization options as follows:

1. Go the personalization settings
2. On the right, click Account picture

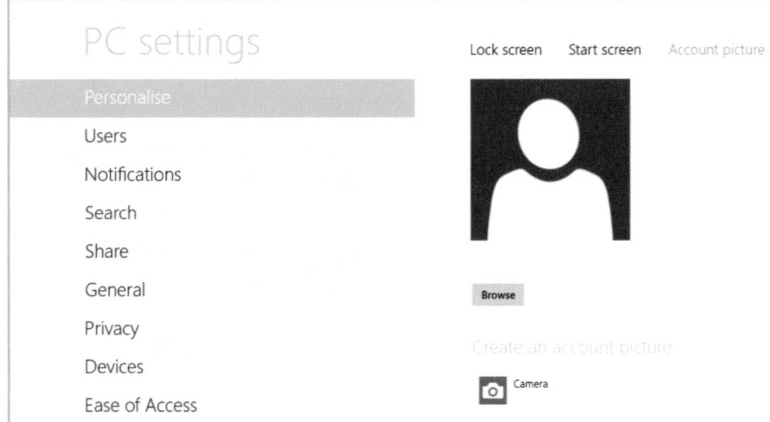

3. Click Browse to search the computer for a suitable picture. Select the picture and click Choose image

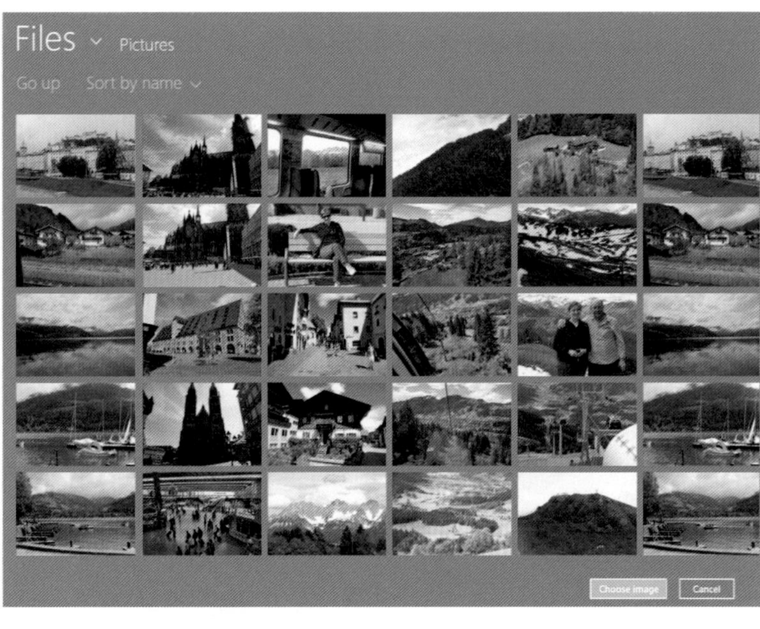

Hot tip 

Under Create an account picture, there is a camera icon. This is not intended for use with a digital camera as might be expected, but rather with a webcam.

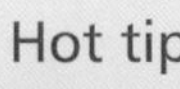 **Hot tip** 

You can use any image for the account picture.

PC settings – users

The new Windows 8 interface provides a range of settings with regard to users. Amongst other things, these include switching accounts and changing account passwords.

Switch accounts

Windows 8 allows two types of account – a Microsoft account, which enables all of Windows 8's features to be used, and a local account, which has restrictions. To switch from one to the other:

1. On the Charms bar, select Settings, Change PC settings
2. On the left, select Users. If you are currently signed in with a Microsoft account, you will see an option to switch to a local account (and vice versa). Click the option

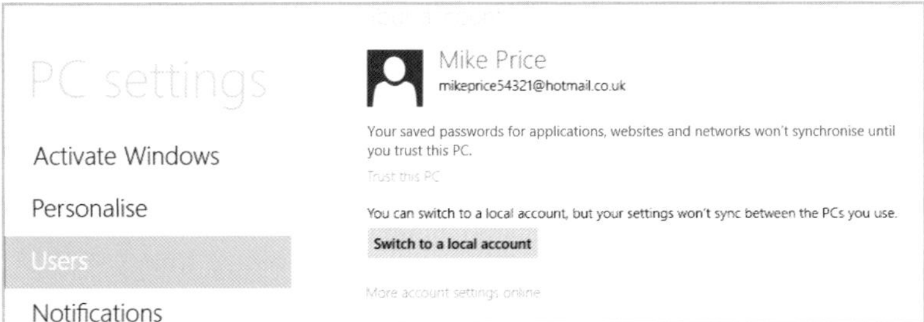

3. In the screen that opens, enter your current password
4. In the next screen, enter a username, password and password hint for the account
5. In the final screen, click Sign out and finish as shown below. You will now be signed out of the account you are using and then be taken to the Lock screen where you will need to log in with the new account's credentials

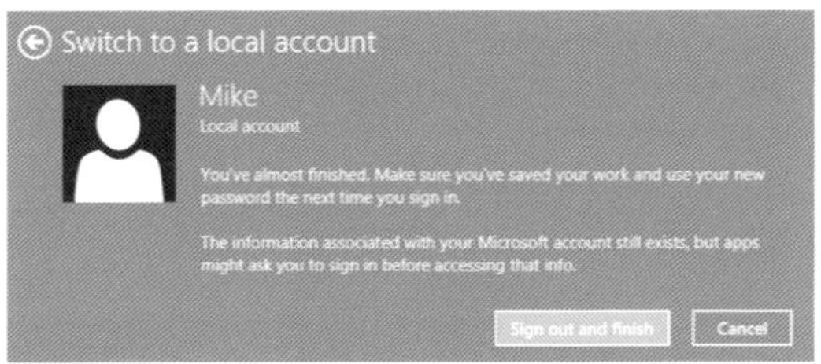

Don't forget

Two types of account can be used with the new Windows 8 interface – a Microsoft account and a local account.

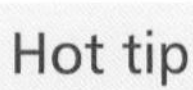

Hot tip

The Switch to a local account option effectively creates a new user account.

...cont'd

Change account password

Should you ever wish to change your account's password, do it as described below:

1 On the Charms bar, select Settings, Change PC settings

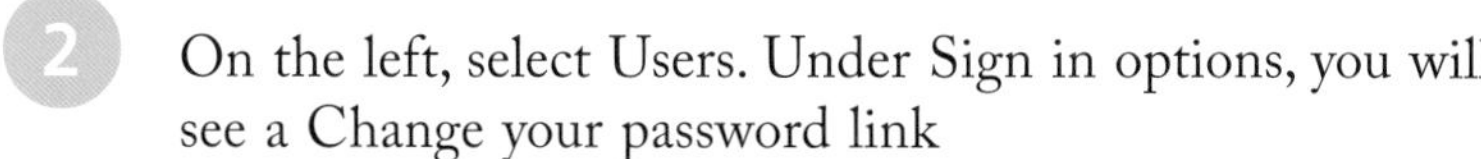

2 On the left, select Users. Under Sign in options, you will see a Change your password link

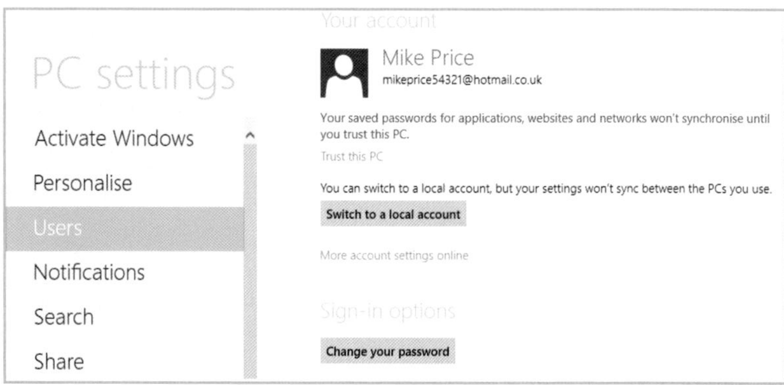

3 Clink the link to open the Change your Microsoft account password screen

4 Enter your old password, your new password, confirm it and then click Next

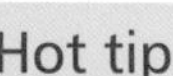

Hot tip

Account passwords can also be changed in the Desktop interface. Go to the Control Panel, User Accounts and Family Safety, and open User Accounts.

Picture password

Windows 8 offers a new twist on security by letting users present their login credentials in the form of a picture password rather than a text password. Set this up as follows:

1. On the Charms bar, select Settings, Change PC settings
2. On the left select Users. Under Sign in options, you will see a Create a picture password. Click it
3. In the screen that opens, enter your current text password
4. At the next screen, click Choose picture. The Picture folder will now open – choose a suitable image and click Open. The picture will open in a new screen – click Use this picture

5. Create three separate marks or gestures on the picture. Each gesture can be a straight line or a circle or a tap

The next time you log in to the PC, you will have the choice of using your text password or the picture password.

Hot tip

Because there are so many possible combinations of pictures and gestures, picture passwords can be more secure than text passwords.

Don't forget

If you make an error when confirming the gestures, you can Try Again and Windows 8 draws the gestures on the screen as guide lines.

PIN code

PIN (Personal Identification Number) codes are another new security feature in Windows 8, and enable users to secure their computer with a four digit code. You may question the need for this as there are already plenty of security options provided, not to mention the fact that a four digit code isn't particularly secure anyway.

The PIN code feature is intended for use on small touchscreen devices

However, the feature is intended for use in tablets and smartphones where the small keyboards provided make it difficult to enter a complex alpha-numeric password.

1. On the Charms bar, select Settings, Change PC settings

2. On the left, select Users. Under Sign in options, you will see a Create a PIN link. Click it

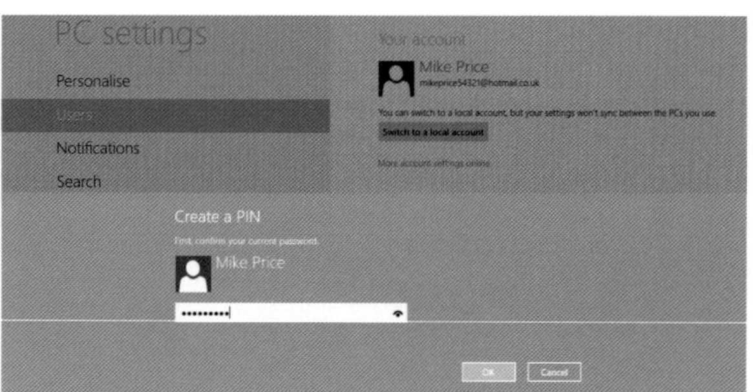

3. Enter your account password and in the screen that opens, enter the four digit PIN. Click Finish

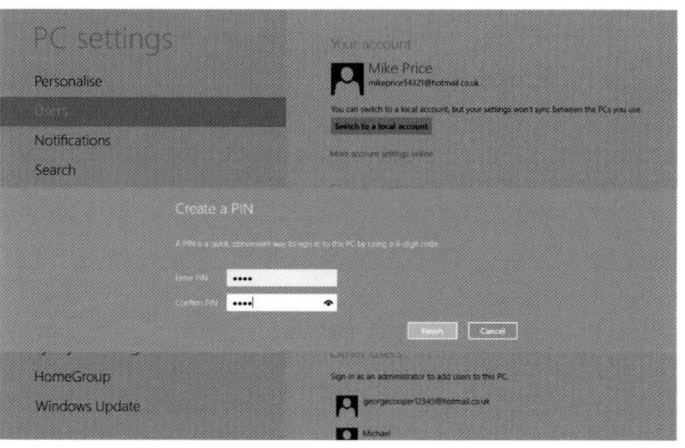

The PIN code option will now be available at the login screen.

Add a user

An important feature in Windows is the provision for setting up more than one user account. This allows a single PC to be shared by a number of people, each with their own computing environment. The procedure for adding a user is as follows:

1. On the Charms bar, select Settings, Change PC settings
2. On the left, select Users. Under Other users you will see an Add a user link. Click it
3. At the next screen, enter an email address to associate with the new account. Click Next

Set up a Microsoft Account
You can use your Microsoft account to sign in to Xbox LIVE, Windows Phone and other Microsoft services.
Email address tom123456789@aol.com
New password ••••••••
Re-enter password ••••••••
First name Tom
Surname Smith
Country/region United States
Postal Code NY 1002

4. At the next screen, you set up a Microsoft account. At the final screen, confirm you're for real with the Captcha security code

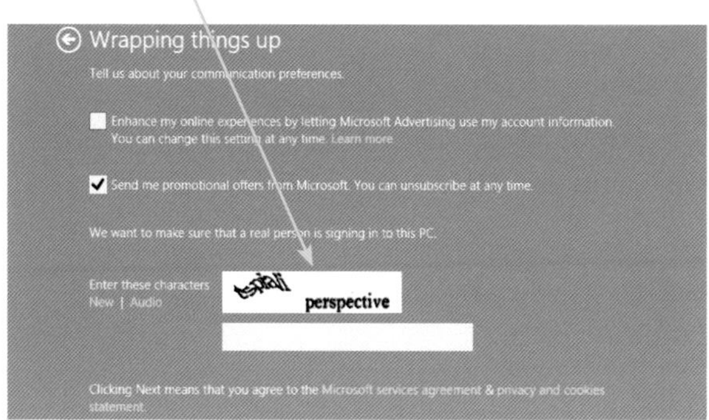

Next time the PC is started, the new user will be able to log in.

When a user is added to a Windows 8 PC, the account type can be either a local account or a Microsoft account.

Close Windows 8

As with many other user options in the new Windows 8 interface, where to go when you want to shut Windows down is not immediately obvious. There are, in fact, three ways to do it:

Settings menu

Activate the Charms bar and then click Settings. Click Power to reveal Sleep, Shut down and Restart options.

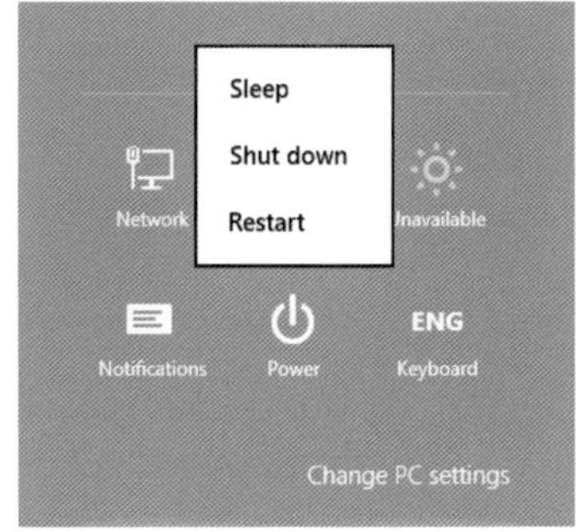

Note that these are the default options. Others, such as Hibernate, can be added in Power Options in the Control Panel.

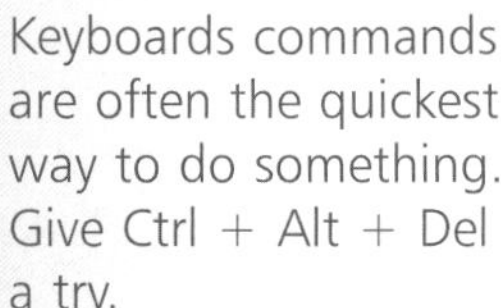

Keyboards commands are often the quickest way to do something. Give Ctrl + Alt + Del a try.

Keyboard

An extremely useful keyboard command that has been around for a long time is still available in Windows 8. This is Ctrl + Alt + Del. Pressing these keys sequentially opens the following screen:

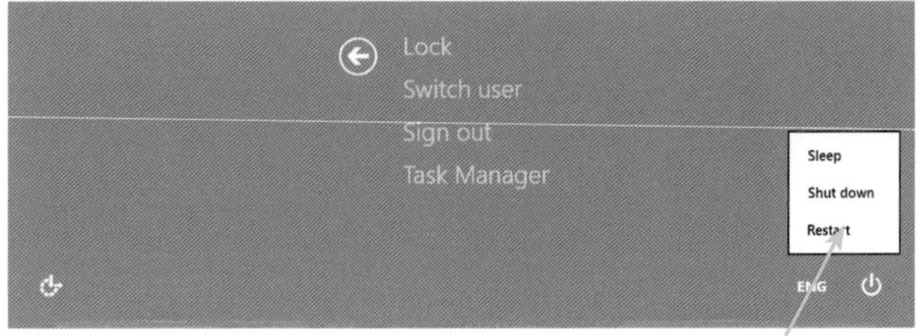

Click the Power icon to reveal the options

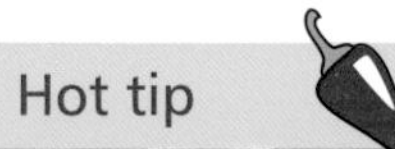

You can also create a Logoff tile. Type logoff on the Start screen. Right-click the result, and on the app bar at the bottom, click Pin to start.

Shutdown/Restart Shortcuts

This procedure lets you create your own power option shortcuts.

1. Create a shortcut named "Shutdown" on the desktop with value shutdown /s /t 0
2. Right-click the shortcut and select Pin to start
3. Repeat to create and pin a shortcut called "Restart" with value shutdown /r /t 0

You will now see Shutdown and Restart tiles on the Start screen.

5 Windows 8 apps

Apps are an integral part of the Windows 8 interface. We explain how they work, how to access their options, plus show some useful tips. We also review all the apps bundled with Windows 8.

Supplied with Windows 8

Windows 8 comes with a number of pre-installed applications, or "apps" as they are commonly known. They cover the most common applications for which a computer is used and so will enable many users to get off to a flying start with Windows 8.

The apps supplied with Windows 8 are:

- Mail
- People
- Messaging
- Calendar
- Photos
- Finance
- Weather
- Internet Explorer
- Store
- Maps
- SkyDrive
- Sport
- News
- Bing
- Travel
- Games
- Camera
- Music
- Video

Don't forget

Several of the bundled apps require the user to be logged in with a Microsoft account.

More apps can be downloaded from the Windows Store (shown below). At the time of writing there is not the huge selection available in the Apple Store and the Android stores, but this will change as time goes on.

Hot tip

If you need apps not supplied with Windows 8, the only place to get them is the Windows Store.

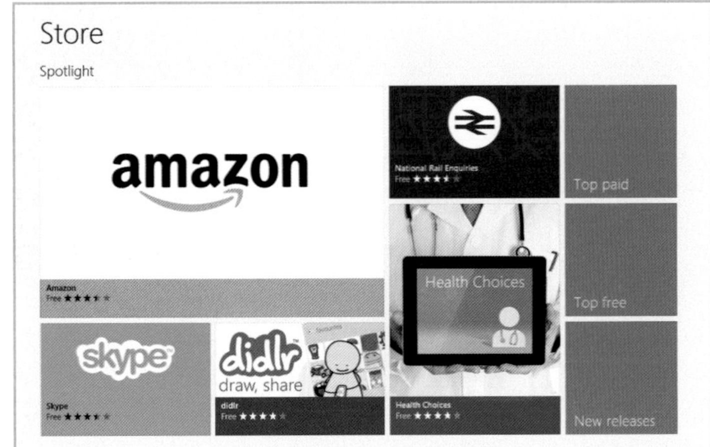

Start apps

We will take a brief look at some of the pre-installed apps – the ones not covered here will be reviewed in later chapters.

People

Windows operating systems have always provided a contact manager, which provided a useful means of keeping phone numbers, addresses, etc., in one place. However, the advent of social media websites, such as Twitter, Facebook and LinkedIn, has seen this type of information stored and used in new ways.

The People app is Microsoft's attempt to update their old Contacts manager to make it relevant to today's needs. It stores the data from your contacts in a cloud-based location, which means they can be accessed from anywhere in the world, and via any of your Windows 8 devices.

Furthermore, the app amalgamates data from all supported networks. Thus, people who use more than one social network will be recognized by the app as being the same person and all their data, whatever the source, is presented as a single contact link.

Hot tip

The People app also integrates with other apps. So from the app, you can send emails via the Mail app, messages via the Messaging app, map addresses with the Maps app, and more.

Messaging

This app is very similar to the Messaging app provided with Windows Phone 8. Essentially, it consists of a threads window for tracking conversations, a messages window that shows all the conversations in the selected thread, and a text box for adding comments to that thread.

Right-clicking on the screen activates an app bar at the bottom, which reveals various options. These include Status (for settings related to your online status), Delete (deletes specified selected threads), Switch (for switching between services), and New (start a new thread).

Calendar

An updated version of a traditional Microsoft application, the Calendar app doesn't really offer anything new. It has been designed to be easy to read, and free of unnecessary distractions. To this end, by default, the content displayed is kept to a minimum. Ease of navigation has been improved, there is a simple interface for adding events, many notification options, and some good advanced scheduling options.

Hot tip

Calendar syncs with Hotmail, Outlook, and Google accounts to bring all your events together for easy viewing.

...cont'd

Finance

The Finance app provides a wealth of finance-related information, with various tabs providing different types of data. You can drill down into items of interest to get more detailed information.

Beware

The Best of the Web feature effectively kicks the user out of the Finance app by switching to Internet Explorer when a suggested item is selected.

A Watchlist feature provides a customizable list of companies that the user wants to keep tabs on. Information that can be monitored includes stock market performance (current and historic), revenue, profit, company profile, and more.

The Currencies tab displays lists of world currencies and provides a handy currency convertor. The Best of the Web tab shows you a list of financial websites relevant to your location.

Weather

The Weather app provides three tabs. The first is the Home screen, which displays weather conditions for the currently-selected location. This includes an overview, an hourly breakdown, and a range of weather related maps.

The Places tab allows more locations to be monitored, each of which can be pinned to the Start screen as a "sub-tile". Thus, a group of locations can be created and monitored directly from the Start screen.

A World weather tab shows a world map that displays weather links for major cities. Clicking the links provides more detailed information.

Sport

Don't forget

The Sports app only covers a few major world sports.

As with the Finance and Weather apps, the Sports app is dynamic and provides updated content in real-time. A number of tabs are devoted to major sports such as American Football, Basketball, Baseball, Ice Hockey, Formula 1, MotoGP and Soccer.

The Favorite Teams feature allows you to specify and monitor teams from various sports. Drilling down enables you to access detailed information such as the latest team news, results, fixture lists, leading players, etc. Favorite teams can also be pinned to the Start screen as sub-tiles.

Currently, this app only covers the sports mentioned above and thus is somewhat restricted in the content it provides.

News

Most people like to keep abreast of what's happening both in their locality and on the world stage. Microsoft's News app provides the conduit.

The app has three tabs, the first of which, Bing Daily, provides headlines covering a range of topics including news (world and local), sport, finance, entertainment, business, politics, science and health.

The My News tab enables you to select any topic under the sun for which you would like news updates, while the Sources tab allows you to specify sources from which to receive information and updates. These are mostly local to your part of the world.

Hot tip

When a news story is clicked, it opens in the website that provides it.

Bing

Clicking the Bing app opens Microsoft's search engine, Bing. The app greets you with a stripped-down version of the home page you'll see by navigating to **Bing.com** in a browser, i.e. with the search bar at the top, and the picture of the day as the background.

Search results are presented in a grid that scrolls to the right – more results appear as you scroll. Unlike the browser version of Bing, related results are restricted to Web and Images.

The number of search results is limited to 100. This may be restrictive if you cannot find what you are looking for fairly quickly. Another drawback is that when a search result is clicked, the site opens in your default browser (so you may as well have done the search from the browser in the first place).

Beware

When a link is clicked in the Bing app, it switches to the default browser. However, the top-left corner hotspot provides a way back to Bing.

Travel

Windows 8's Travel app is a particularly useful app. You can browse through a large list of popular destinations, and also see a number of interesting 360 degree panoramas.

A flight tool is included that lets the user search for flights to and from any international airport in the world. Equally useful is a Hotel tool so that having booked your flight, you can also book somewhere to stay when you arrive.

The Best of the Web feature provides a list of relevant websites.

Apps bar

We mentioned on page 56 that at first glance, the Start screen seems to offer no user options, i.e. no Start button or taskbar. However, it does have a taskbar of sorts and it's called the app bar.

It can be accessed by right-clicking on the screen, pressing Winkey + Z, or swiping from the top and bottom edges of the screen. When you do any of these actions, you'll see the app bar appear at the bottom of the screen:

As the screenshot above demonstrates, it provides just one option – All apps. Clicking this shows not only all the apps installed on the computer but also all the desktop programs. These are differentiated by a different style of tile as shown below:

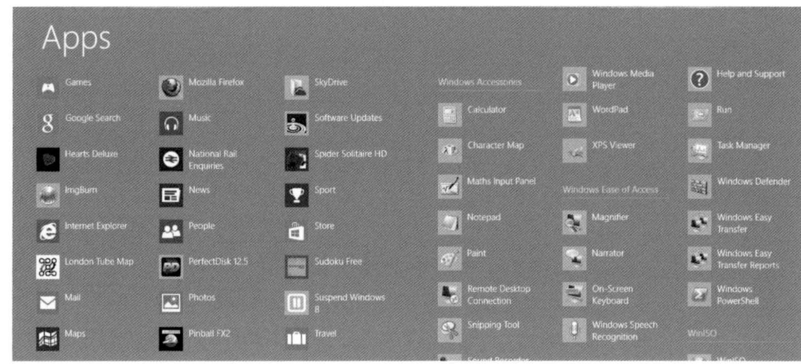

Windows 8 Apps Desktop programs

You find mainly Windows 8 Apps on the left but there are some Desktop programs (e.g. SkyDrive and PerfectDisk 12.5). On the right you see Desktop programs and various system functions, arranged by the folder names under which they were installed.

When in this view, right-clicking on any app reveals two further app bar options. If the app is currently pinned to the Start screen, there will be a Unpin from Start option and an Uninstall option. If the app is not currently pinned to the Start screen, you will see Pin to Start and Uninstall options.

Don't forget

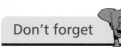

The apps bar is shown (or dismissed) when the user right-clicks on the screen, presses Winkey + Z, or swipes from the top or bottom edge of the screen.

Hot tip

In some apps, such as News, Finance and Sport, an app bar appears at the top of the screen. This provides content-related options.

Right-clicking a traditional Desktop program produces different options. For example, Pin to taskbar, Run as administrator, Open file location, etc.

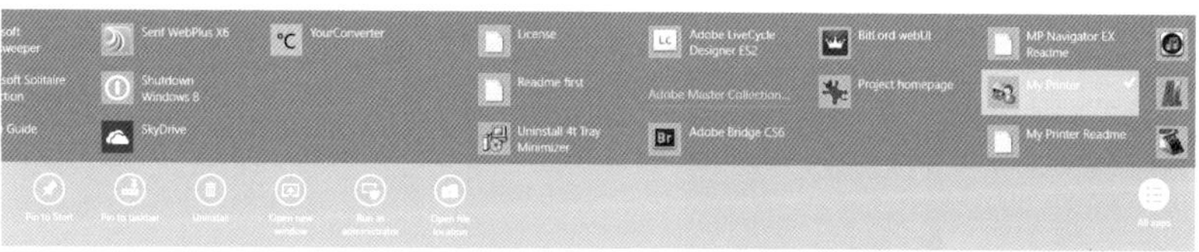

The app bar becomes even more useful when it is used in conjunction with an app. For example, if you right-click on the Calendar app's tile (in the Start screen view, not the All app view) you will see options for: Unpin from Start, Uninstall, Smaller (or Larger) and Turn live tile off. This is shown in the image below:

Selecting Unpin from Start removes the app's tile from the Start screen, Uninstall deletes the app from the computer, Smaller halves the size of the tile (Larger doubles it), and Turn live tile off switches off the tile's live content. Note that these options are common to most apps.

Right-clicking on different apps will reveal different options. Also, activating the app bar from within an open app rather than right-clicking on its tile produces still different options.

Using the Calendar app as an example again, this time we get options for: View (day, week or month), Today (go to the current day), and New (create a new event).

As another example, if you activate the app bar from within the Video or Music apps, you will get various options related to media playback, such as Play, Next, Repeat, Previous, etc. So you can see that the apps bar is contextual and shows related options.

There are no options for resizing the Start screen itself. It runs in full-screen mode only. With regard to the tiles there are just two options – larger and smaller.

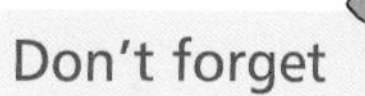

When used within apps, the options offered by the app bar are related to the app in use.

App switcher & Task list

On page 57 we saw how the App switcher can be accessed via the left-hand corner hotspots. This is initiated by touch or with the mouse. However, a keyboard shortcut can also be used to open the switcher.

Don't forget

"Winkey" as in Step 1 refers to the Windows key. This is usually located close to the space bar (see page 60).

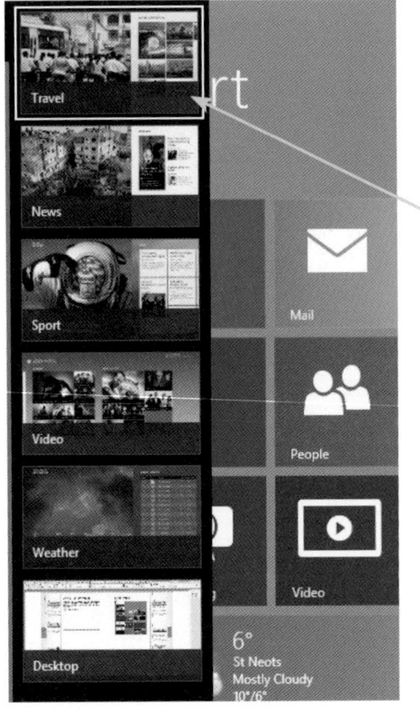

1. Open the App switcher by pressing Winkey + Tab
2. The first app in the list is automatically selected
3. Keeping the Winkey depressed with your thumb, tap the Tab key with your forefinger to move down the list. When the focus is on the desired program release the Winkey

The program will now be moved to the foreground. This shortcut works whether you are on the Start screen or the Desktop.

However, it only works with Windows 8 apps. If you are on the Desktop and need a quick way to switch between programs there, or between apps and Desktop programs, you can use another keyboard shortcut known as the Task list. This is Alt + Tab.

Hot tip

When using the Task list, you can also select programs with the arrow keys.

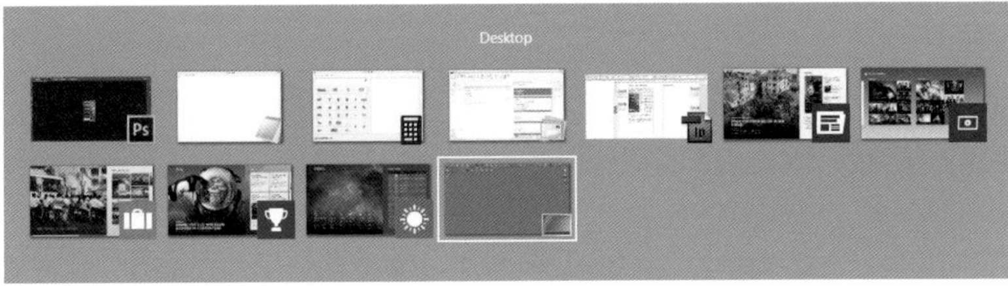

Above, we see open Windows 8 apps and Desktop programs displayed in the Task list. Use the Tab key to quickly switch between them.

Snap apps

Windows 8 apps are what Microsoft describe as "immersive" applications. What this means is that they run in full-screen mode. On a small tablet screen this doesn't present a problem but on a large-wide-screen monitor, it deprives the user of a large amount of space that could otherwise be usefully employed.

A partial solution to this issue is offered by the Snap app feature. This enables two apps to be run side-by-side, with one of them running in a small section on one side of the screen. This is demonstrated below where we see the Bing search app snapped to the left of a Minesweeper game.

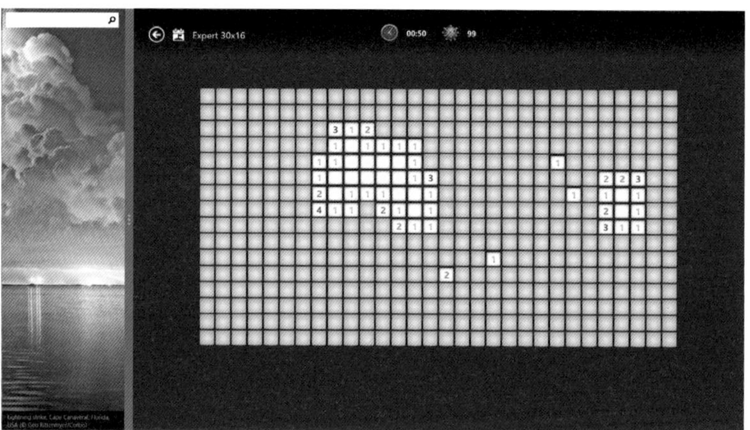

To snap an app to the side of another, open one app, press the Winkey and open the second. Then use Winkey + Tab to open the App switcher. Right-click on the app you want to snap to the side and select either Snap left or Snap right as shown below:

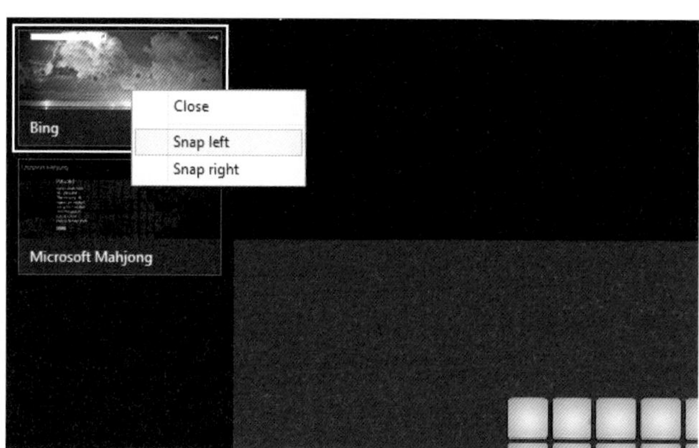

Hot tip

For the Windows 8 Snap feature to work, the display must have a width of at least 1366 pixels. If you are having problems, check this out by going to the Control Panel, Appearance and Resolution, Display, Adjust Resolution.

Hot tip

One way in which this feature may prove to be useful is that it enables a Windows 8 app to be run alongside the Desktop or vice versa. For example, you can use the Desktop to do your work while simultaneously keeping an eye on your emails by having the email app snapped to one side.

Close apps

Closing an app is very simple to do once you know how but, as many users have discovered, the method of doing so is far from obvious.

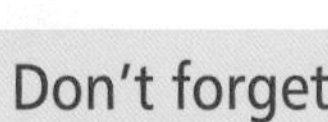

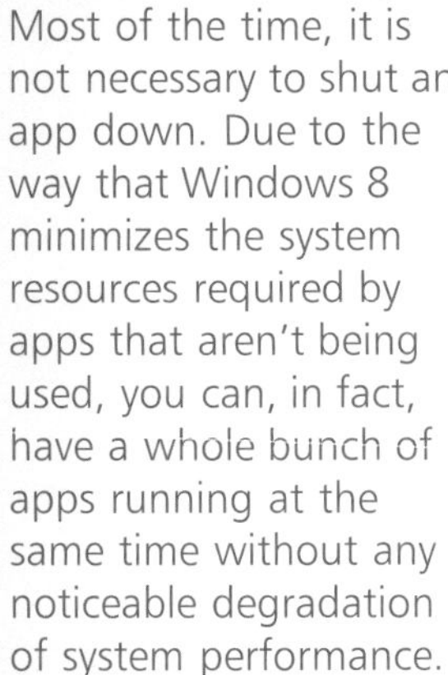

Most of the time, it is not necessary to shut an app down. Due to the way that Windows 8 minimizes the system resources required by apps that aren't being used, you can, in fact, have a whole bunch of apps running at the same time without any noticeable degradation of system performance.

Before we go any further with this, it must be pointed out that usually it is not actually necessary to close apps. This is because when a new app is opened, other running apps are switched to a state of suspension in which they use very little in the way of system resources.

However, there may be situations in which it is desirable or even necessary to close down an app. The following are four ways to do this:

1) Simply press ALT + F4 – this kills the app instantly

2) Hover the mouse at the top edge of the screen and you will see the cursor turn into a hand. Drag downwards and the app window will be reduced to a thumbnail. Simply drag the thumbnail off the bottom edge of the screen

3) You can right-click the app icon in App Switcher and select Close

4) Type task manager while on the Start screen and you'll see the Task Manager icon appear. Click this to open the utility and select the Processes tab where you'll see a list of all running apps and programs as shown below

A quick way of opening the Task manager is to press Ctrl + Shift + Esc.

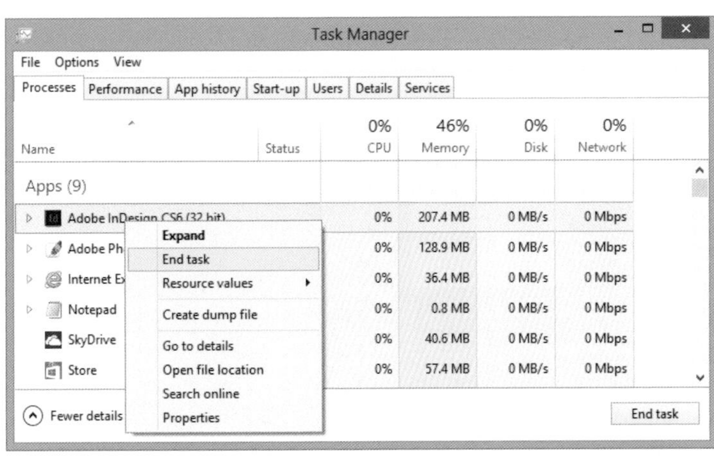

Right-click the app you wish to close and select "End Task".

Reader

Reader is an app provided by Windows 8 that can open PDF files. By default, this app is not placed on the Start screen so you have to go looking for it (or just double-click a PDF file).

Right-click on the Start screen and click All apps at the right of the app bar. Look down the list of apps on the left of the screen and you will see the Reader tile.

As with other Windows 8 apps, Reader runs in full-screen mode and is simple and straightforward in concept. Open a PDF file and that's all will you see – the PDF file. No toolbars or options.

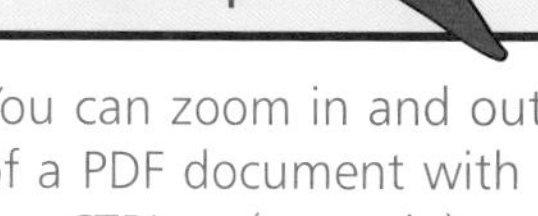

Hot tip

You can zoom in and out of a PDF document with the CTRL + (zoom in) and CTRL – (zoom out) keyboard shortcuts.

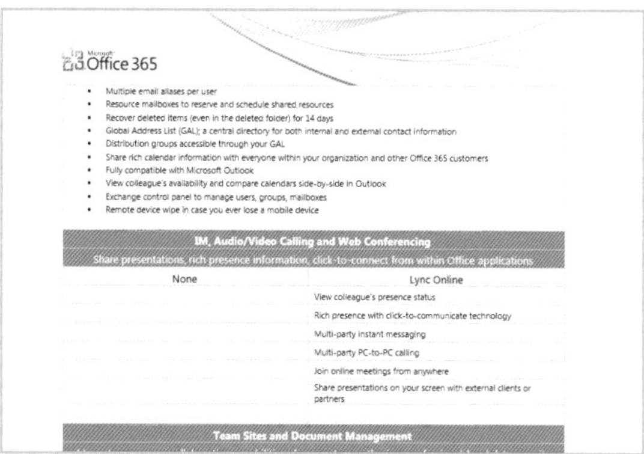

Microsoft Office 365

- Multiple email aliases per user
- Resource mailboxes to reserve and schedule shared resources
- Recover deleted items (even in the deleted folder) for 14 days
- Global Address List (GAL); a central directory for both internal and external contact information
- Distribution groups accessible through your GAL
- Share rich calendar information with everyone within your organization and other Office 365 customers
- Fully compatible with Microsoft Outlook
- View colleague's availability and compare calendars side-by-side in Outlook
- Exchange control panel to manage users, groups, mailboxes
- Remote device wipe in case you ever lose a mobile device

IM, Audio/Video Calling and Web Conferencing Share presentations, rich presence information, click-to-connect from within Office applications	
None	Lync Online
	View colleague's presence status
	Rich presence with click-to-communicate technology
	Multi-party instant messaging
	Multi-party PC-to-PC calling
	Join online meetings from anywhere
	Share presentations on your screen with external clients or partners

Team Sites and Document Management

Right-click on the screen, however, and the app's feature set is revealed.

Reader provides three reading modes: One Page, Two Pages, and Continuous. In One Page view, only one whole page will be seen at a time. In Two Pages view, Reader will display two pages side-by-side.

Hot tip

Reader may be simple but it performs very well. It actually opens PDF files much faster than the native PDF application, Adobe Reader.

Pages can be navigated both vertically and horizontally, depending on the page view being used. It is possible to zoom in and out, and also find specific words with the Find feature.

You can print from the app by pressing Winkey + P to open the Printer list. It is also possible to highlight text, add notes and fill out forms.

SkyDrive

As we explained on page 21, SkyDrive is a Microsoft application that allows users to store data in the cloud via a Microsoft account.

Hot tip

A Skydrive account can be accessed in two ways: directly from a browser and via the Windows 8 SkyDrive app. It is important that you be aware of this because when it is accessed via a browser, many more options are available.

To get started, click the SkyDrive tile on the Start screen and log in with your Microsoft account. If you don't have an account, you will need to create one. Once done, you will be presented with a number of built-in folders:

Hot tip

Microsoft SkyDrive creates a SkyDrive folder that can be placed anywhere – Desktop, taskbar, etc. Any files placed in the SkyDrive folder are automatically uploaded to the cloud.

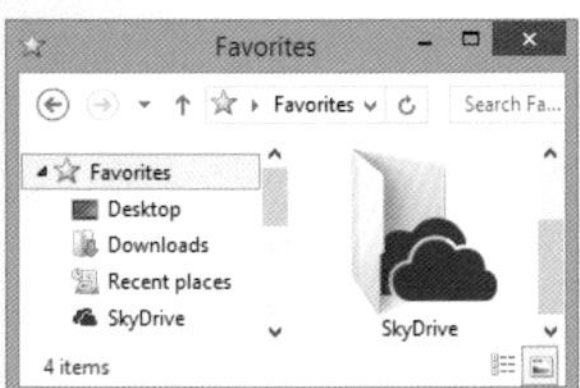

Right-clicking on the screen opens an app bar at the bottom of the screen. This provides various options such as New folder, Upload, and Thumbnails. These enable you to create more folders and, having done so, upload files to them. Right-clicking directly on a folder (or a file within a folder) reveals a Delete option at the left of the app bar.

And that's about it – the SkyDrive app provides little functionality other than the ability to upload and view files in the cloud and download them. Where it does shine, however, is that due to it being integrated with a Microsoft account it can be used to synchronize photos, video, email, documents, etc, across a number of separate devices, such as PCs, smartphones, and tablets.

Note that there is an element of confusion with SkyDrive as there are actually two versions of it, each providing different options: The first is the Windows 8 app discussed above, while the second is Microsoft SkyDrive, a free Desktop app that can be downloaded from **http://windows.microsoft.com/en-US/skydrive/**and installed on any PC (except those running Windows RT).

6 Desktop and Taskbar

You can control how Windows sets up the screen so that it displays text and graphics at the right size. You can also take advantage of multiple monitors if available, and you can choose a Desktop theme with the style, appearance and features that most appeal to you.

Desktop app

As we have seen, Windows 8 provides two interfaces – the new Windows 8 interface and the traditional Desktop that has been around since Windows 95.

However, millions of people, business users in particular, are going to have little or no use for the new interface and will instead want to use the Desktop. The problem here is that Windows 8 insists on parking these people where they don't want to be – on the Windows 8 Start screen.

The Winkey + B shortcut will take you to the Desktop from the Start screen.

It's not a problem getting from there to the Desktop – all you have to do is click the Desktop app tile, which is pinned to the Start screen.

The Desktop app serves one function only – it takes the user to the Desktop. It has no features or options.

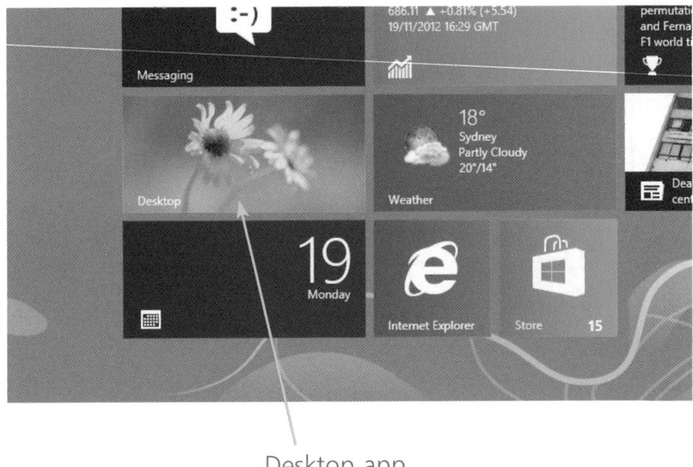

Desktop app

However, for the users who don't need it, it would be better if it wasn't necessary to negotiate the Start screen at all.

While there is no option in Windows for bypassing the Start screen, there are third-party programs that can do this. A good example is Classic Shell. This is a simple application that bypasses the Start screen completely, taking the user directly to the Desktop. The Start screen is still there and can be accessed in the normal way should users wish to do so, but it is not forced on them.

Classic Shell also replaces a number of useful features that have been removed in Windows 8. Examples are the Start button and Start menu.

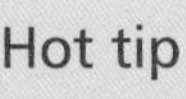

Classic Shell is a free download from **http://classicshell.sourceforge.net** There are quite a few other programs of the same type available as well.

Switching

Carrying on from the previous page, many Desktop users are, of course, going to find some aspects of the new Windows 8 interface useful, and thus will want to switch to it on occasion.

There are two ways to do this:

Windows Key

The simplest method is to press the Windows key. It doesn't matter where you are in the Desktop interface, this key will take you immediately to the Start screen.

Windows key

Start screen picture

Activating the bottom-left corner hotspot while on the Desktop reveals a small representation of the Start screen.

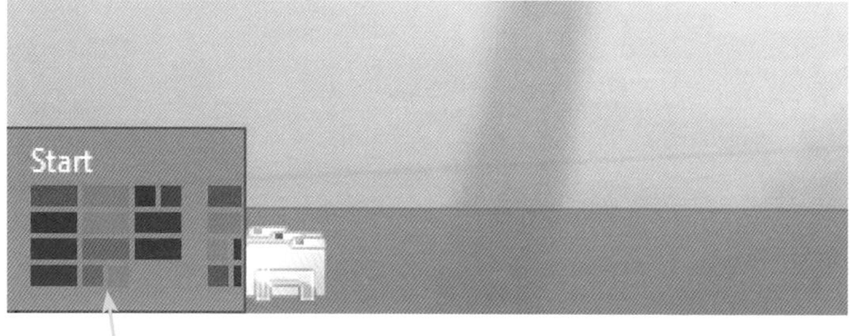

Left-clicking on it will also take you to the Start screen.

Hot tip

When on the Desktop, the Windows key switches the user to the Start screen. When on the Start screen, it toggles between the Start screen and the last app to be opened.

Start Desktop apps

There are various ways of starting an application:

Start screen tiles/Desktop icons

Tiles and icons are actually shortcuts that link to a program's executable file. So, to open a Start screen app, just left-click on the tile; this activates the app, which then opens on the screen. Programs on the Desktop are opened in the same way.

Taskbar icons

Icons on the taskbar are application shortcuts as well. Click one, and the associated application will open on the Desktop.

Search charm

Applications that are located on the Start screen, Desktop and taskbar are easy to locate – they are literally right in front of your eyes. How about programs you can't see though?

Hot tip 

You can open any program on the PC from the Search charm. If it's a Windows 8 app it will open on the Start screen; other programs will open on the Desktop.

Windows 8's Search charm is the answer:

1. Open the Charms bar on the right of the screen
2. Click Search to open the Search charm

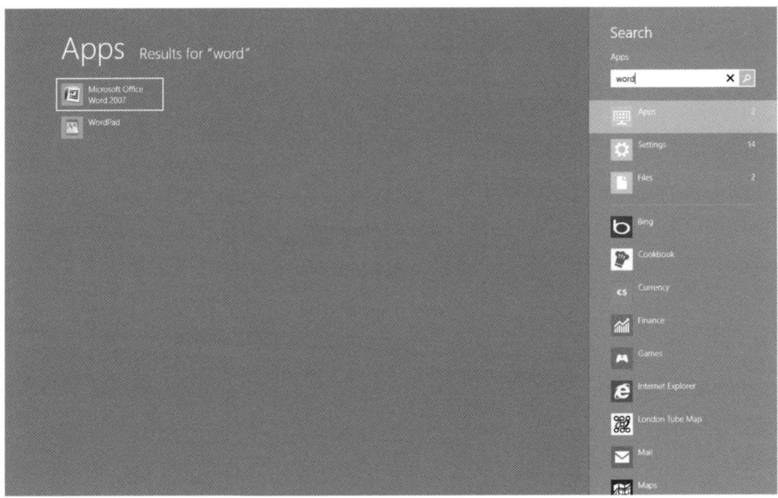

3. Enter the name of the app in the search box
4. On the left you will see the app. Just click to run it

Personalize

You can give your computer a personal touch by changing the computer's window color, sounds, desktop background, screen saver and other aspects. You can change the attributes individually, or select a pre-configured theme.

There are several ways to view and change the current theme:

1. Right-click the Desktop and select Personalize

2. Go to the Control Panel and under Appearance and Personalization, click Change the theme

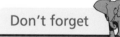

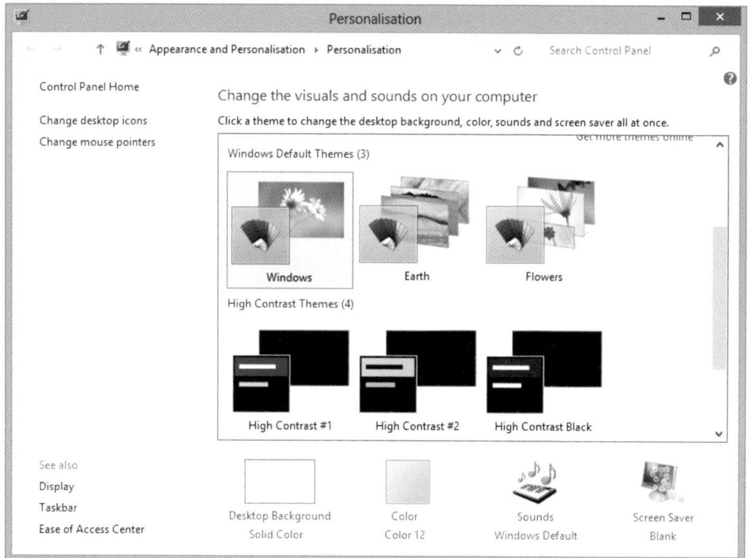

3. You'll see the current theme with its desktop background, Windows color, sounds and screen saver (if any is assigned)

4. Select any of the suggested themes, and it is immediately applied, and its components are displayed

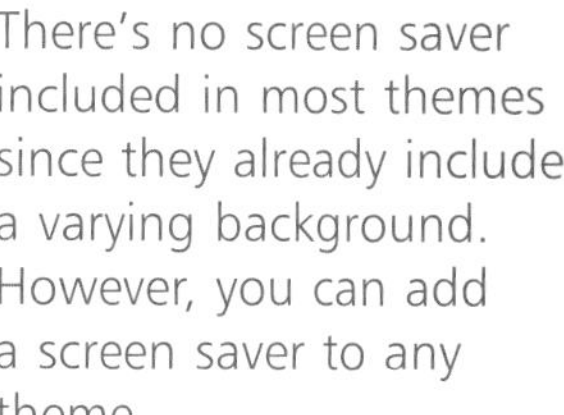

There's no screen saver included in most themes since they already include a varying background. However, you can add a screen saver to any theme.

...cont'd

Hot tip

There will be a theme for the location appropriate to your installed version, for example USA or United Kingdom.

5. In the example below the Windows theme has been selected

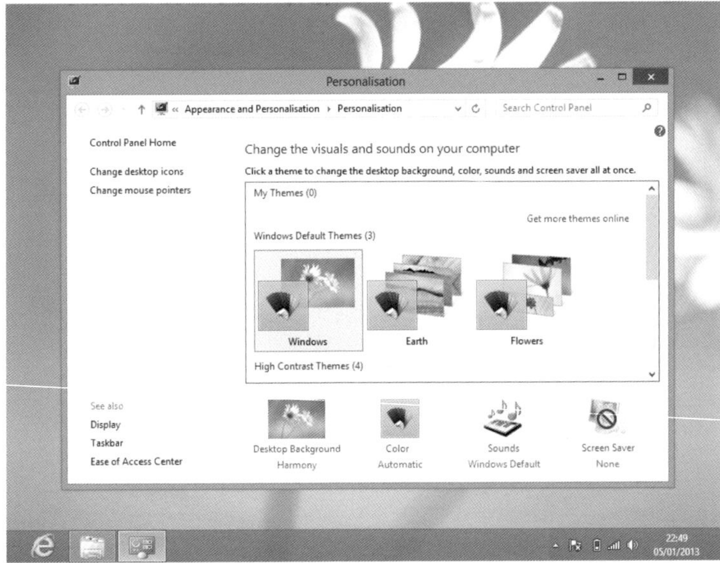

Don't forget

By default, the images will change every thirty minutes, to the next one in sequence. You can adjust the timing, and you can select random order.

6. If you don't like the background image of a particular theme, click Desktop Background to select another. Below, we see the Windows theme as above but now with a different background

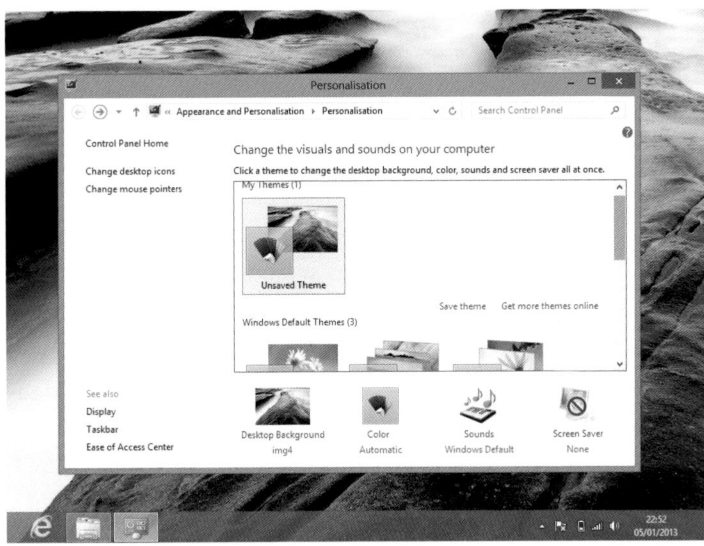

Hot tip

When you change a theme's background, the color of both the Window borders and the taskbar will change as well. If you wish to revert to the original color, click Color and reselect it.

Create a theme

1. Right-click the Desktop, click Personalize, select the existing theme, then select Desktop Background

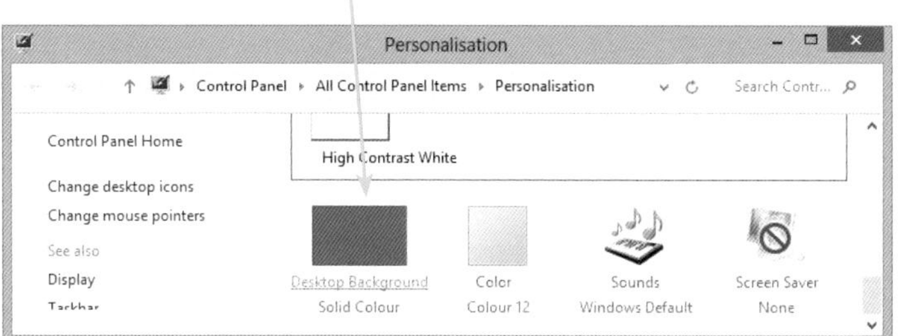

2. Click Browse, select the picture folder containing the images required and click OK

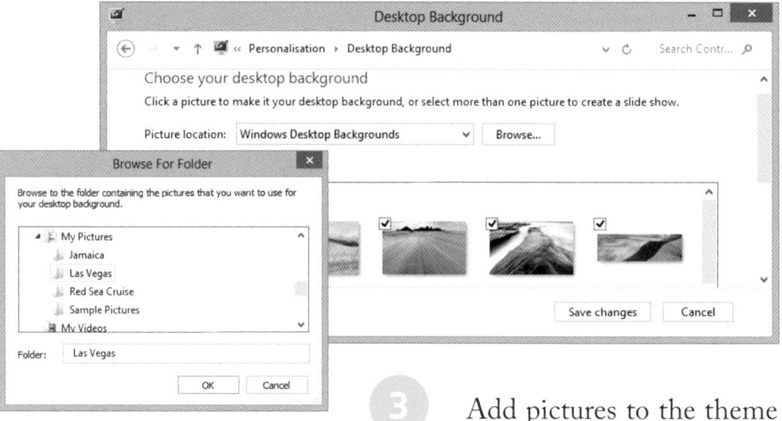

3. Add pictures to the theme

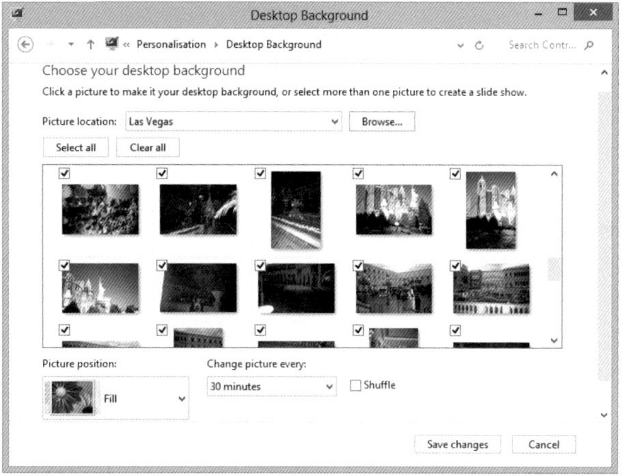

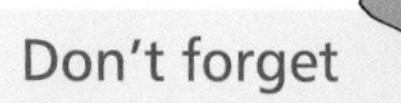

Don't forget

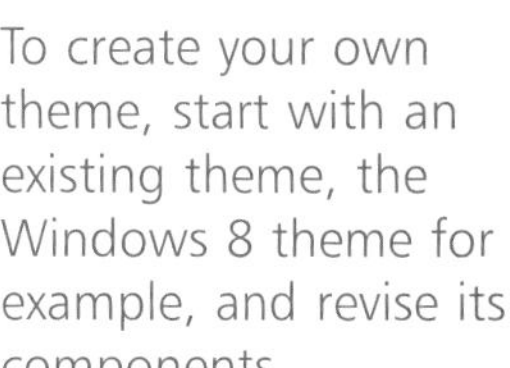

To create your own theme, start with an existing theme, the Windows 8 theme for example, and revise its components.

Hot tip

Select all the pictures or just a selection, set the timing, then click Save changes to add them to the theme you are creating.

...cont'd

The modified theme is added to the My Themes section, as an unsaved theme.

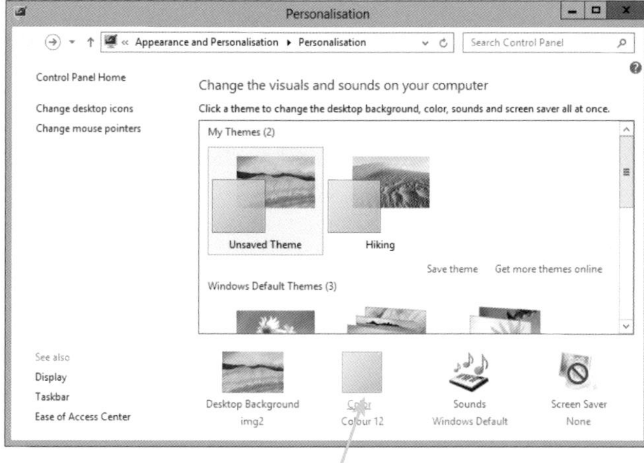

4 Select Color to view Window color settings, and click Save changes, if you make any revisions

You can adjust color intensity. Click Show color mixer, to adjust the hue, saturation and brightness.

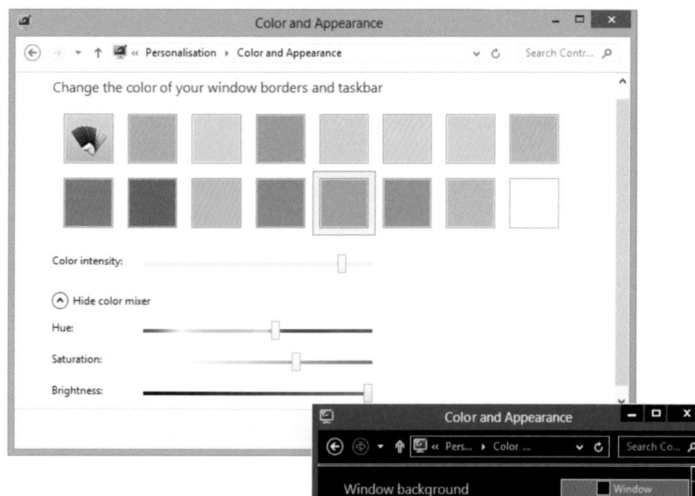

If you are revising a basic or high contrast theme, you will get a different version of the Color and Appearance dialog box when you select the Color link.

Sound scheme

Next, choose a sound scheme:

1. Click the Sounds link for the scheme you are creating, to change the sounds associated with Windows actions

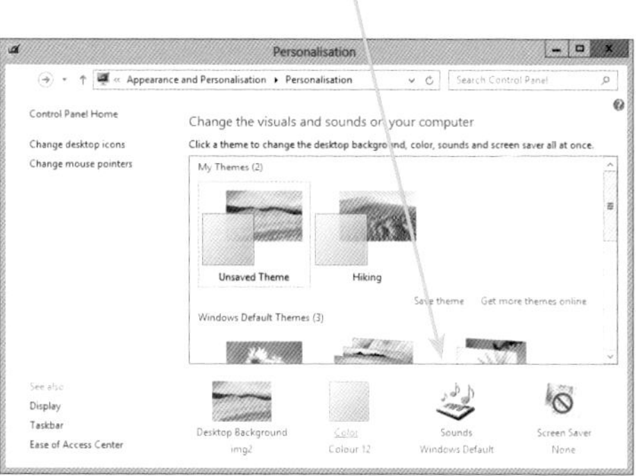

2. Select the Sound Scheme box and choose from the predefined sound schemes to find which you prefer

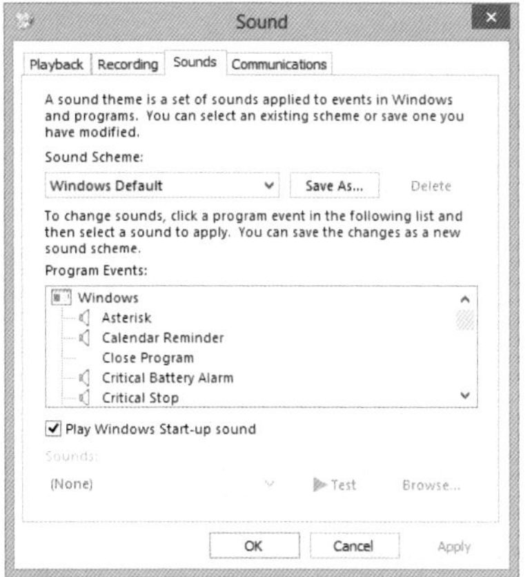

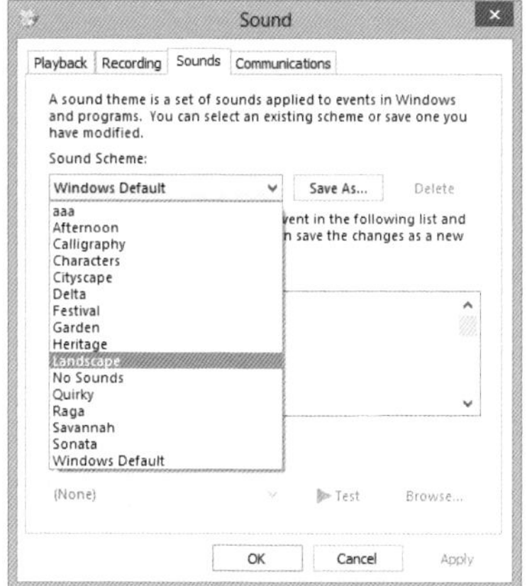

3. Select a program event such as Windows Logon and click Test to listen to the sound

4. Click Browse to choose a different sound file

5. Click Save As to save the revised sound scheme

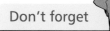

Don't forget

Most of the Windows themes provide their own sound scheme, so you can try these out to see which you prefer.

Hot tip

Click the box Play Windows Startup Sound to avoid sound when Windows starts up. Reselect the box to reapply sound.

Screen saver

These days screen savers are not necessary. However, they do improve security and privacy by hiding your information when you leave the computer. To add a screen saver to your theme:

1. Click the Screen Saver link for your theme

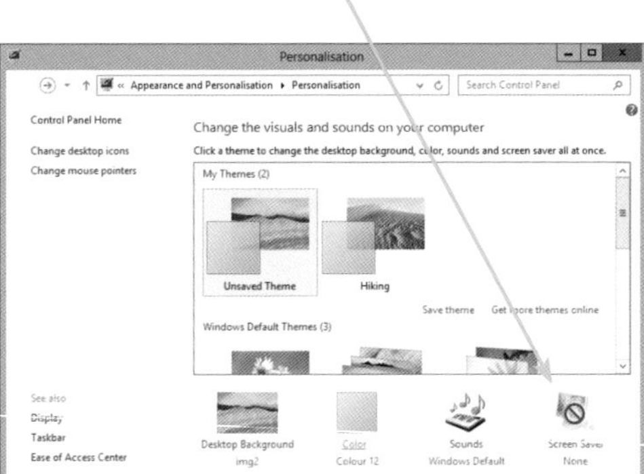

2. Click the Screen Saver box to show the list available

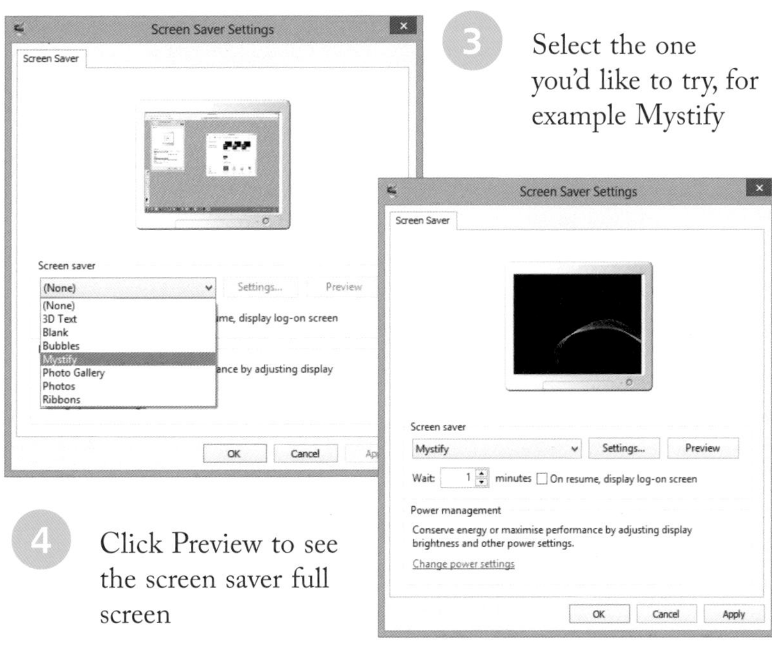

3. Select the one you'd like to try, for example Mystify

4. Click Preview to see the screen saver full screen

5. Set the delay time, click Settings to review adjustments, and click OK to add the screen saver to the theme

Don't forget

To ensure that the password will be required to access the account and applications, select the option On resume, display logon screen.

Save the theme

To save your theme:

1. Select the Save theme option

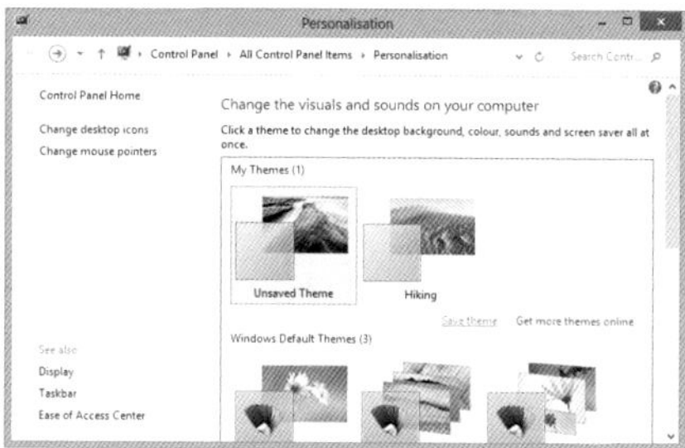

2. Provide a name for your new theme and click Save

3. The theme remains in My Themes, under its new name

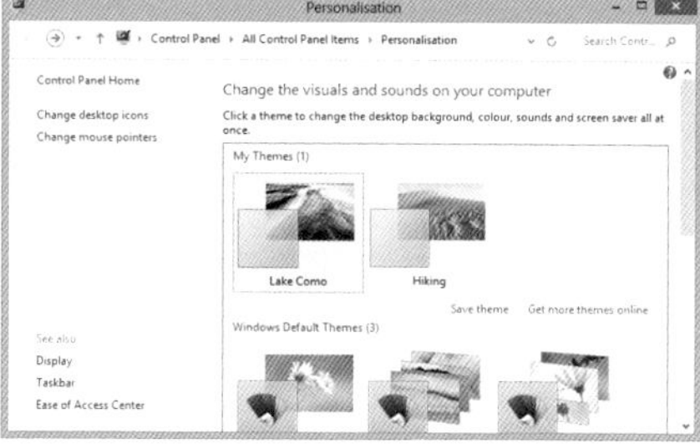

The theme file is stored in the user's applications data area, e.g. C:\users\Michael\AppData\Local\Microsoft\Windows\Themes, along with any Windows themes that have been downloaded.

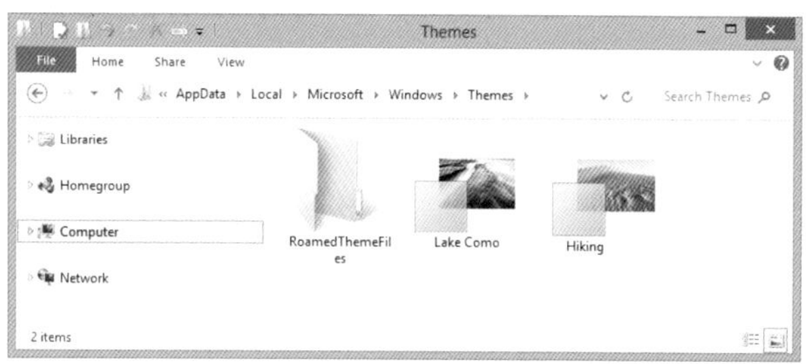

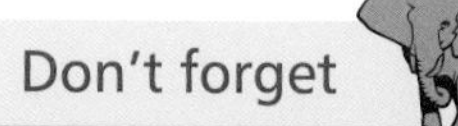

Don't forget

The Unsaved Theme is stored as the Custom theme, until you choose to Save theme.

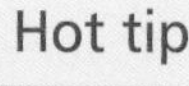

Hot tip

If you cannot see the AppData folder in your User folder, you may need to Show hidden files and folders.

To make the theme available to other users:

1. Right-click the theme and select Save theme for sharing

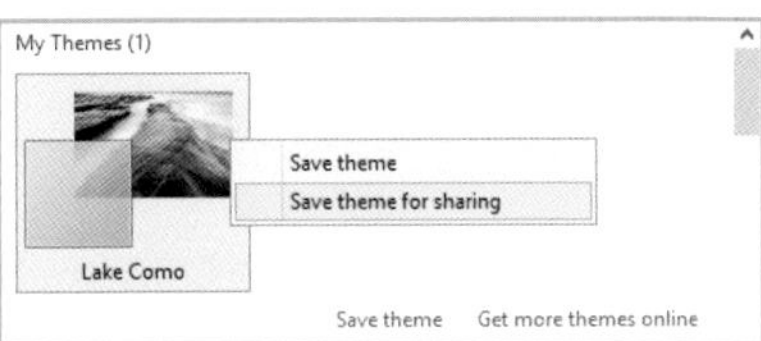

2. Specify the name and folder for the theme and click Save

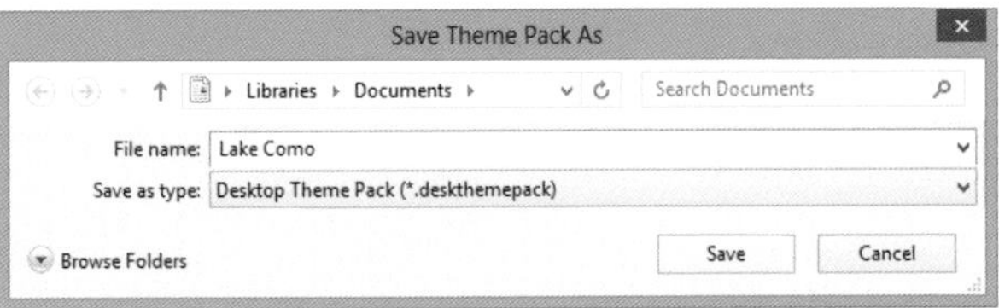

3. The background images, colors, sounds and other settings for your theme are saved in a file of type .themepack

Downloading this file or selecting it on a shared network drive will make the theme available to the other users.

You can remove themes from My Themes when they are no longer needed.

1. Make sure that the theme is not currently selected

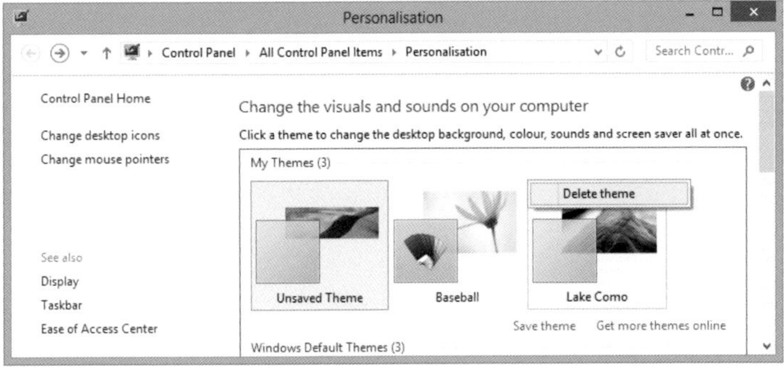

2. Right-click and select Delete theme

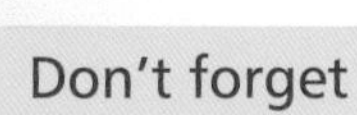
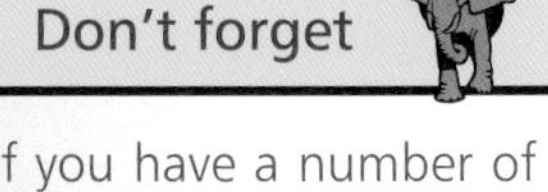

Don't forget

If you have a number of photos as background images, the theme can be quite large.

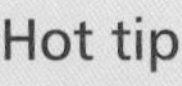

Hot tip

By default, the themepack file will be saved in your documents folder, but you can choose any location, for example a HomeGroup folder.

Screen resolution

To adjust the screen resolution:

1. Right-click the Desktop and select Screen Resolution from the menu

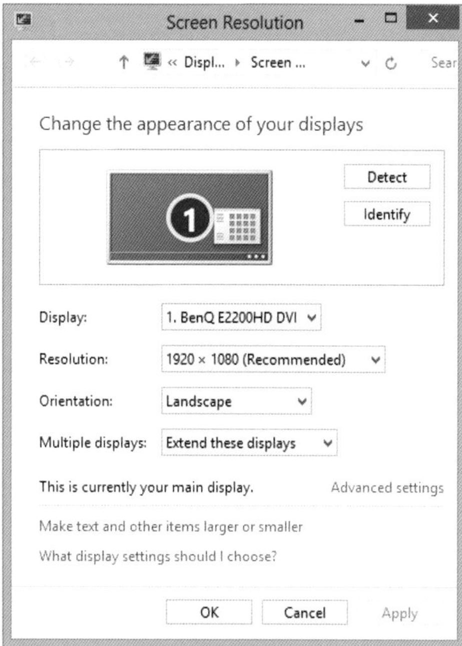

2. Click the Resolution box, select the desired resolution, then click OK to apply

3. Click Keep changes to confirm the revision

The values that are offered depend on the configuration.

The computer screen shown offers four settings at the physical aspect ratio (8 x 5) plus the minimum 800 x 600 and intermediate values at other ratios.

Using these may distort the image, e.g. make circles appear oval.

Screen size	Aspect ratio
1920 x 1200	**8x5**
1920 x 1080	16x9
1768 x 992	16x9
1680 x 1050	**8x5**
1600 x 1200	4x3
1440 x 900	**8x5**
1280 x 1024	5x4
1280 x 800	**8x5**
1280 x 720	16x9
1176 x 664	16x9
1024 x 768	4x3
800 x 600	**4x3**

Hot tip

The screen resolution controls the size of the screen contents. Lower resolutions (e.g. 800 x 600) have larger items so fewer can be displayed. Higher resolutions (e.g. 1920 x 1200) have smaller and sharper items, and more can be viewed on the screen.

Hot tip

Intermediate values will appear individually when you drag the slider to that part of the bar.

Don't forget

You can also change the orientation from Landscape to Portrait, useful for tablet PCs and for a monitor that can be rotated.

Taskbar

The purpose of the taskbar is to launch and monitor running applications. The version provided in Windows 8 has two specific regions – a small section at the right called the Notification area, and the main body of the taskbar on which program icons are displayed.

To explore the taskbar properly and see what it can do, it is necessary to go into its properties (right-click on the taskbar and select Properties).

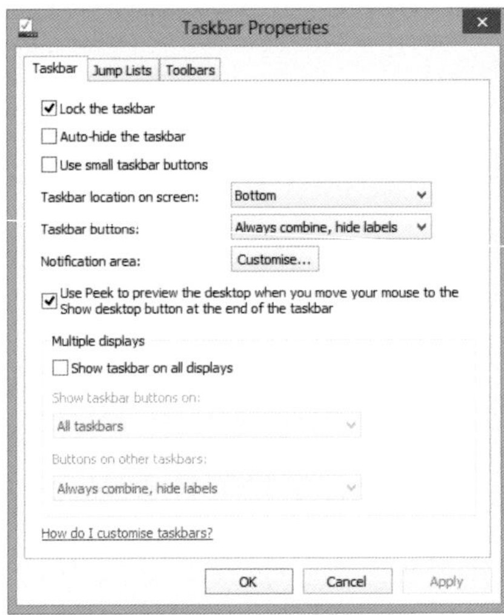

The taskbar tab provides various options. These include:

Locking and unlocking the taskbar. When unlocked it can be moved to any edge of the screen and also its depth can be increased.

Those of you with keen eyesight can reduce the size of the taskbar icons. This enables the bar to hold more of them.

Before you can move or resize the taskbar, it must be unlocked.

You can alter the way taskbar icons are presented. Options include:

- **Always combine, hide labels** – each app appears as a single, unlabeled icon, even if several windows for that app are open
- **Combine when taskbar is full** – each window is shown as an individual icon. When the taskbar becomes crowded, apps with multiple open windows collapse into a single icon
- **Never combine** – each window is shown as an individual, labeled icon, and are never combined regardless of how many are open. As more apps and windows open, icons get smaller, and will eventually scroll

From the taskbar tab, you can also customize the Notification area, e.g. which icons and notifications to display.

Hot tip

When the "Use Peek to preview the desktop..." option is enabled, hovering your mouse at the far-right of the taskbar will return you to the Desktop view, i.e. all open windows will be minimized. To get them back again just left-click.

You will also find options for configuring the taskbar on multiple displays as shown below:

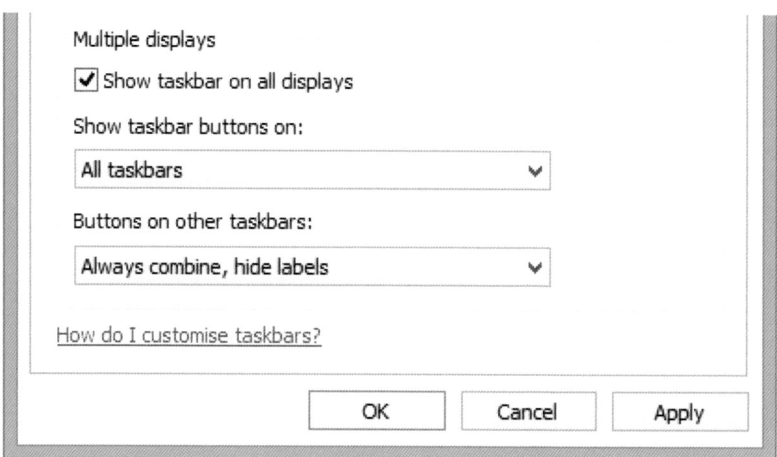

For example, you can choose to have the taskbar showing on all your displays, and also how program icons are displayed.

Jump lists (a list of shortcuts to recently opened files) are an important taskbar feature. You see these when right-clicking on a taskbar icon. The jump list tab provides related options:

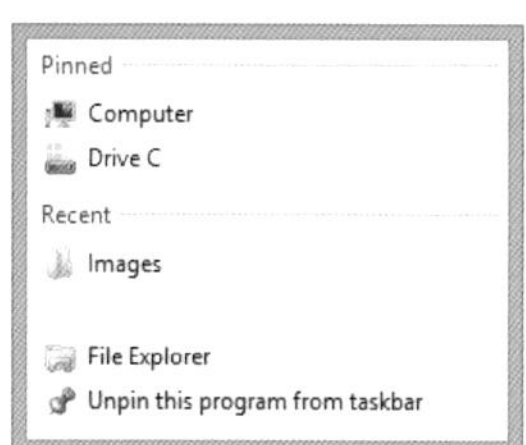

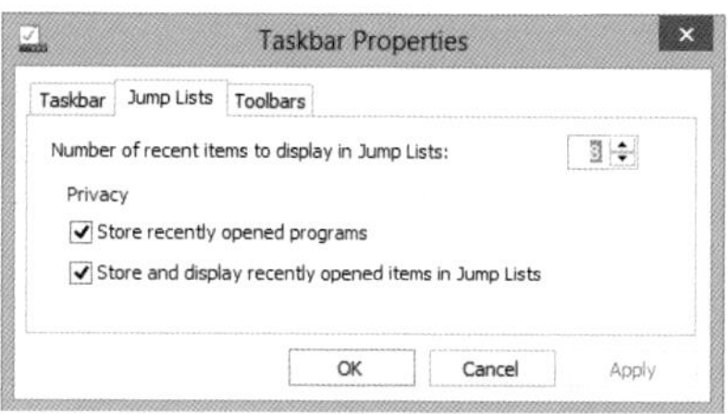

As you can see from the screenshot above, these include the number of recent items to display, and also a Privacy option that prevents the display of recently opened files and/or programs.

Any program can be added, i.e. "pinned" to the taskbar – simply right-click and select Pin to taskbar. Alternatively, you can place it manually by drag and drop.

The final tab in Taskbar Properties is Toolbars. This shows a list of pre-configured toolbars that can be added to the taskbar.

Hot tip

Desktop items can be pinned to the Start screen by right-clicking and selecting Pin to Start.

Hot tip

Folders and files cannot be added to the taskbar. However, they can be dragged to the File Explorer icon on the taskbar and accessed from its jumplist.

Hot tip

By right-clicking on the taskbar and selecting Toolbars, New toolbar..., you can create your own taskbar toolbars.

Power users menu

One of the major changes in Windows 8 is the omission of the Start button, which provided access to many different sections of the operating system in previous versions of Windows.

All is not lost, however – there is a replacement of sorts. Activate the bottom right-hand hotspot to reveal the Start screen picture – see page 85. Instead of left-clicking on it to go to the Start screen, right-click. This will open the Power users menu shown below:

Hot tip 

Another method of opening the Power users menu is to use the Winkey + X keyboard shortcut.

Programs and Features
Power Options
Event Viewer
System
Device Manager
Disk Management
Computer Management
Command Prompt
Command Prompt (Admin)
Task Manager
Control Panel
File Explorer
Search
Run
Desktop

The more useful options include:

- **Programs and Features** – manage the programs installed on the PC, e.g. uninstall, repair
- **Power Options** – this lets you configure a suitable power plan for the PC. Particularly useful for laptop and tablet users
- **System** – provides details about your system plus related links
- **Device Manager** – enables all the PC's hardware to be viewed and configured
- **Disk Management** – provides drive management tools, e.g. formatting and partitioning
- **Computer Management** – tools for advanced system management. These are useful for system administrators
- **Task Manager** – program management tool that provides a range of options regarding the software running on the PC
- **Control Panel** – an important section of the operating system that allows users to view and configure system settings
- **File Explorer** – a combined file manager application and navigation tool. Replaces Windows Explorer
- **Search** – opens the Start screen's Search app. Enables users to locate data, programs, emails, etc.

Multiple displays

The graphics adapter on your computer is probably capable of handling more than one monitor, having for example both VGA (analogue) and DVI (digital) connectors. You can also attach a second monitor to a laptop. To see how Windows handles this:

1. Display Screen Resolution, then attach a second monitor

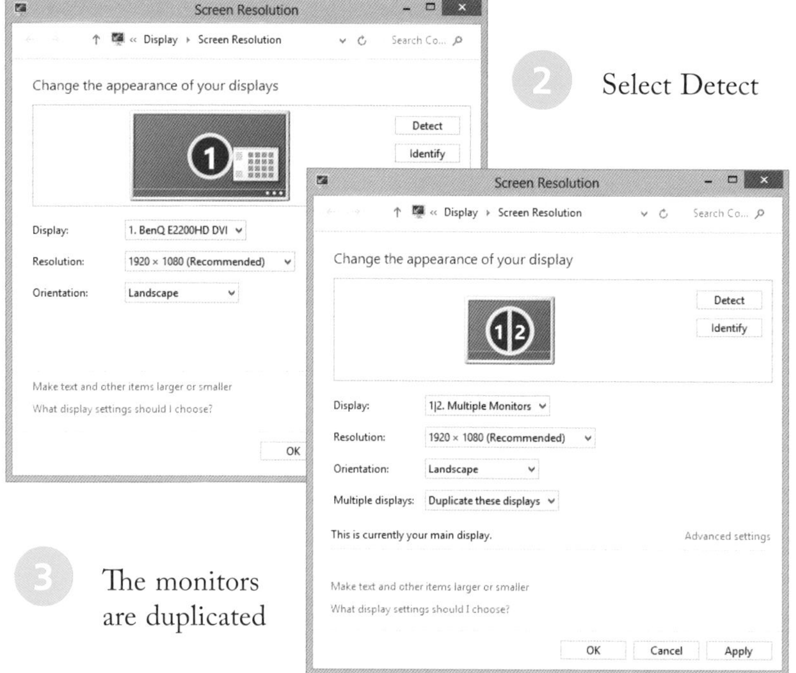

2. Select Detect

3. The monitors are duplicated

Windows resets both monitors to a resolution that both will be able to handle. If you want to continue duplicating the display, you can choose another more suitable resolution that both monitors can support.

1920 × 1080 (Recommended)
High
1920 × 1080 (Recommended)
1600 × 900
1024 × 768
Low

To use the monitors for different information:

1. Select the Multiple displays box and choose Extend these displays

2. Choose the appropriate resolution for each monitor individually - they do not have to be the same

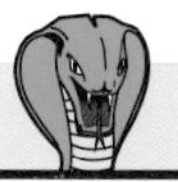

Beware

Your monitor may have both VGA and DVI cables, but you should never attach the monitor to two connections on the same computer.

Beware

If you pick a resolution that is not supported by one of the monitors, you will get a warning message and the change will not be applied.

...cont'd

3. By default, the first monitor is the main display, but you can assign the second monitor instead

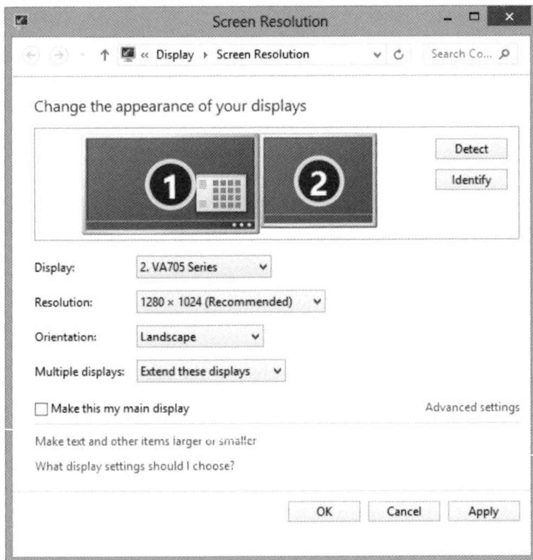

When you click PrtScn with dual monitors, you will capture an image of both monitors, in the positions as arranged.

4. Click Identify to display the numerals 1 and 2. The selected background appears on both monitors, but the taskbar appears on the main display only

You can drag an application window from one monitor to the other, or across both monitors.

5. Drag one of the monitors to rearrange them, stacked, in the reverse sequence or with a different overlap

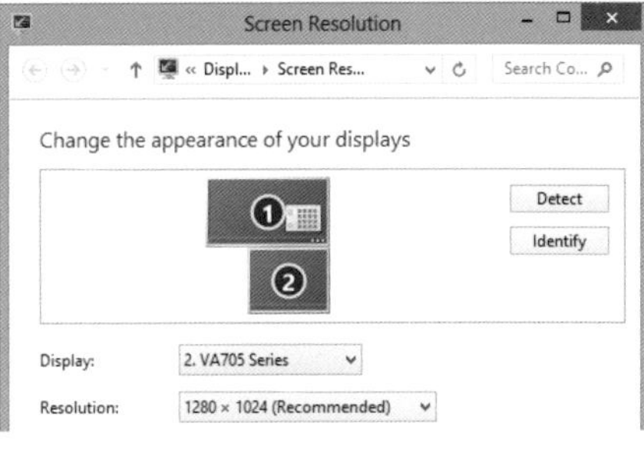

Application windows

A very useful function in Windows is the ability to move and resize application windows. As we have already seen, the apps used in the new Windows 8 interface run in full-screen mode only, and so cannot be moved or resized. Desktop applications, however, can be.

1. To move a window, click the title bar area, hold down the mouse button and drag the window

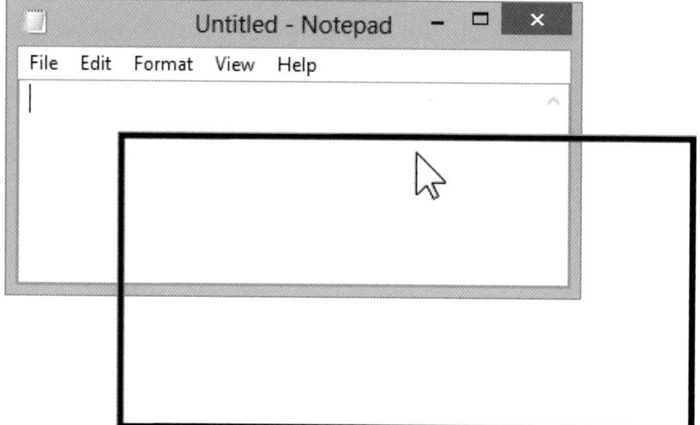

2. To resize a window, move the mouse pointer over any border or any corner until it becomes double-headed. Then click and drag until the window is the desired size

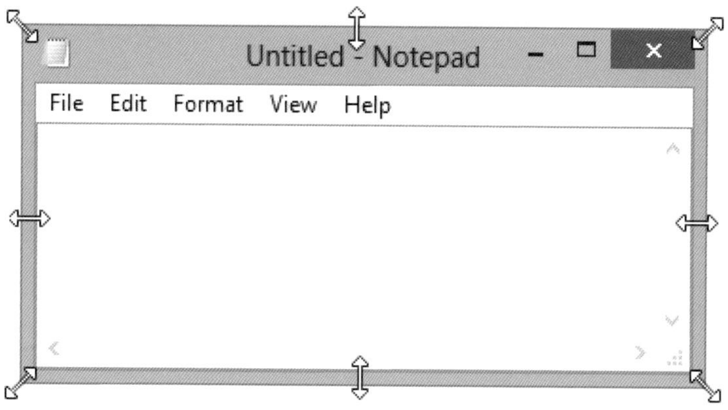

3. To make the window full screen, click the Maximize button. The button will now change into the Restore button – click it again to return to the original size

By default, the window contents show as you drag. To display just the frame, select System Properties, Advanced system settings, and Performance Settings.

When you drag a corner of the window, you can adjust the two adjacent borders simultaneously.

Double-clicking the title bar is an alternative to selecting the Maximize and Restore buttons.

Snap and Shake

Windows 8 includes two neat window manipulation features carried over from Windows 7. These are Snap and Shake.

Snap

Snap is a window docking feature that resizes two windows, each to half the size of the screen, and places them side-by-side. It is almost instant, requiring just two clicks to achieve what previously would need much dragging and resizing. Do it as follows:

1. Drag the title bar of a window to the left or right side of the screen until an outline of the expanded window appears
2. Release the window, which then expands to fill one half of the screen
3. Repeat with another window on the other side of the screen. You will now have two windows of equal size side-by-side and filling the screen as shown below

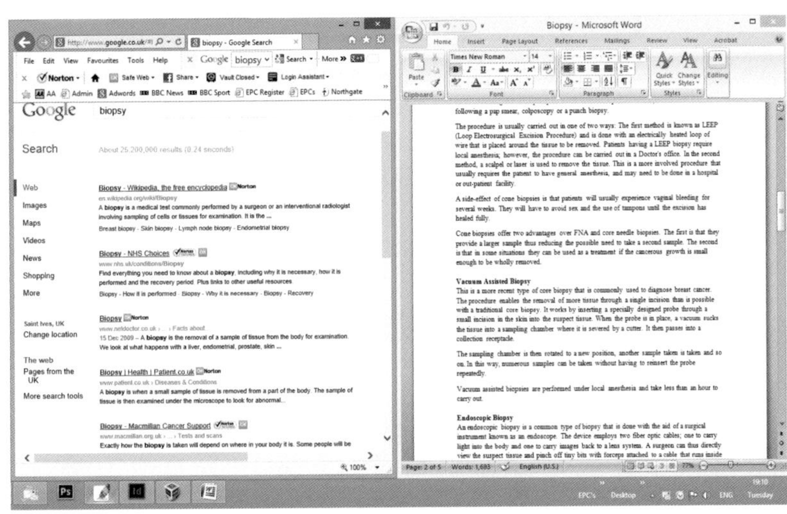

Hot tip 

You can also use Snap to maximize a window to full screen by dragging it to the top or bottom edges of the screen.

Shake

Ever need to cut through a cluttered desktop and quickly focus on a single window? Just click the top of a pane and give your mouse a shake. Voila! Every open window except that one instantly disappears. Shake it again – your windows are restored.

ClearType

ClearType font technology makes the text on your screen appear as sharp and clear as text that's printed on paper. It's on by default in Windows 8, but you can fine-tune the settings.

1. Go to the Control Panel, Appearance and Personalization. Under Fonts, click Adjust ClearType text

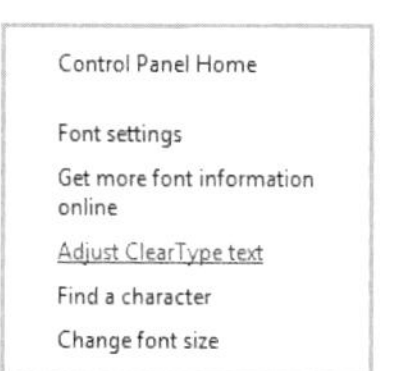

2. Click the Turn on ClearType text box (if not already selected)

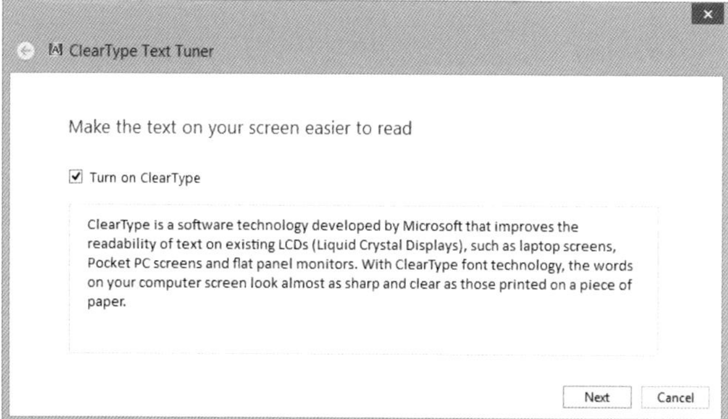

ClearType Text Tuner
Make the text on your screen easier to read
Turn on ClearType
ClearType is a software technology developed by Microsoft that improves the readability of text on existing LCDs (Liquid Crystal Displays), such as laptop screens, Pocket PC screens and flat panel monitors. With ClearType font technology, the words on your computer screen look almost as sharp and clear as those printed on a piece of paper.
Next
Cancel

3. Click Next and Windows checks that you are using the native resolution for your monitor

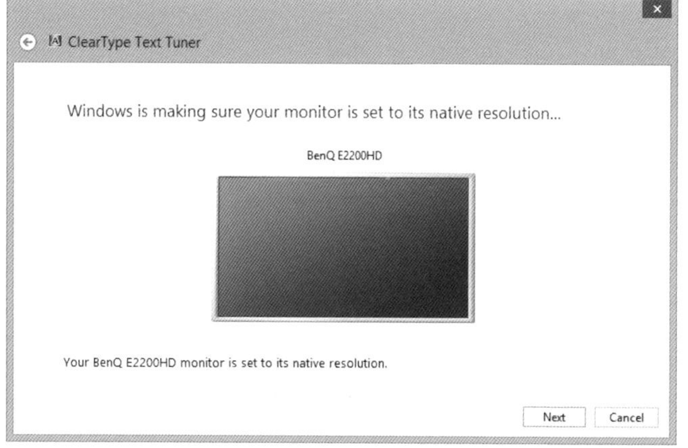

4. Click Next to run the ClearText text tuner

For the full benefit of ClearType, you need a high quality, flat-panel monitor, such as LCD or plasma.

Hot tip

If the monitor is not set to the recommended resolution, you are given the opportunity to change it.

...cont'd

5 Click the text box that looks best to you, then click Next

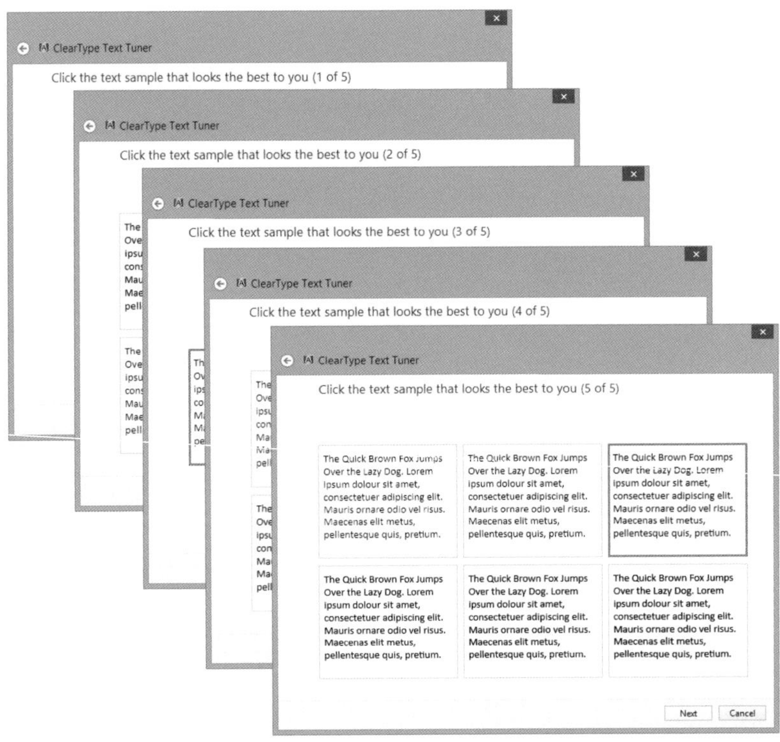

Hot tip

To review the settings on each of the five pages, click Next to accept the default selection.

6 Click Finish to end the ClearText text tuner

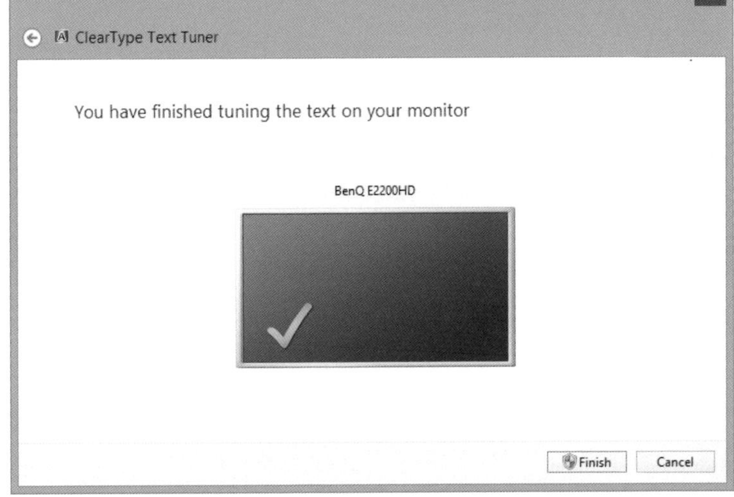

Don't forget

Any changes apply only to the current user. Each user account has its own ClearType settings recorded separately.

7 Built-in programs

There are programs built into Windows to help you in many areas, including text processing, scanning, faxing, image management, and calculations. There are tools to record and process sound and images. There are also special tools available, such as Command Prompt and Windows PowerShell.

All apps

Windows comes with a number of applications, services and functions, the presence of which many users will be completely unaware. Usually, these will be features and programs that they will never need to use. There will be times though, when they miss out on something that would have been useful if only they had known it was there.

To make sure this doesn't happen to you, check to see exactly what is available in Windows 8:

> **Hot tip**
>
> You can see what Desktop programs are installed on the PC by going to the Control Panel and opening Programs and Features.

1. Go to the Start screen
2. Right-click on the screen to open the app bar

3. Click All apps. This opens a screen that shows a miniaturized view of all the apps and programs installed on the computer

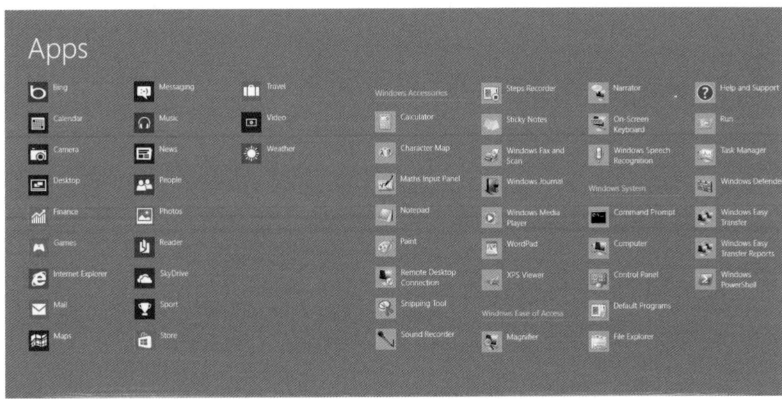

4. Mainly Windows 8 apps are grouped on the left of the screen
5. Desktop programs are grouped on the right of the screen

Desktop apps

Traditionally, Windows has provided a number of basic, but nevertheless useful, built-in applications. Examples include Notepad, Wordpad and Calculator.

While these are all still available in Windows, the method of accessing them is now a protracted procedure that involves opening the All apps view, as explained on the previous page, and then searching through the list of tiles for the required program. Users will rapidly get fed up with having to do this every time.

One solution is to right-click on the program and then from the app bar at the bottom, click Pin to Start (if you want it on the Start screen), or Pin to Taskbar (if you want it on the Desktop). This is demonstrated in the example below where we have searched for Wordpad:

Choose Pin to Taskbar and the program will subsequently be instantly accessible from the taskbar on the Desktop.

If you intend to use the Desktop rather than the Start screen, it will be a good move to pin to the taskbar all the old Windows programs you use. These are likely to include:

- Calculator
- Notepad
- Wordpad
- Sticky Notes
- Command Prompt
- Paint
- Run
- Math Input Panel
- Steps Recorder
- Snipping Tool
- Sound Recorder
- Windows Journal
- Windows Fax & Scan
- Windows Media Player
- Character Map
- Magnifier
- Task Manager
- XPS Viewer

We'll take a look at some of these programs in the next few pages.

Hot tip

Another way round this problem is to install a third-party program that restores the Start button and Start menu. There are several of these available on the Internet (e.g. Classic Shell, see page 84).

Hot tip

If you pin a lot of programs to the taskbar, you may find yourself running out of room. Create more by resizing the taskbar.

Don't forget

Windows RT features special versions of some of these Windows programs, but others are unavailable.

Calculator

While there's no spreadsheet capability built in to Windows, it does offer a handy calculator.

Go to Search on the Charms bar, type calc and click to open it

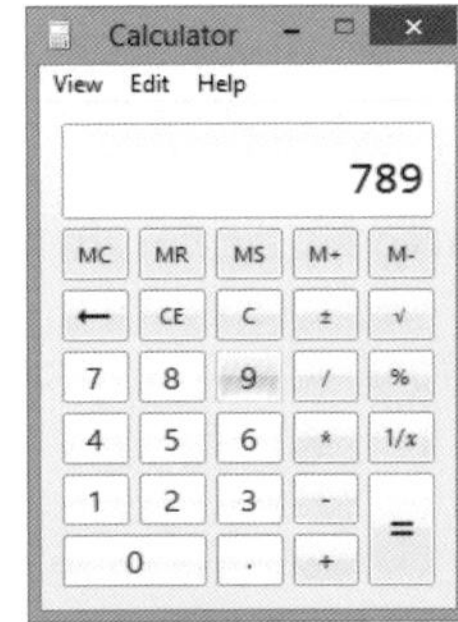

Click calculator buttons or press equivalent keyboard keys, to enter numbers and operations such as Add, Subtract, Multiply, Divide, Square Root, Percent and Inverse.

Don't forget

You can also use the numeric keypad to type numbers and operators. Press Num Lock if it is not already turned on.

2 To complete the calculation, select or press the Enter key

You can also store and recall numbers from memory, and the History capability keeps track of stages in the calculations.

This is just the Standard calculator. You can also choose to use Scientific, Programmer and Statistics versions of the calculator.

1 Open Calculator, select View and choose for example Scientific

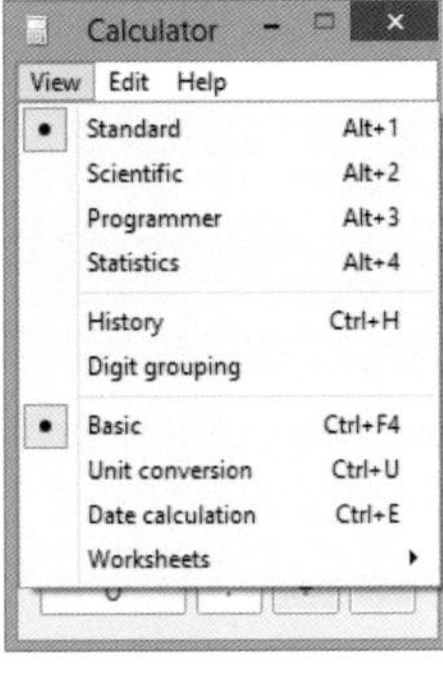

Beware

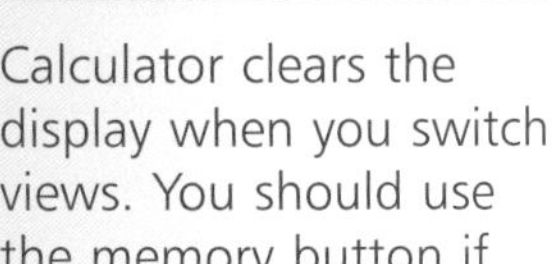

Calculator clears the display when you switch views. You should use the memory button if you need to retain a number between mode switches.

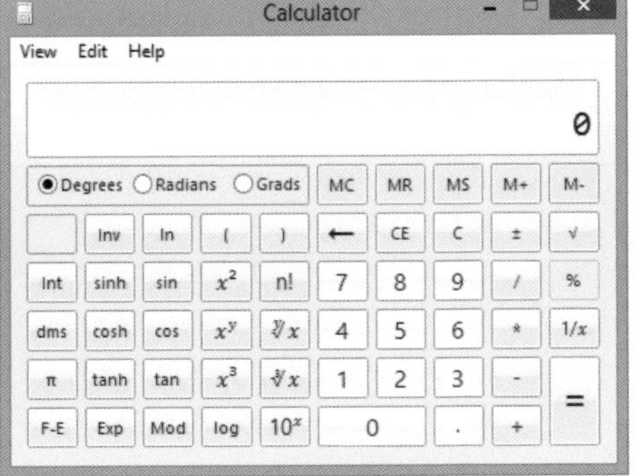

The Scientific calculator includes many functions and inverse functions, including logarithms and factorials.

You can use Calculator to convert between different units of measure. It will subtract dates or add and subtract days from a date. There are also worksheets to calculate fuel economy or lease and mortgage payments.

Notepad

There are several applications that provide various levels of text management capabilities. One of these is Notepad.

The program is a basic text-editing application and it's most commonly used to view or edit text files, usually with the .txt file name extension, but any text file can be handled.

1. Go to Search on the Charms bar, type notepad and open it. Then type some text, pressing Enter to start a new line

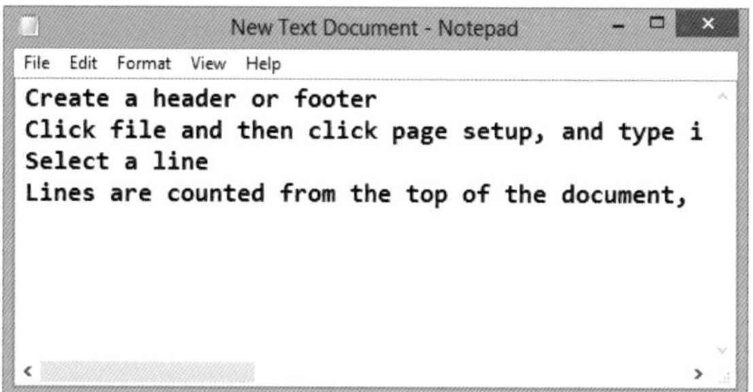

2. Parts of the lines may be hidden, if lines are longer than the width of the window

3. Select Format, Word Wrap to fit the text within the window width

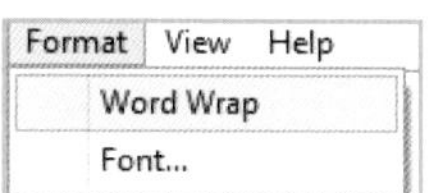

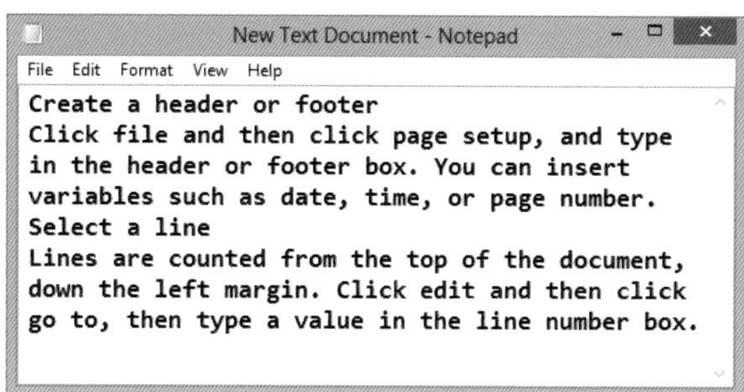

4. Select Edit to cut, copy and paste text, or to insert a Time/Date stamp into the document

5. Select File to save or print the document

Hot tip

Select Format, Font to choose the Font, Font Style and Size. This will apply to all the text in the whole document.

Don't forget

When you print a document, the lines are wrapped between the margins, whatever the Word Wrap setting.

Wordpad

WordPad is a text-editing program you can use to create and edit documents which can include rich formatting and graphics. You can also link to or embed pictures and other documents.

1. Go to Search on the Charms bar, type wordpad and click to open it. Then type in some lines of text

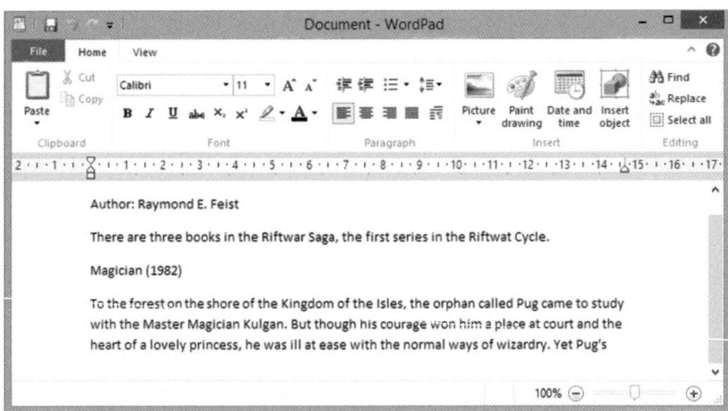

2. Select text and use the formatting bar to change font etc.

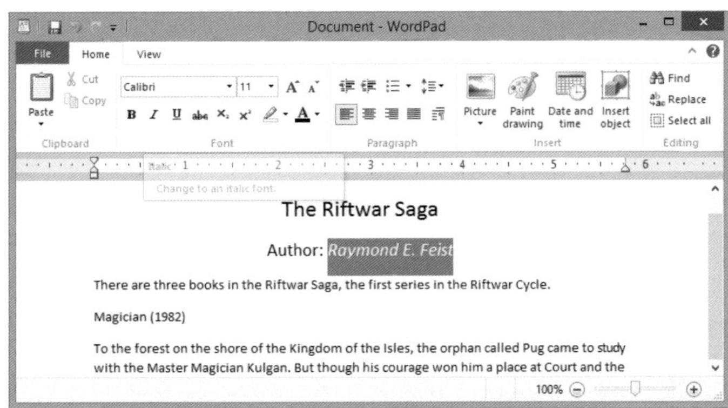

3. Click the Save button on the Quick Access toolbar, type the file name and confirm the file type, then click Save

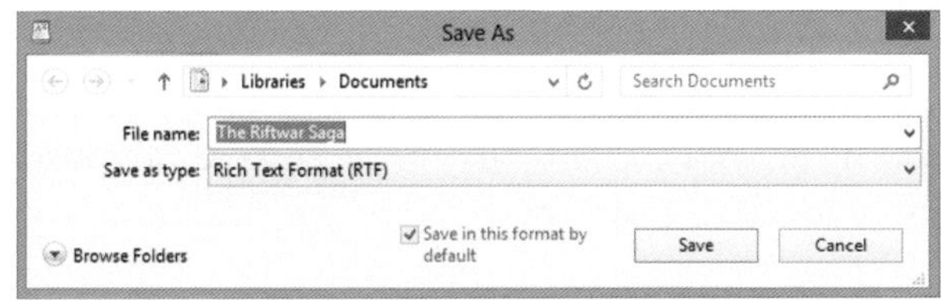

Don't forget

The text automatically wraps as you type, and the Enter key starts a new paragraph.

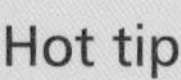

Hot tip

Saving as Rich Text Document (.rtf), Open Office XML (.docx) or OpenDocument Text (.odt) will retain the text styling. However, the other formats save as plain text, and remove images or links.

Paint

Paint allows you to create drawings on a blank drawing area or in existing pictures, photographs or web graphics. Open the program as described below:

Go to Search on the Charms bar, type paint and click to open it. The program opens with a blank canvas

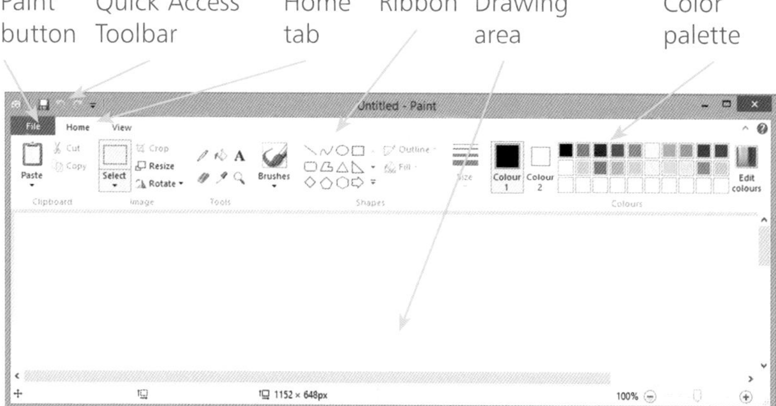

2 Right-click an image file and select Open with, Paint

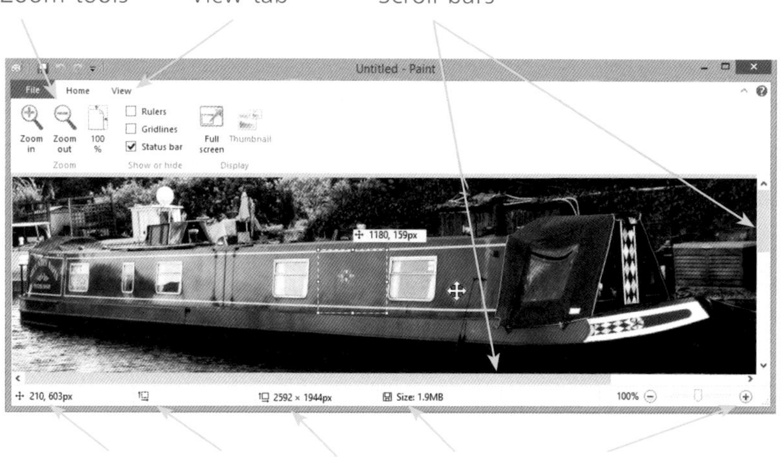

You can zoom in on a certain part of the picture or zoom out if the picture is too large, and show rulers and gridlines as you work.

Don't forget

You may have other image programs on your system, in addition to the ones reviewed here, depending on the products installed and the hardware connected.

Hot tip

When you paste an image onto the Paint drawing area, it will be automatically resized if necessary to fit the whole image.

Don't forget

Paint can open and save as a number of image formats including .bmp, .jpg, .gif, .tif and .png.

Snipping tool

This will capture a screen shot, or snip, of any object on your screen, and you can then annotate, save, or share the image. For example, if there's a window open with information to be copied:

1. Go to Search on the Charms bar, type snipping tool and click to open it
2. Select the arrow next to New to pick the snip type, e.g. rectangular
3. Click a corner and drag to mark out the area you wish to capture

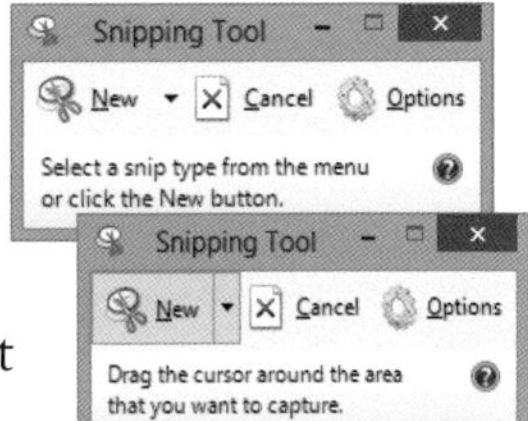

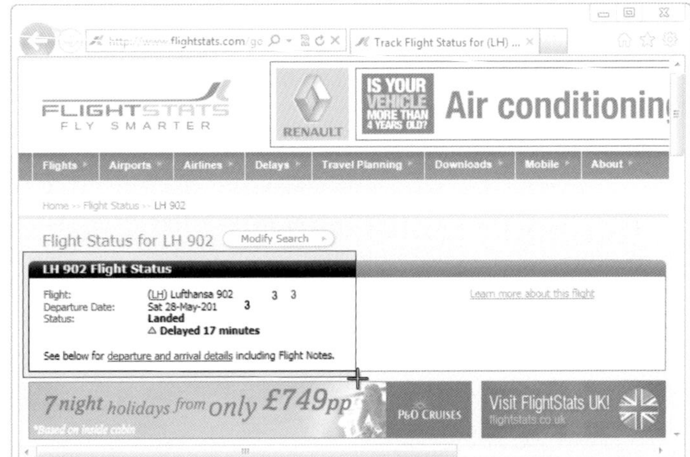

4. Release the mouse, and the snip is copied to the Clipboard and the mark-up window
5. Highlight or annotate the snip if desired then click the Save Snip button, adjust the name and location, then click Save

Don't forget

You can capture a free form area, a rectangular area, a window or the full screen.

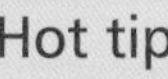

Hot tip

You can save the snip as file type .png, .gif, .jpg or .mht (single file .html). You can then include the saved file in documents or email messages.

Sticky notes

Sticky Notes

You can keep track of small pieces of information such as phone numbers, addresses or meeting schedules using Sticky Notes. You can use Sticky Notes with a tablet pen or a standard keyboard.

To create a new Sticky Note:

1. Go to Search on the Charms bar, type sticky notes and click to open it

2. The new note appears on the Desktop with the typing cursor active

3. Type the text of the reminder that you want to record

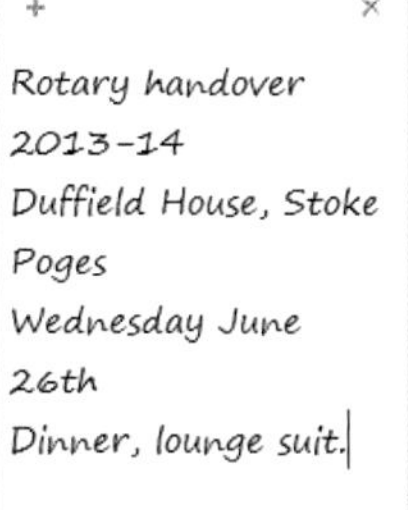
Rotary handover
2013-14
Duffield House, Stoke
Poges
Wednesday June
26th
Dinner, lounge suit.

4. Text wraps as you type, and you can press Enter to start a new line

5. The note is extended in length to accommodate text

6. Drag a corner or edge to resize or reshape the note

Rotary handover 2013-14
Duffield House, Stoke Poges
Wednesday June 26th
Dinner, lounge suit.

You can format text, add bullets to make a list, or change the text size using keyboard shortcuts.

1. Select the text that you want to change

2. Use the appropriate keyboard shortcut to format the text

Ctrl+B	Bold text	Ctrl+Shift+L	Bulleted list
Ctrl+I	Italic text	Ctrl+Shift+L (repeated)	Numbered list
Ctrl+U	Underlined text	Ctrl+Shift+>	Increase text size
Ctrl+T	Strikethrough	Ctrl+Shift+<	Decrease text size

Hot tip

Sticky Notes don't have to be yellow. Right-click the note and choose one of the six colors offered.

Cut
Copy
Paste
Delete
Select All
Blue
Green
Pink
Purple
White
Yellow

Don't forget

To create another note, click the New Note button. To remove a note press the Delete Note button.

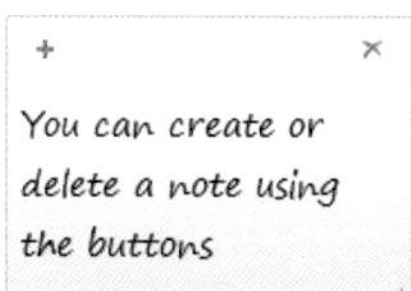
You can create or
delete a note using
the buttons

Fax and scan

Windows provides software to support sending and receiving faxes, but you need a fax modem installed or attached to your computer, plus a connection to a telephone line.

There's also support for scanning documents and pictures, but you need a scanner (or all-in-one printer) attached to your computer.

To start Windows Fax and Scan:

1. Go to Search on the Charms bar, type fax and click to open it

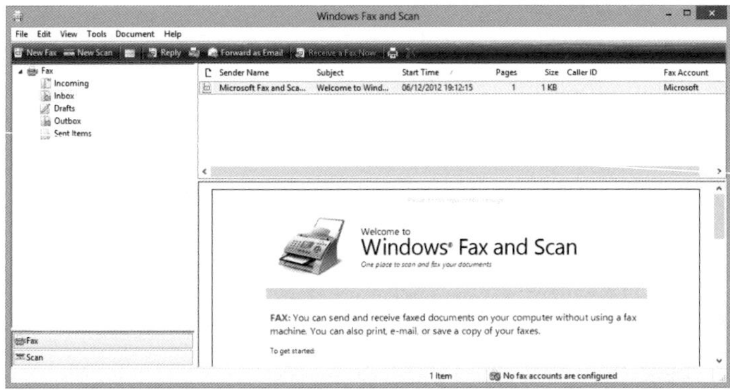

2. An example document is displayed, and this provides guidance for getting started with faxes and scanning

3. To scan a document or picture, click the Scan button then click New Scan on the toolbar, and follow the prompts

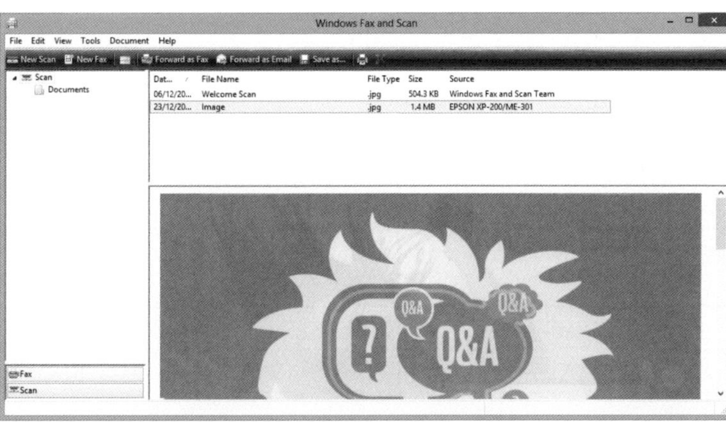

Don't forget

Select View, then Zoom and you can choose a larger or smaller scale, or fit to page or fit to width, as desired.

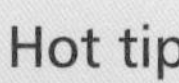

Hot tip

When you have scanned a document or picture, you can forward it as an email or a fax.

Command Prompt

All versions of Windows have included a command line feature for typing MS-DOS commands and other computer commands.

1. Press Winkey + X and click Command Prompt

2. To display a list of commands with a brief description of each, type Help and press Enter

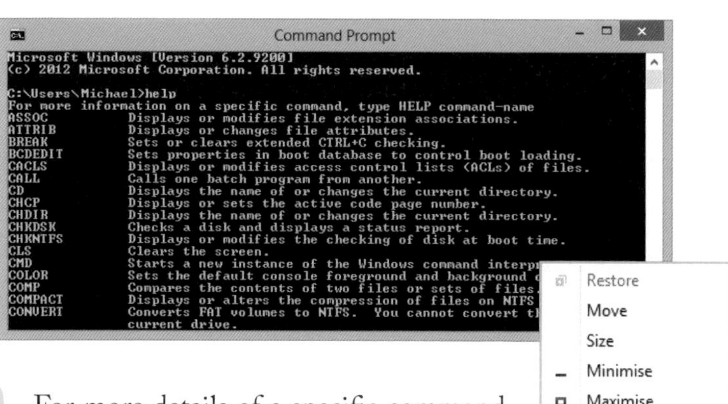

3. For more details of a specific command, type Help Name (or Name /?), for example Help Convert, and press Enter

4. To adjust command prompt options, right-click the title bar and select Defaults (for all command prompts) or Properties (current command prompt only)

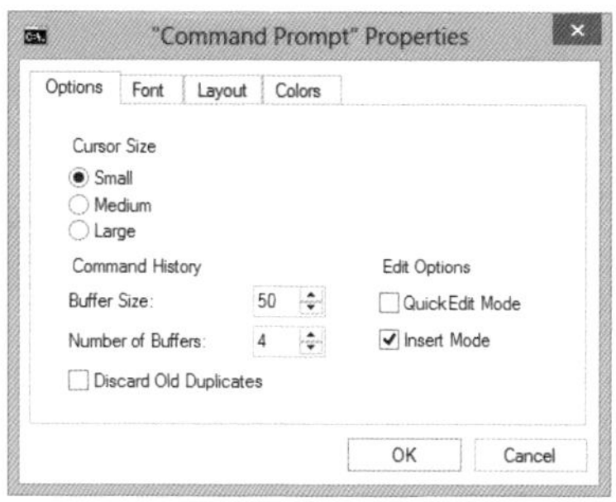

5. To close the command prompt, type Exit and press Enter

Beware

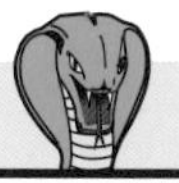

The Command Prompt environment and the MS-DOS and other Windows commands are extremely powerful and should be used with great caution.

Don't forget

If the commands you use require authorization, right-click Command Prompt and select Run as administrator.

Hot tip

Select Edit from the right-click menu, and you can mark, copy and paste text onto the command line.

Windows PowerShell

To support system administrators and advanced users, Windows 8 provides a command-line and scripting environment, far more powerful than the old MS-DOS batch file system.

1. Press Winkey + R to open the Run box. Then enter powershell and press Enter

2. Enter Get-Command for a list of PowerShell commands

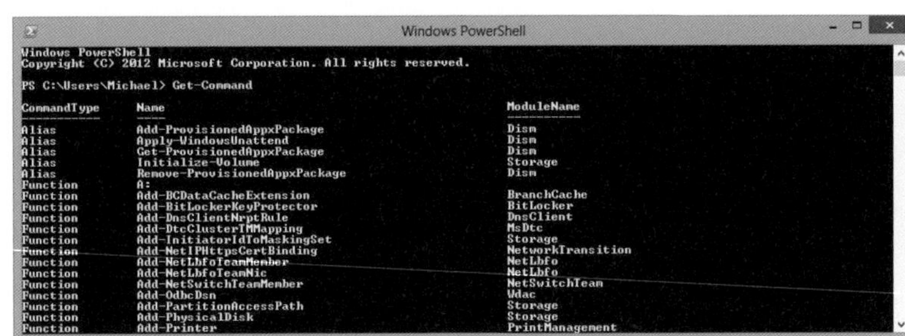

3. Open the Run box again and this time type Windows PowerShell ISE for the Integrated Scripting Environment, and enter the same command

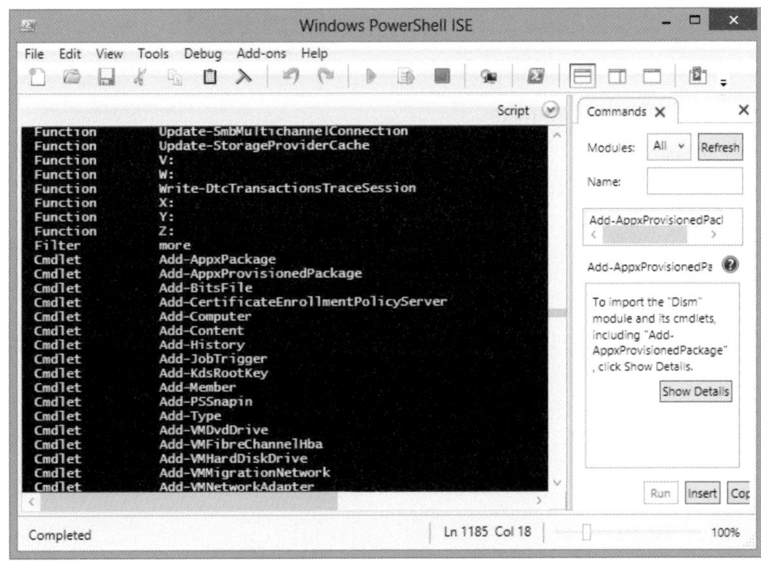

4. For help, go to **http://technet.microsoft.com/powershell**

Windows PowerShell can execute Cmdlets (which are .NET programs), PowerShell programs), PowerShell scripts (file type .ps1), PowerShell functions and executable programs.

You'll find more help in the MSDN library at **http://msdn.microsoft.com/library**

Administrative tools

Administrative Tools are intended for system administrators and advanced users. To see the list available on your system:

1. In the Control Panel, open System and Security, Administrative Tools

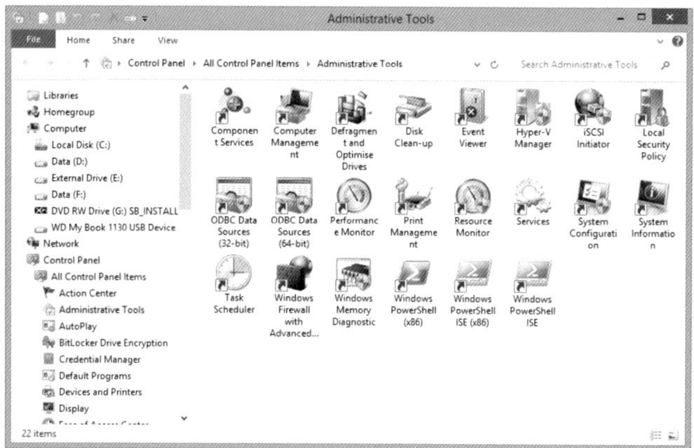

2. Here you see a range of tools that enable you to manage the way the PC is used. For example, click Services and you will see a list of all services running on the PC

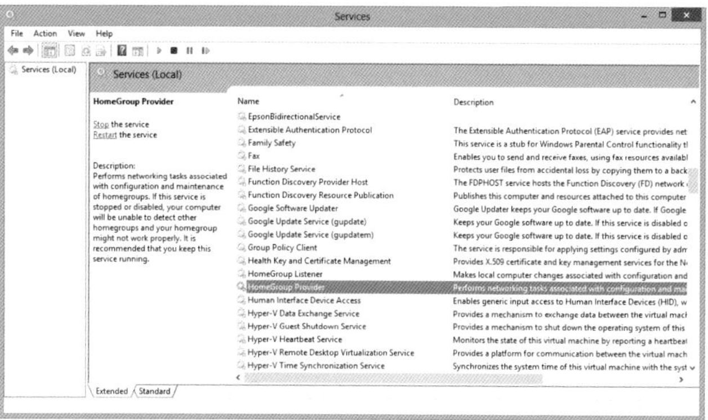

3. Double-clicking a service reveals options for starting and stopping the service. This enables you to disable the ones that aren't necessary. A typical example is network-related services; if you don't use networking, you can safely disable these and gain a small performance boost

Unknown file types

A problem you may come across occasionally is trying to start a program only to be greeted by the following message, or something similar:

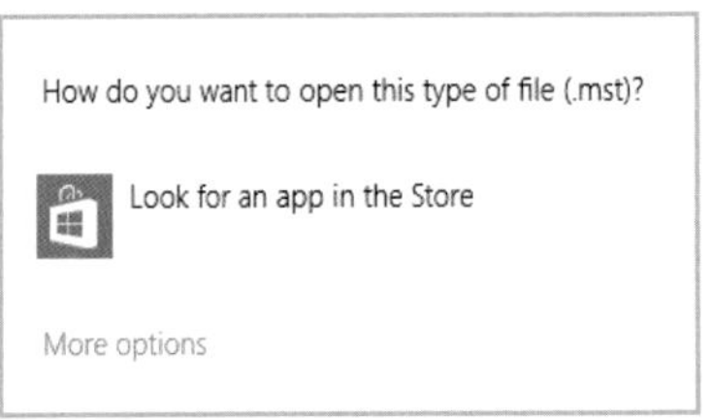

The reason for the message is that Windows hasn't recognized the program's file type and so has no idea what program will open it.

Initially, you are offered one option – Look for an app in the Store. Clicking this will take you to the Windows Store where, if you aren't already, you will have to log in to a Microsoft account. Once done, a search is done automatically for apps capable of opening the file in question.

If one is found, you are offered the option of downloading it – remember, you may have to pay for it. If an app isn't found, you will see this message:

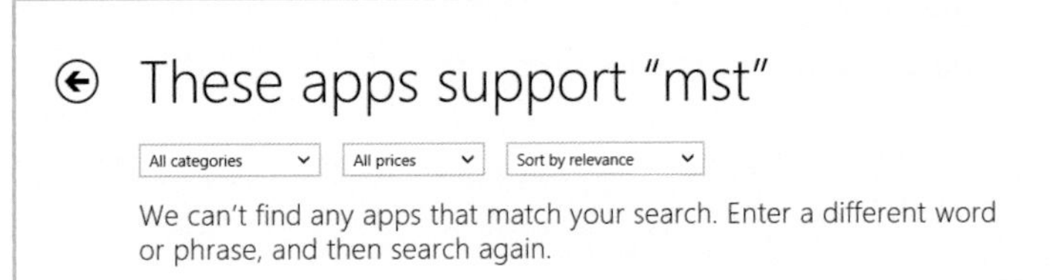

Beware

If you try any of the suggested programs, make sure the "Use this application for all xxx files" option is not selected. Only do this when you are sure the program is the one you want.

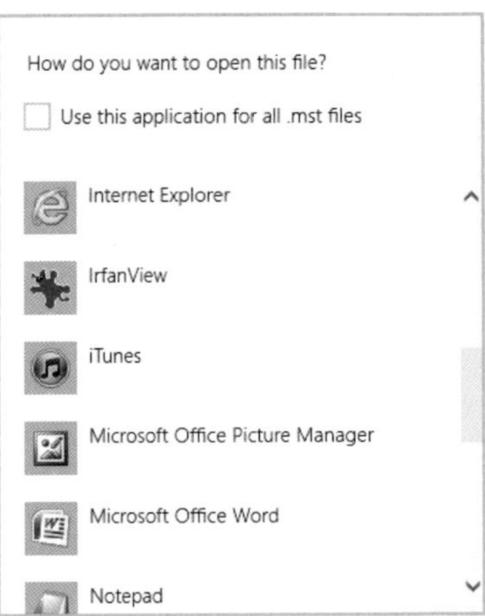

Clicking the "More Options" link will reveal a list of suggested programs to try.

However, if none of these work either, your last recourse is the Internet. There are quite a few sites that provide lists of file types and the programs associated with them.

For example, you can try **http://filext.com**

Change default program

All files are designed to be opened with a specific type of program. For example, graphics files, such as JPEG and GIF, can only be opened by a graphics editing program, e.g. Paint, or with a web browser, such as Internet Explorer.

A common problem that many users experience is when they install a program on their PC that automatically makes itself the default program for opening related files. If the user prefers the original program, he or she will have to reassociate the file type in question. Alternatively, the user might want to set a different program as the default.

1. Go to Control Panel, Programs, Default Programs. Click Associate a file type or protocol with a program

2. Select the file type and then click the Change program button

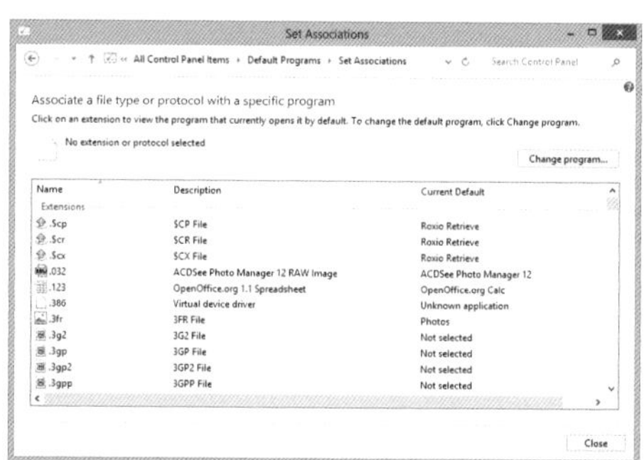

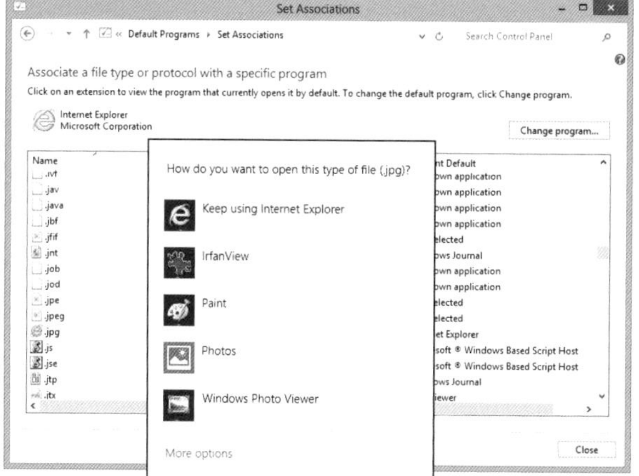

3. You will now see a list of programs on the PC capable of opening the file. Select the one you want

Don't forget

If a newly-installed program has hijacked your files, you can reassociate them with your favored program.

Hot tip

Another way is to right-click a file and then click Properties. Click the General tab and then click Change. Browse to the program you want to open the file with and select it.

Search the Web for software

Hot tip

There will be occasions when a certain program is only needed temporarily. Rather than go out and buy one, download a time-limited trial version for nothing.

Beware

Watch out for phishing sites that imitate those of major manufacturers and rip you off.

Beware

Software acquired from download sites can be poorly coded and thus contain bugs. These can cause problems on your computer.

There was a time when if you wanted a specific program, you either had to visit a store to buy it, or order it online – the instant downloads of today were very rare due to painfully slow Internet connections. Because of this it was almost impossible to "trial" a program – you had to pay for it and hope it did the job.

Nowadays, thanks to broadband, the situation is completely different, and there are several very useful sources of software:

Manufacturers

Without doubt, the best source of software is the manufacturers' websites. The vast majority of them allow users to download time- or feature-limited versions of their products to try out before parting with the cash.

The big advantage here is that the software is guaranteed to be the real deal, and with no unwelcome attachments in the form of viruses and malware. The downside, of course, is that once the trial period is up, you have to pay for the program if you want to keep using it.

Download Sites

Software download sites are set up specifically to provide an outlet for the legions of small software developers. Many of these programs are free (freeware), others are time- or feature-limited, (shareware), while others require up-front payment.

Well known download sites include Download.com, Soft32, ZDNet Downloads, and Tucows. The big advantage offered by these sites is variety – a vast number of programs of all types are available. However, you do have a risk of picking up viruses and malware hidden in the programs, and many of the freeware programs also come with irritating nag screens or ads.

File Sharing

File sharing is a common Internet activity that makes use of peer-to-peer networks. Users install a program that connects to these networks and lets them share designated files on their PC with other users.

This enables all types of data; software, video, images, etc to be downloaded at no cost. The practice is quite legal. However, actually using the data is often illegal. There is also a high risk of virus and malware infection.

8 Windows downloads

Microsoft provides Windows Live Essentials, a set of free applications that supplement and extend Windows, with email, messaging, photos and movie support and security features. Note that Downloads are for Windows 8 only, not Windows RT.

Windows Essentials 2012

1. At **http://windows.microsoft.com/en-US/windows-live/essentials-home** click Download now

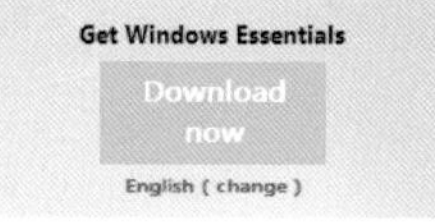

Do you want to run or save **wlsetup-web.exe** (1.18 MB) from **wl.dlservice.microsoft.com**? Run Save Cancel

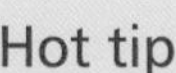

You may receive User Account Control messages to confirm your wishes, during the download and install.

2. Choose to Run the Windows Essentials setup program

3. The setup program is installed and run, and you are prompted to choose the programs that you want to install

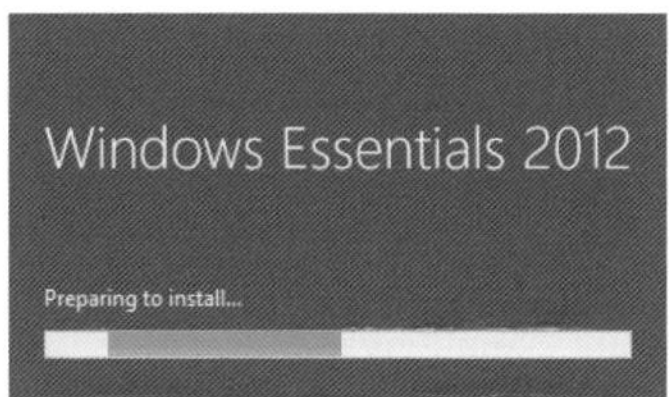

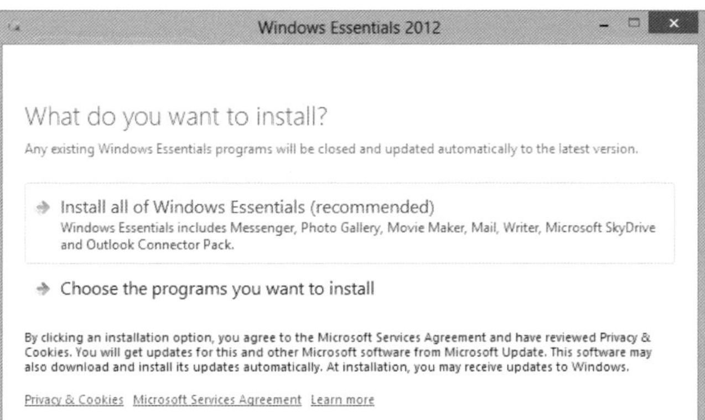

Hot tip

Click View Details for a progress report on the installation.

4. Select to install all the Windows Essential programs, as recommended

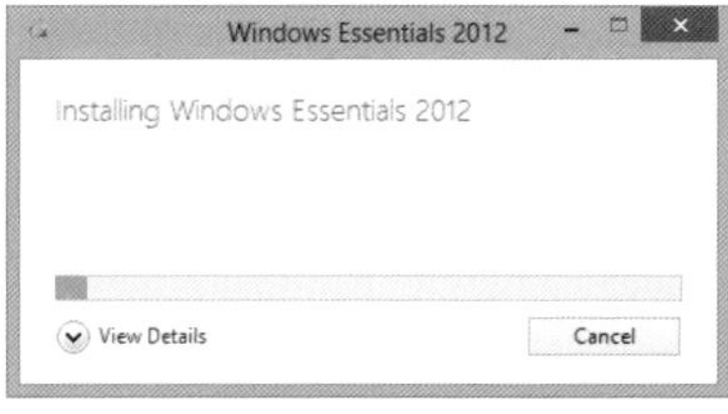

5. The programs are installed in turn

6. Click Close

To install a selection of the programs, run the Setup program and:

1. Click Choose the programs you want to install

2. Clear the box for programs you want to avoid installing

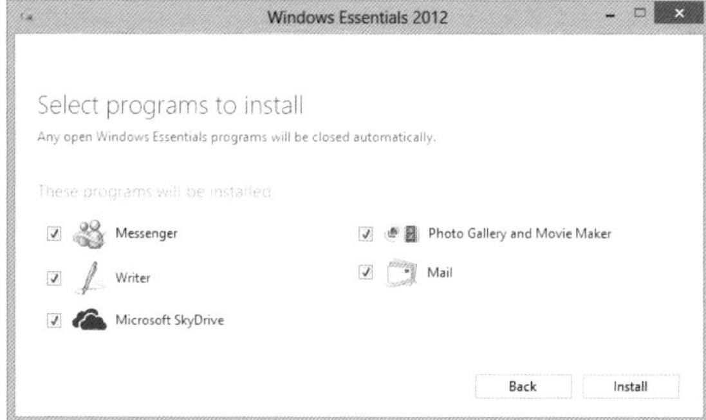

3. The next time, Setup shows which programs are installed

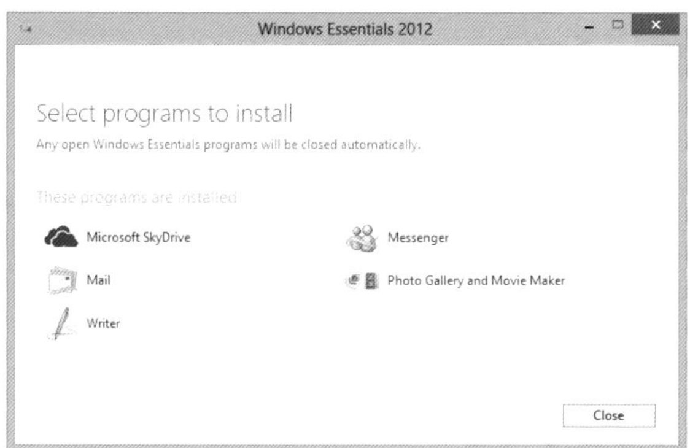

You can choose to install some of the programs, and you will be able to install the others later if you wish.

Applications included

The following applications are included with Essentials 2012:

Mail

Mail is a comprehensive email program that can handle all email accounts. It provides most of the functionality of paid-for programs such as Outlook, including spam and phishing filters, a search facility, storage on SkyDrive, a conversation view, a calendar, and integration with Messenger.

Hot tip

All Essentials 2012 programs are compatible with Windows 7 and Windows 8. Some may not be with earlier Windows versions.

Family Safety

The really neat aspect of this program is that it can be configured and monitored online, and thus from any PC, anywhere in the world. With it, it is possible to manage which sites can and cannot be accessed, and see exactly what a child has been doing online. A number of filters allow the program to be fine-tuned.

Hot tip

When the Essentials 2012 installer is run on a Windows 8 PC, Family Safety will not be offered. This is because the program is already installed in Windows 8.

Messenger

Messenger is an instant messaging program that connects to Microsoft's Messenger Service. It provides common messenger features such as social network integration and the ability to appear offline

Photo Gallery

This application allows users to organize their digital photos. Options here include by date plus tags for people, keywords and locations. The program offers tools for creating panoramas, collages and slide shows. Photos can be shared via several online services, and also published to YouTube, Flickr and Vimeo.

Movie Maker

Movie Maker offers a simple and straightforward way to create and edit home movies. Footage and photos can be imported from a PC or camera. Soundtracks can be added as can transitions and various effects. Completed movies can be published to sites such as YouTube and Flickr.

Hot tip

Microsoft SkyDrive, the Desktop version, is also is also part of the Essentials 2012 suite. We haven't mentioned it here as it is covered elsewhere in this book (see page 82).

Writer

This application is a tool that enables blog posts to be created. It provides all the required formatting tools including links, images and video. A useful preview function helps ensure your blog is perfect before publishing. Writer works with many popular blog service providers such as WordPress, Blogger, and TypePad.

Microsoft downloads

Apart from the Essentials 2012 suite, Microsoft provides other free software for Windows.

Office Viewers

Microsoft Office applications such as Word and PowerPoint are used on millions of PCs all over the world. For businesses, they are essential. They are, however, expensive and occasional users may not be able to justify the cost.

There is a partial solution available for these users. This comes in the form of Office Viewers – programs that can view, copy and print Office documents. These programs are free and there are versions for Word, Excel, PowerPoint, Access and Visio.

1. Go to the Microsoft Download Center. In the search box type the viewer you want, e.g. word office viewer. In the results list, click Word Viewer

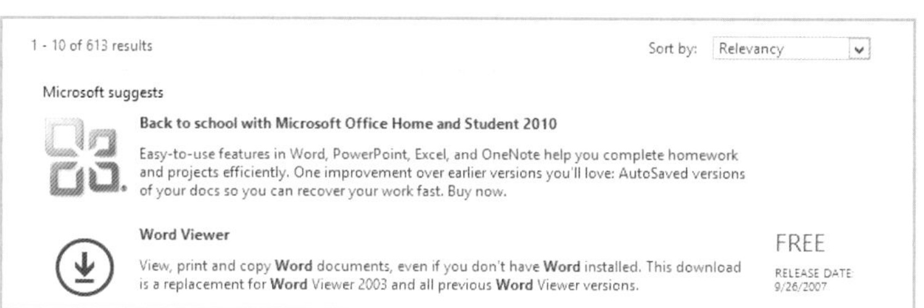

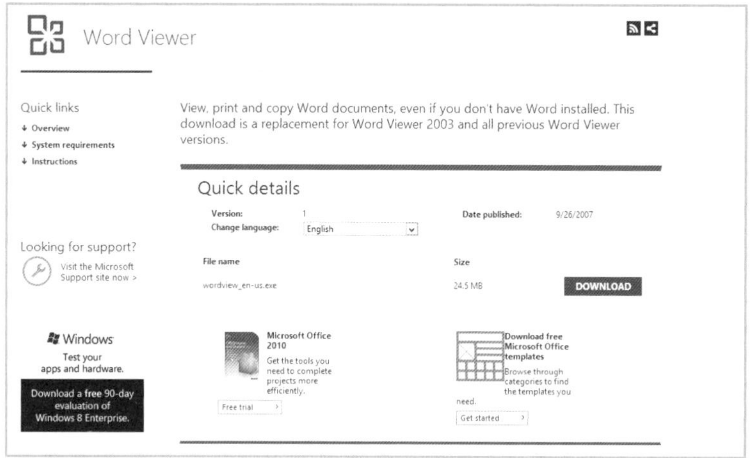

2. In the next screen, click Download

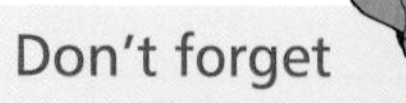

You can only view, copy and print with Office Viewers. You cannot create or save documents.

Microsoft's Download Center is at www.microsoft.com/en-us/download

If you open a SkyDrive account, you will have access to web versions of Word, Excel, PowerPoint and OneNote. These will allow you to create documents as well as read them – all for free.

Other downloads

Don't forget

For every task, there will be many programs available to choose from, for free or for a fee.

There are a number of applications, not included with Windows and not supplied by Microsoft, that are used by thousands of people all over the world. They supplement the existing Windows applications or they fill in the gaps.

The reasons for their popularity are that they are free, good at their intended purpose, and generally well-behaved, i.e. they are free of bugs and malware.

There are, of course, many other programs that do the same things but the ones we are going to highlight in the next few pages tick all the boxes – excellent performance, no malware and absolutely free to use.

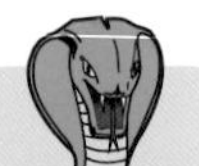

Beware

Not every program offered on the Internet is safe to use. Some are still under development, some may be infected with viruses or malware. Make sure that you check out programs at reliable sources before download.

Category	Program
PDF Viewer	Adobe Reader
Maintenance	CCleaner
CD/DVD Tool	CDBurnerXP
Photo Viewer	Irfanview
Text Editor	Notepad++
Office Apps	OpenOffice.org
Photo Editor	Paint.net
File Sharing	uTorrent

Hot tip

If a program offers to create a Desktop shortcut during installation, accept the option.

All of these programs are available over the Internet, ready for download and installation. In the following pages you'll find the details needed to get started with each of the programs, including:

- Website address
- Brief description
- Installation notes
- Screenshot of application

After installation, each program can be accessed by typing its name in the Search charm.

Adobe Reader

http://www.adobe.com/products/reader.html

Adobe Reader is the worldwide standard for viewing, printing, and commenting on PDF documents of all types.

To install the application:

1. Go to the website and select the Download link

2. Clear the McAfee Security Scan box, then follow the prompts to download and install Adobe Reader

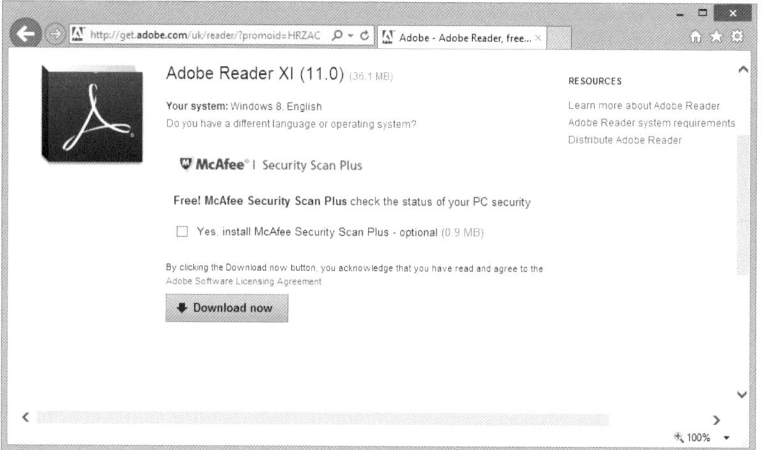

3. Double-click any PDF file to open it in Adobe Reader

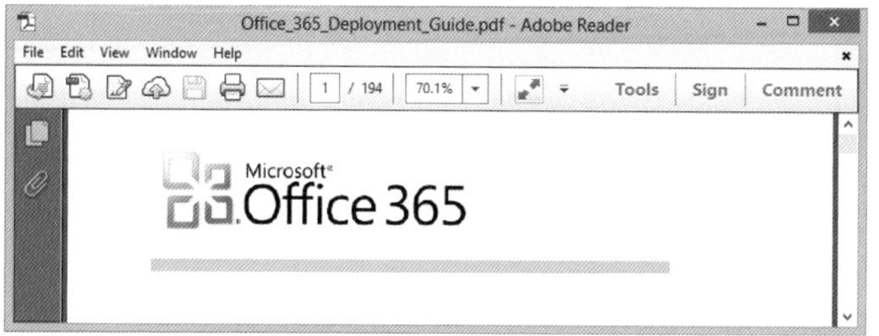

Don't forget

Adobe may use the Adobe Download Manager to install the Adobe Reader and manage updates in the future.

Beware

You may find extras such as McAfee Security being offered. You can usually ignore these unless you are sure they will be needed.

Hot tip

Adobe Reader is not just for viewing documents. Select View, Read Out Loud to set the Reader in narrative mode.

CCleaner

http://www.piriform.com/ccleaner

CCleaner is a utility that cleans out the junk that accumulates over time: temporary files, broken shortcuts, and other problems. The program also protects the user's privacy by clearing the contents of the history and temporary internet files folders.

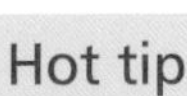

Hot tip

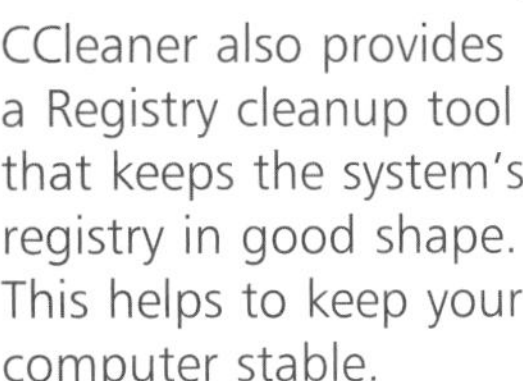

CCleaner also provides a Registry cleanup tool that keeps the system's registry in good shape. This helps to keep your computer stable.

1. At the website, click the Download button

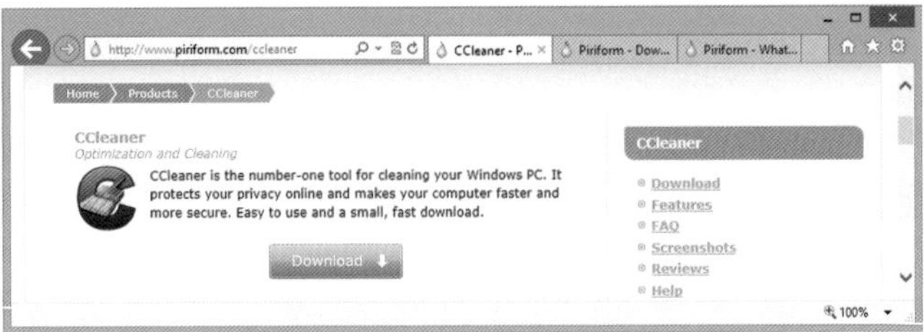

2. Choose the Free download option
3. Run the setup wizard
4. When the installation is complete, click the Analyze button

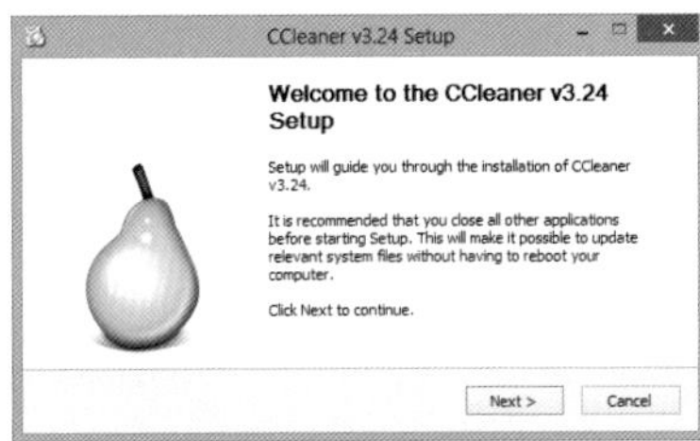

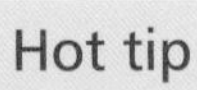

Hot tip

Another very useful tool provided by CCleaner is the Drive Wiper. This enables users to securely remove all the data from a drive.

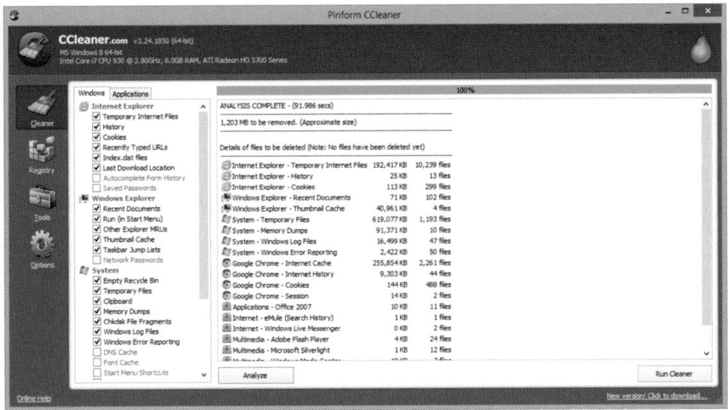

5. You'll see a list of files that can be safely deleted

CDBurnerXP

http://cdburnerxp.se/en/home

CDBurnerXP is a burning utility that enables a wide variety of discs, such as CDs, DVDs, Blu-ray and HD-DVDs to be created. Other useful options include the ability to create ISO image files and bootable discs.

1 Click the Free download button

2 Install the program by running the setup wizard

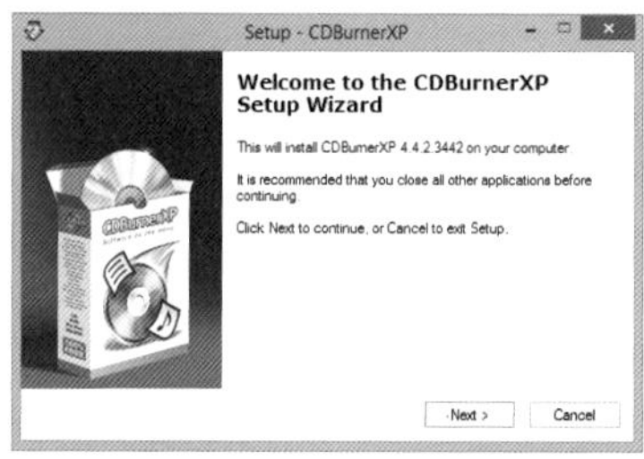

3 You will now see a screen offering to install the Pokki Start Menu. Select I do not accept

4 When the program is run, you are offered various options, e.g. data disc, video DVD, Burn ISO image, etc.

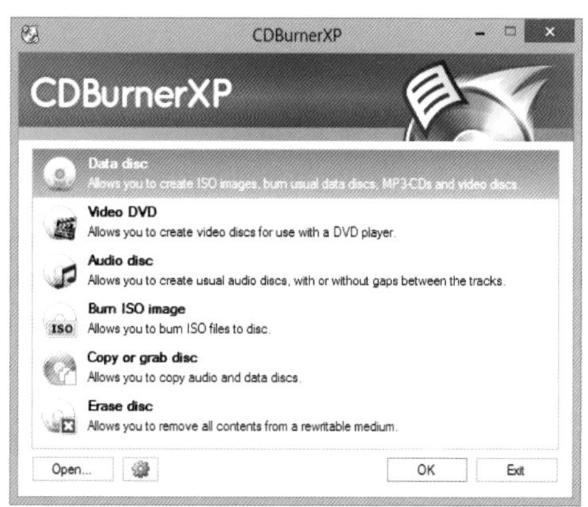

A disc burning utility is not included with Windows 8 so users will have to have to find one themselves – CDBurnerXP is a good option.

The Pokki Start Menu is a freeware application that will also be installed unless you explicitly state you don't want it.

Another free disc authoring utility with a good reputation is ImgBurn, which you download from **http://www.imgburn.com**

IrfanView

http://www.irfanview.com

IrfanView is designed to be simple for beginners and powerful for professionals and is an extremely quick way to scroll through picture folders.

IrfanView is a very fast and compact graphic viewer for Windows that is freeware (for non-commercial use). It supports many graphics file formats, including multiple (animated) GIF, multi-page TIF and videos.

1. Visit the website and select the IrfanView download link

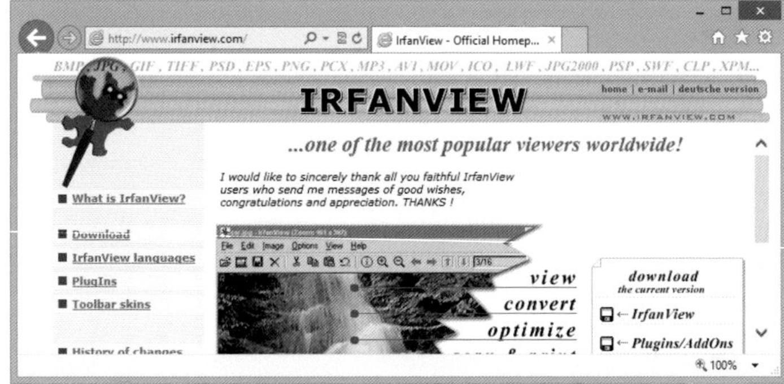

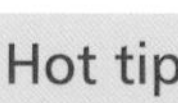

Select the download for Plug-ins/Add-ons to get support for the full set of file formats.

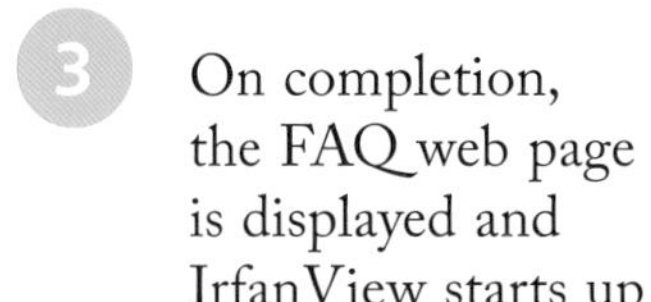

2. Follow the prompts to download and install IrfanView

3. On completion, the FAQ web page is displayed and IrfanView starts up

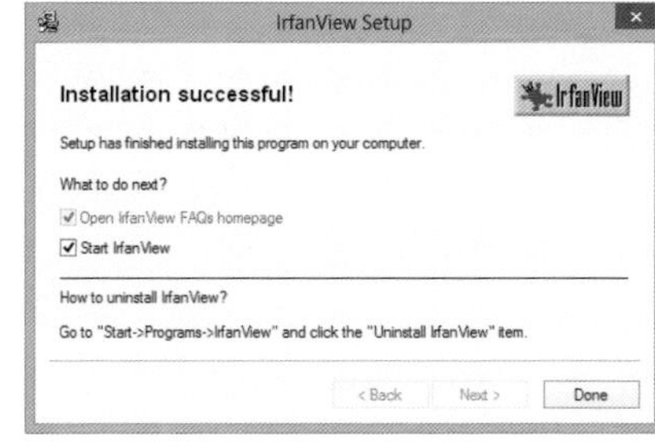
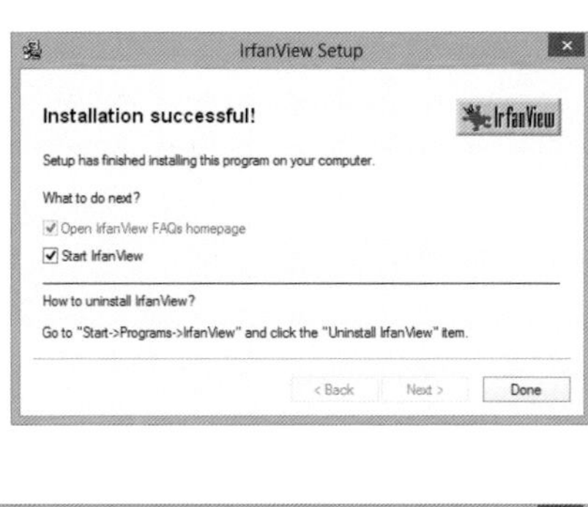

4. In this example, image 16 of 55 is showing

5. Click forward or back buttons to scroll through all the images

Notepad++

http://www.notepad-plus-plus.org

Notepad++ is a free text editor and Notepad replacement that is particularly designed for source code editing and supports over 50 languages, ranging from Ada to XML and YAML.

1. Go to the website and select the Download tab

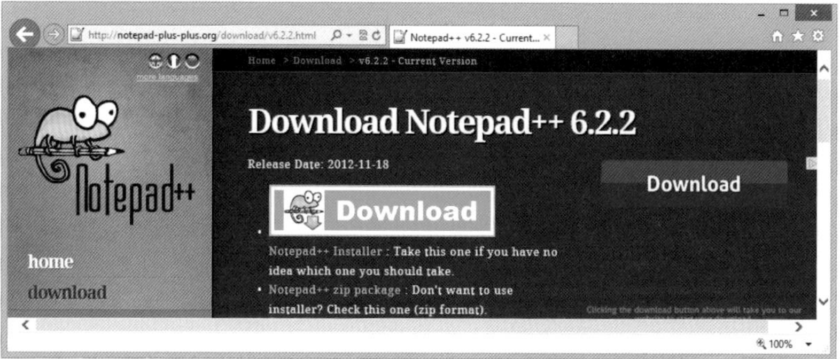

2. Choose to download the current version

3. Follow the prompts to run the Setup Wizard and install Notepad++

4. The program opens with the Change Log, showing new features and fixes

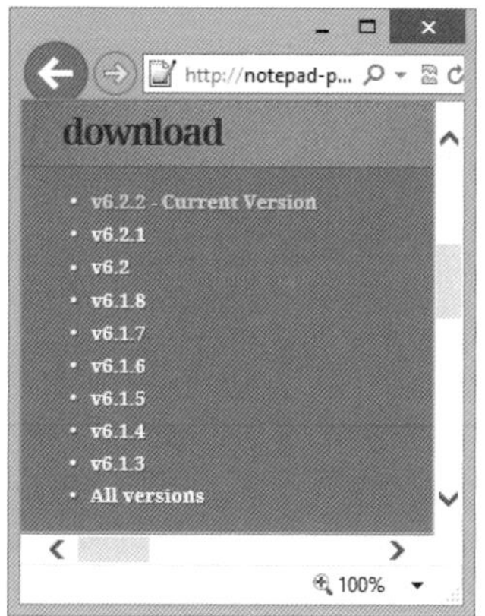

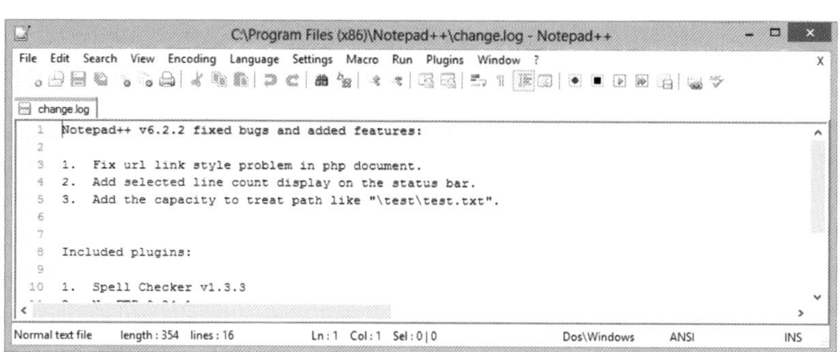

In addition to language support, the main advantage over the built-in Notepad is tabbed editing, which allows you to work with multiple open files.

Hot tip

If you are interested in programming, you can download the source code for this application.

OpenOffice.org

http://www.openoffice.org

Don't forget

This website is the entry point for all aspects of OpenOffice.org, with help, documentation, templates and clipart, as well as installation.

OpenOffice.org is an open-source suite with a powerful set of applications that are very similar to the Microsoft Office, and include techniques such as macros and templates, but have the advantage of being free to use.

1. Visit the website and select Download from the options

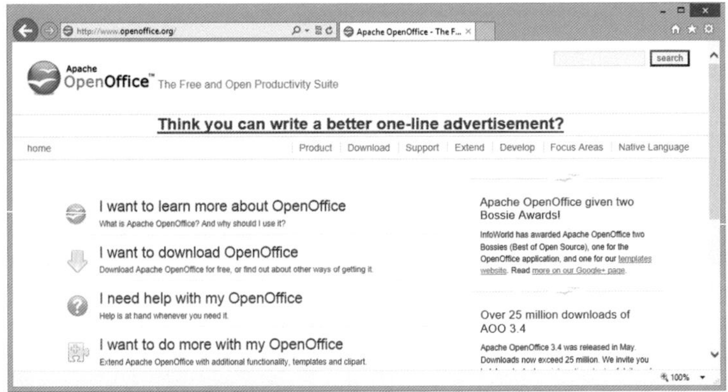

Hot tip

You'll be invited to contribute, but it's your time and effort they want, not your money, since the product is built on user participation.

2. Select Download now to get the version for your system

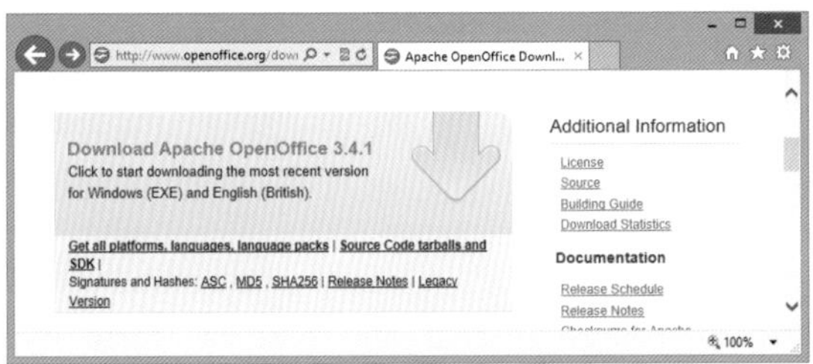

Beware

Because someone else owns the trademark OpenOffice, the correct name for both the open-source project and its software is the full term OpenOffice.org (or the abbreviation OOo).

3. Follow the prompts to unpack and save the installation files ready for the actual installation

4 Provide your name and optionally your organization, as they are to be used in OpenOffice documents

5 Select the Complete setup, and click Next

6 Upon completion, click Finish to end the Wizard

7 Click the shortcut placed on the desktop to start OpenOffice.org 3.3

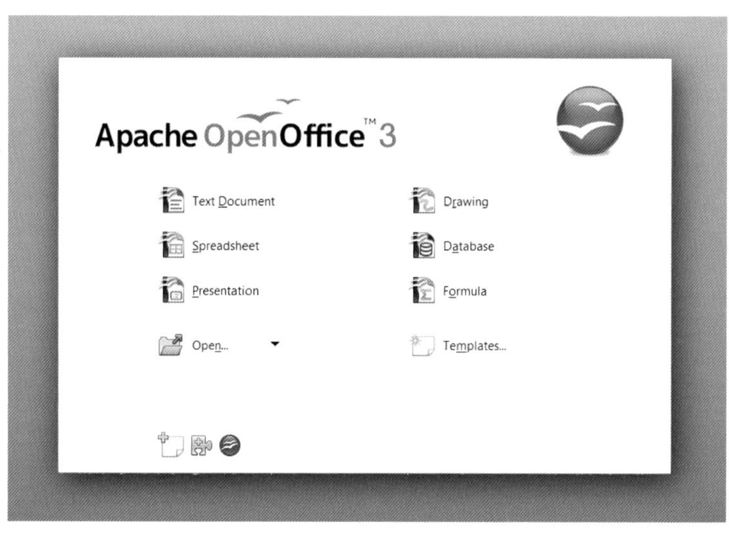

Don't forget

You will also be asked to register your details, the first time you run OpenOffice.org.

Hot tip

OpenOffice.org consists of six components: Writer (word processor) Calc (spreadsheet) Impress (presentations) Draw (vector graphics) Base (database) and Math (formula editor).

Paint.NET

http://www.getpaint.net

Where the built-in Windows Paint doesn't have the power you need, Paint.NET gives you facilities to crop, cut, or edit an image.

It's not equivalent to the full Adobe Photoshop, but it is just what's needed for casual graphic design tasks.

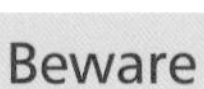

There are many links to lots of programs, such as Facemoods, WhiteSmoke and FLV Player, so make sure that the link you choose does download Paint.NET itself.

1. Click Download or click the Paint.NET v3.5.10 link

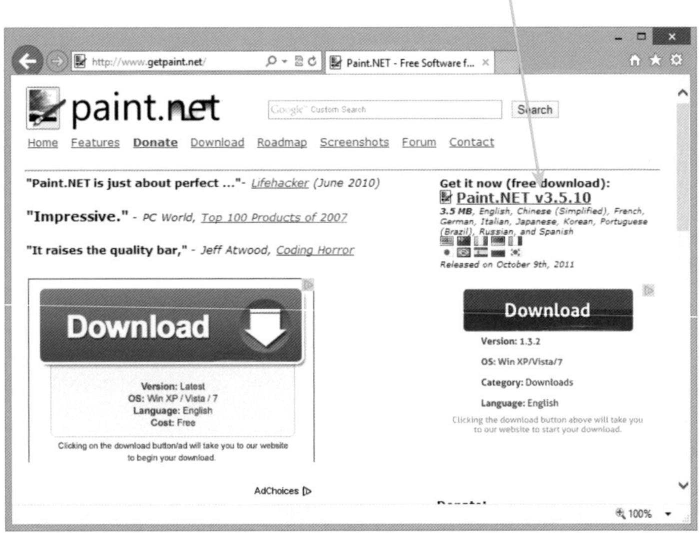

2. Click the Download Now button for Paint.NET

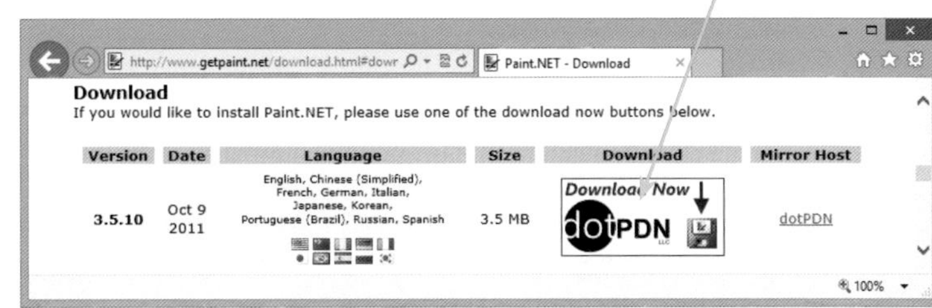

3. Choose to Open the compressed file Paint.NET.3.5.10.Install.zip

4. This expands to the executable file Paint.NET.3.5.10.Install

Free Download Now:
Paint.NET v3.5.10
System Requirements
Windows 7 (recommended), or Windows XP SP3, or Windows Vista SP1+, or newer. 800MHz processor (CPU). 512MB RAM. 1024 x 768 screen resolution. .NET Framework 3.5 SP1 (free download from Microsoft).

5. Choose Quick for the install method and click Next

6. Agree terms and conditions and continue

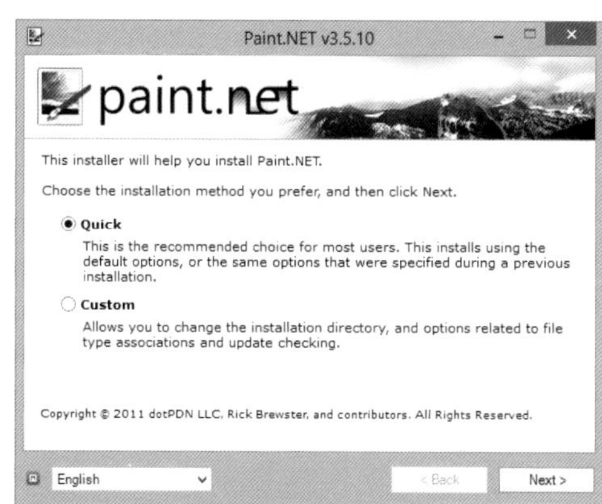

Don't forget

During the installation, Paint.NET will be optimized for best performance on your particular system.

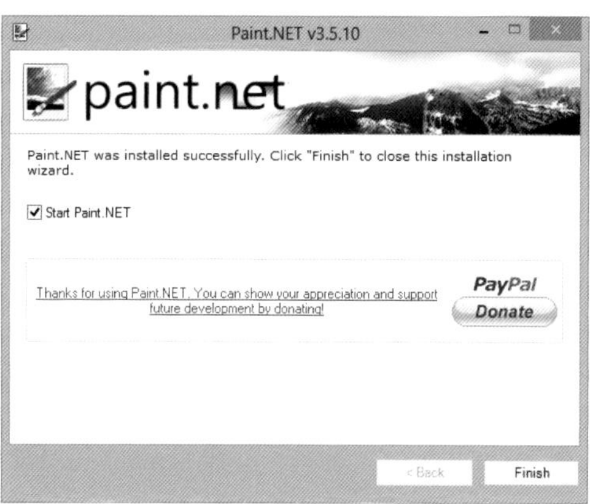

7. Follow the prompts to complete the installation

8. Click Finish, to start Paint.NET

Beware

Paint.NET is free, and you are reminded not to accept any requests for payment. However, you are encouraged to contribute to future development.

Hot tip

Select Effects to see the range offered, Photo for example with Glow, Sharpen and Soften as well as Red Eye Removal. Adjustments also applies various changes to the appearance.

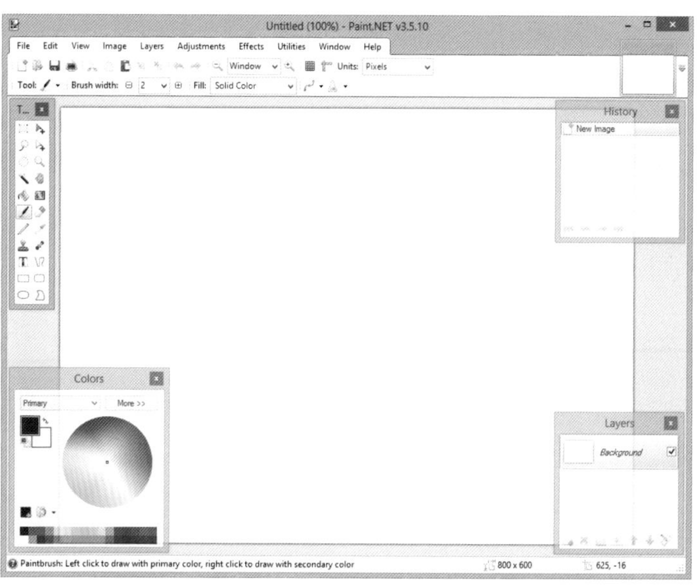

µTorrent

http://www.utorrent.com

Don't forget

A BitTorrent client is a computer program that manages downloads and uploads using the BitTorrent protocol. This is used for peer-to-peer file sharing for distributing large amounts of data.

μTorrent (also referred to as uTorrent) is a freeware, but closed source BitTorrent client. The μ in its name implies the prefix micro, in deference to the program's small size: the program is only 391KB, but it can handle very large downloads, very rapidly.

1. At the μTorrent website click the Free Download button

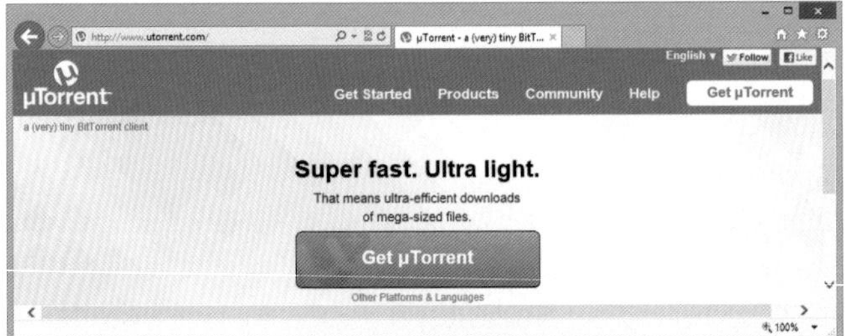

Hot tip

Note that the Windows Store has a *µ*torrent client in the form of a Windows 8 and Windows RT app, at a charge of $1.99. (*Correct at the time of printing.*)

2. Follow prompts to download and run the Setup Wizard

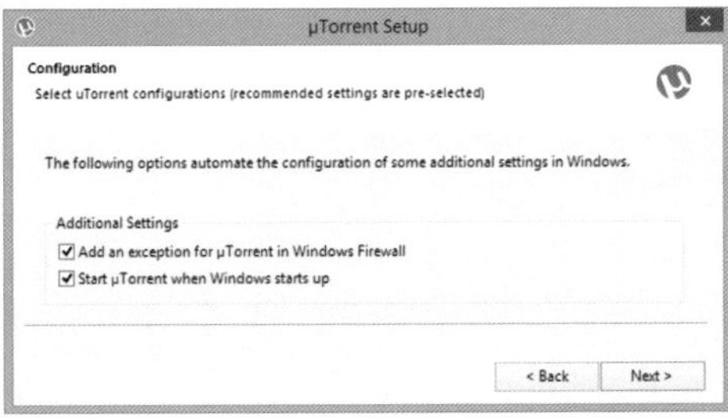

3. When the installation completes, μTorrent is launched

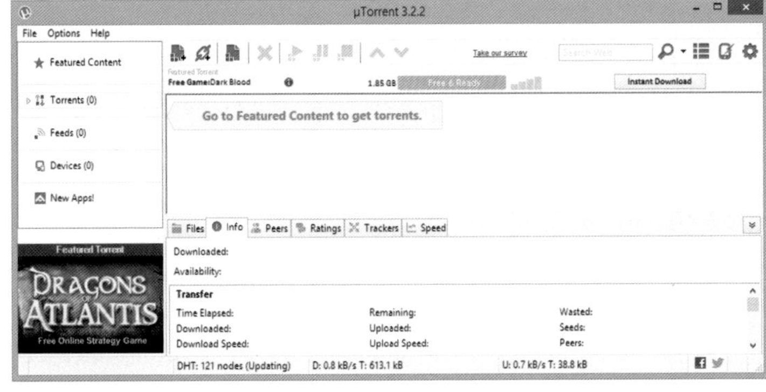

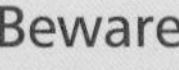

Beware

Make sure that files you select for downloading via *µ*Torrent are in the public domain and not subject to copyright.

9 Windows Store

If you need apps to run on your Windows 8 devices, the Windows Store is the place to go. This chapter shows how to access, search and navigate the Store. You will also learn how to install apps and keep them updated, and how to manage them on the Start screen.

Accessing the Store

When you need apps, the Windows Store is the place to go. It is, in fact, the only place to go – official Windows 8 apps are not available from any other source. To access the store:

1. On the Start screen click the Store tile

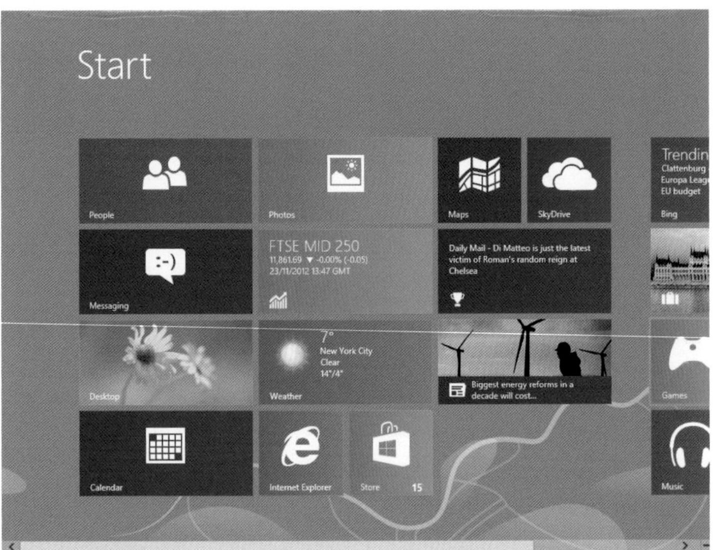

2. The Windows Store will open

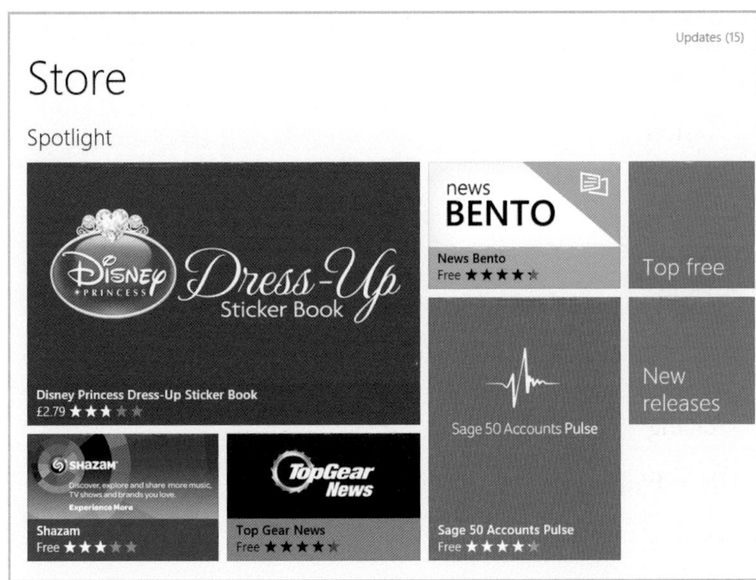

Apps can only be sourced from Microsoft's official Windows Store.

Store categories

As with any online store that stocks a range of different products, the Windows Store organizes its products in specific categories to make it easier for people to find what they are looking for. Currently, in order of access, these are:

- Games
- Social
- Entertainment
- Photo
- Music & Video
- Sport
- Books & Ref
- News & Weather
- Health & Fitness
- Food & Dining
- Lifestyle
- Shopping
- Lifestyle
- Finance
- Productivity
- Tools
- Security
- Business
- Education
- Government

Don't forget

When looking in a category, check to see if there are any sub-categories.

The following categories have sub-categories:

Games

- Action
- Adventure
- Arcade
- Card
- Casino
- Family
- Kids
- Music
- Puzzle
- Racing
- Role Playing
- Shooter
- Simulation
- Sports
- Strategy

Music & Video

- Music
- Video

Security

- PC protection
- Personal security

News & Weather

- News
- Weather

Books & Ref

- E-reader
- Fiction
- Kids
- Non-fiction
- Reference

Navigating the Store

On the Windows Store Home page, initially, there is no obvious means of navigation.

Users with a touchscreen, of course, don't need scroll bars and the like, as they can simply pan to the left or right with a flick of the finger. Mouse users, however, do need them. For these users, all that's necessary is a single movement of the mouse – this activates a scroll bar at the bottom of the screen. Alternatively, they can use the mouse wheel to move backwards and forwards.

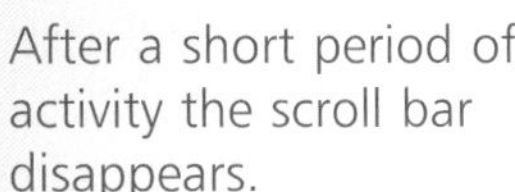

Hot tip

After a short period of activity the scroll bar disappears.

Whichever way you do it though, there are a lot of categories to scroll through. An easy way of reducing the amount of scrolling necessary is to use the keyboard shortcut Ctrl + -. This reduces the size of the tiles thus fitting more into the screen as demonstrated in the images below:

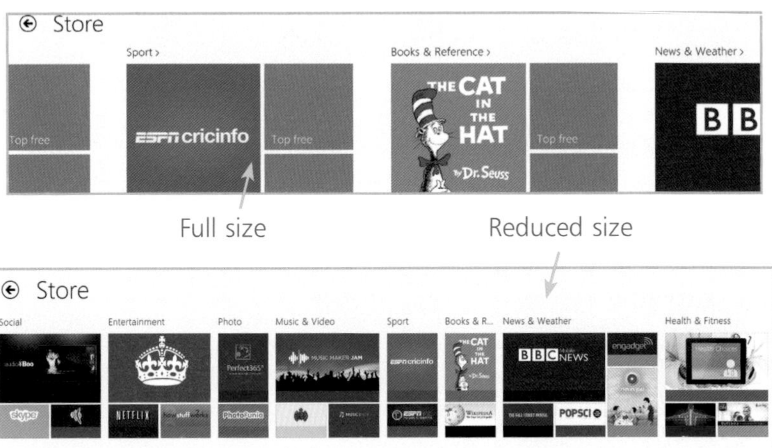

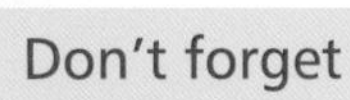

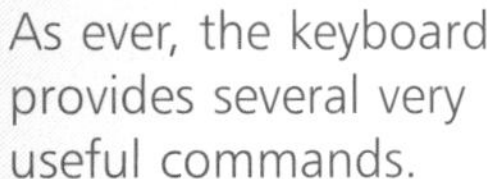

Don't forget

As ever, the keyboard provides several very useful commands.

Ctrl + + restores the full size screen. You can also use the left and right arrow keys to scroll across the screen. The End key takes you to the far right of the screen while the Home key returns you to the far left of the screen.

When actually in a category, however, these keyboard commands do not work so you need to use touch gestures or the mouse as described above.

Move between screens, e.g. a category page and the Home page, by clicking the arrow at the top-left of each screen. Pressing the Backspace key does the same thing. Finally, right-clicking opens an app bar at the top that provides a Home option.

Exploring categories

On the home page, store categories are presented across the top of the screen. Two or three featured apps are shown below – these are apps that are considered to be outstanding examples of their type and thus worthy of display.

To the left of these featured apps are two tiles – Top free and New Releases; the names being self-explanatory.

1. To open a category click its heading

2. On the category page you will the see the heading (Music & Video in the example below) with the number of apps in the category specified at the right

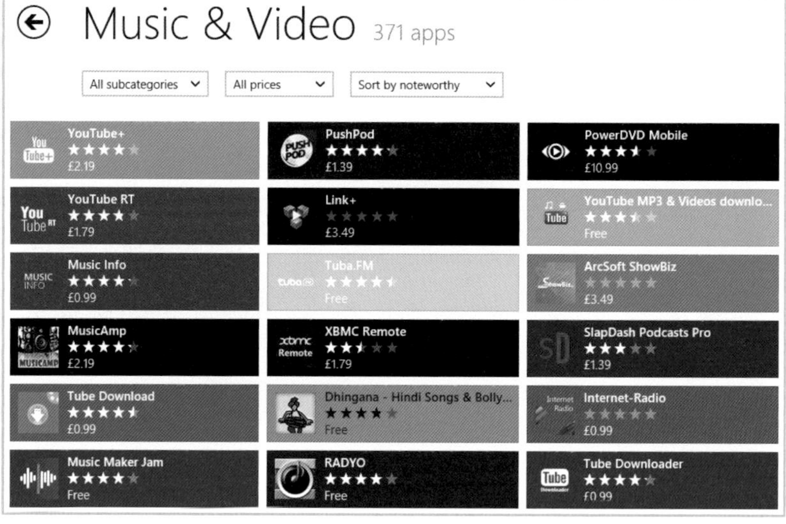

3. Below the heading are the category filters – All subcategories, All prices, and Sort by noteworthy

4. The main body of the page is taken up by the apps. Some of these categories contain quite a few apps and it will require a lot of scrolling to view them all

Hot tip

A quick glance to the right of the heading will show you the number of apps in the category.

Hot tip

The view you see when on a category page is the only view available – its not possible to zoom in or out.

Search the Store

Search is an extremely important component of modern user interfaces and, currently, is one of the most common ways for customers to find things when browsing online stores.

Accordingly, a lot of users get extremely frustrated when they look for a search box in the Windows Store. No matter what page they look on or what view they try, there doesn't seem to be one.

However, there is; they are just going about it the wrong way. The thing to remember here is that the Windows Store is an app just like any other and so is searchable with the Search charm provided by Windows 8. Try the following:

Don't forget 

The Windows Store doesn't have a dedicated search facility so don't waste your time looking for one.

1. When in the Store, simply type your search term – you don't need a search box at all. For example, type video converter and press Enter

2. On the left of the page, you will see the results of your search

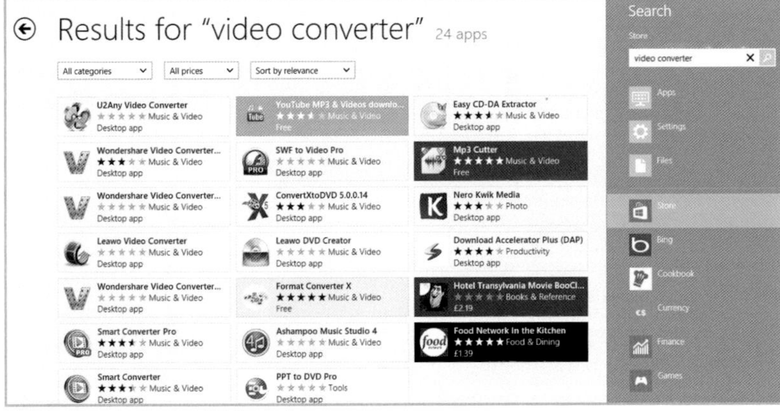

3. If any of the apps shown appear to be of interest, just left-click to open it and get further details

Don't forget 

You don't have to open the Charms bar to access the Search charm – just start typing wherever you are in the new Windows 8 interface and Search will open.

An important aspect of the Search charm is that it is universally accessible. This means you can search for an app (or anything else for that matter) no matter where you are in the new Windows 8 interface. We see how this works on the next page.

In the example shown below, you're using the Internet Explorer app to browse a site about Mahjong. This triggers in you a sudden curiosity to see if there are any Mahjong apps available.

Hot tip

As you type in the search box, suggestions immediately appear in the area below the box.

All you have to do is open the Search charm and type mahjong in the search box. Press Enter, and click Store; you'll now get a page of results related to mahjong.

For general searches, filters are available to narrow the search results down to a more manageable level.

The most important of these is the All categories filter, which will be found in categories that, typically, contain hundreds, if not thousands, of apps. This allows the main category to be split into subcategories.

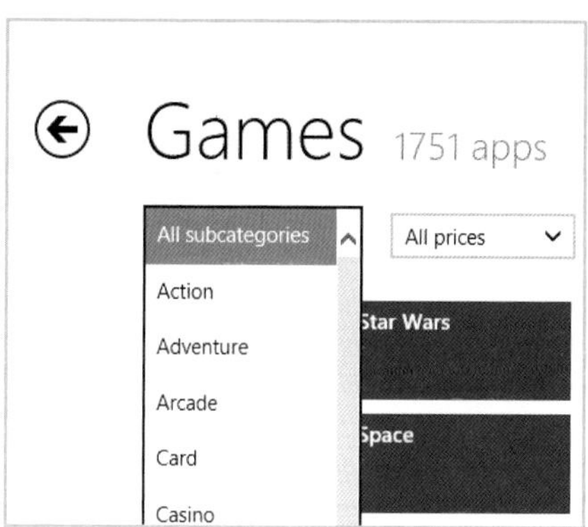

The All prices filter provides three options – Free, Free and trial, and Paid.

Hot tip

Used in conjunction, the three filters provided enable a category containing thousands of apps to be whittled down to a few dozen.

Finally, there is the Sort by noteworthy filter. This enables searches to be categorized by newest, highest rating, lowest price and highest price.

Select an app

To select an app, simply click on its tile. As an example, we have opened the Kindle app as shown below:

At the risk of stating the obvious, before paying for an app it's worth checking out the reviews.

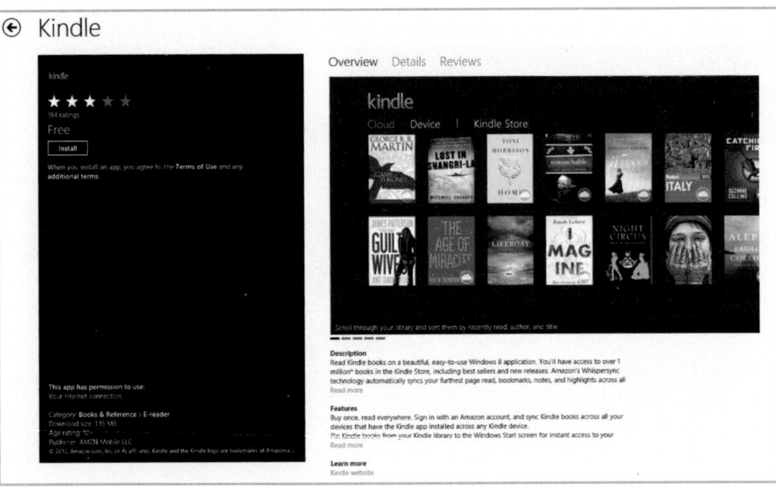

One of the first (and one of the most important if it's a paid app) things you'll see on the left is the app's overall rating. Below this you'll see if it's free, and the Install button. At the bottom is the app's download size, age rating and publisher.

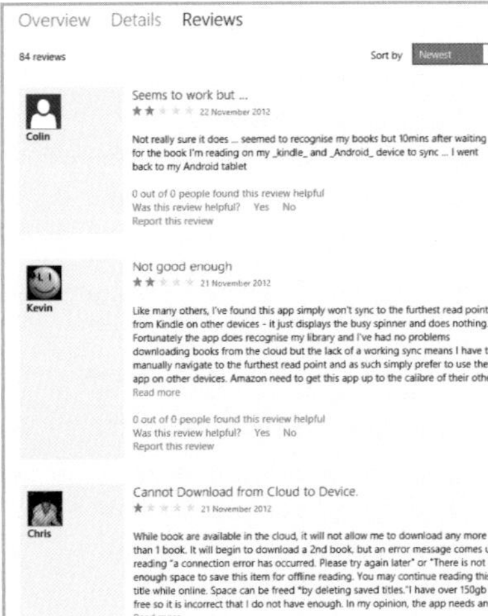

Moving across the page, there are three headings – Overview (the current view), Details, and Reviews.

Overview gives you a quick resume of what the app does and any notable features.

Details, typically, informs you what processors and languages are supported by the app, plus any release notes that may exist.

In the Reviews tab, you see what other users make of the app. A filter is provided in this view, which enables the reviews to be categorized by Newest, Oldest, Highest rated, Lowest rated, and Most helpful.

Download and install

To install an app, click the Install button at the top-left. If you are logged in with a Microsoft account, the download/install routine will begin immediately.

1. At the top-right, you'll see a message that says "Installing xxx" (Kindle in our example)

Installing Kindle...

Results for "kindle" 16 apps

2. When the installation is complete, again at the top-right you'll see a message stating Kindle was installed

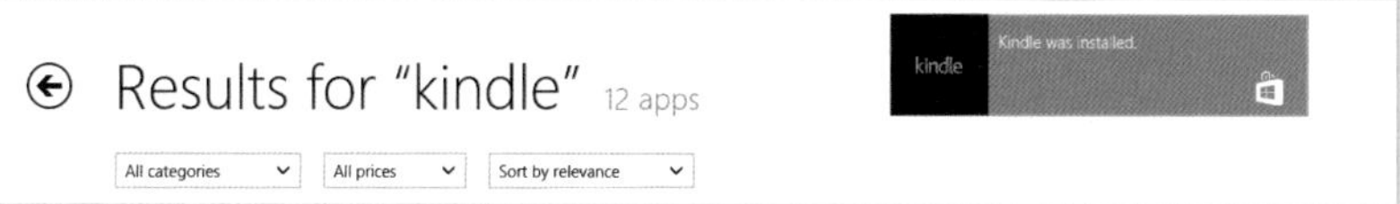

3. Go to the Start screen and at the far right, you'll see the new app

If, however, you are not logged in with a Microsoft account, you will be asked to do so:

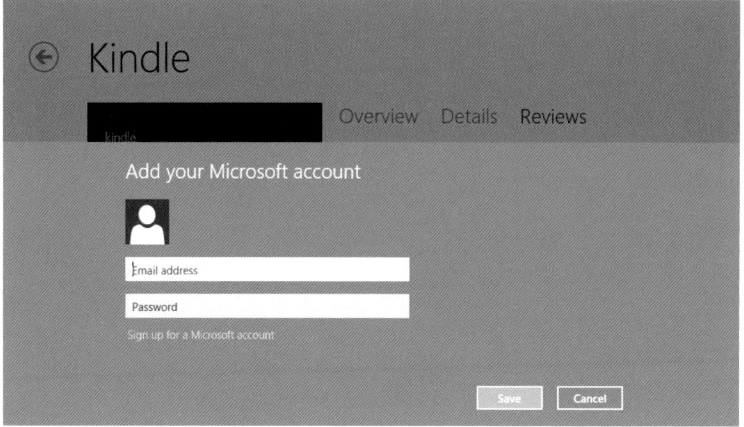

4. Sign in with an existing Microsoft account or create a new one. Then go back to the app and click Install again.

You will not be able to download an app (even a free one) unless you are logged in with a Microsoft account.

Skype

Skype is a service that allows users to communicate by voice, video, and instant messaging. The service is available as an app for Windows 8 and Windows RT, and can be downloaded from the Windows Store.

Don't forget

Calls to other users within the Skype service are free of charge, while calls via landline and mobile networks are charged via a debit-based user account system.

1. When you are in the Windows Store simply type skype. The app opens and at the left you'll see the Install option

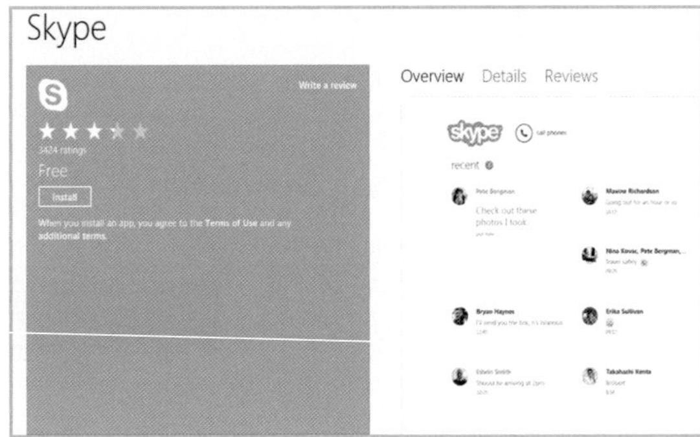

2. When the app is run for the first time you will be asked if it can use your webcam and microphone – click Allow or Block

3. Next, you will be asked if Skype is allowed to run in the background – click Allow or Disallow

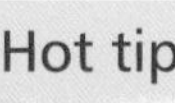

Hot tip

Skype provides additional features, such as file transfer, and videoconferencing.

4. You will now see Skype's Home screen. Before you can make a call you need credit (unless you are calling another Skype user). Click the call phones icon at the top-left of the screen

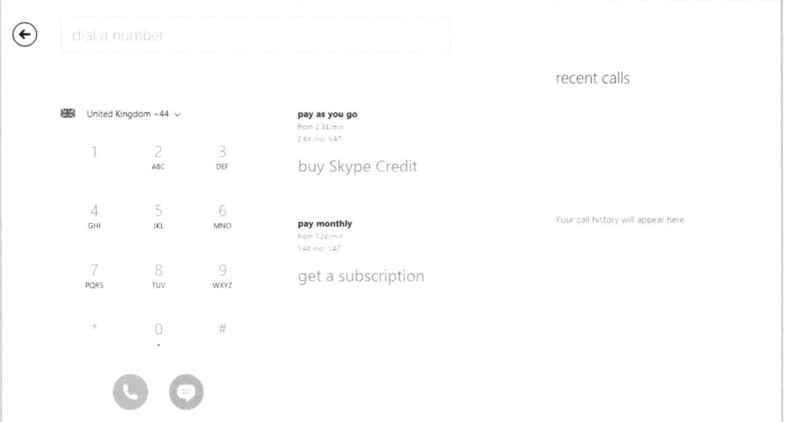

5 At the next screen, you are offered two options – buy Skype Credit and get a subscription. Make your choice by clicking the required option. If you select the latter, for example, you will see the following:

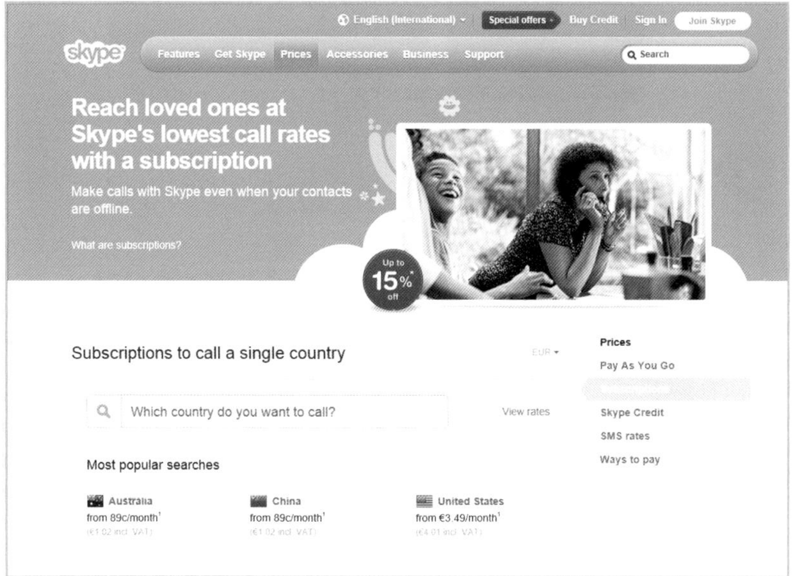

6 Once the financial side of things is sorted out, close the Internet Explorer window. You will be taken back to the app and can start using it

Hot tip

The Skype app can be extremely useful when used with Windows 8's split-screen feature, Snap. This enables a conversation to be had, while at the same time getting on with something else on the main part of the screen.

Hot tip

A feature of the Skype app is that it can be left running permanently without any adverse effect on the computer.

App account

One of the big advantages of logging in to all your devices with the same Microsoft account is that any apps you have bought and installed on one device can be downloaded from the cloud and installed on another device. For example, the author has bought a popular game called Hydro Thunder Hurricane and installed it on his home PC. To install it on his laptop, all he has to do is:

Don't forget

Having paid for an app, you can install it from the cloud on any other devices you use with the same Microsoft account.

1. On the laptop's Start screen, click the Store tile

2. In the Search charm, enter hydro thunder hurricane and click the entry on the results pane

Hot tip

Because the app has already been paid for, the Install button is shown rather than the Buy now button.

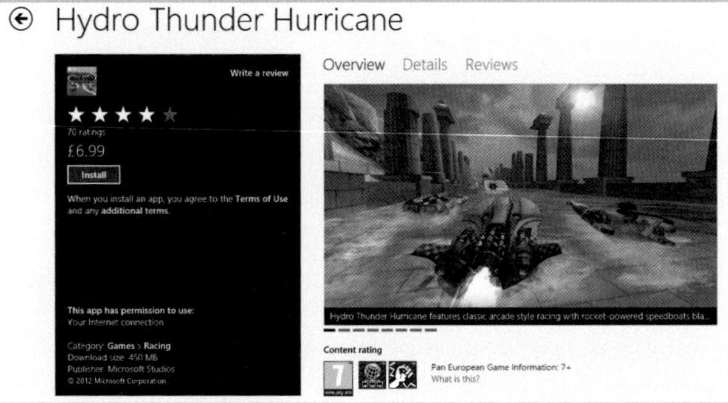

3. When the app opens, click the Install button. The account password is requested

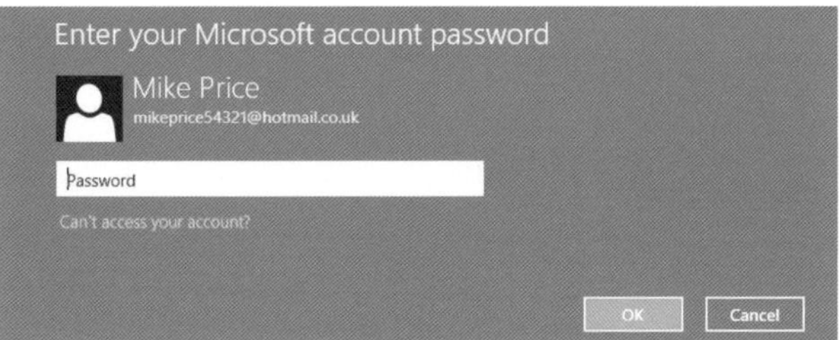

4. The password is entered and the OK button clicked. The app is downloaded to the author's laptop and installed

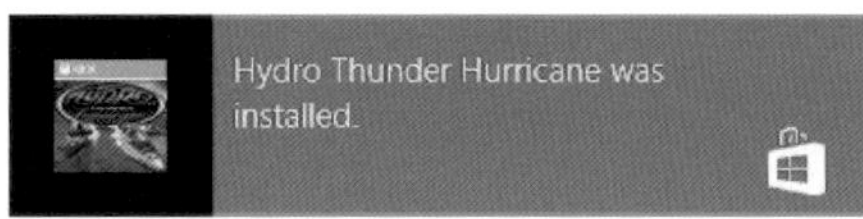

Updates

An important feature in Windows is Windows Update. This enables users to keep the operating system, plus any other Microsoft applications they may have, updated and current.

By default, Windows updates itself automatically. So the operating system is covered, but what about Windows 8 apps?

These are subject to updates, just as regular Microsoft programs are, but the update process here is not automatic. Therefore, it is up to users to do it themselves.

1. Go to the Start screen and click the Store tile

2. When the Windows Store opens, look at the top right-hand corner of the screen

Updates (19)

Store

3. If updates are available, there'll be an indication of how many. Click the indication to open a list of the updates

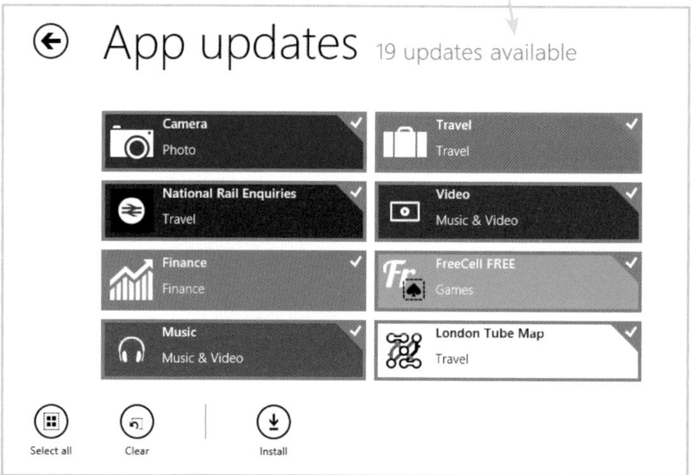

4. By default, all the updates are selected (indicated by a green arrow) – just click the Install button to install them all at once. To deselect them all, click the Deselect button, and to deselect them individually click the tiles

Windows 8 apps need to be updated manually.

Hot tip

The Store tile also shows the number of updates that are available for your installed apps.

Manage apps

App tiles are much larger than traditional desktop icons and so occupy a lot of screen space. The more congested the Start screen becomes, the more sideways scrolling will be necessary to get to a particular app.

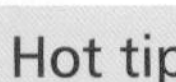

Hot tip

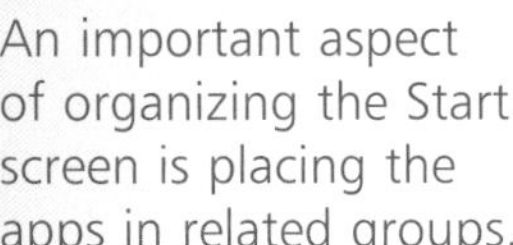

An important aspect of organizing the Start screen is placing the apps in related groups.

Organizing Start screen tiles

So, perhaps one of the first things a user new to Windows 8 will do is to introduce some organization into how the Start screen tiles are presented.

The most important thing is to place your most frequently accessed apps at the left of the screen where they will be on view by default. Do this by left-clicking on the tile, dragging it to where you want it and then releasing it.

Create and organize groups

However, this will be a laborious way of moving large numbers of apps. The answer is to place your apps in groups, which can then be moved about the screen in blocks. Quite apart from making it easier to arrange your Start screen, having your apps in specific and related groups will make it much easier to locate them as and when required.

Hot tip

Another thing you can do is to reduce the size of the large tiles. This will create more space on the Start screen, which reduces the amount of scrolling necessary. Just right-click on a tile to open the app bar at the bottom where you'll see the "Smaller" option.

So how's it done? If you take any tile and drag it across the screen, you'll see a gray bar appear momentarily in certain positions, as shown below. This is the group bar and it splits clusters of tiles into separate groups – drop a tile to the left of the bar and it will be part of the group to the left; drop it to the right of the bar and it will be part of the group to the right.

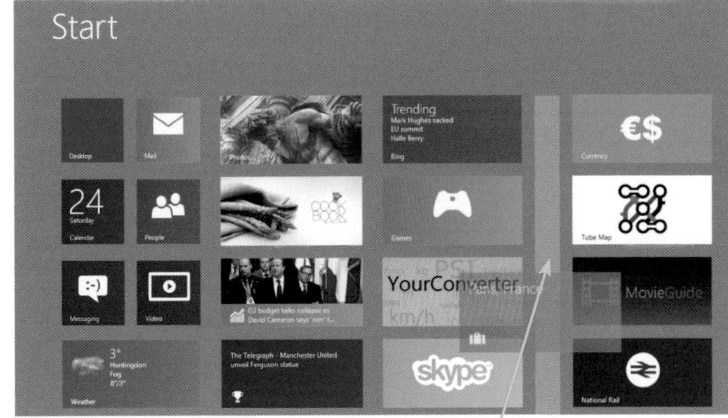

If you want to start a new group, drag an app on to the group bar and release it – the new group is created. Add more tiles to it as already described.

When you have all your tiles arranged in related groups, you can arrange the groups themselves. The way to do this is by making use of Windows 8's Semantic Zoom feature. Touchscreen users can "pinch out" and if you're using a mouse, press the Ctrl button while rotating the mouse wheel. Both actions reduce the size of the Start screen and the installed apps as shown below:

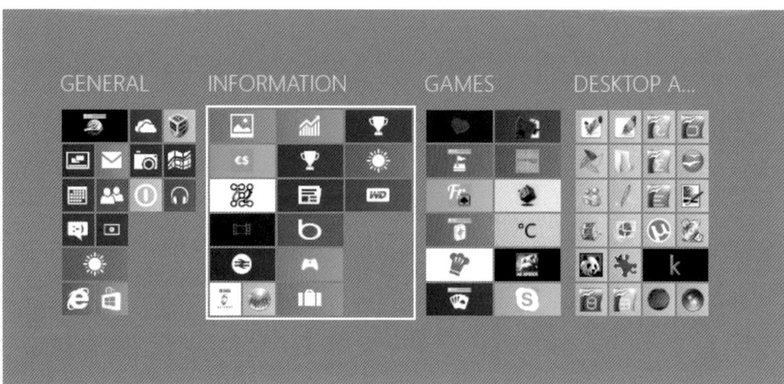

While in this view, you can select entire groups of tiles (the selected group is outlined) and drag them to new positions.

Name a Group

You can also assign names to groups in this view (in the example above, each of the four groups have a name). This is very easy to do – just right-click on a group and click Name group on the app bar at the bottom of the screen.

Enter the group's name in the box and click Name.

You can also zoom out of the Start screen by pressing Ctrl + –.

The Start screen employs a grid structure that keeps tiles neatly aligned.

Desktop apps

An aspect of the Windows Store that causes some confusion is that it is not restricted to Windows 8 apps; it contains Desktop programs as well. Furthermore, the Store handles these programs in a different way than it does the Windows 8 apps.

Hot tip

The link provided for Desktop apps will send users directly to the download page on the publisher's website.

Rather than pay and install through the Store, users have to do these actions at the publisher's website – a link to the site is provided. When you look in a category, or do a search, you will see immediately which are Windows 8 apps and which are Desktop apps – the latter are clearly marked as such.

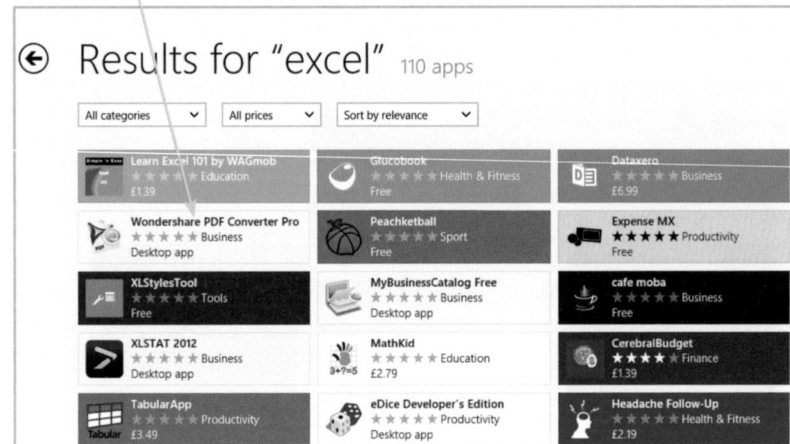

Don't forget

The Windows Store contains both Windows 8 apps and Desktop programs.

When you go to a Desktop app page, you will not be given a Install option. Instead, you will see the link to the website, plus, it will be stated quite clearly that the app has to be obtained from the publisher. We see this in the example below:

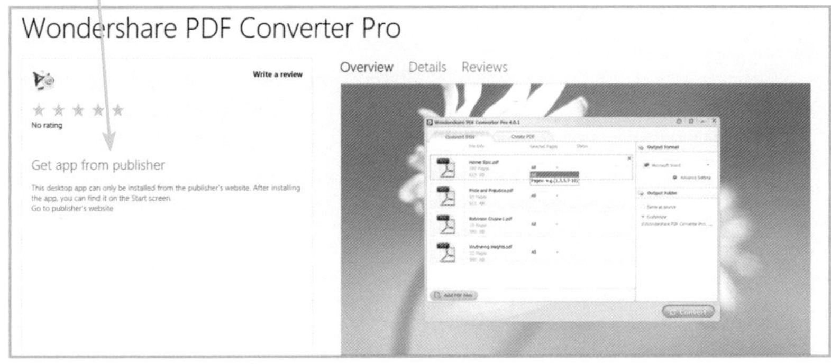

Don't forget

When you buy a Desktop program via the Store, don't forget that updates to the app must be downloaded from the publisher's website – they won't be provided through the store.

10 Search techniques

Windows provides many ways to help you find the programs, utilities and information that you need. There's a search box in every File Explorer folder, and the Search Charm, which is available no matter where you are in Windows.

Start screen search

You're on the Start screen and you need to search for something – how do you go about it? Well, it's remarkably simple in Windows 8 – all you have to do is type. Just put your fingers on the keyboard and type in your search term – you don't need to use a search box at all.

Searches are not restricted to the Windows 8 interface – the Desktop interface is searched as well.

As you begin to type, the Start screen will instantly update to the screen shown below:

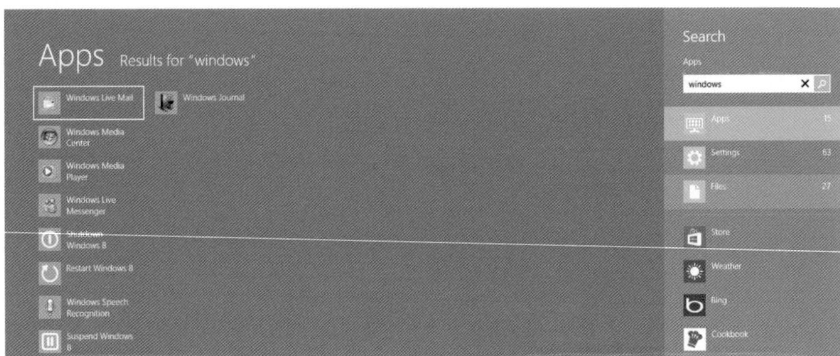

In our example, we've searched for windows. By default, the search results shown are taken from the system's apps and, as we can see above, a number of windows-related apps have been found.

However, it's not just the apps that have been searched – next to Settings on the right, you'll see the number 63. This indicates that 63 settings related to windows have also been found by the search. If you click Settings, you'll see what they are.

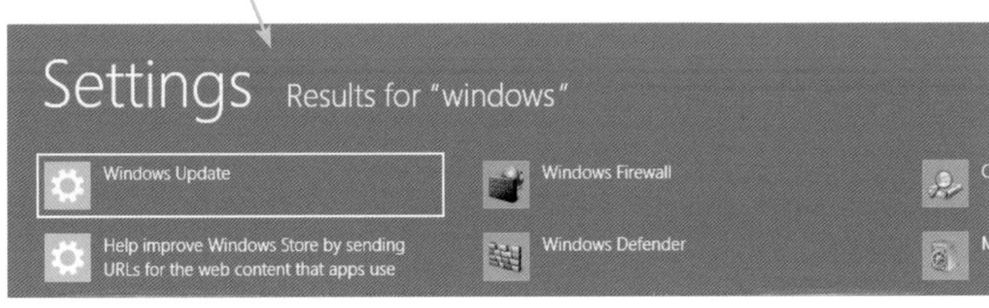

The Search Charm can display results for searches related to specific Windows 8 apps.

Below Settings, you'll see Files. If there are any files related to windows on the PC, they will be indicated here (27 in our example). Underneath Files, you'll see a list of all the Windows 8 apps. Click one to see if a related search result has been found in the app.

Search app

When a search is done in Windows 8, by default, the Apps filter is selected. If this is what you want, fine. Just type your search term and select from the apps results.

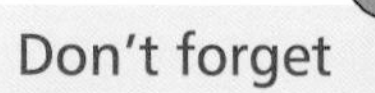

The Windows 8 Search charm provides three primary filters – Apps, Settings, and Files.

However, you may not want this – you may want the search to be done using the Settings or Files filters instead. If so, from an Apps search you could, of course, just click on either of these filters as shown right.

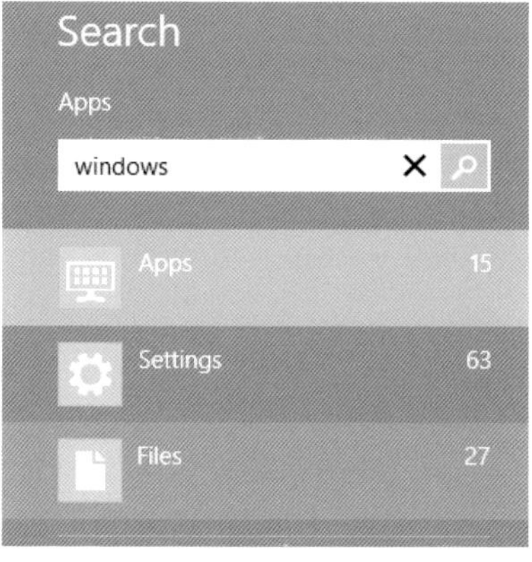

A quicker way, though, is to use a keyboard shortcut that will open the Search charm with the desired filter already selected.

Pressing Winkey + W enables a Settings search to be done from anywhere in Windows 8.

Pressing Winkey + F enables a Files search to be done from anywhere in Windows 8.

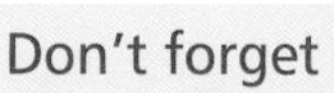

It isn't necessary to be on the Start screen in order to do a search. The Search Charm is universal.

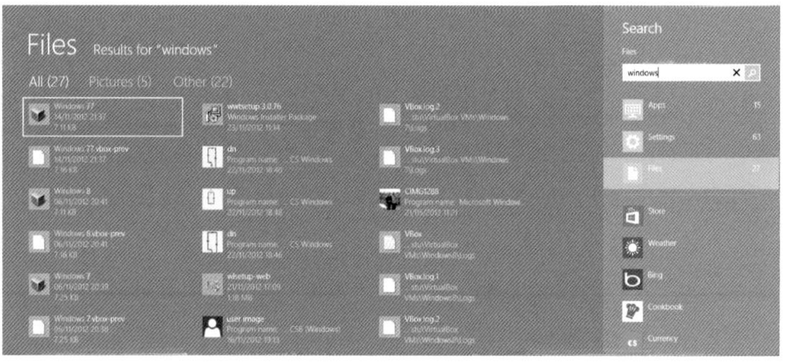

File Explorer search

The Search utility is one of the best features in Windows 8 and provides quick and very comprehensive search results – sometimes too much so in fact. While the Apps, Settings and Files filters help to narrow searches down, general, and system wide, searches can still produce far too many results.

The search facility provided by File Explorer is extremely useful in situations such as these as it enables searches to be restricted to specific parts of Windows, thus producing fewer, but more relevant, results.

Don't forget

Results from a folder search will include any subfolders the folder may contain.

1. Open any Explorer window – it doesn't matter which

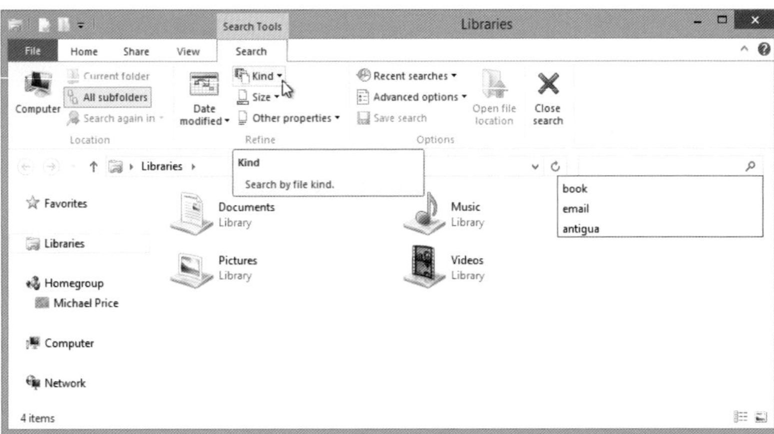

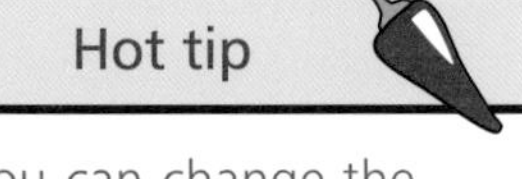

Hot tip

You can change the location from any folder to search anywhere in the computer.

2. At the right, you will see a search box. By default, searches made from this will be restricted to the contents of the folder, plus any subfolders

3. Click in the search box and you'll see a short history of the last three search terms. These can be useful if you need to repeat a search

4. Clicking in the search box also opens the Search tab on the ribbon toolbar

5. The Search tab provides a wide range of options with which to tailor your search – see page 158 for more details of these

Navigation pane

At the left of the window, you'll see the Navigation pane. By default, this shows links for Library folders, Computer and Network. These links enable any folder or drive on the computer to be accessed and thus searched. Do it as follows:

1. Move the mouse pointer over the Navigation pane and triangles appear alongside the section names. Click a white triangle to expand a list or a black triangle to collapse a list

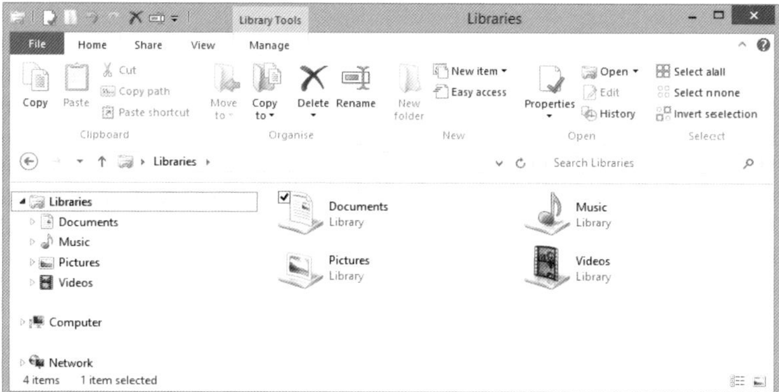

2. Select a folder name to display its contents and find files. For example, you can explore the drives, folders and files in the Computer folder

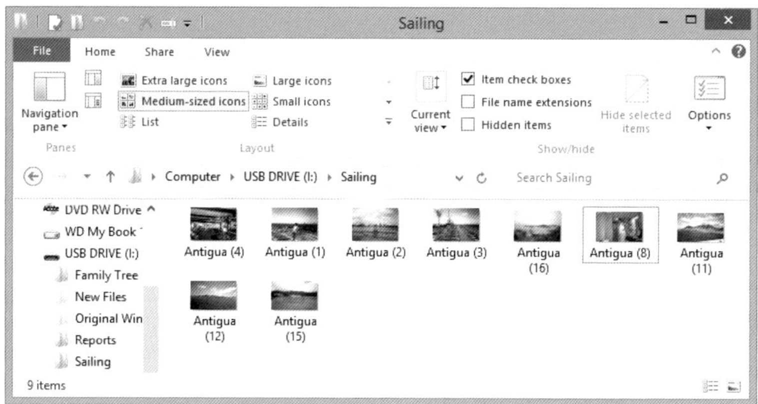

3. At any point, you can use the folder search box to search a particular folder

Hot tip

Double-click any name to expand that folder and display its contents with the one action.

Don't forget

You click the triangles or double-click the names to expand and collapse the entries.

Search tools

Windows provides a number of filters with which folder searches can be made even more relevant. These can be accessed from the ribbon toolbar found at the top of File Explorer folders.

This is a toolbar that provides options related to the task at hand, i.e. it is contextual. We'll take a closer look at this later on but for now we'll see what it has to offer in the way of search options.

Open a folder you want to search and click in the search box. The Search tab on the ribbon toolbar will immediately reveal the search tools. We'll take these as they appear on the toolbar:

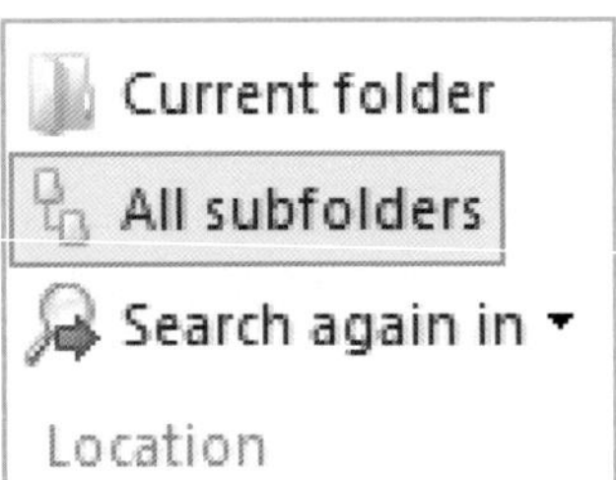

Current folder – restricts the search to the current folder

All subfolders – includes subfolders in the search

Search again in – list of locations in which to repeat the search

With the Date modified filter, it is possible to search specific dates or ranges of dates. Options provided are: Today, Yesterday, This week, Last week, This month, Last month, This year and Last year.

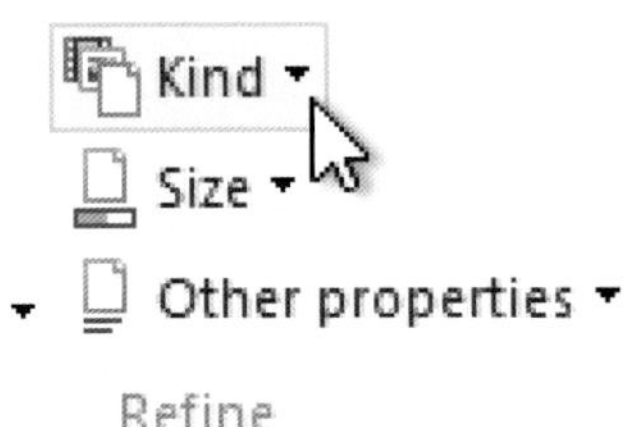

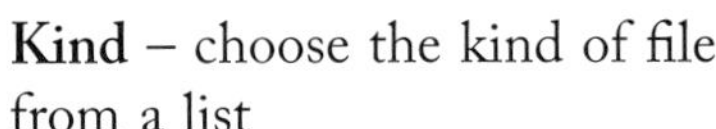

Kind – choose the kind of file from a list

Size – choose from a list of sizes ranging from tiny to gigantic

Other properties – choose from Name, Type, Folder path & Tags

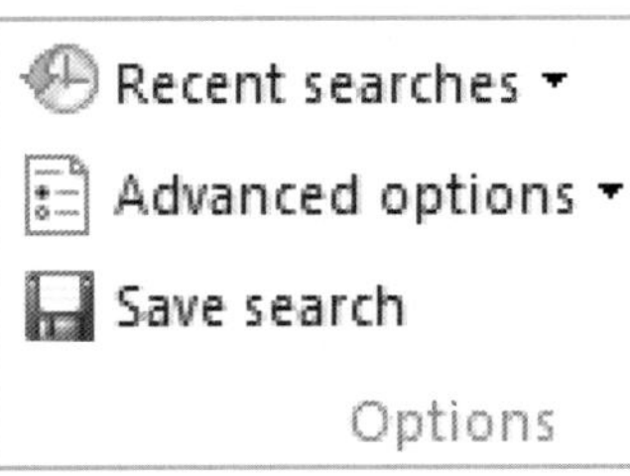

Advanced options – searches can be set as exact or partial matches, and to include compressed folders, and file contents

The Recent searches and Save search options are not filters.

Favorites

The Navigation pane includes a section where you keep shortcuts to the locations on your system that you may often need to review. To view your File Explorer favorites:

1. Open any folder, right-click in the Navigation pane and select Show favorites

2. A Favorites link now appears at the top of the pane. Select it and you will see it has three default shortcuts – Desktop, Downloads and Recent Places

3. Select a folder that you would like to add to Favorites

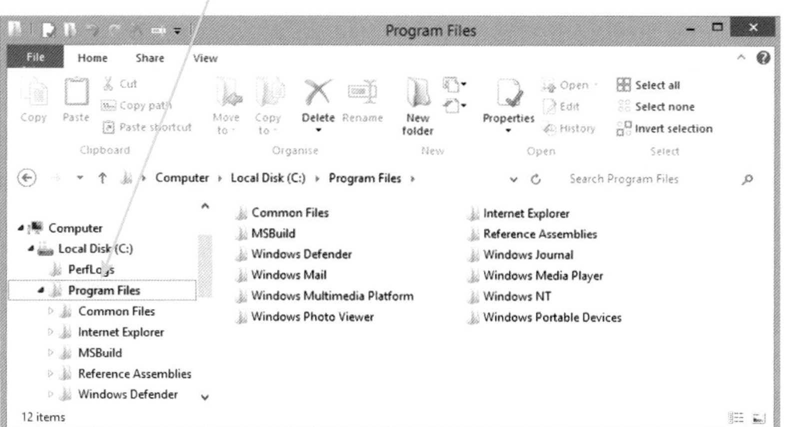

4. Right-click Favorites in the Navigation pane and select Add current location to Favorites

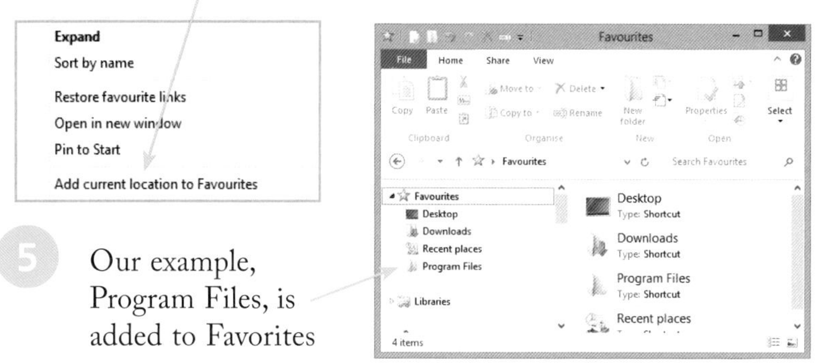

5. Our example, Program Files, is added to Favorites

Favorites can also be used to save searches that you may want to use again.

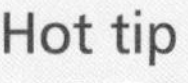

You can use this menu to sort the Favorites, or to restore the defaults if you have removed any of them. To remove a Favorite, default or new, you right-click the name and select Remove.

Folder and search options

You can change the way files and folders function and how items are displayed on your computer using Folder and search options.

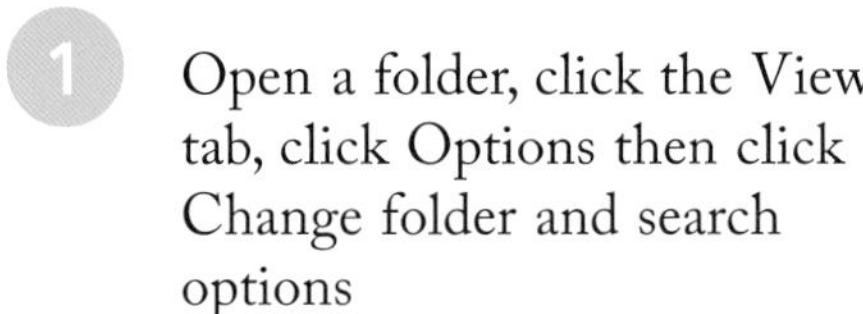

1. Open a folder, click the View tab, click Options then click Change folder and search options

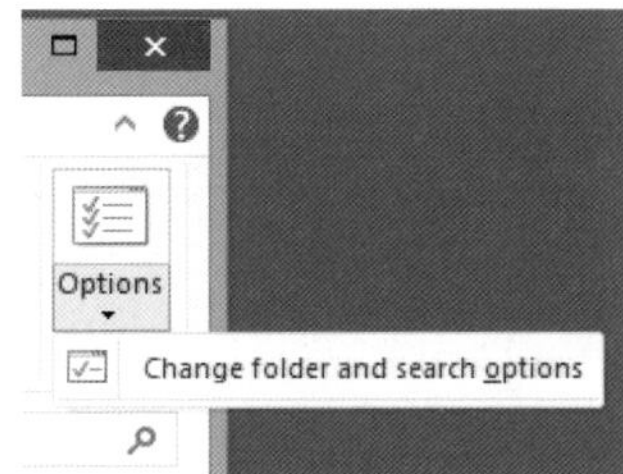

2. When Folder Options displays, select the General tab

From this panel you can:

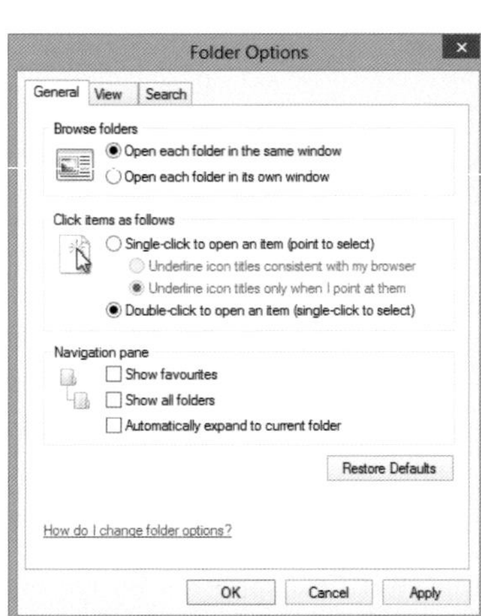

- Choose to open each folder in the same window, or in its own window
- Use double-click to open an item, or use the browser style single click to point and select items
- Control the operation of the Navigation pane
- Restore defaults after previous changes

3. Select the View tab

From here you can:

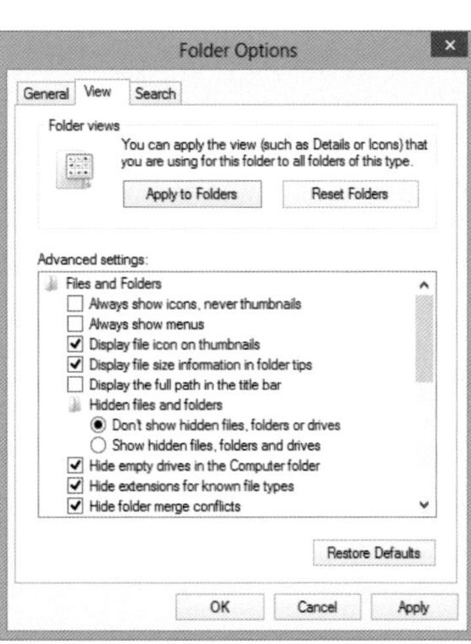

- Apply the View for the current folder to all folders of the same type
- Reset folders
- Apply advanced settings to files and folders
- Restore defaults after making changes

Don't forget

You will also find Folder Options under Appearance and Personalization in the Control Panel.

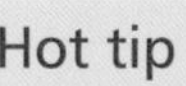

Hot tip

You can choose to hide or show hidden files, folders and drives. You can also hide or reveal file extensions.

Scroll down to reveal the remaining settings

Among these settings are options to:

- Automatically open the folders that you were using when you last shut down Windows whenever you start your computer, thus restoring your work session
- Hide or show file tips that display when you point to files
- Use check boxes to select items
- Hide empty drives in the Computer folder

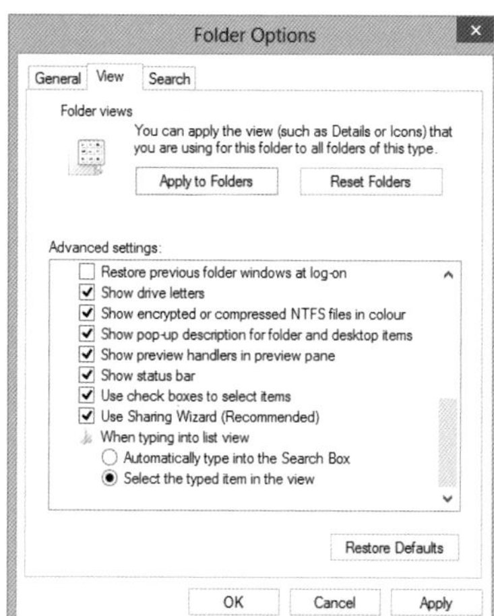

Don't forget

Make a note of the options that you would normally prefer since the Restore Defaults will undo all changes not just recent changes.

Select the Search tab

The Search settings let you manage what to search and how to search.

- Find partial matches
- Don't use the index when searching file folders for system files
- Include system directories
- Include compressed files
- Search file names and contents

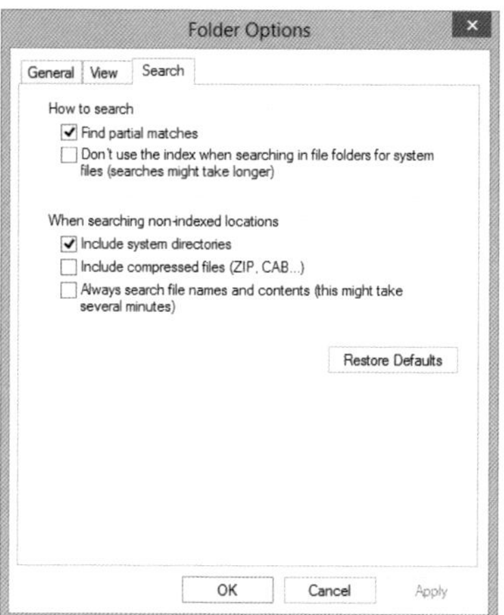

You can click the Restore Defaults button to undo any changes that might previously have been applied.

Indexing options

When you add a folder to one of the libraries, that folder will automatically be indexed. You can also add locations to the index without using libraries.

Don't forget

Windows uses the index for fast searches of the most common files on your computer. By default, folders in libraries, e-mail and offline files are indexed but program and system files are not indexed.

1 Go to the Control Panel and click Indexing Options

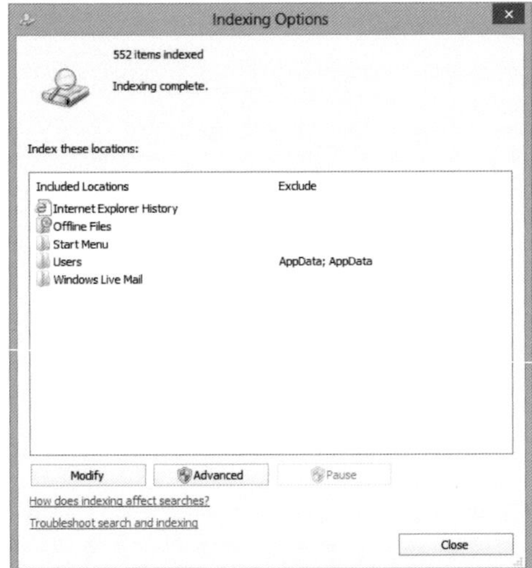

2 Click Modify then expand the folder lists and select new locations to index, for example Book, and click OK

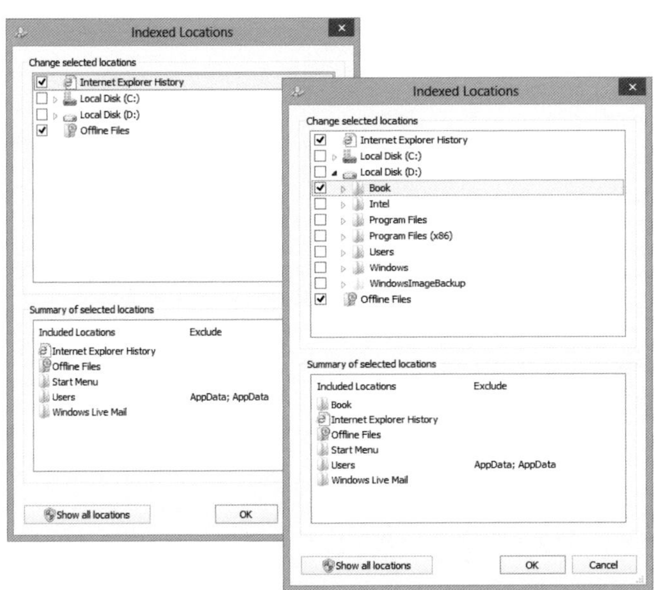

3 The contents of the new locations are added to the index

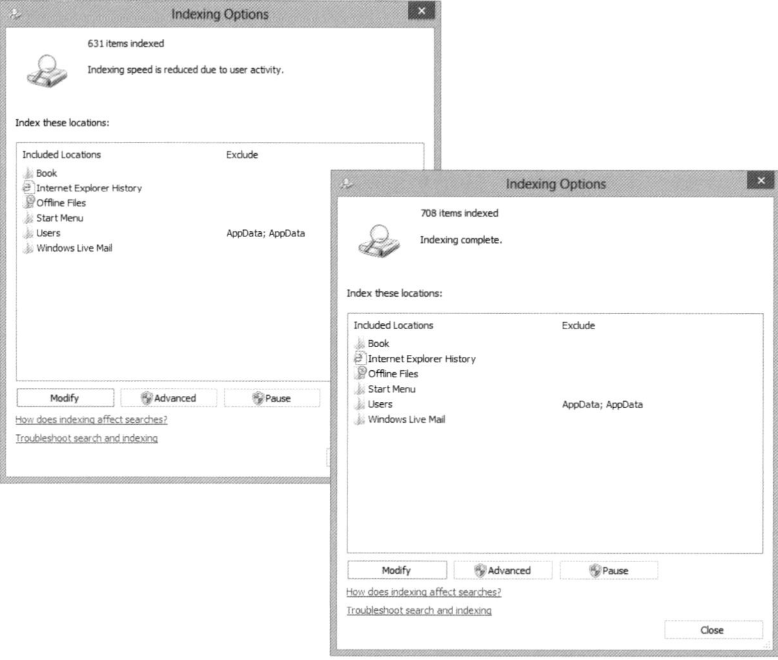

4 To make changes to the settings for indexing, click the Advanced button and select the Index Settings or File Types tab

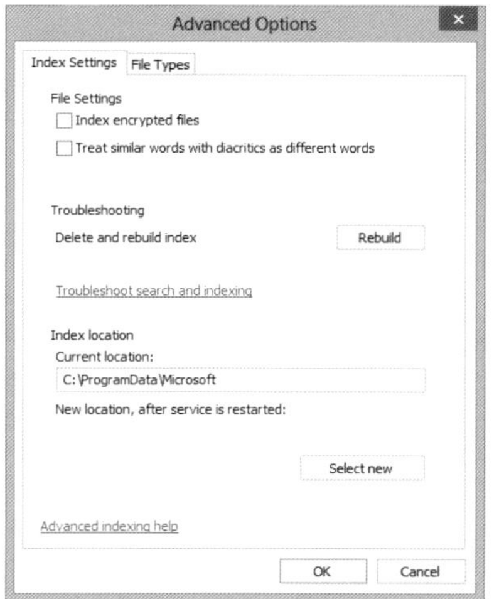

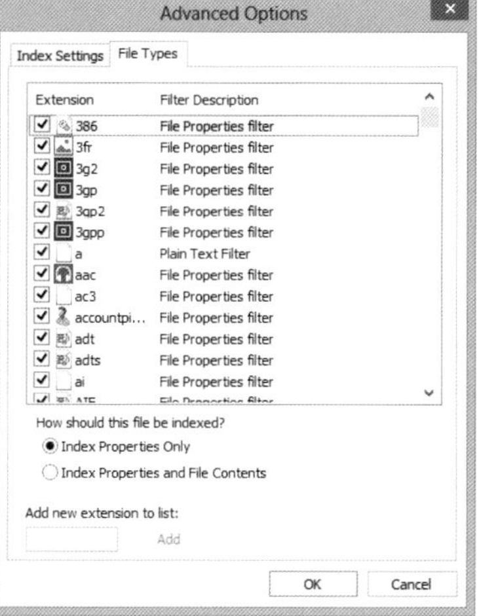

Don't forget

Indexing proceeds in the background, and may slow down during periods of user activity.

Beware

If required, you can press Pause to suspend indexing, but you are recommended to do this for no more than 15 minutes at a time.

Hot tip

You can choose to index encrypted files, ignore accents on characters for matching, change the index location, or delete and rebuild the index. You can also specify file types that are indexed by properties only or contents plus properties.

Address bar

The address bar at the top of the folder contains the location path of the folder or library, and you can use this to check the actual folder path and to switch to other libraries and folders.

1. Click the space in the address bar to the right of the location names (and left of the down-arrow)

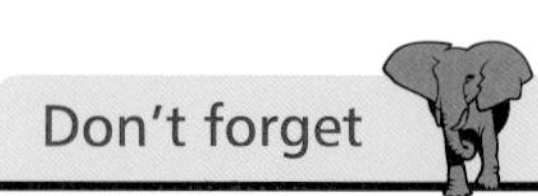

If a library rather than a folder is being displayed, you'll see a library path rather than a drive.

2. The current location is shown in the standard drive and folder path format

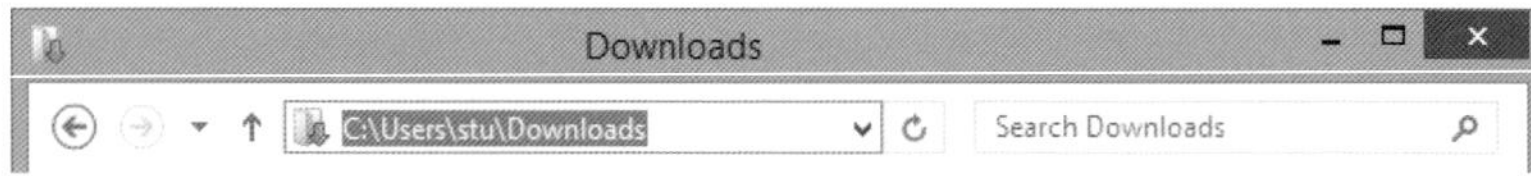

3. Click anywhere in the folder to revert to the location path

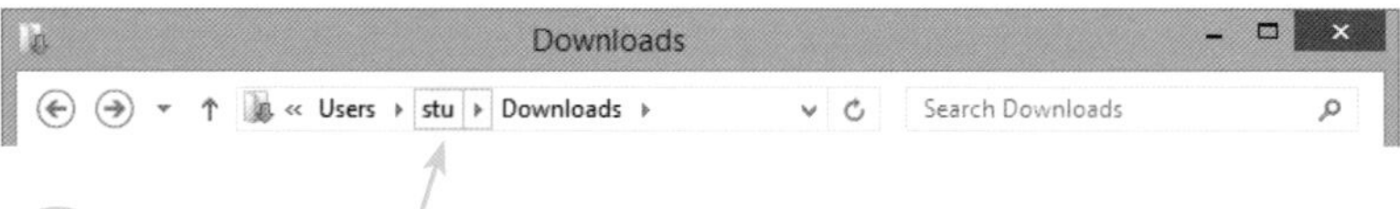

4. Click a location name, for example the user name, to switch to that location

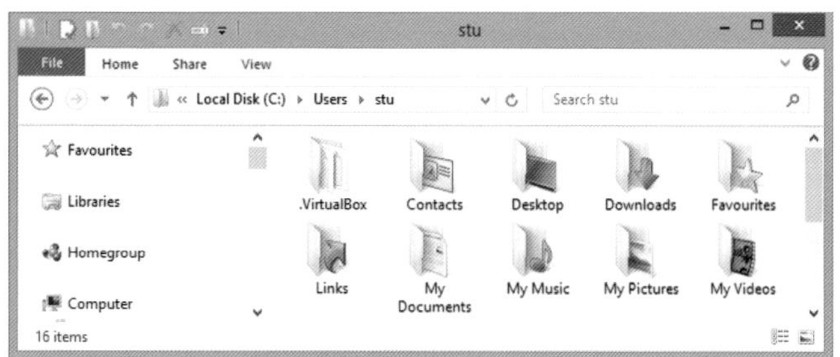

Click the arrow to the right of the location name to show all the folders that are stored within that location.

5. Click the arrow to the right of a location name, for example Users, to display all the folders in that location

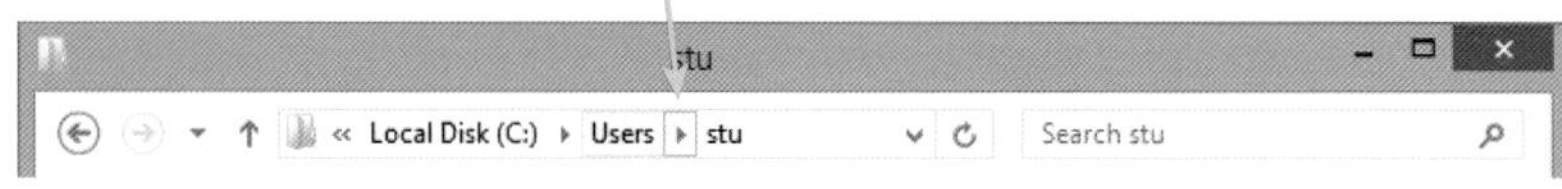

6. When the folders are displayed, you can select any folder to switch to that location

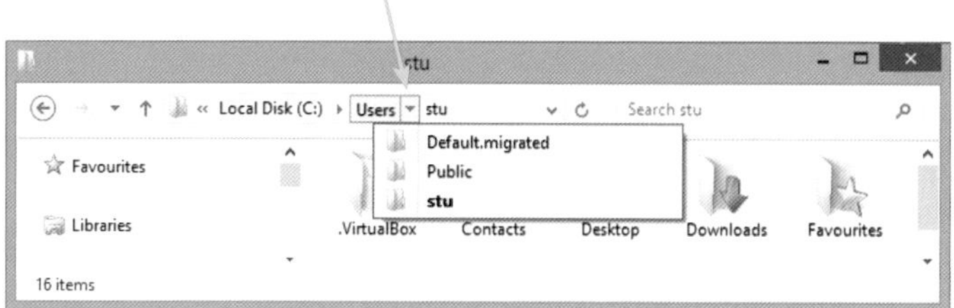

7. Click the back arrow to redisplay the previous folder

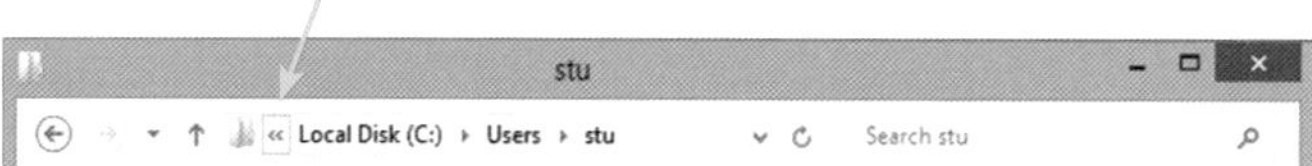

8. If the address bar entry is truncated to the left (indicated by a double bracket, you'll need to widen the window to see the missing portion

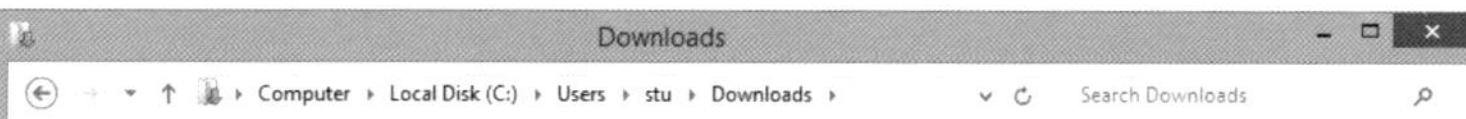

9. Click the arrow at the left to see the top level locations

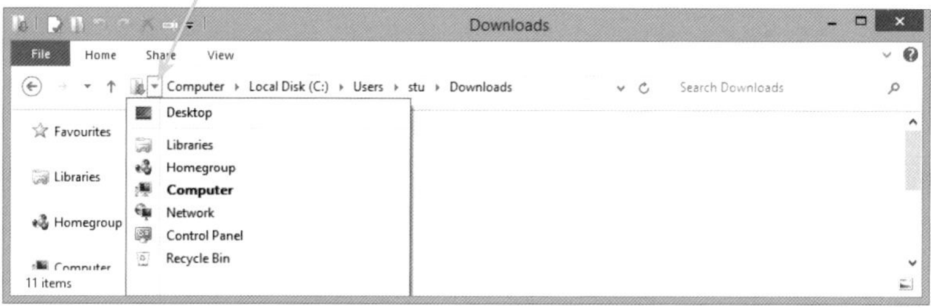

10. Select Desktop to see the complete structure of your system components

The current folder location, in this case the active user, is shown highlighted in the list.

Hot tip

As this illustrates, the libraries, user folders, network folders, etc. are included as special folders in Desktop, along with Computer and the desktop icons. Note that File Explorer is also used to display the Control Panel.

Save searches

Don't forget

Save a search, and the next time you want to use it, you just open the saved search, and you'll see the most current files that match the original search.

If you regularly search for a certain group of files, it might be useful to save your search. To save a search:

1. Carry out a search as previously described

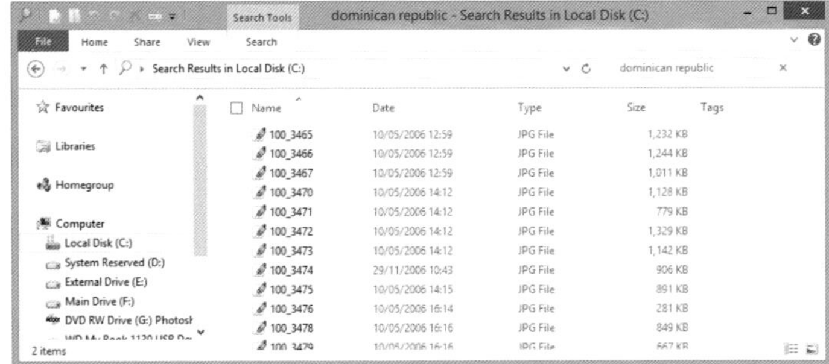

2. When the search is complete, click Save search

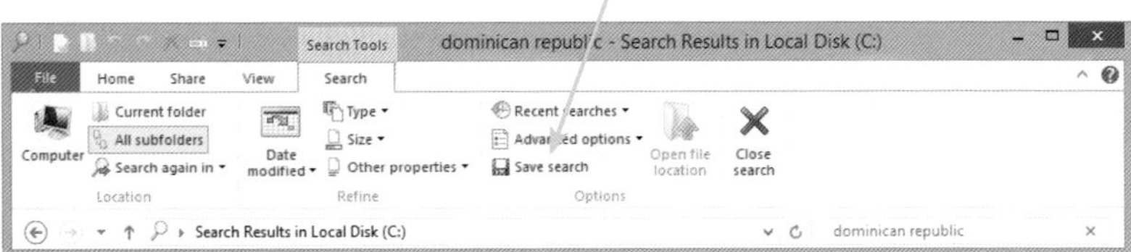

3. Type a name for the search, and then click Save. A shortcut to the saved search will be added to the Favorites section of the Navigation pane

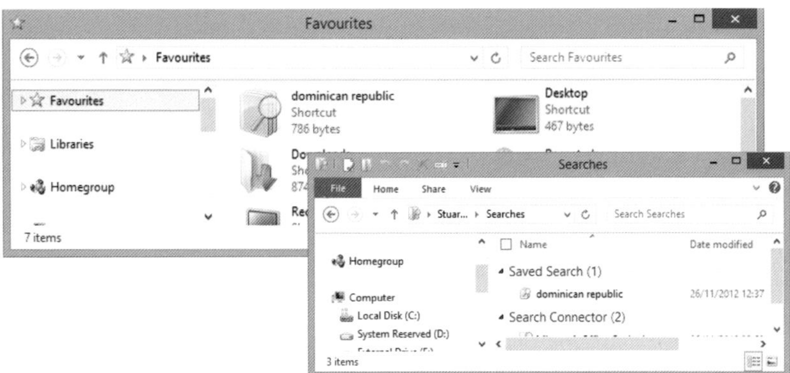

4. The search itself will be saved in the Searches folder, which you will find in your personal folder

Move and copy

You can use the Search results and the Navigation pane to help move or copy files and folders from their original locations.

1. Use Search to display the items you wish to copy or move (in this case all Word files in Users named Minutes)

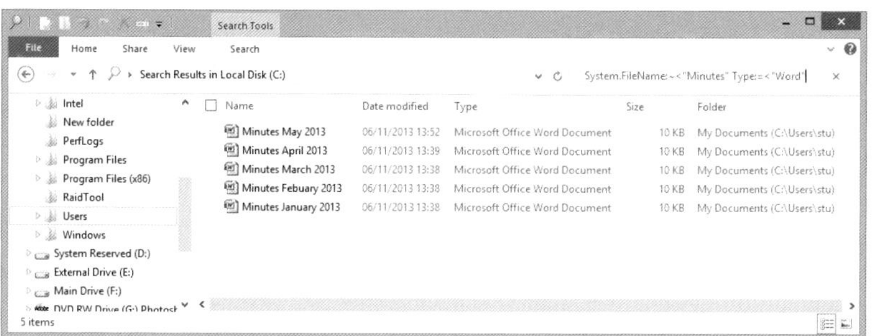

2. Select the items to copy, using Shift or Ctrl as necessary

3. Expand the Navigation pane (clicking the triangles, not the folder names) to show the target folder

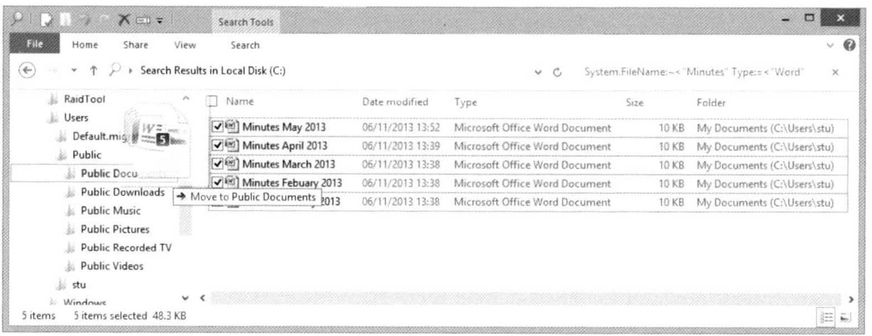

4. Right-click part of the selection and drag the items onto the Navigation pane, over the name of the target folder

5. Release the mouse and click Move here or Copy here as appropriate, and the files are added to the destination

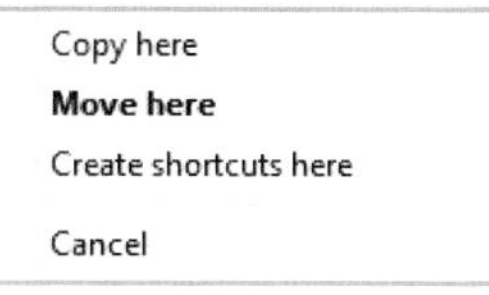

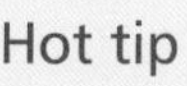

Select the first item, then press Shift and select the last in a range, or press Ctrl and add individual items to the selection.

Don't forget

If the destination is on the same drive as the selected items, the default is Move, otherwise the default becomes Copy. However, you can still make your preferred selection.

6. As soon as the move takes place, Windows Search adjusts the search results, in this case showing Public documents

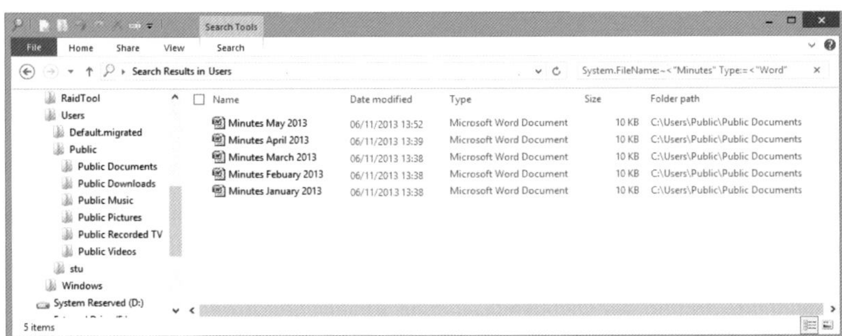

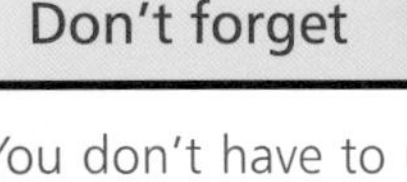

You don't have to use Search, you can Move or Copy from the original location using the same techniques.

7. Select the target folder, and you'll see all the items added

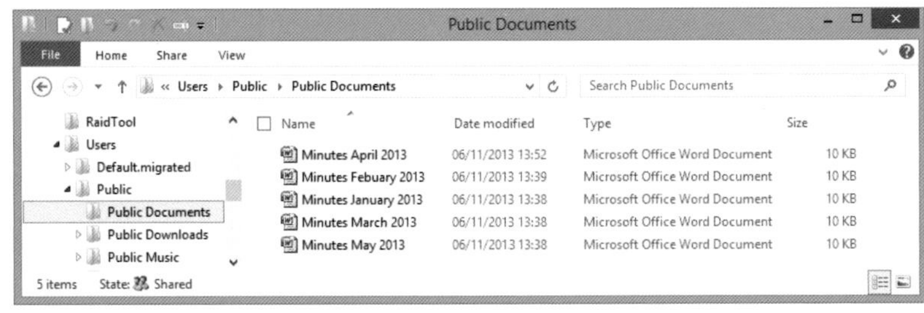

Drag with left mouse button

1. Left-click and drag, then release the mouse button over the destination, and Windows will Move or Copy immediately, with no menu

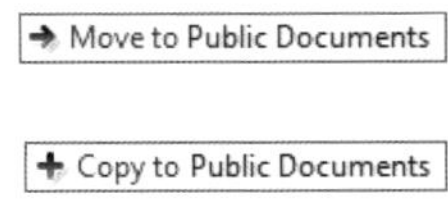

Don't use the left-click option unless you are very familiar with it, since there's no opportunity to confirm the action.

Force move or copy

With either left-click or right-click, you can force the action you want, whether the same or different drives are involved.

1. Press Shift as you drag and Move becomes the default

→ Move to Public Documents

2. Press Ctrl as you drag and Copy becomes the default

+ Copy to Public Documents

11 Manage files and folders

Use File Explorer to manage your files, folders and libraries, sorting and organizing the contents and linking to the locations that hold the required data. Windows provides libraries for documents, music, pictures and videos but you can define your own libraries for your projects or to manage information such as family history.

Files, folders and libraries

Don't forget

Windows uses the NTFS file system for disks and large storage devices. One of the older FAT file systems is normally used for smaller storage devices such as memory cards and flash drives.

Data storage devices are defined as blocks of fixed-size sectors. These are managed by the file system, which defines a root folder with lists of file names and folder names. Each folder can contain further file and folder names. This gives a hierarchical structure.

Files of the same or related types will usually be stored in the same folder. For example, your main hard drive will be organized along the following lines:

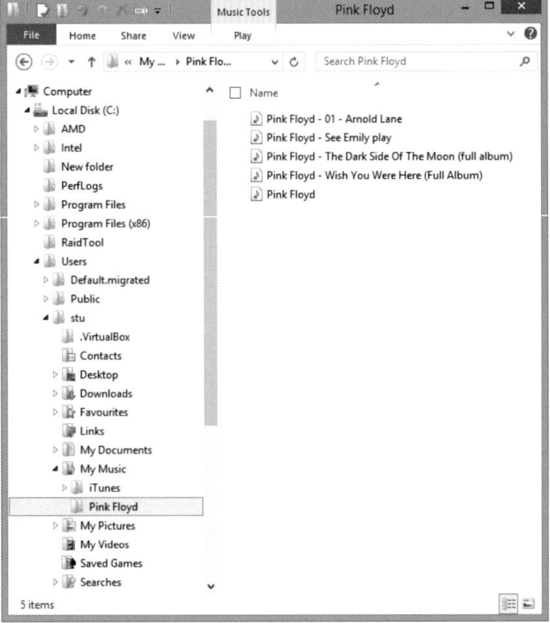

Hot tip

Each file has a starting block and links to the subsequent blocks, with the last link being the end of file marker. The blocks are not necessarily allocated in sequence, hence the potential for fragmentation.

The root folder includes the Program Files folder which contains applications installed on your system, and the Users folder which contains the folders and files associated with each user account. In your user account folder, you will see a number of folders including your Music folder. The example shows the files and folders associated with a particular artist.

Windows 8 goes a stage further and associates folders with similar content into Libraries. The folders included in the library may actually be stored separately on the disk, or may be on a different disk on the computer or elsewhere on the network.

To manage the files, folders and libraries, Windows uses the File Explorer application.

File Explorer

There are several different ways to start File Explorer or change the particular files and folders being displayed.

1. Click the File Explorer shortcut icon on the Taskbar, or open the Power user menu and select File Explorer

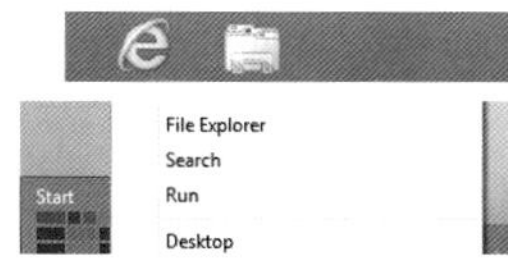

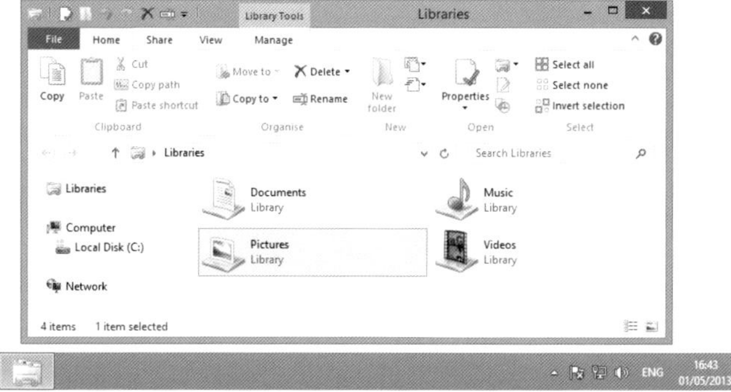

2. The Libraries folder is displayed, and the taskbar shortcut becomes an active task button

3. Click an entry on the Navigation pane to display those contents instead, for example select Computer

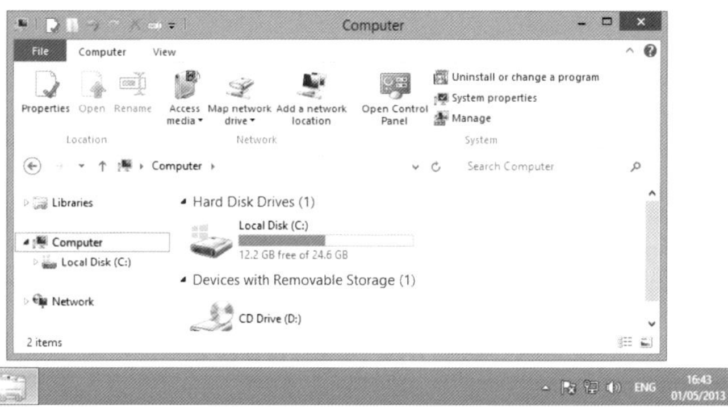

4. To retain the current entry, and open another, right-click the newly-required entry and choose Open in new window

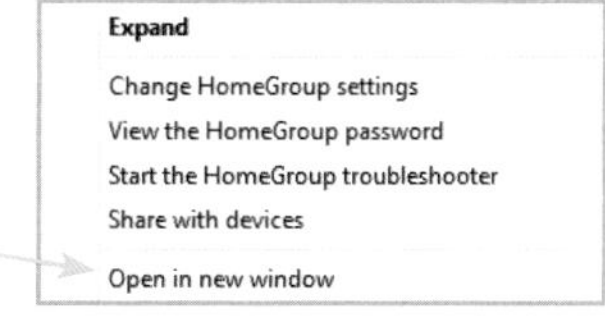

Hot tip

Press Winkey + E, to open File Explorer with Computer.

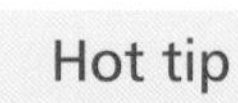

Hot tip

You can press Winkey + X to open the Power user menu. Then click File Explorer.

...cont'd

The taskbar button for the program initially shows a single icon. When you open a second window, another icon is stacked. When you open three or more windows, a third icon added.

1. Move the mouse pointer over the task button, and thumbnails for the open windows are displayed as shown below:

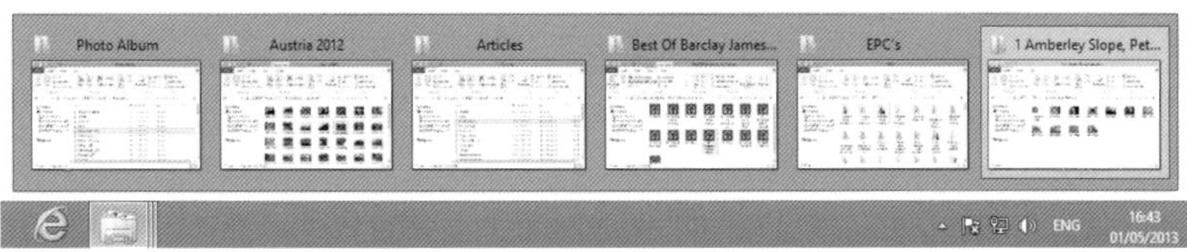

2. Click on a thumbnail to open that window in File Explorer

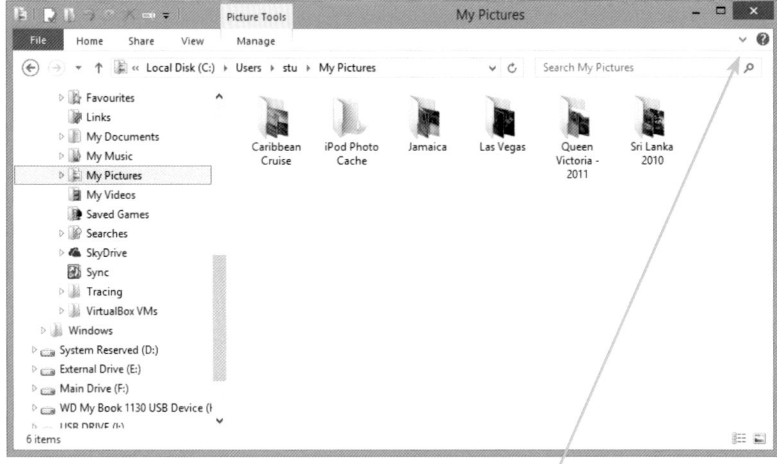

3. Click the down arrow to open (or close) the File Explorer ribbon toolbar

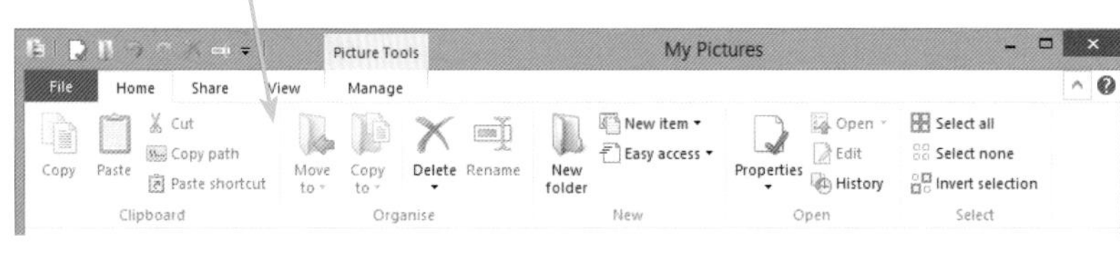

Hot tip

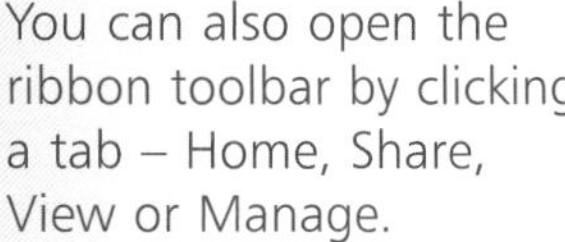

You can also open the ribbon toolbar by clicking a tab – Home, Share, View or Manage.

File Explorer layout

This shows all the elements for File Explorer, apart from the ribbon toolbar, which we look at on page 174.

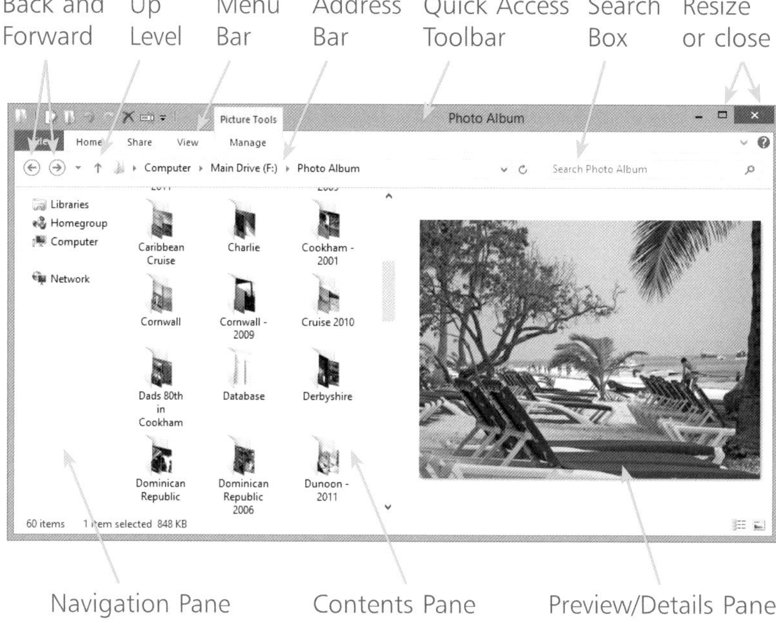

File Explorer preview

The type of preview displayed depends on the file type. For documents and PDFs, you will see part of the first page. For music files, you'll get a Play link.

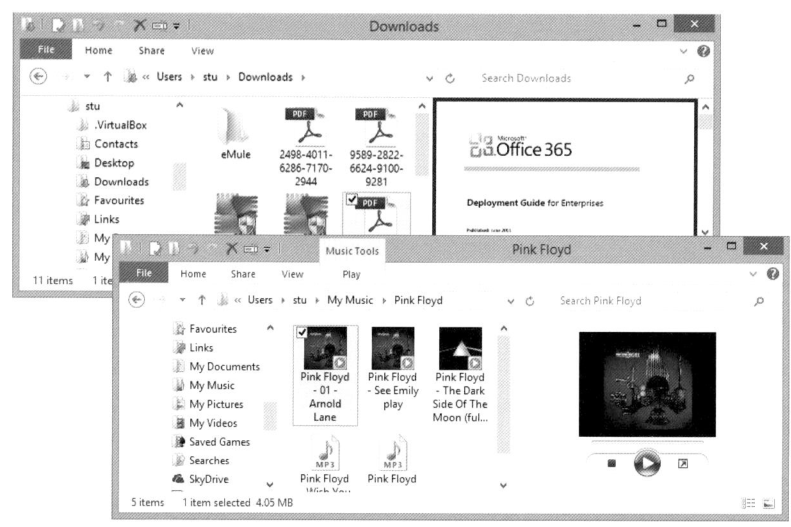

Beware

For file types Windows does not recognize, or when a folder is selected, you will see a message saying: No preview available.

File Explorer ribbon

A new feature in Windows 8 is the File Explorer ribbon toolbar, which is situated at the top of every File Explorer folder. By default it is hidden; to reveal it just click the down-arrow located just under the red X close button at the top-right.

In essence, the ribbon consists of a File menu plus three core tabs – Home, Share and View – that are always visible. Other tabs include Manage, Computer and Network. The ribbon also shows colored contextual tabs, the display of which depends on the type of object selected by the user. For example, when a video folder is opened or a video file is selected, the Video Tools tab appears and provides related options, such as Play, Stop, Pause, etc.

This system of core and contextual tabs enables the ribbon toolbar to offer some 200 different management commands. The user gets the required options as and when required without having to wade through unrelated toolbar menus, right-click menus, etc.

Hot tip

The File tab offers a variety of options.

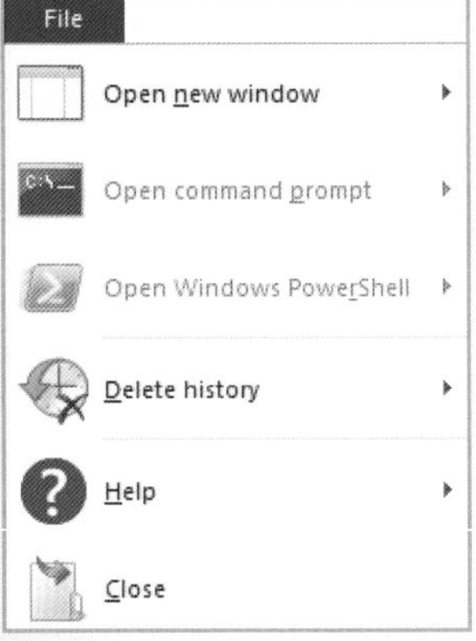

Home tab

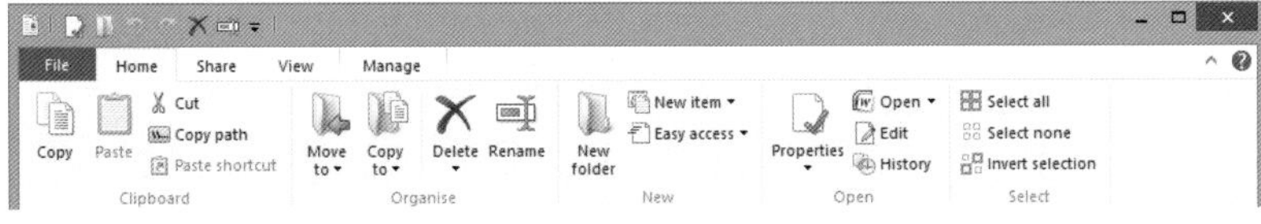

View tab

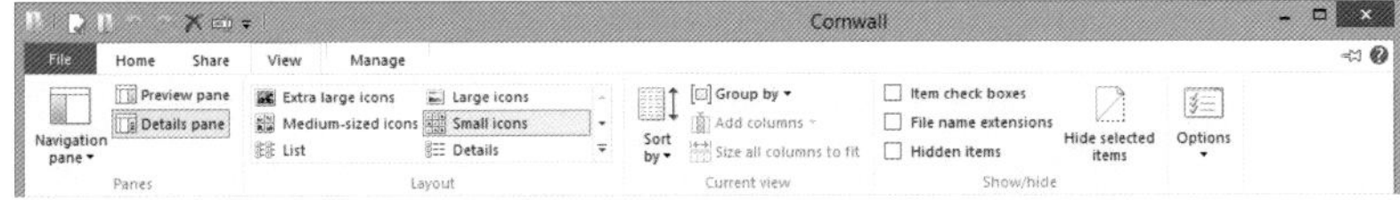

Computer tab

Share tab

Manage tab

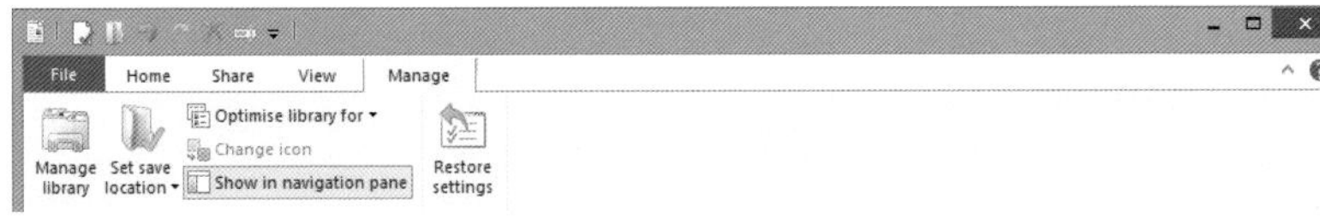

Folder contents

You'll also find that the way in which the contents of folders are displayed varies depending on the type of file involved.

In these example views, the Navigation, Details and Library panes have been hidden, to put the emphasis on the Contents pane.

Documents

Details view:
- Name
- Date modified
- Type
- Size

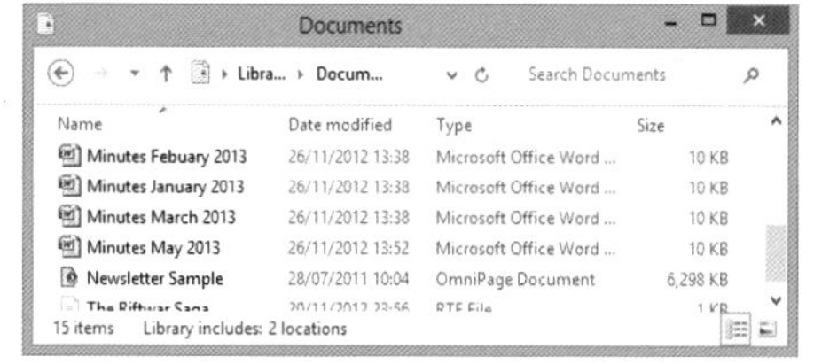

Music

Details view:
- Name
- Contributing artists
- Album
- Track number
- Title

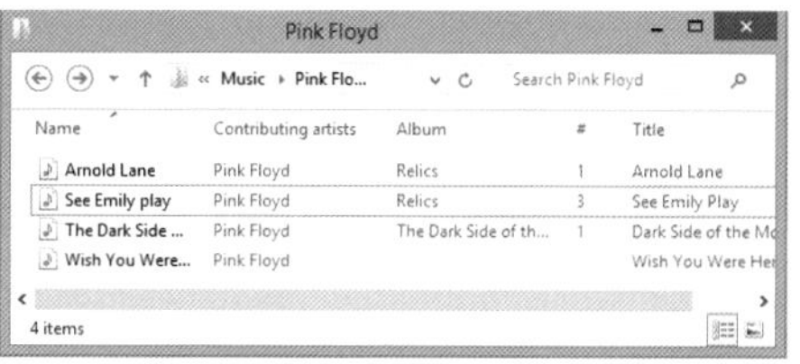

Pictures

Large Icons view

Data Folders

Medium Icons view

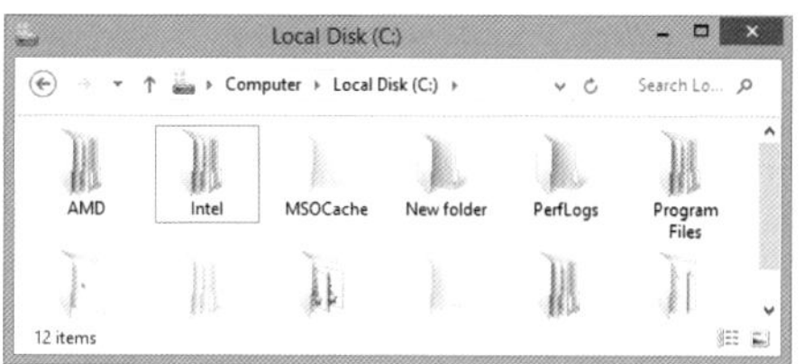

Libraries

Tiles view

Since views can easily be varied, you may find the setup for some of the folders on your system may be different.

Don't forget

Documents and Music both use the Details view, but the fields displayed are appropriate to the particular file type.

Hot tip

The Videos library also uses the Large Icons view, while Network and Computers use the Tiles view, the same as Libraries.

Change view

Hot tip

While the View menu option available by right-clicking in a folder provides a quick way to change a folder's view, the View menu on the ribbon toolbar offers more, and more easily accessible, options.

1. Open the folder whose view you want to change, and right-click in an empty part of the folder

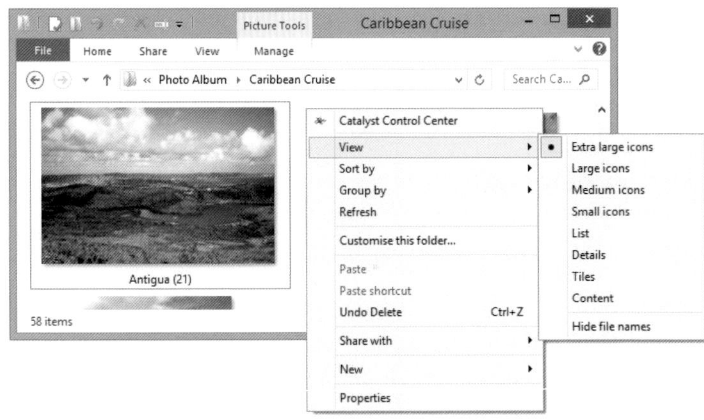

2. Hover the mouse on the View menu option and then select the required view. Using our example above, we are changing the view from Extra large icons to Medium icons. You can see how the view has changed below

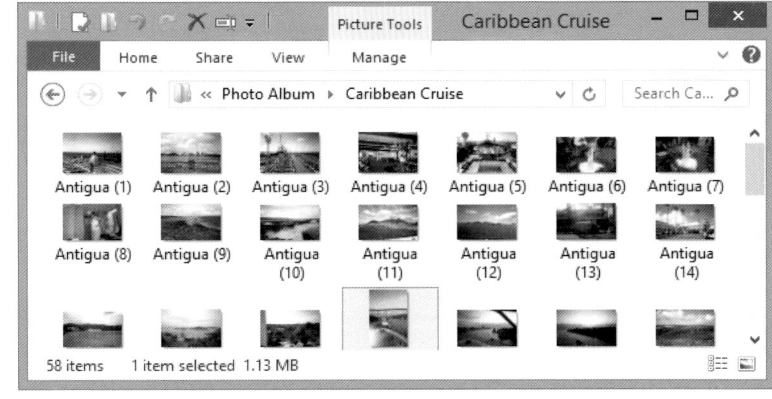

Beware

The information provided in the Content view depends on the file type. For example, Pictures has Date taken, and Music has Track length.

3. The same commands, and more, are also available from the View tab on the File Explorer ribbon toolbar

Sort contents

You can sort the contents of any folder by name, date, size or other attributes, using the Details view. You can also group or filter the contents.

1. Open the folder and select the Details view

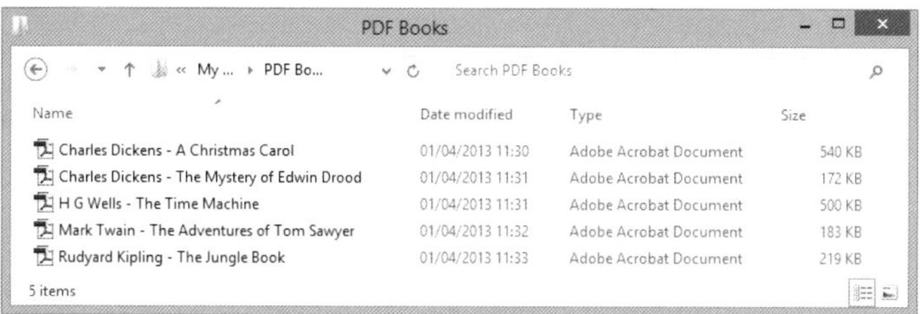

2. Click on a header such as Size and the entries are sorted

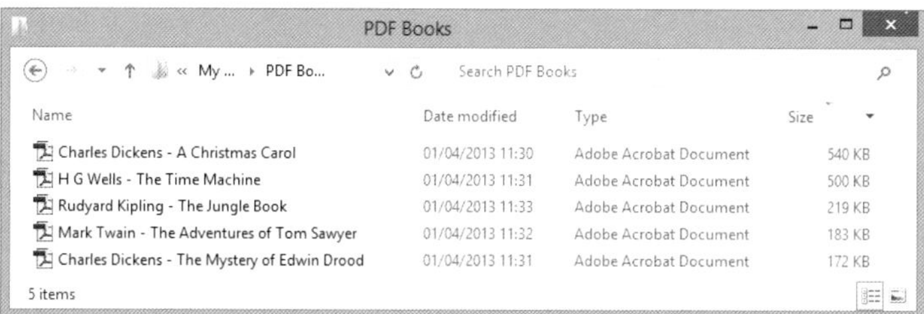

3. Click the header again, and the sequence is reversed

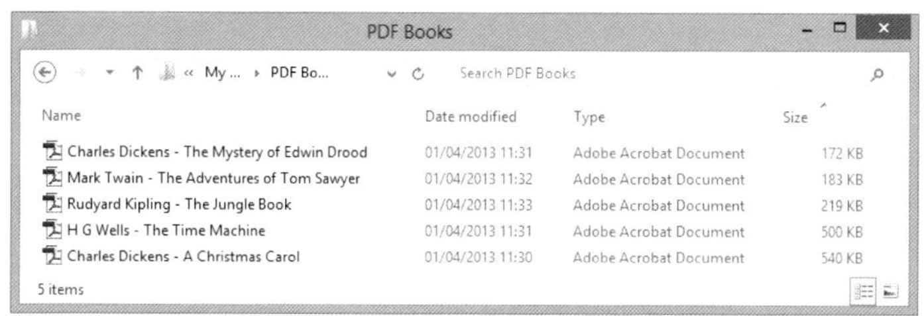

4. Change the view, and the sequencing that you have set up will be retained for the new view

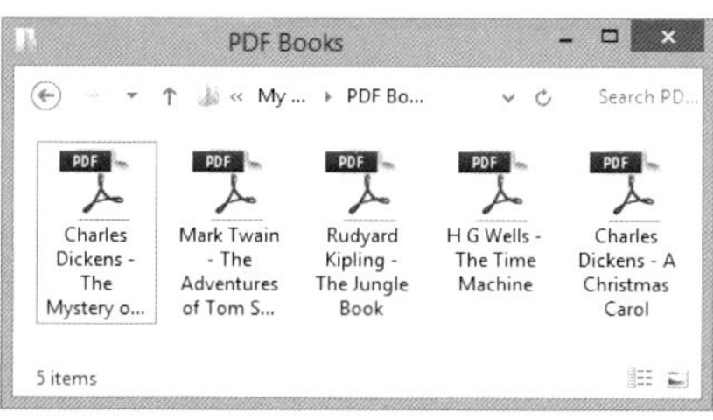

Don't forget

On the first selection, alphabetic fields such as Name or File Type are sorted in ascending order. Number fields such as Date or Size are sorted in descending order.

Hot tip

Click the arrow next to the Change your view button, to group the entries in ranges. By excluding some of the ranges, you can filter the contents displayed.

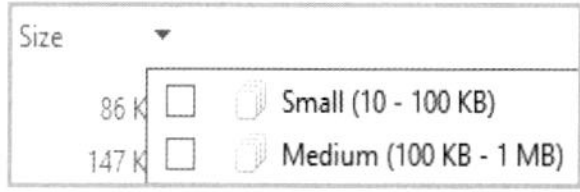

...cont'd

You can reorganize the contents from views other than Details.

1. Open the folder, and right-click an empty part of the Contents, being sure to avoid the icon borders

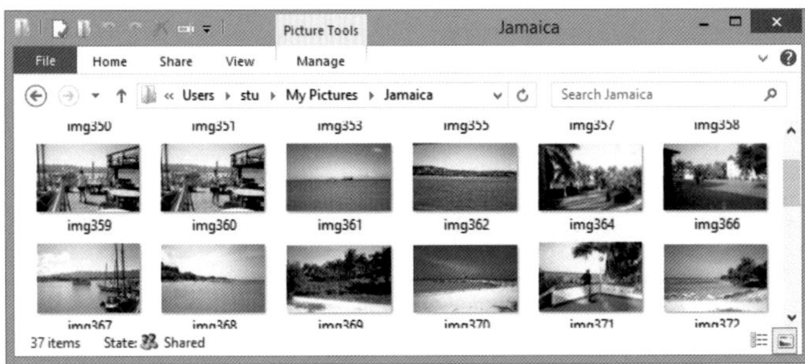

The space between icons can be very narrow, so you must take care to choose an empty area.

2. Select Sort by, to change the sort field or sequence

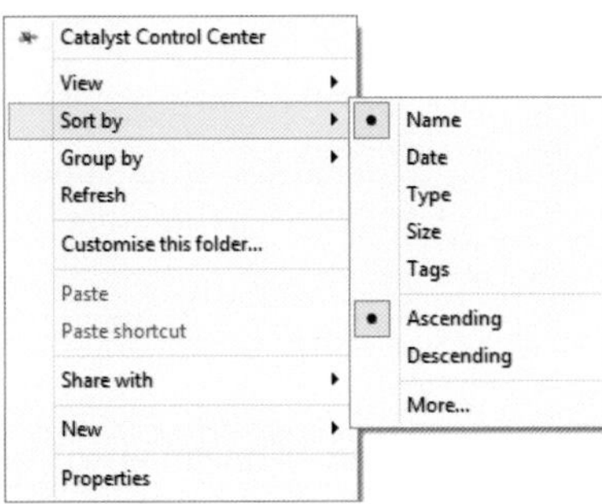

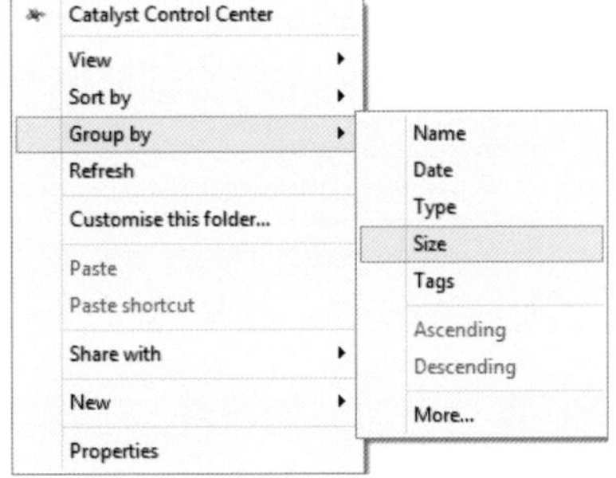

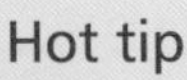

Click More to add other attributes that can be used for grouping or sorting. The selected fields would also appear on the Details view.

3. Select Group by, and select the field (for example Size) by which you want to arrange the entries in ranges

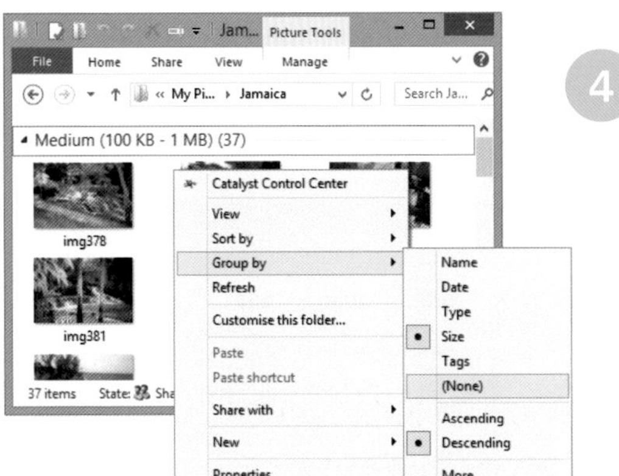

4. To remove the grouping, select Group by and then (None)

Windows 8 libraries

At install, Windows 8 has four libraries each with two locations:

- Documents — My Documents, Public Documents
- Music — My Music, Public Music
- Pictures — My Pictures, Public Pictures
- Videos — My Videos, Public Videos

1. Open File Explorer to show libraries

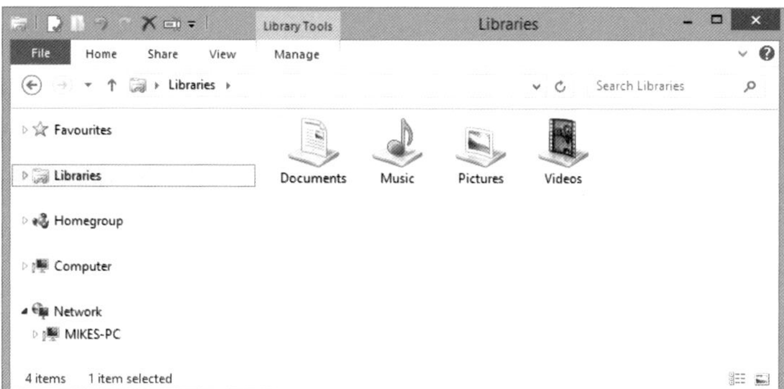

2. Double-click a library, for example Pictures, to open it

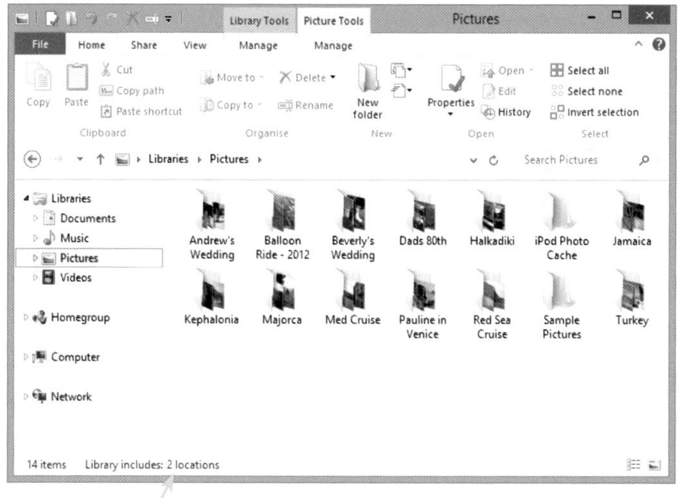

3. Here we can see the library includes two locations. The folders in each of these locations are listed

Don't forget

You can include other locations in the existing libraries, and you can also create your own libraries.

Hot tip

You can also open the Pictures library from the Navigation pane.

Manage library

Hot tip

The File Explorer ribbon Library options don't appear automatically – you have to select a library and then click the Library tools tab.

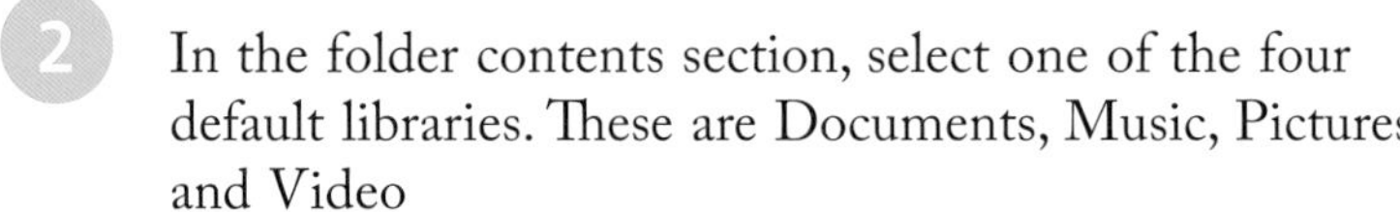

1. Open the Libraries folder and click the down-arrow under the red X close button to reveal the File Explorer ribbon toolbar

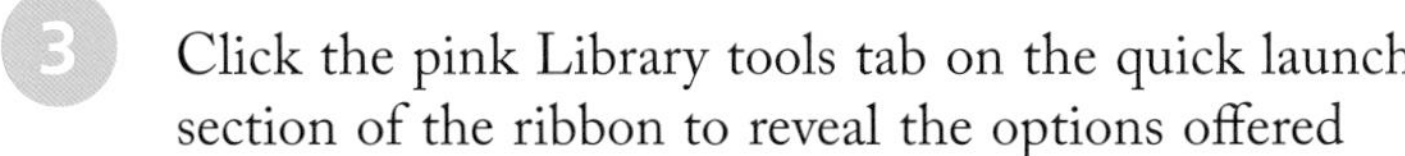

2. In the folder contents section, select one of the four default libraries. These are Documents, Music, Pictures and Video

3. Click the pink Library tools tab on the quick launch section of the ribbon to reveal the options offered

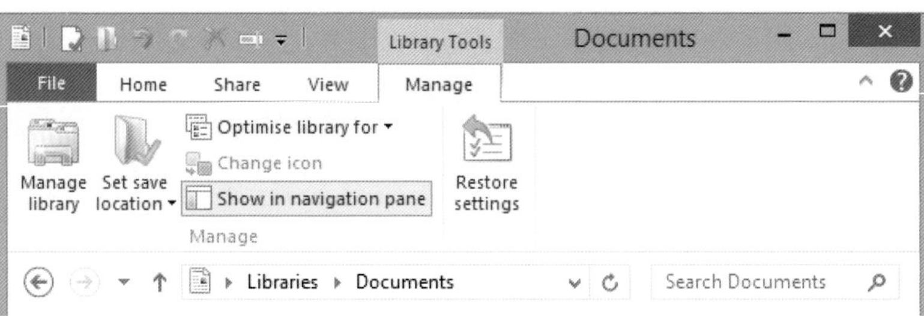

Manage library – the Manage library link enables you to add new locations to an existing library – see pages 181-182 where we look at how to do this.

Set save location – this allows you to specify a default save location within a library. For example, if one of your libraries has two or more locations, you can set one of them as the default.

Optimize library for – the four default libraries all have different arrangement options. You'll see this when you right-click in a library and select Arrange by. For example, the Documents library offers Folder, Author, Date modified, etc, while the Videos library offers Year, Type, Length, etc. Should you create a new library, the Optimize library for link enables you to quickly set suitable arrangement options for the content of that library.

Show in Navigation pane – this lets you hide or show the Libraries link in the Navigation pane.

Restore settings – Click this link to undo all configuration changes made to the Libraries feature.

Add a location

1. Open the Libraries folder and access Library tools as described on page 180. Then click Manage library

2. Click the Add button next to Library locations

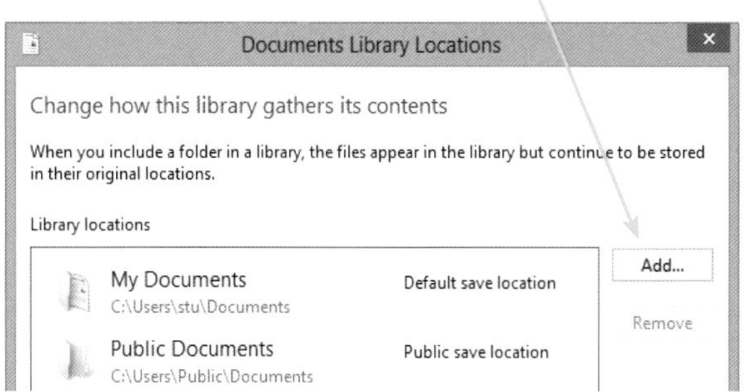

3. Open the drive the required folder is located on

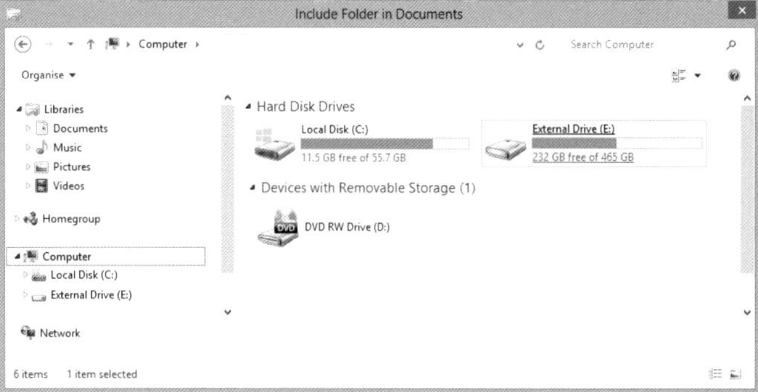

4. Select the folder and then click Include Folder

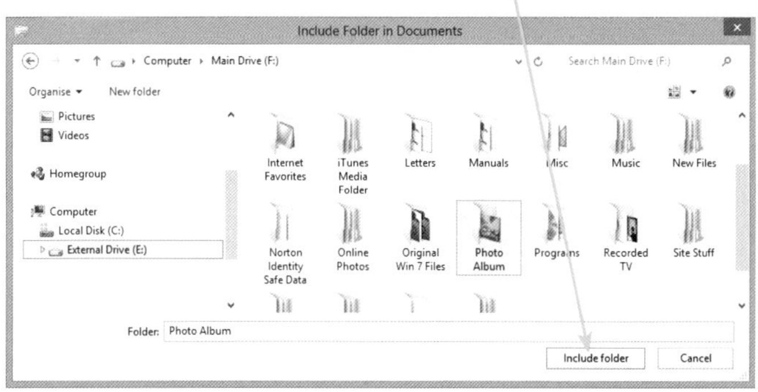

Don't forget

This lists the currently defined locations and indicates the default save location, where new files would be added.

Hot tip

You could select folders from your hard drive, a second internal hard drive if available, or an external hard drive, as in this example.

Don't forget

The folder you select must be shared. If this is not already the case, you'll be prompted to allow sharing.

5 The selected folder becomes a new location in the library

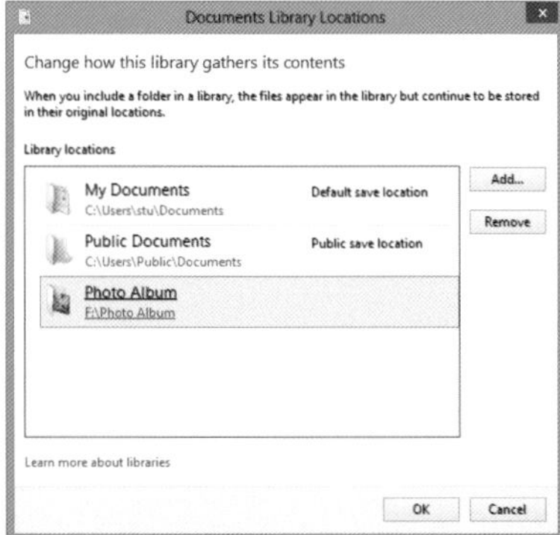

6 Click OK and the contents of the location are displayed

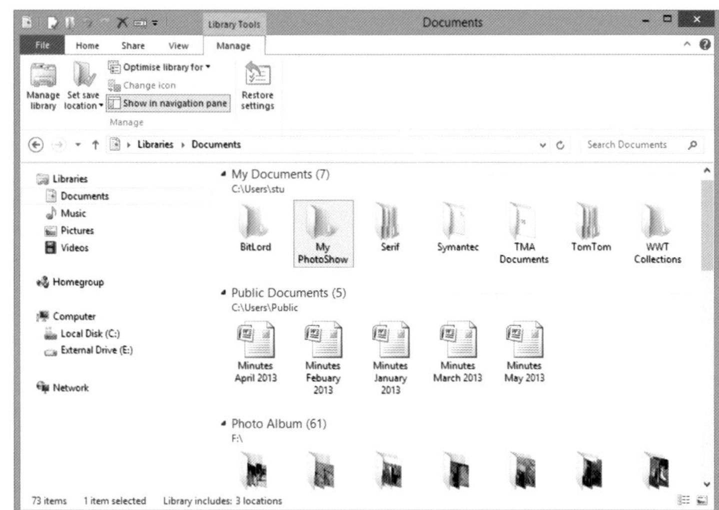

Beware

You cannot use folders from Devices with Removable Storage. You can add folders from removable drives, but only if they appear in the Hard Disk Drive section.

Removable drives

1 Select a folder on a DVD or on a USB flash drive, then click Include Folder

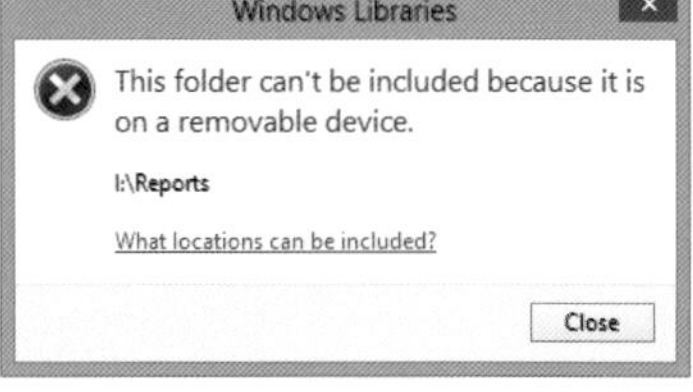

2 You are warned this folder cannot be included

Arrange library contents

Library contents are usually organized by location and folder, but you can change this if you wish.

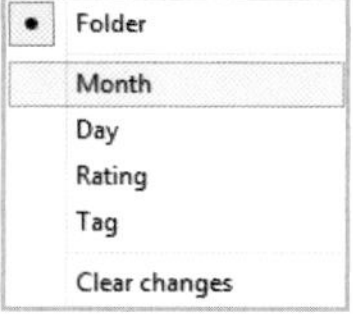

1. Click the Arrange by box, initially Folder, and select an alternative, e.g. Month

2. The contents of all the folders are gathered together in groups by month and displayed as stacks

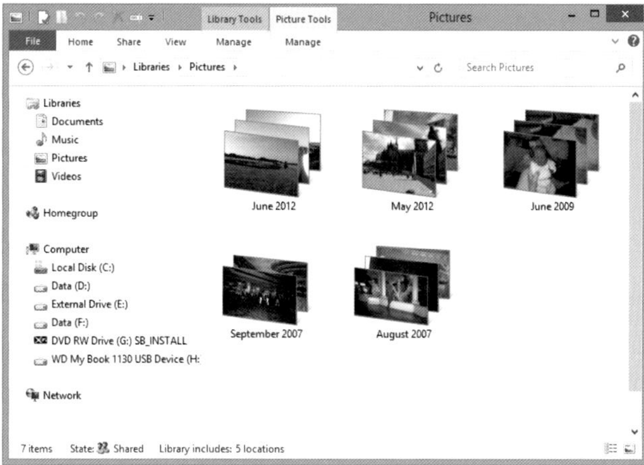

3. Select a stack and press Enter (or double-click) and the contents of that stack are displayed, grouped by Day

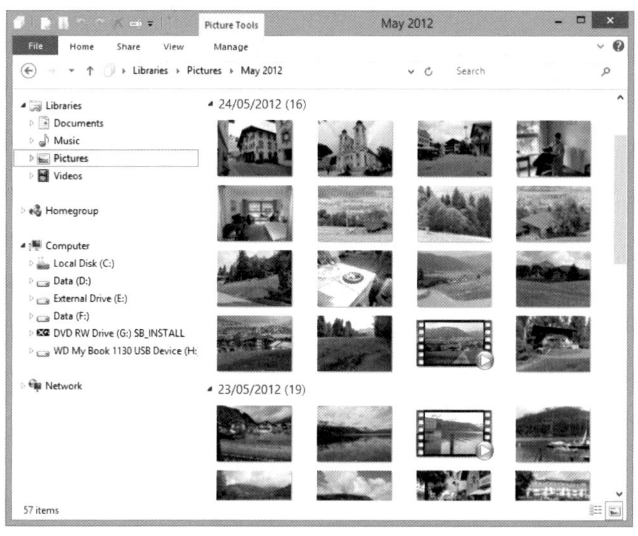

Don't forget

There is an option to Clear Changes which removes any sorting or grouping and reverts to the default display.

Hot tip

The Details pane shows the number of pictures in the selected stack. If no stack is selected, it shows the total number of stacks.

Beware

When you've selected an arrangement, there's no Clear changes, but you can select Folders and that option will be restored.

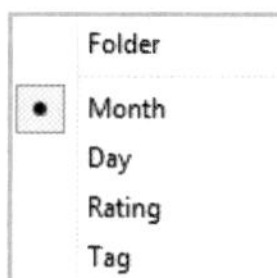

Create a library

You can create a library of your own to manage other collections, for example project plans, or family history.

1. Open the Libraries folder, right-click in the folder and select New, library

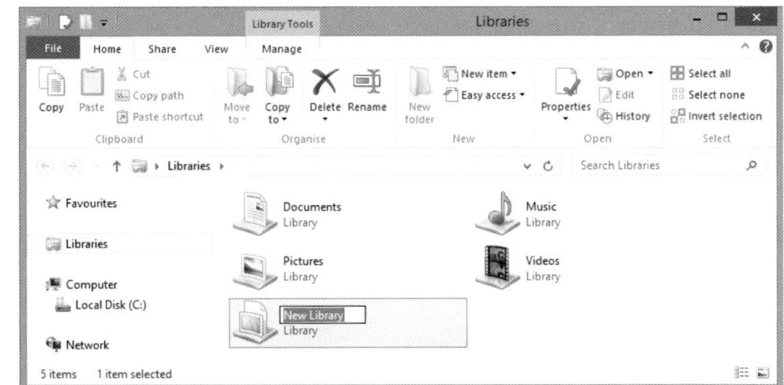

2. Type the library name, e.g. Projects, and press Enter

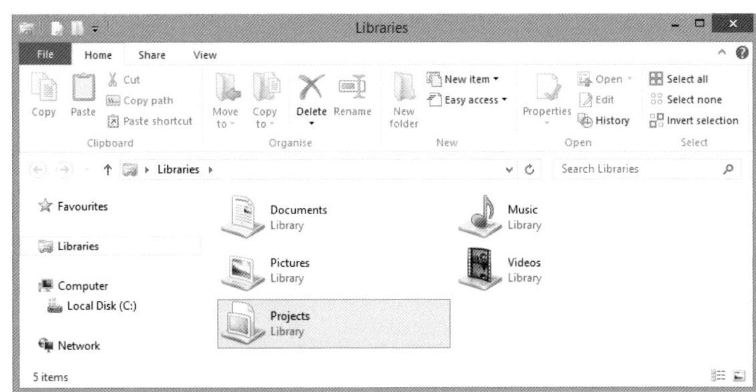

3. Double-click the new library to open it, and you'll be invited to add folders

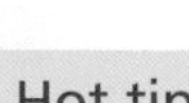

The first folder that you add will be assigned as the save location, but you can change this later if you wish.

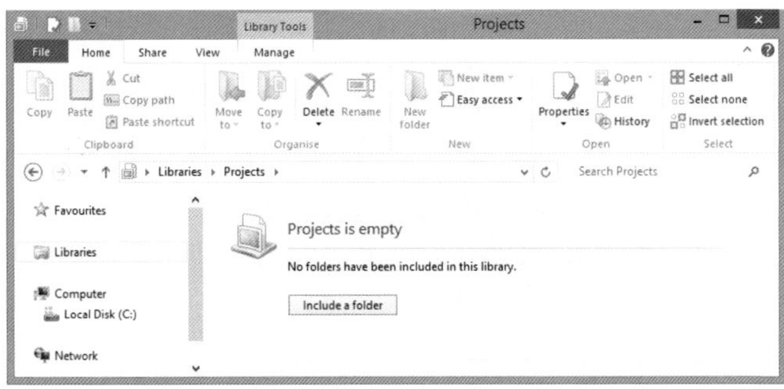

Adjust properties

When you've added folders, the library appears on the Navigation pane and shows locations and folders, just like default libraries.

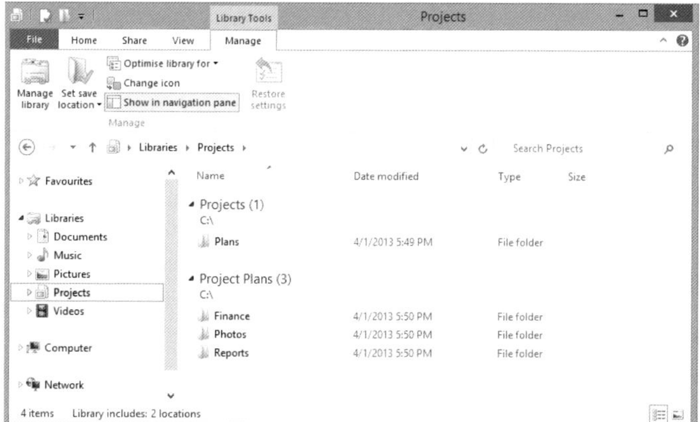

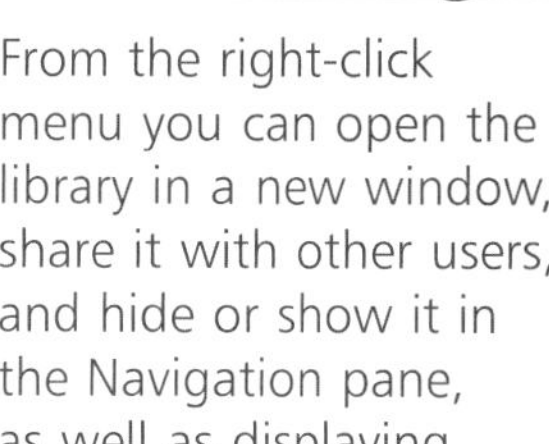

Don't forget

From the right-click menu you can open the library in a new window, share it with other users, and hide or show it in the Navigation pane, as well as displaying properties.

1. Right-click the library name in the Navigation pane or in the Libraries folder and select Properties

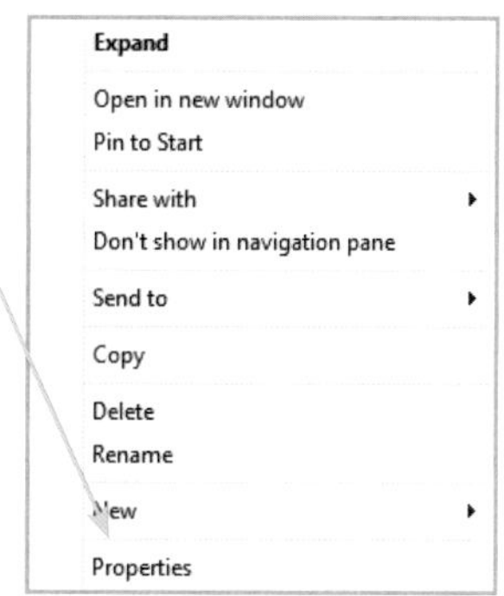

From here you can:

- Select a location and click Set save location
- Include a new folder or location
- Remove an existing location
- Hide or show in Navigation pane
- Check Sharing status
- Restore defaults after making changes
- Apply the changes you make

2. Click OK to save your changes, or click Cancel to abandon your changes

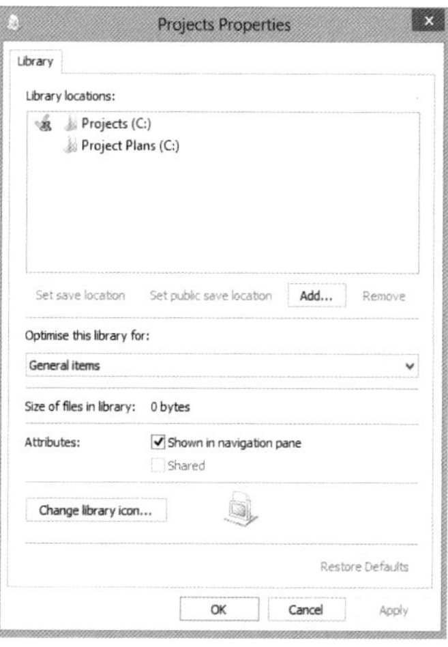

Hot tip

By default, the library will be optimized for the type of file it contains, or for general items if the file types are mixed. However, you can choose a particular file type if you prefer.

Customize folders

Don't forget 

To customize a folder in a library, access it from your hard disk or right-click the library folder and select Open file location.

1. Right-click the folder and select Properties

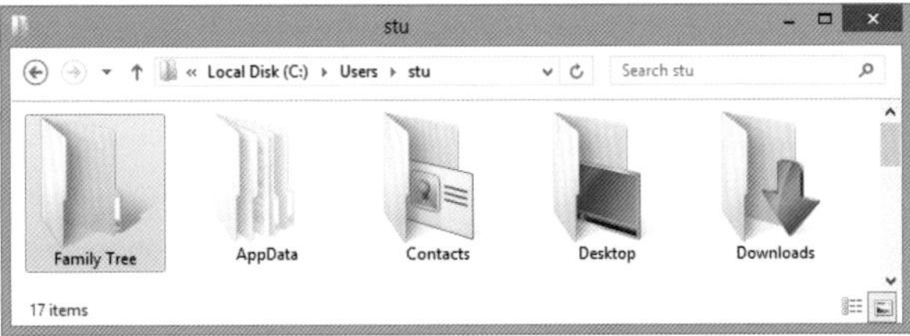

2. Click the Customize tab on the Properties panel
3. To specify a folder picture, click the Choose File button
4. Find and select the picture image and click Open

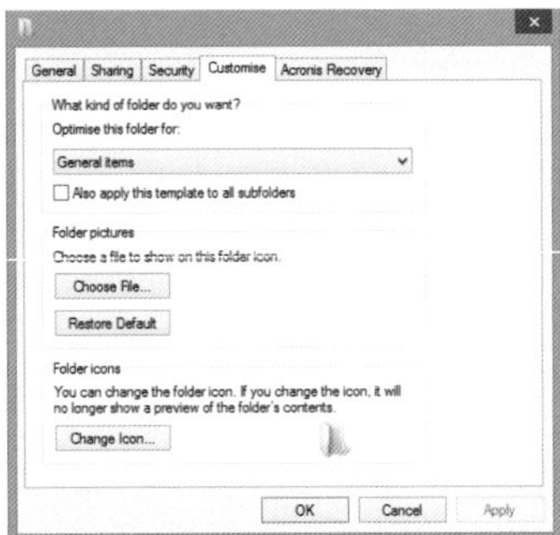

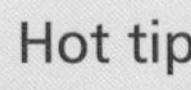

By default, the folder will be optimized for general items, but you can choose a specific file type if you wish.

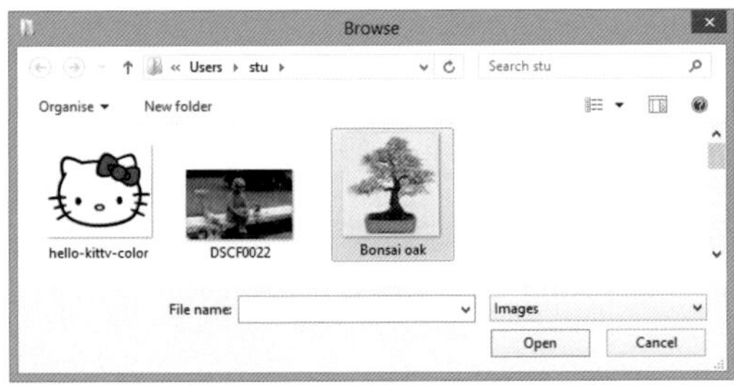

5. Click OK on the Properties panel to add the image
6. The folder image is inserted and displayed

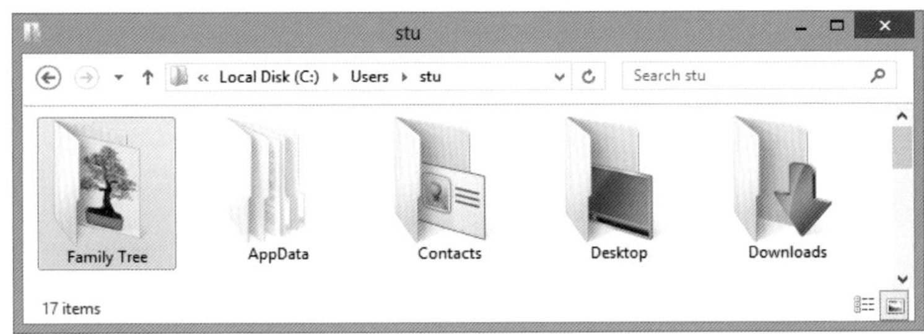

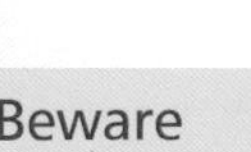

You can only add images on drives defined with the NTFS file system with its extended attributes. They cannot be added to drives defined with a FAT file system.

12 Email and messaging

You can use the communications tools built in or added to Windows to communicate with others, sending messages and attachments to individuals or groups of contacts. The Calendar facility helps you manage appointments and tasks. You can also receive more general communications, in the form of newsletters and information feeds.

Email

You can use email (electronic mail) to receive and send messages and files, to individuals or groups of people. You can send messages at any time of day or night. The recipients don't have to be at their computers, since they find the messages waiting the next time they check their email. However, if they are at their computer (or using their smartphone) they'd get the messages immediately and could respond straightaway.

This is much more efficient than regular mail or telephone services, and it is free, no matter how far away the recipients might be. The only cost is for your Internet connection, though you also need an email program or web-based email service.

Don't forget 

To connect your computer to the Internet, you must sign up with an Internet service provider (ISP), who provides a modem or router that gives access over phone line or cable.

Web mail

You can register for a free web-based email service, such as Gmail, Windows Live Hotmail, or Yahoo! Mail. These services allow you to check your email using a web browser, on your own computer, or on any computer connected to the Internet, for example a friend's computer, or a computer in a public location such as a library or hotel.

Email programs

On your own computer you can also check your email using an email program, from Microsoft or another supplier. Email programs often have more features and are faster to search mail than most web-based email services.

Hot tip 

To set up your email program you must obtain details from your ISP, such as your email address, password and names of your incoming and outgoing email servers.

In previous versions of Windows, Microsoft supplied an email program as an integral component, either Outlook Express or Windows Mail. There's no built-in Desktop email program for Windows 8, but you can use the Mail app included in Windows 8, or download Windows Live Mail as part of the Windows Essentials. We will use the latter as the example product for Windows email.

Microsoft Outlook

Microsoft also provides an email program named Outlook, which is part of the Microsoft Office system. This provides similar functions to Windows Live Mail, but it must be purchased as a separate product or as part of the Microsoft Office Suite.

Don't forget 

An email address consists of a user name (or a nickname), the @ sign, and the name of your ISP or web-based email provider, for example: sue29@gmail.com.

Mail app

The Mail app provided by Windows is, like all the apps, a fairly basic affair. It lets you send and receive email but little else – it does not offer the range of features found in traditional Desktop email programs.

However, one noteworthy feature that it does have is that it is integrated with the People, Messaging and Calendar apps. For example, when you add an email account to the Mail app the contacts are added to People, and the meetings and other events are added to Calendar.

Set up the email app as follows:

1. Click the Mail tile on the Start screen
2. Sign in with your Microsoft account
3. At the bottom-right of the opening screen, you'll see a list of email services. Click the one you want

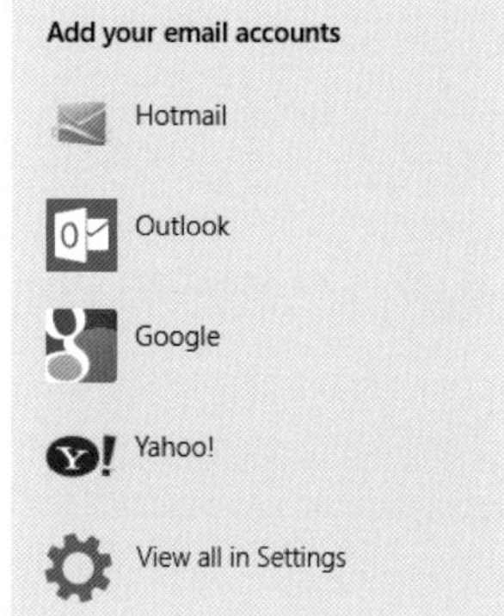

4. When prompted, enter your email address and password in the boxes

Add your Google account

Enter the information below to connect to your Google account.

Email address

Password

Include your Google contacts and calendars

Connect Cancel

5. Assuming your email address and password are valid, your account will now be set up with no further input necessary

Used in conjunction with the People, Messaging and Calendar apps, the Mail app will take care of all your private communications.

If your email provider is not in the list, click View all in settings. Here, you can configure your account manually.

...cont'd

6 Your account folders and emails are downloaded

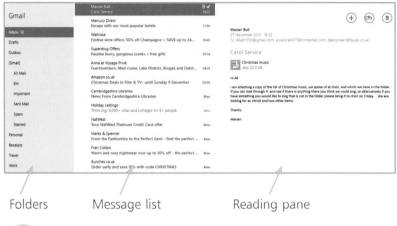

Folders Message list Reading pane

7 To send an email, click the ⊕ icon at the top-right

8 Enter the email address

9 Click Add a message and type in your message text

10 Right-click on the screen to open an app bar at the bottom. This offers the following options:

- Save drafts
- Attachments
- Copy
- Font
- Bold
- Italic
- Underline
- Text color
- Emoticons
- Bullet lists
- Numbered lists
- Undo/Redo

Hot tip

The Mail app comes with a nice list of emoticons.

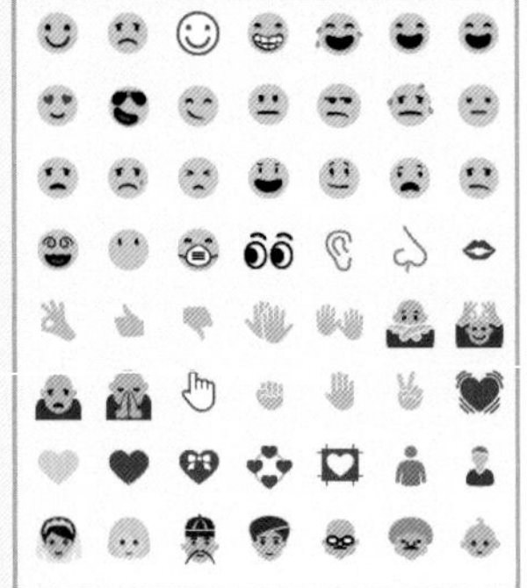

Beware

The Mail app doesn't provide many of the features users take for granted.

Windows Live Mail

As already stated, Windows 8's email app provides few configuration options for the more advanced email user. If this is you, you will need to install a third-party program.

Mozilla, authors of the FireFox web browser, provides the free Thunderbird email client, while another free email program with a very good reputation is Eudora. Both of these are good choices and can be downloaded from the manufacturers' websites. If you do an Internet search, you will also find a multitude of other email programs. This might be a good time to try out a few and see how you get on with them.

Alternatively, you can opt to stay with Microsoft. Their current free offering is Windows Live Mail, an updated version of the Windows Mail program that was provided with Windows Vista.

If you are migrating from Windows Vista or Windows 7 and used Windows Mail, you will probably decide to go with Windows Live Mail. This can be downloaded from the Windows Essentials 2012 website at **www.download.live.com**

When the installation is complete, start Mail as follows:

1. Type windows mail in the Search charm and press Enter

2. OK the licence agreement by clicking Accept

3. Windows Live Mail starts and you see the splash screen as shown below

Windows Live Mail 2012

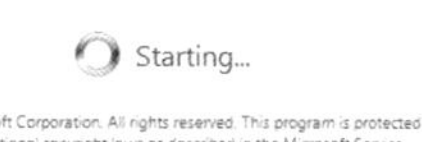

Starting...
© 2012 Microsoft Corporation. All rights reserved. This program is protected by U.S. and international copyright laws as described in the Microsoft Service Agreement.

Hot tip

If you are likely to use Windows Live Mail frequently, pin it to the Start screen or taskbar as previously explained.

Sign in to Windows Live Mail

When the splash screen closes, the Add your email accounts dialog box will open.

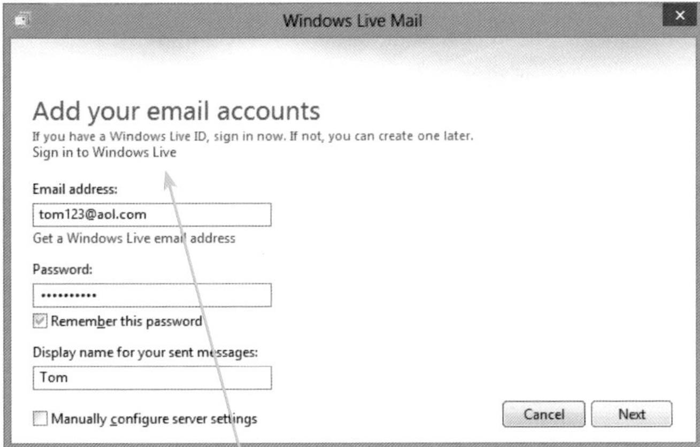

1. If you already have a Windows Live ID, click the Sign in to Windows Live link

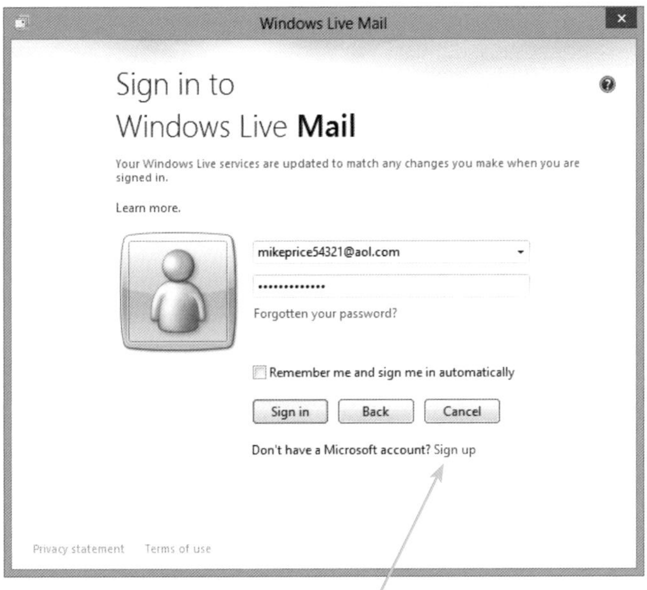

2. If you don't have a Windows Live ID, click the Sign up link and fill in the web form to create one

Hot tip

If you have a Hotmail or MSN email address, this acts as a Windows Live ID. Otherwise, use an existing email address, e.g. Gmail, Yahoo or an ISP email.

You can also choose to create a Windows Live ID immediately, and use this in Windows Live Mail.

Add email accounts

1. In Windows Live Mail, enter the email address and password, and type the display name for messages

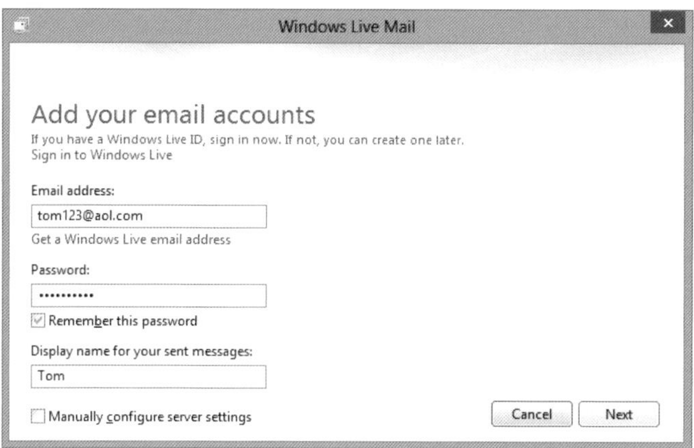

2. If this is a Windows Live ID, you should sign in to Windows Live

3. Your email account will be added to Windows Live Mail

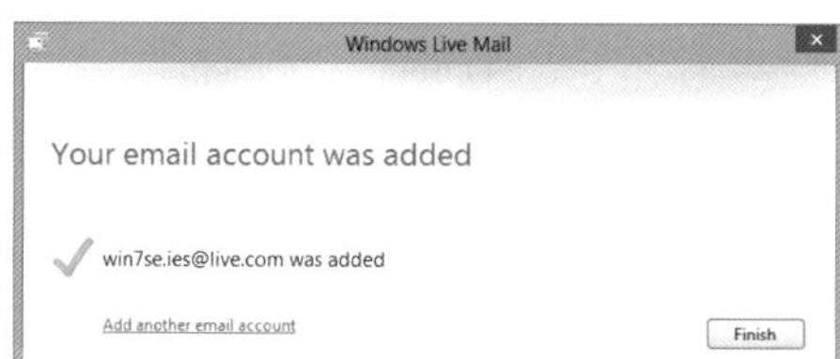

4. Available messages will be downloaded from the server

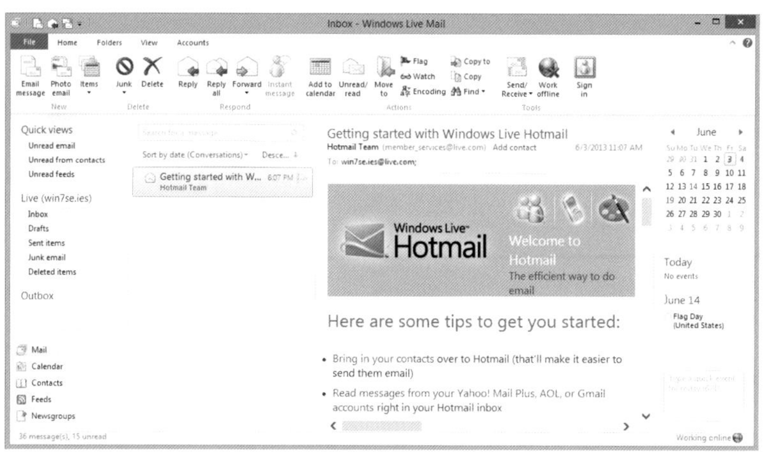

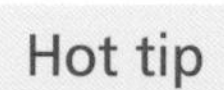

Click the link to Add another email account, if you have others you want to define.

Hot tip

By default, the message in the Inbox is opened and displayed in the reading pane. However, this can be switched off.

To add another email account:

If more accounts are required, add them as follows:

1. Select the link to Add another email account or select Accounts, Email in Windows Live Mail

2. Type the email address and other details, and click Next

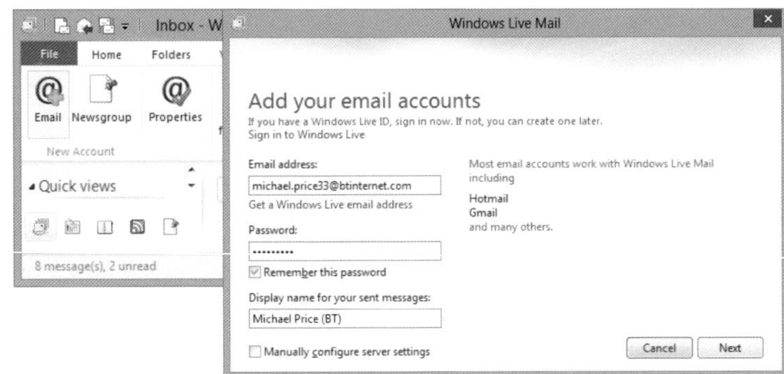

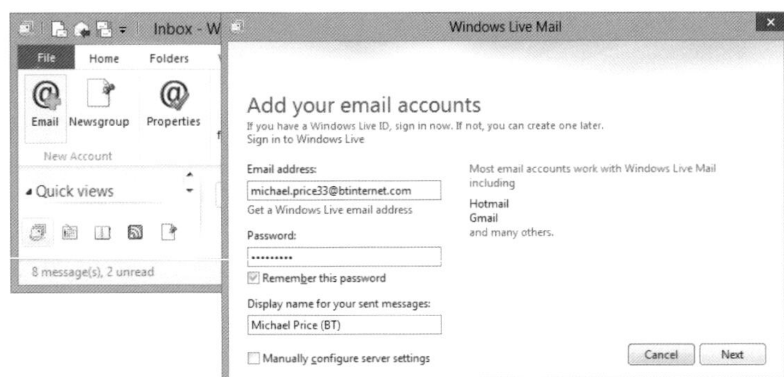

3. Select the Server type, and enter Server addresses and other details (as provided by your ISP) then click Next

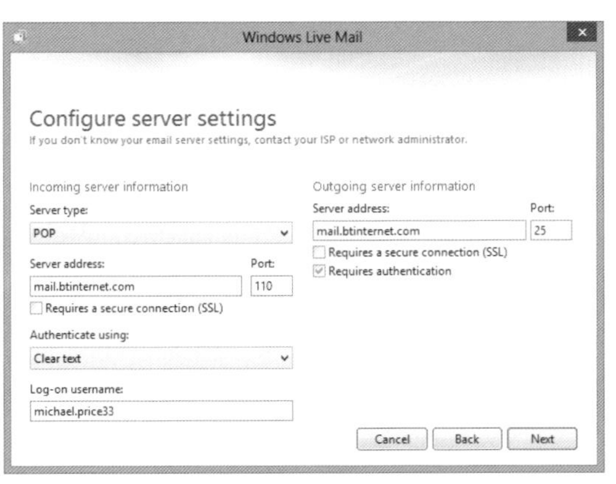

4. This email account is also added to Windows Live Mail

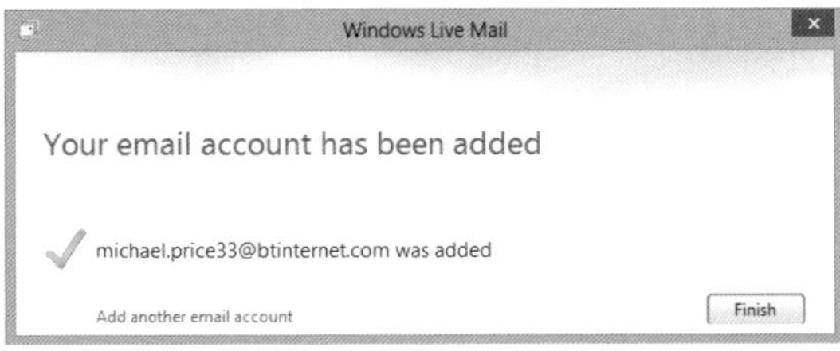

Don't forget

If Windows Live Mail does not have the server information required for the email account, you will be prompted to supply them.

Hot tip

You can define three server types: POP (used for most ISP accounts), IMAP (used for web-based accounts such as Gmail) and Windows Live Hotmail (for Windows Live IDs).

5 The messages for the specified email are downloaded from the server to the Inbox for the account

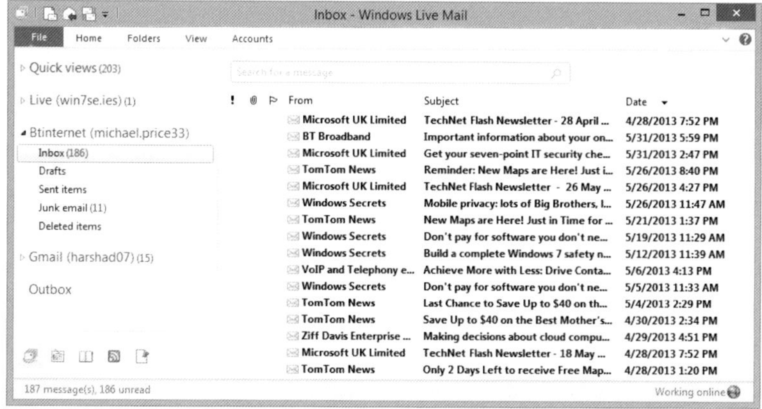

Don't forget

The layout of Windows Live Mail in these examples has been adjusted to allow more room to display the list of messages.

6 You may find that some messages are identified as junk email and automatically moved to the Junk email folder

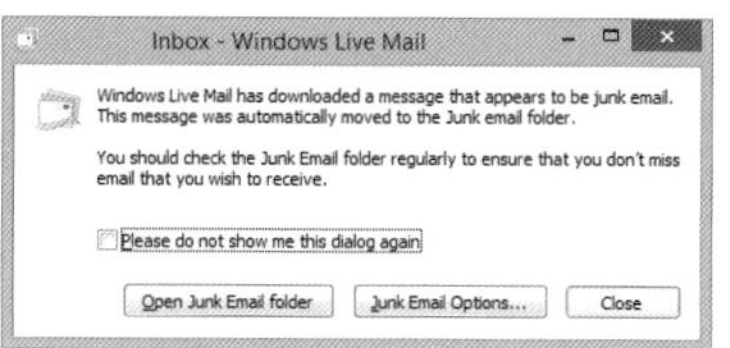

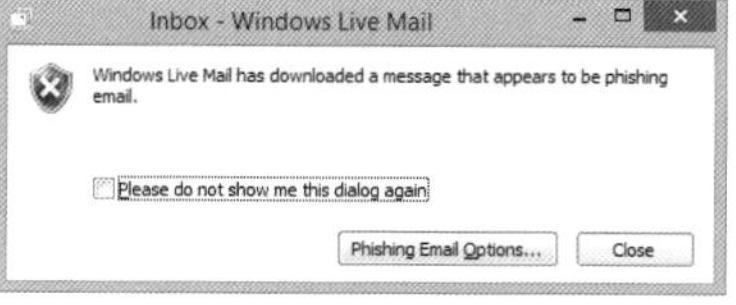

7 Some messages may be identified as phishing email, trying to deceive you into giving personal information, and these are also moved to the Junk email folder

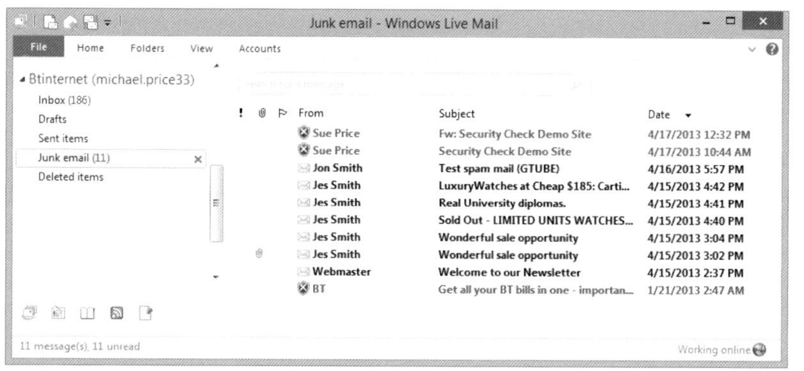

Beware

Not all of the messages identified as junk email are necessarily invalid. One phishing message for example is a genuine communication that happens to be addressed to Dear Customer, which raised the warning.

Mail layout

1. Open Windows Live Mail, and it typically has Mail selected, with folders, Inbox, preview and calendar

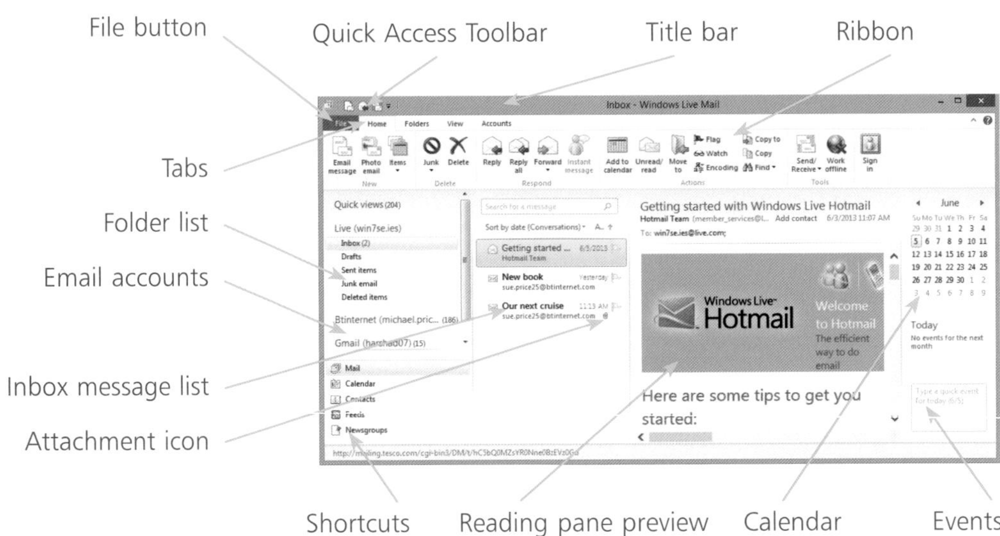

The Home tab displays the commands on the ribbon that you require for working with messages you send and receive.

2. Click the Folders tab to create, copy or move folders

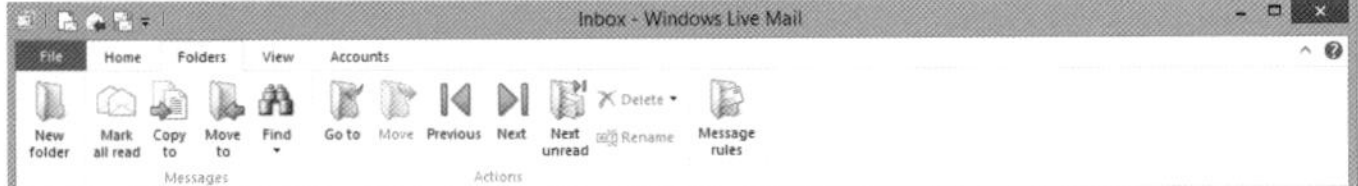

3. Click the View tab to change the window view and layout

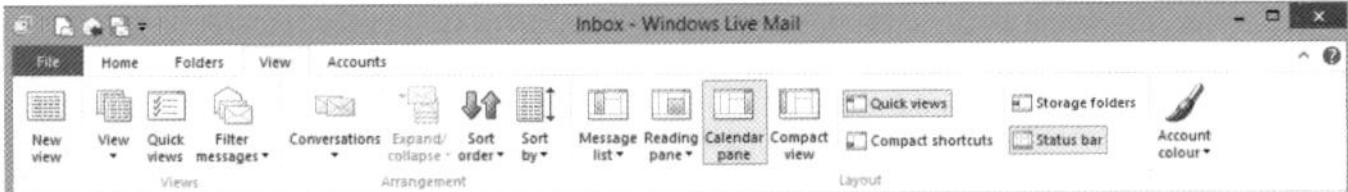

4. Click the Accounts tab to add accounts or view properties

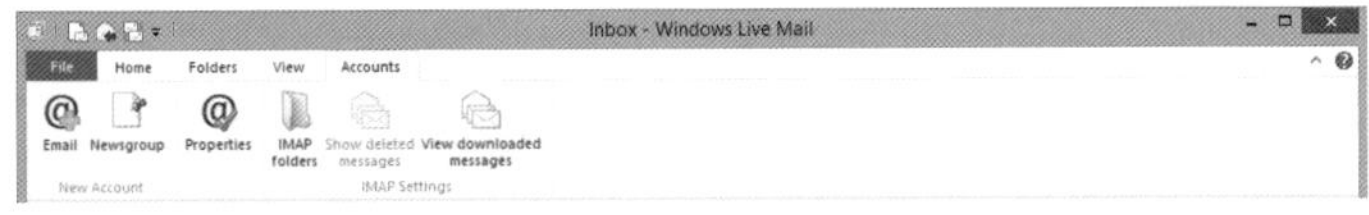

Don't forget

When you switch to Calendar, Contacts, Feeds or Newsgroups, the Home tab displays a different set of commands appropriate to the chosen function.

To change the view and layout of the Mail window:

1. Open Windows Live Mail, select the Mail function and click the View tab

2. Click Reading pane, and select Off to avoid showing a preview of the selected message

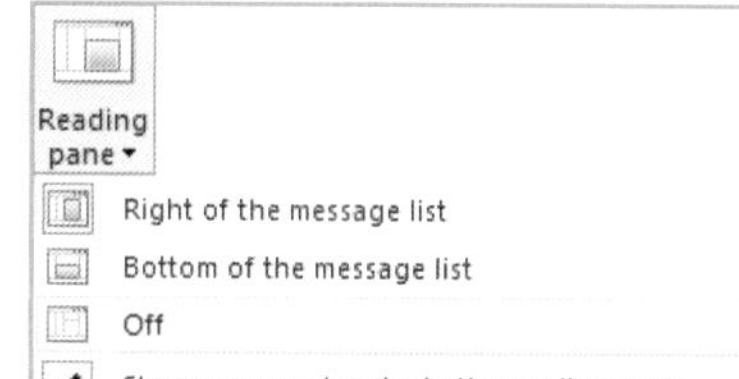

3. Click Calendar pane, which operates as a toggle to hide or show the calendar

4. Click Compact shortcuts, to show the functions as a set of icons

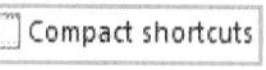

5. Right-click the ribbon and select Minimize the Ribbon, to hide it

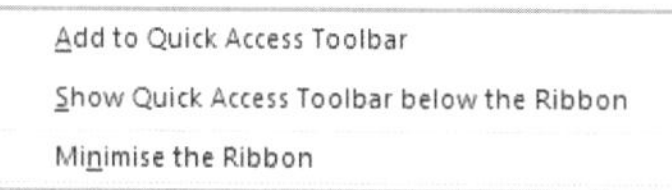

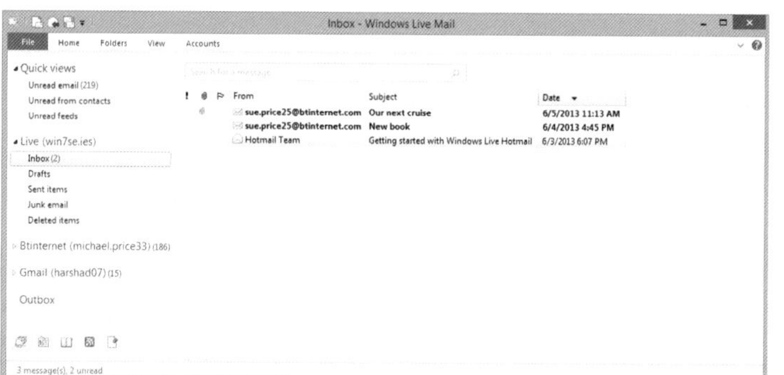

6. To redisplay the ribbon temporarily, so you can select a command, simply click the appropriate tab

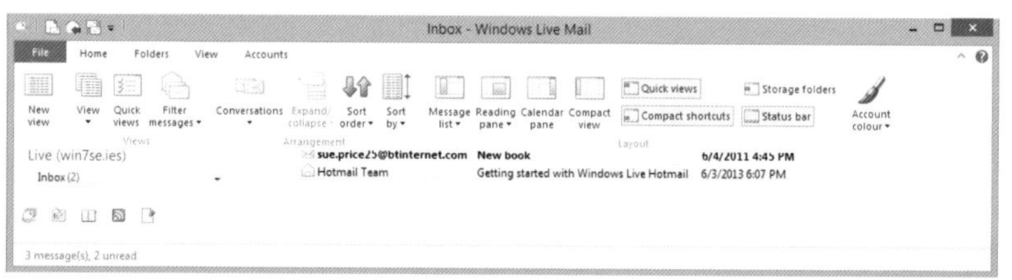

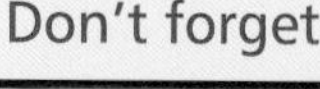

Don't forget

Click the toggles Quick views or Status bar, to hide or show the respective items.

Hot tip

Click Add to Quick Access Toolbar to add the command that's currently selected on the ribbon.

Hot tip

Right-click the Tab bar and select Minimize the Ribbon to redisplay it permanently.

Messages

To see the messages that are available for any of your accounts:

1. In Windows Live Mail, select Mail and click the account

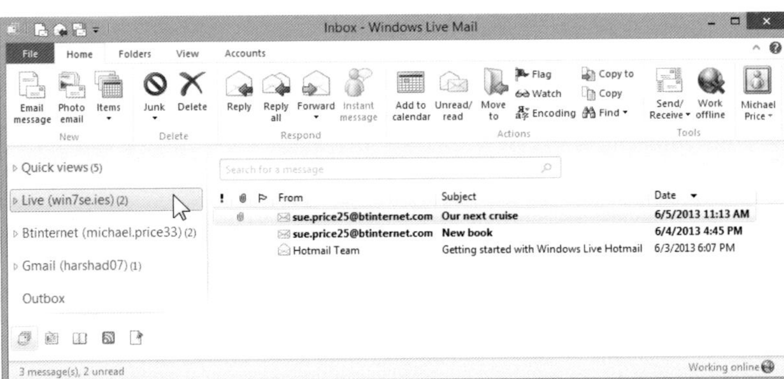

2. To see mail for all the accounts defined, click Quick views

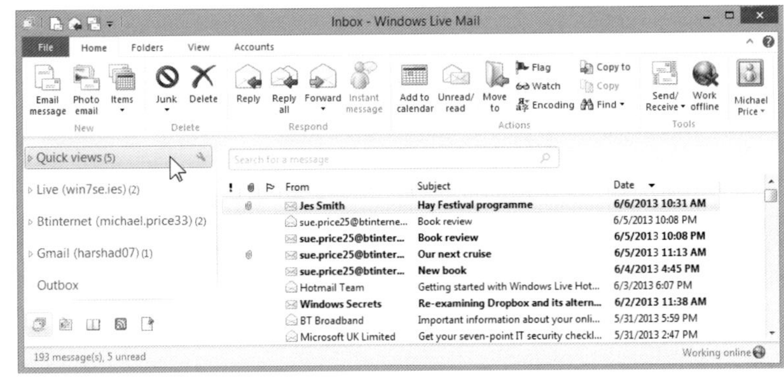

By default, Windows Live Mail will check on the server for new email messages, at startup and then every 10 minutes.

1. To change the delay time, select the File tab and select Options, Mail. Then click the General tab

2. Enter the new time required and click OK

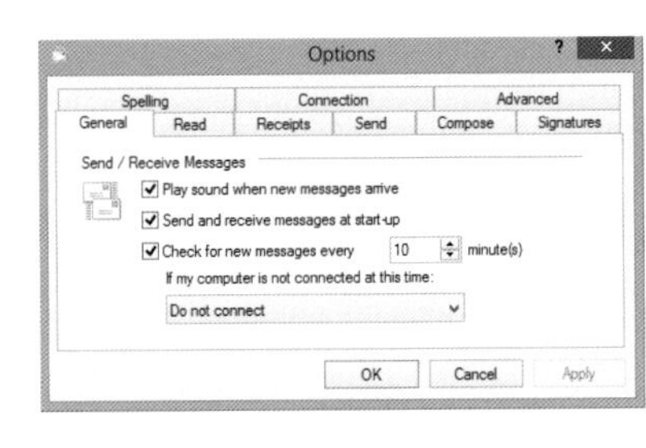

Hot tip

Unread messages are shown highlighted, and the count of unread messages appears in brackets after each account name. The count for Quick views shows the total number of unread messages across all the accounts.

Don't forget

You can click the Send/Receive button at any time to check if there's any mail waiting at the servers for your accounts.

To read an individual message in the account or Quick views list:

1. Double-click an entry in the list (or select the entry and press Enter) to open the message

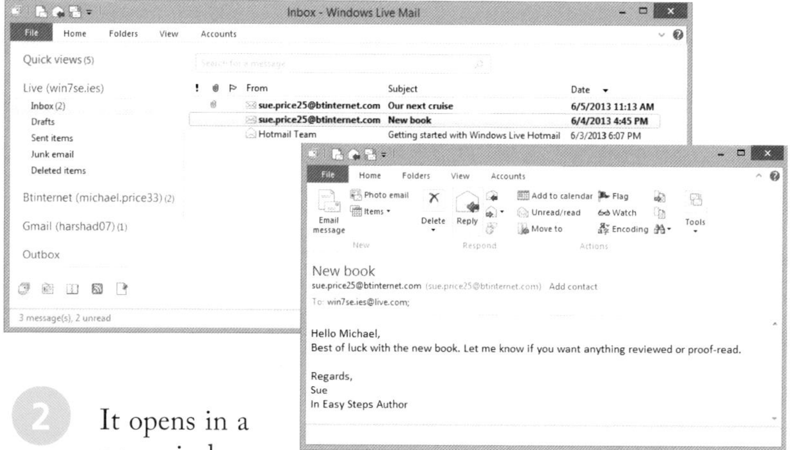

2. It opens in a new window

3. Click Reply and type the response

4. Click the Send button

5. The reply is moved to your Outbox, from where it is sent to your mail server

6. A copy of the reply is saved in your Sent items folder

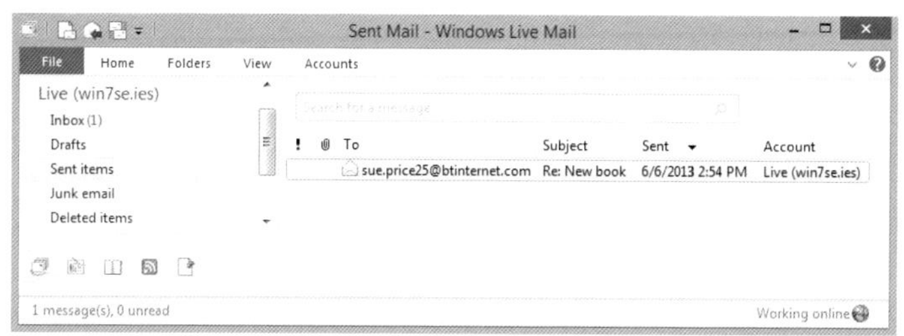

Don't forget

Click the white triangle next to the account name to display the folders - Inbox, Drafts, Sent items etc.

Hot tip

You can reply to the sender, reply to all addressees, or forward the message to one or more other users.

Beware

You may receive a message requesting confirmation. Click the Verify link, or type the characters and select OK.

Attachments

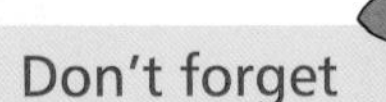

Some messages have files attached, as shown by the paperclip icon on the Inbox entry.

1. Select and open a message with an attachment

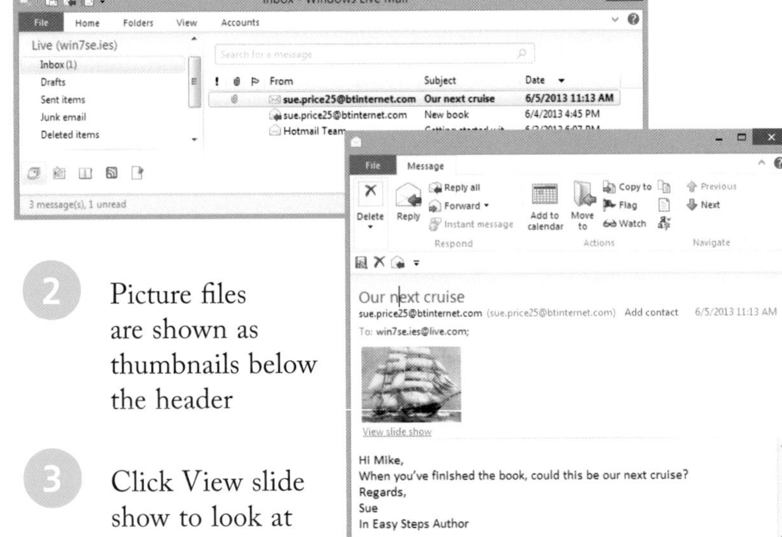

2. Picture files are shown as thumbnails below the header

3. Click View slide show to look at the images

4. Right-click the thumbnail or file icon and select Save as (for just that attachment) or Save all

5. Confirm the folder location and click Save to write the attachments to disk

Hot tip

When you receive other file types such as documents and spreadsheets as attachments, they will be shown as file icons.

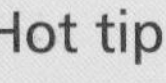

Alternatively, you can click the Windows Live Mail button, select Save then Save Attachments, and choose which attachments to save.

To add an attachment to your messages or replies:

1. Type the message then click Insert, Attach file

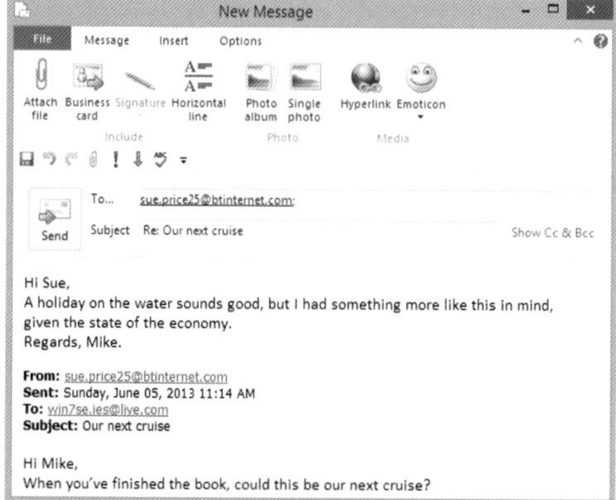

2. Locate the required folder, select the file and click Open

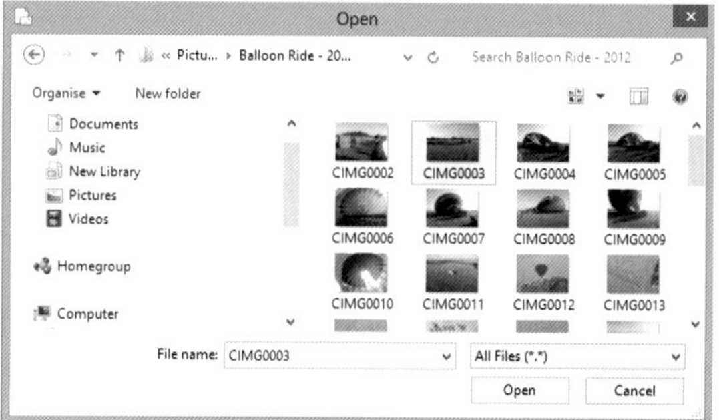

3. The file is added as an icon below the message header

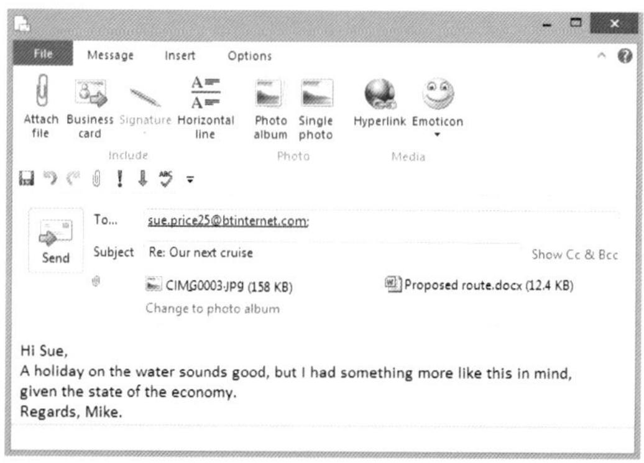

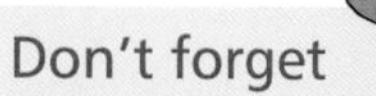

Select Insert, Single photo to add the picture as an image in the message, positioned at the current location of the typing cursor.

Hot tip

You can add other file types, for example a Word document. Click the Send button when you've finished typing the message and adding attachments.

Contacts

Don't forget

You can save contact details in the Windows Live Mail Contacts folder, which acts as an address book, with personal and business information.

1. When you receive an email from a new contact, right-click the Inbox entry and select Add sender to contacts

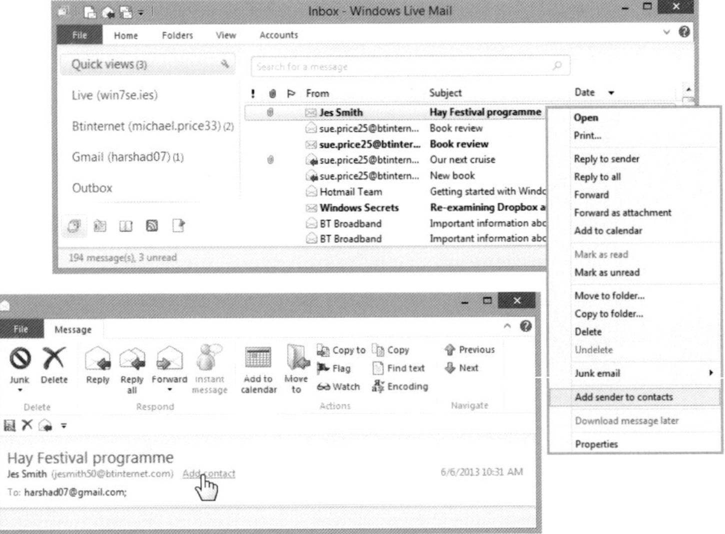

Hot tip

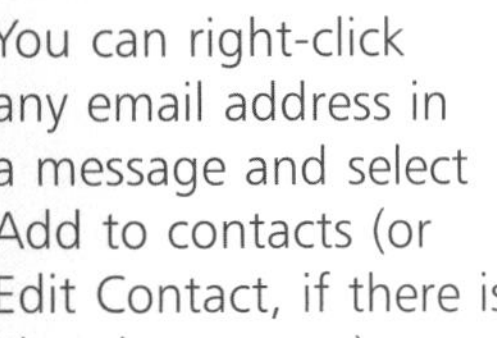

You can right-click any email address in a message and select Add to contacts (or Edit Contact, if there is already an entry).

2. Alternatively, open the message and click the Add contact link next to the sender name (unless already in Contacts)

3. In either case, the available details are displayed

4. Add any further information and click Add contact

Hot tip

Click the Contacts icon or shortcut to view the contents of your Contacts folder, and add, edit or delete entries.

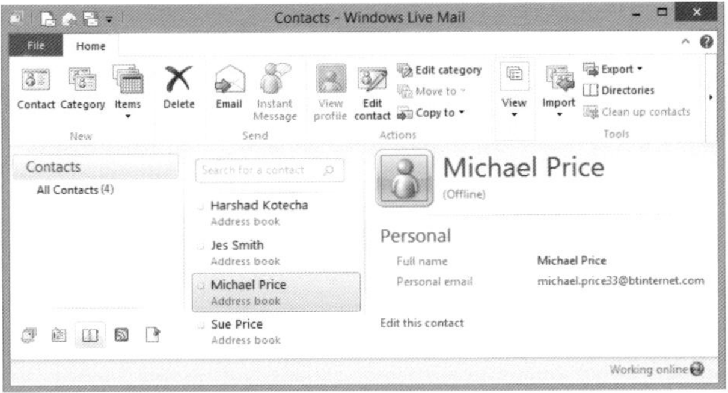

Junk email

Junk email, or spam, is unsolicited mail that is sent to lists of email addresses. Your ISP will provide filters to filter spam so that it doesn't actually reach your computer. Your antivirus program may redirect suspect mail. For spam that gets past these checks, Windows Live Mail lets you set up rules to block suspect senders and redirect junk mail.

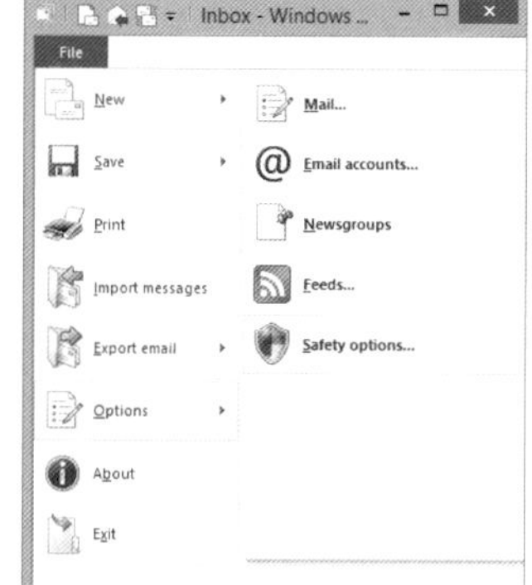

1. Select the File tab, select Options and then choose the Safety options
2. Click the Options tab
3. Review the option selected and adjust if appropriate

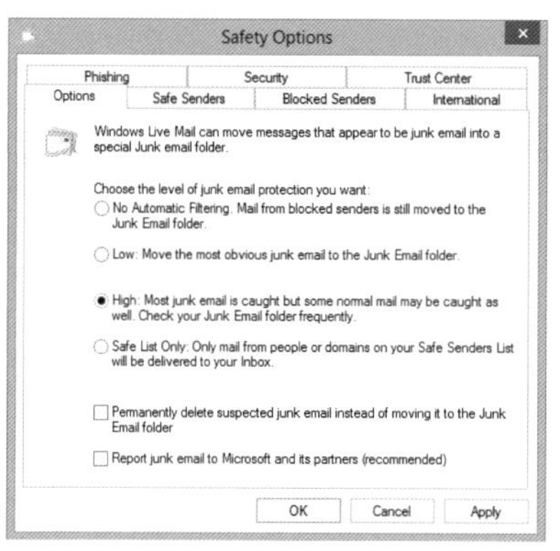

4. You can permanently delete junk mail, but this risks deleting valid mail which has been inadvertently redirected
5. Decide if you want to notify Microsoft of junk mail detected
6. Click the Safe Senders and the Blocked Senders tabs, to add particular email addresses or domain names
7. Click the Phishing tab to enable or disable the protection against phishing attacks
8. Click the International tab to block messages from specific countries or in a particular language group

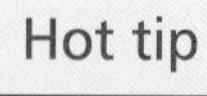
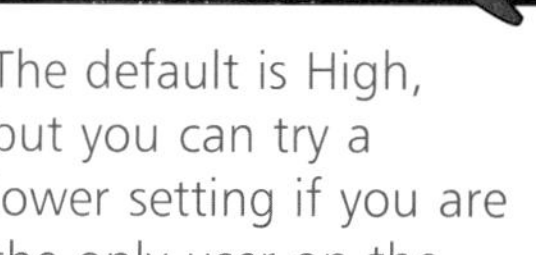

Hot tip

The default is High, but you can try a lower setting if you are the only user on the computer.

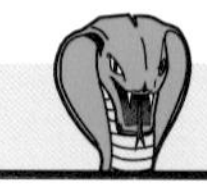

Beware

You may find that your email is filtered before it gets downloaded, so sign on to your account at the appropriate website and check the junk mail folder there, in case valid messages have been trapped by error.

People app

While on the subject of contacts, Windows 8 provides three apps that are related to, or make use of, contacts (apart from the Mail app). The first of these is the People app. While this is essentially a contacts manager for storing information such as email addresses, phone numbers, addresses, etc., it does have one powerful feature in its armory.

This is the ability to amalgamate all your contacts across a range of different email services and social media websites. It also provides some basic social networking tools, such as tweets and comments that can be used without having to leave the app.

Don't forget

People lets you access all your contacts, regardless of where they are, from one convenient location.

1. On the Start screen, click the People tile

2. If you are signed in to the computer with a Microsoft account, the Home page will open. If not, you will be asked to sign in

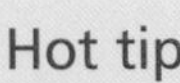

Hot tip

People can link the same contacts from different networks under one profile. There is also an option that allows you to link contacts manually.

3. On the Home page, you can view your Profile details. On the profile details page, right-clicking reveals an Edit link, which opens your Microsoft Live page from where you can edit your account details

Still on the Home page, click your account and then click the Go to settings and connect your Facebook, Twitter and other accounts link

4 This opens a new screen from where you can choose the accounts you want to add to People from the list provided

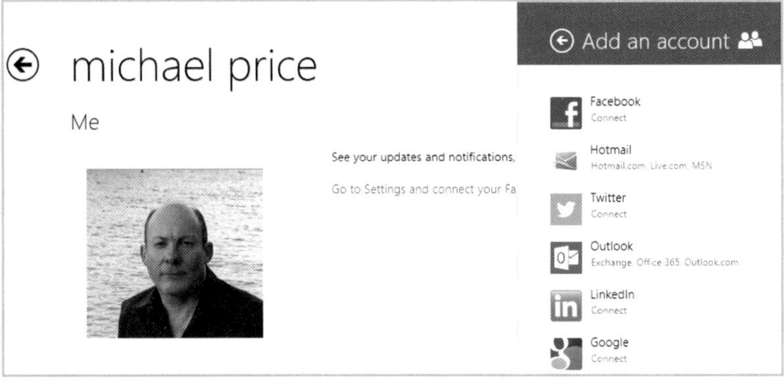

5 The Home page is now populated with your contacts

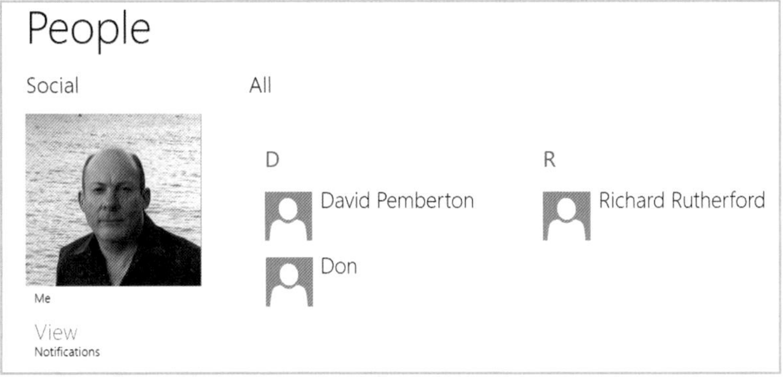

6 Click a contact to see what's new from them. At the bottom of the screen, you'll see options to add the contact to your favorites, retweet their posts and to reply to them

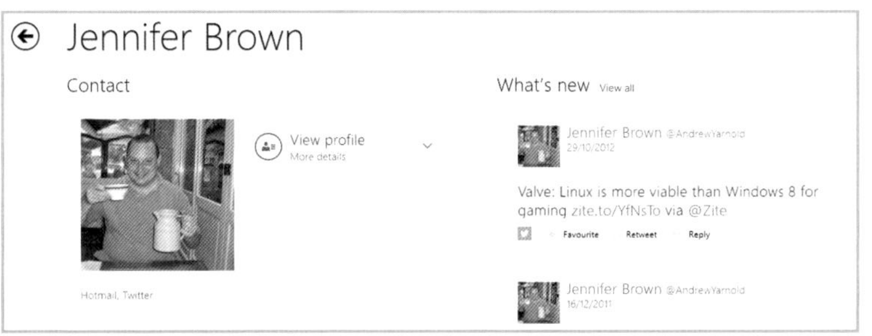

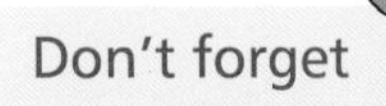

Don't forget

While in the People app, clicking Settings from the Charms bar provides related options.

Hot tip

Right-click on the screen to open the app bar. Click Online only to restrict the contacts displayed to those who are online.

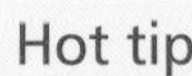

Hot tip

The People app can be used to open the Messaging app to initiate a chat session with a contact. It can also be used with the Maps app to plan a route to a contact's address.

Mail calendar

There's full calendar capability included in Windows Live Mail.

1. Open Windows Live Mail and select the Calendar icon

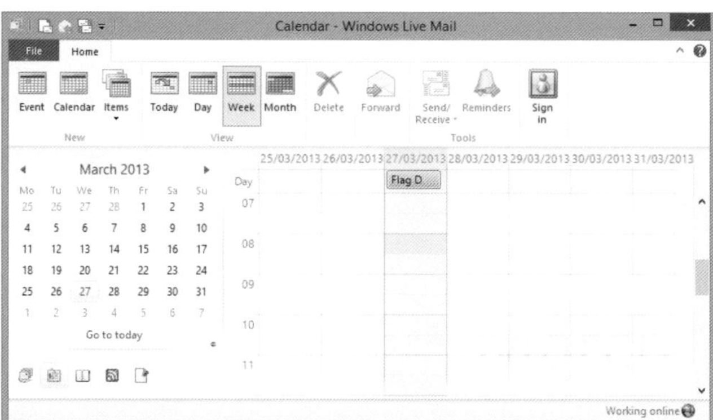

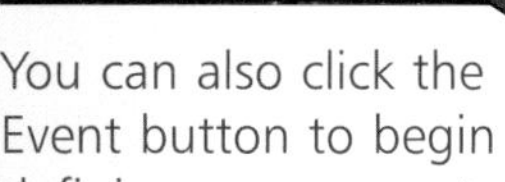

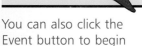

Hot tip

You can also click the Event button to begin defining a new event.

2. Select a date, double-click a time period and define an event start time, end time and reminder time

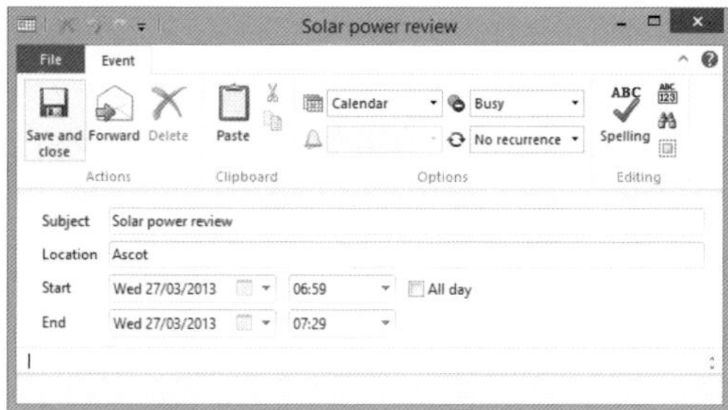

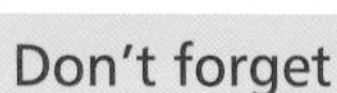

Don't forget

You can specify an all day event or a multi-day event, and you can specify that an event is recurring, e.g. weekly, monthly or yearly.

3. Click Save and close, to add the event to the calendar

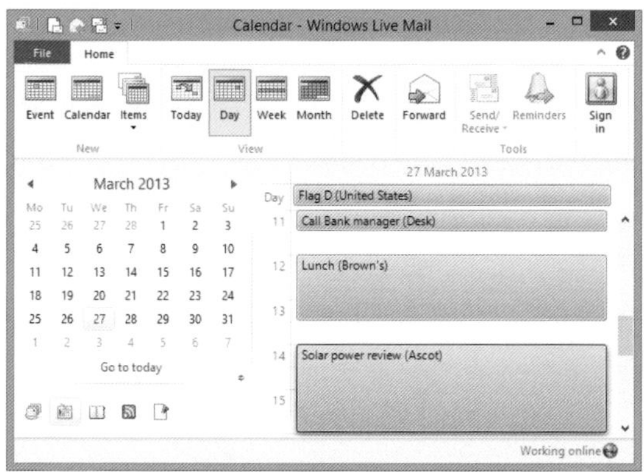

Calendar app

An alternative to Windows Live Mail's calendar is the Calendar app supplied by Windows 8.

The app is powered by the Exchange ActiveSync (EAS) technology that is the backbone of Microsoft services such as Hotmail, Exchange, and Office 365. It can also connect to other EAS-based calendars, which include Google Calendar.

As with other Windows 8 apps, Calendar uses a browser-like form of navigation. When using a mouse, you'll see small navigational arrows appear near the top-left and top-right of the screen. Or you can use the keyboard – Ctrl + left arrow and Ctrl + right arrow to move left and right respectively.

A cool feature is that moving backwards or forwards in time is done within the context of the current view. For example, going back while in week view takes you back a week. Going forward while in day view takes you forward to tomorrow.

1. Click the Calendar tile on the Start screen

2. If you are signed in to the computer with a Microsoft account, the calendar will open in monthly view. If not, you will be asked to sign in

3. Initially, the calendar has no entries. Create one by double-clicking on a day to open the Details page

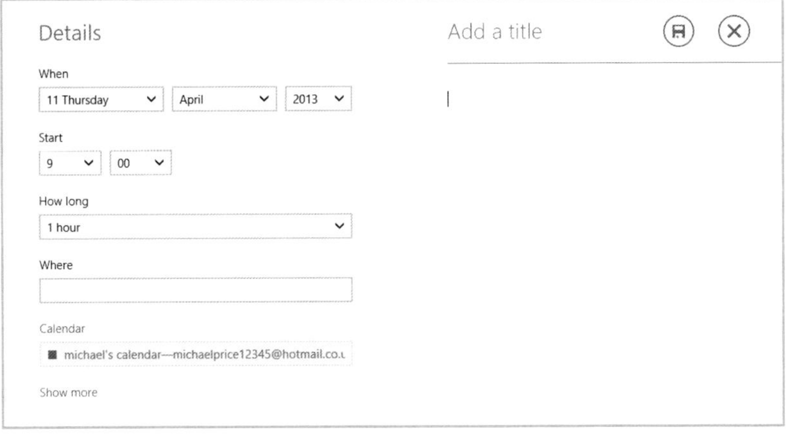

Calendar works well when snapped to the side of another app. It provides a thumbnail view of the month and the current day's events.

Calendar can show detailed information regarding your next event on the lock screen.

...cont'd

Hot tip

You can import calendars from Hotmail, Outlook and Google by clicking Add an account from Settings on the Charms bar.

4. Under Details there are a range of options:

- **When** – select a day for the event to take place on
- **Start** – set a start time for the event
- **How long** – specify a time period for the event
- **Where** – specify where the event is to take place

Clicking the Show more link reveals a list of further options, such as how often the event is to take place, reminders, status, etc.

5. At the top-right of the screen click on Add a title. Type in the title text, the first few characters of which will be the heading on the calendar page. Then, add details of the event in the Add a message section

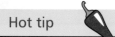

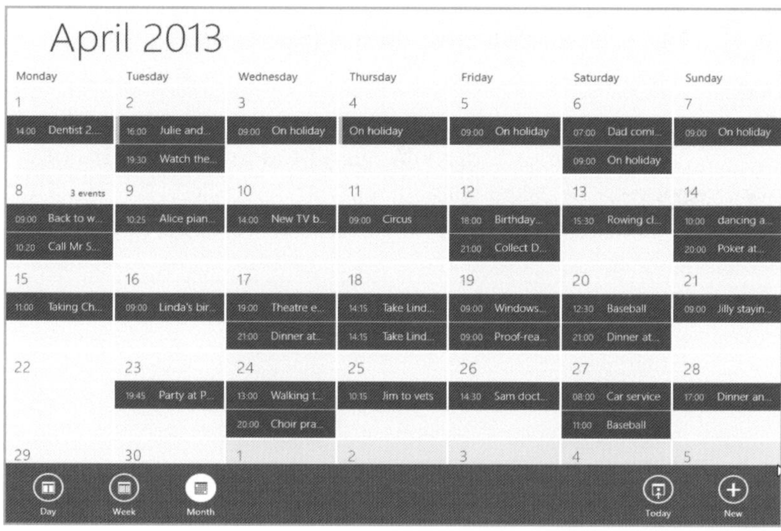

6. Right-click on the calendar to open the app bar. This lets you change the view to Day, Week or Month

Messaging app

The Messaging app supplied by Windows 8 is a fairly basic example of this type of software. It is similar to the Messaging app on Windows Phone 8, and provides many of its features such as being able to swap between services on the fly.

The layout is very simple; the Home page consisting of two panes that show ongoing conversations on the left-hand side, with the current active conversation being displayed on the right.

Note that at the time of writing, the app only supports two services – Windows Messenger and Facebook Chat.

Hot tip

Contacts that are currently online have a green bar next to their name or photo.

1. Click the Messaging tile on the Start screen
2. If you are signed in to the computer with a Microsoft account, the Home page will open. If not, you will be asked to sign in
3. You see the Home page welcome message

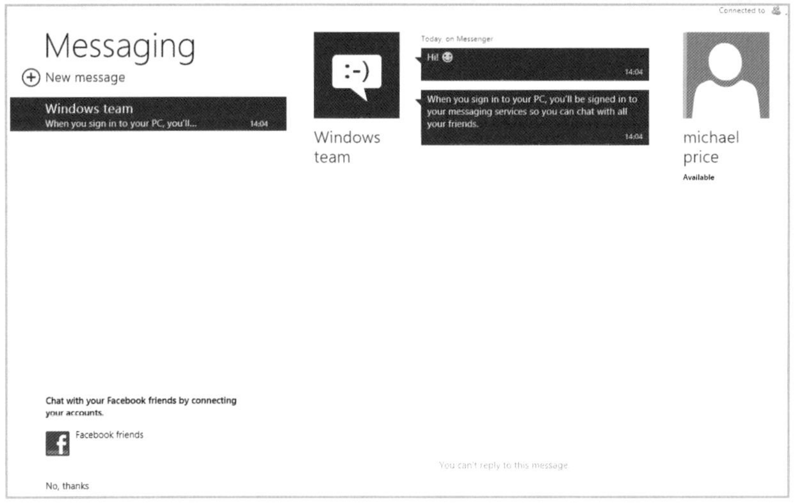

4. The left-hand pane shows a list of ongoing conversations
5. The right-hand pane shows the current conversation. This can be viewed in a "conversation" view

Hot tip

With the Messaging app, it is possible to place notifications on the lock screen.

...cont'd

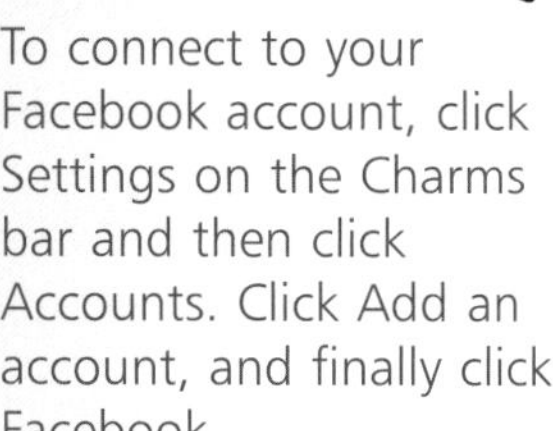

Hot tip

To connect to your Facebook account, click Settings on the Charms bar and then click Accounts. Click Add an account, and finally click Facebook.

6. To start a conversation, click New message at the top-left of the Home page

Messaging
New message

7. Windows now switches to the People app so you can select a contact to add to the Home page

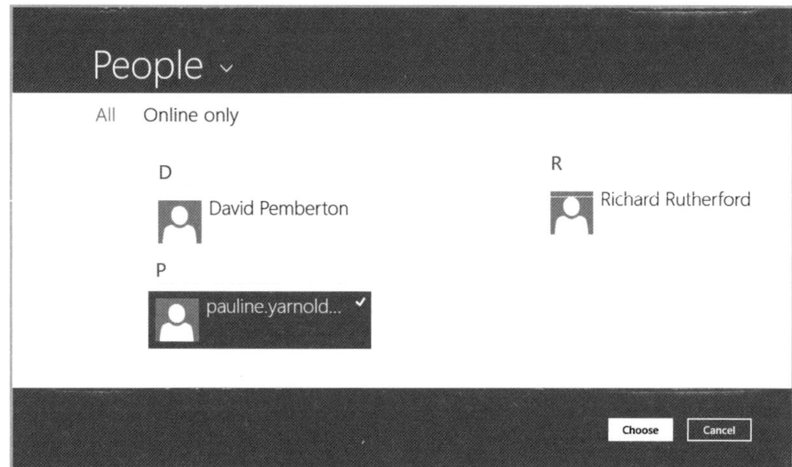

8. Select a contact and click Choose. The contact is added to the Home page. Select it and then type your message in the box at the bottom of the screen

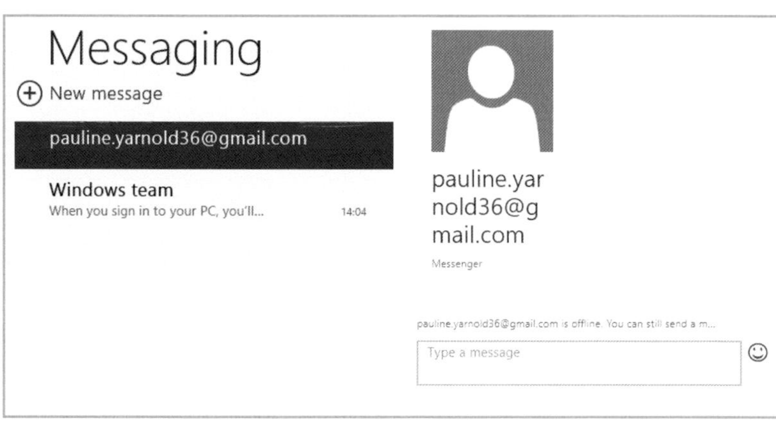

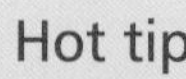

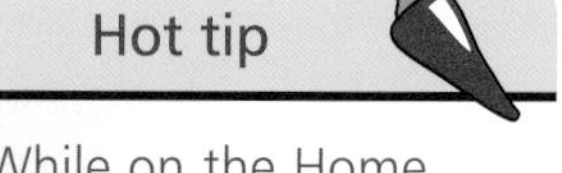

Hot tip

While on the Home page, the app bar provides an Invite link. This lets you add a new friend to Messenger.

Newsgroups

To take part in a discussion, you need to access the appropriate newsgroup server and subscribe to the particular newsgroup.

To specify the newsgroup server in Windows Live Mail:

1. Choose the Newsgroup shortcut icon, then select the Accounts tab and click Newsgroup in New Account

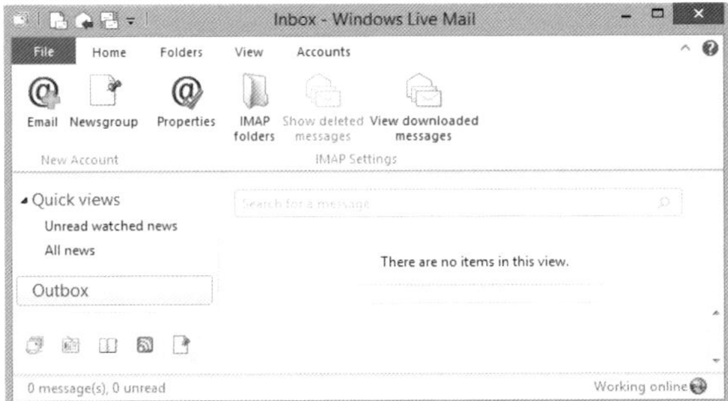

2. Supply the display name or nickname that you want others to see and click Next

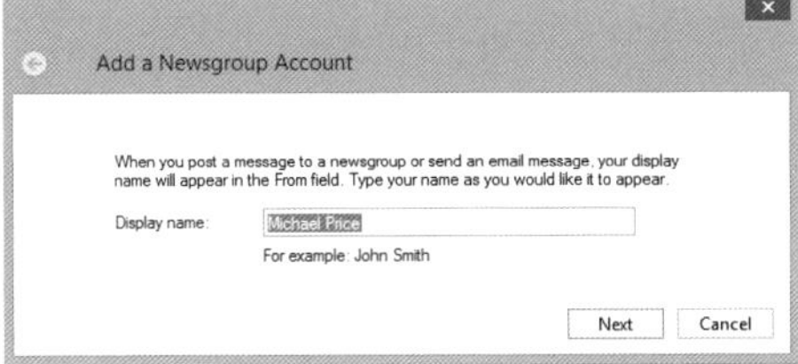

3. Provide your email address for personal replies

You could make a deliberate error in the email address, such as putting "at" rather than @. This will be obvious to a human reader, but would help avoid your email address being detected by robots that search the Internet for email addresses to use for spam.

Hot tip

Windows Live Mail also includes Newsreader capability, so that you can participate in online discussion groups.

Hot tip

If you do mistype the address, accidentally or deliberately, you'll get a warning but will be allowed to enter the address as typed.

...cont'd

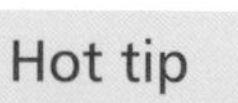

Hot tip

This is a free news server and has no requirement for log on. If you choose a paid service, you'd be given a user ID and password and you'd specify My news server requires me to log on.

4. Name the newsgroup server you have decided to use, for example: freenews.netfront.net

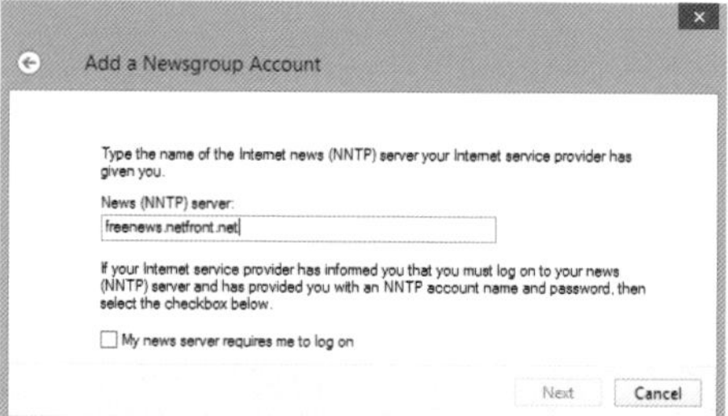

5. Click Next then click Finish to add the account

6. The names of the newsgroups will be downloaded – there are over 40,000 in the list for the example newsgroup server

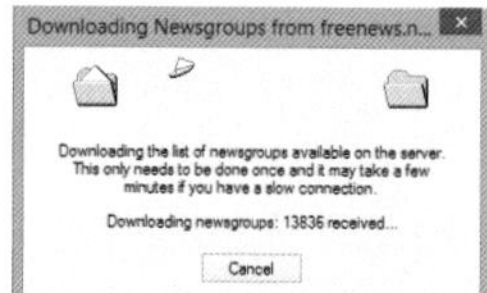

Hot tip

You can search the Internet to find the newsgroups and servers that cover your interests, or other enthusiasts may suggest their favorites.

7. Type keywords related to your interest, e.g. Bridge, to list only those newsgroups that are relevant

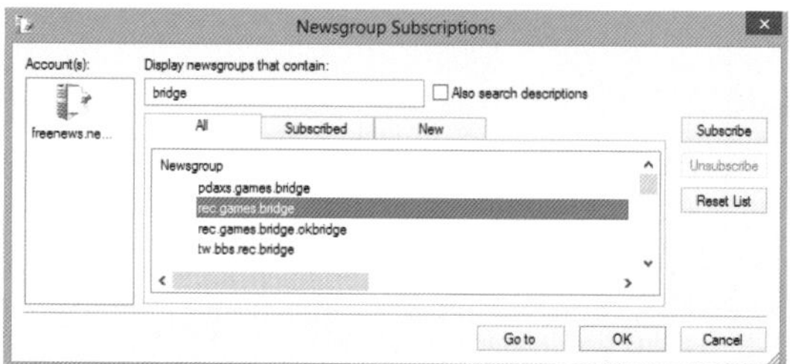

8. Select a particular newsgroup, click Subscribe and Go to

Hot tip

If you decide that you do not wish to receive any future postings from that newsgroup, you can choose Unsubscribe.

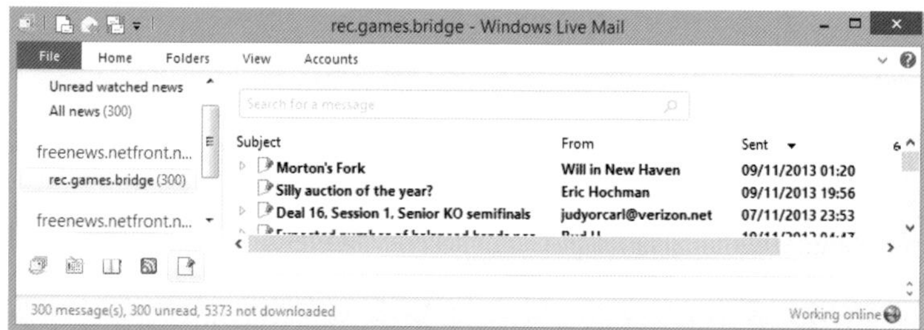

13 Internet Explorer

Windows includes Microsoft Internet Explorer as the default browser. Version 10, the latest release, takes advantage of hardware acceleration on graphics adapters, manages the effects of add-on applications and includes improved tabbed browsing facilities. There is also an app version of Internet Explorer, which is available from the Start screen. Like all apps, this is a no-frills application.

Windows 8 versus Desktop

Hot tip

The advantages of not supporting add-ons and plug-ins are much increased speed, stability and security – all essential in a browser designed primarily for use with a tablet.

A unique feature in Windows 8 is the provision of two different versions of Internet Explorer – Desktop Internet Explorer and the Internet Explorer app. While they look completely different, in reality, the app is basically a stripped-down version of Desktop Internet Explorer and so provides much less in the way of features and options. However, they both run on the same underlying architecture.

For example, they share the user's browsing history, cookies, passwords, and temporary files. If any of these items are deleted from one version, they are also deleted from the other.

As might be expected, Internet Explorer 10 offers a number of improvements over its predecessor, Internet Explorer 9. These include:

- Native Flash integration
- Improved performance
- Improved standards support, e.g. HTML5 and CSS3
- An upgraded JavaScript engine
- Security improvements

The improvements apply to both versions of Internet Explorer 10.

Don't forget

For a speedy full-screen experience, use the app. For more demanding use, the Desktop version will be better.

Where the app version differs markedly is the way it is presented to the user. Instead of the traditional array of toolbars, menus and buttons, the app has a clean, uncluttered interface that runs full-screen – the only thing that is visible on the page is the app bar at the bottom. As soon as you click on the page, even this disappears (to get it back, just right-click on the screen).

The only other options offered are forwards and backwards arrows, a Refresh button, Pin site, Find, Favorites, Tabs, and View on Desktop Internet Explorer.

The other major difference between the two versions is that, with the exception of the built-in Flash, the app does not support any plug-ins or add-ons, e.g. no Java, Silverlight, Shockwave, etc. If you need to use a plug-in or add-on, you will have to switch to the Desktop version.

Screen layout

When the Internet Explorer app is opened, it shows just the Home page and an app bar at the bottom. The only other element that can be displayed is the Tab bar at the top of the screen. This is opened by right-clicking anywhere on the page.

The image below demonstrates what elements are available:

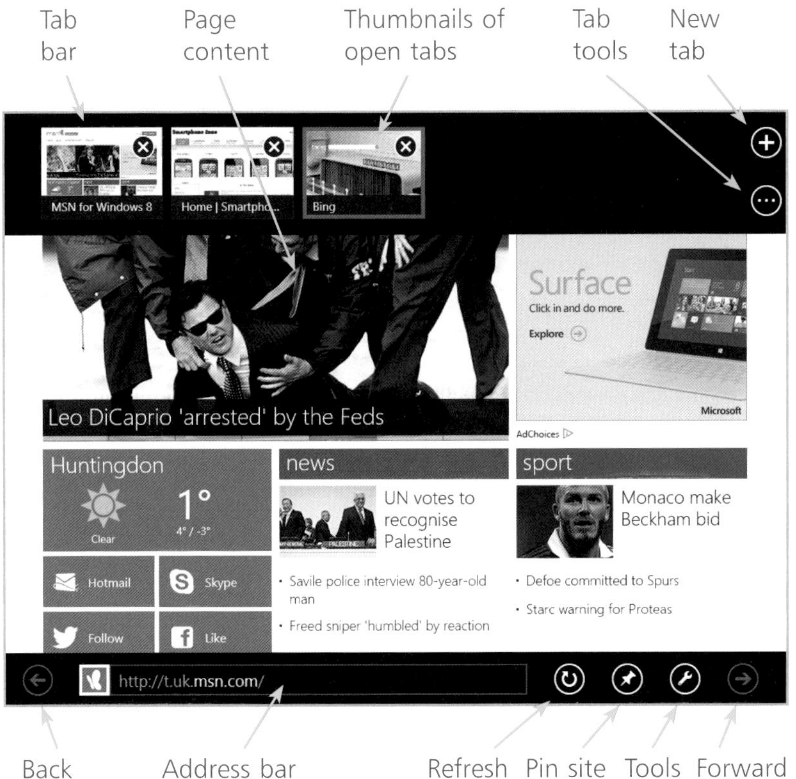

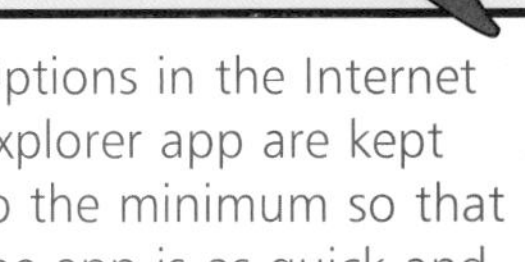

Options in the Internet Explorer app are kept to the minimum so that the app is as quick and responsive as possible.

When browsing the Web, the user will also see two semi-transparent arrows appear in the middle of the screen on either side of the web page.

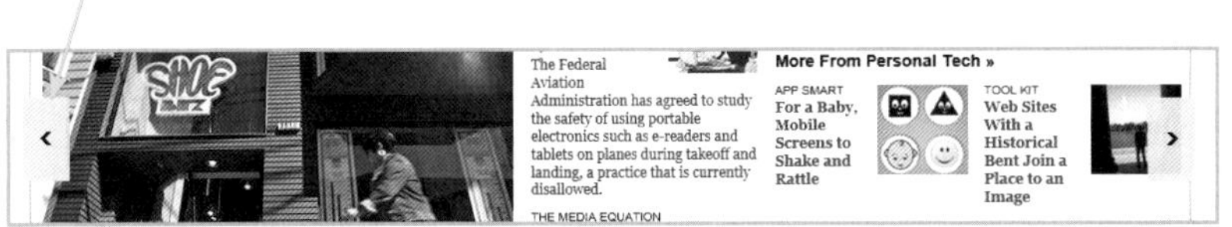

Hot tip

Flip Ahead does not work with Desktop Internet Explorer – just with the IE app.

This is a new feature in Internet Explorer called Flip Ahead. See page 231 for more details on this.

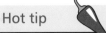

App bar

When you open the Internet Explorer app, an app bar is present at the bottom of the screen. It provides the majority of the user options available with this version of Internet Explorer.

The ones we are going to look at here are Pin to Start, Add to favorites and Page tools:

Hot tip

Rename your pinned site by clicking in the box above the blue Pin to Start button.

Pin to Start

You've found a site you are likely to use frequently. The app bar provides two ways of quickly accessing it:

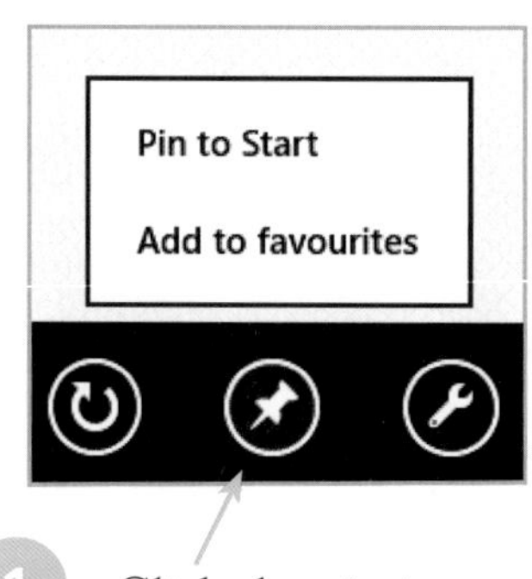

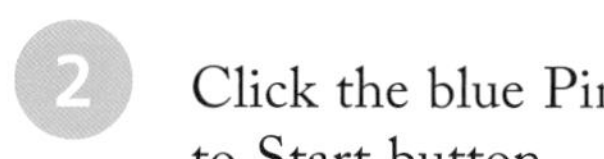

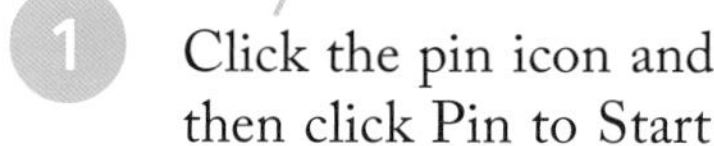

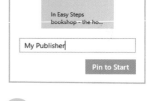

1 Click the pin icon and then click Pin to Start

2 Click the blue Pin to Start button

3 On the Start screen you'll now see a tile for the web page

Hot tip

As soon as you left-click in a page, the app bar disappears. Just right-click to get it back.

Add to Favorites

If you just want to add a page to your favorites list, do as described in Step 1 above, but this time click Add to favorites.

Page Tools

The Page tools link provides the user with two options:

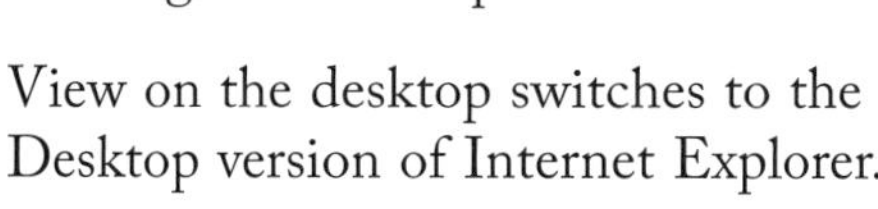

View on the desktop switches to the Desktop version of Internet Explorer.

Find on page opens a Find toolbar. This enables you to search for specific words or phrases in the current web page.

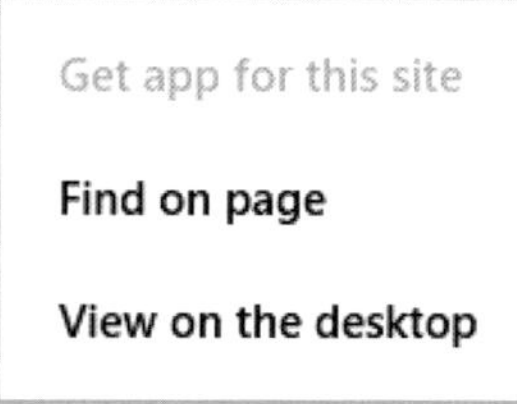

Don't forget

If you need to switch to the Desktop Internet Explorer, right-click on the page and click Tools.

Open web page

To open a web page with the Internet Explorer app, you have several options:

Address box

To the left of the app bar is the address box – use this to type in a web page address.

You can also do a search from the address box – just type your search term and press Enter. As you type, a list of suggested sites will appear as shown below:

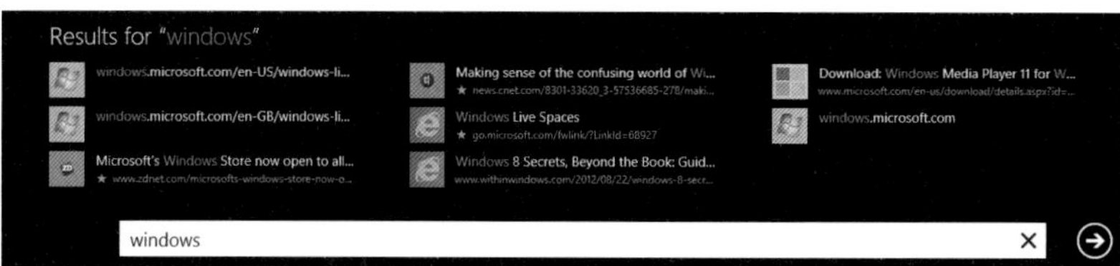

Pinned pages and favorites

If you've pinned a page, you can open it in two ways:

1. Go to the Start screen and scroll across the screen until you see the page's tile. Click the tile to open the page
2. Left-click anywhere in the address box to extend the app bar. Pinned pages will be listed under Pinned. To the right of the pinned pages, you'll see your Favorites

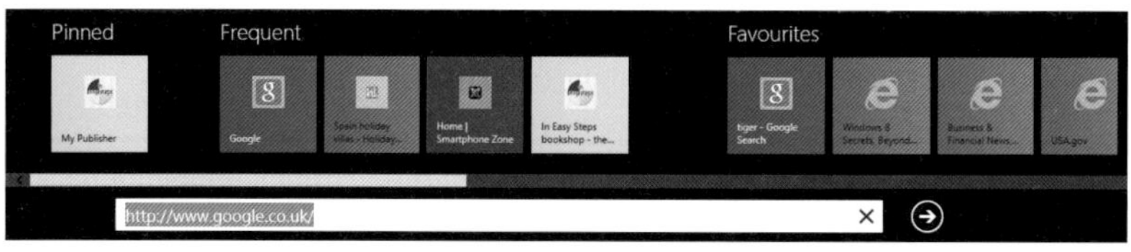

3. You will also see a list of frequently accessed pages under the heading Frequent. Click the tiles to open the pages

Hot tip

The address bar also doubles as a search box. Just type your search term and press Enter. As you type, a list of suggested sites will appear.

Open in new tab

Tabs are an extremely useful feature in modern browsers that allow the user to have a number of pages open simultaneously, and quickly switch between them.

At first glance, the tab feature doesn't appear to be present in the Internet Explorer app – it is there though, you just have to activate it.

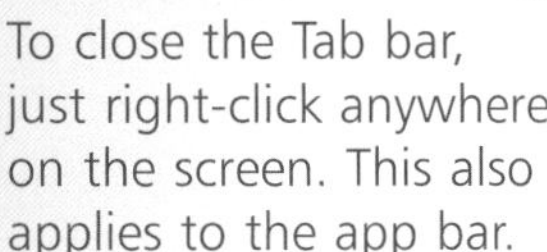

Hot tip

To close the Tab bar, just right-click anywhere on the screen. This also applies to the app bar.

1. Right-click anywhere on the screen

2. A black bar appears at the top of the screen – this is the Tab bar. At the left are thumbnails of open tabs. To switch to one, just click on the thumbnail. To close it, click the X at the top right

3. At the far right, you'll see a + icon. Click this to open a new tab

4. Open a page in the tab with any of the methods described on page 217

5. Below the New tab icon is Tab tools. This provides two options: The first, Close tabs, is self-explanatory

   The second, New InPrivate tab, enables you to open an InPrivate browsing session (no records of the session are kept) in a new tab

   New InPrivate tab

   Close tabs

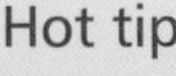

Hot tip

InPrivate Browsing enables you to surf the Web without leaving a trail in Internet Explorer. This helps prevent anyone else who might be using your computer from seeing what you looked at on the Web.

Desktop Internet Explorer

There are two ways to open Desktop Internet Explorer: the first is to switch to it from the app version as explained on page 216. The second is explained below:

1. On the Desktop, at the far left of the taskbar, you'll see the Internet Explorer icon

2. Click it to open Internet Explorer

The first time you run Internet Explorer it will open the MSN website for your region as shown below:

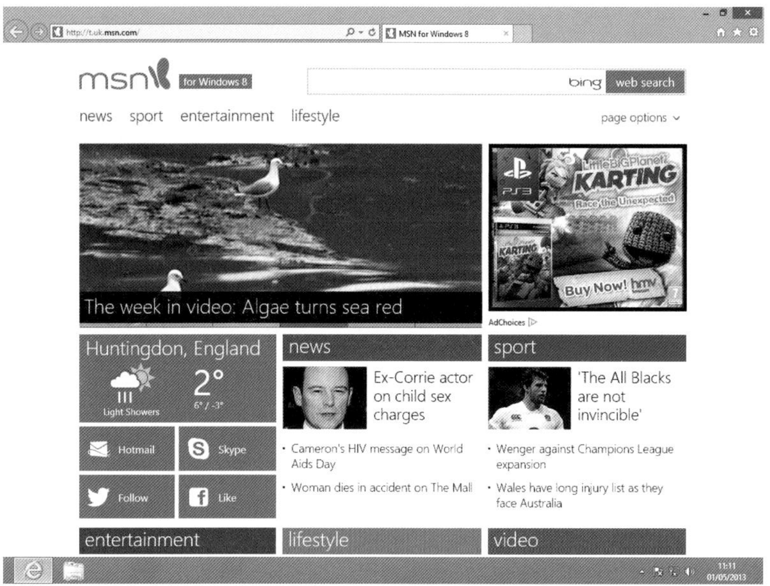

This is probably one of the first things you will want to change.

1. Press Winkey + X to open the Power users menu and select Control Panel

2. Click Network and Internet and under Internet Options, click Change your homepage

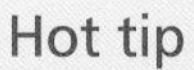 

Hot tip

You can also access Internet Options from Internet Explorer. Click the Tools icon at the top far-right and select Internet Options.

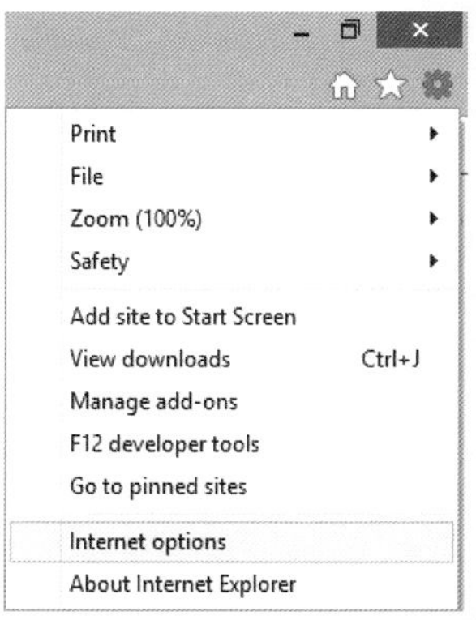

Default Internet Explorer

In the preceding pages, we have seen how to manually open both versions of Internet Explorer. However, there are situations where clicking a link (in an email for example) will launch the browser automatically. When this happens, which version do you want the link to open in? You can configure this as follows:

You can open Internet Explorer's menu bar temporarily by pressing the Alt key.

1. Open the Desktop version of Internet Explorer and press the Alt key. This opens the toolbar at the top of the screen. Click Tools and then Internet Options

2. Click the Programs tab

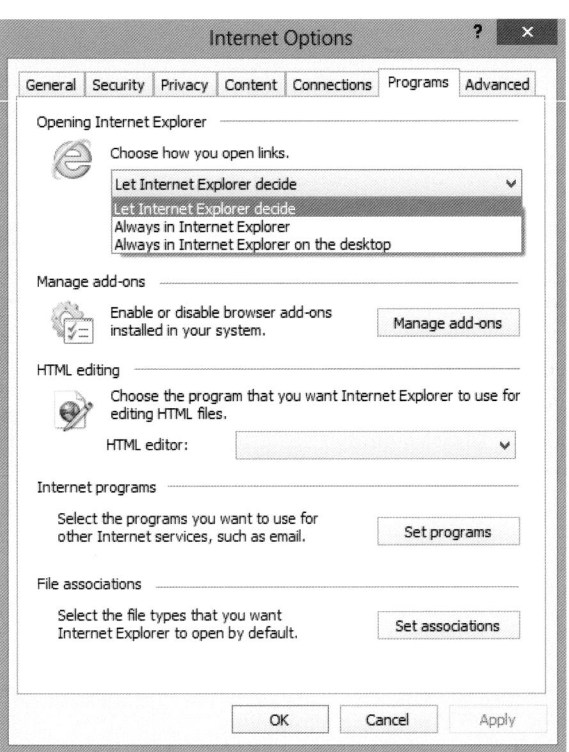

3. At the top of the dialog box there is an option to choose how you open links. If you want them to open with the Internet Explorer app, select Always in Internet Explorer, and for the Desktop version, select Always in Internet Explorer on the desktop

Window layout

When you open Desktop Internet Explorer, it displays the Home web page in a simplified view with these components included:

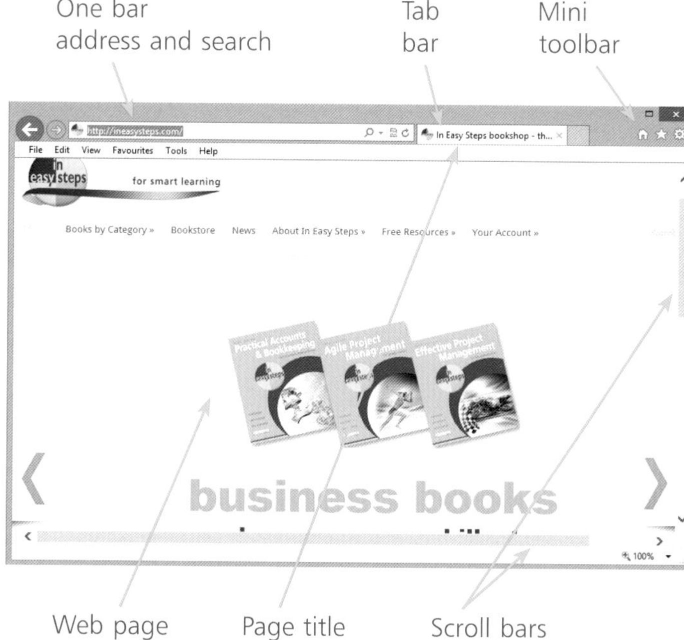

Don't forget

You can change the Home page or add extra pages.

1. To show the other bars (hidden by default), right-click alongside the Tab bar and select Favorites bar. Right-click again for the Command, Status or Menu bar

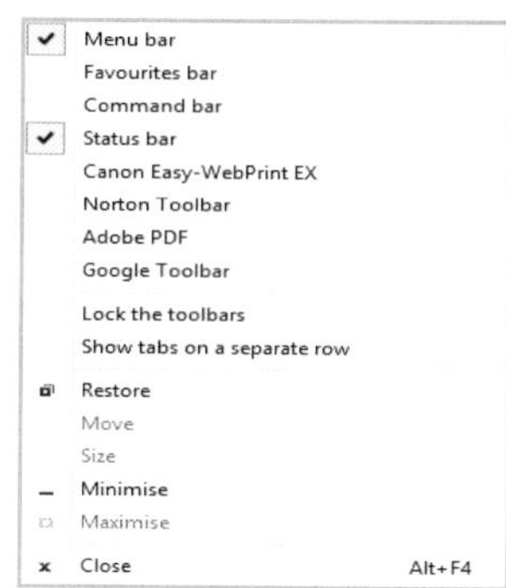

Hot tip

You select one bar at a time, and it is added and then marked with a tick, Select again to remove the tick and hide the bar. You can also set Show tabs on a separate row.

...cont'd

Don't forget

Click in the address box to display the typing cursor and make adjustments to the existing address.

2 Click the One box to highlight the website address

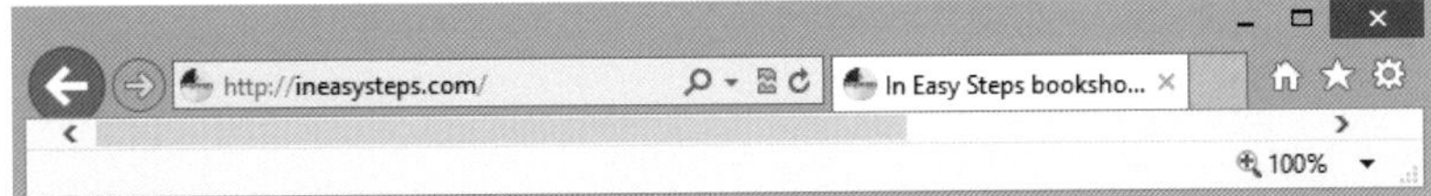

3 Start typing to delete the old address and enter the new

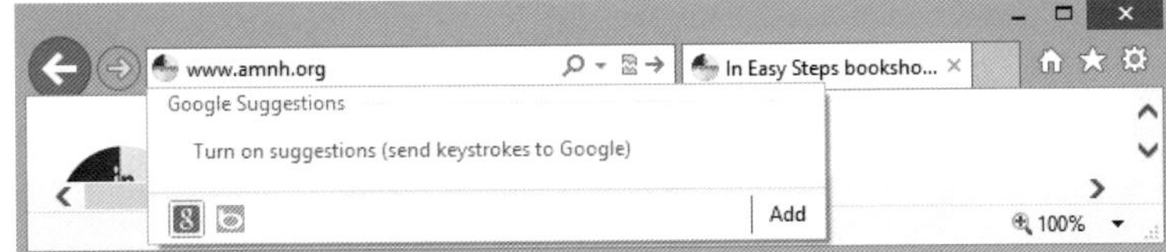

4 Press Enter to display the website required

Hot tip

Hyperlinks to other pages may be text or graphics. When you move the mouse over a link, the pointer changes to a hand, and the link is often underlined or otherwise highlighted.

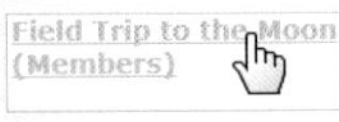

5 Select a hyperlink to display another web page

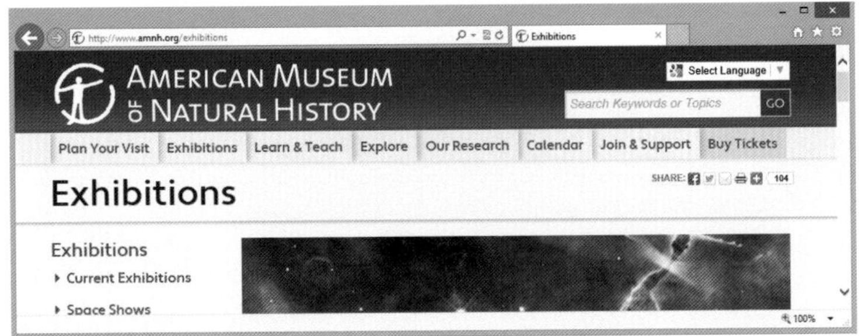

Tabbed browsing

Tabbed browsing enables you to open multiple web pages in a single browser window and switch between them by clicking the appropriate tab. To open a new tab:

1. Click the New Tab button on the tab row or press Ctrl + T

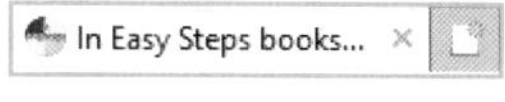

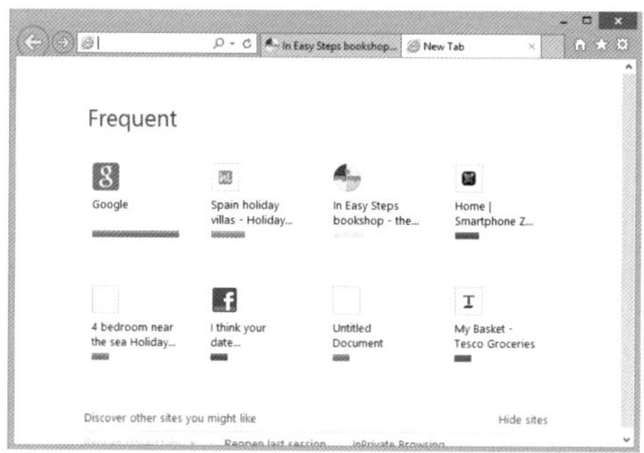

On the new tab page, you can type a web address into the Address bar, open previously closed tabs or browsing sessions, or select one of your regular sites.

2. Press Ctrl as you click a link to open it in a new tab, or right-click the link and then click Open in New Tab

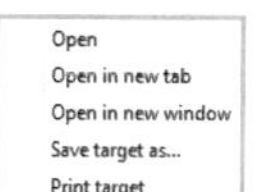

When you open links on a web page in new tabs, these tabs are grouped, in the same color as the page they were linked from.

If you have multiple tabs open, you can also use Quick Tabs (Ctrl + T)to easily switch to other tabs.

If you have a mouse with a wheel, you can click a link with the wheel to open it in a new tab.

Favorites and History

You can ask Internet Explorer to remember web page addresses.

Don't forget

The Favorites button opens the Favorites Center, which contains the Favorites, Feeds and History lists.

1. With the required web page open, click the Favorites button, select Favorites and click Add to Favorites

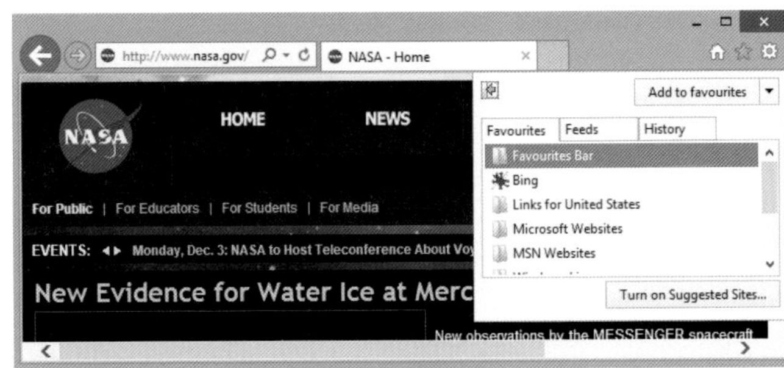

2. The name is the page title, but you can revise this as needed

3. Use the Favorites folder, or create a new folder

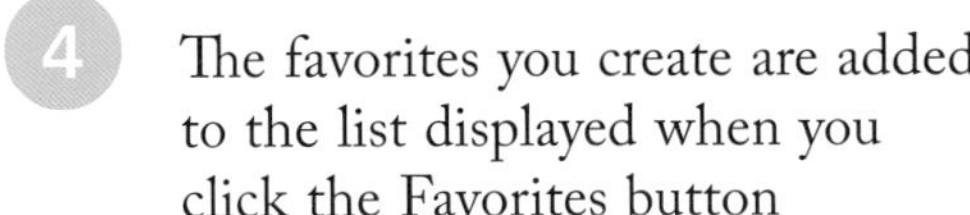

4. The favorites you create are added to the list displayed when you click the Favorites button

5. Click the green arrow to fix the list, so you can explore the folders

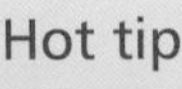

Hot tip

The list will continue to be displayed, even when Internet Explorer restarts, until you click the X at the top right to close the Favorites Center.

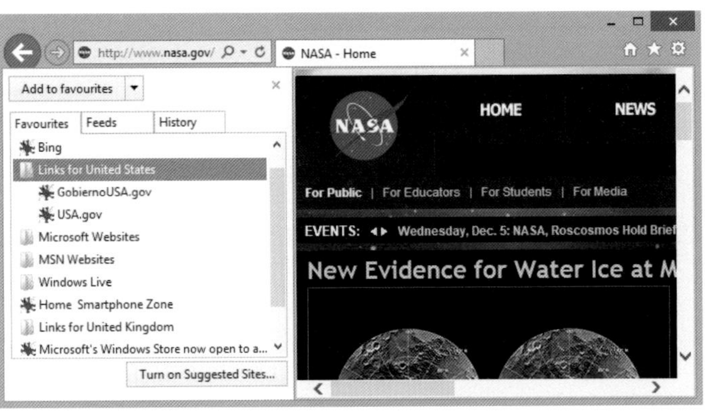

You can review the websites and web pages that you have visited previously.

1. Click the Favorites button and select History from the tabs in the Favorites Center

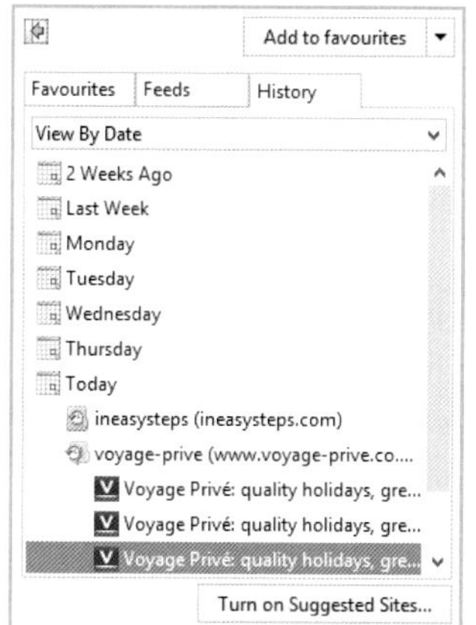

2. Click a period (day or week) to display the websites viewed

3. Click the website name to display the list of web pages viewed at that site

4. Select a web page to view its contents (and remove the History list from view)

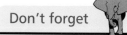

Don't forget

You can select Add to Favorites to add any of the History web pages that you select. You do not have to select the Favorites tab.

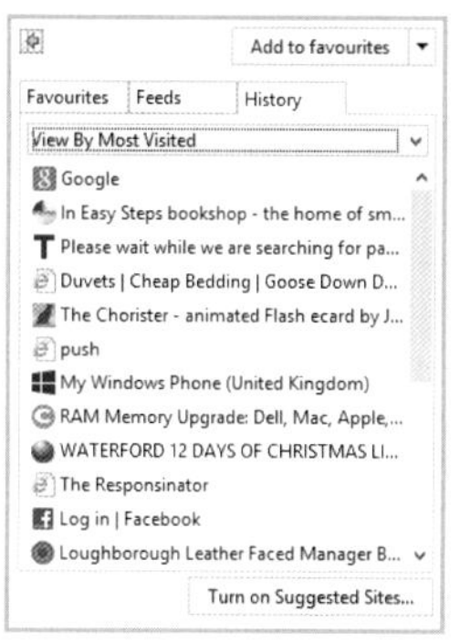

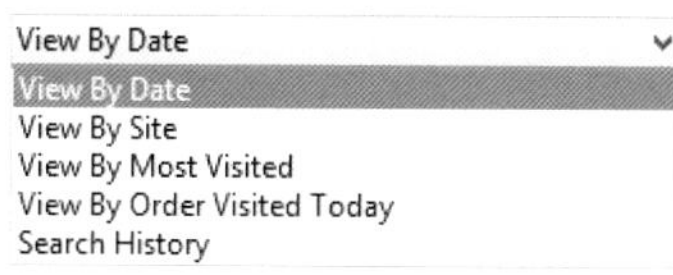

Hot tip

To keep the History list in view while you select web pages, click the green arrow. Click the Close button to remove the list.

5. To change how the History gets displayed, click the arrow next to the View By Date button and select, for example, View By Most Visited, and the list contents (and the button name) are changed

6. You can also View By Site, or View By Order Visited Today

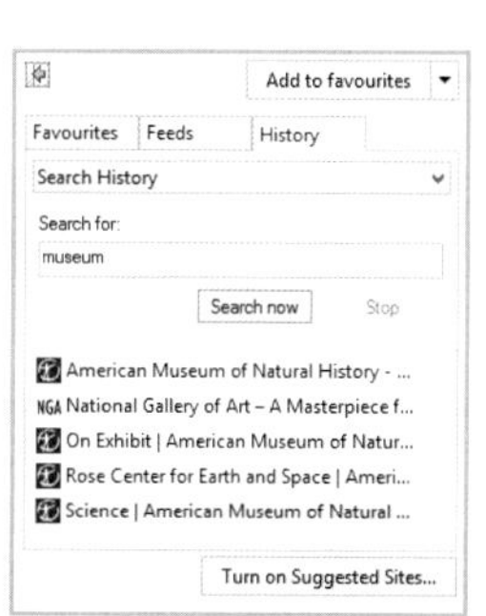

7. Choose Search History and type appropriate keywords, then click Search Now

8. Previously-visited web pages with those keywords included in their titles are listed

RSS feeds and web slices

You may be able to keep up-to-date with frequently changing websites, without having to visit the sites to check for updates. Many sites offer RSS feeds or web slices to notify you of changes.

Internet Explorer can detect when RSS feeds or web slices are available, and will draw your attention to these with an icon. This is on the Command bar, so you'll need to make this available.

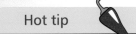

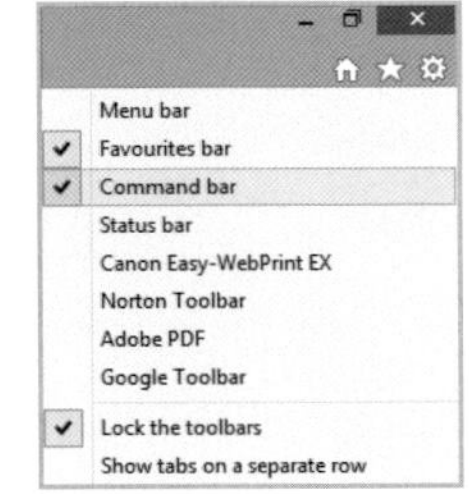

1. Right-click the toolbar and select Command bar

2. When you visit a website, Internet Explorer automatically searches for RSS feeds and web slices

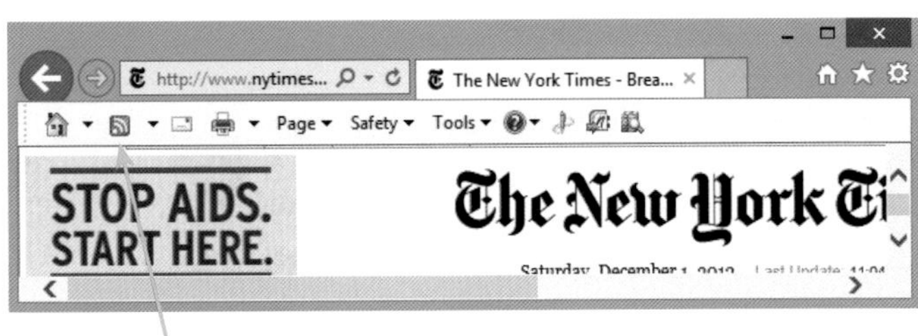

3. An orange RSS icon means feeds have been detected

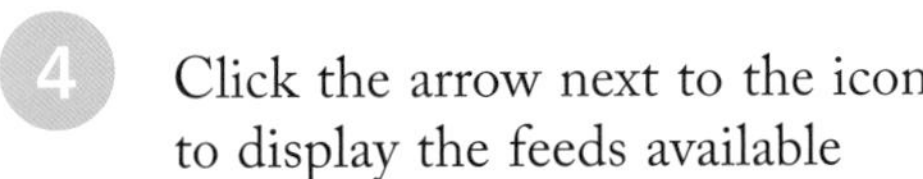

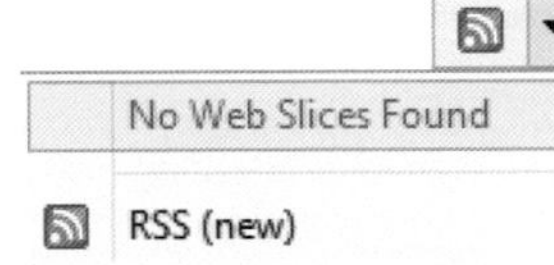

4. Click the arrow next to the icon to display the feeds available

5. A green RSS icon means that web slices (with or without feeds) have been detected on that web page

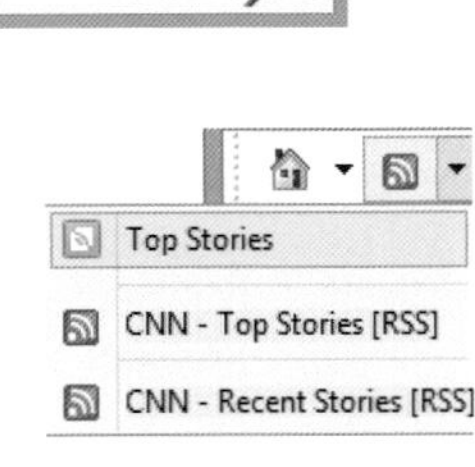

Hot tip

The RSS stands for Really Simple Syndication, a method of distributing lists of headlines, update notices and additions. A Web Slice is a way to subscribe to a specific portion of a web page.

Don't forget

When the RSS icon on the Command bar is grayed, it means that no RSS feeds or web slices have been detected.

6 Click the arrow next to the RSS icon to show the feeds

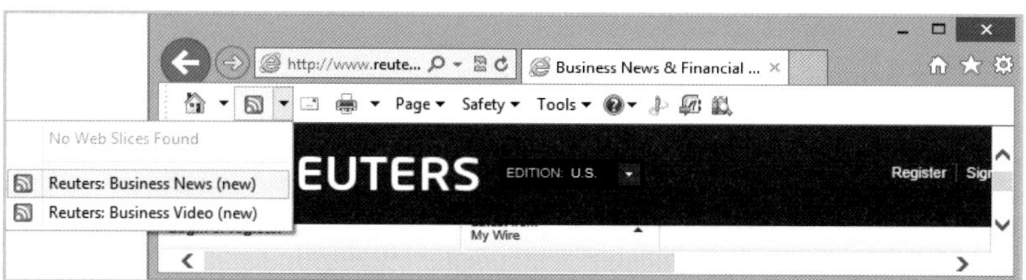

7 Select the name of an RSS feed to view the current items

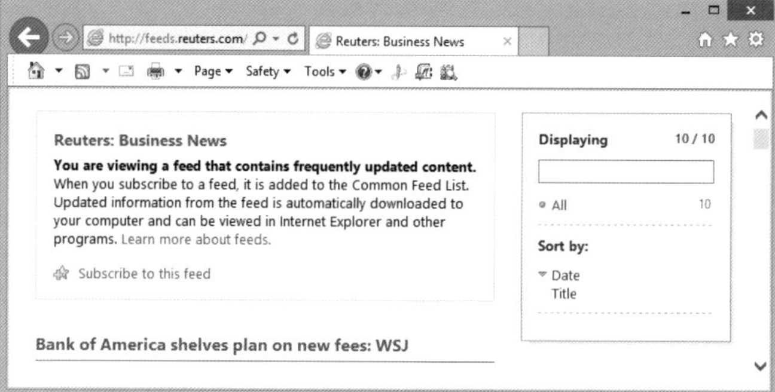

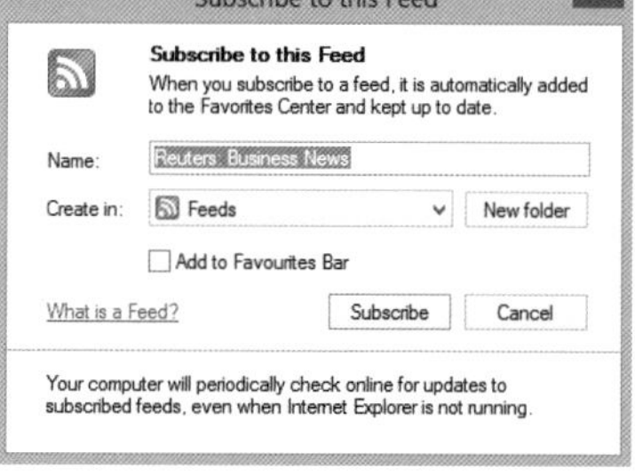

8 Click Subscribe to this Feed, and click the Subscribe button, to add the feed to the set of feeds being managed by your browser

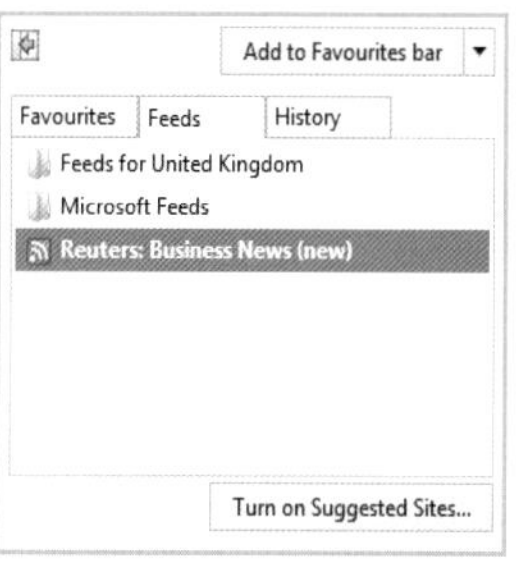

9 Click the Favorites button and select the Feeds tab to see the list of feeds in your browser

10 Select a feed to see the list of updates available

You see an invitation to subscribe, plus a list of current items. You can sort these by date or alphabetically.

Hot tip

As when you add your Favorites, you can create a folder to organize your various RSS feeds.

Don't forget

The names of feeds that have new entries available will be highlighted.

Change search provider

1. Click the One box and start typing an address

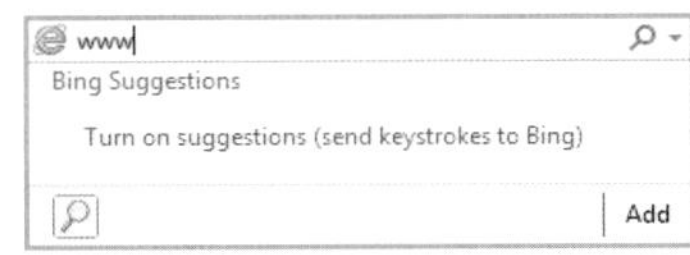

2. Click the Add button to add a search provider

Don't forget

You will be shown the latest entries for the Search category. If you cannot find the provider you want, click Search to explore all the entries in the gallery.

3. The Internet Explorer Gallery displays on a separate tab. Select the search provider you want and click Install

4. Choose to make this your default if desired, and click Add

Add Search Provider

Do you want to add this search provider?

Name: "Google"
From: www.iegallery.com

Make this my default search provider
If an address I type in the address bar can't be found, open the top search result
Use search suggestions from this provider

Add | Cancel

Search provider names can be misleading. Only add search providers from websites you trust.

5. Select the One box and start typing

6. You could add further search providers, e.g. Yahoo, and your preferred choice will remain as the default

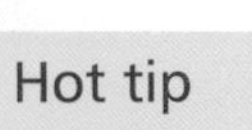

Hot tip

Select the Tools icon and select Manage Add-ons if you want to remove any of the search providers.

Open in new window

To follow a series of links without discarding an existing sequence of pages, you can open a new browser window. There are several ways to do this:

1. Open the Charms bar, type internet in the Search charm and press Enter

2. Right-click the Internet Explorer shortcut on the taskbar, and select Internet Explorer on the Jump list

3. Press Ctrl + N to open a new window with the same web page, then select the web link required

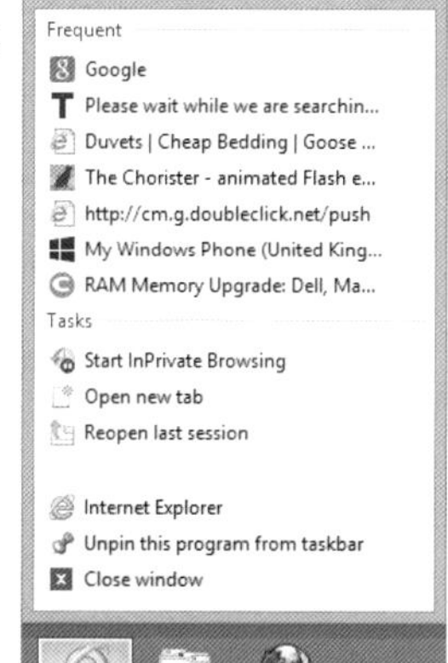

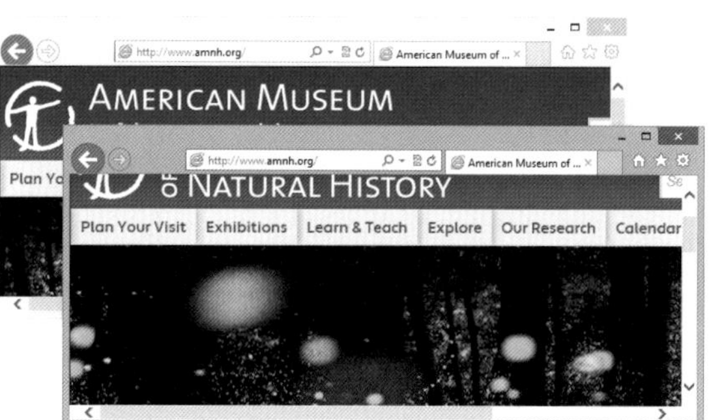

4. Right-click the required link and select Open link in new window to display that web page in its own browser window

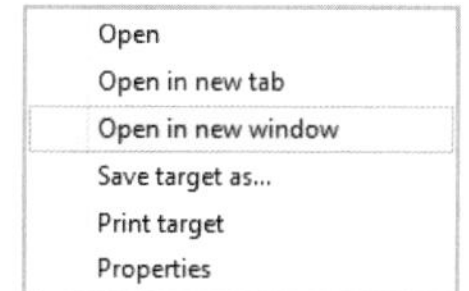

Don't forget

Each time you select Internet Explorer from Search or the taskbar Jumplist, it opens a new browser window at the Home page.

Hot tip

You can switch between the separate Internet Explorer windows by clicking the Internet Explorer shortcut on the taskbar and selecting the appropriate thumbnail.

Pinned sites

Internet Explorer has a useful way to help you access frequently used websites – you can pin them to the taskbar.

1. Drag the icon from the address bar

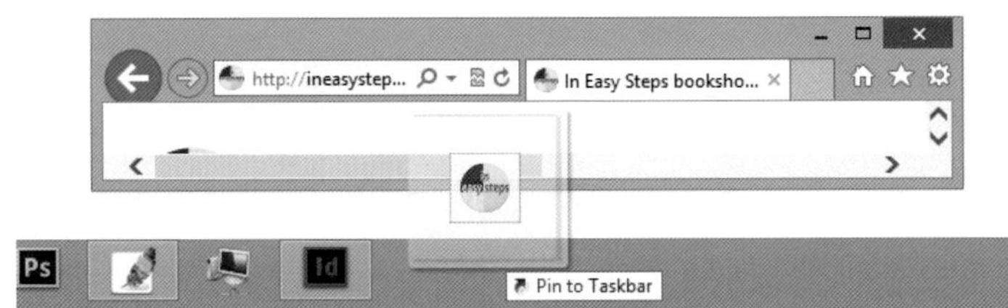

2. Release the mouse button to drop the icon on the taskbar,

3. Click the Pinned Site icon to display the web page

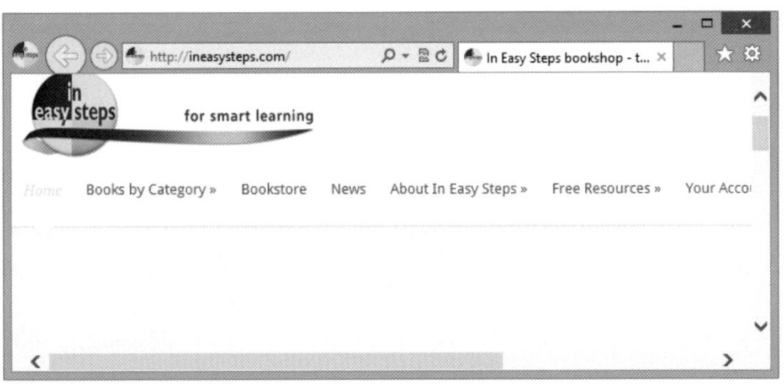

The window is different from the normal Internet Explorer window. The Home button has been removed from the toolbar, and the Pinned site icon added next to the Back and Forward arrows, which are colored to match the icon.

Clicking the icon returns to the Pinned site web page, which acts as a custom Home page for this instance of Internet Explorer.

Don't forget

Alternatively, you can drag a tab from the Tab bar, or an icon from the New Tab page, to drop onto the taskbar.

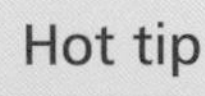

Hot tip

All windows and tabs opened from the Pinned Site are in the same group on the taskbar, and the Jump list can include related functions.

Flip Ahead

Internet Explorer 10 introduces a new browsing feature called Flip Ahead, which is designed to make browsing multi-page articles, or search results, an easier experience.

It works by placing a forward and back button on either side of the browser window in an easily accessible position. The buttons are only visible when the mouse is moved to either side of the window – this prevents the feature being intrusive.

Flip Ahead is only active in web pages that contain a link to "go forward" to another page. The image below shows how the buttons look.

Go backwards

Flip Ahead

Be default, Flip Ahead is disabled. To enable it go to Control Panel, Network and Internet, Internet Options. Click the Advanced tab, scroll down to Enable flip ahead and check the box.

You can also enable it in the new Windows 8 interface. Open the Internet Explorer app and then access the Charms bar by pressing Winkey + C. Click Settings, click Internet Options, scroll down to Flip ahead and enable it.

Note that Flip Ahead only works in the Internet Explorer app.

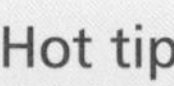

Flip Ahead automatically loads linked pages so when the user clicks the forward button, the page loads instantly.

Hot tip

Flip Ahead works with the majority of websites. However, there are some with which it doesn't.

Don't forget

Flip ahead does not work in Desktop Internet Explorer.

Caret browsing

When selecting text in a web page it can be difficult to select precisely what you want without also selecting adjacent text, and objects such as images and tables, as shown below:

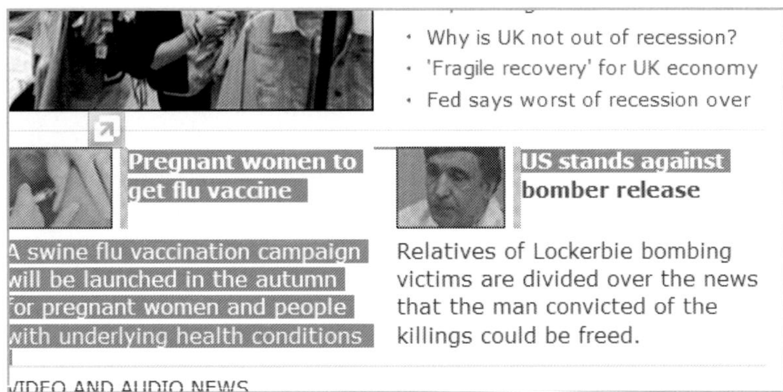

Internet Explorer's Caret Browsing feature has been introduced to solve this problem. This enables you to use the keyboard instead of the mouse to make selections, and it offers much more precise control.

To activate Caret Browsing, press F7. Then place the cursor at the beginning of the text block you want to select, press and hold down the Shift key and highlight the text with the arrow keys.

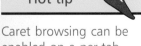

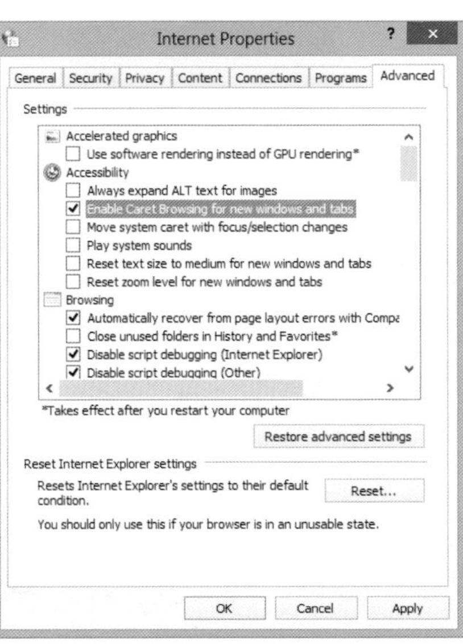

Some users may find this feature so useful that they might want to have Caret Browsing permanently enabled. This is very easy to do:

1. On Internet Explorer's menu bar, click Tools, Internet Options. Then click the Advanced tab and check Enable Caret Browsing...

Hot tip

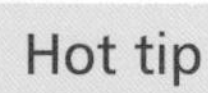

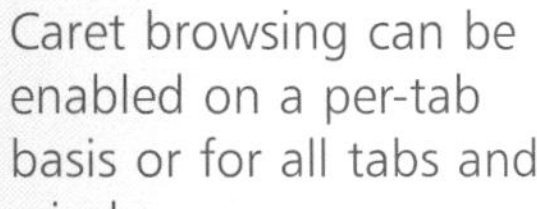

Caret browsing can be enabled on a per-tab basis or for all tabs and windows.

14 Digital images

The computer is the ideal way to manage and organize the digital images you capture with your still camera, camcorder or cellphone. You can edit and print photos, create slide shows, or turn your photos and videos into movies that can be displayed on the TV or published to the Internet, to share with your family and friends.

Digital images

Digital images may be created in a graphical application, using a scanner or with digital still and movie cameras. The images are defined in terms of picture elements or pixels. The location, color and intensity of each pixel is stored in the image file. The images can then be displayed, enhanced, printed and shared using software on your computer or on specialized websites.

Cameras also have Digital zoom, which magnifies the picture by cropping it to select only the specific area after it has captured it as pixels. This would reduce the saved image size. However, it is usually better to edit and crop on your computer, using software supplied with the camera or included in Windows.

The size of the file depends on the image resolution (the number of pixels used to represent the image) and the color depth (the number of color variations defined). For example:

Pixel size	Bytes	Colors	Name
8-bit	1	256	
16-bit	2	65,536	hicolor
24-bit	3	16,777,216	trucolor

Another factor that influences the image size is the degree of zoom that the camera utilizes. Cameras use the capabilities of the camera lens to bring the subject closer, enlarging the image before it is stored as pixels. This is known as Optical zoom.

High resolution cameras can take images of say 4000 x 3000 pixels in trucolor. This works out at 36 million bytes per picture. Various image file formats have been developed to store such large images. These incorporate image compression algorithms to decrease the size of the file. The algorithms used are of two types: lossless and lossy.

Lossless compression algorithms reduce the file size without losing image quality, though they will not be compressed into as small a file as a lossy compression file.

Lossy compression algorithms take advantage of the inherent limitations of the human eye and discard information that does not contribute to the visible effect. Most lossy compression algorithms allow for variable quality levels (compression) and as these levels are increased, the file size is reduced. At the highest compression levels, the deterioration in the image may become noticeable, and give undesirable effects.

Image file formats

BMP (Windows bitmap)

This handles graphics files within Windows. The files are uncompressed, and therefore large, but they are widely accepted in Windows applications so are simple to use.

Don't forget

These are the main image file format types you will encounter in dealing with digital photographs and website images.

GIF (Graphics Interchange Format)

This is limited to 256 colors. It is useful for graphics with relatively few colors such as diagrams, shapes, logos and cartoon style images. The GIF format supports animation. It also uses a lossless compression that is effective when large areas have a single color, but ineffective for detailed images or dithered images.

JPEG (Joint Photographic Experts Group)

The JPEG/JFIF filename extension is JPG or JPEG, and it uses lossy compression. Nearly every digital camera can save images in the JPEG format, which supports 24-bit color depth and produces relatively small files. JPEG files suffer generational degradation when repeatedly edited and saved.

PNG (Portable Network Graphics)

This was created as the successor to GIF, supporting trucolor and providing a lossless format that is best suited for editing pictures, where lossy formats like JPG are best for final distribution of photographic images, since JPG files are usually smaller than PNG. PNG works with well with web browsers.

Don't forget

You should save originals in the least lossy format, and use formats such as PNG or TIFF to edit the images. JPEG is good for sending images or posting them on the Internet.

RAW image format

This is used on some digital cameras to provide lossless or nearly-lossless compression, with much smaller file sizes than the TIFF formats from the same cameras. Raw formats used by most cameras are not standardized or documented, and differ among camera manufacturers. Graphic programs and image editors may not accept some or all of them, so you should use the software supplied with the camera to convert the images for edit, and retain the raw files as originals and backup.

TIFF (Tagged Image File Format)

This is a flexible format that saves 24-bit and 48-bit color, and uses the TIFF or TIF filename extension. TIFFs can be lossy and lossless, with some digital cameras using the LZW compression algorithm for lossless storage. TIFF is not well supported by browsers but is a photograph file standard for printing.

Photos app

Hot tip

The Photos app provides a very basic photo acquisition function for importing photos.

The Photos app provides links to the photo collection on your PC, as well as your photos on SkyDrive, Flickr, and Facebook, plus any other connected PCs and devices.

As with the People app, which can amalgamate all your contacts from a variety of sources, the Photos app does the same with all your pictures. So, while they may be scattered about on various websites, computers, portable drives, etc, the app pulls them all together into one location from where they can be quickly accessed.

1. Start the app by clicking the Photos tile on the Start screen

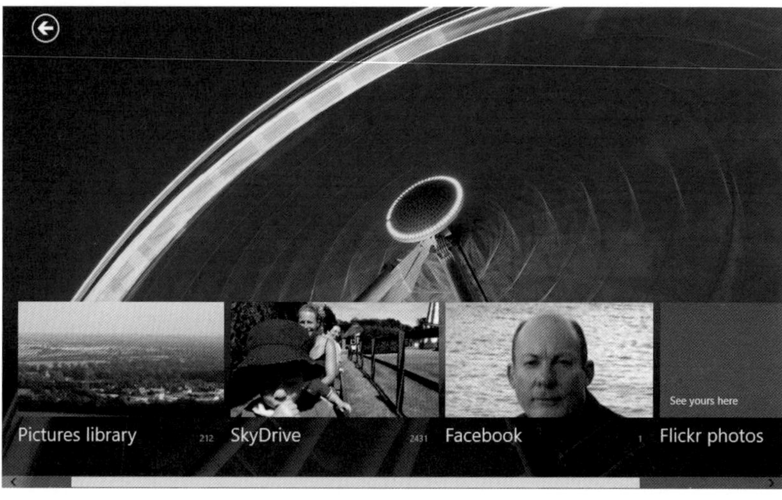

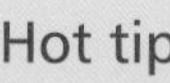

Hot tip

You can set which accounts to show in the Photos app by going to options on the Charms bar.

2. Get started by putting your local pictures into the Pictures library – these will then be available from the first section of the app

3. Continue the process with SkyDrive, Facebook, and Flickr. Note that these all require you to be signed in with a Microsoft account. Once done, all pictures on these accounts can be viewed from the app

4. The Devices section enables you to add pictures from other devices, e.g. a PC, tablet, USB drive, etc.

5. You can zoom in and out by pressing the Ctrl key while rotating the mouse wheel. Below we see the contents of a folder while zoomed out to the maximum

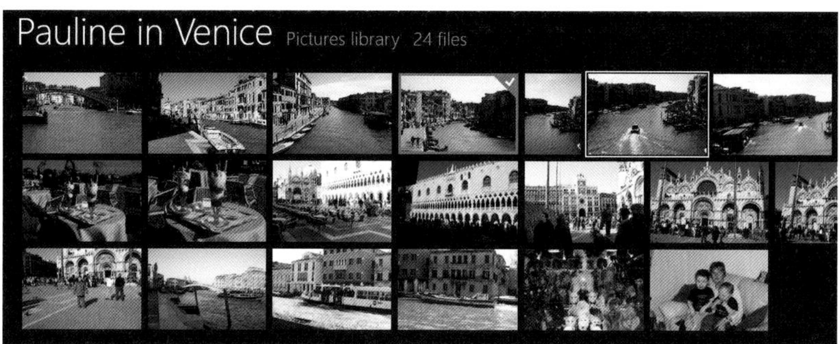

6. To share your photos, select the desired pictures by right-clicking on them and then go to Share on the Charms bar. You will see the sharing options available to you

7. You can change the default background image of the app itself, or the app's tile. Do this by opening the desired picture and right-clicking on it. From the app bar, select Set as and choose the required option

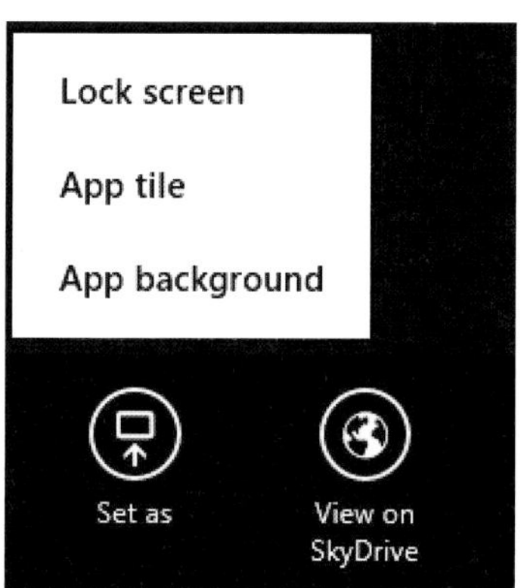

The Share options available to you depend on what accounts you have set up in the app, what other apps you have installed, and how they are configured.

You can turn the contents of a folder into a slide show. The option to do this is on the app bar. Note that you must have a folder open.

Import photos

There are a number of ways to import pictures into a Windows 8 PC (they can also be imported from different types of device). We'll start with the Photos app:

Beware

If you import two or more picture folders, the folders themselves will not be imported – just the pictures. These will be "lumped together" and placed in the Pictures library.

1. Connect the device containing the pictures to your computer

2. Right-click in the app and on the far right of the app bar, click Import

3. You'll see a list of the devices connected to your computer. Choose the one that contains the pictures to be imported

Choose a device to import from
If you can't see your device listed, make sure your device is turned on and connected to your PC.
USB DRIVE (E:)
WD My Book 1130 USB Device (H:)

4. A thumbnailed list of all the pictures on the device is shown. Select the ones you want to import and click the Import button

Import with Windows

Windows AutoPlay offers another method of importing pictures to a computer.

1. Connect the device to the PC – a camera for example. Windows AutoPlay will open at the top-right of the screen and ask what you want to do with the device

2. Click on the message window and then click Import photos and videos

3. This opens the Photos app. Click Import at the bottom-right

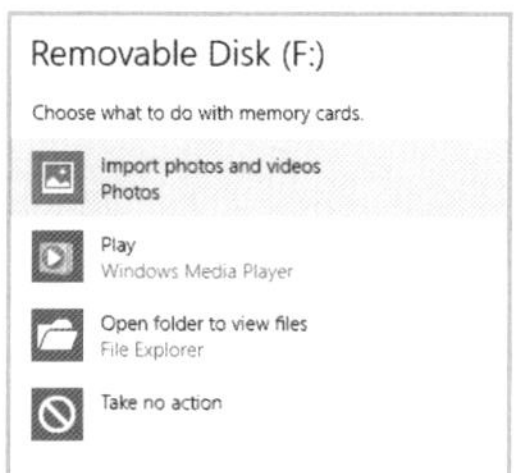

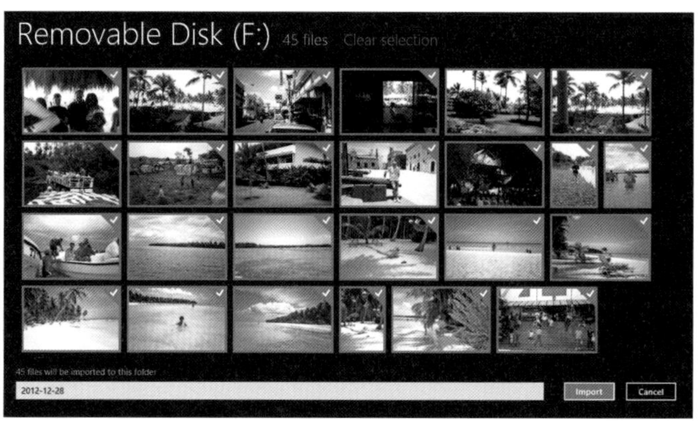

4. The pictures are imported and saved in the user's Pictures folder

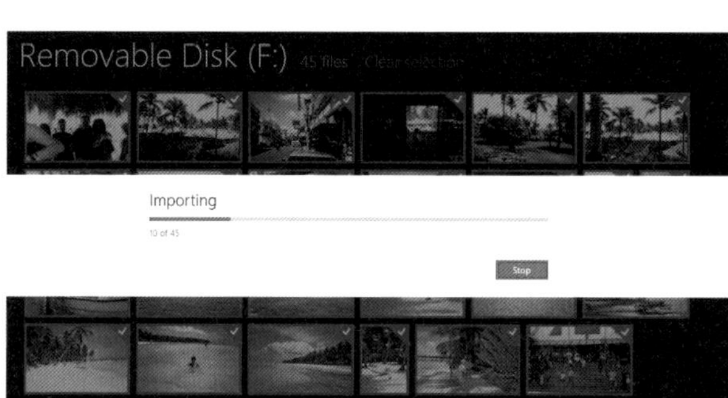

Hot tip

New pictures are selected by default. If there are any that you do not want to import, deselect them.

Don't forget

The next time that you import from this device, Windows will only select new items and tells you when there is nothing to transfer.

...cont'd

Import with Windows Live Photo Gallery

Imaging applications also offer picture import options. In this example, we are using Windows Photo Gallery from the Windows Essentials 2012 suite.

1. Connect the device containing the pictures

2. Open Windows Photo Gallery and click Import at the far-left of the ribbon menu

Hot tip

If you have Windows Essentials installed on your system, you can use Windows Photo Gallery to import your pictures.

3. Select the required device and click the Import button

4. Add tags if desired, then click Next

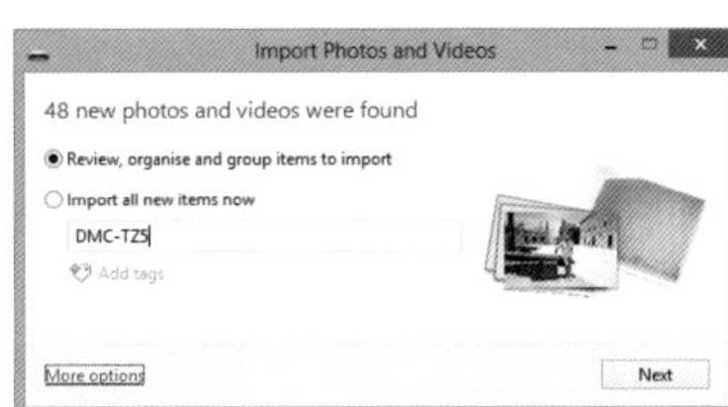

5. The image files are transferred to the folder specified

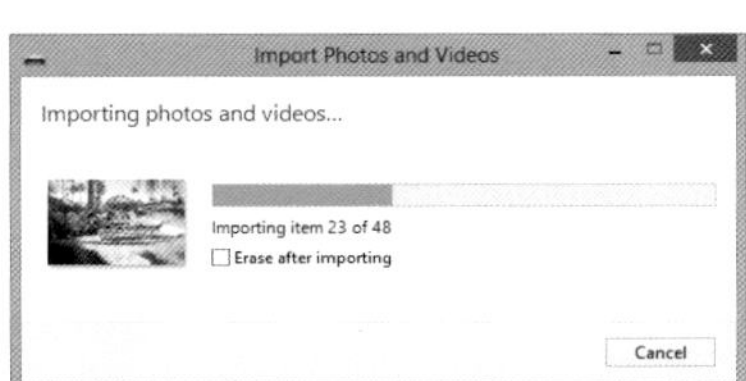

Hot tip

If the pictures cover a variety of events, you can choose Review, organize and group items prior to import.

6. Windows Live Photo Gallery displays the contents of the folder, grouped by month and year taken

Camera app

Of all the apps bundled with Windows 8, the Camera app is one of the most basic. The first thing to note here, and it's something that confuses many users, is that the app only works with webcams – connect a digital camera to it and absolutely nothing will happen.

Beware

You cannot use a digital camera with the Camera app – it works with webcams only.

1. Connect your webcam to the PC
2. Open the Camera app from the Start screen
3. You will be asked to approve the app using your webcam and microphone

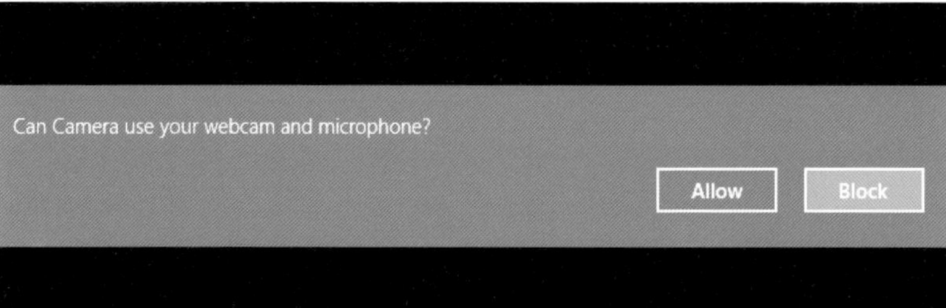

4. When the camera is on, you'll see an app bar offering three options – Camera options, Timer, and Video mode

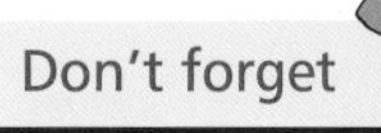

Don't forget

To get the best picture, set up your device in Camera options.

5. The first thing to do is set up your camera. Click the first option on the app bar, Camera options

...cont'd

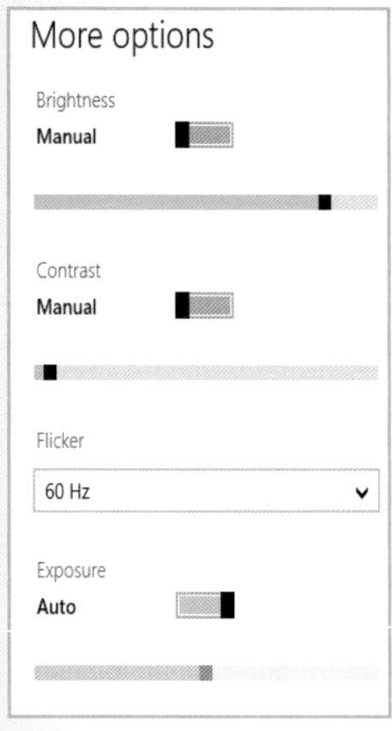

6 Choose the required camera resolution, set up your microphone, and switch video stabilization on or off

Click the More link to open further options. These include controls for Brightness, Flicker, Contrast and Exposure

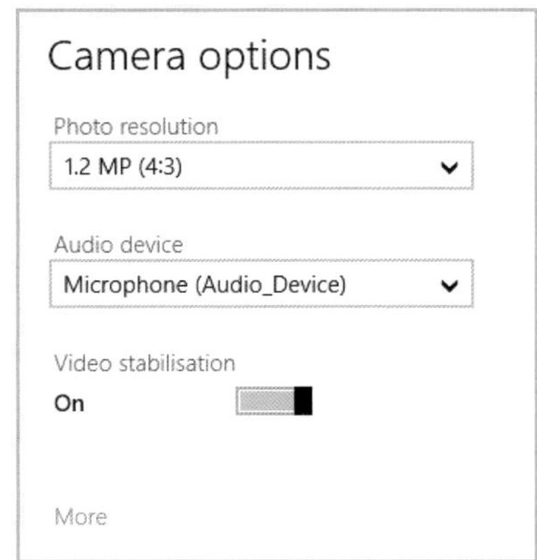

7 To take a picture, just tap or click on the screen

8 To make a video, click Video Mode (it will turn white) and click on the screen to start the recording – this starts the timer. To stop the recording, click on the screen again

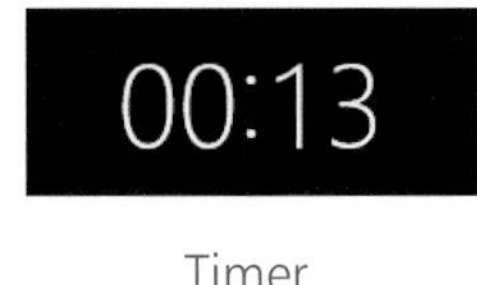

Timer

9 Once you have taken a few pictures, you can browse through them by clicking the left and right arrows that appear on the screen

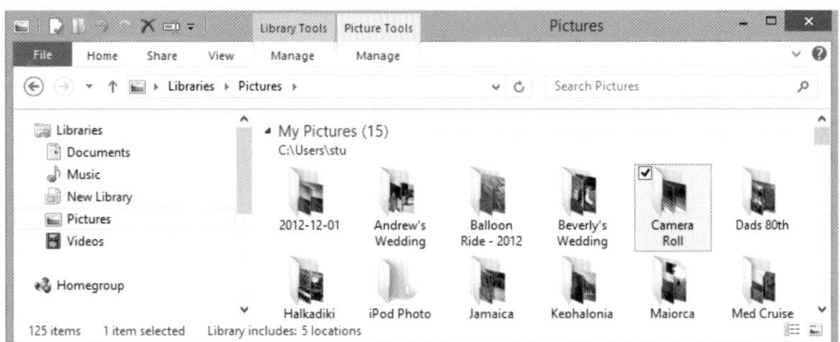

10 Alternatively, go to your My Pictures folder. Open the Camera Roll folder to see your images and videos

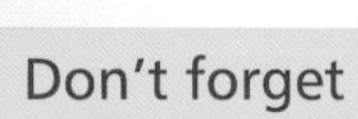

Pictures and videos taken by the Camera app are saved by default in the My Pictures folder.

Windows Photo Viewer

By default, Windows 8 uses the Photos app to open pictures. This, of course, automatically switches you over to the new Windows 8 interface. However, there is another way to view your pictures – Windows Photo Viewer.

1. Right-click on the picture you want to open and from the menu select Open with > Windows Photo Viewer

2. The picture will now open in Windows Photo Viewer

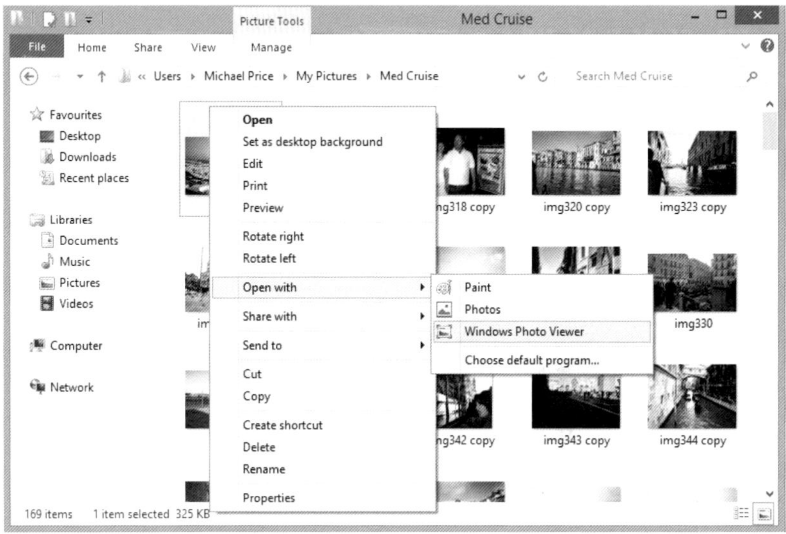

Don't forget

The options shown on this page are also available from the ribbon toolbar.

However, the next time you open a picture, it will again open in the Photos app as it is the default viewer. If you are happy with this, fine. If not, you need to set Windows Photo Viewer to be the default viewer.

1. Repeat Step 1 above but this time select Choose default program rather than Windows Photo Viewer

2. You will now see a list of programs on the PC that are capable of opening the picture

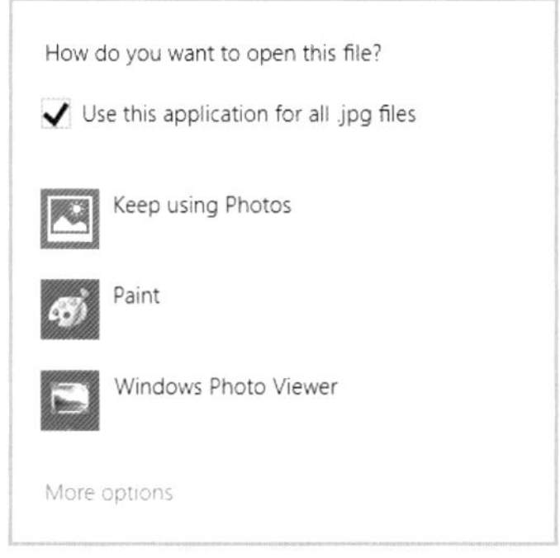

...cont'd

3. Check the Use this application for all .jpg files box

4. Select Windows Photo Viewer

Using the above example, all jpg image files will now open in Windows Photo Viewer by default. However, this won't apply to other image formats such as TIFFs and PNGs. Therefore, you will have to repeat the procedure for each file type as described above.

As a general note, Windows Photo Viewer does just what its name suggests – it lets you view pictures but little else. Such features as it has include:

- Zoom – move in and out of the picture
- Previous and Next – move backwards and forwards through a folder of pictures
- Rotate – rotate a picture clockwise and anti-clockwise
- Print – print a picture
- Email – attach pre-sized pictures to a email message

Don't forget

You have to associate image file types with Windows Photo Viewer individually.

Hot tip

When you email an image file as an attachment, you can specify the size, or send it at the original size.

Medium: 1024 x 768
Smaller: 640 x 480
Small: 800 x 600
Medium: 1024 x 768
Large: 1280 x 1024
Original Size

Photo Gallery

The Photos app and Windows Photo Viewer are just two of hundreds of imaging programs. A free alternative is Photo Gallery, a program included in Microsoft's Essentials suite. This has the added advantage of offering many more options, which makes it a far more capable program.

1. Download and install it from the Live Essentials website

2. Right-click on the picture and select Open with > Photo gallery

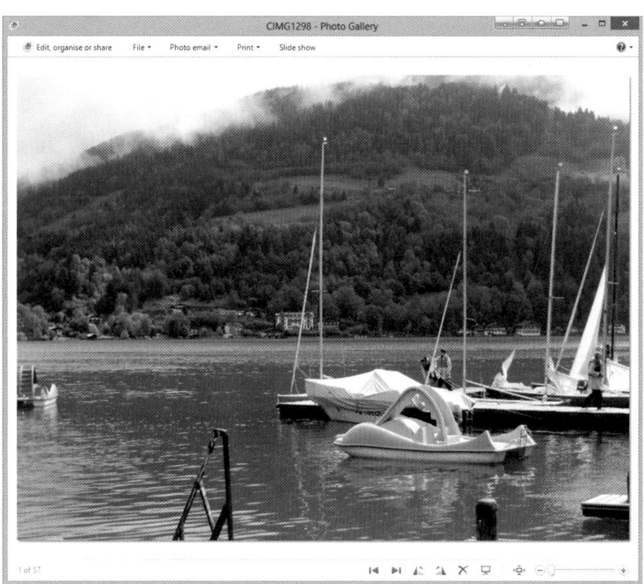

3. The options offered by Photo gallery in its initial view, as shown above, are almost identical to those of Windows Photo Viewer, i.e. Previous and Next, Rotate, Zoom, etc. These are fine if you just want to view the picture

4. If you need more features and options, however, click Edit, organize or share at the top-left of the window

5. A new window opens, at the top of which is a ribbon toolbar. This offers a multitude of image-related features and options. These are accessible from five section tabs – Home, Edit, Find, Create and View

Don't forget

If you are looking for a fully-featured imaging program to edit and organize your pictures, Photo Gallery is highly recommended.

Hot tip

On the Home tab you will find tools that let you share your pictures with social media sites such as Facebook and YouTube.

Home

The Home tab enables you to import pictures and videos, manage and manipulate pictures, plus, organize, find, and share.

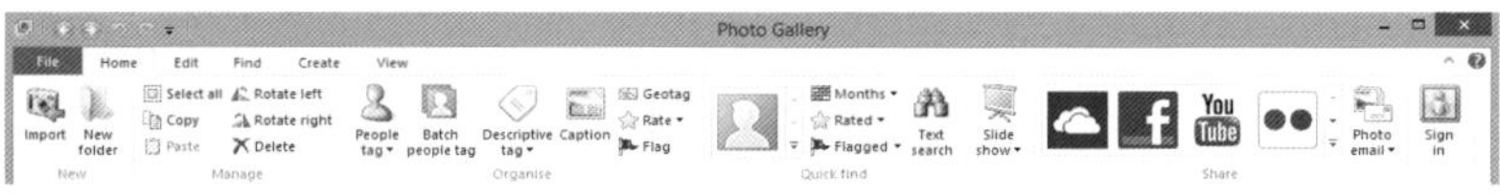

Edit

The Edit tab offers more managing and manipulating options, plus Properties, Quick adjustments, and Effects.

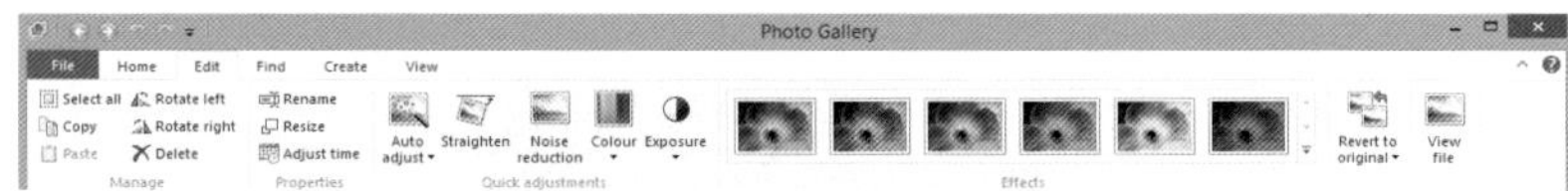

Find

Options provided by the Find tab include a wide range of filters such as date, people, rated, tags, flagged, and file details.

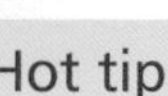

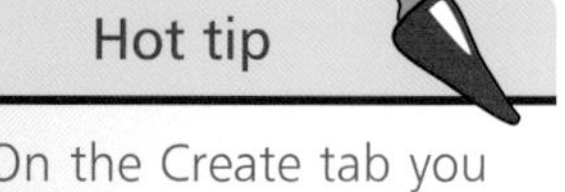

Hot tip

On the Create tab you will find a Panorama option that lets you stitch a series of photos together to create one wide panoramic image.

Create

Users looking to do something with their pictures will appreciate the options on the Create tab. These are grouped into three sections – Tools, Share, and Publish.

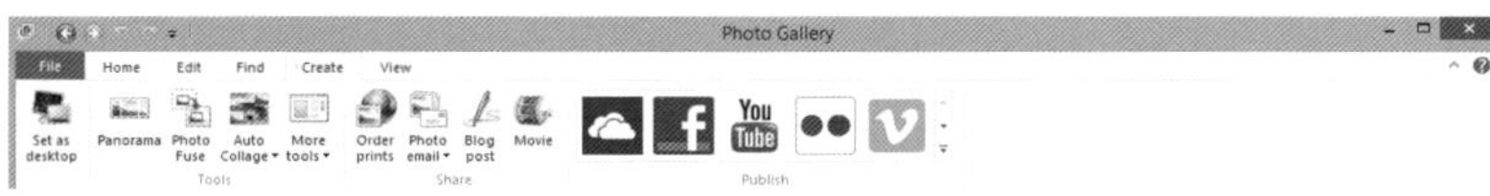

View

The View tab provides various viewing options, plus image details, ratings, media type and more.

Edit photos

1. Double-click the image in Photo Gallery and check that the Edit tab is selected

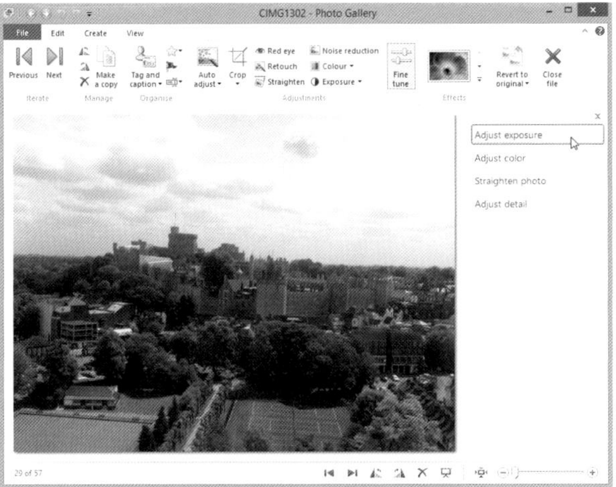

2. Select Fine Tune, and click Adjust Exposure

3. Slide pointers either way until you get the desired effect

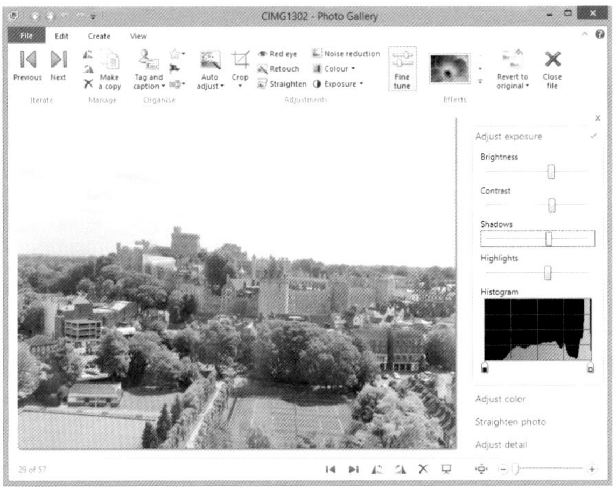

4. To keep the revised image, select Close File and changes are automatically saved back into the folder

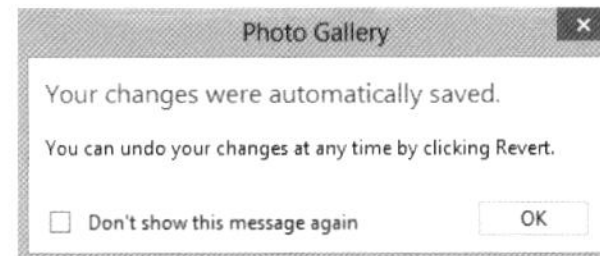

Hot tip

The software provided with your camera gives similar facilities to Photo Gallery. For more powerful and professional editing, use a program such as Adobe Photoshop.

Don't forget

Successive changes may degrade the image, so you might want to click Revert to original to undo changes that proved unhelpful, and start over.

...cont'd

Hot tip

You can apply any of the editing tools, such as Red eye, Retouch, Straighten or Auto adjust, and the original photo will be preserved and available for recovery if needed.

At any time, even after saving the changed image and closing the file, you can still retrieve the original picture.

5. From Photo Gallery, Edit the picture and select Revert to original

6. Click Revert, and the original is recovered, and all changes are nullified

Revert to original

Are you sure you want to revert to the original version of this photo?

If you revert, all changes you have made to this photo will be lost.

Revert Cancel

You can check the contents of the Original Images folder where the initial copies of images are stored:

1. Select the File tab for Photo Gallery and select Options then click the Originals tab

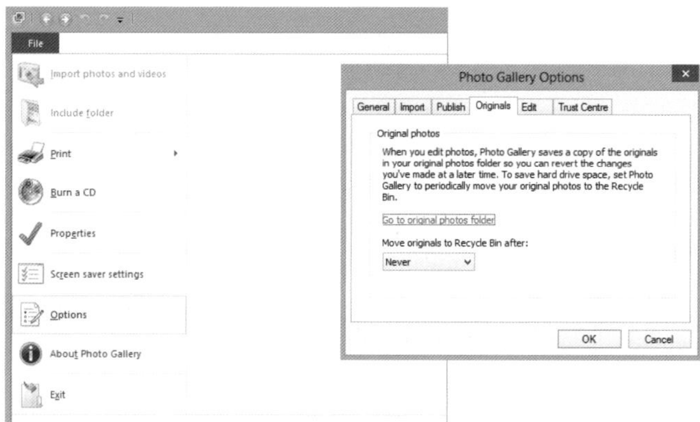

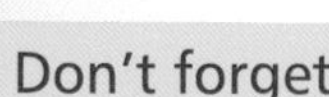

Don't forget

Photo Gallery keeps the initial files in the Original Images folder, but the naming and organization isn't helpful. You might prefer to make separate copies of the photos you want to change, and edit those copies, so you can keep proper track of the originals.

2. Click Go to original photos folder, and click the Address bar to show the file path for the folder

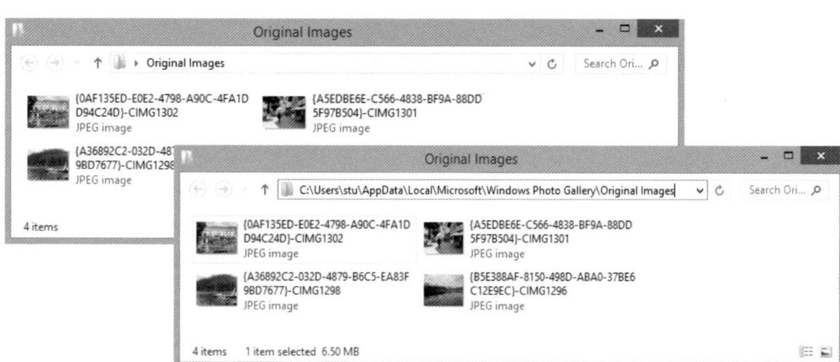

Print photos

1. Open Photo Gallery and select pictures to print, using Ctrl or Shift to select multiple files

2. Select the File tab, select Print, and Print again

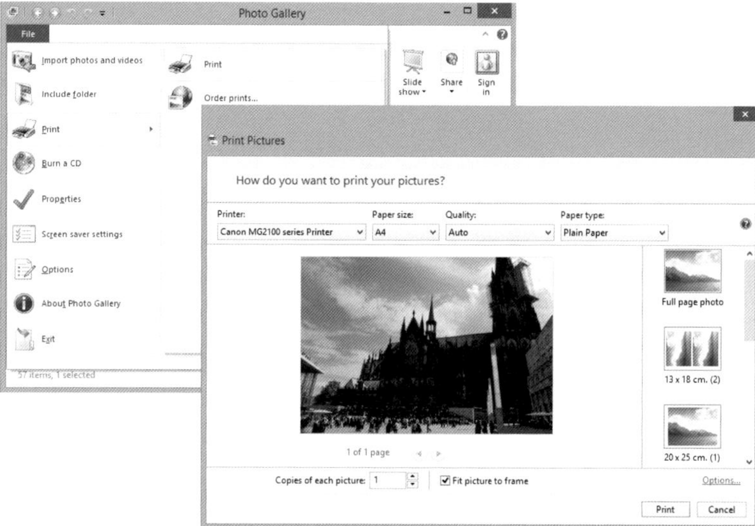

3. The default is to print one picture per page. Scroll down to view the variety of layouts offered

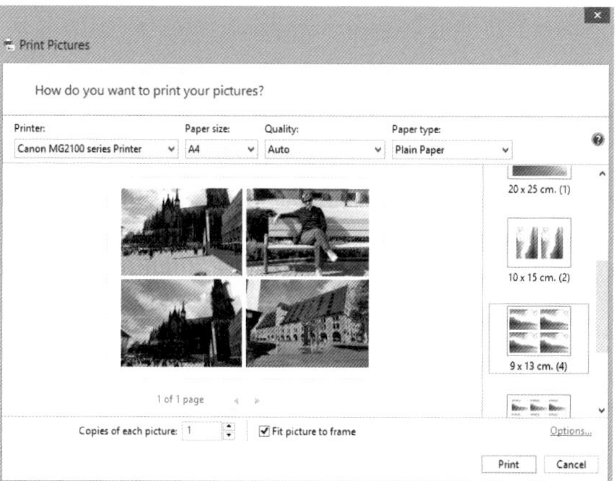

4. Check the print quality and the paper size and type, then confirm the printer selection and click Print

If you Select Print, Order prints, Windows will access the Internet to locate online print services in your region.

Video app

As with photo viewers, Windows 8 provides two video players – an app for use with the Windows 8 interface and a program for the Desktop interface. The Video app is what we're going to look at here.

Hot tip

You will need to be signed in with a Microsoft account to rent or buy videos.

1. Open the app by clicking the Video tile on the Start screen

2. The app opens with Microsoft's xbox video service in a prominent position

3. Here you'll see a list of featured videos. Scroll to the right to see the movies and television stores. Click the headings to open the full list of available movies and TV shows

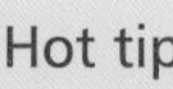

Hot tip

A wide range of filters are provided. These include new releases, featured, top selling, genres, and studios.

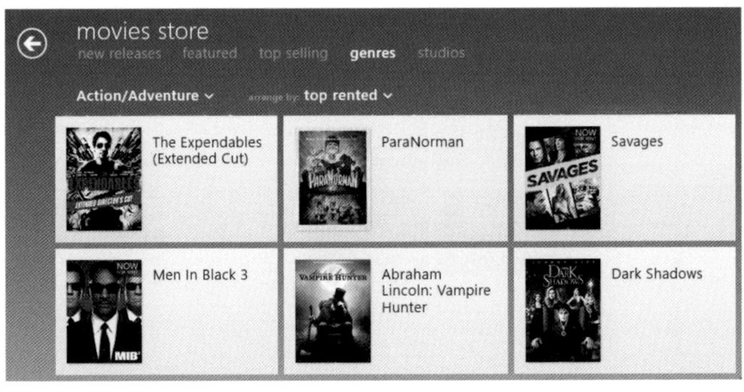

4. With the aid of the filters at the top of the screen, select a movie or TV show and click on its tile

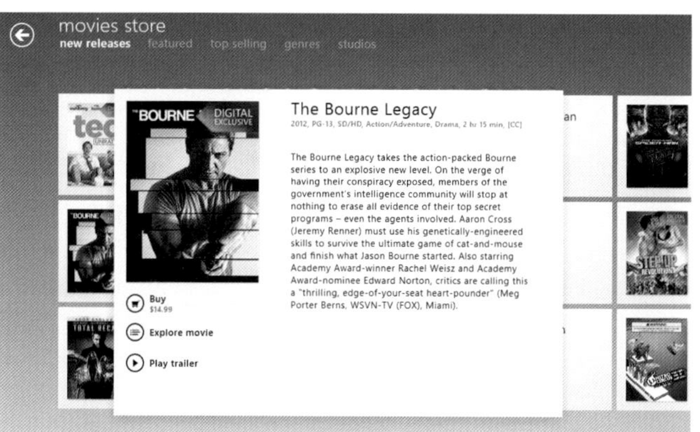

Hot tip

Trailers are available for most movies. The Explore movie option provides an overview of the movie.

5. Options include Buy, Rent, Play trailer, and Explore movie. These vary according to the movie or TV show

You may not be looking to spend any money though; you may just want to play one of your own videos. If so, do the following:

1. On the Home page, right-click and select Open file on the app bar
2. Browse to where your video is located, select it and click Open at the bottom right to play the video

Note that videos accessed in this way are not "remembered" by the app – it will only remember the last opened video folder. If you want your videos to be always accessible from the app, you have to place them in your My Videos folder.

Video controls such as Play, Pause, Previous, and Next can be accessed from the app bar at the bottom (right-click to open it).

Don't forget

Only videos placed in the Video library will be accessible from the Video app.

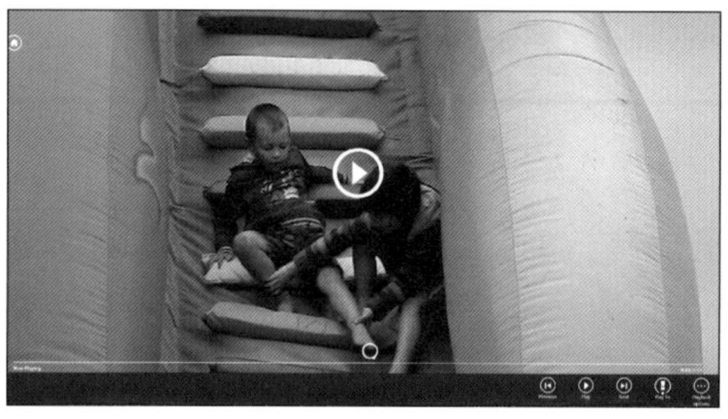

Movie Maker

Microsoft's Essentials software suite provides a program called Movie Maker. With this, it is possible to create and edit movies.

Don't forget

You can choose to speed up or slow down the video clip, if you want to create a special effect.

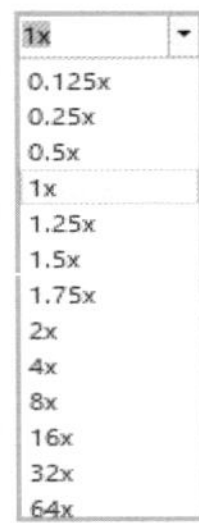

1. Open the program by typing movie maker in the Search charm. Click Add videos and photos on the menu bar, browse to your video clip, select it and click Open

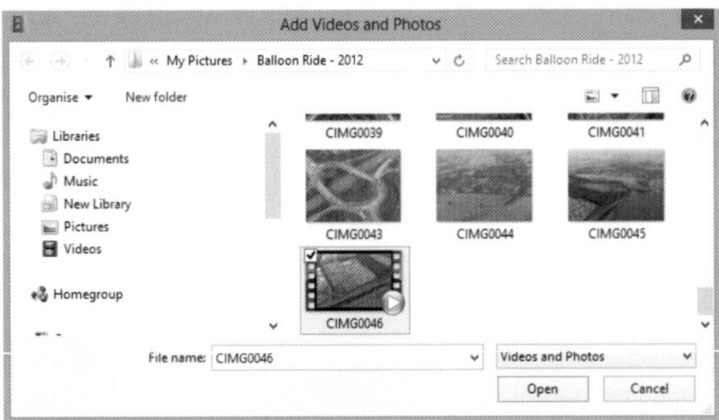

2. On the menu bar click Video Tools, Edit

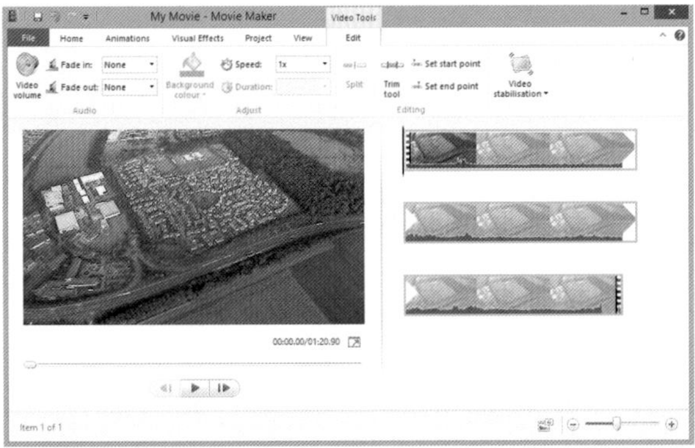

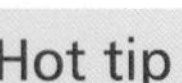

Hot tip

You can add music and captions and make other changes. These only affect the project movie. The original video clip is unchanged.

From here, you can set a new start point or finish point, split the video or trim sections out of the video. When you've finished:

3. Select the File tab and select Save project as

4. Amend the name and click Save

Create a movie from photos

Movie Maker can be used to give a professional appearance to your photos by adding transitions and effects, music and voice-over, titles and credits. When finished, you can save the photos as a movie, and write it to DVD to watch it on the TV, or email it to friends and family, or share it on the Web.

You start with your imported collections of photos.

1. Open Photo Gallery, select the folder and choose the items you want to include in your movie

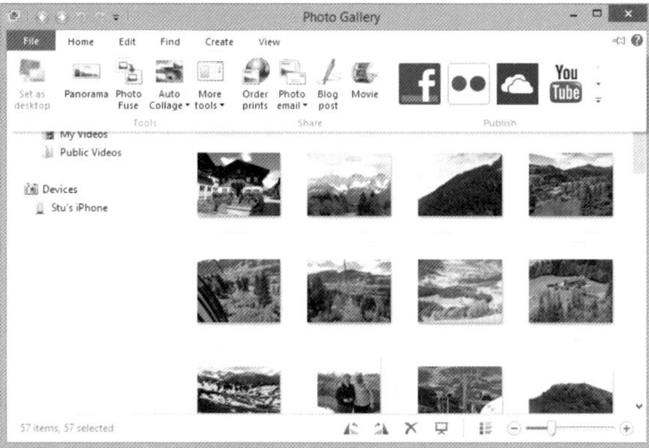

2. Select the Create tab and click the Movie button

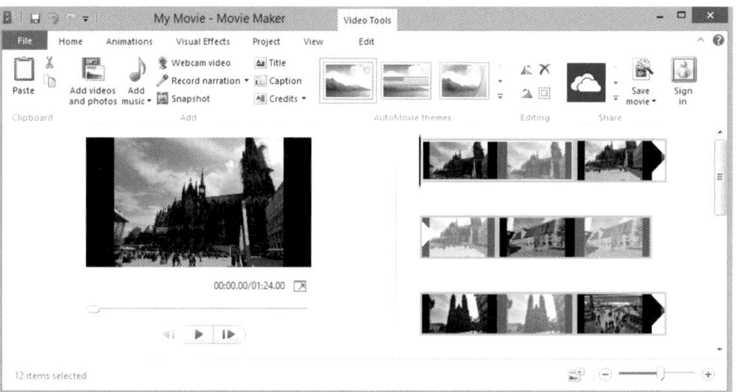

3. A new project, again called My Movie, is generated as a slide show, with a delay of seven seconds between slides, and initially with no transition between slides or other effects

Don't forget

You can include video clips (edited as desired), as well as photos to create your movie.

Hot tip

To select a range of photos, click the first one, press shift and then click the last. To select individual photos, hold down the Ctrl key as you click. Press Ctrl + A to select all the photos in the folder.

Don't forget

Move the mouse pointer over any slide to see the settings that are currently applied.

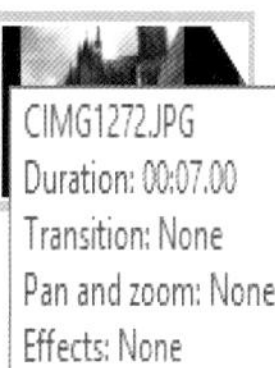

...cont'd

Don't forget

The AutoMovie themes have the more commonly-used settings predefined, but you can apply your own choice, using the Animations and Visual Effects tabs.

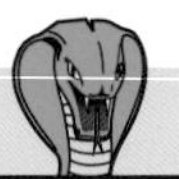

Beware

Save your project from time to time, preferably using a different name than My Movie. The resulting .wlmp file is relatively small, since it doesn't contain the actual image files or audio tracks.

Hot tip

You can add more photos and videos, create captions, and fit music to the slide show.

4. Move the mouse pointer over one of the AutoMovie themes, and you'll see the effects immediately displayed

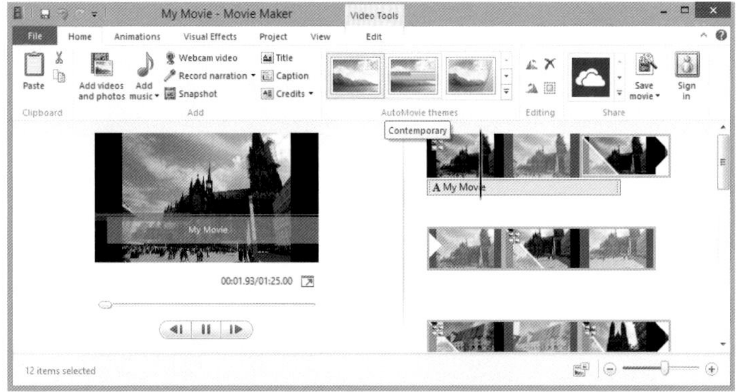

There are seven themes – Default, Contemporary, Cinematic, Fade, Pan and Zoom, Black and White, and Sepia. Review each in turn to decide which is most effective.

5. Click the desired theme, to apply it to your movie
6. Click the Play button to run the movie
7. Click Preview full screen (or press F11) to see the movie full size
8. Drag the slider to move ahead, or click the Pause button to stop playing
9. Select Video Tools, Edit to adjust the time delay between slides

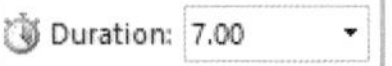

Save and publish your movie

1. Select the File tab and select Save movie, then choose a setting, e.g. high definition (1440 x 1080)

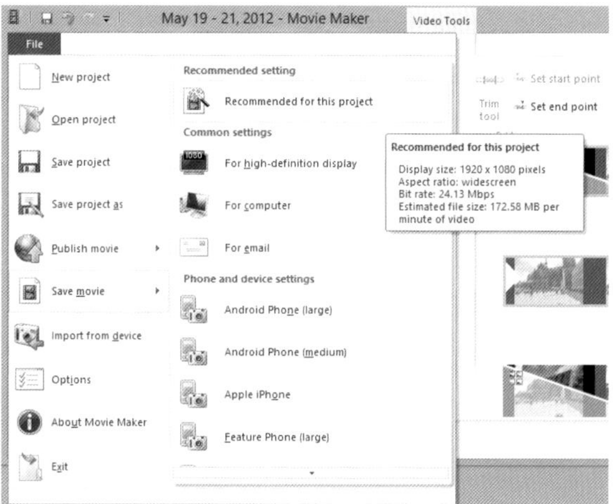

Hot tip

You can save the movie in the format best suited to the device where it will be played. There are formats for TV, computer and mobile devices such as Windows Phone, and lower resolution versions suitable for email.

2. The project is saved in .wma video format, and includes copies of all the pictures, video clips and audio files

Hot tip

The estimated file size is shown in the Tool tip when you move the mouse pointer over the setting for each device.

3. Select Publish Movie to prepare the movie for the Internet

4. You can save the movie on your SkyDrive or select a service, e.g. Facebook, YouTube or Flickr

5. Click Exit to end Movie Maker

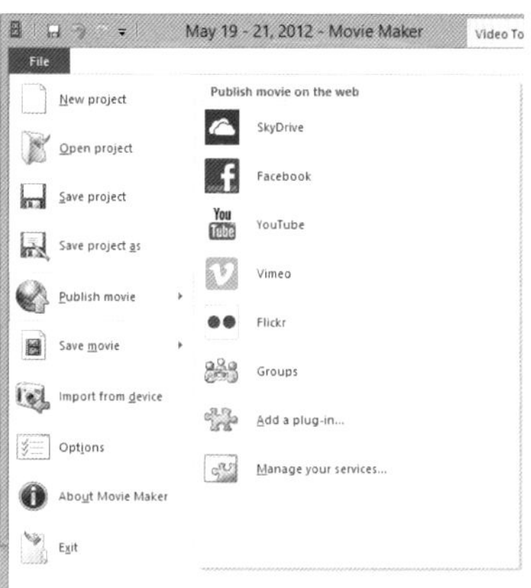

Hot tip

Select Add a Plug-in to find other web services that may be made available for publishing movies online.

Photo apps at the Store

If the Photos app described on pages 236-237 does not meet your requirements, a large selection of other photo apps are available in the Windows Store.

1. Open the Store from the Start screen
2. Open the Search charm and type photo
3. Click Store on the right-hand side of the screen

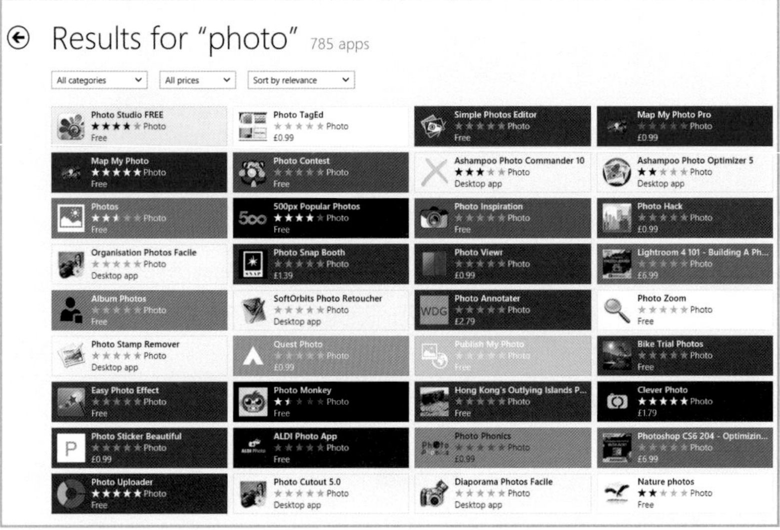

Many of these apps provide image-related options other than just organizing and sharing. For example, you will find apps that:

- Map pictures to specific locations, i.e. geo tagging
- Create photo albums
- Provide editing tools
- Provide camera functions
- Import pictures from other devices
- Create slide shows

15 Windows games

Traditional Windows games such as Freecell may be missing from Windows 8 but there is a huge number of games available in the Windows Store. We take a look at some popular ones.

Games support

Gaming has always been a very popular use of computers and, in recognition of this, Windows operating systems have traditionally provided a selection of games with which users can amuse themselves.

However, with Windows 8 this has come to a stop – Microsoft has decided that mobile devices are the way forward. This means bundled applications now have to be lightweight and thus sparing of system resources – in other words they have to be optimized for use on tablets and smartphones.

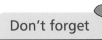

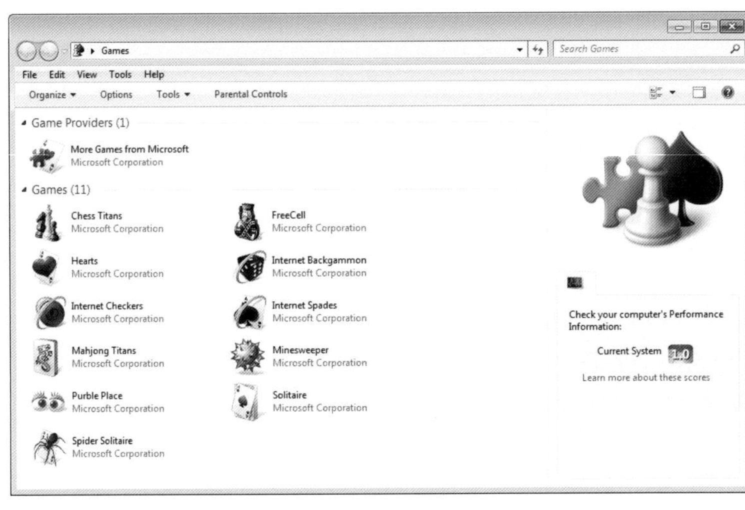

Traditional games such as Hearts and Freecell are missing

Don't forget

If you want to play games in Windows 8, you have to download them from the Windows Store.

Beware

Many of the free games have advertisements or nag screens (or both).

Beware

Not all the old Windows games are available in app versions – some have gone for good.

Therefore, users who wish to play these games now have to go to the Windows Store and download app versions of them. While this may be a nuisance, there is a plus side.

The Store contains a vast number of games that have been designed specifically for Windows 8 and so haven't previously been available. So, not only should you be able to find app versions of your favorite Windows games, you will now have many more to choose from.

Another advantage of the move to games in app form is that they are optimized to run in full-screen mode – as a result, many are easier to play, and also offer more user options.

Games app

Those of you looking for games can also try the Games app. Not only can you download Windows 8 games from here, you can also get overviews of the games and other useful information.

When the app starts, you'll see several sections. Center-screen is Spotlight, which basically highlights some well rated games. Next to that is an empty section with the heading Game Activity (details of the games you play are displayed here). Then there is Windows Games Store and, finally, Xbox 360 Games Store.

1. Click on the Windows Games Store section heading

2. Use the New Releases and Genres filters to find a game

3. Click on the game's tile

Hot tip 

As you start playing games, the games activity section populates with a list of the games most recently played across all of the platforms on which Xbox Live is supported.

Hot tip 

Many of the games in the Windows Store have trailers. These can help decide if the game is worth paying for.

...cont'd

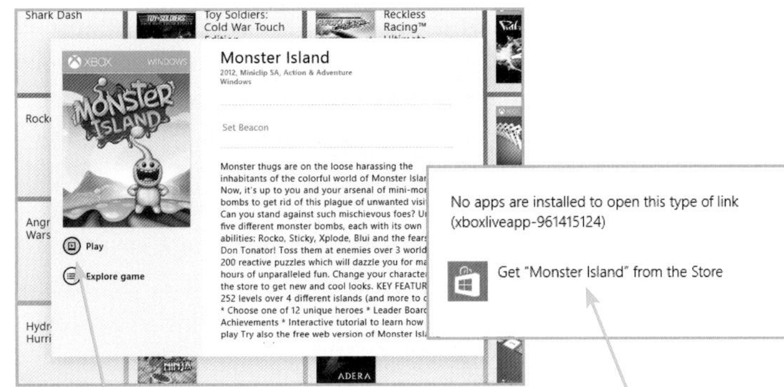

4 Click Play

5 Click "Get xxx from the Store"

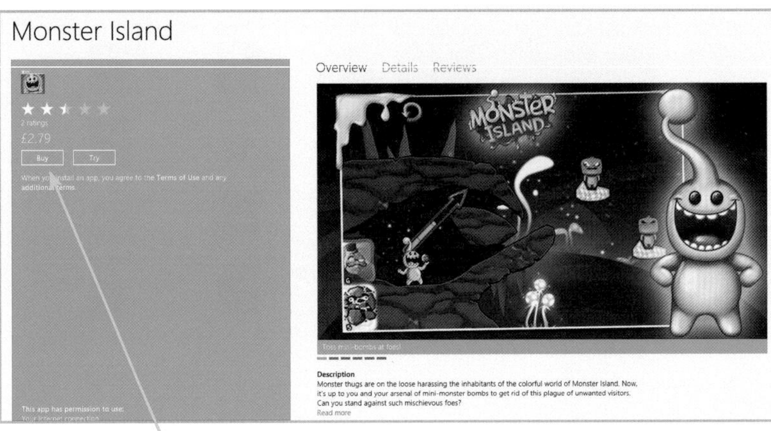

6 If the game is free, you'll see an Install button. If not, click the Buy button

7 Enter your Microsoft account password

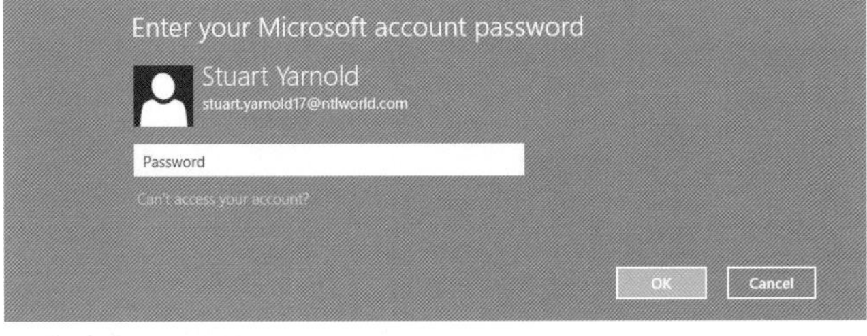

8 On the payment and billing page, pay for your game

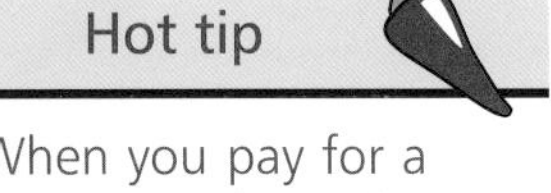

Hot tip

When you pay for a game, you have the option to save your payment details so you don't have to re-enter them for future purchases.

Quite apart from games for Windows 8, it is also possible to buy games for the Xbox 360 via the Games app. You won't be able to play them on Windows 8 but the next time you turn on your console, you can download them from the cloud and install them.

To help you make the right decision when choosing games to buy, useful information about them is available.

1. Click on the game's tile
2. Click Explore game

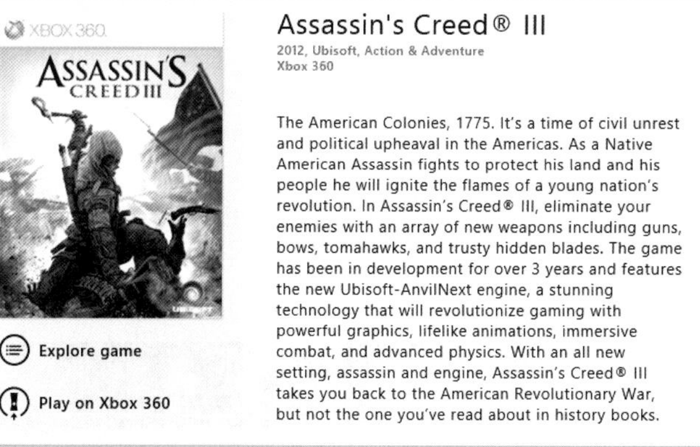

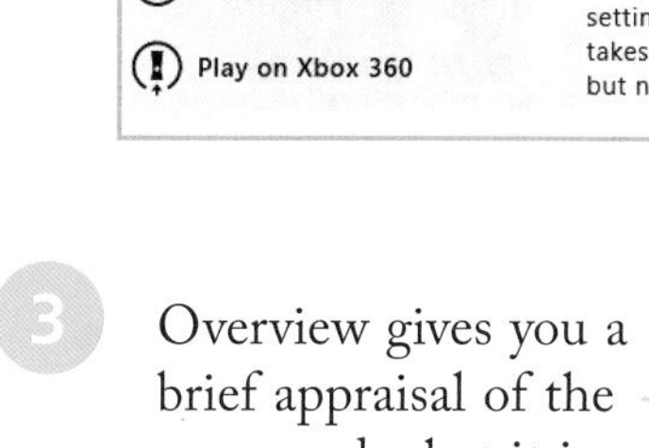

3. Overview gives you a brief appraisal of the game and what it is about
4. Below the overview are details of the online features offered by the game
5. Extras provides links to game videos, add-ons, themes, avatar items, and more

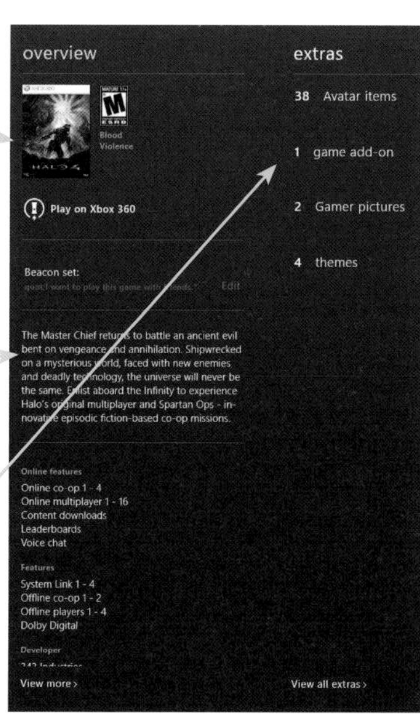

Hot tip

If you buy an Xbox game through the Games app, you will be prompted to download Xbox SmartGlass from the store. This app turns your PC or tablet into a second screen that interacts with your Xbox.

Hot tip

The Games app acts as a front-end to the Xbox LIVE gaming platform.

Games at the Windows Store

The Windows Store contains some twenty different categories of software. Let's see what it has to offer to gamers.

1. The second section on the Home page is Games. You'll see several tiles that link to featured games, plus Top free and New releases. You may want to check these out first

2. Click the Games heading to open the full list of games

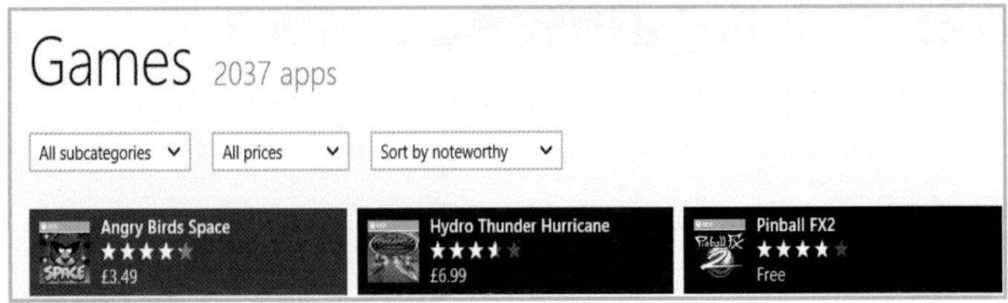

3. Above the list are three filters. Use these to narrow your search

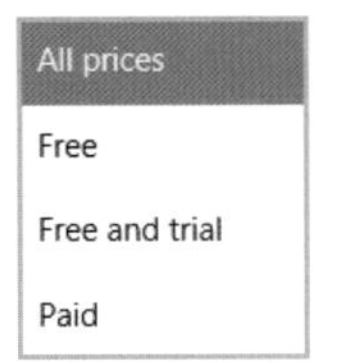

All subcategories
Action
Adventure
Arcade
Card
Casino
Family
Kids
Music
Puzzle

At the time of writing, over 3000 games can be downloaded from the Windows Store.

Explore Pinball FX2

We'll take a look at some of the free games available in the Windows Store. One of the most popular is Pinball FX2, which can be played on a Windows 8 PC, the Xbox 360, and online.

1. Go to the Windows Store and type pinball into the Search charm. Pinball FX2 will appear in the Recommendations section. Click to open it

2. On the game's Home page you will see 19 tiles under My Collection, each of which represents a different pinball table. All but the first one (Mars) are grayed out, which means they are not available

3. At the bottom is an app bar that provides links for Help & Options, Achievements, Leaderboards, Tournaments, and Restore tables

4. To the right is a main section that provides an overview of the selected table. The tiles surrounding it provide options related to scores and leaderboards

5. Click the Help & Options link. This opens a list of options that include How to play, Controls, Settings, Credits, and About. Of these, the only two you really need to look at are Controls and Settings

Hot tip

The only table provided with Pinball FX2 is the Mars table. All the others have to be paid for and then downloaded. Currently, there are 18 of these.

Hot tip

Many of the options in Pinball FX2 relate to online play.

...cont'd

Don't forget

By clicking on a control, you can select the key that activates it. For example, for Ball Launch, you can choose from the down arrow, number 2, number 0, and Enter.

6. Control options are provided for keyboard and mouse, Xbox 360 controller, and touch control. Below, we see the options for keyboard and mouse

7. A default set of controls are provided. For example, the left flipper is operated with the left Ctrl key. However, if the default key for any particular control doesn't suit you, you can cycle through a list of alternative keys by clicking repeatedly on the control in the menu

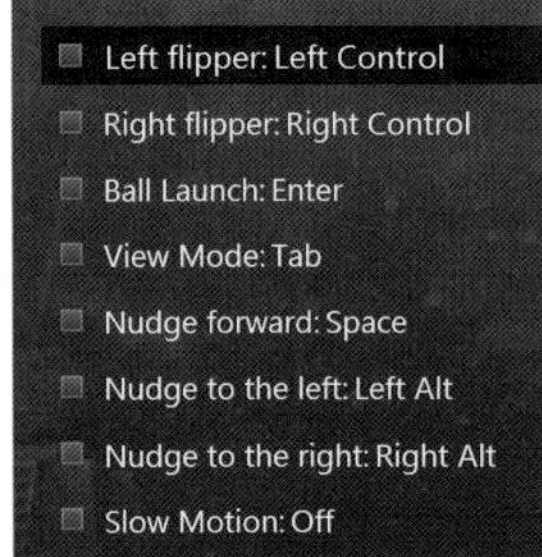

Hot tip

During a game, you can zoom in and out. Tables can be viewed from different angles as well.

8. Settings provides three main options – Audio, Video and Graphics. On the right we see the audio settings – volume controls for different types of sound used in the game

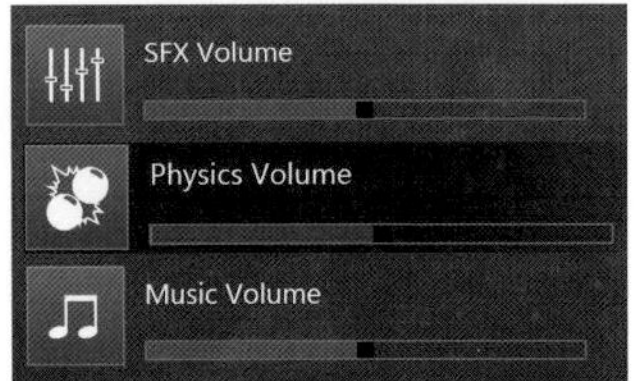

9. When you are ready to play, you can choose from Single Player or Hotseat mode. The latter enables two, three or four players to play a game

Hot tip

During the game, you can click the pause button – this opens a list of options that include Table Guide. This will explain the "mission" of the game.

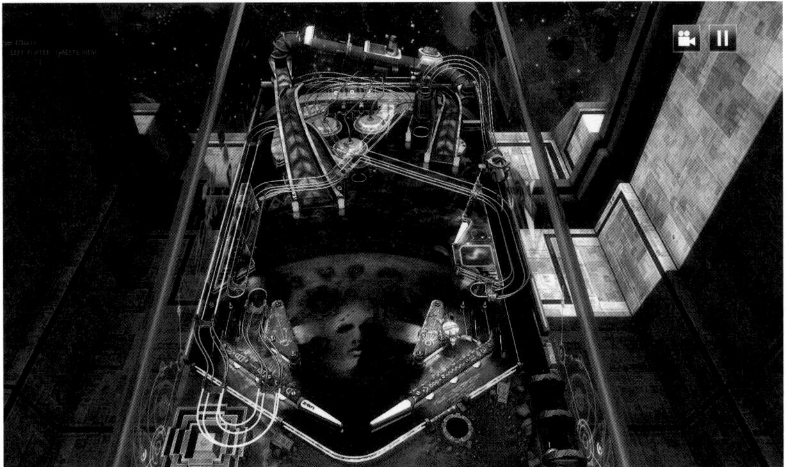

PuzzleTouch

PuzzleTouch is all about jigsaws and is a game that will appeal to jigsaw buffs and children. A number of jigsaws are supplied with the program but it is also possible to create them from your own pictures.

1. The available options are presented on the Home page. Make your choice from the three skill levels – Easy, Intermediate or Challenging

2. Select a jigsaw from the ones provided. There are ten for each skill level

3. Or, create your own. Clicking Create a puzzle from your photo album will open your My Pictures folder. Choose a picture and the program will cut it up into jigsaw pieces

4. Complete the puzzle by rearranging the pieces

Hot tip

If you lose your way in the jigsaw, right-click on the screen. From the app bar that opens, click Box Image to see a complete picture of the jigsaw.

Hot tip

If you have a webcam connected to the PC, you can create a puzzle from that by clicking Create a puzzle from your camera.

Mahjong Solitaire

Mahjong Solitaire is a Microsoft game that can be played on the PC, a tablet or online. The purpose of the game is to remove all the tiles from the board by matching them with identical tiles.

1. The Home page shows a number of sections – Choose Puzzle, Daily Challenges, Awards, Leaderboards, Statistics and How to Play

Hot tip

If you play a lot, the Statistics section on the Home page will be interesting.

2. If you are new to Mahjong, click How to Play. The various options will tell you everything you need to know to play the game

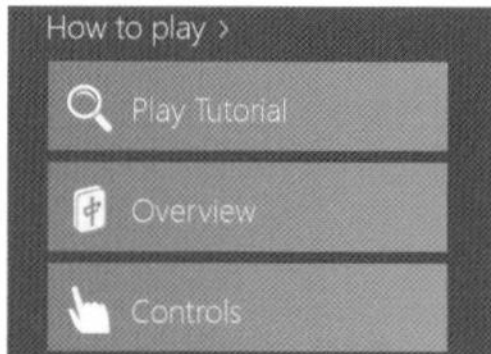

3. When you are ready to play, click Choose Puzzle

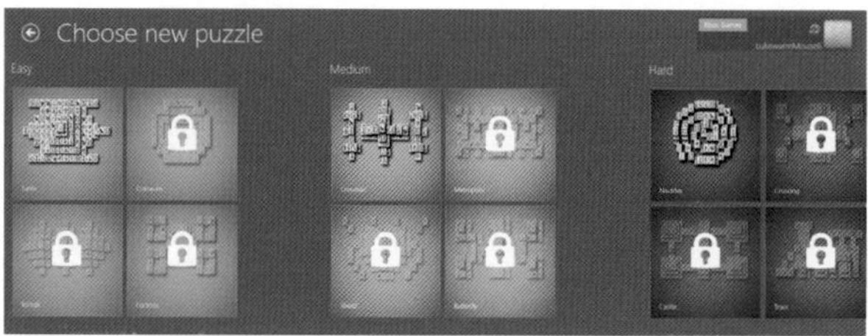

4. Select your skill level – Easy, Medium, Hard or Expert. Initially, you are restricted to the first game in each level; when you have completed this, you can move up to the next one

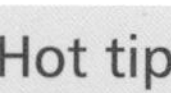

Hot tip

If you get stuck or just want to take a break, open the app bar. Clicking Hint will reveal a matching pair. Click Pause to stop for a while.

5. Click pairs of matching tiles to remove them from the board. Clear the board completely to win

Minesweeper

Minesweeper is a another Microsoft game. The purpose is to uncover all the empty squares in a grid while avoiding the mines.

1. On the Home page, select your skill level – Easy, Medium or Expert. There is also a Custom option, which allows you to set your own degree of difficulty

2. At the top of the screen are a timer and the number of mines on the board

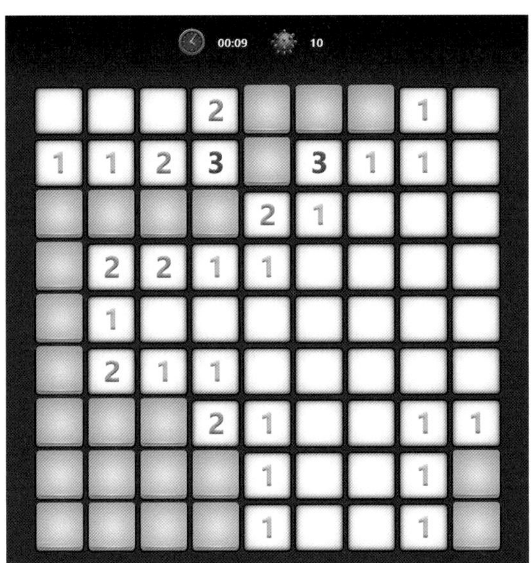

3. As you reveal empty squares, numbers appear on them. These indicate how many mines are touching that square and thus help you determine which squares are mined

4. If you hit a mine, that's it – the game is over

5. When all the empty squares are uncovered, you win

Hot tip 

The more difficult the skill level you choose, the more squares and mines there are on the board.

Hot tip 

Right-clicking on a square that you suspect contains a mine will put a warning flag on the square.

Compatibility Center

So far we've looked at ways of acquiring games via Microsoft sources, i.e. the Windows Store and the Games app. One of the advantages of doing it this way is that the game is guaranteed to be compatible with Windows 8.

Hot tip 

You can check all types of both software and hardware for compatibility with Windows 8.

However, games designed to play on the Desktop may not be compatible. Therefore, it will be a good move to check out a game before paying for it. This can be done at the Microsoft Compatibility website.

1. Go to **http://www.microsoft.com/en-us/windows/compatibility/win8/compatcenter/home**

2. From the Apps on the toolbar select PC gaming. Do a search for your game and see if it is listed. If it is, it will be categorized as either Compatible, Not compatible, No Info, or Action Recommended

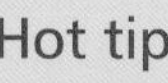 

Hot tip

Several factors are considered when determining product compatibility. These include Windows certification requirements and user feedback.

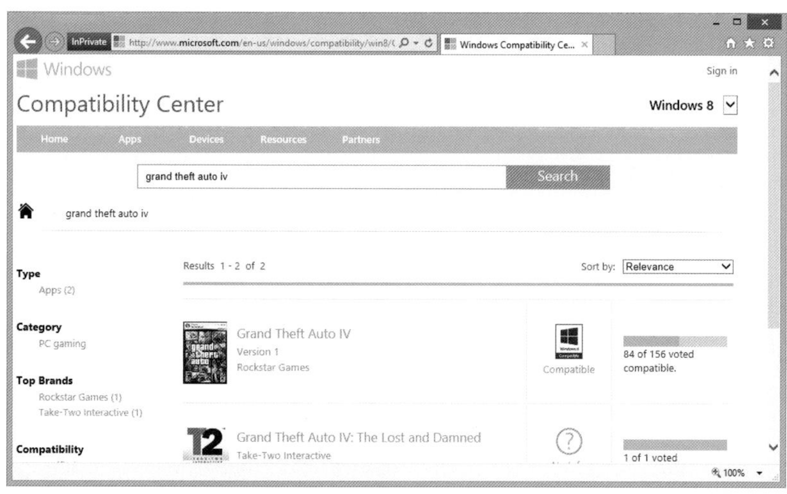

3. You can also browse the site by using the filters on the left of the screen

16 Music and sound

The sound card in your computer lets you play music, listen to internet radio or play videos with audio tracks. You can also share your media files with others on your network. With a microphone, you can dictate to your computer. Of course you need suitable software to do all this and Windows 8 provides the Music app and Windows Media Player.

Audio connections

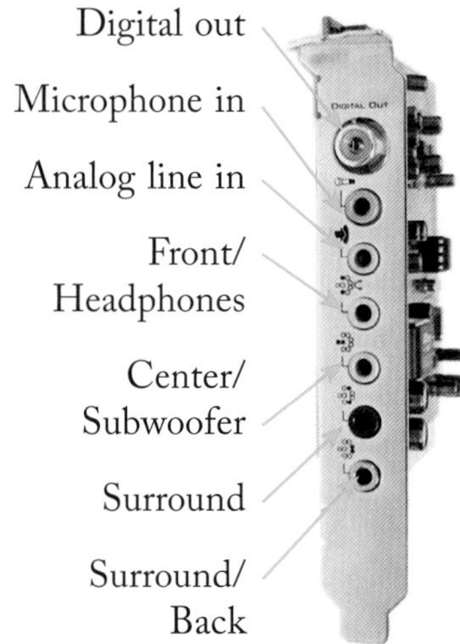

Desktop and laptop computers are equipped with audio facilities that can produce high fidelity audio playback. On desktop machines, the soundcard can provide the connections for various types of speakers ranging from simple stereo speakers to multiple speaker sets with surround sound.

For a laptop or notebook, the options are often limited to microphone and headset sockets, though some laptops include more sophisticated connections such as the SPDIF (Sony Philips Digital Interface) used for home theater connections.

Hot tip

On a desktop computer, the soundcard may be incorporated into the motherboard or provided as a separate adapter card, as shown here.

You may have speakers attached to your computer, or built into the casing of portable computers. To check the configuration:

1. Go to the Control Panel, Hardware and Sound, Sound, and then Manage audio devices (from the Sound section)

2. Select Speakers and click Configure, then select your configuration, click Next and follow the prompts to Finish and save the speaker specification

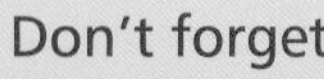

Don't forget

The configurations listed depend on the features of your soundcard. To check the operation of each of your speakers, click the Test button. Note that some software will only use the main speakers, especially with tracks that are two-channel stereo only.

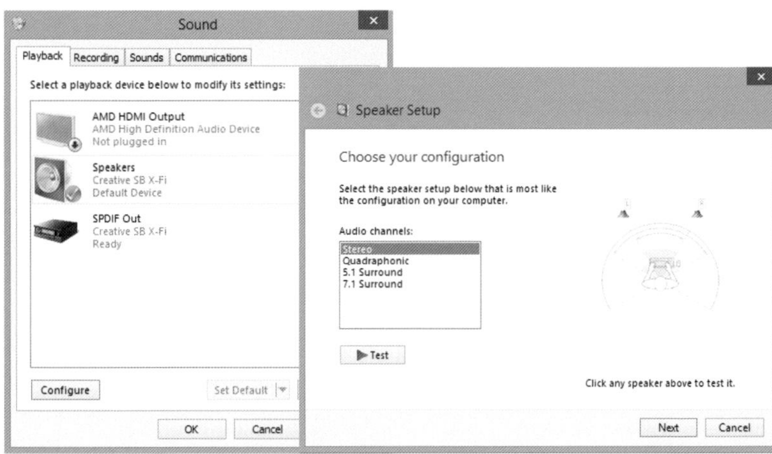

Music app

The Music app is one of the better apps in Windows 8. Not only can you play your own music from it, you can also access a huge range of artists and genres from Microsoft's Xbox Music service.

1. The first thing to do is place all your music in the My Music folder. It will then be accessible in the app

2. Open the Music app and scroll to the left. Your music will be listed under my music

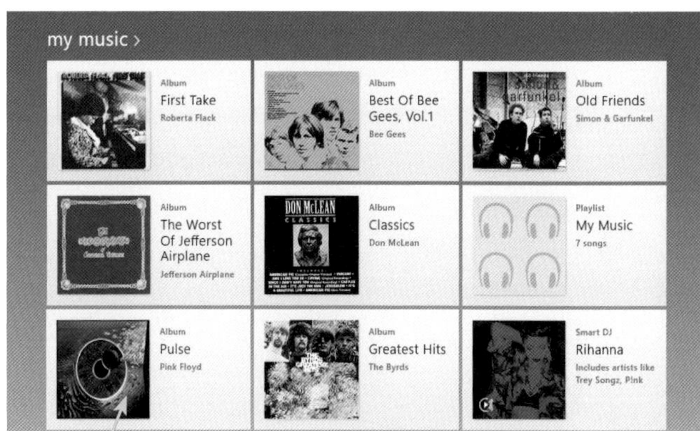

3. Click a music tile to open it

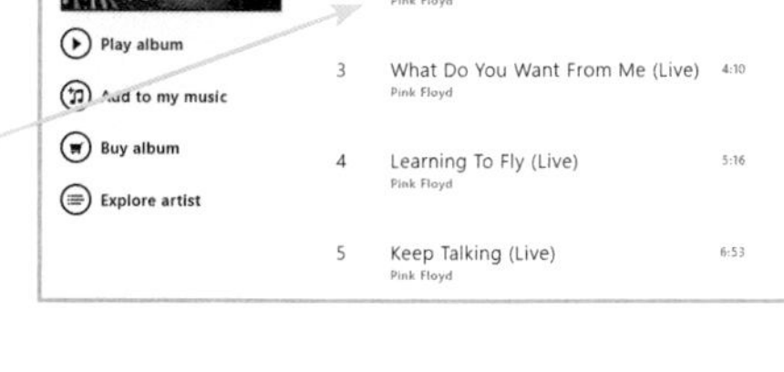

4. Click a music track to play it

5. Right-clicking on a music tile or track will open an app bar at the bottom of the screen

This provides a variety of playback options, such as Play, Pause, Add to Playlist, etc.

Clicking on the my music heading will give you a filtered view of your music, e.g. date added, Albums, Artists, and Songs. You can also create playlists while in this view.

Having created a playlist, you can easily add to it via the Add to Playlist option on the app bar.

Download media files

Due to the quantity and variety of music available through the Windows 8 Music app, you may find your own music taking a back seat.

Hot tip

With the Music app open, open the Settings charm and go to Preferences. You'll find a number of related options here.

1. On the app's Home screen, to the right of my music, you'll see two sections – all music and top music. These both feature various artists – take a look at these first

2. If there is nothing of interest there, click on a section heading to see the full range of available music

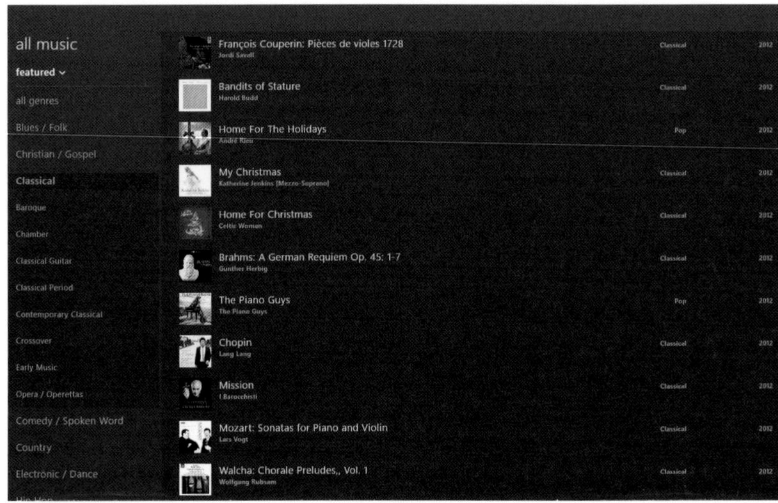

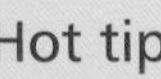

Hot tip

The Explore Artist link provides a lot of useful info about an artist. For example, a biography, a chronological list of albums made and more.

3. Clicking an item reveals options to Play album, Add to my music, Buy album, and Explore artist

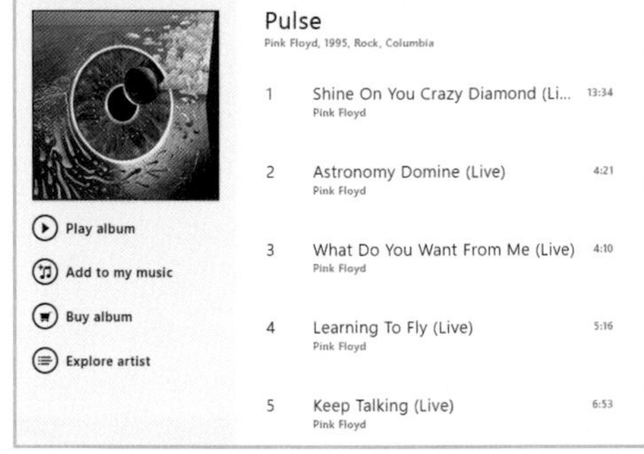

4. Click Add to my music and then go to the my music section at the left of the Home page. The item will be available from my music as long as you have an internet connection

5. In the example below, we have added the album "Pulse" by Pink Floyd to my music

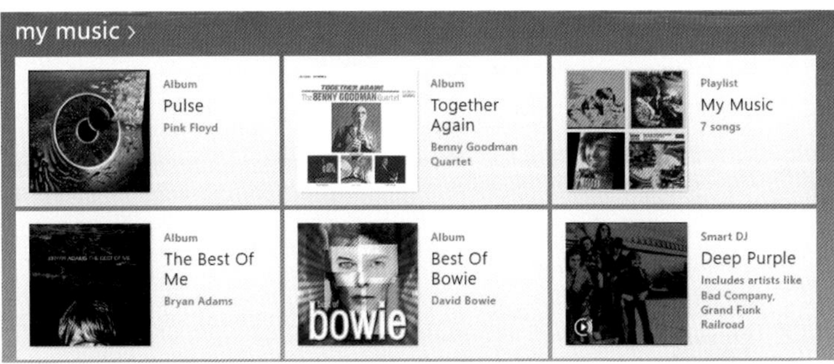

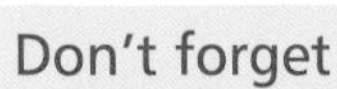

Don't forget

Music added by the Add to my music link will only be be available while you are connected to the Internet.

There is, however, a catch. While you can listen to music in this way without having to pay for it, you will be subjected to advertisements. If this is something you can do without, it is possible to buy an Xbox Music Pass for $9.99 a month *(correct at the time of printing).*

You may decide you like a piece of music well enough to pay for it. If so, do the following:

1. Find the album you want to buy, as described on the previous page
2. Click on the item to open the options screen. Select Buy album and follow the prompts to pay for it
3. You also have the option of buying individual songs from an album – you don't have to buy the whole thing. Simply right-click on a song and select Buy song on the app bar that opens at the bottom of the screen

Hot tip

To buy an Xbox Music Pass, go to the Charms bar, click Settings and then Account.

Note that if you have an Xbox Music Pass, you will be able to download some songs free of charge.

Windows Media Player

Hot tip

Windows Media Player supports an extensive list of media codecs. This ensures it will play most types of media.

Windows Media Player (WMP) has long been one of the best applications in Windows and the version supplied in Windows 8 is no exception. Unfortunately WMP is excluded from Windows RT.

WMP can handle just about any media-related task that can be asked of it.

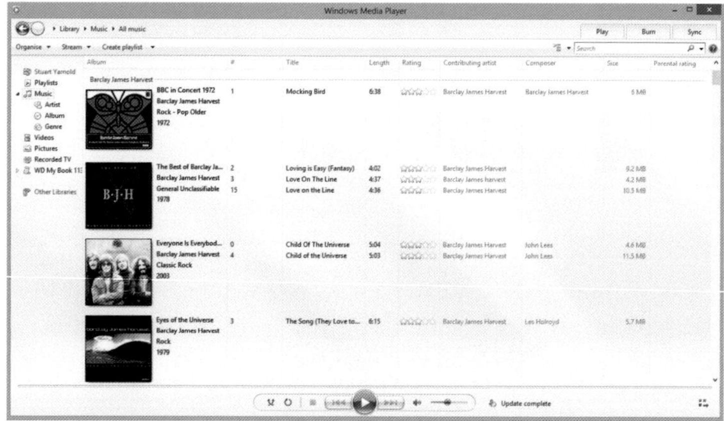

These include:

- Playing music
- Viewing your pictures
- Playing video
- Streaming media on home networks
- Ripping music
- Burning media to disks
- Downloading media files
- Listening to music on the Internet
- Creating playlists
- Synchronizing media on the user's devices
- Accessing online media sources to rent or buy music

Hot tip

Windows Media Player features brightness, contrast, saturation and hue adjustment controls. It also provides a 10-band graphic equalizer with presets and SRS WOW audio post-processing system.

Play CDs

Assuming you have a CD/DVD drive on your computer, you can use your soundcard and speakers to play an audio CD.

1. Insert the disc in the drive, and AutoPlay asks what you want to do

DVD RW Drive (E:) Audio CD
Tap to choose what happens with audio CDs.

2. Select Play audio CD Windows Media Player

DVD RW Drive (E:) Audio CD
Choose what to do with audio CDs.
Play audio CD
Windows Media Player
Take no action

The CD begins to play, as an unknown album and showing no details other than the track numbers and their durations.

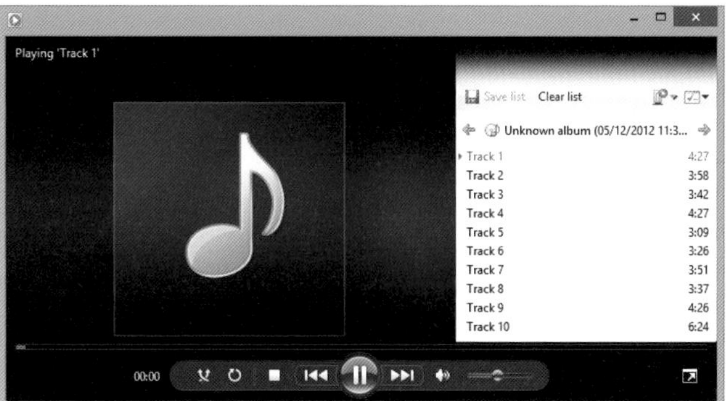

If you are connected to the Internet, Windows Media Player will locate and download information about the CD, and display the album and track titles. You can also change the Visualization to display the album cover image.

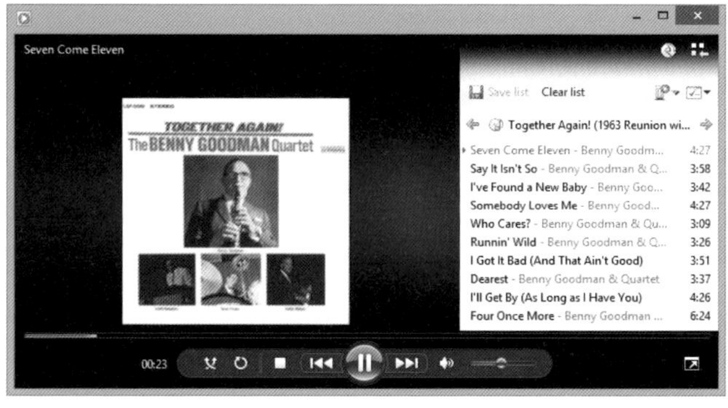

Click the box Always do this for audio CDs, and the selected option is carried out automatically in future, whenever an audio CD is identified.

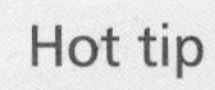

Right-click the window and select Visualization to choose the effects to display, for example the Album art (cover image).

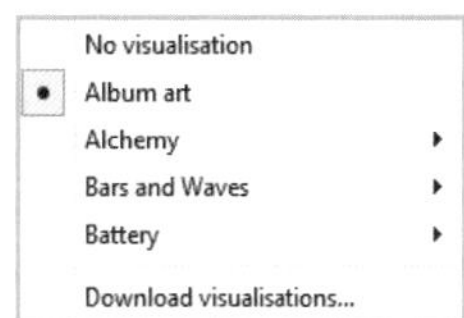

Copy CD tracks

Beware

Your Media Player may be set to automatically begin ripping when you insert an audio CD, so it might be better to choose the format before inserting the CD.

Don't forget

You can listen to the CD while you are ripping it, or play other content from your library. To cut short the copy, click Stop rip.

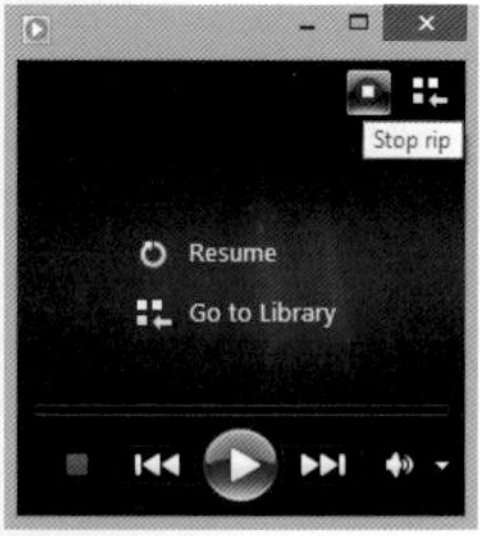

Hot tip

You'll be offered the option to copy protect your files so they can be played on one computer only. Choose No, if you want to be able to play the tracks on any computer on your network.

You can copy songs from an audio CD, an action known as Ripping the CD, where Media Player makes file copies that get added to your library. To specify the type of copy:

1. Right-click the Media Player window and select More options

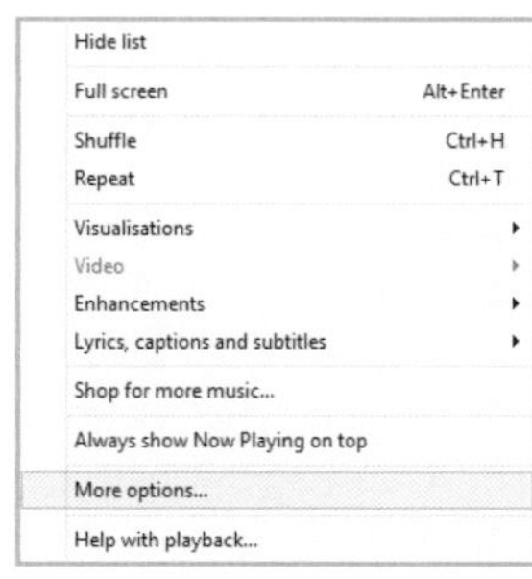

2. Click the Rip Music tab

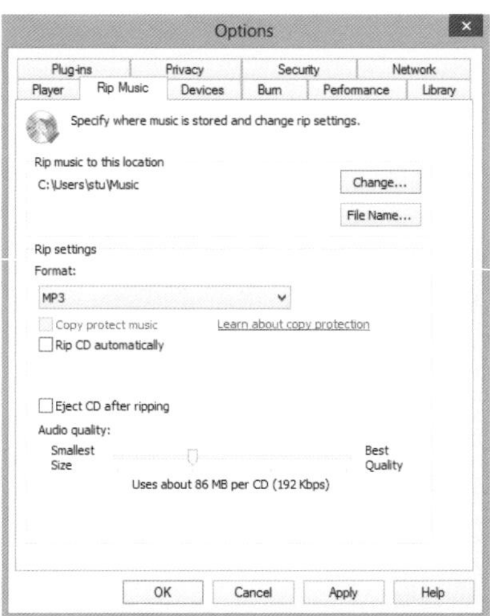

3. Set Format as one of the Windows Media Audio (WMA) file formats, or select the MP3 format for greater flexibility

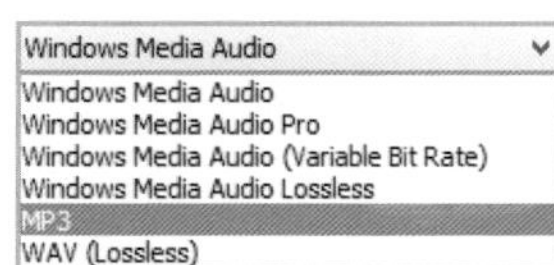
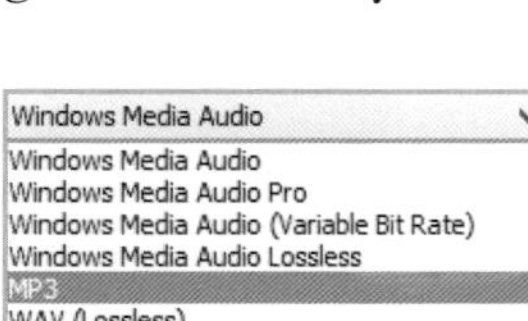

4. Select the bit rate - higher bit rates will give much better quality but will use up more disk space

5. Click the Rip CD button to extract and compress the tracks

6. The tracks are added to your Music library, and stored with a folder for each artist, and a subfolder for each of their albums

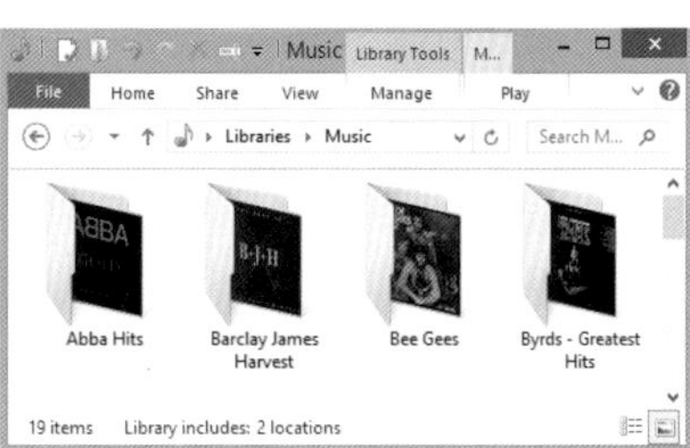

Media Player library

1. When the CD has been copied, select Go to Library (or click the Switch to Library button)

2. Select Music to display the Music library, by artist and track

3. Select Artist or Genre to group all the associated albums

4. Select Album to display the albums alphabetically by title

Don't forget

The Windows Media Player library displays the contents of the Music, Videos and Pictures libraries for the current user, with links to the libraries of users who are online and members of the HomeGroup.

Hot tip

Click Organize and select Customize navigation pane, to group music by other properties, such as year, rating or composer.

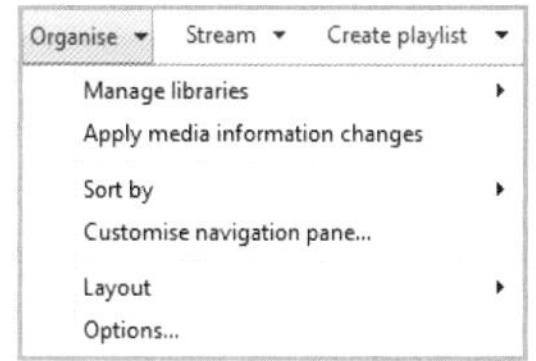

Hot tip

Double-click a group to display the individual tracks that it contains, arranged by album.

Internet radio

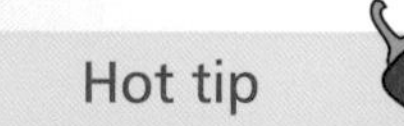

Approximately 60,000 stations worldwide can be listened to on TuneIn Radio.

A popular feature in Windows Media Player allows users to listen to internet radio stations. However, this functionality has been removed from the version of WMP in Windows 8. It is not provided in the Music app either.

The solution, therefore, is to download a third-party program. Go to the Windows Store, and from the Search charm search for internet radio. You'll see a number of results. One we have tried and can recommend is TuneIn Radio, shown below:

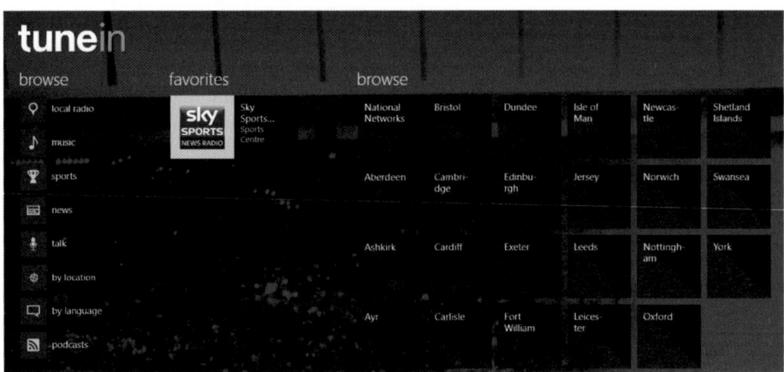

The app knows your geographical location so when you start it, the Home screen will show regions in your country. Click on these to open a list of local stations.

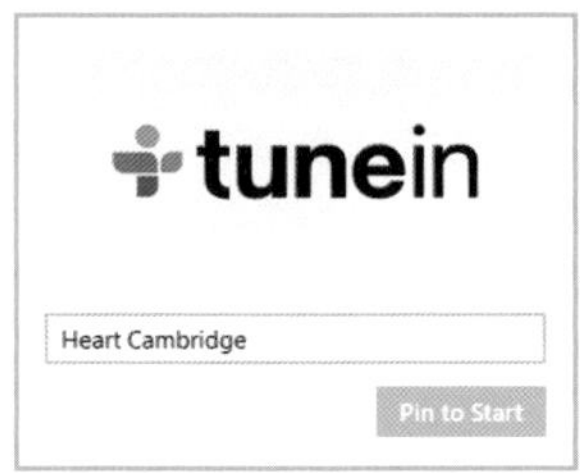

With a station open, right-click on the screen to open the app bar. You'll see two options: Click Add to add the station to your favorites, and click Pin to pin it to the Start screen.

The Home page provides a number of options. The Sports, Music, News, and Talk links open lists of related stations. If you fancy extending your horizons a bit, click By Location. Starting with the major world regions, you can drill down to local regions in virtually every country in the world.

By Language lets you choose radio stations broadcasting in specific languages. You can also search for podcasts – pre-recorded audio programs that are available on the Internet.

Home media streaming

Anything that you can play in Windows Media Player, you can share with other computers and devices on your home network.

1. Open Windows Media Player, select the Library view and click the Stream button

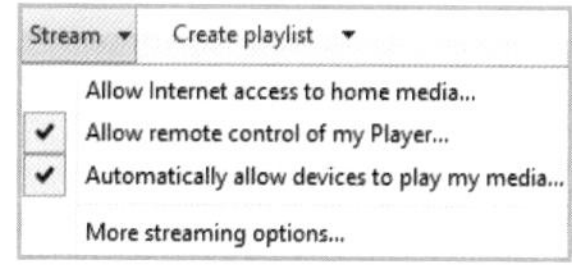

2. This should show Allow remote control, Automatically allow devices to play, and More streaming options

With these settings, your Windows Media Player will have access to Other Libraries, in particular the media libraries that were shared when the computers on your network joined the HomeGroup.

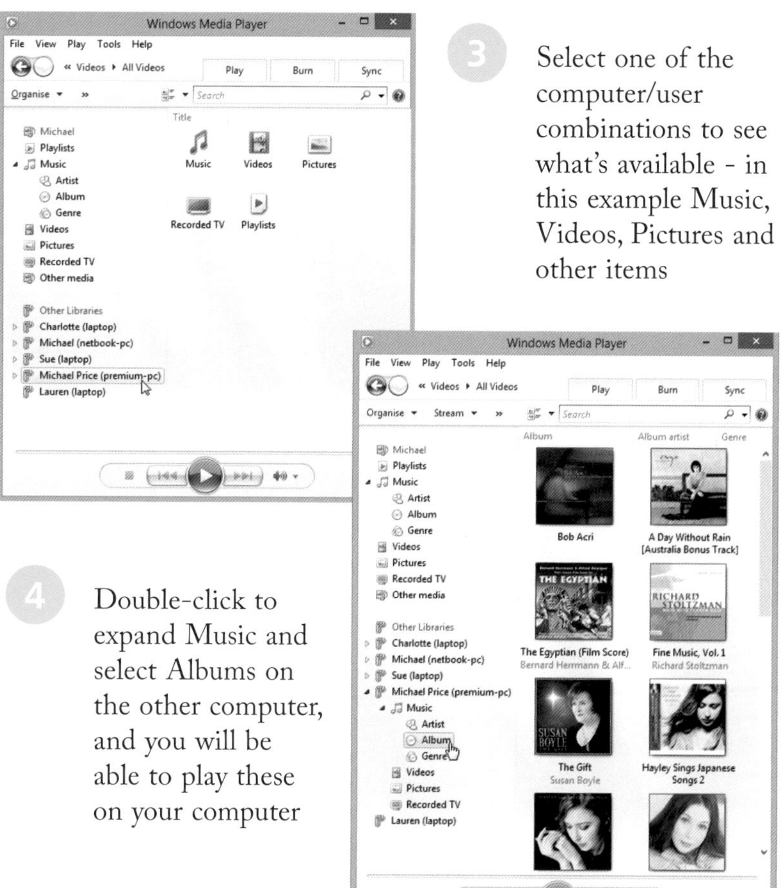

3. Select one of the computer/user combinations to see what's available - in this example Music, Videos, Pictures and other items

4. Double-click to expand Music and select Albums on the other computer, and you will be able to play these on your computer

Hot tip

These are the default for Windows Media Player and HomeGroup, but if necessary, turn on media streaming, and select the options to Allow remote control and Automatically allow devices to play.

Don't forget

You may have to wait a few moments as the list of contents is transferred from the other computer.

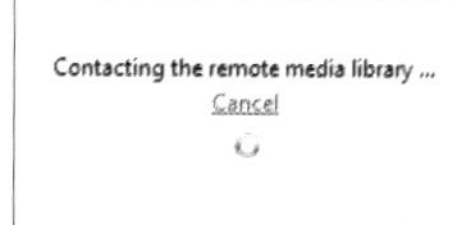

Play to device or computer

You can also use media streaming to play items from your computer on another computer or device on the network.

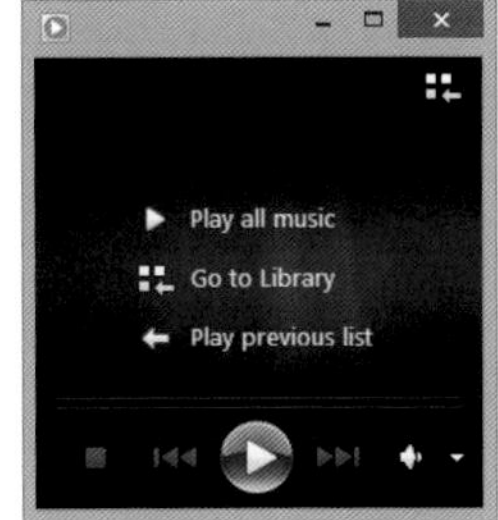

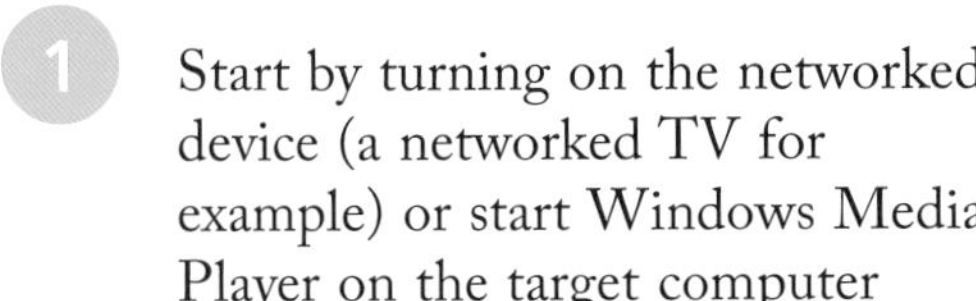

1. Start by turning on the networked device (a networked TV for example) or start Windows Media Player on the target computer

2. Open Windows Media Player on your computer and ready the items for playing but press the Pause button

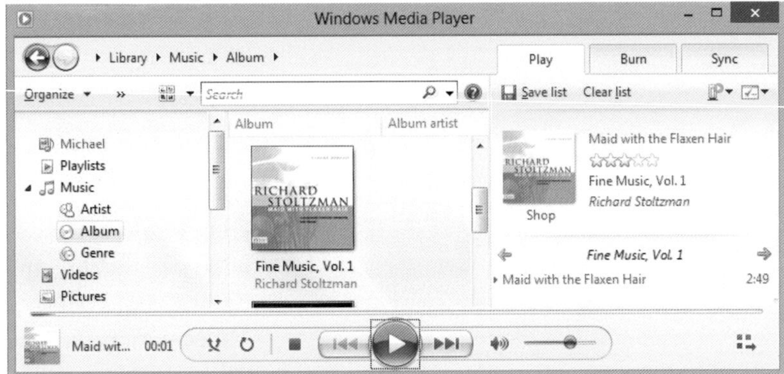

3. Click the Play to button and select the device or computer you want to use

4. Windows Media Player contacts the device and initiates playing the selected media files. You can the control the operation from either computer

Hot tip

The Play to function is supported by Windows Phone 8, which can also stream media files to networked devices or computers running Windows Media Player.

Don't forget

You don't have to use Windows Media Player to initiate Play to. You can simply highlight a group of files in one of the library folders, then right-click the files, select Play to and click the target device.

Dictate to your computer

One way to interact with your computer is to simply tell it what you want, with Windows Speech Recognition.

1. Go to Control Panel, Ease of Access, Speech Recognition

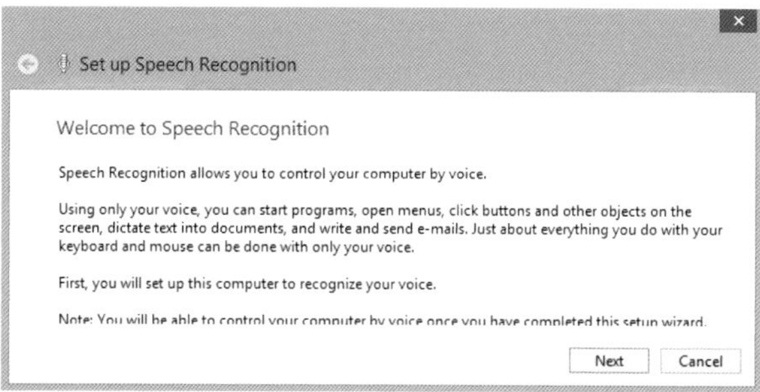

2. Select the type of microphone that you'll be using, a headset microphone being best for speech recognition

3. Follow the advice to position the microphone effectively then read text aloud so the microphone volume can be set

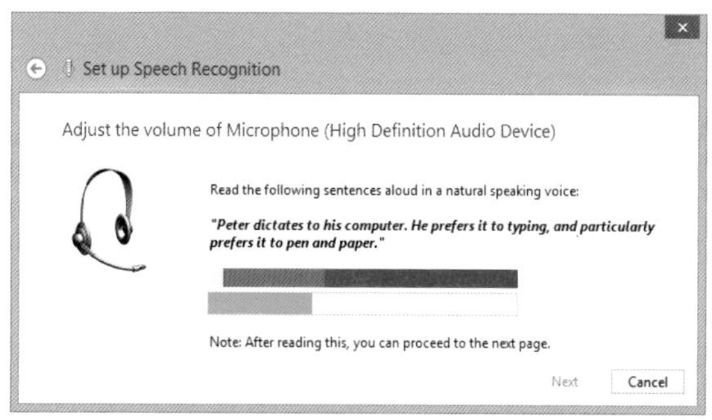

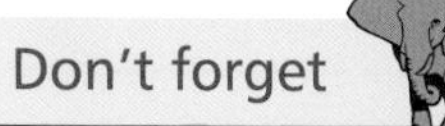

Speech Recognition is supported in all editions of Windows 8 and is available in the English, German, French, Spanish, Japanese and Chinese languages.

The wizard takes you through all of the steps that are required to set up Speech Recognition on your computer.

...cont'd

Don't forget

Use Manual activation mode unless you are planning to always control your computer by voice.

4. Following the prompts, choose Manual or Voice activation mode, and run Speech Recognition when Windows starts

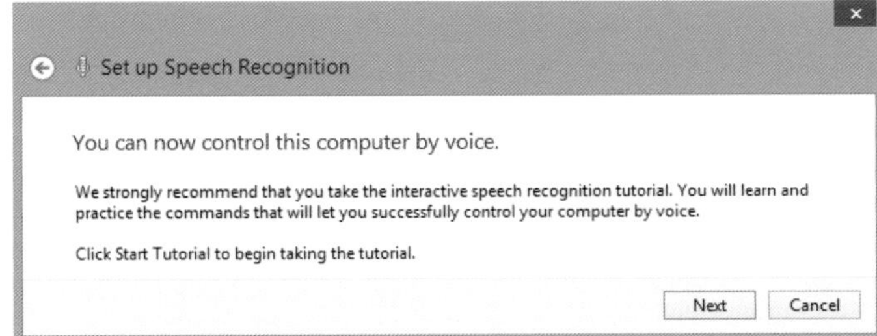

Hot tip

All the users on the computer should carry out their own training sessions, so that each has a separate profile.

5. Click Start Tutorial to learn about the basic features and to Train your computer to better understand you

When you start Windows, Speech Recognition will start up and switch itself into Sleeping mode, or Turn listening off (depending on the activation mode you have set).

1. If it is Off, right-click the Speech Recognition bar and select Sleep
2. Say "Start listening" (or click the button on the bar)
3. Say "What can I say?" to view the Speech Reference Card

Don't forget

You can print this guide so that you have it to hand when you are practicing with the system.

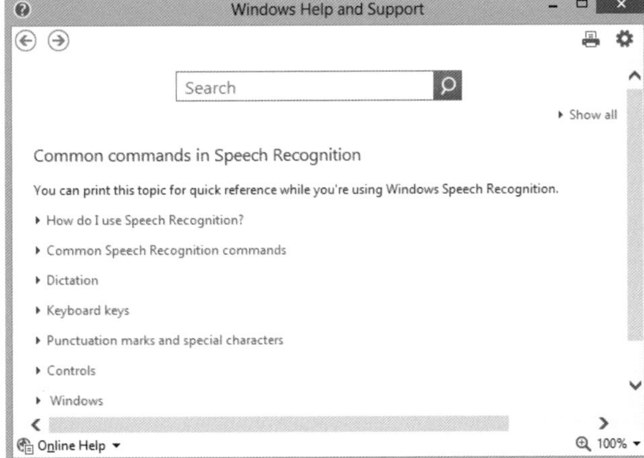

Text to speech

You can let the computer talk to you, using the text to speech facilities of the Narrator application.

1. Press Winkey + U to open the Ease of Access Center and select Narrator (or press Spacebar when Narrator is highlighted)

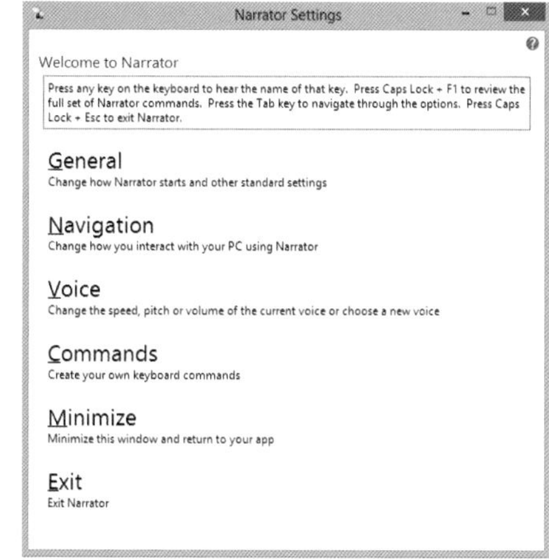

2. Narrator starts up and you can configure the main settings to set up the program

3. Click Voice to adjust the voice settings. Adjust the speed, volume and pitch to suit your preferences. Narrator will read the contents of the screen, including the text content of programs such as Notepad, WordPad, and Windows Help and Support

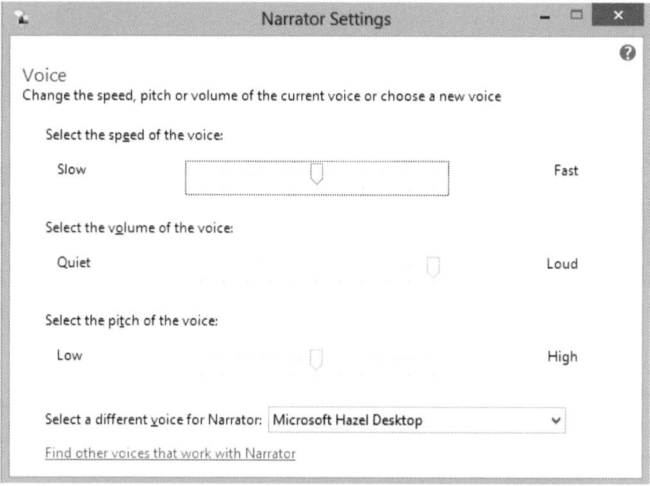

4. Click the Help icon at the top-right of the narrator window to get some useful hints

Don't forget

From the Ease of Access Center select Use the computer without a display and choose Turn on Narrator, to have the program start automatically when you start Windows.

Beware

Narrator does not read the text content of programs such as Internet Explorer and Microsoft Word, so its value is somewhat limited, in comparison to Speech Recognition.

Windows Media Center

Users of Windows 8 Pro can install Windows Media Center (WMC) as we explained on page 18. If you use your PC as a home entertainment system, this program provides another way to manage your media files and functions.

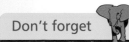

Windows Media Center is not bundled with Windows 8. However, users of Windows 8 Pro can install it as an extra.

1. Open WMC from the Search charm

2. The Media Center includes pictures & videos, music, movies and TV (live, recorded and internet)

3. Click Search for details of the free streaming internet TV video service, with TV shows, movies, trailers and clips

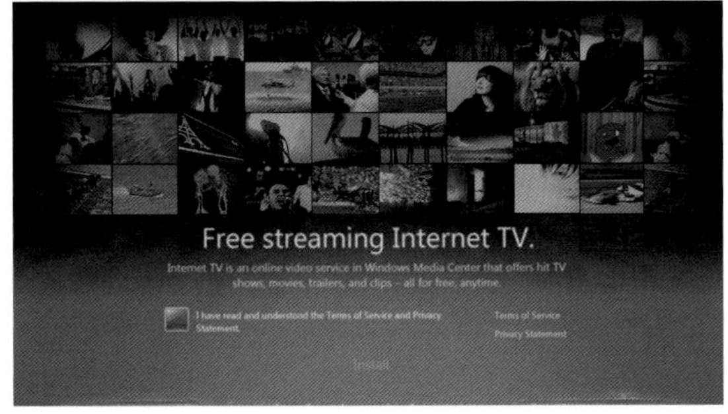

The first time you run this program, you may see Get Started setup. Select Express for the recommended options, or Custom to personalize the settings.

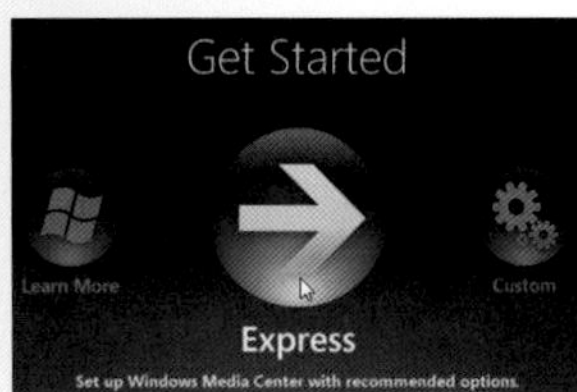

4 View pictures, slide shows and videos from your libraries, and view or input media files from a removable device

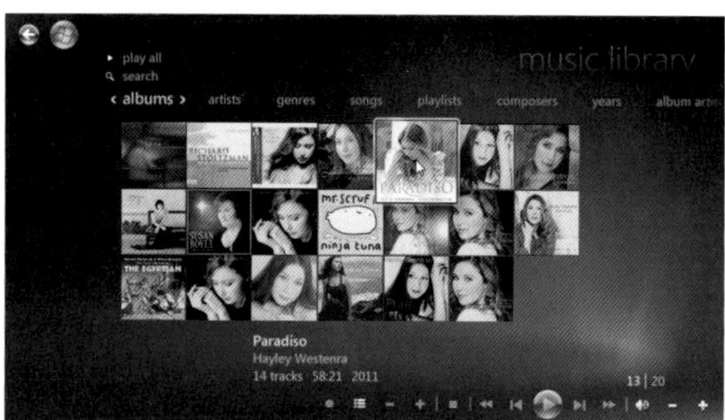

5 You can play music, create playlists, watch slide shows while playing music, or copy music from CDs and DVDs

6 From Tasks, you can burn to CD/DVD, sync your devices and even shut down your computer

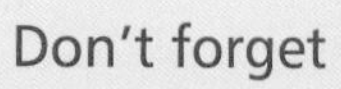

Don't forget

Like Media Player, Media Center displays the contents of your Music folder, plus any other media folders that you selected during setup.

Hot tip

With a TV Tuner fitted, Windows Media Center turns your PC into a Digital Video Recorder, so you can pause and rewind live TV or record shows for viewing later.

Recording

To record stuff on your computer, you need a microphone and also a program to do the recording. Searching the Windows Store we found several free recording apps. These included Tape Recorder, Simple Audio Recorder, Pocket Recorder, and Quick Sound Recorder. Of these, we liked Quick Sound Recorder the most.

Hot tip 

A paid version of Quick Sound Recorder is available. This provides more functionality.

1. Start a recording by clicking Start Recording – this starts the timer below. Click again to stop recording

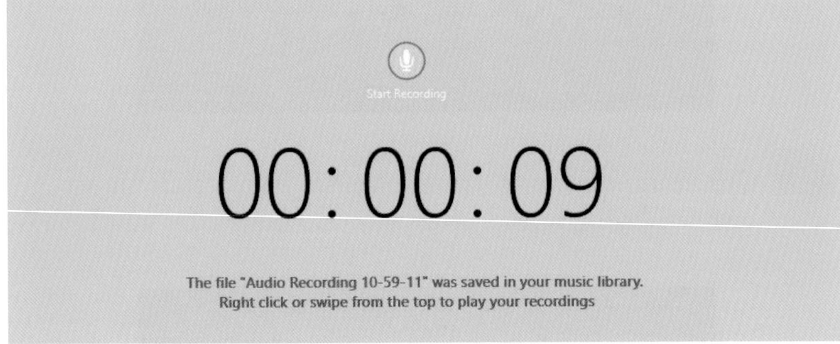

2. Right-click on the screen to open an app bar at the top. Click View Recordings

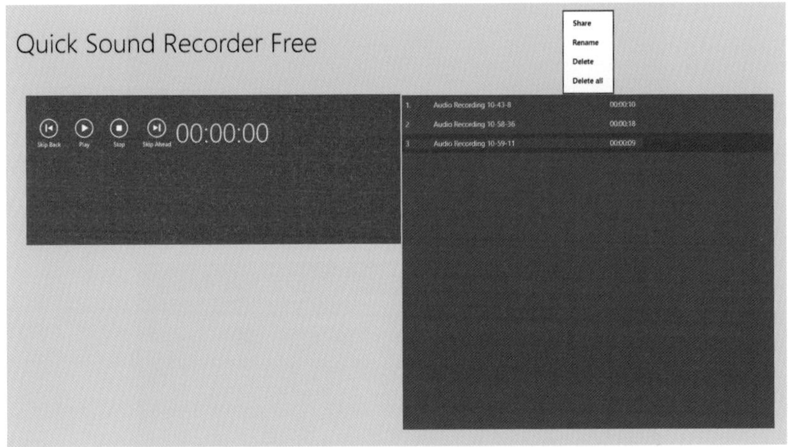

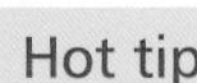

Hot tip 

By default, recordings are saved in the Music library.

3. Playback controls are at the left of the screen. At the right is a list of all the recordings you have made. By right-clicking on a recording, you get options to Share, Rename, Delete, and Delete All

17 Devices and printers

Learn how to manage your devices in the new Windows 8 interface and also the Desktop. You can add various types of printers and scanners to your PC, and Windows usually provides the drivers needed to manage the devices.

PC settings – devices

Windows has always had a device management utility called Device Manager with which users can manage the devices on their computer. The new Windows 8 interface provides a much simpler option that helps users to add and remove devices, troubleshoot device issues, and more.

Hot tip

You can also manage your devices on the Desktop. Go to the Control Panel and click View devices and printers.

1. On the Charms bar, select Settings and then click Change PC Settings

2. Select Devices on the left side of the window

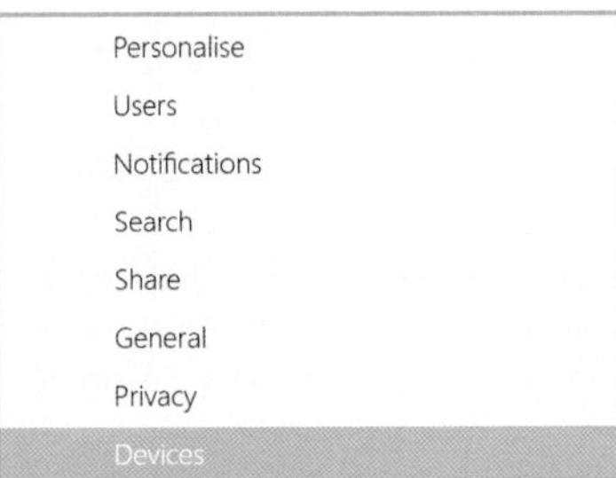

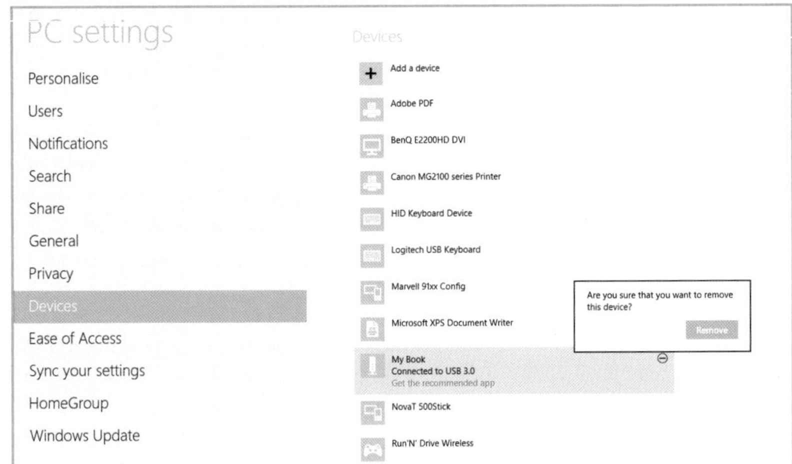

Hot tip

It is important to remove devices from your PC in the correct way. Simply disconnecting them can cause problems.

3. On the right you will see a list of all the devices connected to your computer

4. Left-click on an entry to see the options for that device. For example, the entry highlighted above shows that a Western Digital My Book external hard drive has an app available for it – clicking the link will take you to the app's Install page

5. Clicking the – icon opens a Remove link. This allows you to remove the device safely

Add a device

These days most hardware devices are very easy to install. Simply connect it to the computer and switch on. Windows will see the device as a new addition to the system, locate the drivers from its in-built driver database, and then install it.

Things don't always happen as they should, though. If you experience any problems, try the following:

1. Open PC Settings, Devices as described on the previous page

2. Check if the device you are trying to install is listed under devices. If it is, you may see a message that explains the problem, as shown below

3. If you don't see your device in the list, click Add a Device at the top of the screen. Windows will now look for rec... ...lded devices

... a list of the ... lows has

... device is ..., click on it and then follow the prompts

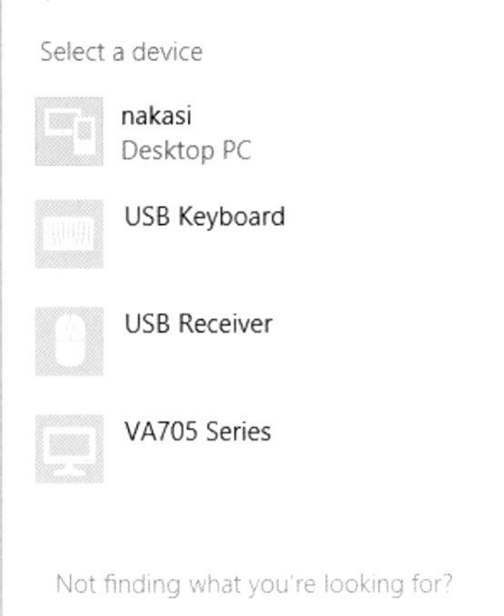

6. If the device isn't listed, click Not finding what you're looking for? at the bottom

7. A Help page will open offering advice on why the device isn't being found, plus measures you can take to resolve the issue

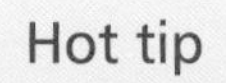

Hot tip

The most common reason for Windows not seeing a device is that it simply hasn't been switched on.

Control Panel devices

Device management can also be carried out via the Desktop – good news if you don't like the new Windows 8 interface!

1. Go to the Control Panel, Hardware and Sound, and click View devices and printers

2. You will see icons for all the devices on your computer

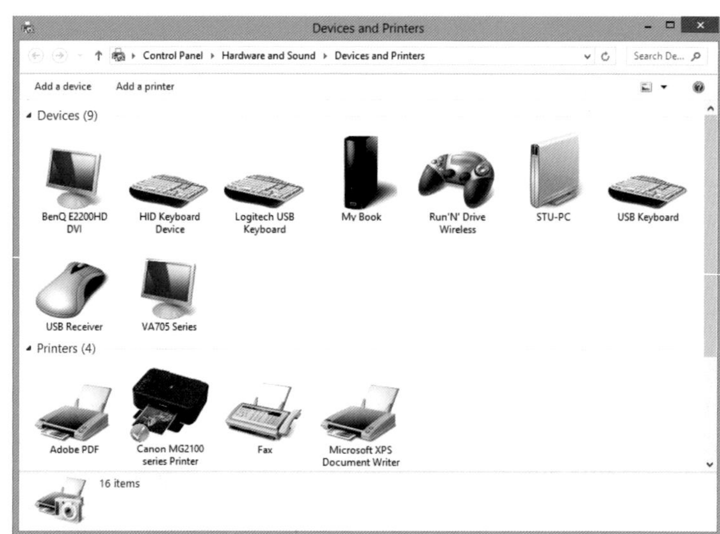

3. Click Add a Device to install a new hardware device. If the device being added is a printer, click Add a printer

4. Left-click on a device to see its Properties. Right-clicking will open a menu with options related to that particular type of device

5. Here we see right-click options for a printer. Other devices will have different options

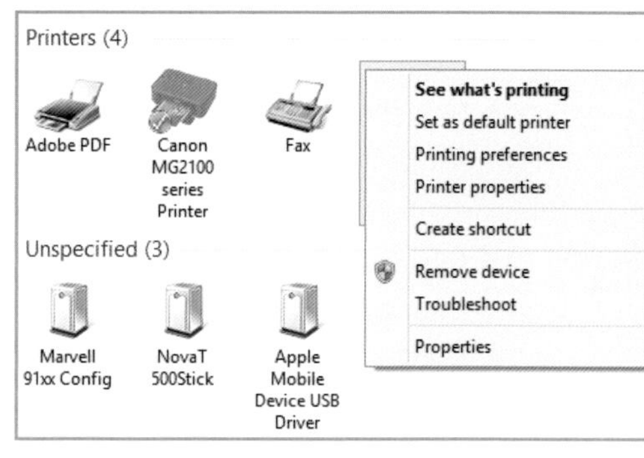

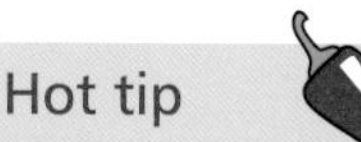

In comparison with the Windows 8 interface, the Desktop offers more management options.

Update device driver

To check the date for your printer driver:

1. Go to Control Panel and open Devices and Printers. Right-click the printer and select Properties, Hardware tab, Properties and, finally, the Driver tab

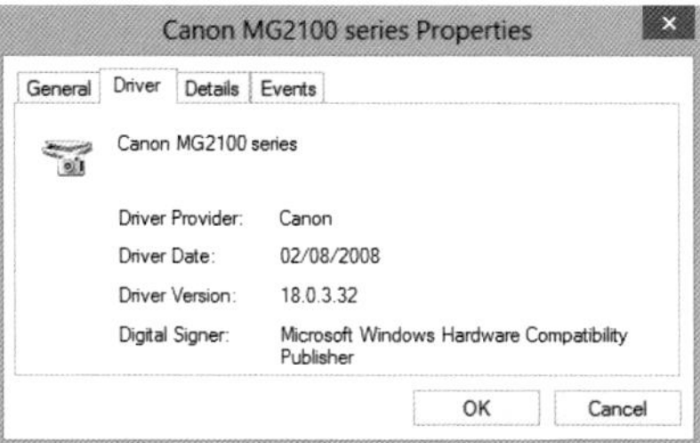

2. In the example above the driver is dated 02/08/2008, so it is well out of date

3. To check for the latest driver visit the manufacturer's website, e.g. **www.canon.com**, and select Support

4. Enter the device's model number in the search box and click Search

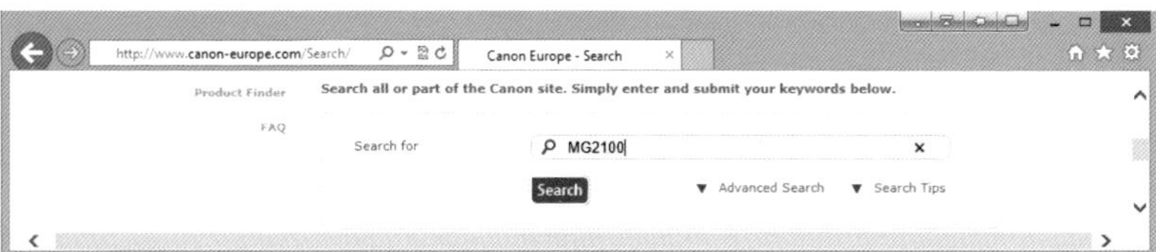

5. The support site has a Windows 8 driver that supports this printer

8. **MG2100 series MP Driver Ver. 1.01a (Windows 8/8 x64/7/7 x64/Vista/Vista64/XP)**
File version: 1.01a
Operating system(s): Windows 8, Windows 8 (x64), Windows 7, Windows 7 (x64), Windows Vista, Windows Vista (x64), Windows XP
Language(s): English, Français, Español, Italiano, Deutsch, Dansk, Suomi, Nederlands, Norsk, Svenska, Русский, عربية, Čeština, Ελληνικά, Magyar, Polski, Português, Türkçe, Bahasa Indonesia, 日本語, 한국어, 繁體中文, ไทย, 简体中文
Description:This file is a driver for Canon IJ multifunction printers.

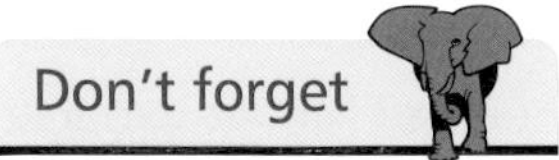

Don't forget

Normally, Windows will have an up-to-date driver for the printer, but this is not always the case, so if in doubt, check with the manufacturer.

Hot tip

Follow a similar process at the website for your printer, to search Support for possible updates to the driver.

...cont'd

Don't forget

You can run the program immediately, but if you save it to disk and then run the program, you can retain a copy for backup purposes.

6. Click the Download button and follow the prompts to save the driver installation file on your system

Do you want to run or save **mp68-win-mg2100-1_01a-ea24.exe** (21.0 MB) from **gdlp01.c-wss.com**? Run Save Cancel

7. Run the installation program to start Setup

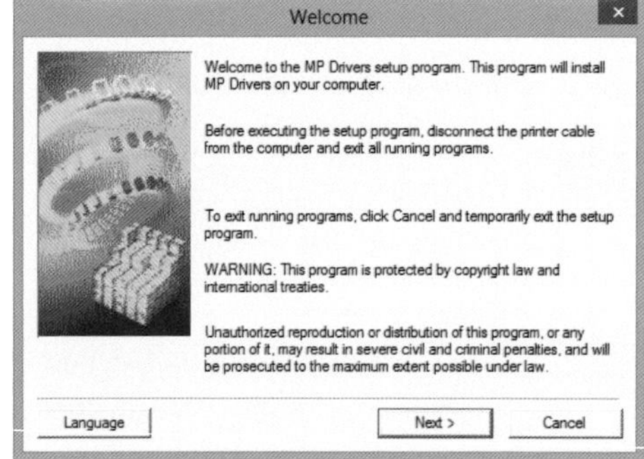

Hot tip

You may be required to accept terms and conditions, and you may be asked to specify if this is to become the default printer.

8. Follow the prompts to configure the printer

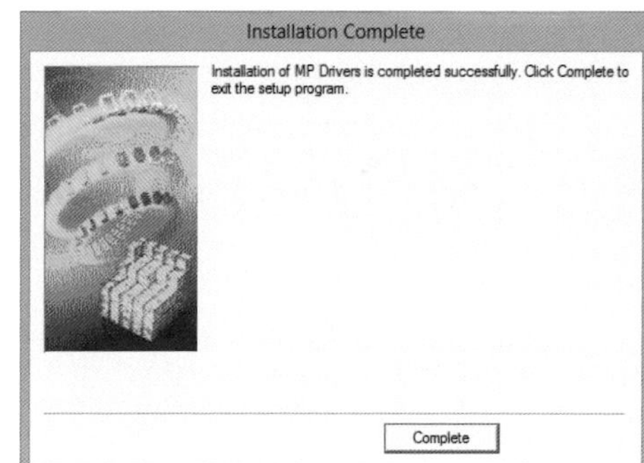

9. The new driver will be added to Devices and Printers

Hot tip

The printer will now be managed by the up-to-date driver software.

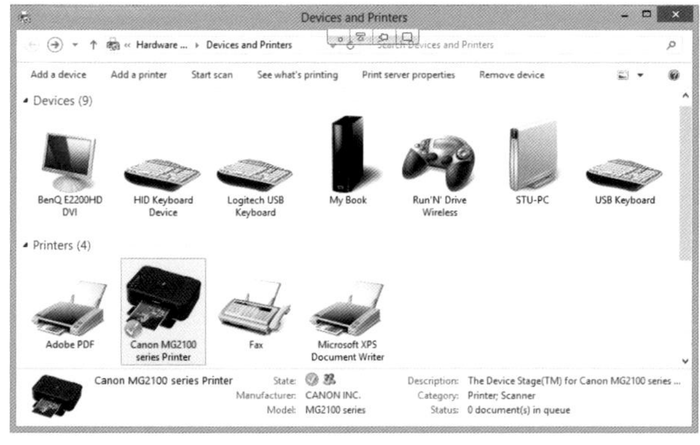

Wireless printer

1 Go to the Control Panel, Hardware and Sound, and click View devices and printers. Click Add a Printer

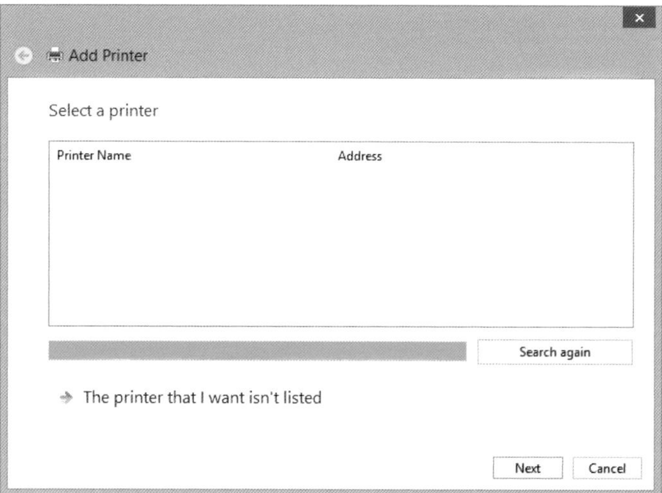

2 Windows will attempt to find your networked printer. If it does, select it and click Next to install it. If it doesn't, however, you will see a blank dialog box. In this case, click "The printer that I want isn't listed"

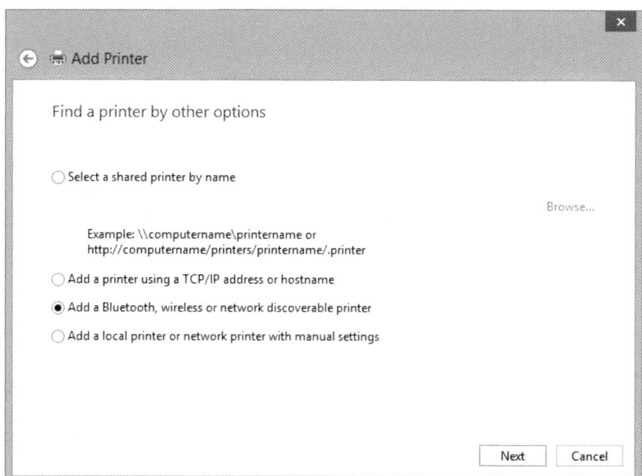

3 Select Add a Bluetooth, wireless or network discoverable printer and click Next

Don't forget

If you have a wireless printer set up on your network, you can add it to your Windows 8 computer.

...cont'd

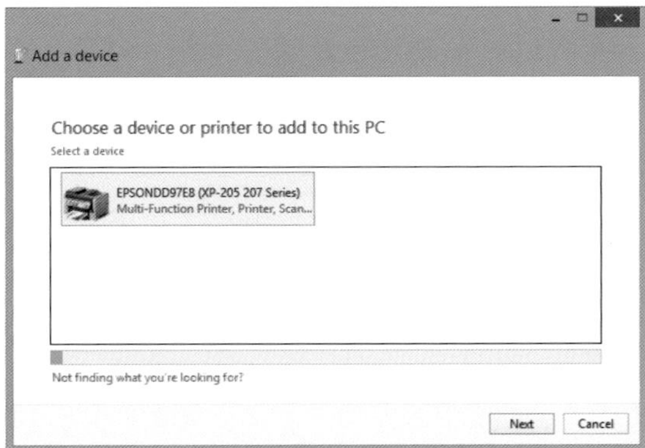

4. This time Windows should find the printer. Select it and click Next

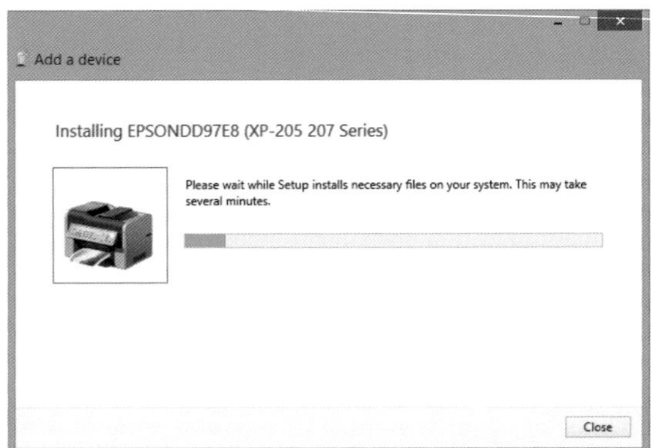

5. Windows installs the printer

Beware

Adding a new printer often results in a change to the default printer, so you need to check this and ensure the right printer is specified.

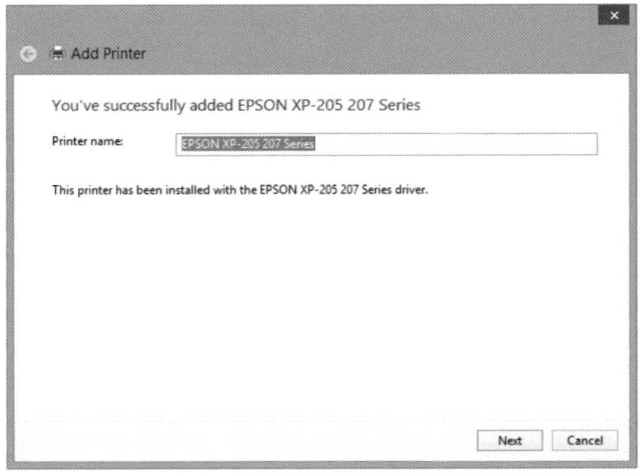

Virtual printers

You may have some items in Devices and Printers that are not physical devices but are software programs that act as virtual printers. To see how these could be used:

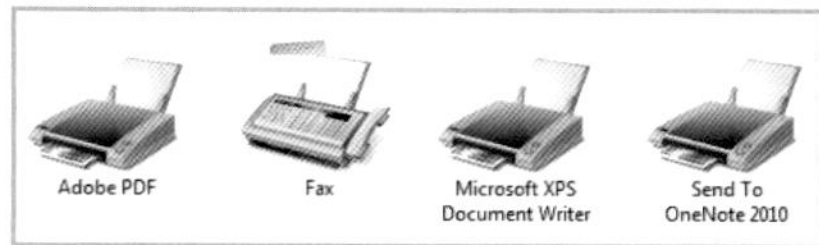

1. Open a document with text and graphics in WordPad

2. Open the File menu and click Print

3. Choose one of the virtual printers, for example Adobe PDF as shown below. Click the Print button

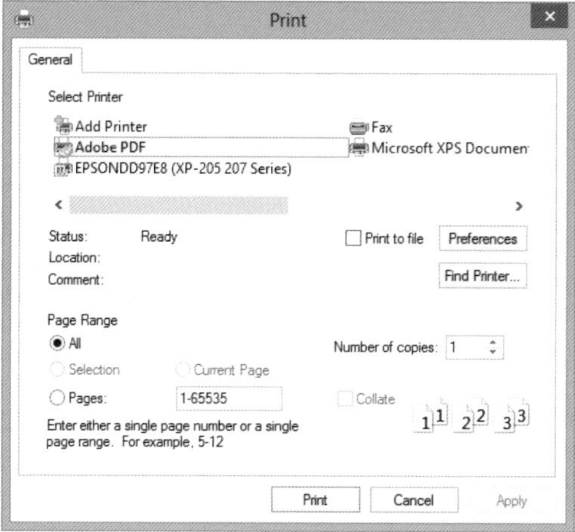

4. You'll be asked to confirm the location and file name, and a PDF version of the document is saved

WordPad is chosen since it supports text and graphics, but you could use any Windows program.

...cont'd

Alternatively:

1. Select Microsoft XPS Document Writer as the printer

2. Provide a name, and the document will be saved in XPS format

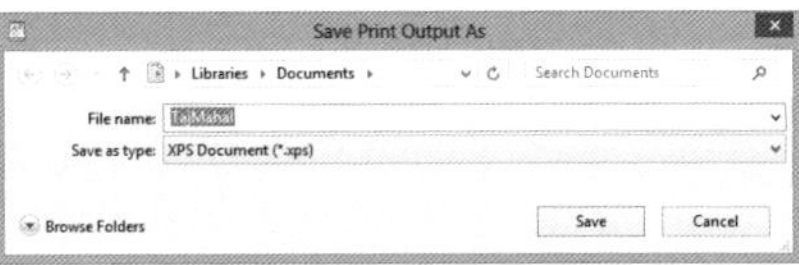

Some printer drivers pass control on to other programs:

1. Select Fax as the printer and Fax Setup is started

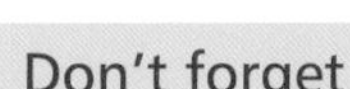
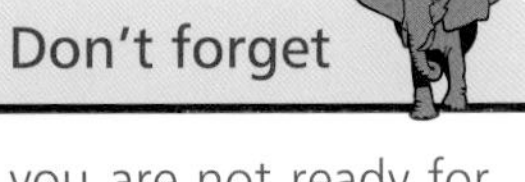

Don't forget

If you are not ready for Fax Setup, click Cancel and you can create a fax and save it as a draft to send later.

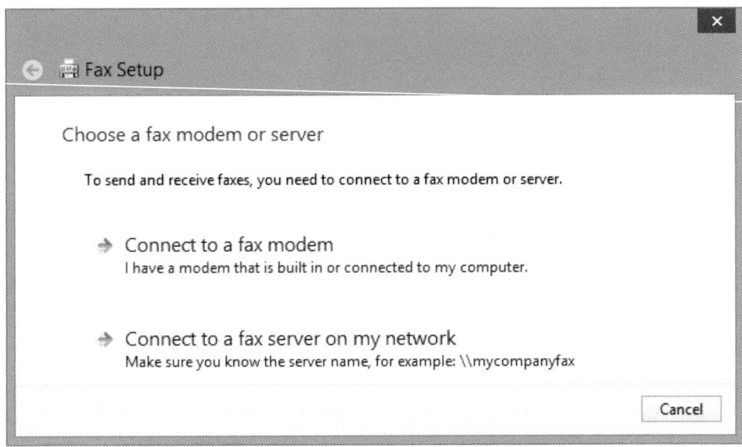

2. Choose your setup, then complete the cover page, and send your document as a .tif image file

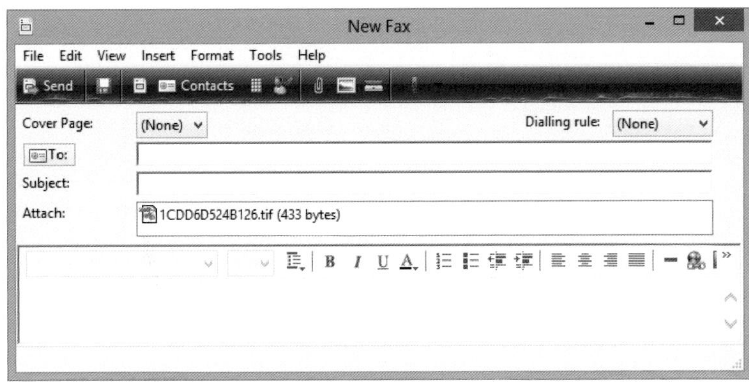

Generic/text only printer

To create a generic/text only printer:

1. Open Devices and Printers, click Add a printer and then click The printer that I want isn't listed

2. Tick Add a local printer or network printer with manual settings

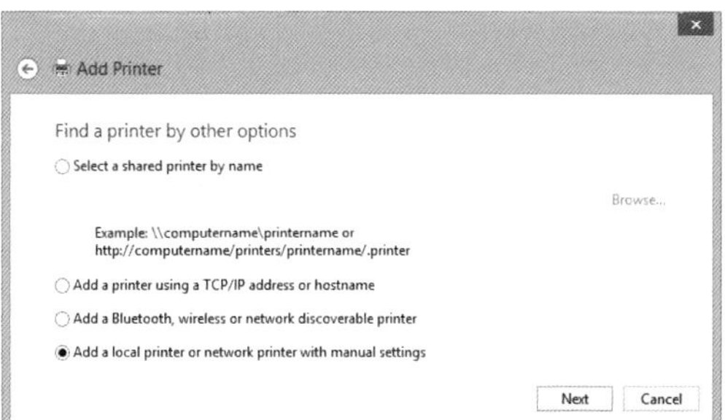

3. Select Use an existing port and choose FILE: (Print to File) and click Next

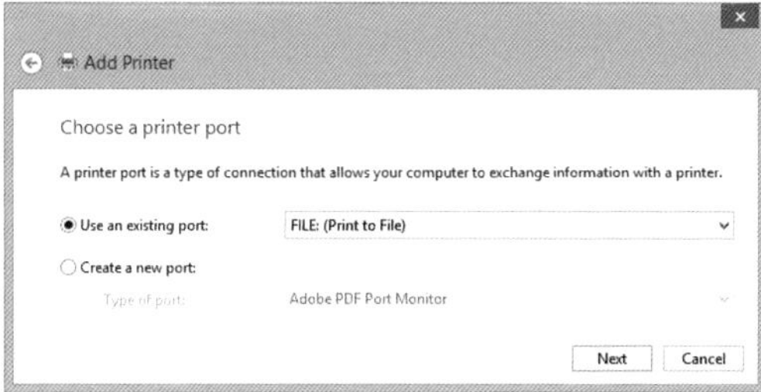

4. In the Manufacturer field select Generic and in the Printers field select Generic/Text Only then click Next

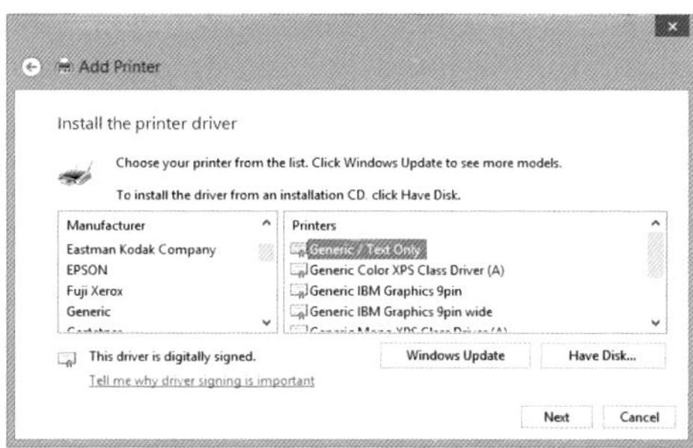

You can install a generic/text only printer driver in Windows 8 as a way to capture text information in a file, or for use with an application that requires this type of printer driver.

If you are creating support for an old printer, you'd choose the port it uses, COM1: for example.

...cont'd

5. Accept or amend the suggested name and click Next

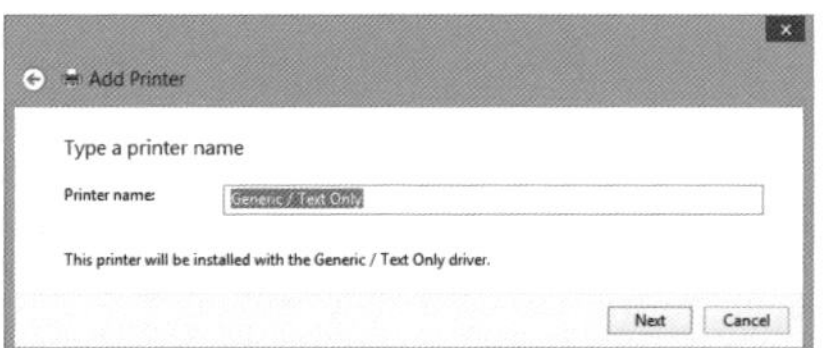

Don't forget

Since this printer creates files on your system, it is best to avoid making it shareable.

6. Select Do not share this printer and click Next. Ensure the printer is not set as default, and finally click Finish

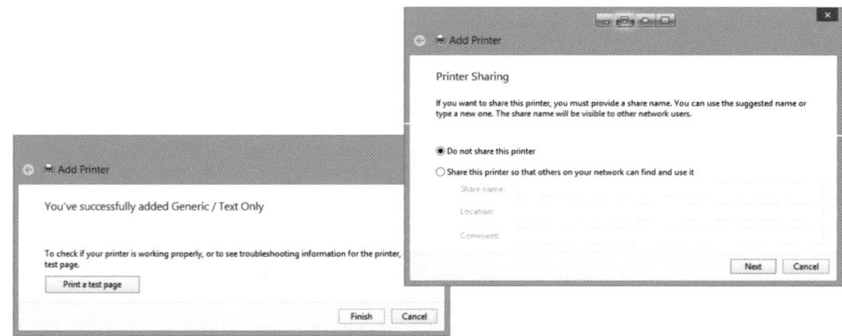

7. The printer is added to Devices and Printers

To check out the operation of this printer:

1. Create a simple document using Notepad – it is helpful to use plain text for the initial testing

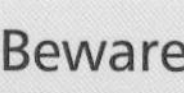

Beware

When you print from a formatted source, the graphics and formatting will be stripped out. You may find the resulting text disorganized, especially since a default line of 80 characters is assumed.

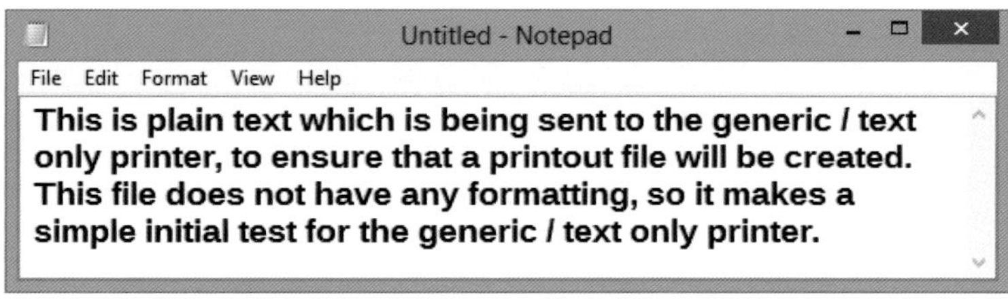

2. Select Print and choose the Generic/Text Only printer

3. Provide the file name (type .prn is usual for printouts) and click OK

Add a scanner

You can install a scanner to the Devices and Printers folder.

1. To install a USB-connected scanner such as the Epson Perfection 1260, insert the USB cable and switch on
2. If the driver is available, the scanner will be installed
3. If the driver is missing, an error message displays
4. An Action Center message gives the solution – download and install the driver from the Seiko Epson Corporation

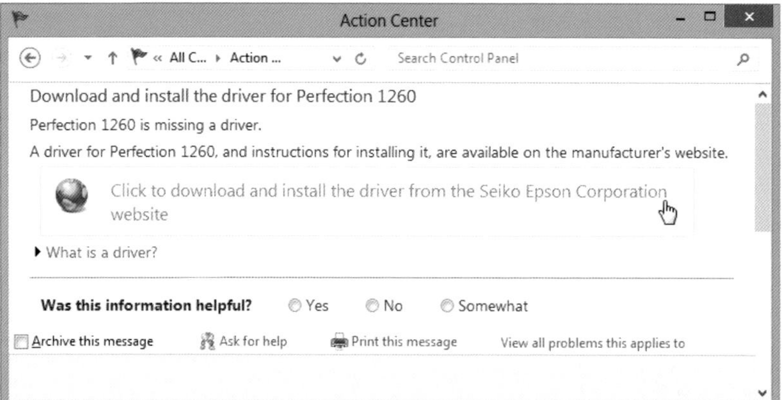

5. Select the link and at the manufacturer's website select your operating system, e.g. Windows 32-bit

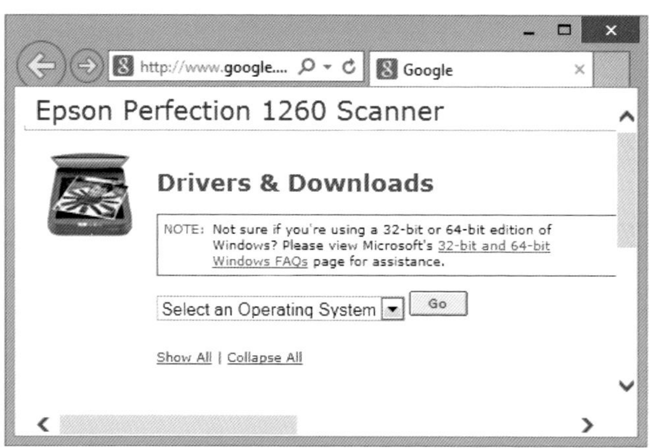

Don't forget

Windows 8 will have the drivers for many scanners, but may not include older devices.

Hot tip

Windows checks its compatibility database and identifies where to find the missing driver.

...cont'd

Don't forget

The downloaded file is self-extracting and contains the drivers for a number of Epson scanners, including the Perfection 1260.

6. Installation instructions for the selected system are shown

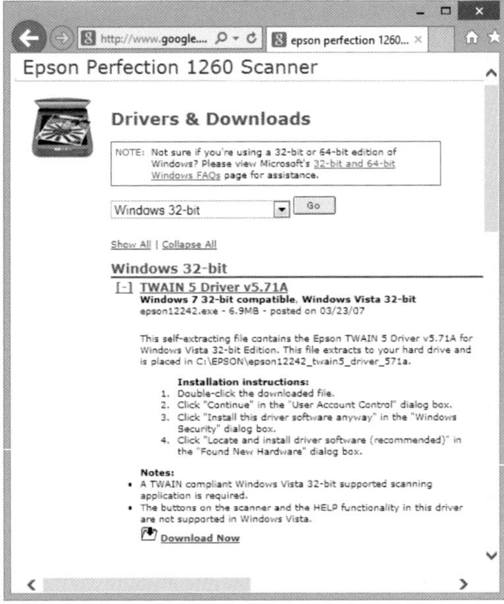

Hot tip

You may find it best to unplug the scanner before installing the software. When you reconnect the scanner, Windows will now recognize and add it.

7. Click Download Now, and choose to Run or Save the file

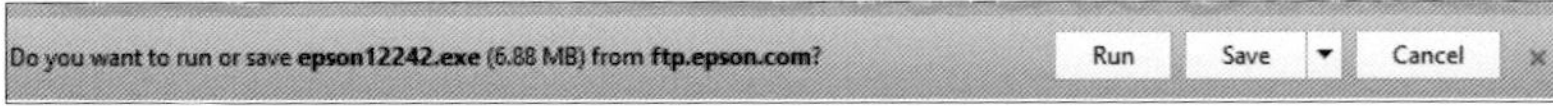

8. When you do run the downloaded file, it will start the installation process, and the scanner will be added

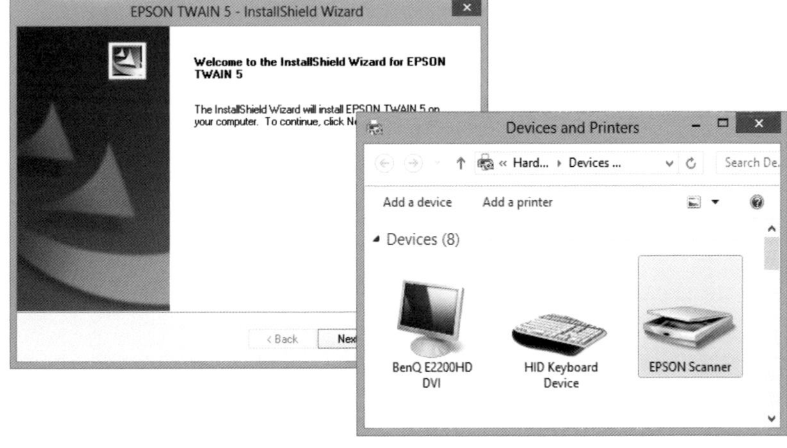

Using the scanner

1. Open Devices and Printers, right-click the scanner device and select Scan Properties

2. Click the Events tab, and select the Start button

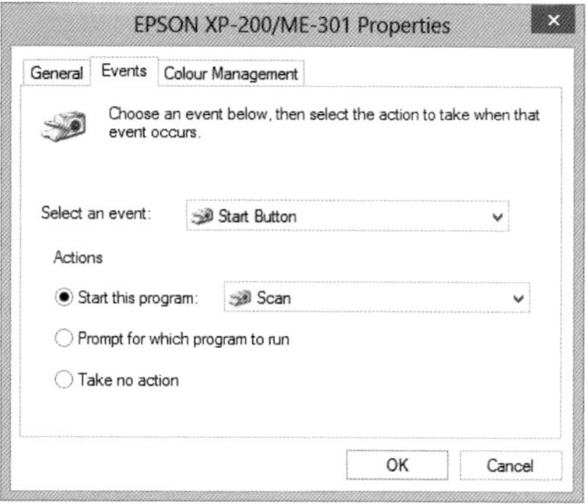

3. Choose Start this program and select Scan

4. Insert a document and press the Start button

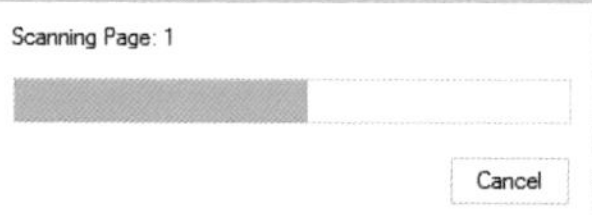

5. The document is scanned and the image is imported

6. View the image in the Pictures library

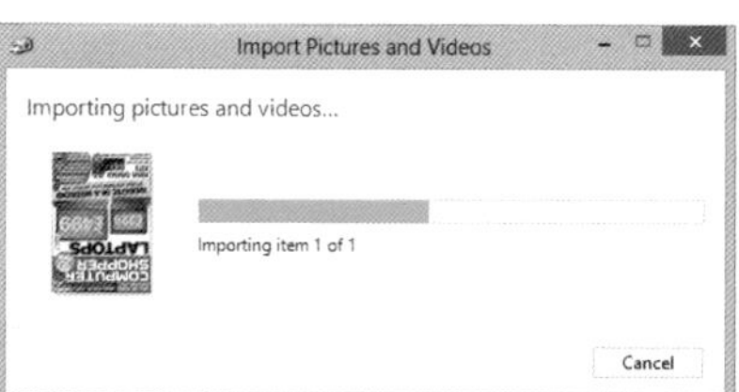

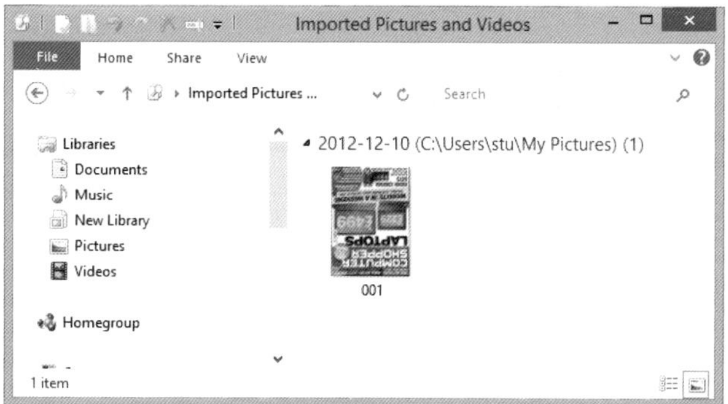

Hot tip

You can invoke the Scan program when you want to import an image, or the Windows Fax and Scan Application.

Don't forget

The images are stored in a folder with the name set to the date that they were scanned.

Add a storage device

Adding a storage device to a Windows 8 computer couldn't be easier – Windows does the hardware configuration for you. In this example we are adding a Western Digital My Book external hard drive to the system.

As with most current devices, the drive uses a USB connection. If your device uses USB 3.0, connect it to a USB 3.0 socket (if available) rather than USB 2.0 (USB 3.0 is much faster than USB 2.0 so the drive will perform much better.)

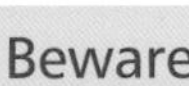

Beware

You can run a USB 3.0 device from a USB 2.0 socket but it will not operate at its maximum performance level.

1. Drive connected to a USB socket
2. Switch on the drive
3. Windows automatically installs the device (adding any device driver software needed)

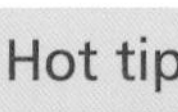

Hot tip

If you are unsure which of your USB sockets are USB 3.0, look for any that are colored blue – these are USB 3.0; USB 2.0 are black.

4. Go to Devices and Printers

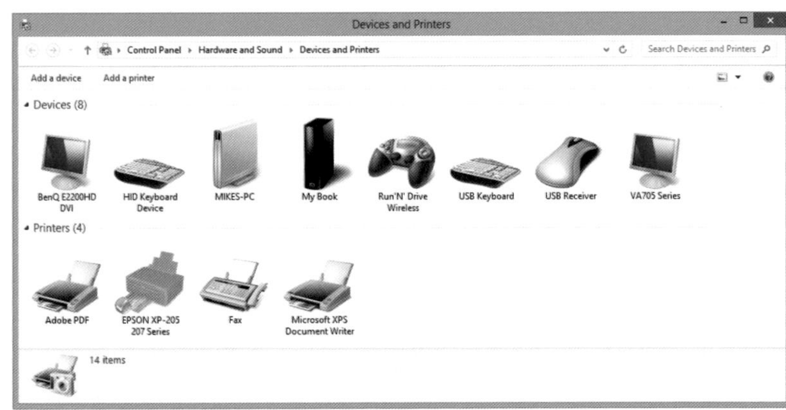

5. The Western Digital MyBook is installed

18 Networking Windows

If you have more than one computer, even just a laptop and a desktop machine, you can connect them with cables or wireless, and share information between the computers. Windows makes it easy to set up and manage the network that you create. This chapter explains all you need to know.

Create a network

Don't forget

Most routers will offer both wired and wireless connections, as well as internet access, or you may have individual devices for each of these functions.

A network consists of several devices that exchange information over a cable or via radio waves. A computer plus internet router forms a small network. If you have other computers, they can be added to share the internet connection and perhaps share data information with each other, creating a larger network.

To be able to connect to the network, each computer requires an Ethernet (wired) network adapter plus cable, or a wireless network adapter. The flow of data between the computers and the router is managed by Windows.

To start a new network using a wired network adapter:

1. Install a network adapter in the computer (if required)

2. Start the computer and on the Charms bar click Settings and then the Network icon. You will see that Windows recognizes there is a network adapter with no connection

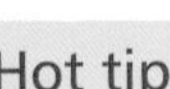

Hot tip

You can't create an ad hoc network in Windows 8 and Windows RT, but you can connect to an ad hoc network if one is in range (unless your PC is running Windows RT). There are third-party tools for creating ad hoc networks, if you need to do this.

3. Connect the adapter to the router using a network cable

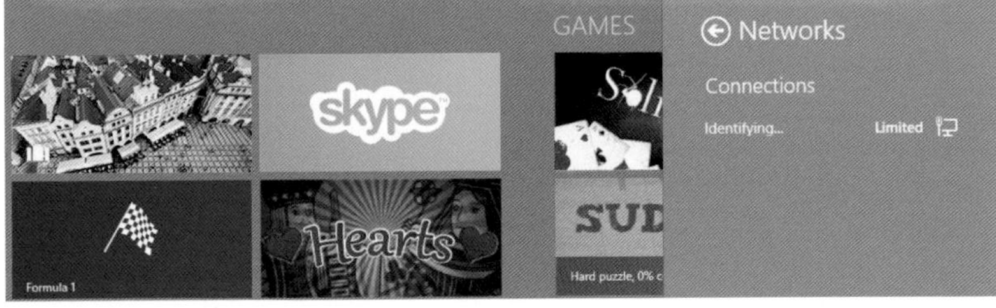

4. Windows will now automatically detect and identify the new network

5 Windows will ask you if you want to turn on network sharing between PCs, and connect to network devices such as printers

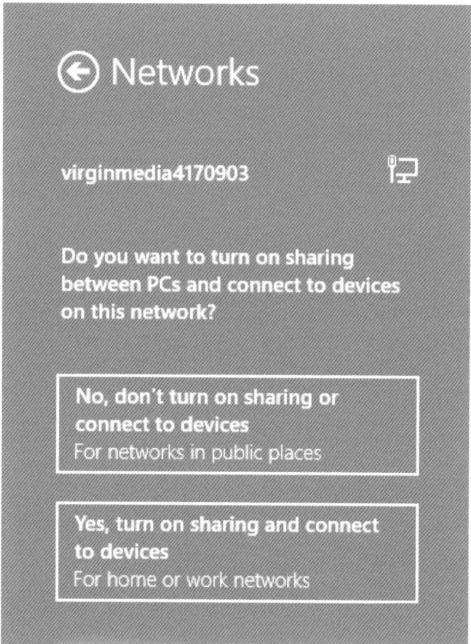

6 Choose No, don't turn on sharing or connect to devices for networks in public places (such as coffee shops or airports), or when you don't know or trust the people and devices on the network

Hot tip

The first time you connect to a network, you'll be asked if you want to turn on sharing between PCs and connect to network devices such as printers. Your answer automatically sets the appropriate firewall and security settings for the type of network that you connected to.

7 Choose Yes, turn on sharing and connect to devices for home or work networks, or when you know and trust the people and devices on the network. This setting allows your computer to connect to devices on the network, such as printers

Hot tip

The setting formerly known as network location (Private/Public or Home/Work/Domain) is now called network sharing. You turn this setting on or off as part of the process of connecting to a network.

8 Your new network is created and your computer is connected to it

Network classification

Two main types of network are possible in Windows 8 – Private and Public. If you are going to get involved in networking, it is important to understand the differences between them.

Hot tip

Network Location Awareness allows programs that use network connections to apply different behaviors based on how the computer connects to the network. In conjunction with Windows Firewall with Advanced security, you can configure specific firewall rules that apply only when connected to a specific network type. By default, the first time you connect to any network, the network is designated as Public unless you assign it to another category.

Public

A public network is one that is directly connected to the Internet. Typical examples include your computer, and airport, coffee shop, and library wireless networks. Because they use public Internet Protocol (IP) addresses, devices on these networks are visible to other devices on the same network, and also on other networks.

This has advantages and disadvantages. The main advantage is that their "openness" allows data to be freely and easily shared between connected devices. This is the basis of the Internet. The disadvantage is that the lack of security makes it very easy for these networks to be hacked.

Private

Private networks tend to be smaller and much more exclusive. Examples are home networks and corporate intranets. Because members of these types of network are usually known to each other, and often are not connected to the Internet, security is much less of an issue.

The most common use of private networks is in the home since most Internet Service Providers (ISPs) only allocate a single IP address to each residential customer. In homes that need to have several computers connected to the Internet, the answer is to network them so they can all share a single internet connection.

1 Public network

2 Private network

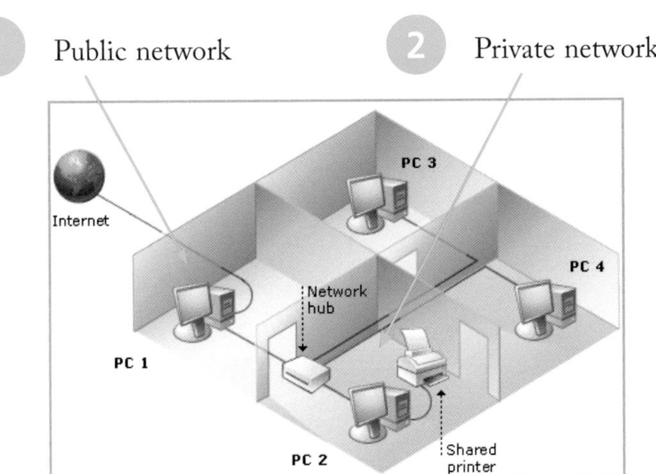

Create HomeGroup

1. Go to the Control Panel, Network and Internet. Then click Homegroup

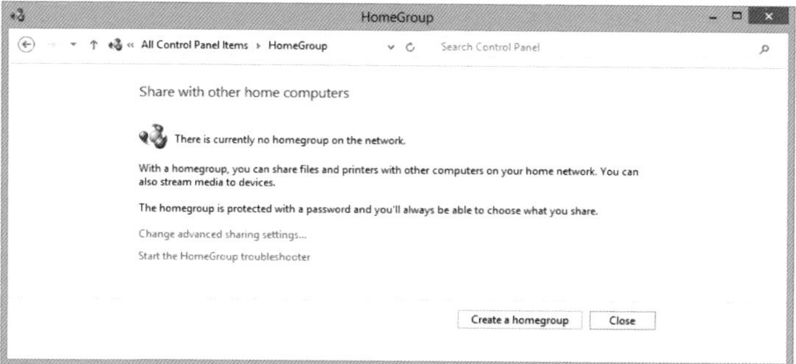

2. Click Create a homegroup and in the next window click Next. You'll then see the window below from where you can choose what to share on the network

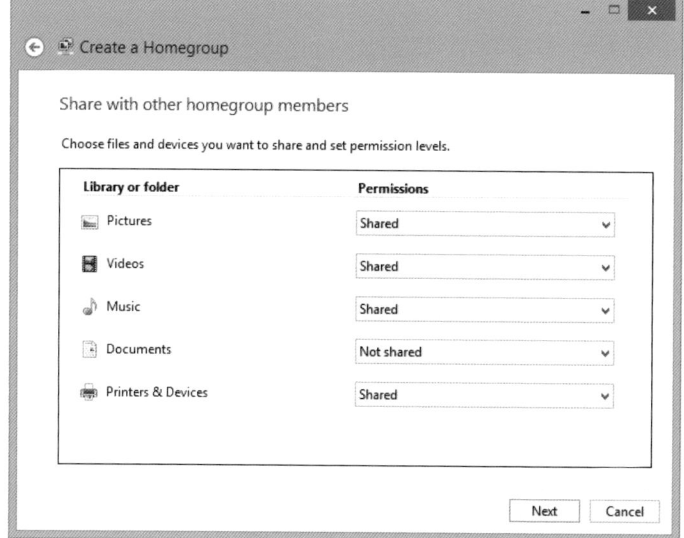

3. You will now see a screen that provides the password needed for other computers to join the HomeGroup

4. Record the password and click Finish. A HomeGroup has been created

Don't forget

When there is already a HomeGroup on the network, you will be invited to participate.

Hot tip

You can view or change the password from the Network and Sharing Center or from the Control Panel.

Join the HomeGroup

When you connect to a Home network which already has a HomeGroup, you are invited to join.

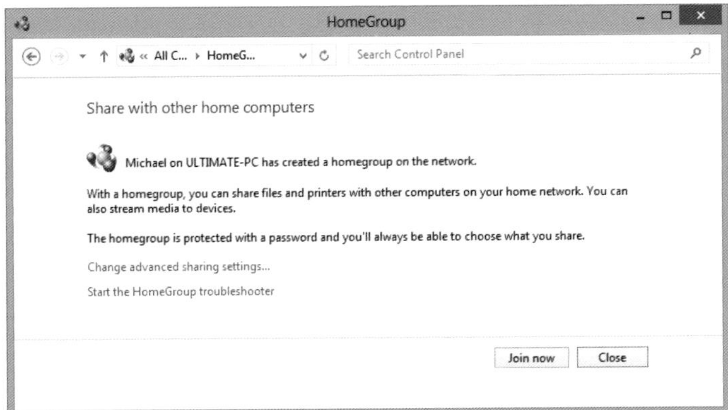

1. Click Join now
2. Select what you want to share and click Next
3. Type the password and click Next

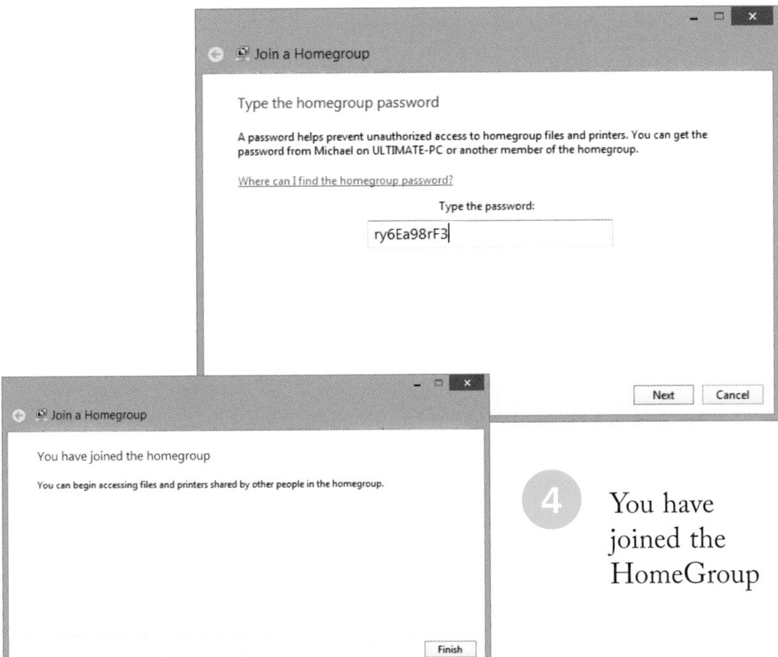

4. You have joined the HomeGroup

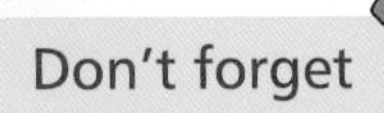

You will only be invited to join the HomeGroup if you specify your network location as Home when you connect to the network.

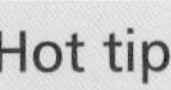

If the HomeGroup was created by another user on the network, you must be given the password to be able to participate.

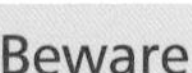

Everyone on the network who joins the HomeGroup will be able to share everything that you make available.

Network settings

Settings related to networking can also be found in the new Windows 8 interface.

1. Open the Charms bar and click Settings

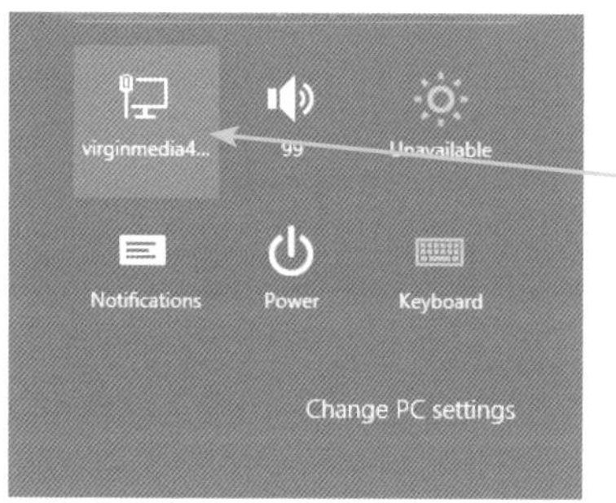

2. Click the Network icon

Network setting options are available in both Windows interfaces.

3. Details of all your connections are shown. In the example on the right, there is the main internet connection plus a number of WiFi connections

4. Left-click on an entry for connection options

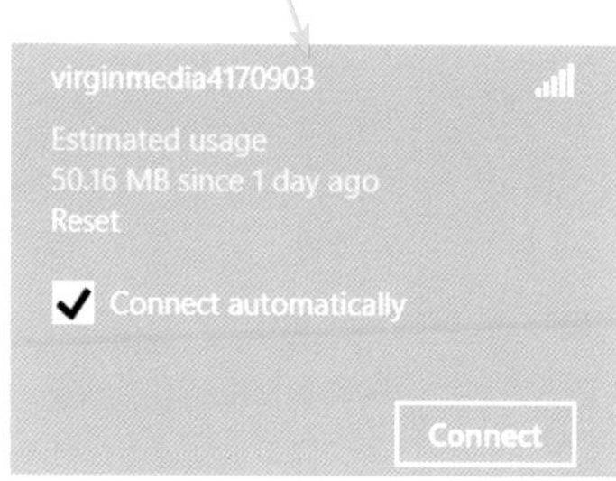

5. Right-click on an entry for other options

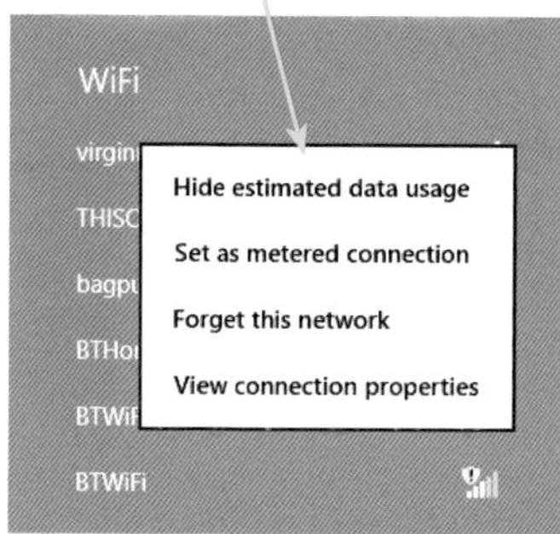

Connect to wireless network

Don't forget

If you have a netbook or laptop PC, and your router supports wireless access, you can connect to a wireless network.

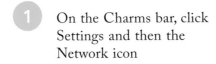

1. On the Charms bar, click Settings and then the Network icon

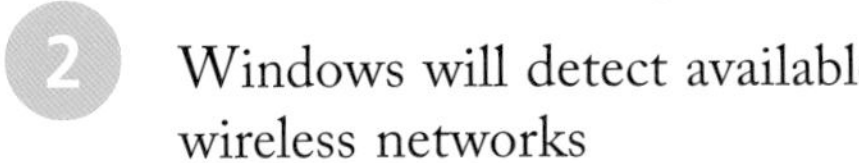

2. Windows will detect available wireless networks

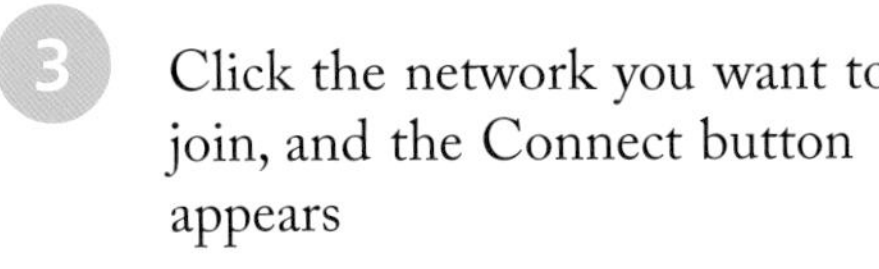

3. Click the network you want to join, and the Connect button appears

4. Check the Connect automatically box – this connects the PC whenever the network is in range

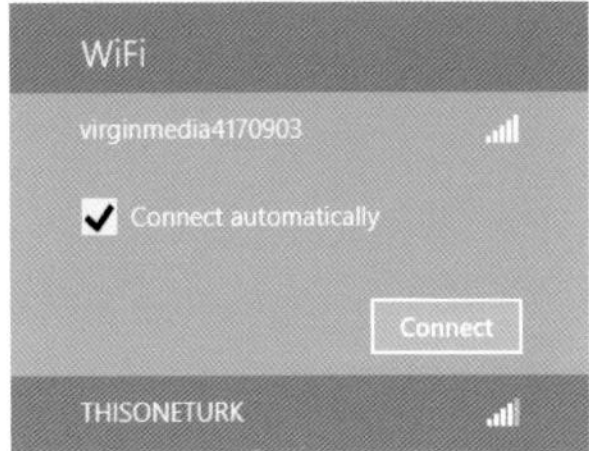

5. You are prompted for the security key. Click Next to continue

6. Windows connects to the network and validates the security key

7. The computer is shown as connected to the network

8. Internet access will be indicated if it is available on the network

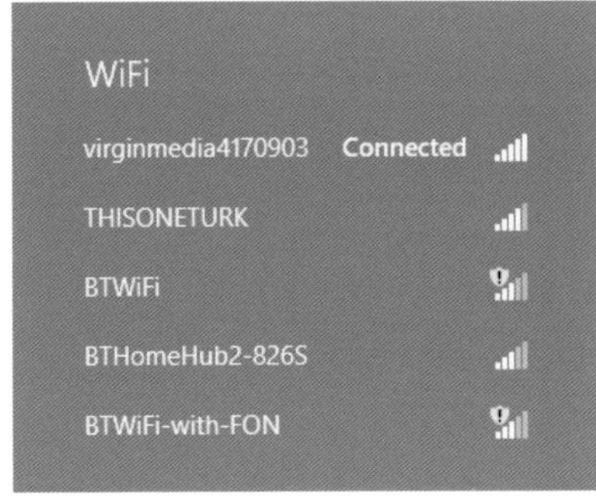

9. Go to the Control Panel, Network and Internet. Click Network and Sharing Center

10. Network information for the PC's networks is displayed

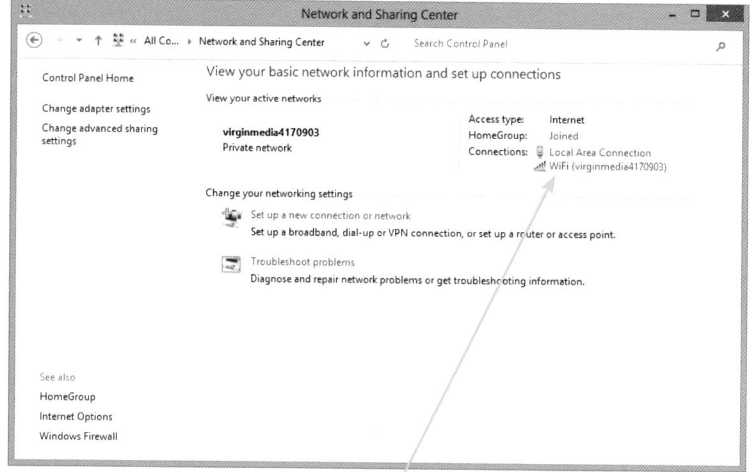

11. Click the WiFi connection to display the status of the wireless network

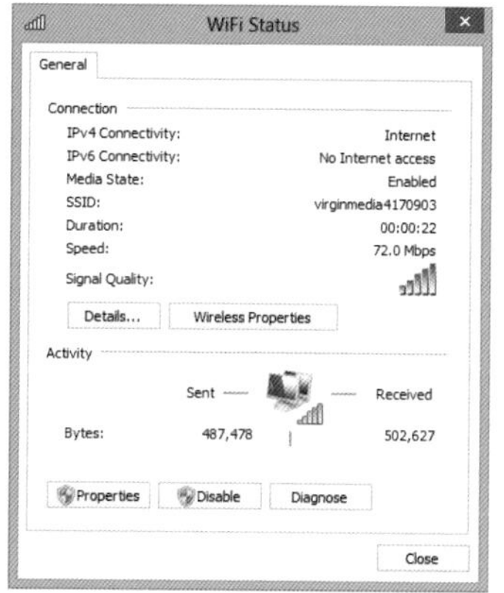

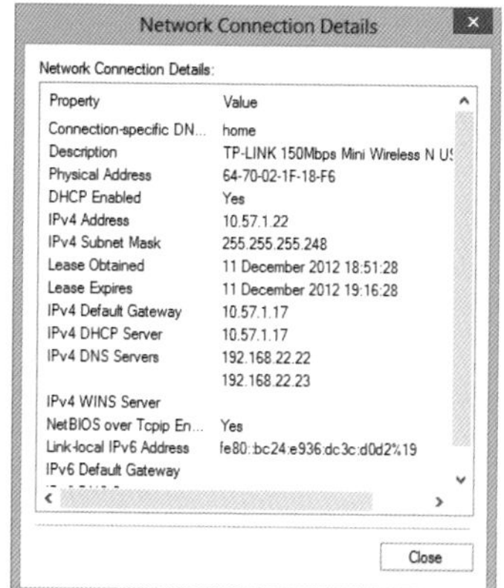

12. Click the Details button for the wireless network connection details

13. Click Close then Close again to return to the Center

In the example on the left, the wireless network shares the same router gateway address for internet access as the wired network.

View network devices

Many networks contain a lot of devices and keeping track of them all can be somewhat tricky. To assist with this, Windows provides a location that lets you view all the devices on your network.

Hot tip

The Network dialog box can also be opened by searching for "View network computers and devices" with the Search charm. It will be available under Settings.

1. Open any File Explorer window and select Network at the bottom of the Navigation pane

2. The Network dialog box opens

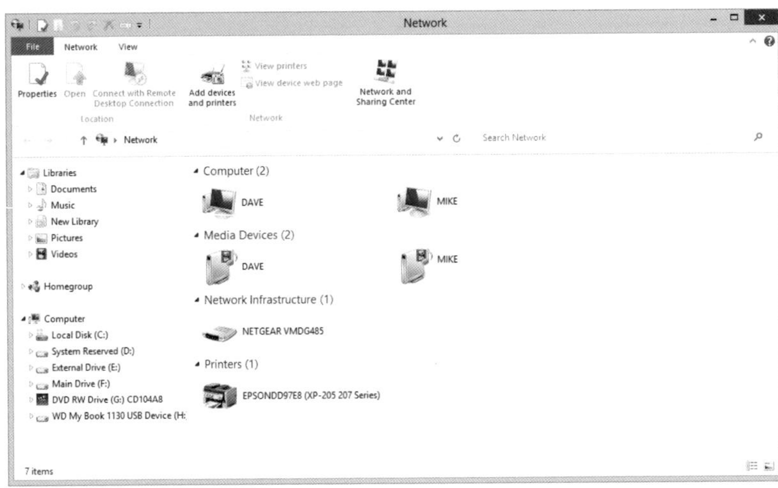

Here, you will see all the devices in your network. In the very basic network shown above, at the top are the networked computers – Dave and Mike. Click on either of these and you see all the files on the respective PCs that have been designated for sharing.

Don't forget

If you need to know exactly what devices are on your network, Network is the place to find out.

Below are media devices, a Netgear wireless router and an Epson multi-function printer.

Right-clicking on the various devices reveals related options. For example, right-clicking on a computer provides an option to pin it to the Start screen for quick access. Right-clicking on the router reveals options to disable network connectivity and also to open the device's configuration web page.

At the very top, you can open the ribbon toolbar. This provides further network-related options.

View HomeGroup

Another way of seeing what PCs are being shared on the network is by viewing the networked computers in HomeGroup.

1. Open any File Explorer window and select HomeGroup on the Navigation pane

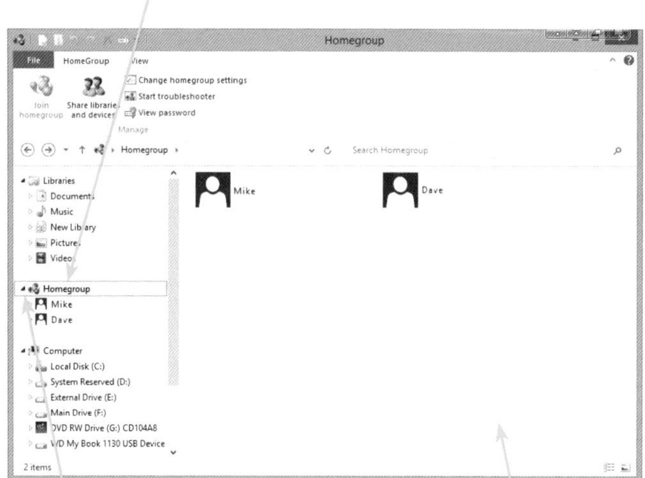

2. Click the arrow before HomeGroup to reveal the PCs in the network

3. Click HomeGroup to show the networked PCs in a new window

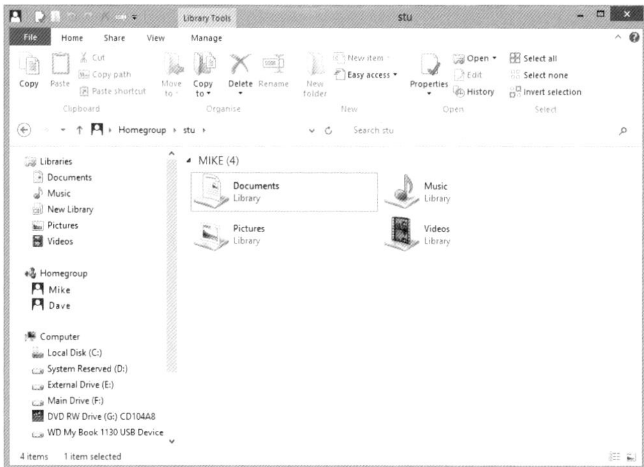

4. Click on a networked computer to browse its content

By clicking the arrows in the Navigation pane, you can access the contents of a networked PC without leaving the current folder.

Network and Sharing Center

Hot tip

Select the Network location, in this case Home network, if you need to switch to an alternative network location.

1. Right-click the Network icon in the Notification area and click Open Network and Sharing Center

Troubleshoot problems
Open Network and Sharing Center

2. Your basic network information is displayed

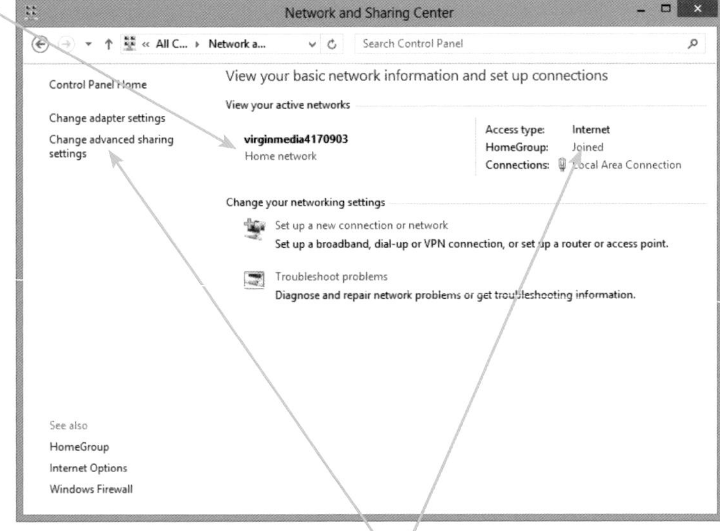

3. Click the HomeGroup status, or select the link to Change advanced sharing settings

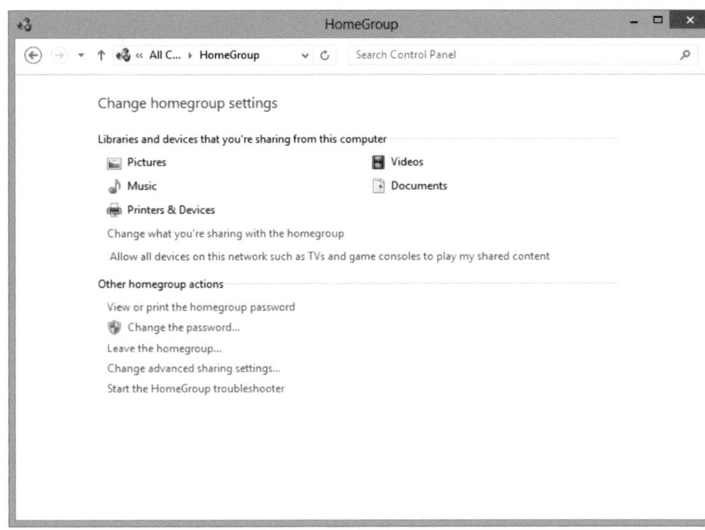

Select View or print the HomeGroup password, if you need a reminder or if you want to share it with another user on the network.

1. For detailed information, click Local Area Connection

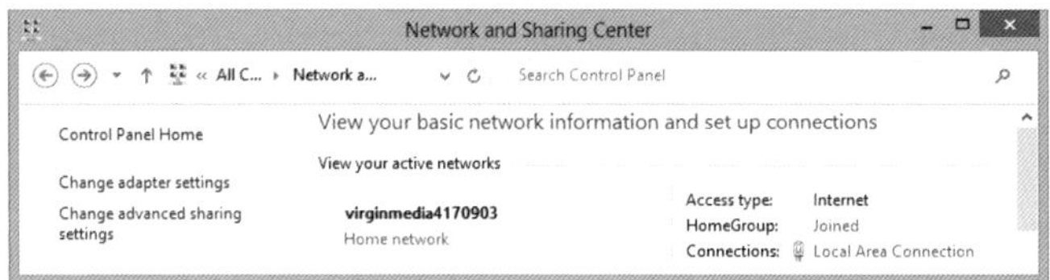

2. The connection status is displayed. Click the Details button for network connection details, including addresses

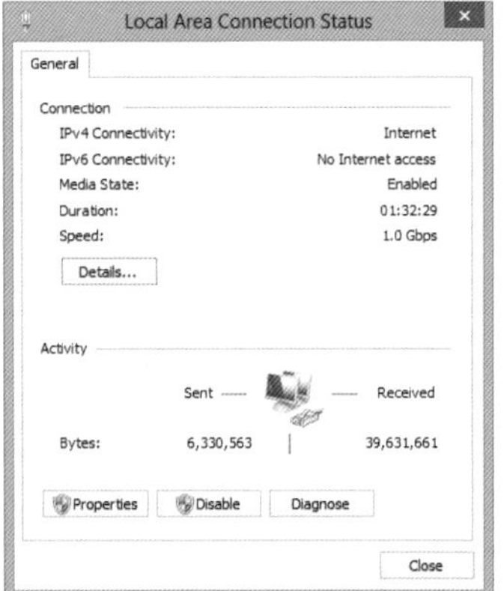

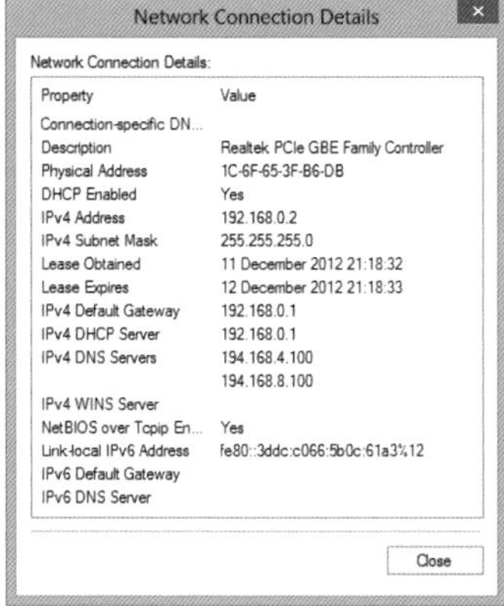

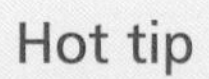

Hot tip

The Status panel shows the adapter speed and the amount of data transfer activity. The Details panel shows the addresses for the adapter and router components.

3. Click Close then Close again to return to the Center

4. Click Change adapter settings, on the left hand menu to view the adapter status and make changes to the settings

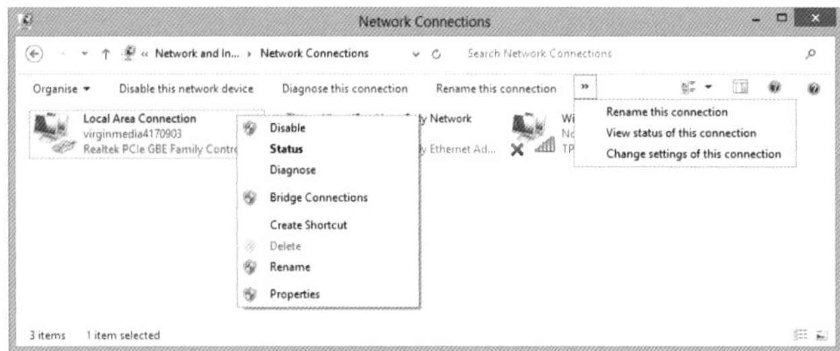

Don't forget

You can also view the local area connection properties from the Status panel.

5. Click the toolbar buttons, or right-click the adapter icon to select one of the options or to view the properties

PC settings

HomeGroup and network sharing options are also available from the new Windows 8 interface.

Hot tip

Windows 8 HomeGroup PC Settings do not provide as many configuration options as the Network and Sharing Center in the Desktop interface.

1. Open the Charms bar and select Settings, Change PC Settings. Click HomeGroup. If you are already a member of a HomeGroup, you will see the following:

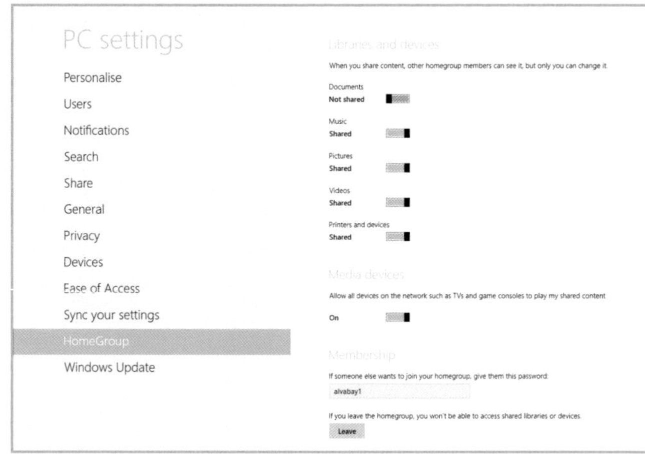

2. Sharing can be turned on and off for Documents, Music, Pictures, Videos, and Printers and Devices. To do this, just click in the boxes. In the same way, you can allow or disallow media devices on the network from playing shared content

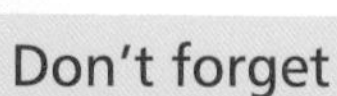

If you are not part of a HomeGroup, you will not see any of these options.

3. Under Membership you'll see the password for the HomeGroup. If someone wants to join the network they will need this

4. The final option allows you to leave the HomeGroup

5. If you are not a member of a HomeGroup and one is available, you will be invited to join

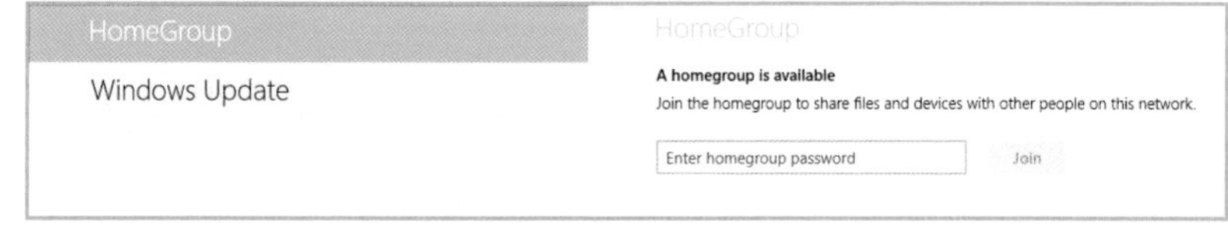

Monitor network

Windows provides several tools to monitor the activities on your network.

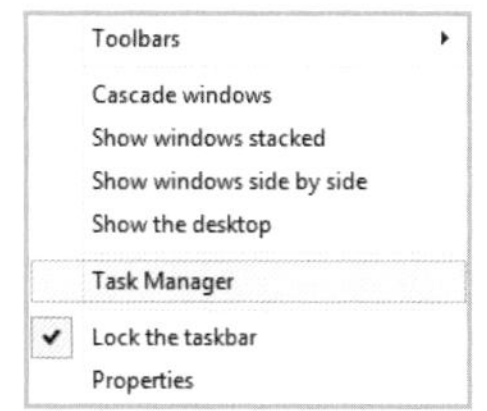

1. Right-click on the taskbar and select Task Manager

2. Select the Performance tab to see activity charts for the network adapter or adapters (wireless and wired)

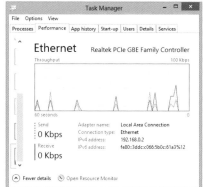

3. At the bottom of the window click Open Resource Monitor

4. Comprehensive tables and charts are displayed, giving a real-time view of all of the networking activity

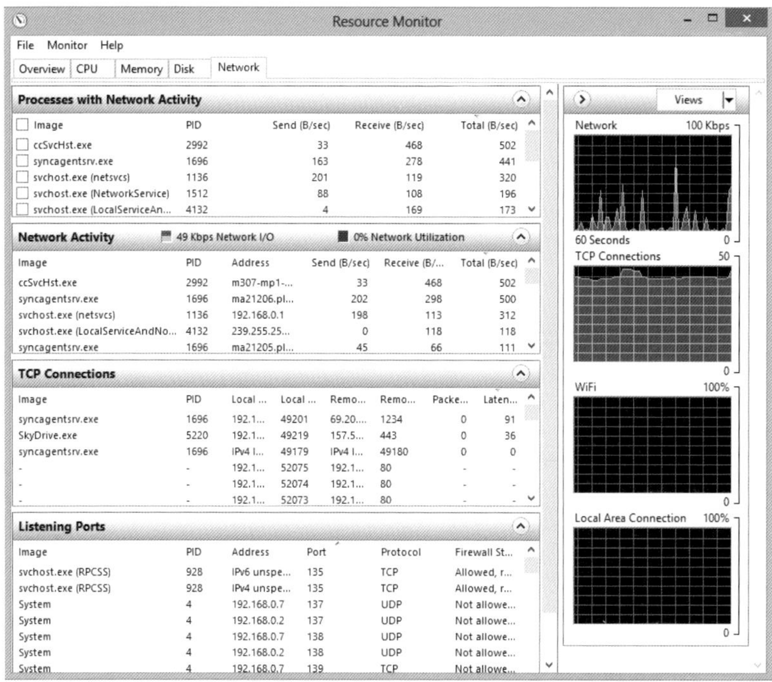

Don't forget

Network monitors can help you identify the causes of unexpected or excessive network activity on your system.

Sharing folders

Don't forget

The HomeGroup makes it easy to share libraries and printers with other computers on the network, but there are some situations it doesn't cover.

Hot tip

You can type a user name that you know is defined on the computer, or click the down-arrow and select from the list.

If you want to share a file or folder that is not in a library, or if you want to share with computers running other operating systems, you need the file sharing wizard.

1. Open File Explorer and locate the required file/folder

2. On the ribbon toolbar, click the Share tab and select the appropriate share option

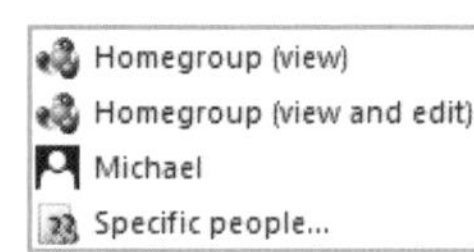

3. Type a user name and click Add to include that user

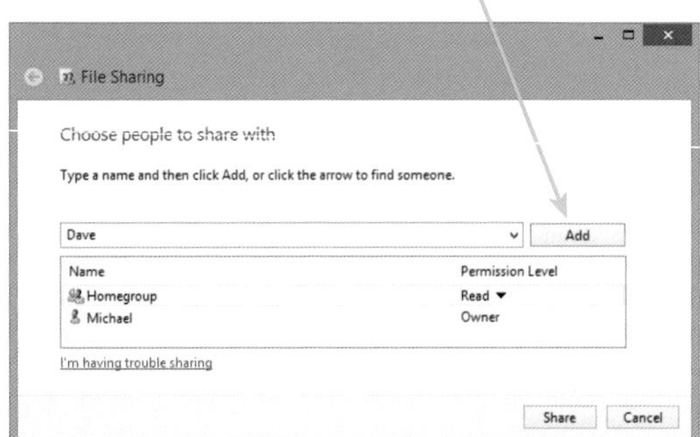

4. Click the user names to change the permission from the default Read to Read/Write (or Remove)

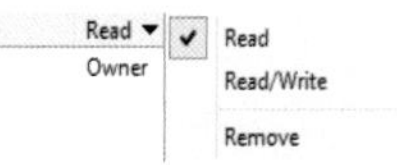

5. Click the Share button to assign the folder permissions granted

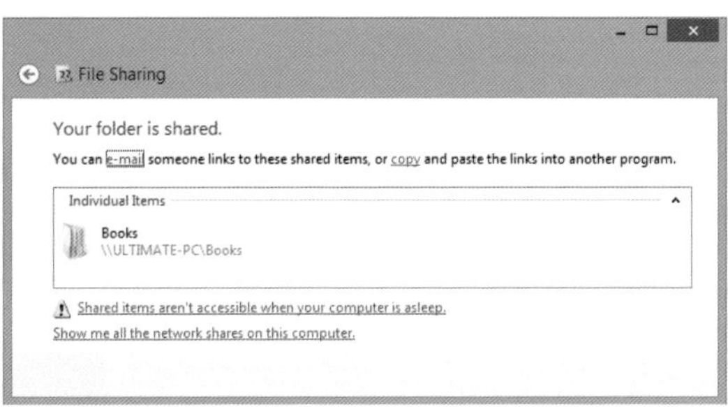

The folder is shared, and you are given the options to email the links for the shared item, or to copy the link into a program.

19 Control Panel and Mobility Center

The Control Panel is a major component in Windows and most aspects of the computer can be administered from it. This chapter explains how to find your way around in it. We look at user accounts and how they can be used for a number of purposes. The Mobility Center is useful for portable computer owners.

Start Control Panel

The Control Panel is a part of the Windows interface that enables users to view and adjust system settings and controls via applets. For example, adding and removing hardware and software, managing user accounts, and changing accessibility options.

You can open the Control Panel in two ways:

Many Control Panel applets can be accessed in other ways. For instance, Folder Options is available on the ribbon toolbar of any Explorer window.

1 While on the Desktop interface, hover the mouse over the bottom-left corner hotspot

When the Start screen icon appears, right-click on it and select Control Panel

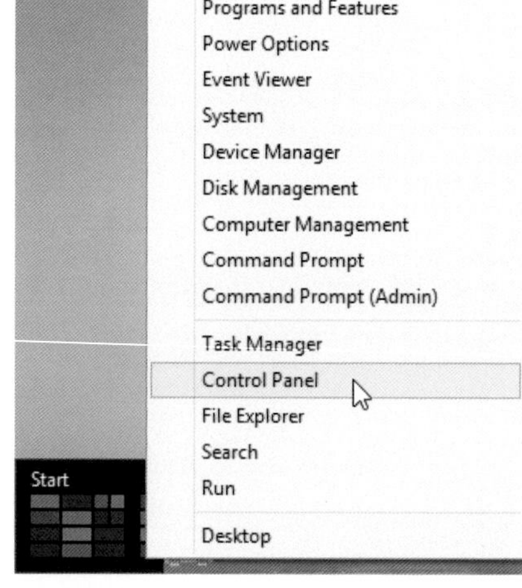

2 While on the Start screen, just type control panel

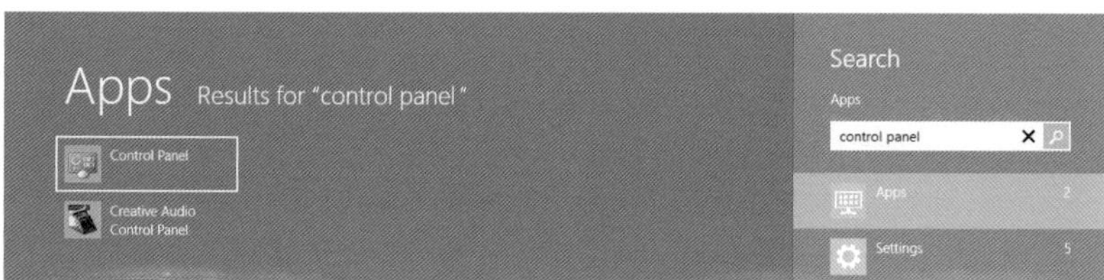

The Control Panel doesn't run in the new Windows 8 interface.

Press Enter and the Control Panel will open. If you are likely to access it frequently, you can pin it to both the taskbar and the Start screen. Just right-click on Control Panel and select the required option from the app bar.

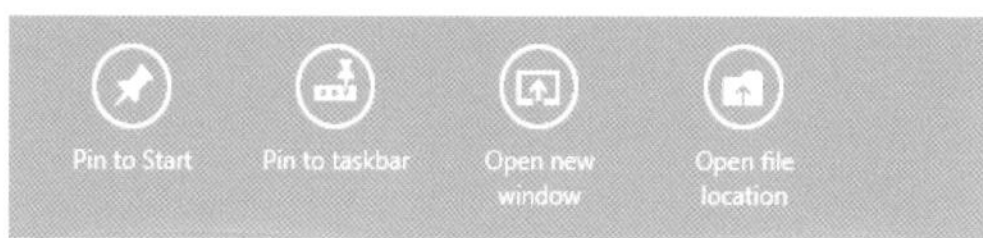

We recommend that all users take a look at the Control Panel – many useful options and features are available here.

View by categories

There are some 50 applets in the Control Panel so locating the one you want can take a while. For this reason, by default, the Control Panel opens in Category view as shown below:

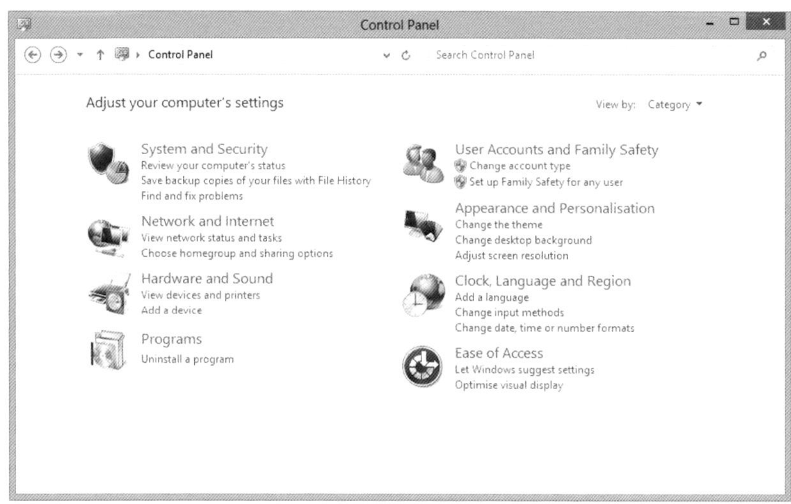

Hot tip

If you are interested in applets of a specific type, e.g. the Internet, the category view allows you to just see related applets.

In this view, there are eight categories:

- System & Security
- Network & Internet
- Hardware & Sound
- Programs
- User Accounts & Family Safety
- Appearance & Personalization
- Clock, Language & Region
- Ease of Access

Hover the mouse over the green category headings to open a pop-up that gives a brief description of what the applets do. If you click on the headings, you will see a complete list of the applets within the category. Below the category headings are blue links that lead to the more important applets in the category.

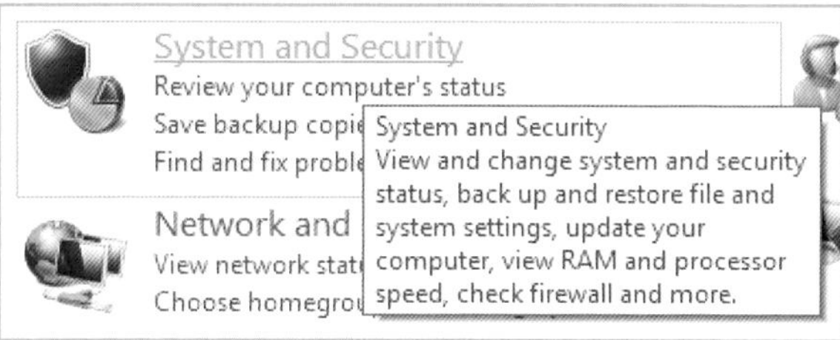

View by icons

If you want to view all the Control Panel's applets in the same window, you need to switch to an icon view. To do this click the Category link at the top-right of the window. You are given two options: large icons and small icons.

Hot tip

Right-clicking on a Control Panel applet provides options to pin the applet to the Start screen, and also to create a Desktop shortcut.

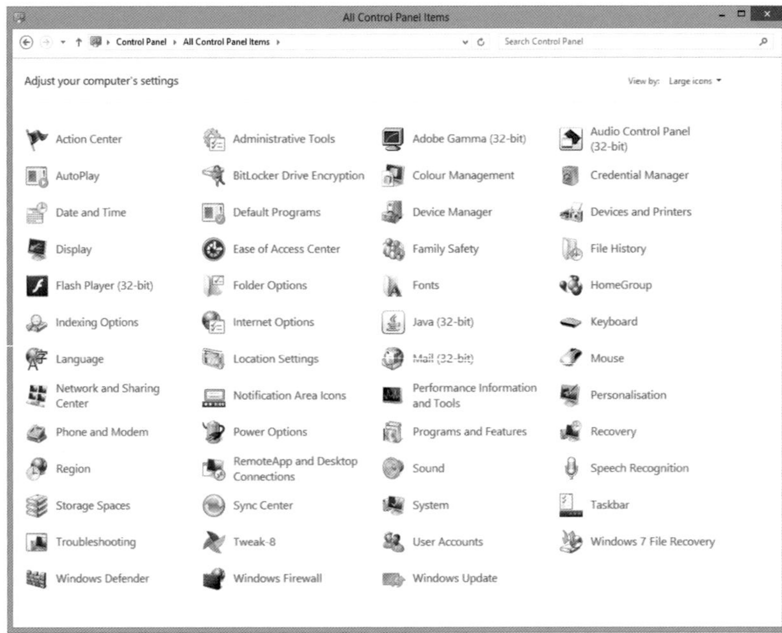

Hot tip

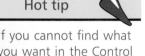

If you cannot find what you want in the Control Panel, try doing a search from the search box at the top-right of the window.

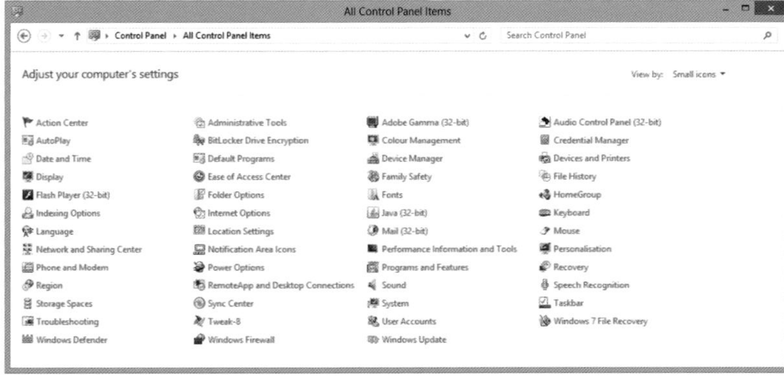

In either view, hovering the mouse over an applet opens a pop-up window that provides a brief description of what the applet does.

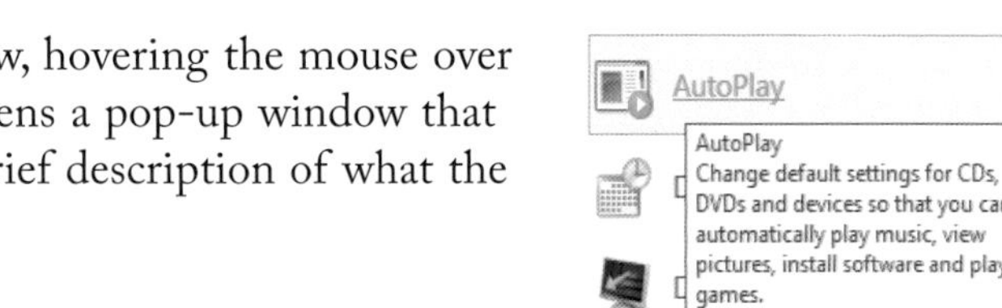

User accounts and Family Safety

Windows allows the setting up of any number of user accounts, each of which can be individually configured in many ways. For example, users can personalize their computing environment with different wallpaper and colors, they can install software that's only accessible from their account, and even hardware.

The ability to do this is particularly useful in a home environment where several family members all use the PC. By giving each their own account, which they can customize to suit their specific requirements and tastes, a single PC can be used sensibly and without conflict.

It can also be useful in a single-user environment by enabling a user to create accounts for specific purposes. For example, one account can be set up for photo-editing with shortcuts to all the relevant programs placed on the Desktop or Start screen. Another account can be set up as a home office, etc.

Another useful application of user accounts is to password-protect the main account and then create standard accounts for the kids. They can use the PC but won't be able to compromise its security or performance due to the limitations placed on standard accounts.

The Internet is a minefield that can expose gullible and trusting kids to many different types of threat. All responsible parents will want to minimize, if not eliminate completely, the risks their children are exposed to. User accounts play a big role here. By creating a separate account for each child and setting up software to monitor and restrict their activities while using their accounts, an element of protective control can be introduced.

There are many commercially available programs available for this purpose, such as Net Nanny, CyberPatrol, etc. The best of these applications enable parents to control and monitor literally every aspect of what the typical child might want to do on a computer and the Internet.

Before you try any of these though, take a look at the Family Safety utility provided by Windows 8 – see page 327.

Hot tip

When two or more accounts are created, one of them must be an Administrator account. The person running this account will be able to set restrictions on what other account holders can and cannot do.

Change account type

When Windows 8 is installed on a computer, an administrator account is created by default. However, the user has the option of creating and using a standard account instead. Lets take a look at both types and see what the pros and cons are:

Hot tip

A Windows 8 computer must have at least one administrator account.

Administrator

The administrator account has complete access to the computer and can make any desired changes.

Most people use it for two reasons:

- It's already there
- It allows them to do whatever they want on the computer

Note that any program that is run on an administrator account also has complete access to the computer. This is how malware, viruses and rootkits get on to a user's system. It is also possible for the user to cause unintentional damage to their system due to having access to system tools like the Windows Registry and the System Configuration utility.

Standard Accounts

Standard accounts are much safer as they do not allow users to make unauthorized changes that affect the system. If a standard account user tries to install a program for example, they will get a User Account Control (UAC) prompt to provide an administrator password before being allowed to do so.

Don't forget

Doing your day-to-day computing with a standard account will help protect your PC from viruses and malware.

However, while they may not be able to install programs, make changes to global settings, etc, they will be able to do just about anything else. Therefore, on a day-to-day basis, using a standard account will present no problems to the average user.

The ideal setup then, is to create a standard account for daily use. This helps protect the user from viruses and malware as they are not allowed to run. Should the user need to make a change that requires administrator permission they don't even need to log out and then log back in as an administrator – they simply provide the administrator password in the UAC dialog box that appears.

It is also possible to run programs under the administrator account by right-clicking the file to be run and select Run as administrator from the context menu.

Before you can use a standard account, you need to create one. Do it as described below:

1 Go to the Charms bar, select Settings, Change PC Settings, and then click Users

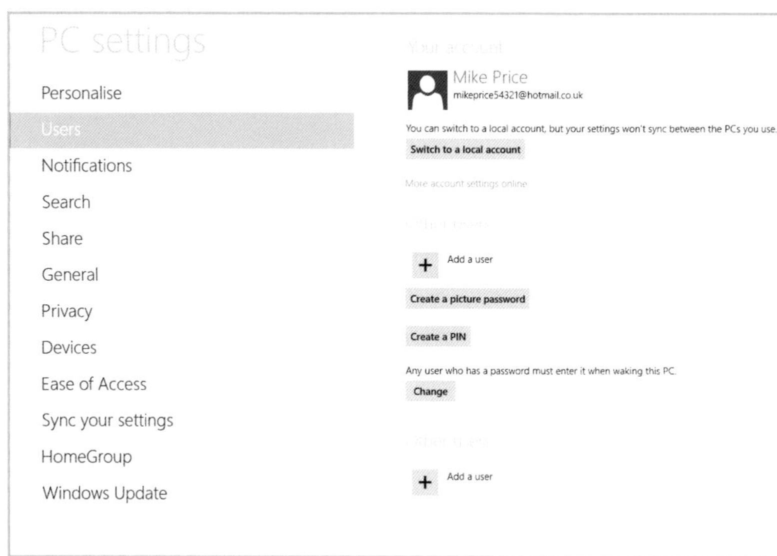

Hot tip

Accounts are created in the Windows 8 interface. Managing them is done in the Desktop interface.

2 Click Add a user. In the window that opens you can opt for the user to sign in with a Microsoft account or a local account. In this example, we are using a local account

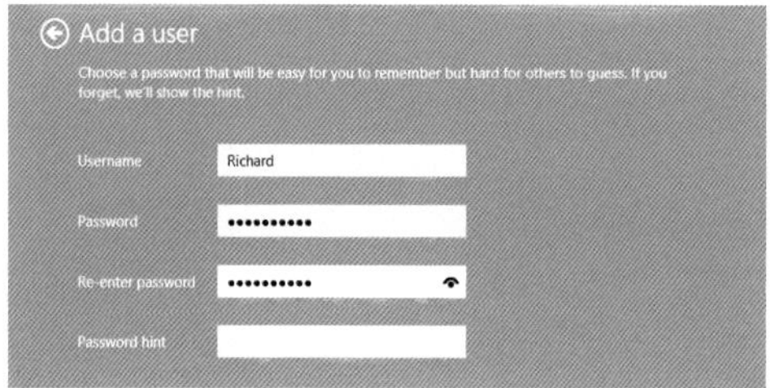

3 Enter the username and password (if required)

Hot tip

If you don't enter a password in Step 3, the PC will boot directly to the Start screen.

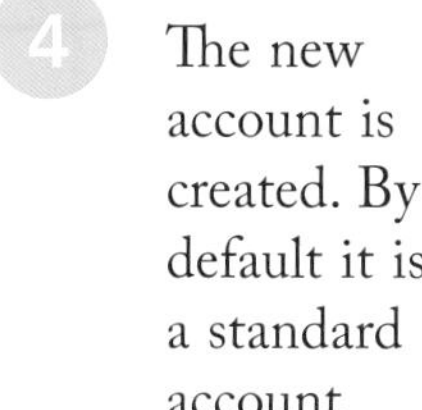

4 The new account is created. By default it is a standard account

Hot tip

By default, when an account is created it is a standard account.

...cont'd

You may, at some point, wish to change an administrator account to a standard account, or vice versa. This is done in the Desktop interface.

Standard account holders cannot make changes in User Accounts.

1. Go to the Control Panel, User Accounts and Family Safety. Click User Accounts, Manage another account

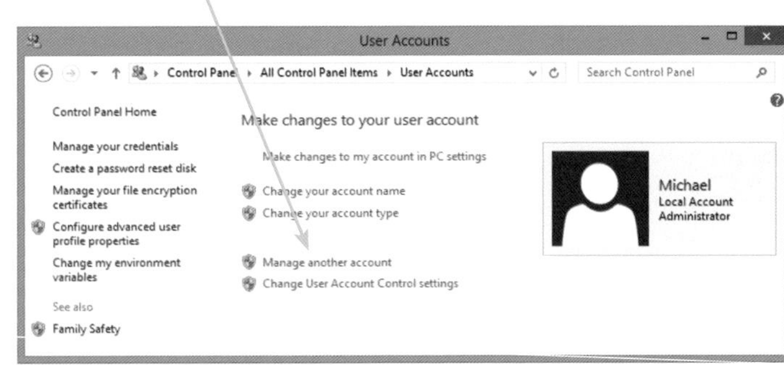

2. Select the account you want to change and then click Change the account type

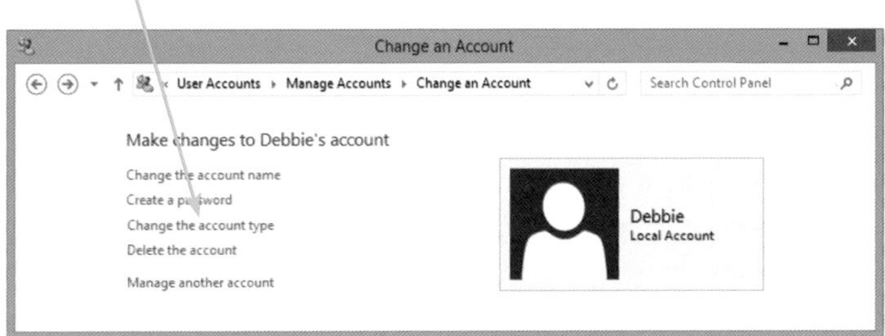

3. Select Administrator and click Change Account Type

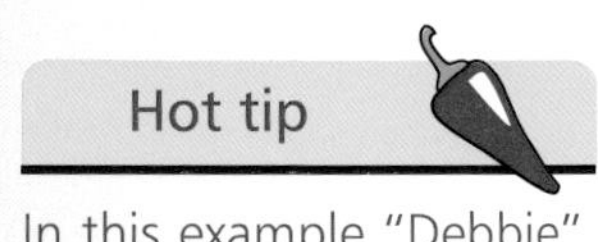

In this example "Debbie" is now an administrator.

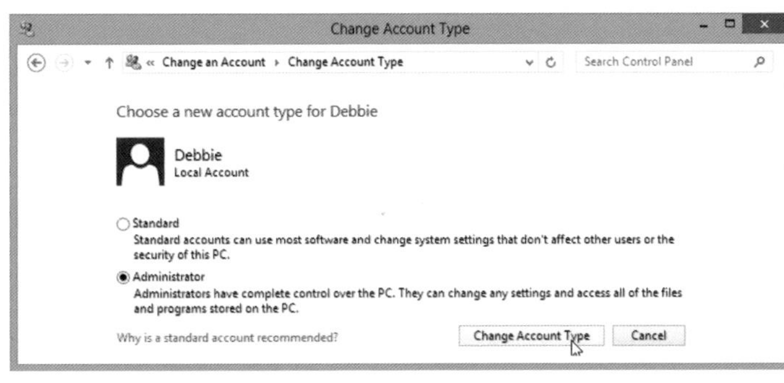

Set up Family Safety

We saw on page 323 that user accounts and child protection utilities go hand-in-hand. To see how they combine in order to monitor and restrict a child's computer activities, we will demonstrate how to set up the Family Safety utility provided by Windows 8.

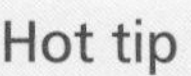

The Family Safety utility can only be used with standard accounts.

1. Create a standard user account for each child

2. In Control Panel, click Set up Family Safety for any user

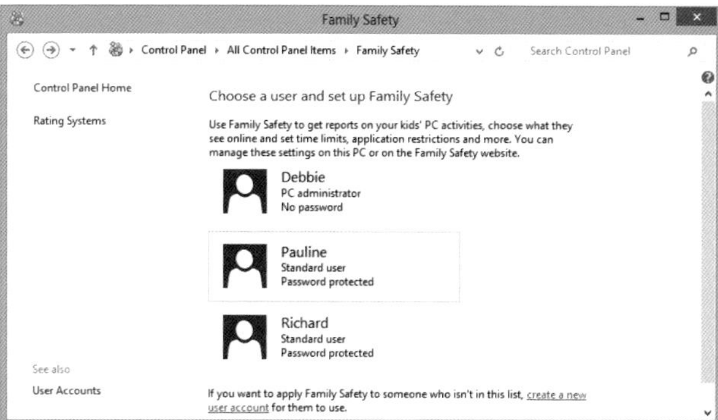

3. Click the account to be protected. This opens the User Settings screen where you can set parameters such as time limits, game ratings, program restrictions and PC usage

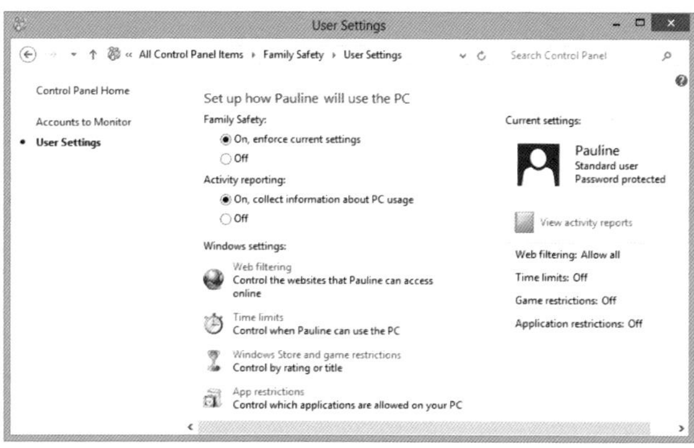

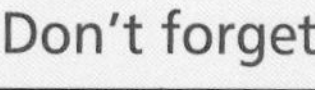

You can monitor and control your children's internet activities from the Family Safety website.

4. Log in to your account at **https://familysafety.microsoft.com** and you will be able to administer the Family Safety utility online – very handy when you are away from home

Add guest account

A third type of account available in Windows 8 is the Guest account. This is an account for users who don't have a permanent account on the PC. It allows them to use it but without having access to personal files, or being able to install software or hardware, change settings, create passwords, etc.

An example of when a guest account may be used is allowing a babysitter to use the computer while you are out for the evening.

Users of guest accounts are extremely restricted in terms of what they can do on the PC.

1. In Control Panel, click Change account type under User Accounts and Family Safety

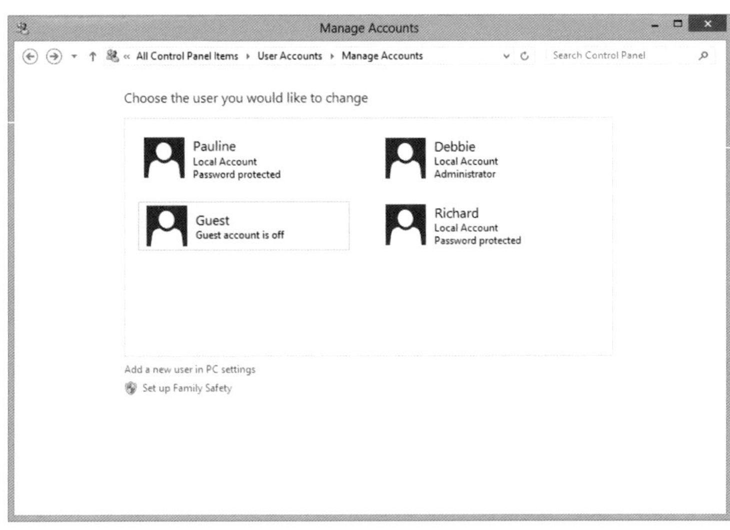

You don't need to create a guest account – one already exists. It just needs to be turned on.

2. You will see that a Guest account already exists but that is turned off. Click on it to open the settings screen

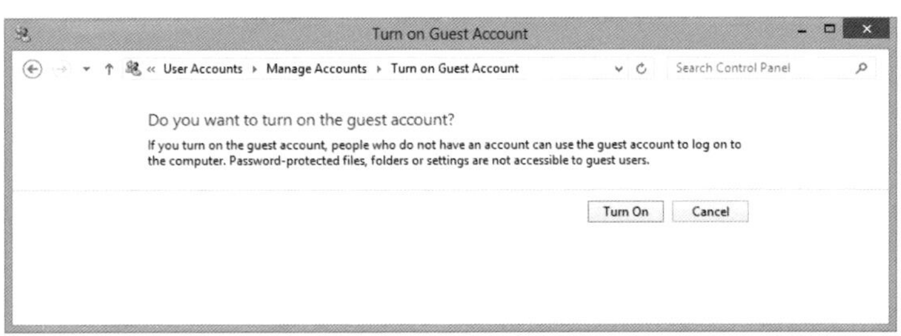

3. Click the Turn On button to activate the Guest account. It will now be available at the Windows log in screen

Ease of Access

Windows 8 provides a number of accessibility options designed to help users see, hear, and use their computers. These options are all available in the Ease of Access Center.

1. Go to the Control Panel, Ease of Access and click Ease of Access Center

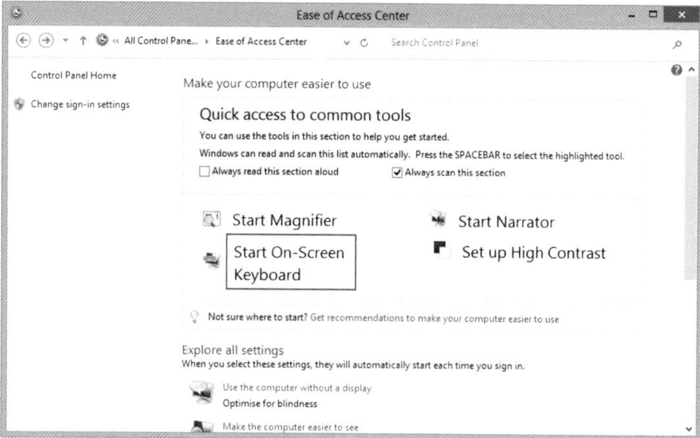

2. Click Get recommendations to make your computer easier to use

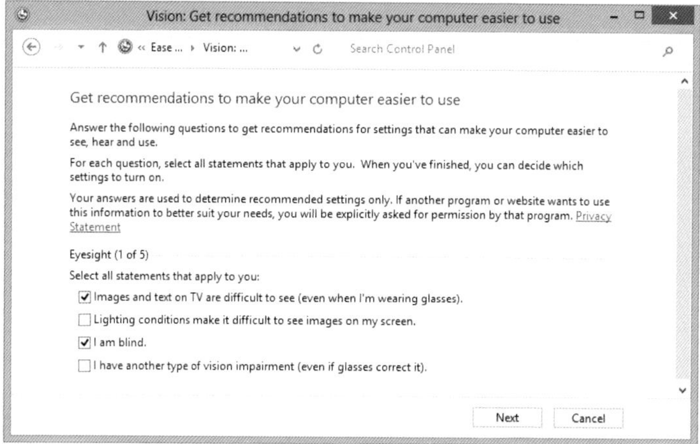

3. A wizard will open and it will walk you through five screens in which you are asked questions about your eyesight, dexterity, hearing, speech, and ability to reason

Hot tip

Ease of access tools are not just for those with disabilities. PC users with no impairments may find some of these tools useful in everyday computing.

Hot tip

Mouse keys are a particularly useful tool. They can also keep you going if your mouse stops working for some reason.

...cont'd

4. When the wizard is finished, click OK. You will then be presented with a list of settings that Windows thinks will help you to use the computer

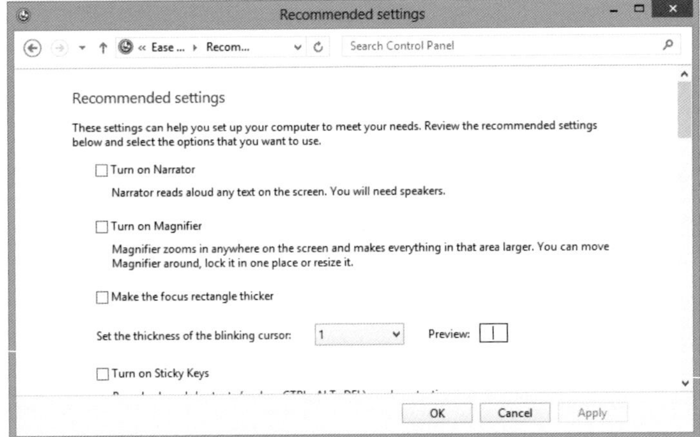

5. None of the suggestions are actually implemented – it's up to you to read the list and select the ones you want

6. If you don't need advice from Windows, just choose from the available options on the Home screen. These include using the PC with a display, without a keyboard or mouse, using text alternatives for sounds, and more

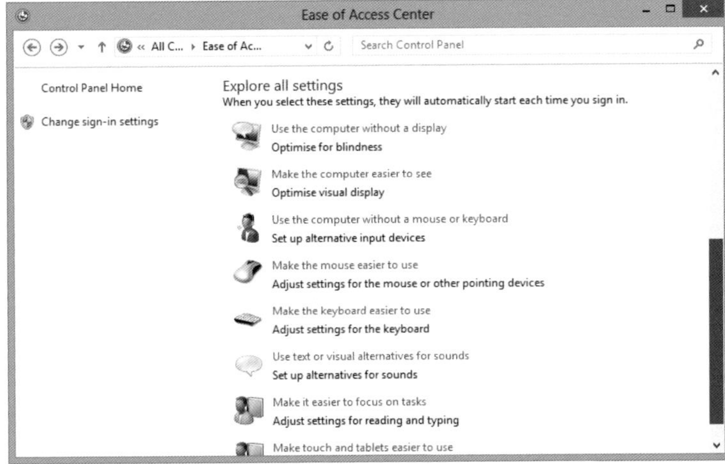

Hot tip

Another useful tool is Magnifier. This gives you an enlarged view of specific elements on the screen.

Start Mobility Center

You'll find Windows Mobility Center (WMC) on any portable computer, though not usually on a desktop or all-in-one computer. The utility is basically a control panel that provides all the Windows options specific to portable computers in one easily accessed location.

There are several ways to open Windows Mobility Center. These include:

1. Press Winkey + R to open the Run box. Type mblctr and press Enter

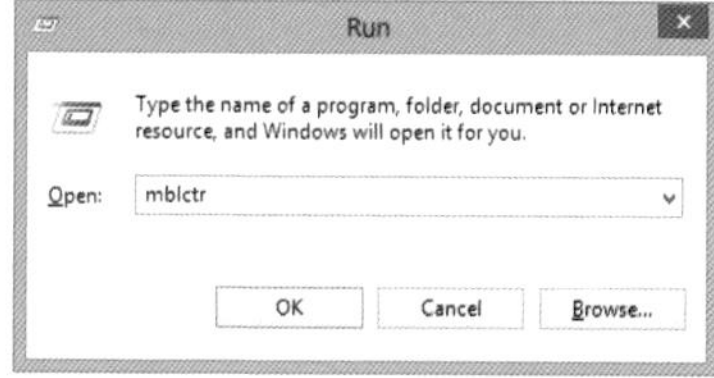

2. Go to the Control Panel > Hardware and Sound. Then click Windows Mobility Center

3. You get a link to Windows Mobility Center when you right-click the battery icon in the Notification area

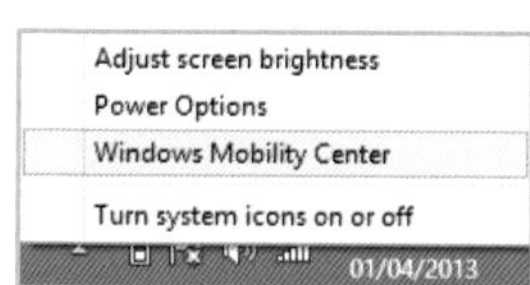

4. When the utility opens, you will see the following window

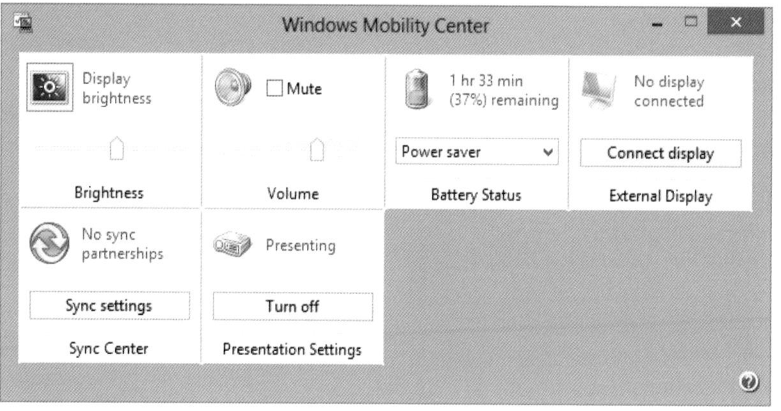

5. The options offered depend on the type of computer and the hardware it is using

If you are using a desktop PC, Windows Mobility Center will not be accessible.

The options in Windows Mobility Center may differ from PC to PC.

Screen management

Windows Mobility Center provides several options related to screen management.

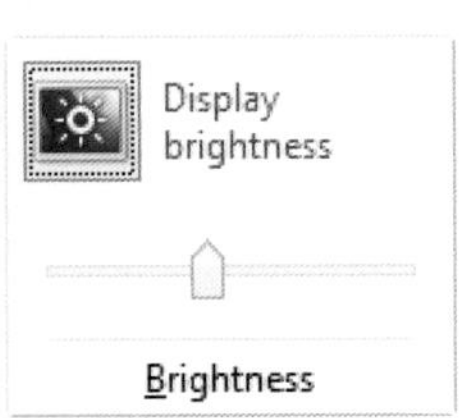

Brightness

The first is display brightness. This is an important setting with laptops as the higher it is set, the quicker the battery will run down. The Mobility Center provides a quickly accessible way of adjusting the setting. If you click on the icon, you will open the computer's Power Options utility from where you can make changes to various settings including the display brightness.

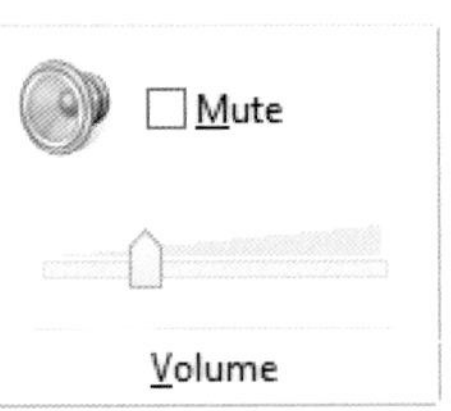

Volume

As with the brightness setting, the higher the PC's volume level, the greater the load on the battery. You can adjust it with the slider, check the Mute box, or click the icon to open the Sound utility for more options.

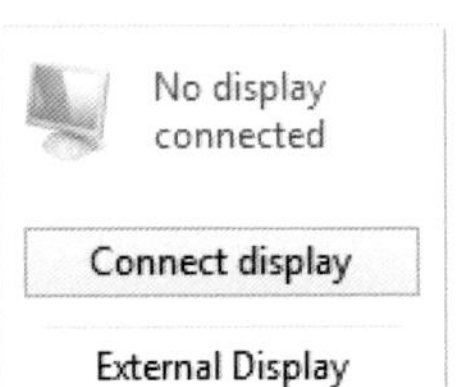

External Display

The External Display option allows you to connect your laptop to a different monitor, duplicate the display, or extend the display.

Click the icon and the Desktop Screen Resolution utility will open. If you click Connect display, you will open Second screen in the Windows 8 interface. Both offer the options mentioned above.

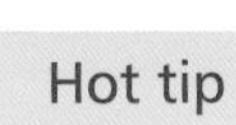

Hot tip

Many people connect their laptops to the main PC monitor to take advantage of the larger, and usually better, displays these offer.

Presentation Settings

Laptops are often used in business to give presentations. With this in mind, the Presentation Settings option makes it possible to pre-configure a laptop's settings in terms of volume, screen saver, and background so that they will not detract from the presentation. To do this, click the icon and make your adjustments as shown on the right. Click OK, and then click the Turn on button.

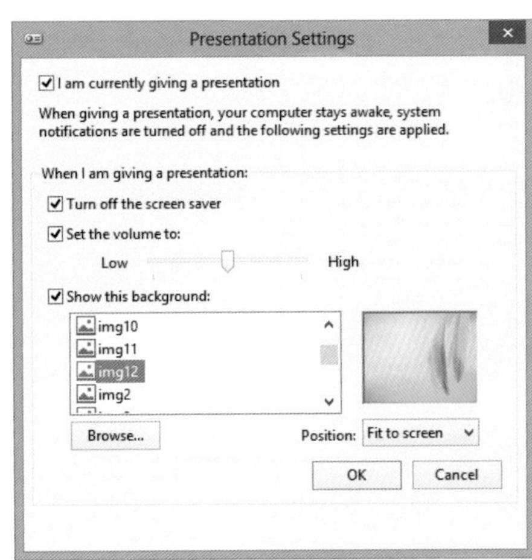

When the presentation is finished, you can revert to the normal settings by clicking the Turn off button.

Battery status

The main drawback with portable computers such as laptops is the constant need to conserve battery power. To this end, the Windows Mobility Center provides options that help to manage this aspect of portable computing.

All the settings described on page 332 affect to some degree the length of time the battery will last. Users looking to conserve battery power will benefit by lowering these settings as far as possible.

A related option provided by Windows Mobility Center is battery power monitoring, or status. This tells the user the percentage of power remaining in the battery and also how much longer it will last before requiring a recharge.

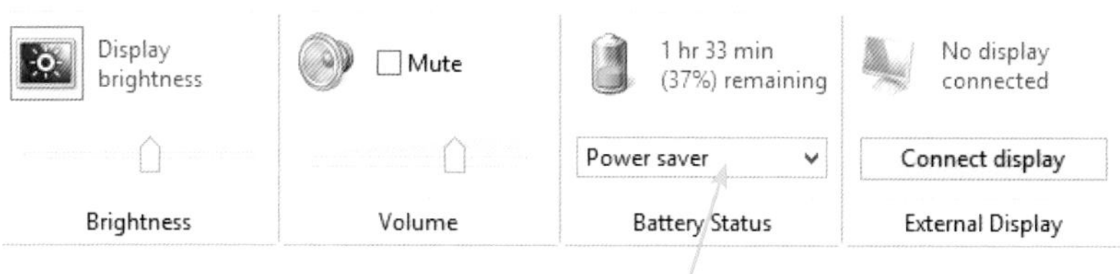

The drop-down box provides three basic options:

- **Power saver** – this option will extend battery life
- **High performance** – this option reduces battery life
- **Balanced** – this option is a compromise between performance and battery life

Clicking the battery icon opens the Power Options dialog box, which provides settings with which to fine-tune the Power saver, High performance and Balanced options.

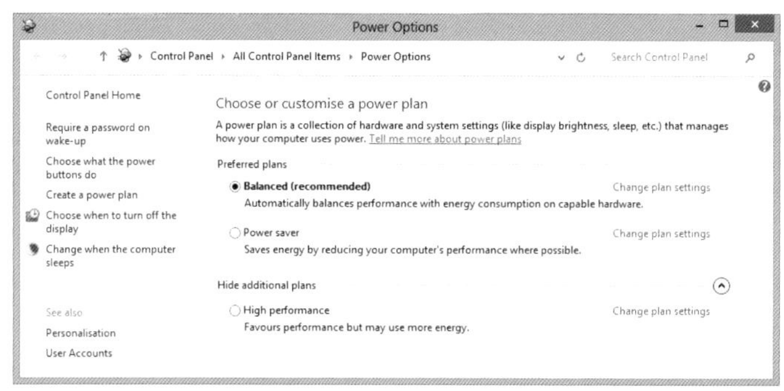

Hot tip

You can also see the battery status from the battery icon in the Notification area. If the battery is fully charged, the icon will look like this:

If it is running low, it will look like this:

Hover over the icon and you will see the percentage of power remaining and also how much longer the battery will last:

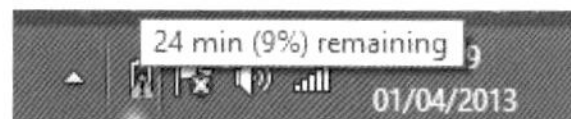

Power options

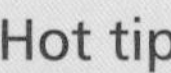

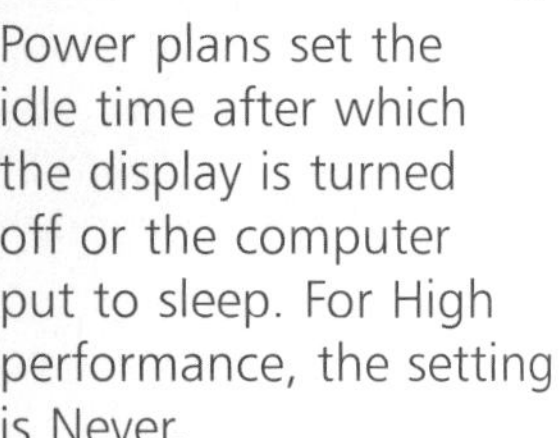

Hot tip

Power plans set the idle time after which the display is turned off or the computer put to sleep. For High performance, the setting is Never.

This feature is provided for all types of computer, though it takes on particular significance for battery powered PCs.

On a mains powered computer such as the HP TouchSmart 610:

1. Go to the Control Panel, Hardware and Sound. Then click Power Options

2. You can select one of the power plans offered, or create a power plan (based on an existing power plan)

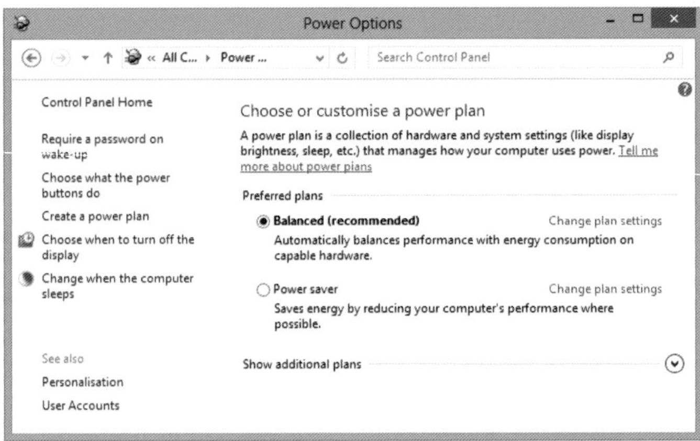

3. Select the action Choose what the power buttons do, to specify Do Nothing, Hibernate, Sleep or Shutdown when you press the power button on your computer

Hot tip

Not all computers support Hibernation, so this option does not always appear.

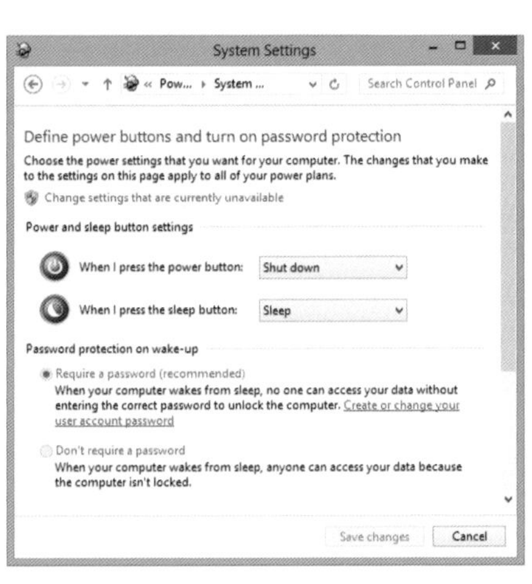

4. On some keyboards there is a Sleep button, for which you can specify Do Nothing, Hibernate or Sleep

20 Troubleshooting

When an error occurs on your PC, Windows attempts to identify the issue. It also provides a set of troubleshooters and a problem step recorder. Other facilities include allowing a friend to remotely connect to your computer. There is also support for improving program compatibility.

Windows error reporting

Don't forget

Windows identifies errors and problems and attempts to find solutions for you.

When an error occurs on your system, Windows collects debug information (a memory dump) and offers to send this over the Internet. If you agree, the data goes to a website where the developer of the problem product can review the data and hopefully develop solutions. If a solution already exists, it is sent back so that you can apply it to your system.

To see how Windows checks for problems and provides solutions:

1. Select the flag in the Notification area to click Open Action Center

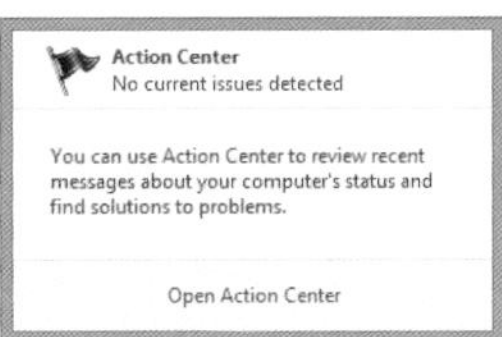

2. Here you can review messages and resolve problems

Hot tip

The Action Center also monitors security issues as well as the maintenance and troubleshooting issues discussed in this chapter.

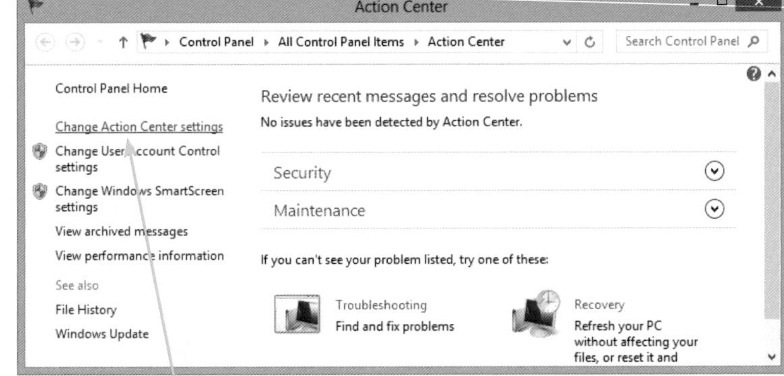

3. To see what areas are being checked for problems, select Change Action Center settings

4. To choose when to check for solutions to problems, click Problem reporting settings

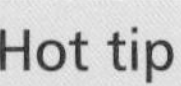

Hot tip

If you manage some tasks manually, Backup for example, you'd clear the associated box.

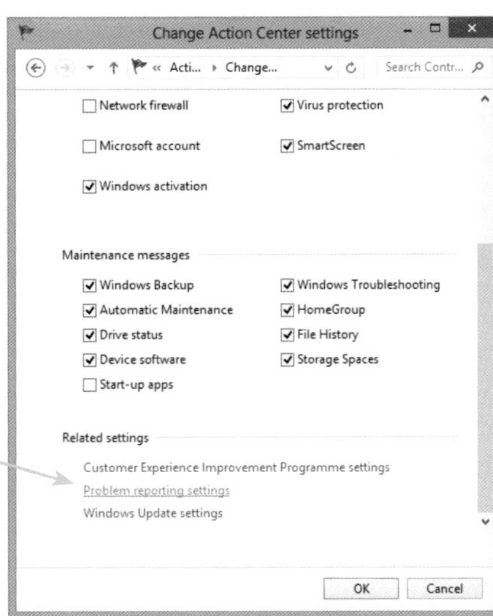

5. Automatically check for solutions is recommended, but you can turn off the check or ask to be prompted

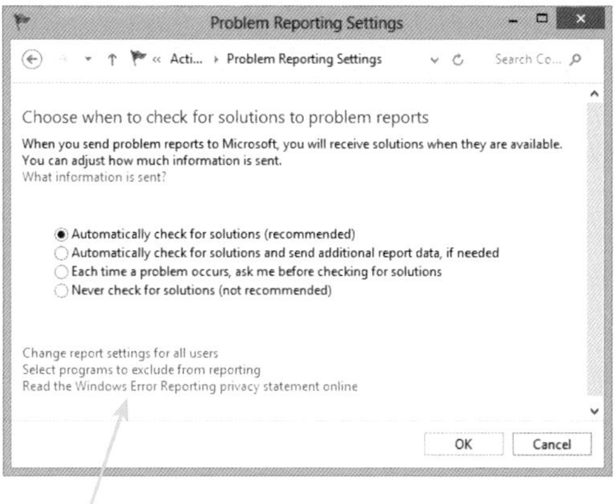

6. Specify programs that you want excluded from reporting, for example programs that deal with sensitive information

When there are messages waiting at the Action Center, the Flag icon notifies you.

Solve PC issues: 1 important message

1 important message

Network firewall (Important)

Open Action Center

1. Click the icon for more details and select Action Center to view the full message

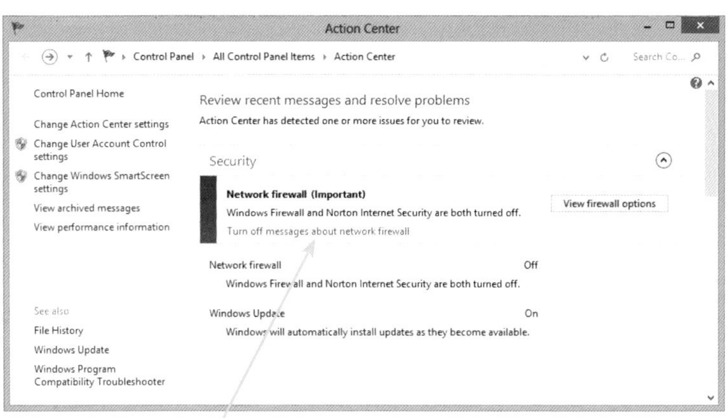

2. Select Turn off messages about Windows Firewall if, for example, you are already aware of the issue

Hot tip

If you are concerned about the information being sent, review the Windows Error Reporting privacy statement to see how the information you send is managed and protected.

Don't forget

Click Options for the actions. In this case, it suggests Turn on Windows Firewall.

Troubleshooting settings

Don't forget

Entries will only appear here when there are problems that Windows has identified and for which solutions are available.

1. Expand the Maintenance section, to review the status of the monitoring that is being applied

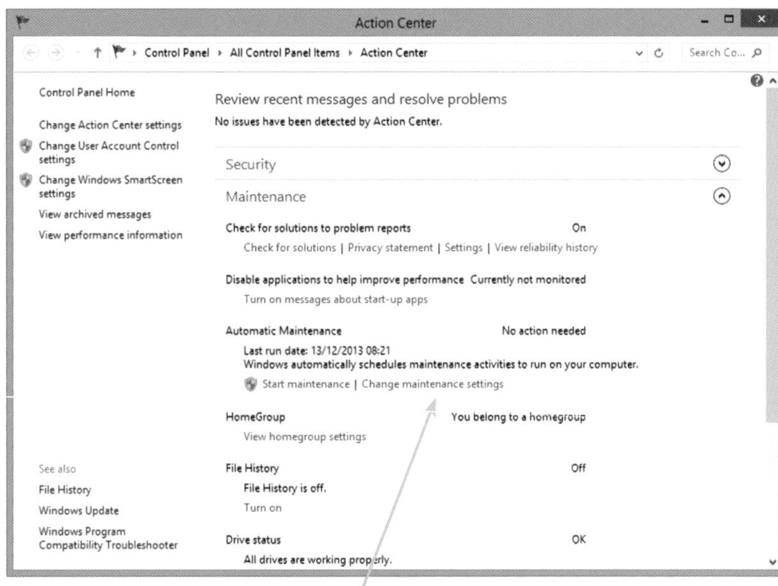

2. Click Change maintenance settings to specify the scope of problem analysis and maintenance allowed on your system

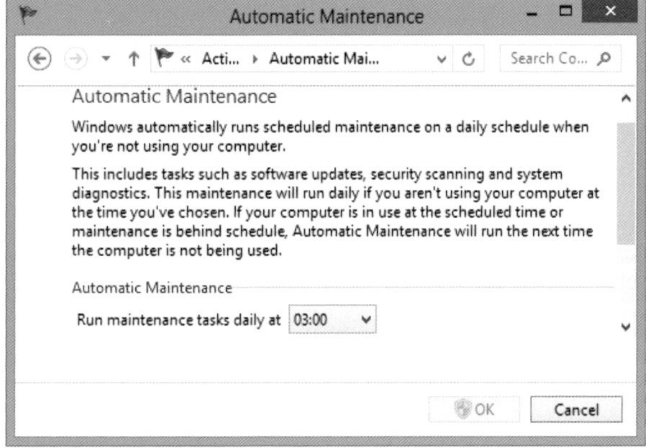

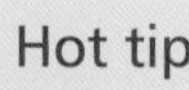

Hot tip

You may want to turn off these options for a system that is being operated by an inexperienced user, so they won't have to deal with troubleshooting responses.

3. By default, Windows will remind you when the System Maintenance troubleshooter can help fix problems, and will also allow users to browse for online troubleshooters

Windows troubleshooters

1. Open the Action Center and select Troubleshooting

2. This lists categories and the troubleshooters available within these to handle common computer problems

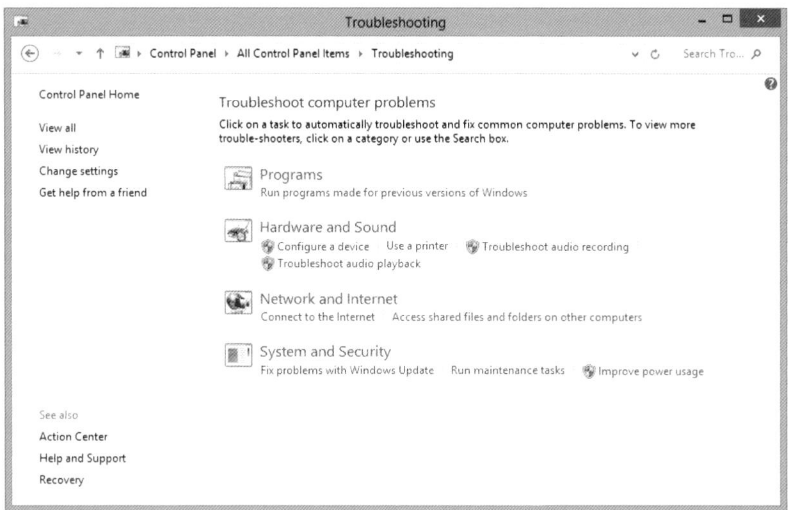

3. Select a task that appears to match the problem you have

4. If there's no suitable task, click the most appropriate category

5. Windows searches online to find any troubleshooting packs in that category

6. The troubleshooters are listed by their subcategories

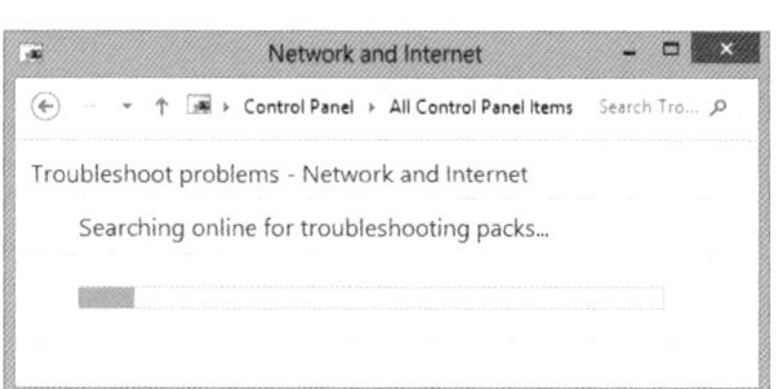

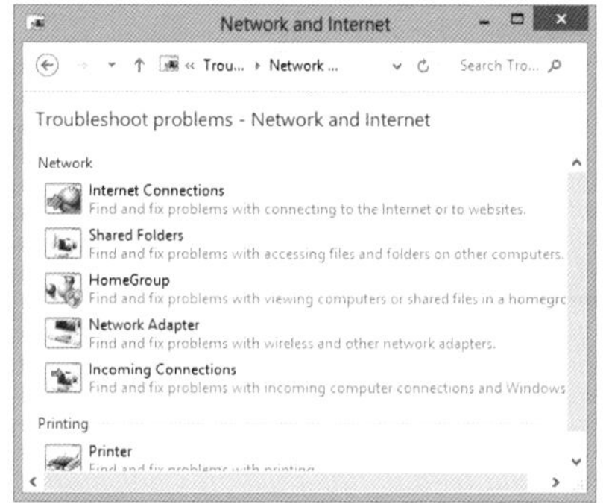

Don't forget

If you encounter a problem, and find no related messages in the Action Center, you can try the troubleshooters provided by Windows.

Hot tip

Depending on the category you select, you should find one or more troubleshooters online, ensuring that you have the latest support for the problem area.

Troubleshooter in action

1. To illustrate, select Connect to the Internet, in the Network and Internet category

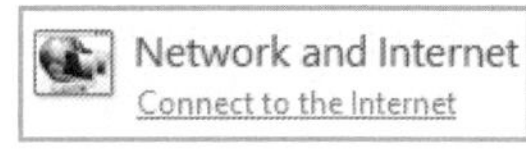

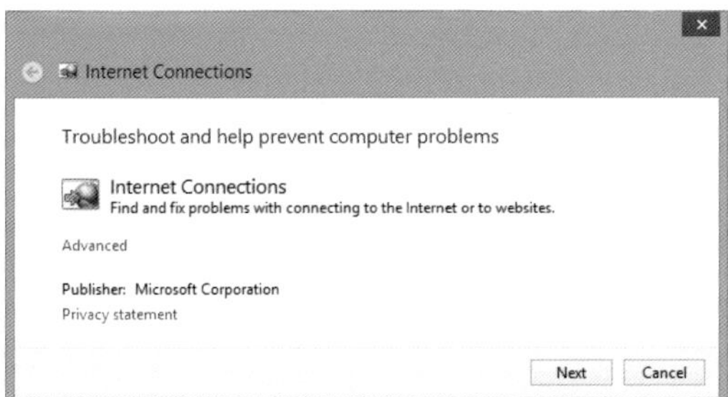

2. Click Next to run the troubleshooter, which carries out a series of checks to detect any internet connection issues

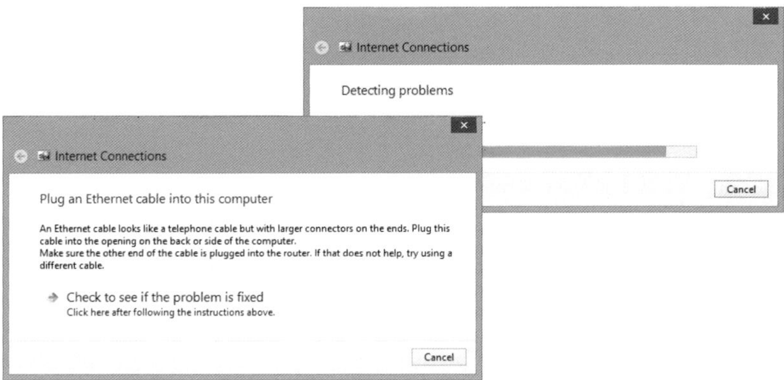

3. In this case the problem is identified as a unplugged Ethernet cable. You are advised to check that the cable is connected both to the PC and to the router

4. Check the cable and then click Check to see if the problem is fixed

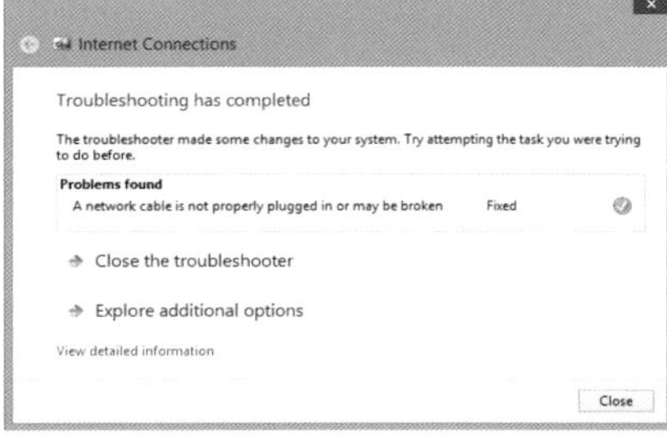

5. Confirmation that the problem is fixed

Problem Steps Recorder

If troubleshooting doesn't help, and you need to report the problem, you can use Problem Steps Recorder to automatically capture the steps you take, including a text description of where you clicked and a screen shot during each click. You can save the data to a file that can be used by a support professional or a friend helping you with the problem.

To record and save the steps:

1. Open Control Panel and type record steps in the search box. Then click Record steps to reproduce a problem

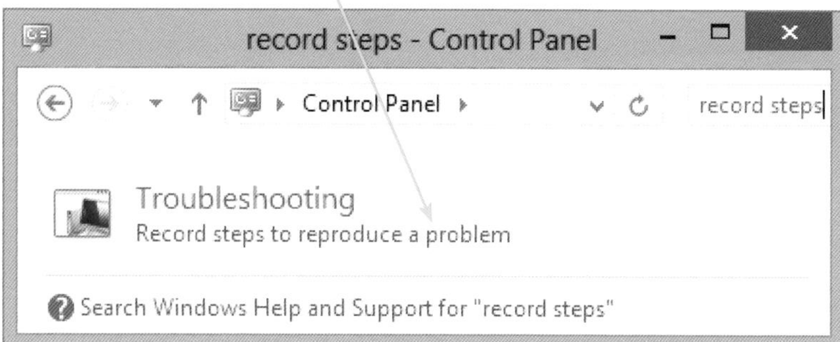

2. When Problem Steps Recorder is open, click Start Record

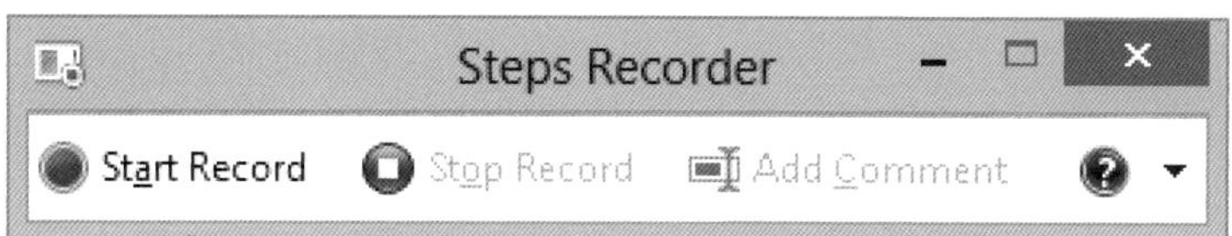

3. Go through the steps to reproduce the problem. You can pause the recording at any time, and then resume it later

4. Click Add Comment whenever you want to make notes about any step in the process you are recording

Beware

Some programs, for example a full-screen game, might not be captured accurately or might not provide useful details.

Hot tip

If you want to record any activities that need administrator authority, you must run the Program Steps Recorder as an administrator, in elevated mode.

...cont'd

5 Type your comments in the box that opens at the bottom right of the screen

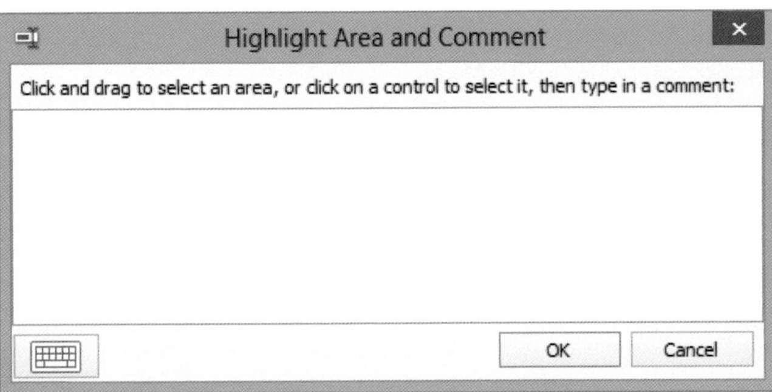

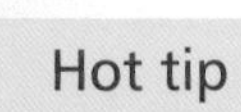

When you record steps, anything you type will not be recorded. If it is relevant to the problem, use the comment option to note what you type.

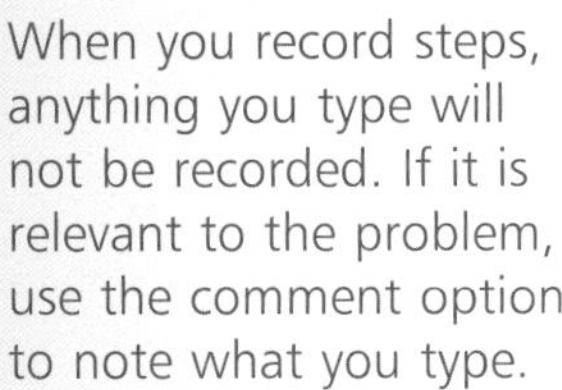

6 Click Stop Record when you have finished all the steps

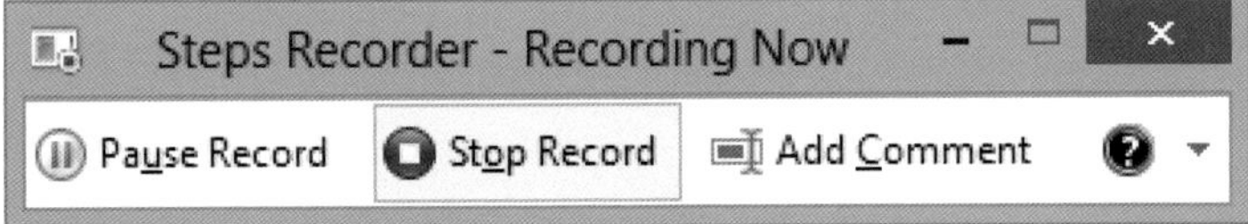

7 Provide a name and folder for the report and click Save

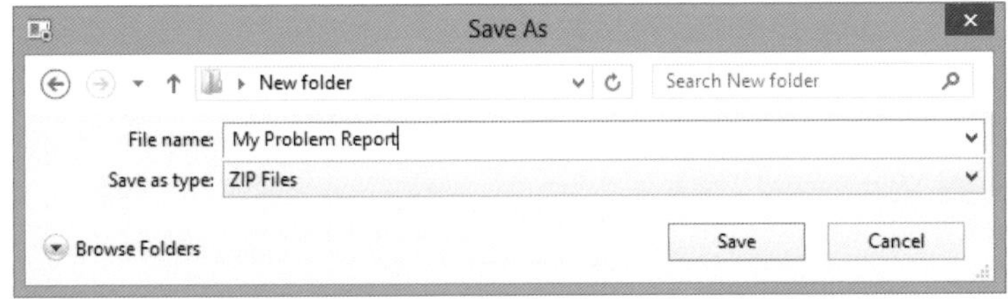

8 The report is saved as a compressed ZIP file in the folder

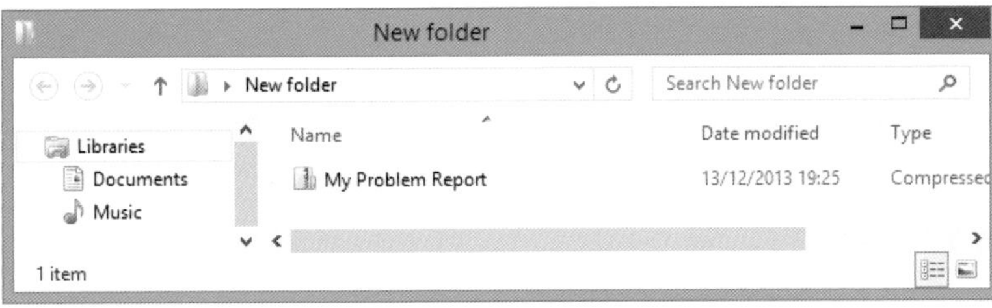

View the report

1. Double-click the compressed ZIP file, then double-click the MHTML document that it contains

2. The report opens

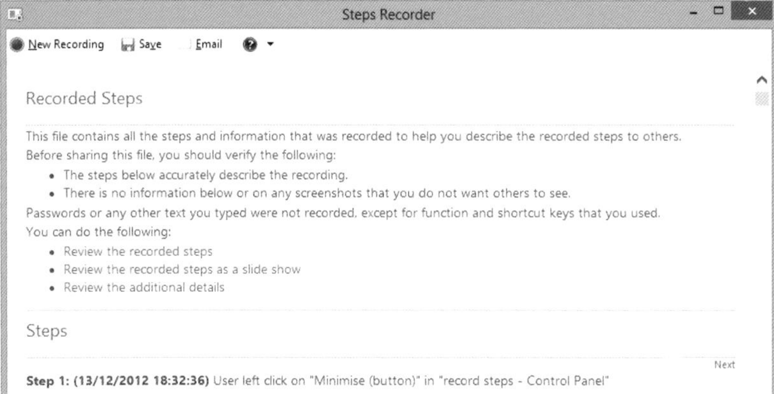

3. Each step has a description of the action taken, plus a screenshot of the full screen at that point

Hot tip

There is a summary of the contents, and links to the individual steps and to additional details, which contain technical information intended for advanced users.

Don't forget

You can view the actions and screenshots as a slideshow, which proceeds automatically, showing a new step every few seconds.

Get help from a friend

Don't forget

You can ask a friend to look at how your system is working, even if they are away from you, by connecting your computers.

1 Go to Control Panel. Click Find and fix problems under System and Security, then select Get help from a friend

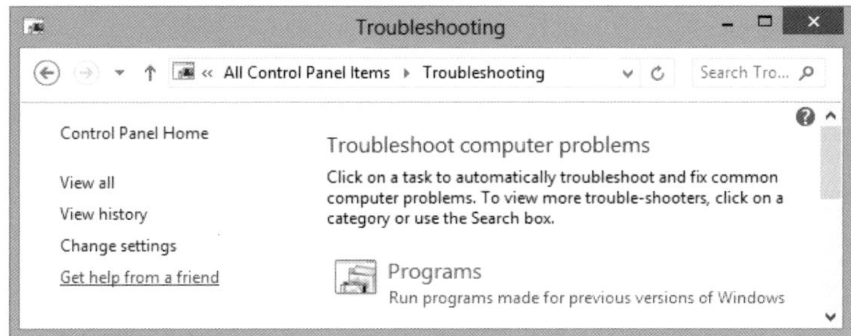

2 Click the option to Invite someone to help you

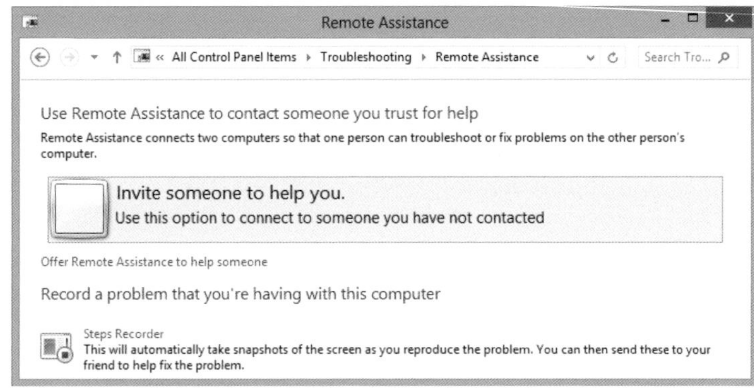

3 Select, for example, Use email to send an invitation

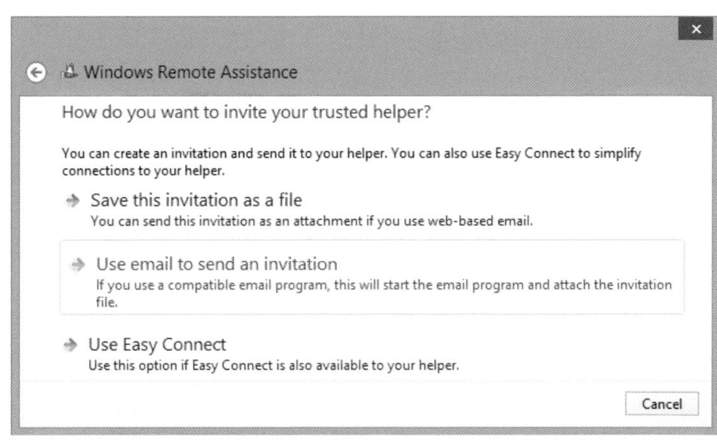

Hot tip

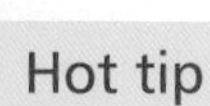

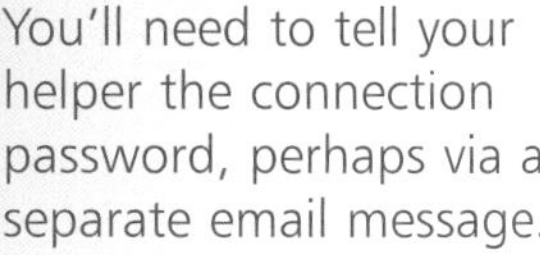

You'll need to tell your helper the connection password, perhaps via a separate email message.

4 Amend the message, adding the helper's name and email address, and click the Send button

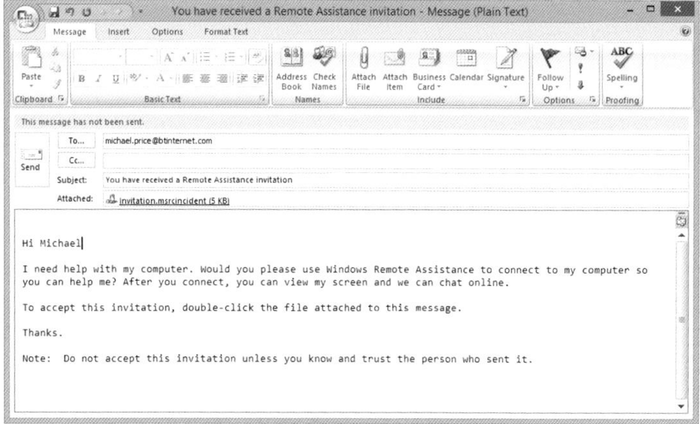

5 Remote Assistance provides a password for you to share, then waits for an incoming connection

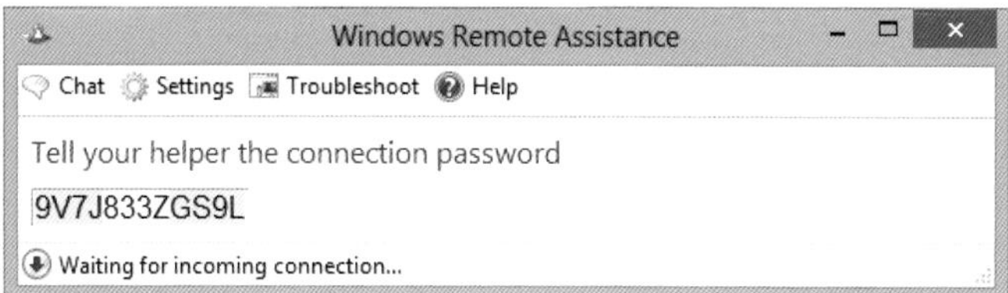

6 Your helper receives and opens the message and, if willing to help you, double-clicks the attached invitation file

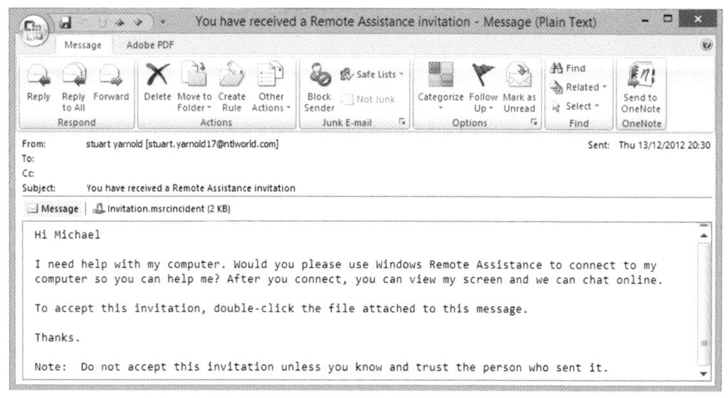

Don't forget

You can change the contents of the message however you wish, to make it appropriate for the person you are contacting.

Hot tip

You'll need to tell your helper the connection password, perhaps via a separate email message, or via instant messaging.

Send and respond

1 Your helper opens the invitation file and enters the connection password

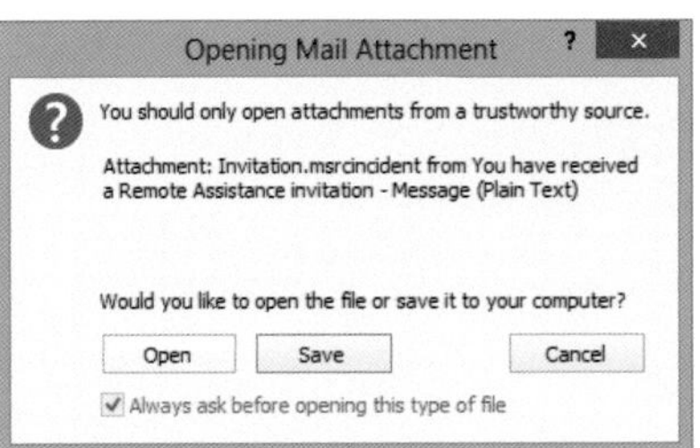

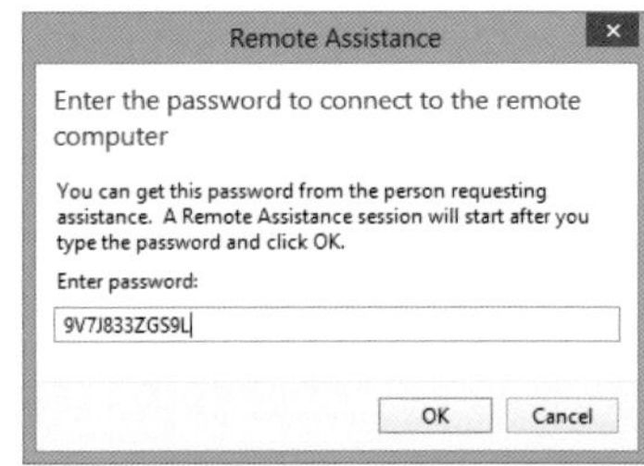

Don't forget

When your computer is connected this way, you are giving full access, so you should be sure it is a trusted friend that you have contacted.

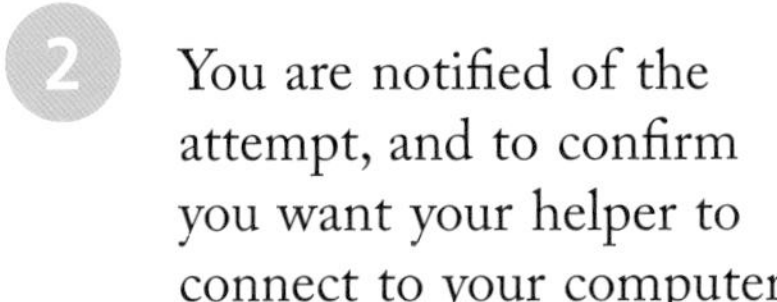

2 You are notified of the attempt, and to confirm you want your helper to connect to your computer

3 Your helper can now see your Desktop on his monitor, and observe any actions that you take

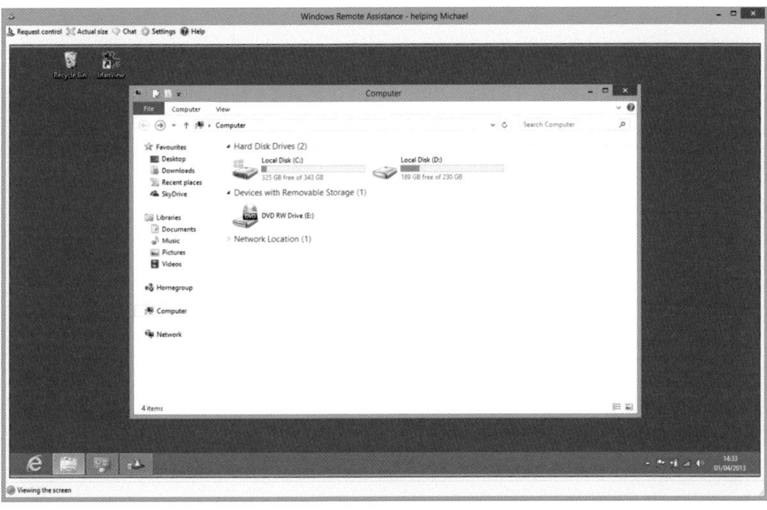

4 Your helper can click Request control, asking to operate your computer using his mouse and keyboard

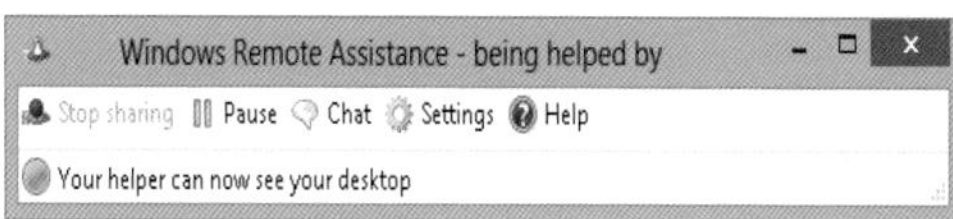

5. When you receive the request, click Yes to allow your helper to share control of your desktop

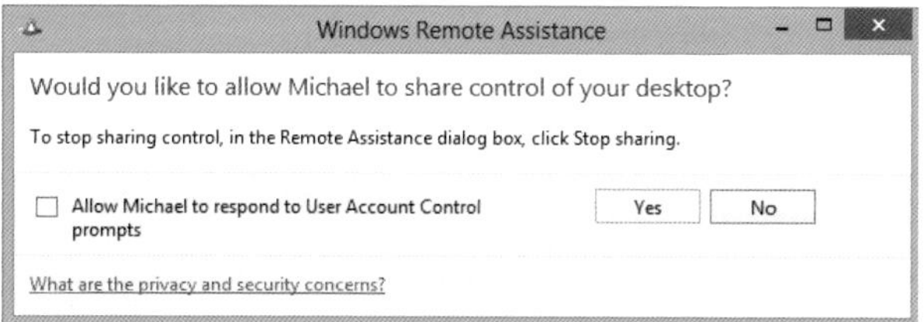

6. Now either you or your helper can operate the computer using mouse and keyboard

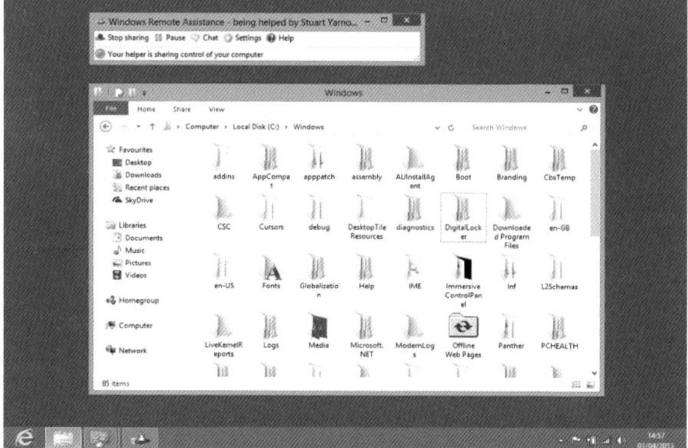

7. Click Chat to communicate via instant messaging, or click Stop sharing to retrieve full control

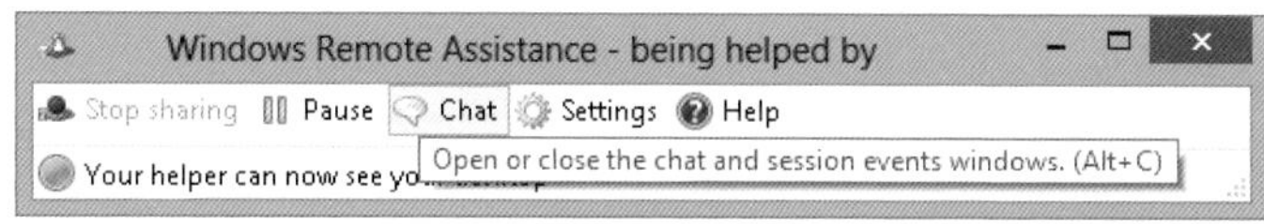

8. Close Remote Assistance when you have finished

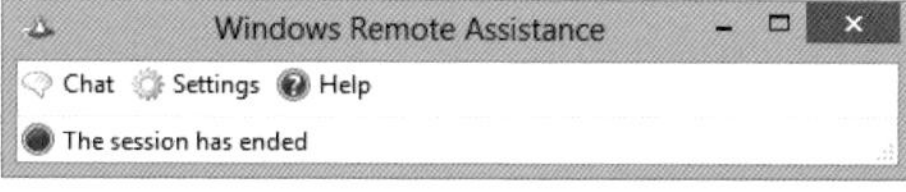

Hot tip

Click the box to allow your helper to respond to User Account Control prompts.

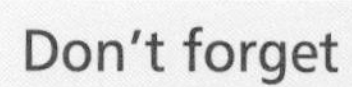

Don't forget

Click Pause if you want to temporarily stop the remote assistance session, for example to carry out a separate task.

Use Easy Connect

Don't forget

If you believe you are likely to connect with the same computer on a frequent basis, and it is using Windows 7 or Windows 8, then you can use the Easy Connect method.

1. Invite someone to help you (see page 344) and select Use Easy Connect

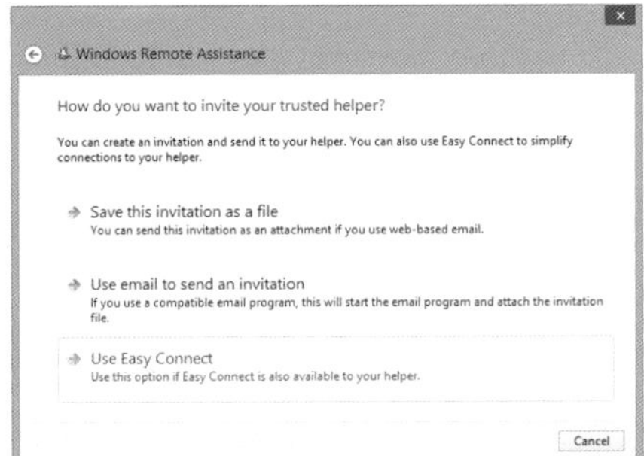

2. Remote Assistance will generate an Easy Connect password which you must supply to your helper

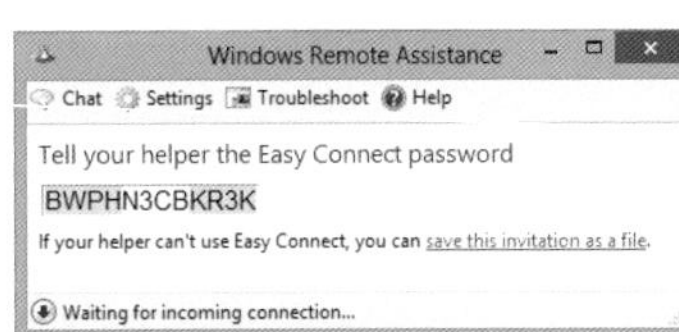

3. Your helper will open Troubleshooting and select Offer Remote Assistance to help someone, then select Easy Connect and enter the password provided

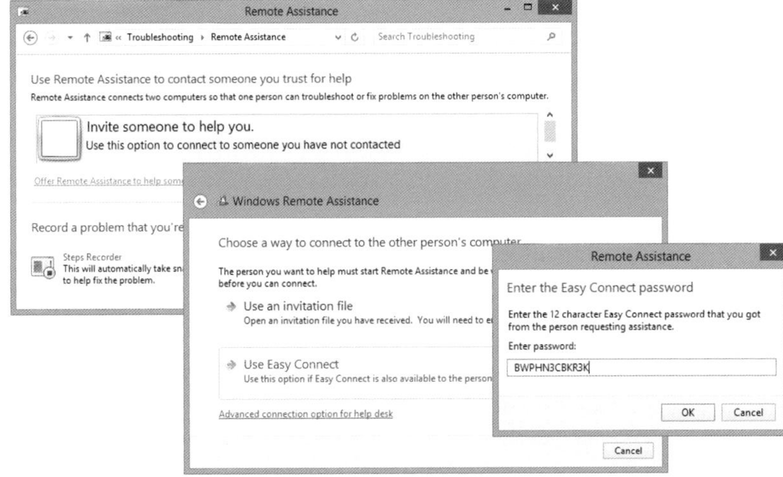

When the connection is made, contact information is exchanged between your computer and your helper's computer that will allow you to quickly connect in the future without using the password.

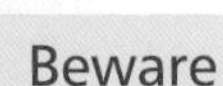

Beware

If you have problems connecting, such as issues with the firewall or router, try the Troubleshooting option at either computer for suggestions, or switch to the Invitation method.

System Restore

If problems arise due to recently added drivers or updates, you can use System Restore to return the computer to an earlier position.

1. Open the Action Center and select Recovery

2. Open System Restore by clicking Next

3. Choose the recommended restore, or choose a different restore point, to go back to an earlier state, and click Next

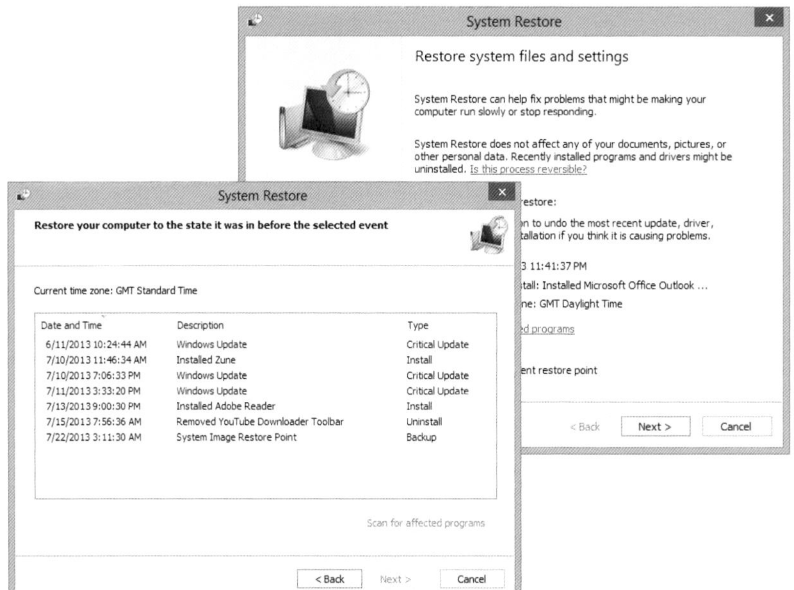

4. If you've displayed more restore points, select the one that predates the problems, and click Next

Hot tip

System Restore will suggest the option to undo the latest change to your system. Choose this if problems have only just appeared. You can still try another restore point later.

...cont'd

5. Confirm your restore point and select Finish

Beware

If System Restore is being run in safe mode or from the System Recovery Options menu, it cannot be undone.

6. Click Yes to continue and carry out the system restore

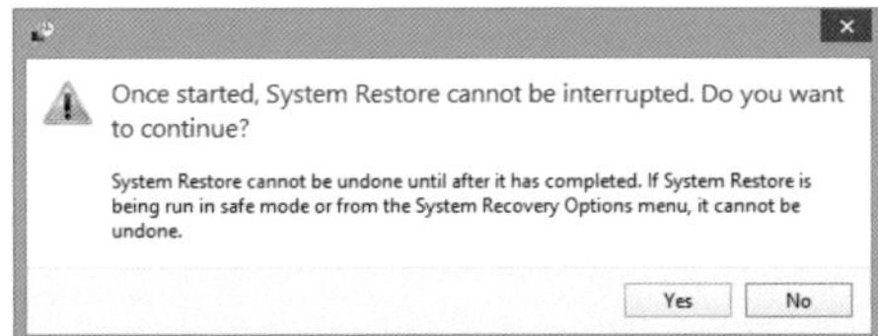

7. Windows will close down and restart, and the system files are restored to the required versions

8. If this does not fix the problem, you can Undo System Restore, or Choose a different restore point

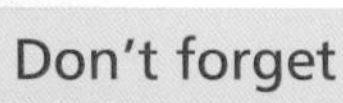

Don't forget

Once started, you must allow System Restore to complete. You can then Open System Restore and select Undo, if you want to revert to the initial state.

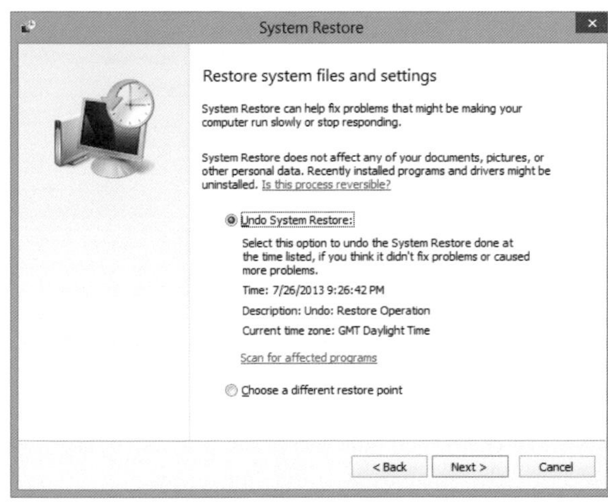

Start in Safe Mode

1. Open the Charms bar and select Settings, Change PC Settings, General
2. Scroll down to Advanced start-up and click Restart now
3. Click Troubleshoot > Advanced options > Startup Settings
4. Click Restart to reboot the computer

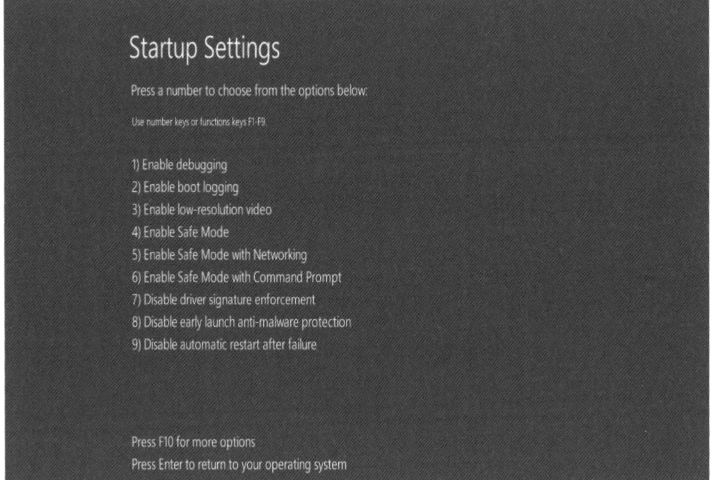

5. When the Startup Settings screen appears, press the F4 key or the number 4 key to select Safe Mode. The computer will now reboot into safe mode

Note that Startup settings replaces the advanced boot menu found in previous versions of Windows. Unlike the advanced boot menu, Startup settings cannot be initiated while the PC is booting by pressing the F8 key.

It can only be initiated from within Windows as described above, from a Windows 8 installation disk, or a Windows 8 Recovery drive. Also, Startup settings options cannot be selected with the mouse or keyboard – a specific key is allocated to each option.

Hot tip

Safe Mode starts Windows with a limited set of files and device drivers, without the usual startup programs and services. This validates the basic settings.

Don't forget

Safe Mode cannot be initiated by pressing the F8 key as with previous versions of Windows.

Program compatibility

When you install programs on your Windows 8 PC, you may come across one or two that refuse to run: this will be due to an incompatibility issue with Windows 8. A possible solution is the Compatibility Mode wizard. This will recreate the Windows environment for which they were designed and will, in most cases, get them running.

1. Click the flag icon in the Notification area to open Action Center. Then click Windows Program Compatibility Troubleshooter

2. Click Next and after a few moments you will see a dialog box showing you a list of all the programs on the PC

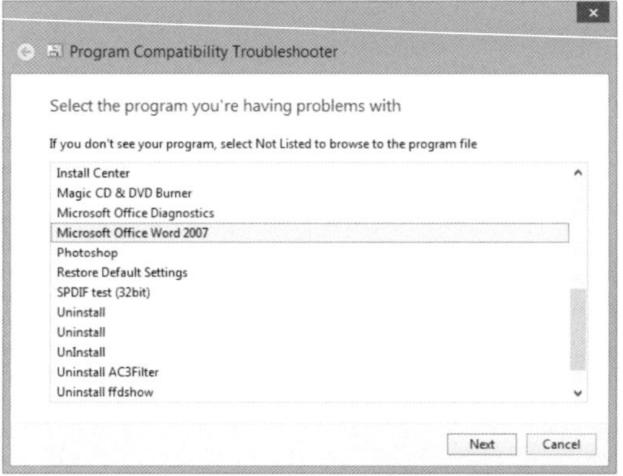

3. Select the one you're having trouble with and click Next

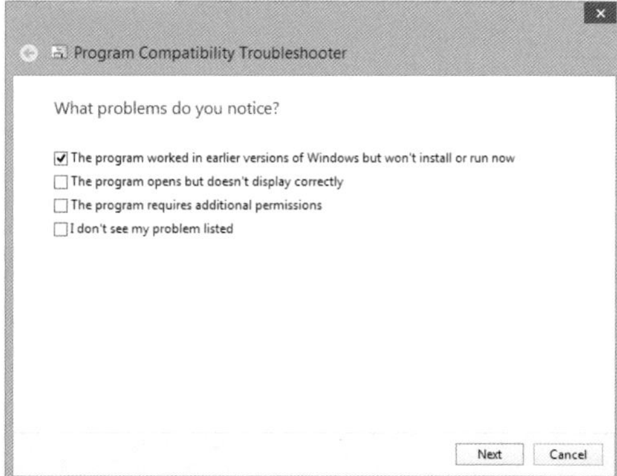

4. Choose the appropriate problem from the list and click Next

5. Windows will try to fix the issue. If the problem hasn't been resolved, click No, try again with different settings to repeat the procedure with other possible causes

Hot tip

Another way of applying compatibility settings is to right-click the program's executable (setup) file. Click Properties and then open the Compatibility tab. From here, you can choose an operating system that the program is known to work with.

Hot tip

If a program won't install at all, the method described on the right won't work. In this case, do it as described above.

Hot tip

Once a program has been successfully set up, it will use the compatibility settings every time it is run.

21 Backup and recovery

You need to keep safe copies of your data and other information so that in the event of problems you can recover your system. Windows provides ways to make backups of the system and data, and helps you restore the copies should it be necessary.

Sync settings and share

Hot tip 

If you have full synchronization turned on, your data will be accessible on all devices logged in to with a Microsoft account. Also, your settings, e.g. backgrounds, colors, etc., will be replicated on all the devices.

An important feature in Windows 8 is the ability to synchronize your settings across all your devices. This means that when you change your desktop background, for example, the change is replicated on all your devices.

Because your settings are stored on the cloud, not only are they synchronized, they are thus also automatically backed up. Furthermore, the backup is dynamic as it is done in real-time.

The synchronization feature is enabled by default, so you may wish to review exactly what is being synchronized, and thus backed up.

1. Open the Charms bar and select Settings, Change PC Settings. Then click Sync your settings

2. On the right, you'll see all the settings on your PC that can be synchronized. At the top, under Sync settings on this PC, you can turn off synchronization altogether

Beware 

If you have critical or confidential files on SkyDrive, you may want to think carefully about synchronizing passwords.

3. You can toggle individual settings on and off by clicking on them

4. When you have made your selections, click Share. This allows you to choose what to share

Sync to SkyDrive

While the synchronization feature makes it possible to automatically backup your settings, it cannot backup your files and folders. For this, you need the Desktop SkyDrive program that is supplied with the Essentials 2012 suite.

1. When you have installed it, open the Charms bar and type skydrive in the search box. You will see two results on the left of the screen. The top one is the Windows 8 SkyDrive app. The second one is the Desktop SkyDrive

2. SkyDrive opens on the Desktop as a regular folder with a number of pre-configured subfolders

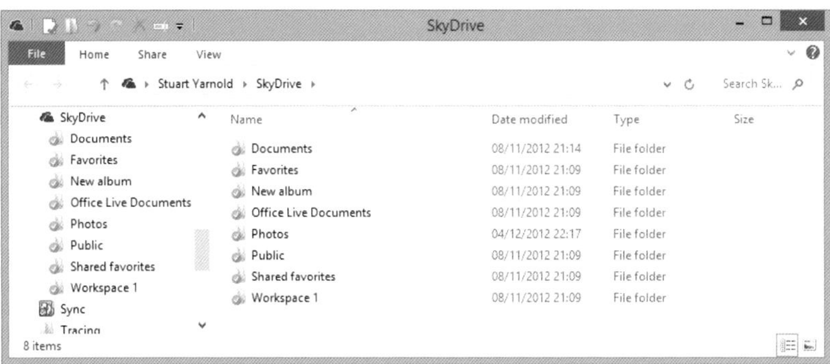

3. These folders exist in the cloud and are the same ones you'll see in the Windows 8 SkyDrive app. You can keep them as they are, add more, or delete them and create your own folder structure

4. To backup a file or folder, just save it anywhere in the SkyDrive folder – it will be automatically uploaded to the cloud

5. You can save files to the SkyDrive folder from some programs' Save As menu. Another way is to browse to the file or folder in the Navigation pane and simply drag it across to the SkyDrive folder

The SkyDrive folder works just any File Explorer folder – files can be added, deleted, renamed, etc.

Don't forget

The Desktop SkyDrive program is not the same as the Windows 8 SkyDrive app.

Hot tip

Some programs provide a Save to SkyDrive menu option. An example is Microsoft Office 2013.

Copy data

Don't forget

Protecting your files can be as simple as copying the files onto a USB flash drive, but there are more sophisticated methods available.

When you create documents or other files on your computer, it is wise to take precautions to protect your work, in case problems arise with the original version.

To illustrate the options and the considerations, we'll look at an example computer (running Windows 8 Pro).

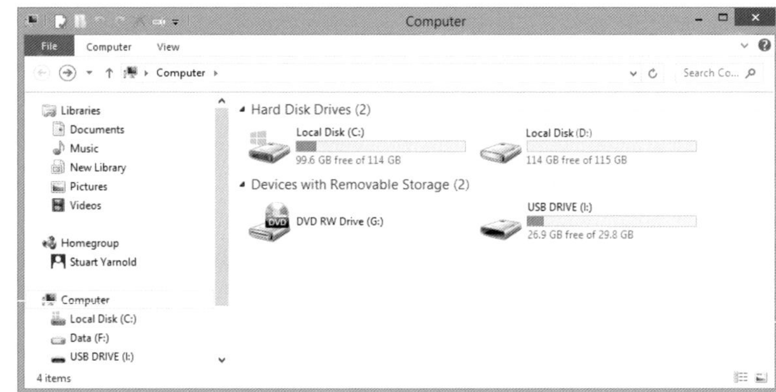

1. Press Winkey + X and select File Explorer to view the storage devices:

- Local Disk (C:) containing the system and the library files
- A second hard drive Local Disk (D:) which is empty
- USB Drive (I:) which is nearly empty
- A DVD RW Drive (G:) is available, but with no media

2. Go to Control Panel and click Change account type under User Accounts and Family Safety, to see the accounts

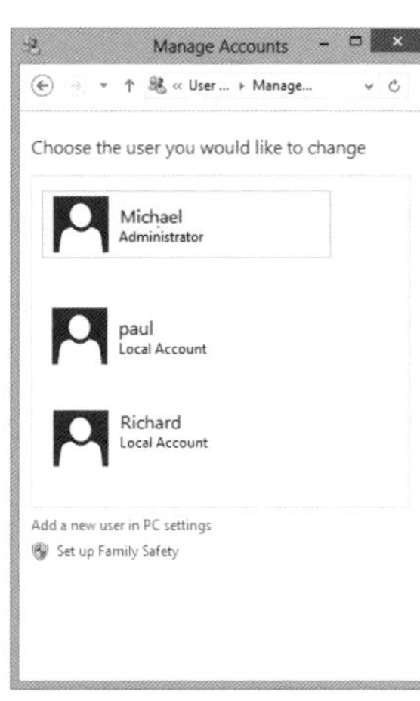

- Michael (administrator)
- paul (standard user)
- Richard (standard user)

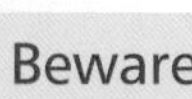

Beware

The standard user accounts have no password assigned. As administrator, you could select the accounts from this panel and create passwords for them.

To make a copy of a file on the USB drive:

1. Navigate to the folder containing the file

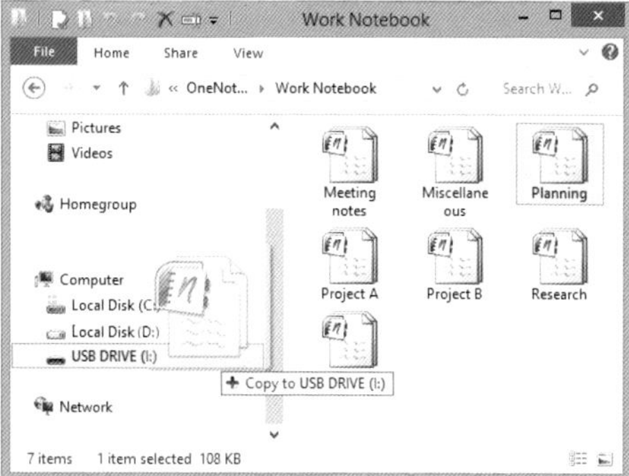

2. Left-click and drag the file onto the drive name in the Navigation pane, and release it there

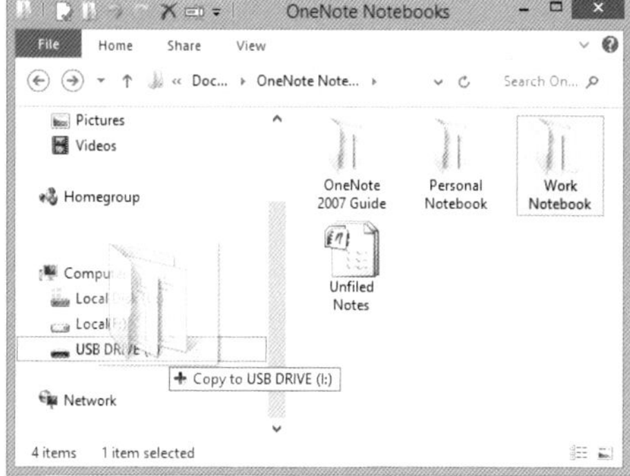

3. You can also drag a folder to copy the whole contents

Repeated copies

Note that a repeated copy at a later date to the same removable drive would over-write the initial copy. To keep a history of changes, you need to copy to a folder, perhaps named for the copy date, or use a separate removable drive each time.

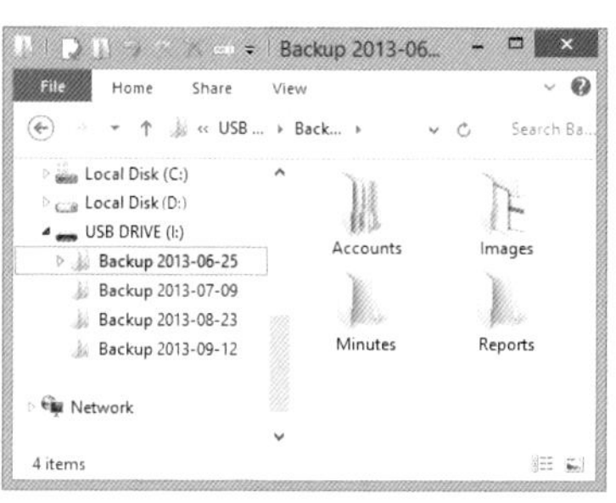

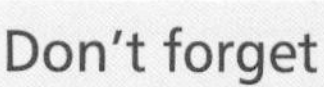

You could also right-click a file or folder and select Copy, then right-click the destination drive and select Paste (or use the Ctrl + C and Ctrl + V keyboard shortcuts).

Beware

If you right-click as you drag, you will Move rather than Copy the files to the destination drive.

Copy libraries

Suppose you want to save the whole contents of your libraries:

1. Open the Libraries in File Explorer

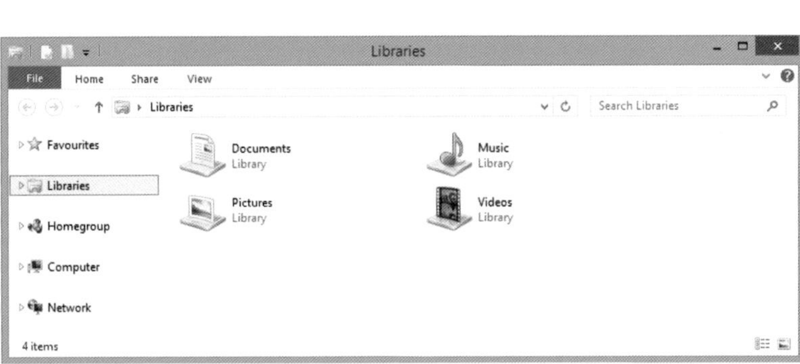
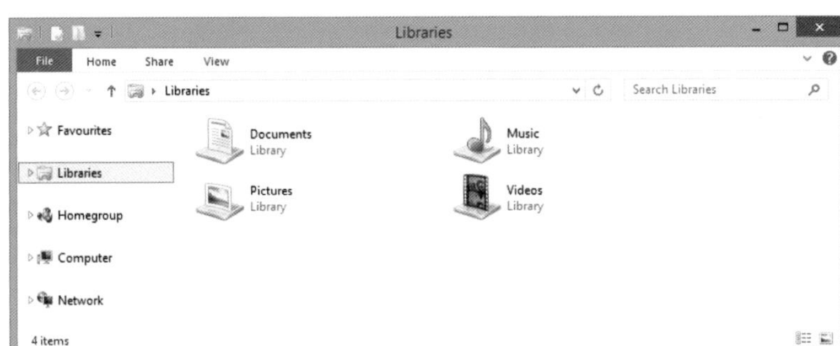

2. Click the arrow to the left of Libraries and select Desktop to show the Libraries folder

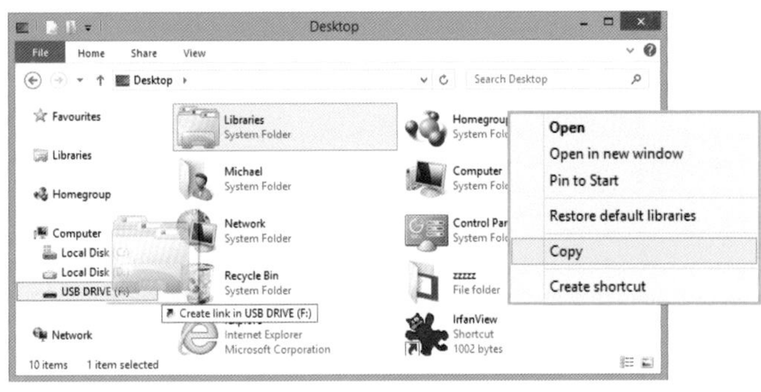

3. Rather than drag & drop, right-click the Libraries folder and select Copy

4. On the Navigation pane, select the removable drive to open it

5. Right-click the Contents pane and select Paste

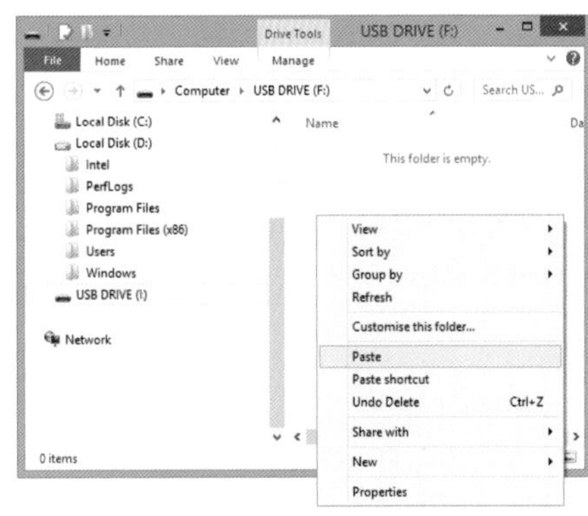

Don't forget

You can Show all folders in the Navigation pane to display the Desktop and the Libraries folder.

Beware

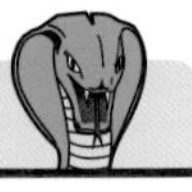

Dragging and dropping the Libraries folder creates a link to the original folder, rather than the copy as made for files and folders.

6. The contents of the libraries are copied to the removable drive

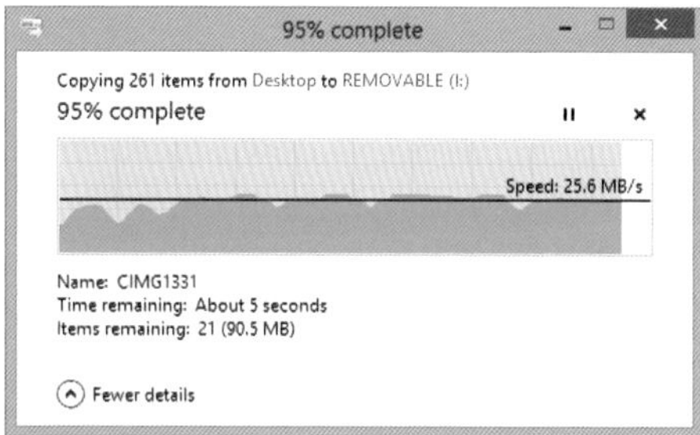

7. Expand the Navigation pane entry for the removable drive, and you'll see how the contents are arranged

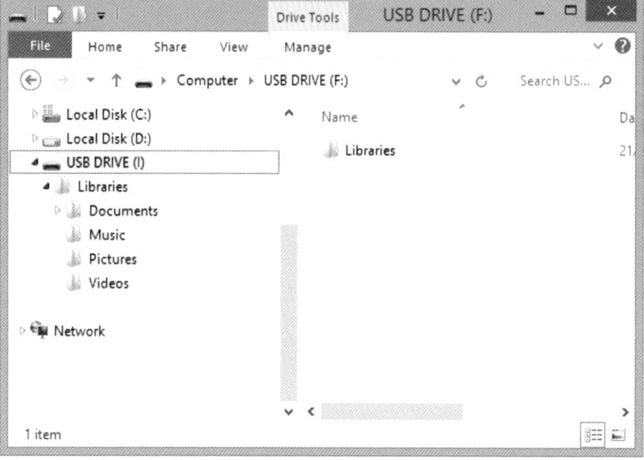

Note that each library folder on the copy contains the merged contents of the Current user and the Public libraries. This can lead to difficulties when restoring files and folders.

When you copy libraries, you'll also have problems with over-writing older copies with new copies.

Other users

You may encounter problems accessing user folders, if you are required to make backup copies on behalf of other users with accounts on your computer.

Hot tip

The files and folders that are listed in the libraries may be stored in separate locations on your disk.

Beware

You will find that various problems arise when your copying activities are more complex. They can all be resolved, but it may be much easier to use Windows 7 File Recovery to manage the requirements.

Refresh your system

Like everything else in life, Windows depreciates with use. It develops faults, slows down and may become unstable. Windows 8 provides a utility that will quickly restore it to an "as new" condition.

Hot tip

Virtually all problems that occur with Windows can be repaired. However, it is almost always easier to simply revert the system to a state prior to the fault manifesting itself. The Refresh utility is one way of doing this.

1. Go to the Charms Bar > Settings > Change PC Settings. Then click General. Scroll down to Refresh your PC without affecting your files and click Get Started

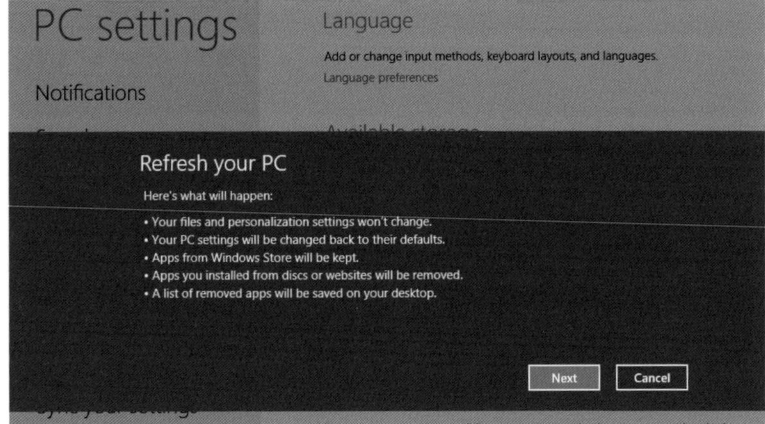

A new screen opens and it tells you what will happen if you run the utility:

- **Your files and personalization settings won't change** – this means that your data will not be deleted, and that any changes you have made to the default personalization settings will be retained. The former is the big plus here as it means you do not have to make a backup of your data and then reinstall it afterwards
- **Your PC settings will be changed back to their defaults** – this means that Windows 8 will be deleted and replaced by a new copy. Any configuration changes made to Windows settings will be lost
- **Apps from Windows Store will be kept** – Windows 8 apps installed from the Windows Store will not be deleted
- **Apps you installed from discs or websites will be removed** – All third-party software will be deleted.

Hot tip

You might be prompted to insert your Windows 8 installation disc, or recovery media, that came with your PC.

2 Having read and understood what the utility will do, click Next

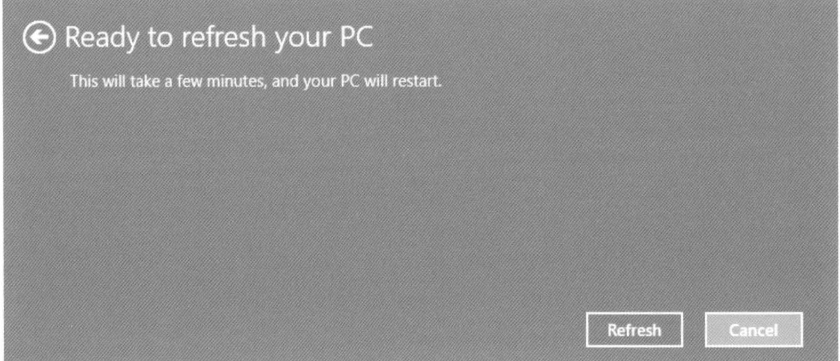

Hot tip

A big advantage of the Refresh utility is that it is quick. It will reinstall Windows in a fraction of the time taken by the original installation.

3 Click Refresh

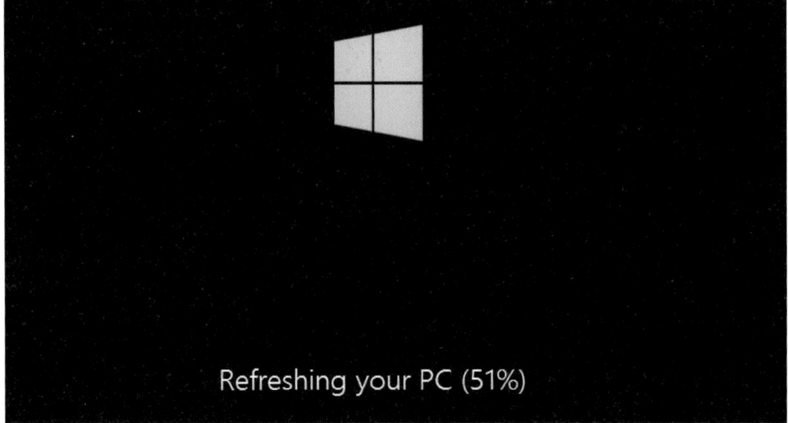

4 The computer will reboot and the Refresh procedure takes place

Effectively then, the Refresh utility will install a new copy of Windows 8 while retaining the user's Windows 8 apps, data and personalization settings. Everything else will be deleted.

The big drawback is that users will have to reinstall/reconfigure probably most of their software, and reconfigure various Windows settings.

Reinstall your system

Hot tip

The Reset utility provides an ideal way of securely deleting your data on a computer you are going to sell or scrap.

The traditional method of completely restoring a Windows PC to its factory settings is to do a clean installation. This wipes the drive clean of all data, after which a new copy of Windows is installed. The procedure is done by booting the PC from the installation disk, and is something that most users will be wary of trying.

Windows 8 provides a much simpler method of restoring Windows to its factory settings. This is courtesy of its Reset utility. It works as described below:

1. From the Charms Bar go to Settings > Change PC settings > General > Remove everything and reinstall Windows. Click Get started

2. At the first screen, click Next. At the second, you will be presented with two options as shown below

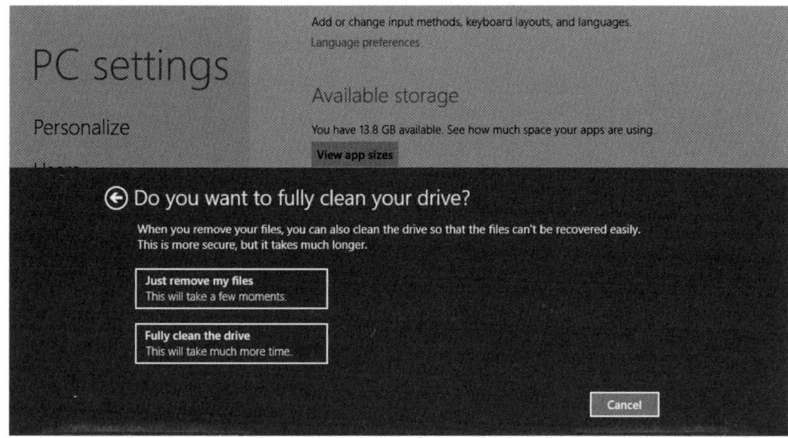

Hot tip

When you click the Reset button, the computer will reboot after which the Reset utility will run.

Choose the first option, Just remove my files, if you just want to start again from scratch. All the data you have put on the PC will be deleted leaving you with a "as new" copy of Windows.

The second option, Fully clean the drive, does the same but also wipes the drive securely so the data can not be subsequently recovered.

3. Select the required option and then sit back as Windows is restored

Enable File History

Windows 8 provides some very useful backup utilities. One of these is File History, which is located in the Control Panel. With it users are able to quickly restore individual files that have been modified, damaged or even deleted.

It works by making automatic backups (every hour by default) of all files stored in the following folders: Contacts, Desktop, Favorites, and the Documents, Music, Pictures and Video Libraries. By default, File History is turned off. Enable it as follows:

1. Connect an external drive to the PC. This will be a USB flash drive or external hard drive

2. Go to Control Panel, File History. Assuming you have connected an external drive, you will see the following

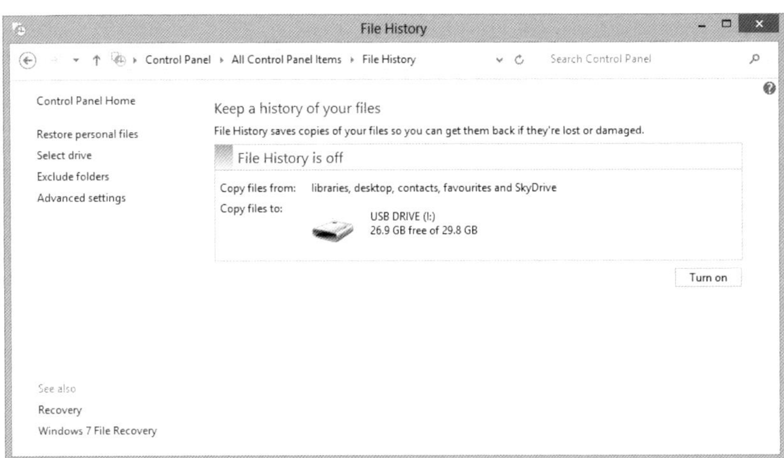

3. Click Turn on

All files in the above mentioned folders will now be automatically backed up every hour. Note that existing backups are not over-written by new ones – each backup is kept so over a period of time, a file history is created. This enables a file to be restored from a backup created at a specific time and day.

To restore a file, click Restore personal files from the link at the top-left of the window. Then browse to the required backup.

Hot tip

The only way to backup folders other than the ones mentioned on the left with File History is to add them to a library.

Hot tip

By default, backups are made every hour. However, this can be changed in Advanced settings.

Hot tip

If you have two or more removable drives in your system, you can select the one to save the backups on by clicking Select drive.

Windows 7 - style backup

Another useful backup utility in Windows 8 is the somewhat incongruously entitled Windows 7 File Recovery. This makes copies of data files for all those using the computer.

By default, these backups are created on a regular schedule, but you can create backups manually at any time. The utility keeps track of the files and folders that are new or modified and adds them to your backup. To set up Windows 7 File Recovery:

Hot tip

If your data is critical, we suggest backing it up to two separate mediums and keeping them in different locations.

1. Go to the Control Panel and select an icon view. Open Windows 7 File Recovery and then click Set up backup

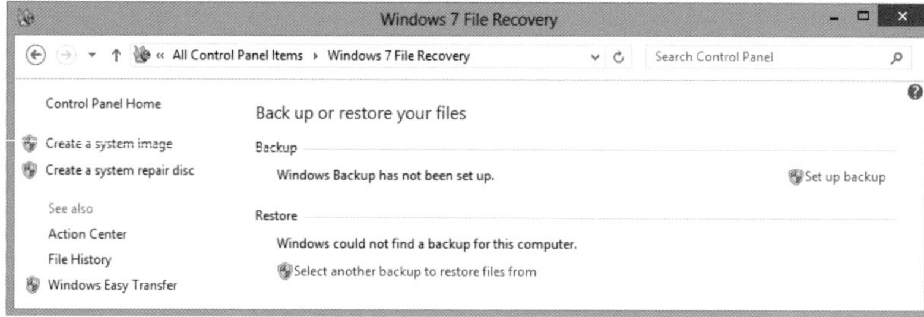

2. Windows Backup starts and searches for available devices

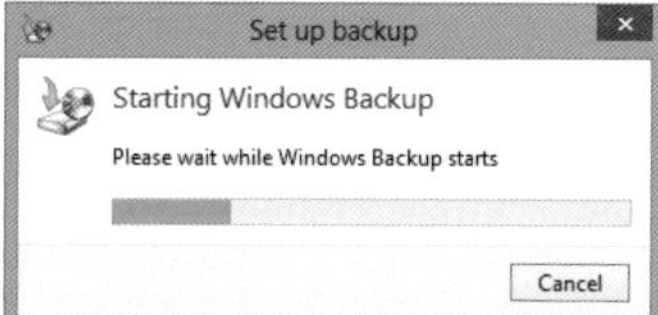

3. The available backup devices are listed, and Local Disk (D:) is recommended

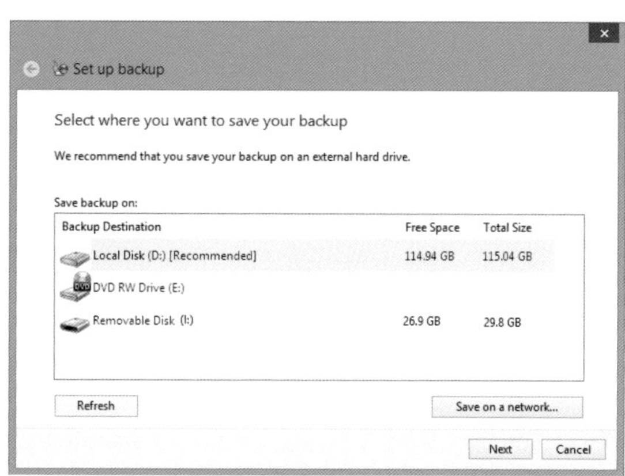

Choosing the backup device

Windows prefers an external drive if available, or any hard drive other than the system drive. It lists the writable DVD drive, though you'd need multiple discs for a full backup.

It also lists the USB flash drive, since it is greater than 1GB.

To continue the setup:

4. Select the device you want to use and click Next

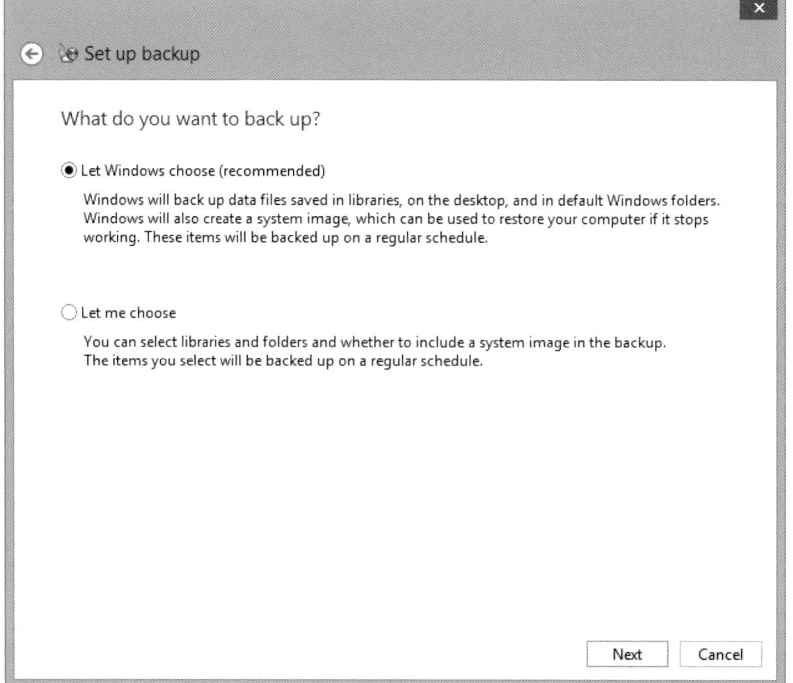

5. Windows now asks you what data you want to back up. The first option, let Windows choose (recommended), backs up the data stored in commonly accessed folders, such as libraries and the Desktop. The second, Let me choose, allows you to specify exactly what data to back up

6. Make your choice and then click Next

Don't forget

You could also select Save on a network and choose a shared folder or drive from another computer on the local network.

Hot tip

If you don't have a second drive, or one of sufficient capacity, we suggest you create a second partition on your existing hard drive (from Control Panel >Administrative Tools > Computer Management > Disk Management) and use this as the backup location.

...cont'd

The first backup

When you've chosen what to backup, you can run the first backup:

1. Review the details, and click Save settings and run backup

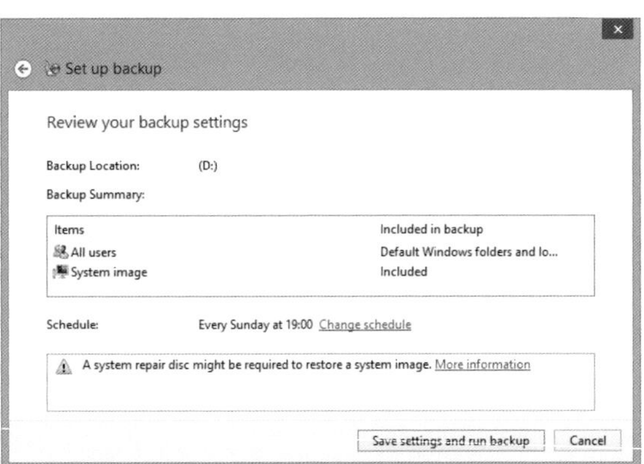

2. Backup commences, and the progress is displayed in the Home screen

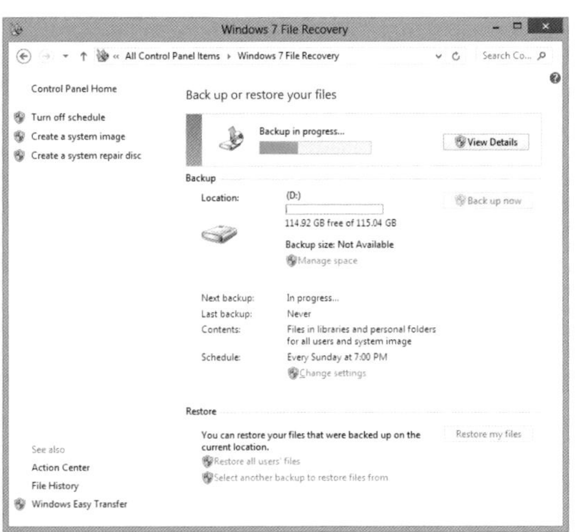

As indicated, there has been no previous backup, and future backups are scheduled to run weekly, every Sunday at 7:00 PM – though you can change the schedule (see page 369).

3. Click View details for a closer look at the backup actions that are taking place

You are warned that a system repair disk (see page 376) may be required to restore the system image.

From the Home screen, you have full access to all the functions and you can change settings and schedules as necessary.

4. The details panel shows the percent complete and the current action taking place

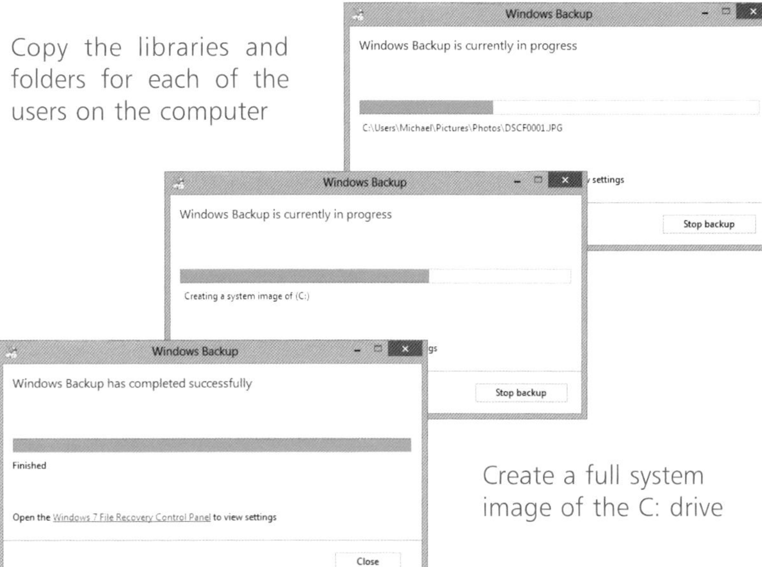

Copy the libraries and folders for each of the users on the computer

Create a full system image of the C: drive

5. Upon completion, the Home screen shows backup size, and date and time for the next backup

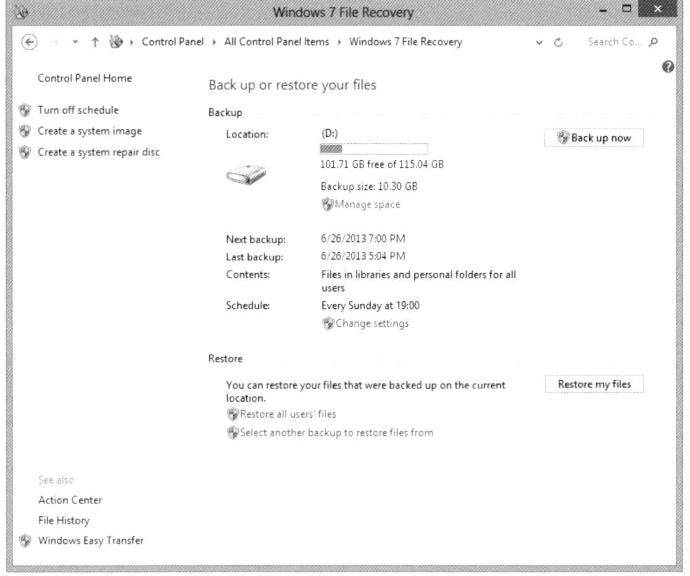

Don't forget

You can see from the file and folder paths being displayed which items are being copied at any time during the backup.

Hot tip

Even if you close the progress panel and the Home screen, you can see from the icon in the Notification area that backup is in progress.

...cont'd

After the backup

To see details of the backup:

1. Press Winkey + X and click File Explorer. Check the drive the backup was saved to – Local Disk (D:)

2. There is now only 101GB free, compared with the initial 115GB available before Backup was run

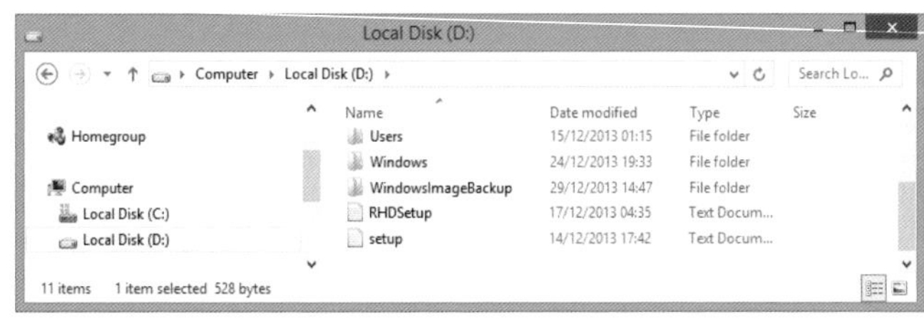

3. Open the drive and you see the contents, but when you move the mouse pointer over the folders, they appear to be empty

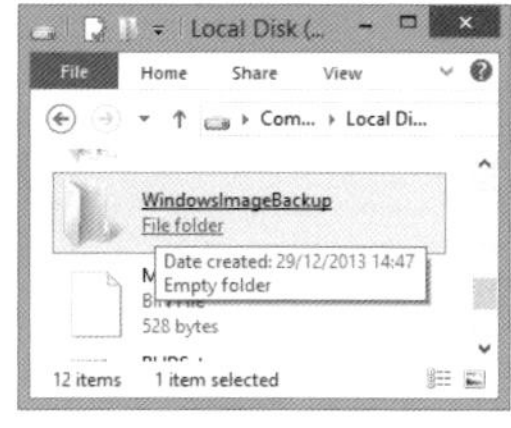

4. Double-click a folder and you'll be prompted for permission

5. Open the next couple of folders, and you will eventually find a file of substantial size which is evidently the system image

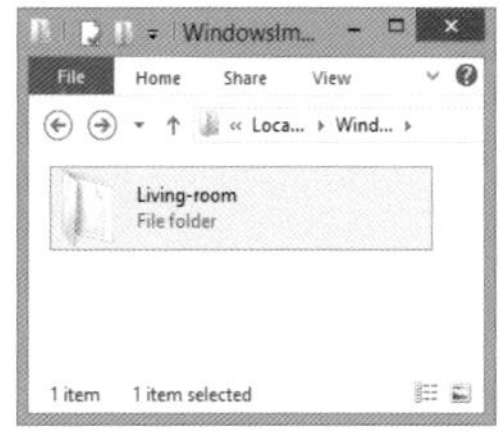

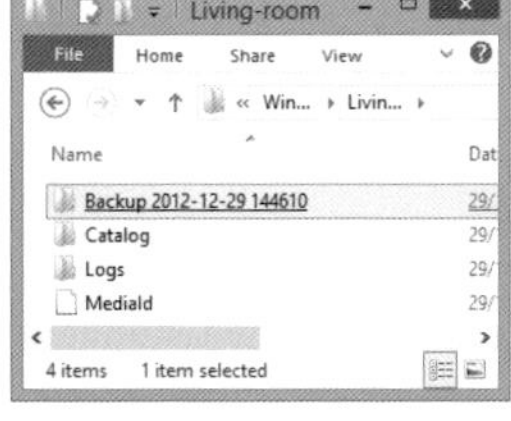

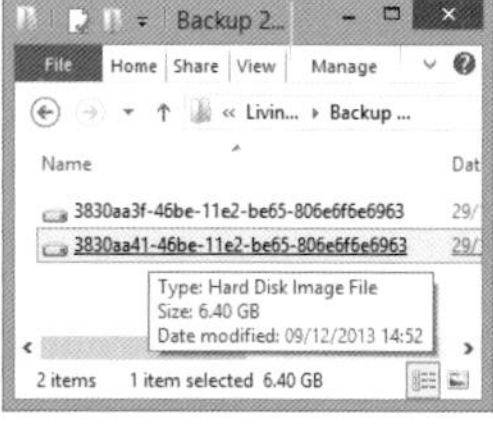

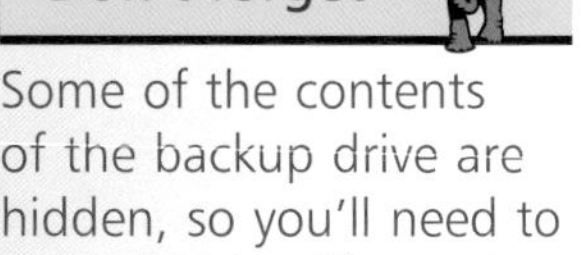

Don't forget

Some of the contents of the backup drive are hidden, so you'll need to Show hidden files and folders.

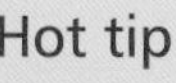

Hot tip

The contents of the backup drive or folder are protected, and cannot really be dealt with directly.

Scheduled backup

You can configure a backup schedule:

1. After the next scheduled update, display the Home screen, and you'll see just minor changes

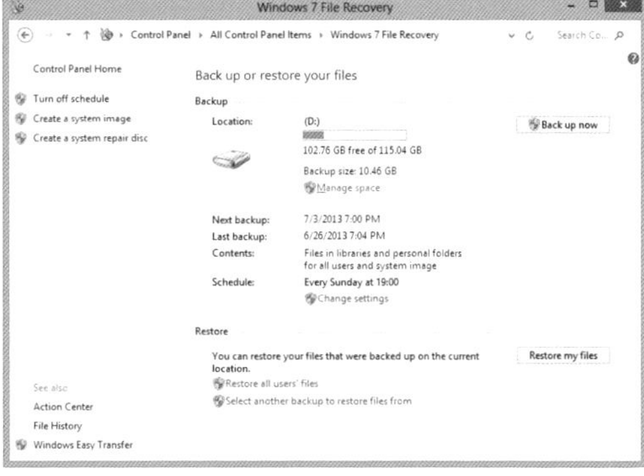

2. To change the schedule, click Change Settings and follow the prompts, until asked to Review your backup settings

3. Select to Change schedule

4. Choose How often, What day, What time

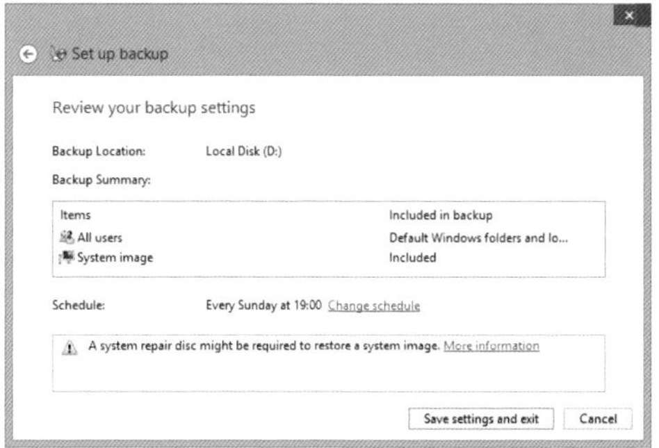

Set up backup

How often do you want to back up?

Files that have changed and new files that have been created since your last backup will be added to your backup according to the schedule you set below.

☑ Run backup on a schedule (recommended)

How often: Weekly

What day: Sunday

What time: 19:00

OK Cancel

5. Select OK then click the Save settings and exit button

Hot tip

After the first update, the utility only saves changes to the files, and so there is usually very little to record.

Don't forget

You can schedule updates daily, weekly or monthly, and choose any time of day or night.

Beware

If it's time for your regularly scheduled backup and your computer is off, sleeping, or hibernating, Windows 7 File Recovery skips the backup and waits for your next scheduled backup.

Create a manual backup

If you make changes to your files, and want to ensure you have saved copies, you can run Backup manually.

1. Open the Home screen and select Backup now

2. The backup as defined in Setup is initiated, and progress displayed, as described for the first backup (see page 366)

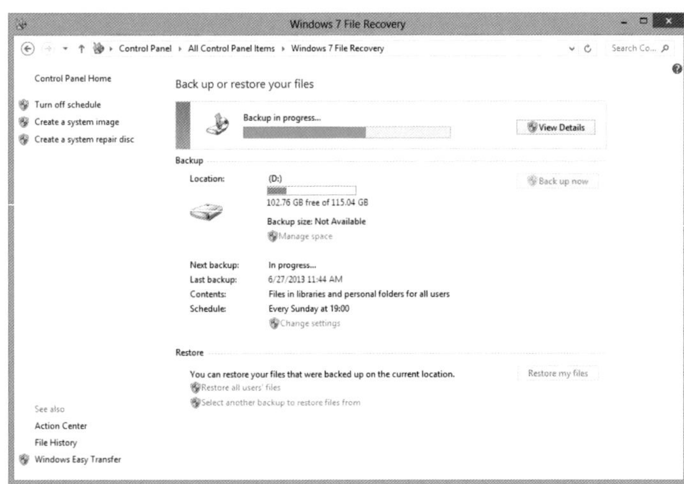

3. The changes to files and the user libraries are copied, then the system image is created

4. When the backup completes, the Home screen shows changes in backup size, and next backup date

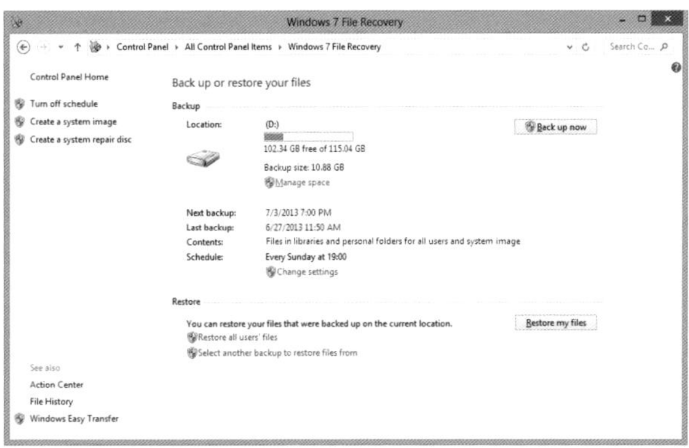

You can use manual backup if you find that scheduled backups have been missed, for example because the machine was turned off or hibernating at the scheduled time.

Manage space

Windows 7 File Recovery allows you to view the way the space on your backup device is used, and how much free space there is.

1. Go to the Home screen and select Manage space
2. The summary shows how the backup space is allocated

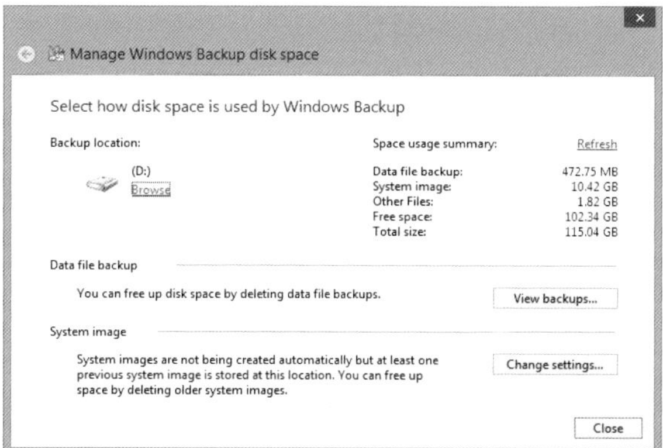

3. Click View backups to see or delete backup periods

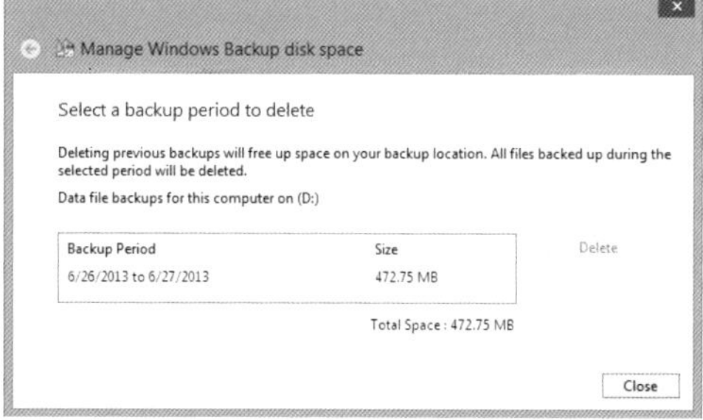

4. Click Change settings to say how system images are kept

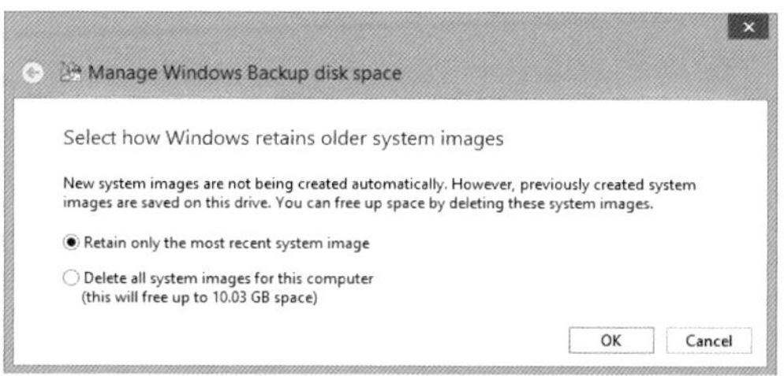

Don't forget

Windows 7 File Recovery backs up all selected folders the first time it's run and then it only backs up files that are new or have been modified since the last backup.

Hot tip

If you let Windows manage the space, it will save as many system images as will take no more than 30% of the backup disk, then delete older system images. You can instead choose to keep only the most recent system image. This is always the case for a network backup location.

Restore files

Don't forget

With backups created, you can restore files and folders that have been lost, damaged, or changed accidentally.

1 Open the Home screen, to show the current backup location, and scroll down to the Restore section

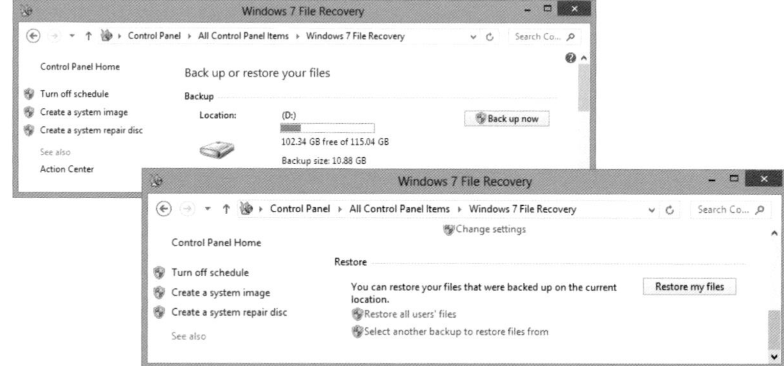

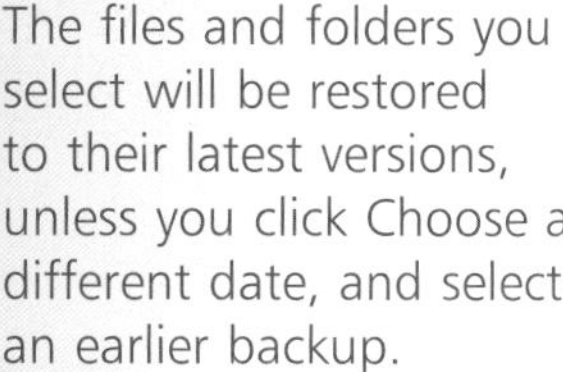

Hot tip

The files and folders you select will be restored to their latest versions, unless you click Choose a different date, and select an earlier backup.

2 Select Restore my files, and select Browse for files

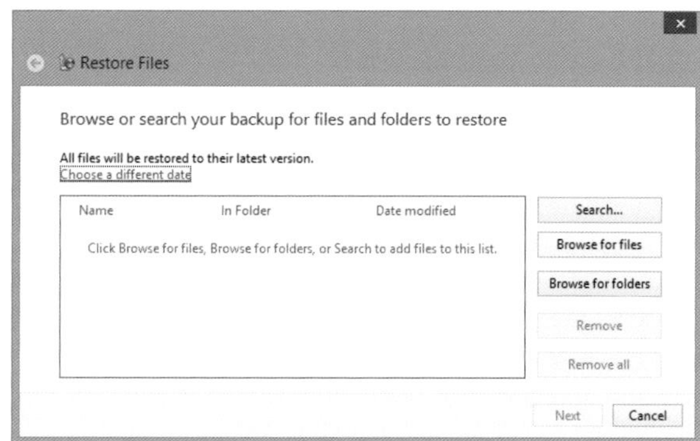

Hot tip

You can also click Search to look for files in the backup folders by name. Select Browse for folders, when you want to Add folders to the restore list.

3 Explore the backup folders, select files and click Add files

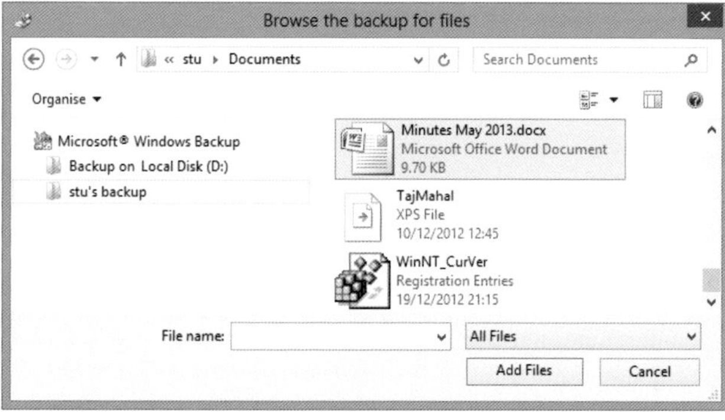

4 You can Remove any files or folders selected by mistake, then click Next to begin restoring your final list

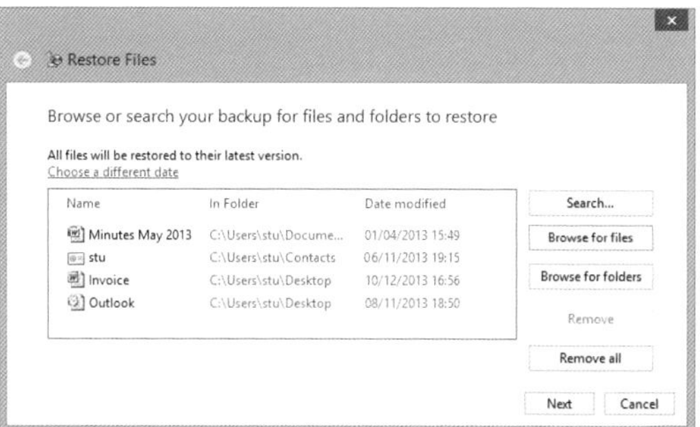

5 Restore to the original location or select another folder

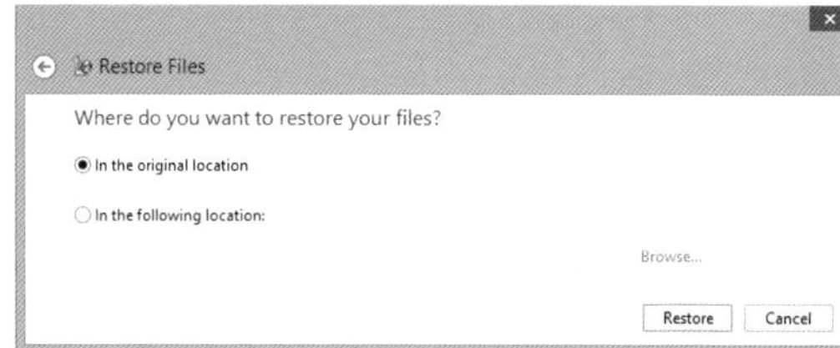

6 The files and folders are restored to the specified location

7 The log file shows any problems that might arise

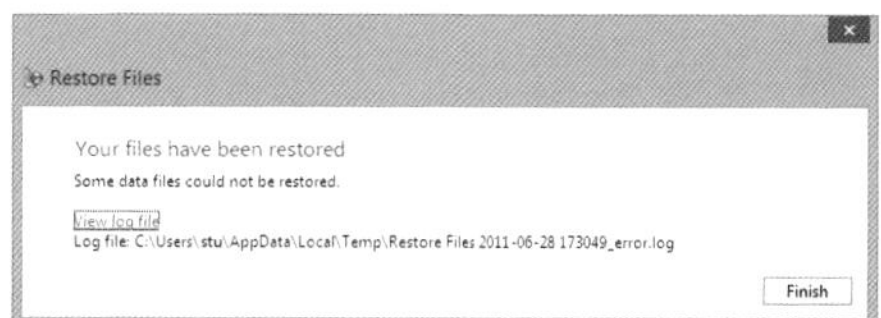

Don't forget

If you have administrator authority, you can select Restore all users' files, and recover files for any user on the system.

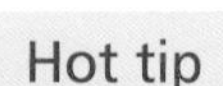

Hot tip

If the file that's being restored already exists in the location, you can copy and replace, copy and rename or just skip that copy.

Create a system image

A system image is an exact copy of a drive. By default, a system image includes the drives required for Windows to run. It also includes Windows and your system settings, programs, and files.

Should the imaged computer subsequently develop a problem that cannot be repaired, it can be restored from the image.

There are many third-party utilities of this type, a well known one being Acronis True Image, but Windows 8 provides its own.

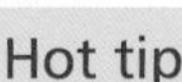

Hot tip

A system image will restore the PC to the state it was in when the image was built.

1. Open Windows 7 File Recovery from the Control Panel and click Create a system image

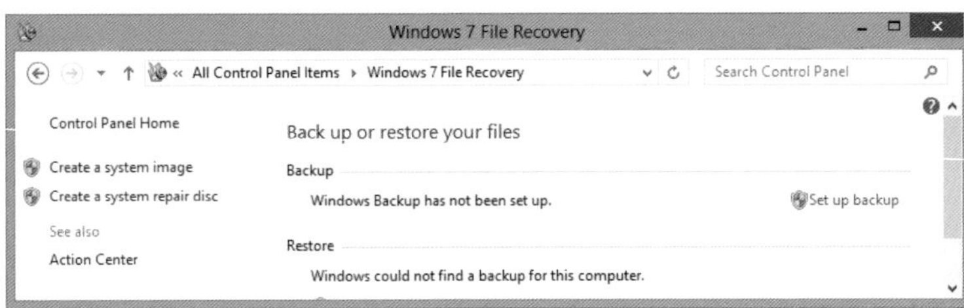

2. Select a location for the backup. Options include a hard disk, DVDs or a network location

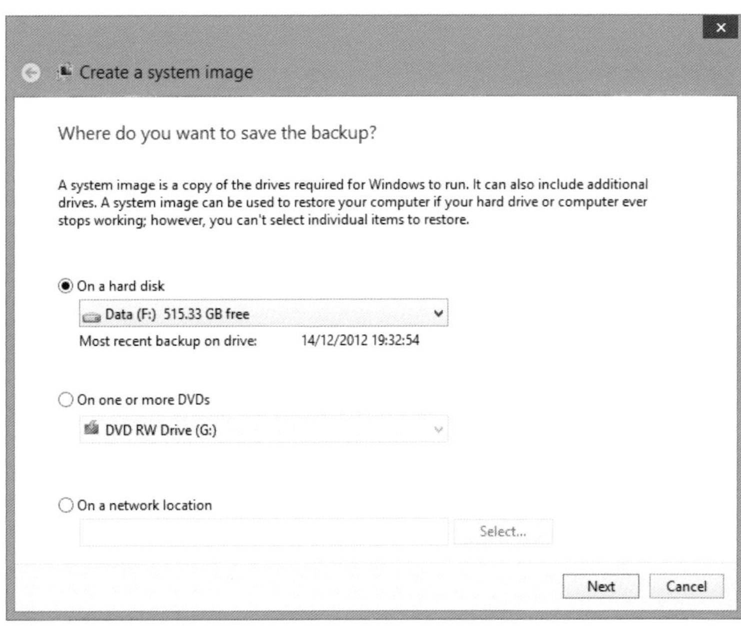

Create a system image
Where do you want to save the backup?
A system image is a copy of the drives required for Windows to run. It can also include additional drives. A system image can be used to restore your computer if your hard drive or computer ever stops working; however, you can't select individual items to restore.
On a hard disk
Data (F:) 515.33 GB free
Most recent backup on drive: 14/12/2012 19:32:54
On one or more DVDs
DVD RW Drive (G:)
On a network location
Select...
Next
Cancel

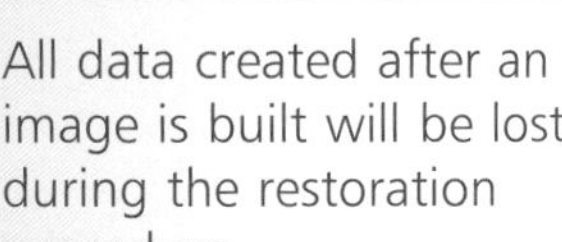

Beware

All data created after an image is built will be lost during the restoration procedure.

3 Select the drives to include in the image

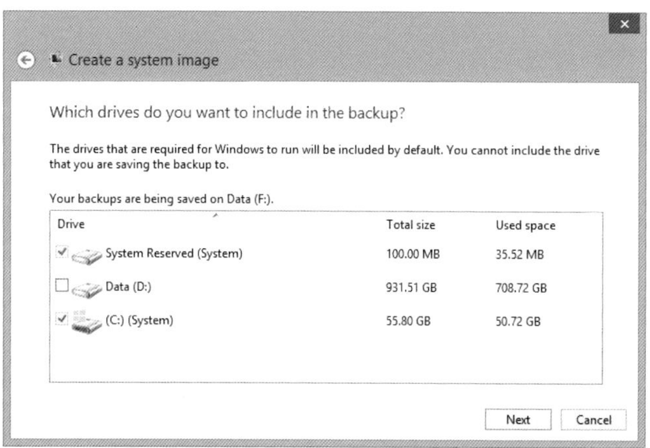

4 Review your settings and then click Start backup

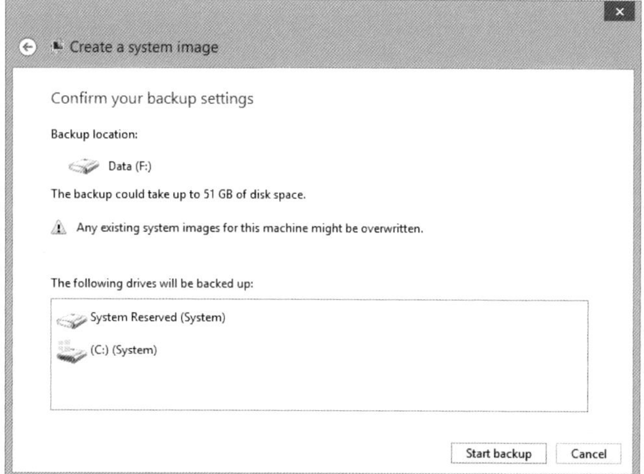

5 Windows creates the system image

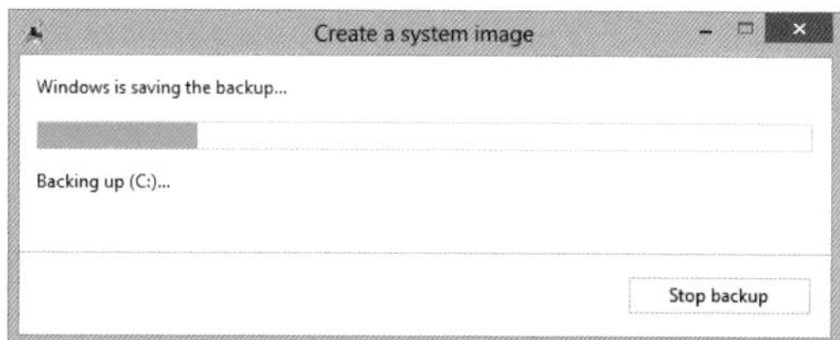

Hot tip

Images cannot be saved on the boot disk (where Windows is installed). You must use a different drive or partition

Hot tip

If you don't have a second drive, you can create a second partition on your C: drive for the image.

System repair disc

There will be occasions when it is impossible to get into Windows for some reason – damaged startup files is a typical example. For this reason, recovery and troubleshooting utilities have to be accessible from outside the Windows environment.

To be able to use the Windows utilities in this type of situation, they have to be first placed on removable media.

1. Open the Search charm and enter recdisc. Open the utility by pressing Enter

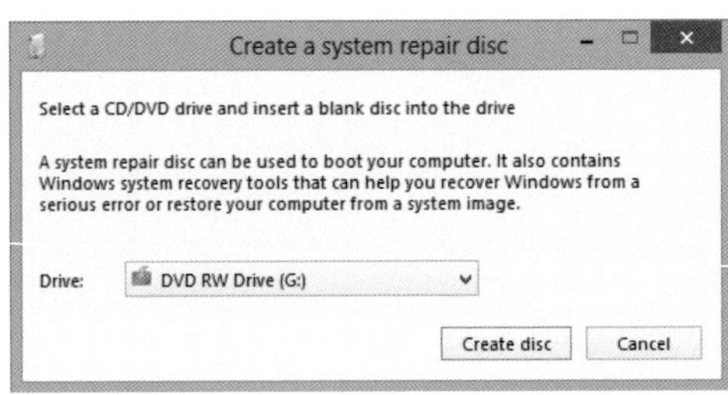

2. Place a DVD in the DVD drive and click Create disc

3. The system repair disc is created

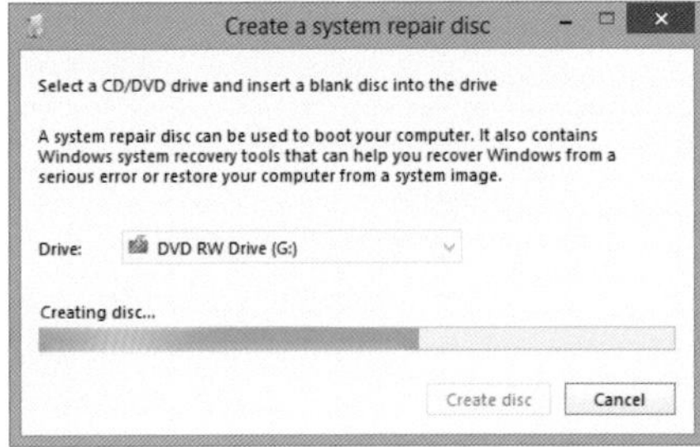

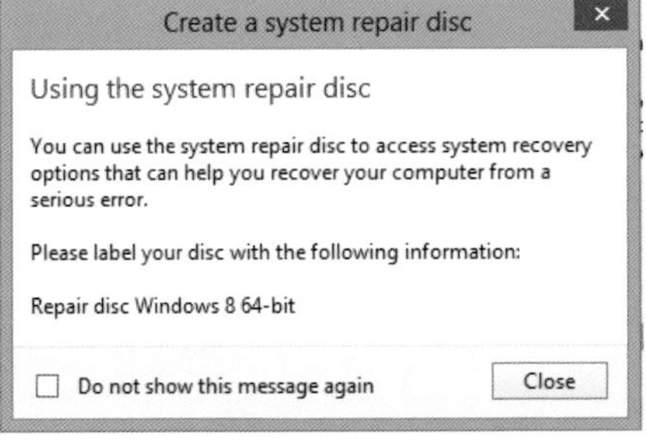

4. You are prompted to label the disc

If you don't have a DVD drive or would just rather use a USB flash drive, go to the Control Panel and open Recovery. Then click Create a recovery drive and follow the prompts. The recovery drive will contain exactly the same utilities as the system repair disc.

Hot tip

Create a system repair disc now – if you leave it until you need it, it will be too late.

You can also create a repair disc with a USB flash drive. This is done with Recovery in the Control Panel.

22 Security and encryption

If your system or your storage devices contain sensitive information, you can protect the data even if the device is lost or stolen, using the various encryption facilities that are included in Windows 8.

User account management

There are several ways to manage user accounts on your computer. The primary option is User Accounts in the Control Panel. This is used to create or remove user accounts, change the account types, add or change passwords, or change the pictures associated with accounts.

Don't forget

User Accounts is in the Control Panel.

If you have several users sharing your computer, you might want to enable Secure Logon. To set this up, you need the alternative User Accounts dialog.

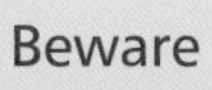

Beware

This alternative User Accounts is very powerful and should only be used with caution.

1. Press Winkey + R to open the Run box

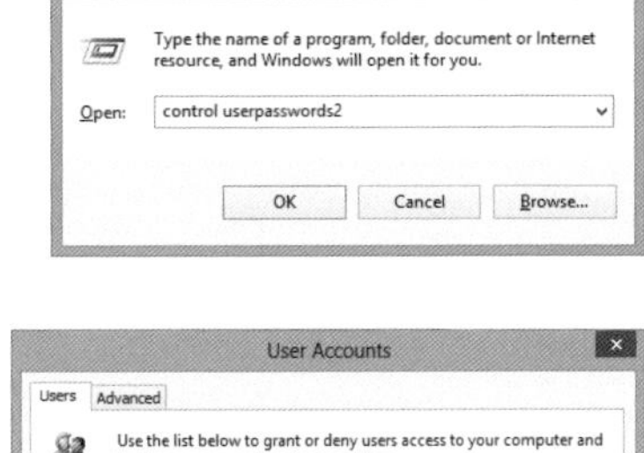

2. Type the command control userpasswords2 and press OK

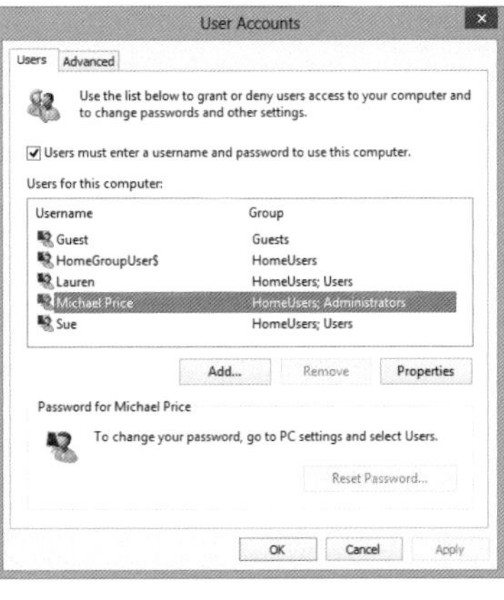

3. Select the Advanced tab to show Secure Logon

Hot tip

Setting Secure Logon guarantees that the sign on prompt is genuine, not an external program trying to discover your password.

4. Click the box that will Require users to press Ctrl + Alt + Del

In the Pro and Enterprise editions of Windows 8, you can manage user accounts with the Local Users and Groups policy editor. There are several ways to display this. For example:

1. From the Advanced tab of the second User Accounts option, click the Advanced button

2. Press Winkey + R, type lusrmgr.msc and press Enter

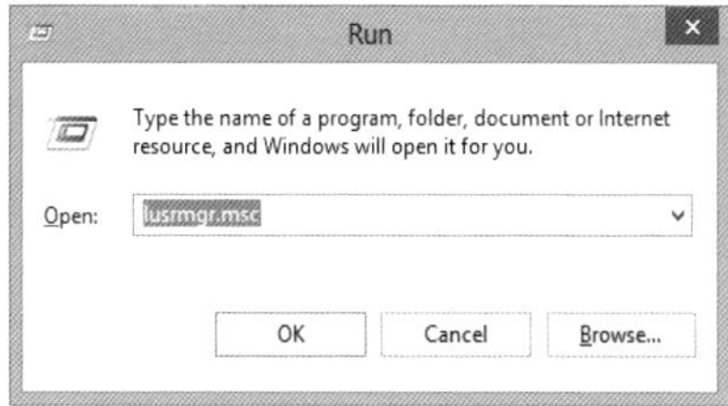

3. When the panel opens, click Users and you will see an extra user Administrator, not shown in User Accounts

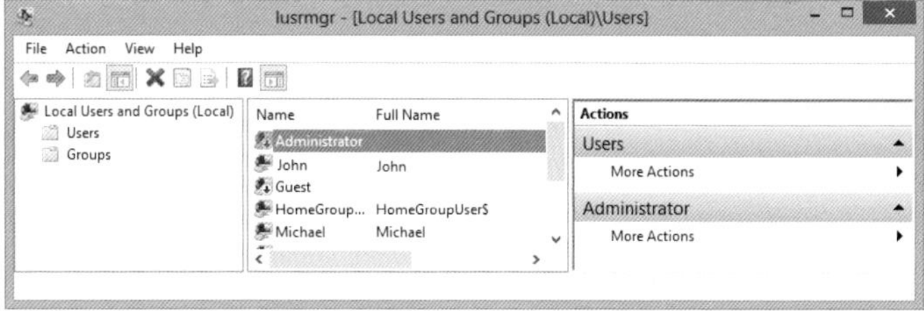

4. Double-click user account Administrator to display its Properties, and you'll see it is disabled by default

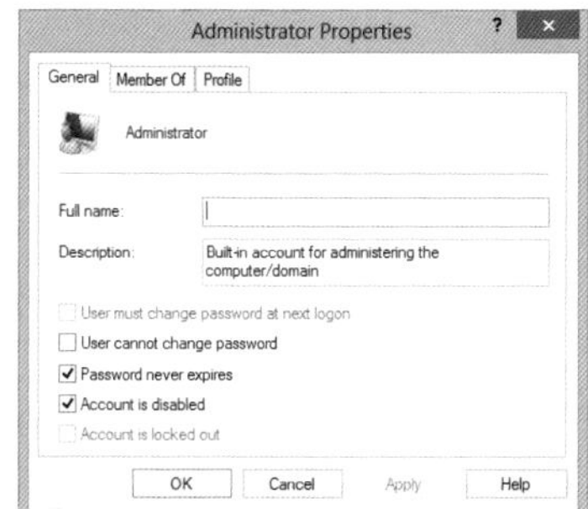

Set Password...
All Tasks
Delete
Rename
Properties
Help

5. If you do enable this account, make sure to select More actions, then Set password

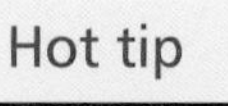

Hot tip

This is a built-in account that is automatically created but not normally used. If you do choose to use it, make sure to set a password.

Set password to expire

By default, your password can remain the same for always, but you are recommended to change it on a regular basis. Windows can be set to ensure that this happens.

You can also double-click the user name to open Properties.

1. Open Local Users and Groups (see page 379), select your user name and click More Actions, Properties

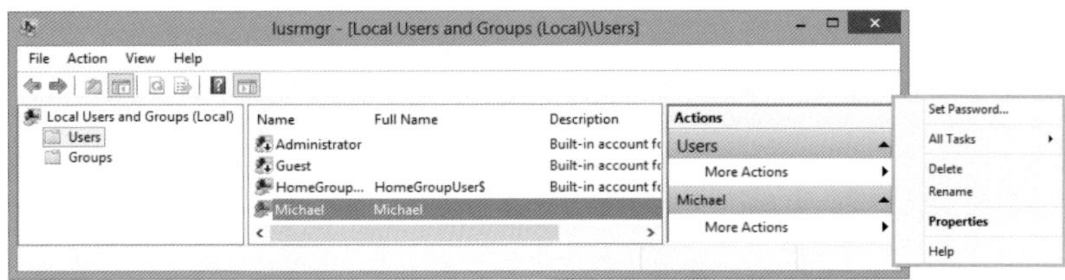

2. Clear the box for Password never expires and click User must change password at next logon

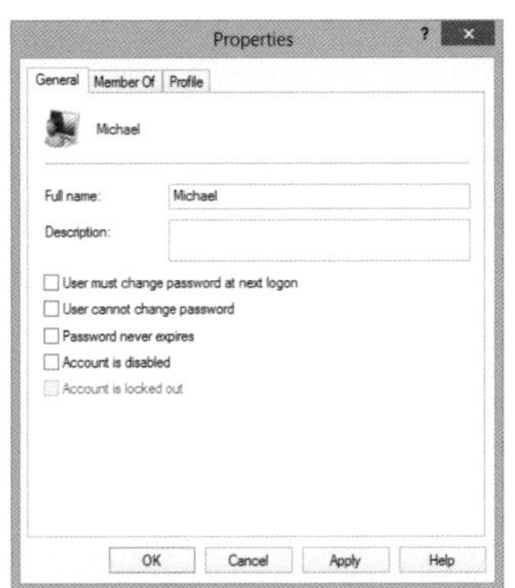

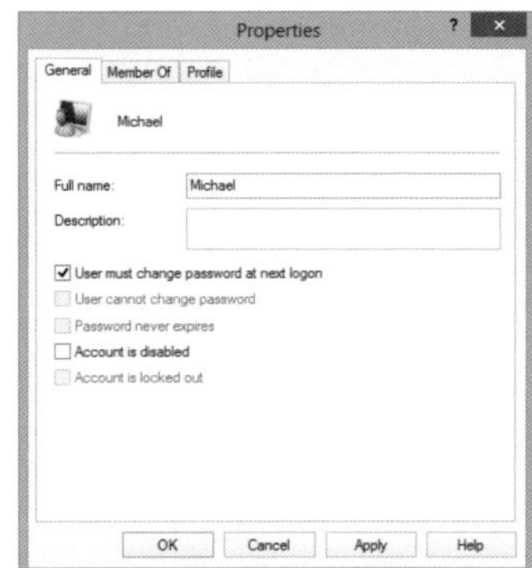

3. Close Local Users and Groups, then open Local Security Policy (see page 379) and expand Account Policies

You could change the maximum password age to 182 days, and then you would get a new password twice a year.

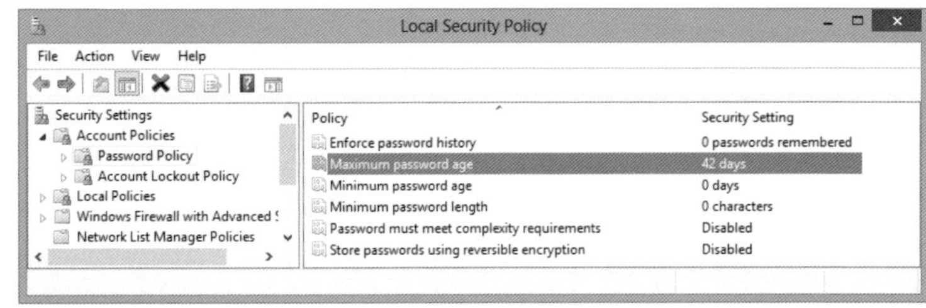

4. Select Password Policy, and then Maximum password age

5 When you next sign on to the computer, select your account name as usual and enter your current password

6 You are told your password has expired. Click OK

7 Enter your existing password, then the new password and then confirm the new password and continue

8 Windows changes the password and confirms the change

9 Click OK and Windows starts. The password is reset, and future sign ons will proceed without interruption

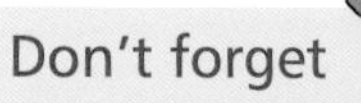

When you enter a new password, Windows reminds you that you can create a password reset disk. However, it is only needed once, not every time you change your password.

Beware

When the specified period has passed, Windows will again notify you that the password has expired and require you to provide a new password.

Hide user list

Whenever you start Windows, logoff or switch users, the Account selection screen displays the list of users defined for that computer.

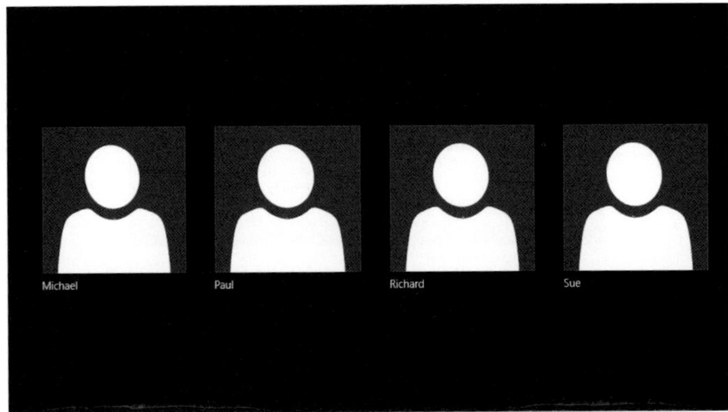

Don't forget

You'd make changes like this if you have to leave your computer unattended, for example when running a presentation at a meeting or show.

You might feel it would be more secure for the names to remain hidden, especially if you are using your computer in a public area. You can do this using the Local Security Policy.

1. Press Winkey + R and type secpol.msc, then press Enter to open Local Security Policy

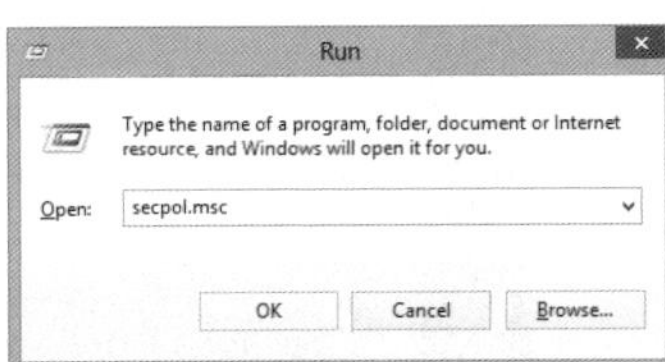

2. Expand Local Policies, select Security Options and locate Interactive Logon: Do not display last user name

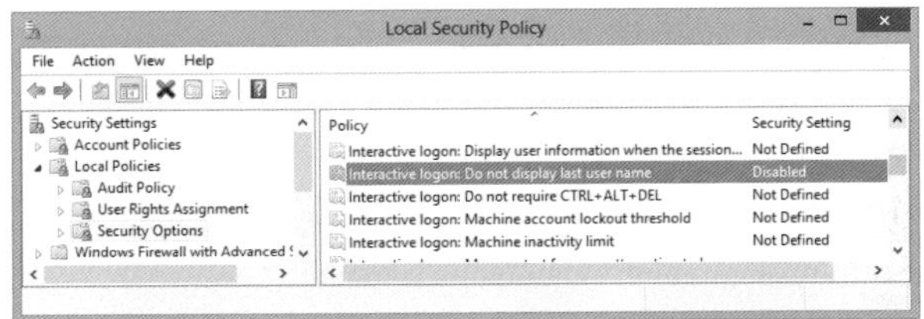

3. Double-click the entry to display the Properties, select Enabled, and then click OK

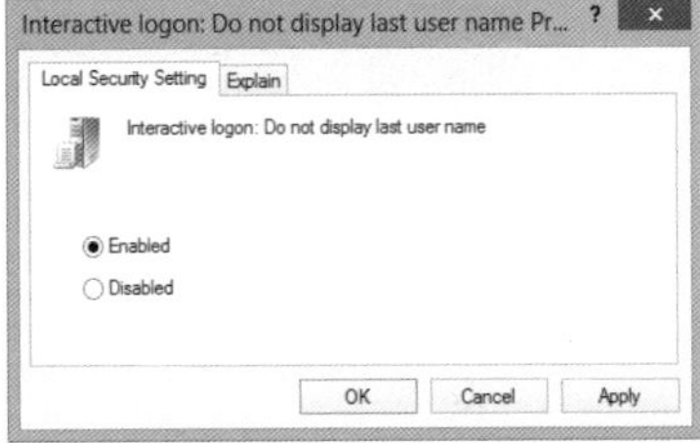

4. The entry will now be shown as Enabled, so click File, Close to save the change

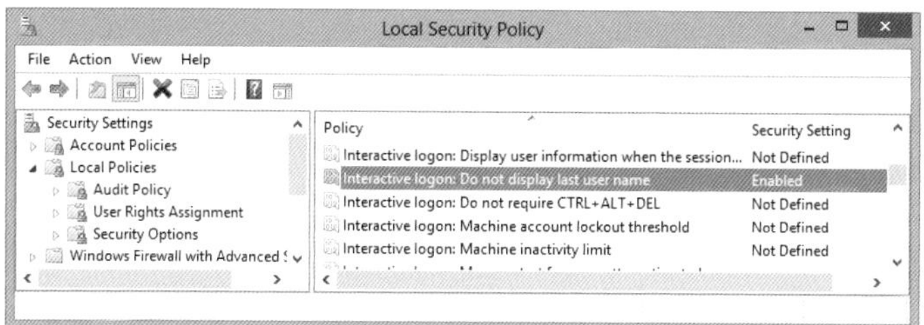

5. The next time you restart, log off or switch users, the Sign on screen is displayed, with no user name specified

6. Type your user name and your password to sign on

7. If you make a mistake, you are just told the user name or password is incorrect, and you must click OK and try again

If you have other users on the computer with administrator accounts, they can of course view the list of users in User Accounts, or make changes to Security Options to reverse the setting.

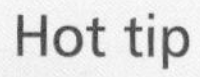

There's no user picture, and no Switch Users button. If you enter a wrong value, there's no clue and the password reminder is not offered, to preserve the security.

Encrypting files

Don't forget

Anyone getting hold of a copy of the files won't be able to access their contents. Even another user logged on to your computer is unable to access the files.

You might be storing personal, financial or other information on your computer that you wouldn't want others to read. Some editions of Windows include encryption tools that can help protect confidential data. There are three components:

- **Encrypting File System (EFS)** – with this your sensitive files and folders can be encoded so that they can only be read when you log on to the computer with the associated user account
- **BitLocker Drive Encryption** – this is used to encrypt an entire hard disk volume. The encryption is linked to a key stored in a Trusted Platform Module (TPM) or USB flash drive
- **BitLocker To Go** – this provides BitLocker encryption for removable media

Hot tip

TPM hardware will normally be found on business machines rather than home computers. However, a USB flash drive can be used in place of TPM.

Windows editions with encryption

EFS is available in the Pro and Enterprise versions of Windows 8 and the Professional, Enterprise and Ultimate editions of Windows 7. You must have Windows 8 Pro, Windows 8 Enterprise, Windows 7 Enterprise or Windows 7 Ultimate to encrypt a drive using BitLocker or BitLocker To Go.

There are no facilities to encrypt files in the Home Premium, Home Basic or Starter editions. However, when you encrypt a USB flash drive with BitLocker To Go, you can add, delete, and change files on that drive using any edition of Windows 7.

Systems running Windows XP and Windows Vista can, with the appropriate authentication, open and read the files on an encrypted drive using the reader program that is included on the drive itself. However, files cannot be changed or added.

Beware

You need a system partition in addition to the Windows volume. This system partition is normally set up when Windows is installed.

Hardware requirements

For Bitlocker drive encryption of the whole system, the Windows partition and the System partition must both have NTFS format.

You can use BitLocker to encrypt additional fixed data drives, and BitLocker To Go to encrypt your removable data drives. These drives must have at least 64MB available space and can be formatted using FAT or NTFS (unless intended for Windows XP or Windows Vista, when FAT will be required).

Using EFS

You can encrypt individual files, whole folders, or entire drives using EFS. However, it is best to encrypt by folder (or by drive) rather than by individual file. This means that the existing files would be encrypted, and new files that get created in that folder or drive will also be encrypted, including any temporary files that applications might generate.

To encrypt the contents of a folder on your hard drive:

1. Locate the folder in File Explorer

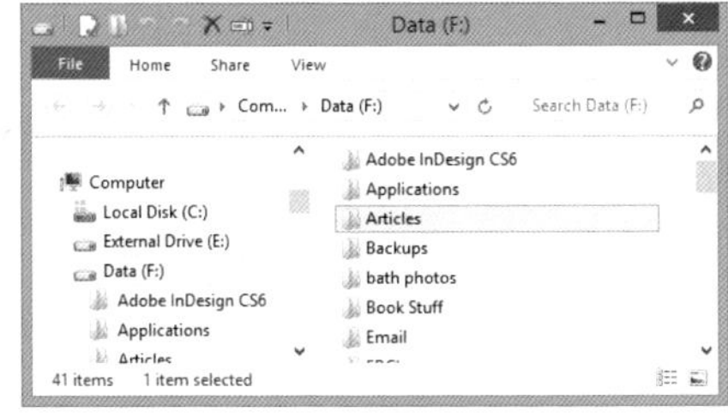

2. Right-click the folder icon and select Properties and the General tab

3. Click the Advanced button to display the Advanced attributes

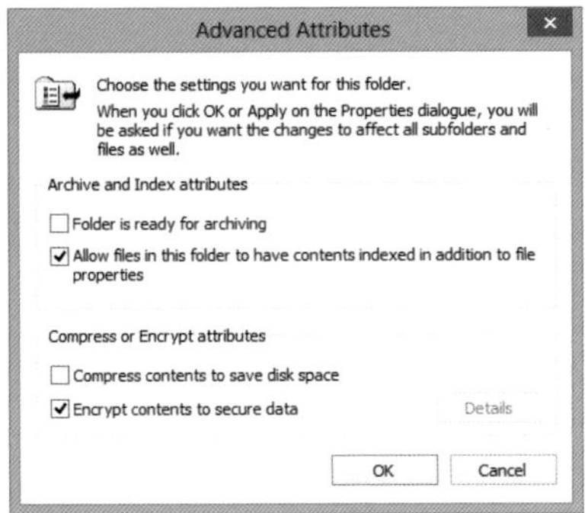

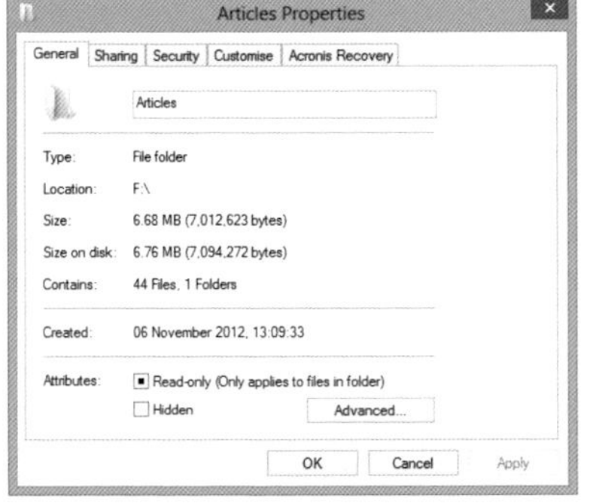

4. Select Encrypt contents to secure data, then click OK

5. Click OK in Properties to apply the change

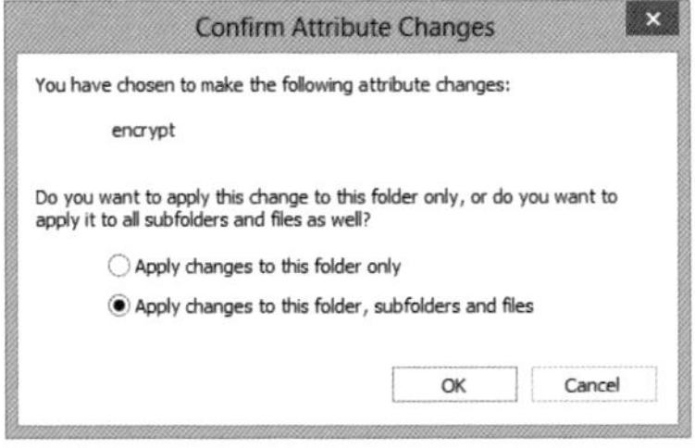

6. Select Apply changes to this folder, subfolders and files, then click OK to continue

Don't forget

If you allowed encryption of individual files in a folder, temporary files created there would be unencrypted, even though they could contain copies of the information you are trying to protect.

Hot tip

If the folder is on a drive that is not formatted as NTFS, there will be no Advanced button, and EFS encryption will not be available.

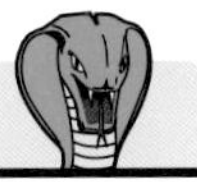

Beware

If you choose Apply changes to this folder only, only new files will be encrypted, not existing files.

...cont'd

7. Your encryption certificate is created, and the folder and its contents are encrypted

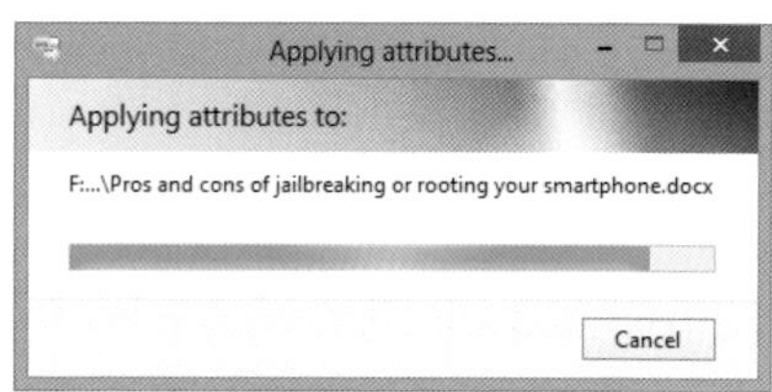

8. As encryption proceeds, a message is displayed, reminding you to Back up your file encryption key

When encryption completes, check the folder in File Explorer, and you'll see the name text for the folder and its files has been recolored as Green, whether you display the contents as Tiles, List or any other view.

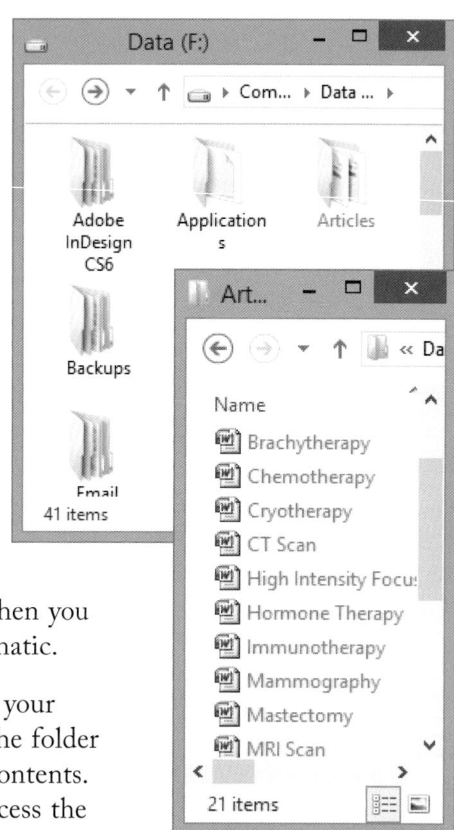

When you work with encrypted files from your user account, that's the only visible difference. Windows will decrypt your files as you use them and will re-encrypt them when you save, and it is all fully automatic.

Another user logging on to your system may be able to see the folder and open it to display the contents. However, any attempt to access the files will give an error message from the associated application, saying that access is denied.

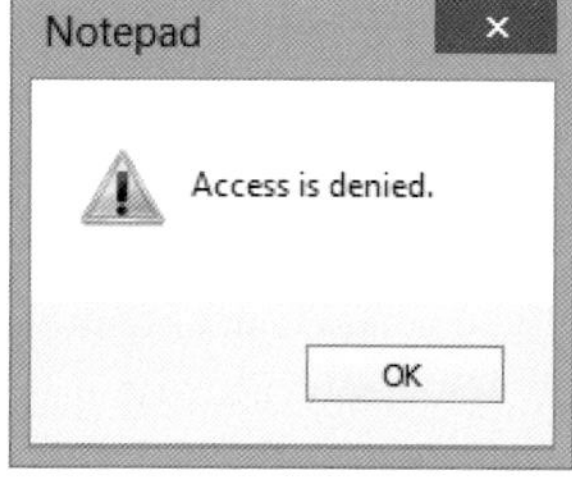

Similarly, Copy or Move of encrypted files will be denied. Even administrator user accounts will be denied access.

Hot tip

If you'd chosen the other mutually-exclusive attribute, Compress contents to save space, you would see the name text recolored as Blue.

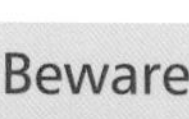

Beware

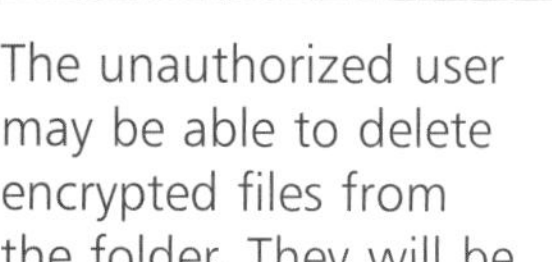

The unauthorized user may be able to delete encrypted files from the folder. They will be transferred to the recycle bin, but will still be classed as encrypted.

Backup encryption key

1. Press Winkey + R, and enter certmgr.msc

2. Expand Personal and select Certificates

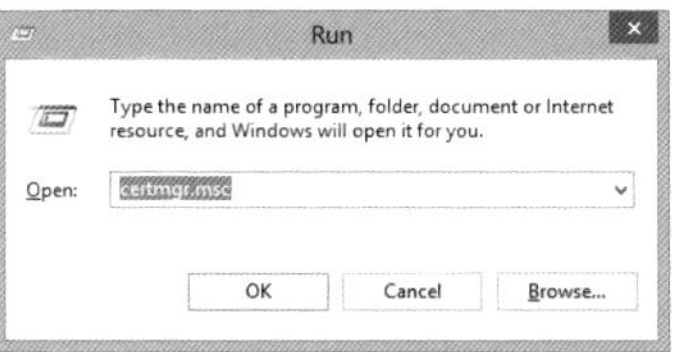

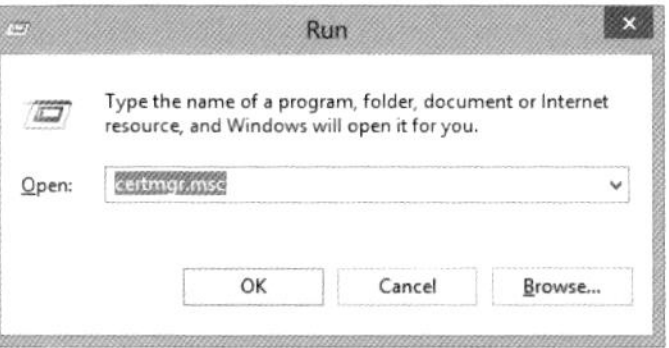

Don't forget

If you lose the certificate, perhaps due to a hard disk failure, you won't be able to use your encrypted files. That's why you are advised to create a backup.

3. Select the certificate for the Encrypting File System

4. Select Action and choose All Tasks, Export

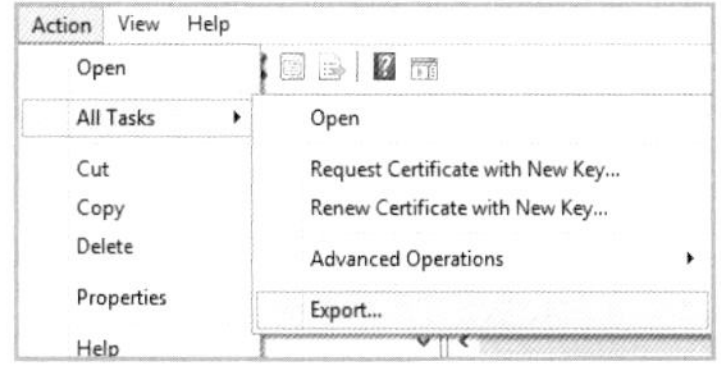

Hot tip

You'll need a removable device such as a USB flash drive, which is not encrypted and which can be kept physically secure.

5. The Certificate Export Wizard starts. Click Next

6. Click Yes, export the private key with the certificate then click Next

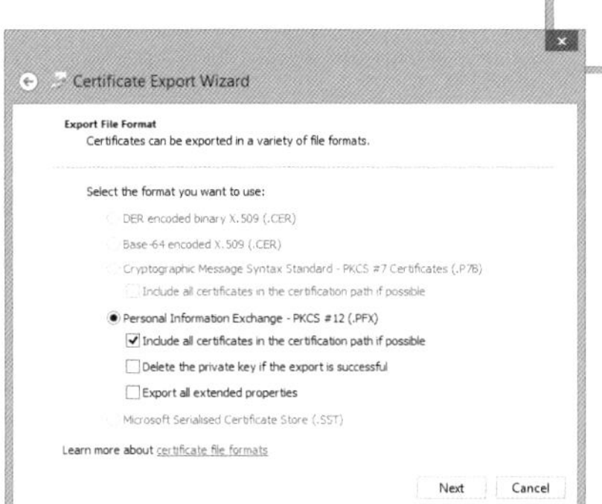

7. Select the Personal Information Exchange (PFX) file format, and click Next

...cont'd

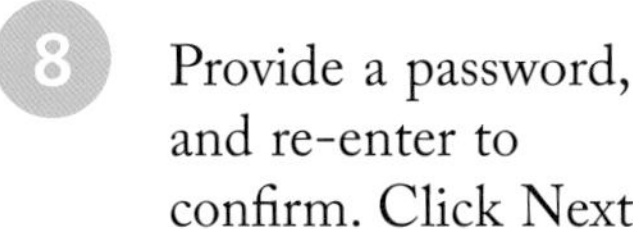

8 Provide a password, and re-enter to confirm. Click Next

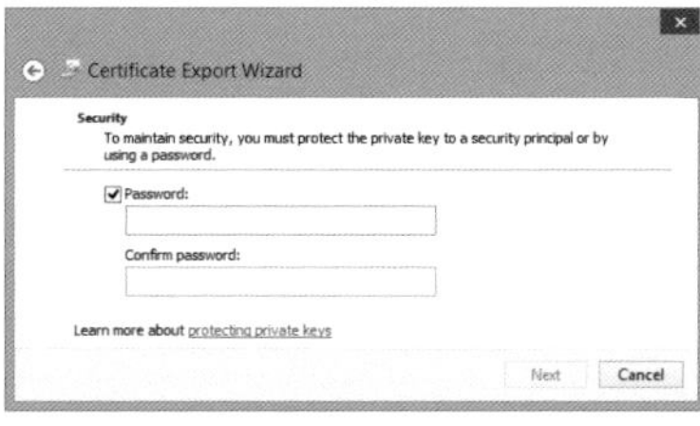

9 Click Browse to choose the destination drive

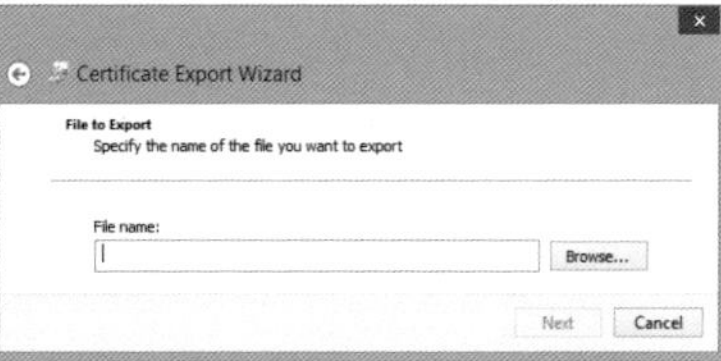

10 Select the storage device, enter the file name, and Save

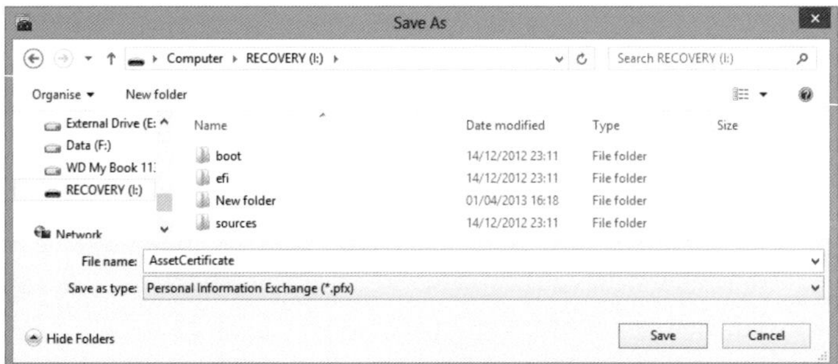

11 Click Next to confirm name and location

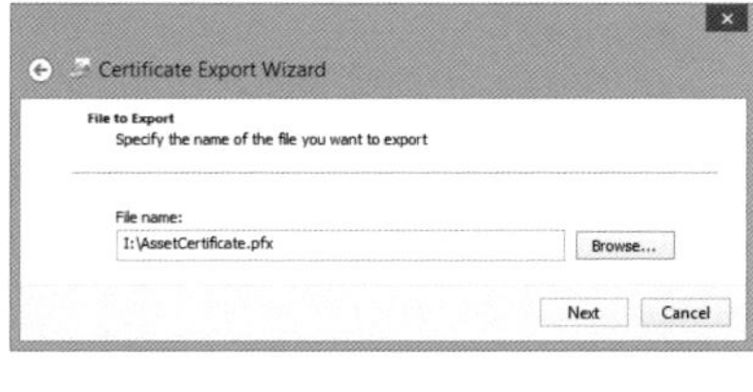

12 Click Finish to complete the Wizard

To restore the certificate, you'd insert the backup media, run certmgr.msc to open Certificate Manager, select Personal, and then Action, All Tasks, Import, and follow the prompts from the Certificate Import wizard.

Hot tip

You could use the same device as you use to create a password reset disk, since it has the same security requirements.

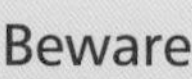

Beware

Remove the storage media and store it in a safe location, since it can enable anyone to access your encrypted files.

BitLocker To Go

To encrypt a removable drive:

1. Connect the drive and press Winkey + X to open the Power users menu. Select File Explorer

2. Right-click the drive icon and select Turn Bitlocker on

3. Choose how you want to unlock this drive – password or smart card

4. Select password and enter your password, enter it again to confirm, then click Next

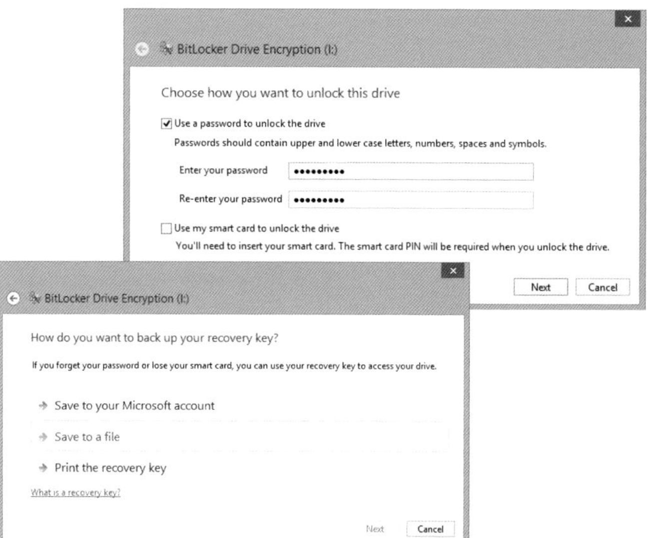

5. Click Save the recovery key to a file, the file name is provided, and you specify the drive and then click Save

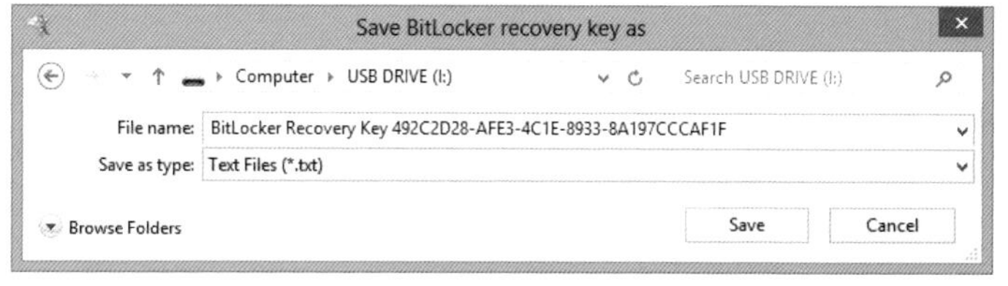

Large organizations use smart cards for network authentication and have computers with smart card readers that can access the cards and store information there.

A good choice might be the USB flash drive being used as the password reset disk and for your EFS certificate.

...cont'd

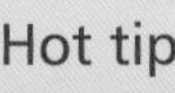

Hot tip

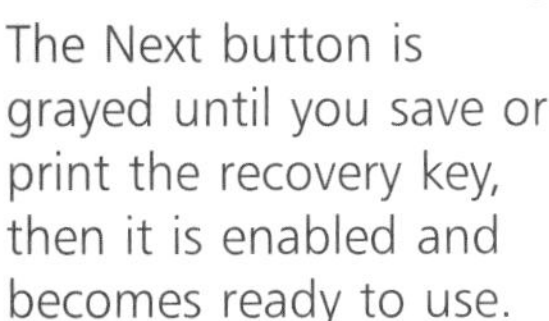

The Next button is grayed until you save or print the recovery key, then it is enabled and becomes ready to use.

6. You can also choose to print the recovery key. When the key has been saved or printed, click Next

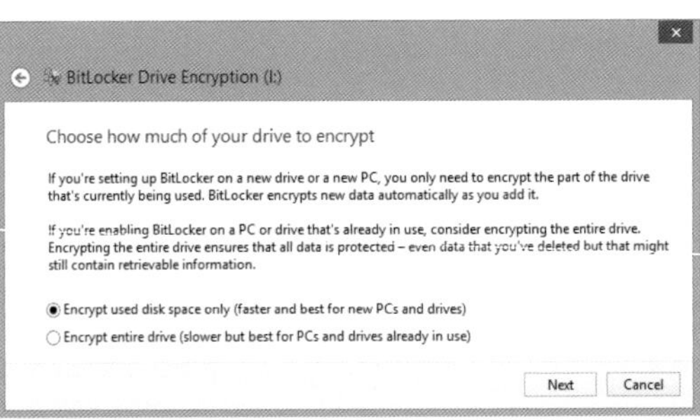

7. Choose how much of the drive to encrypt

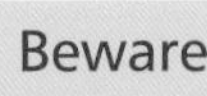

Beware

If for any reason you need to remove the drive before completion, click Pause to interrupt the processing, or else files could be damaged.

8. Click Start Encrypting and the files on the removable device are processed

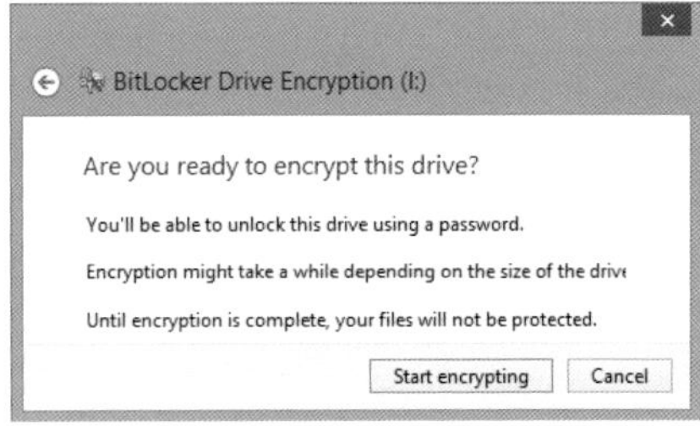

9. Click Close when encryption completes

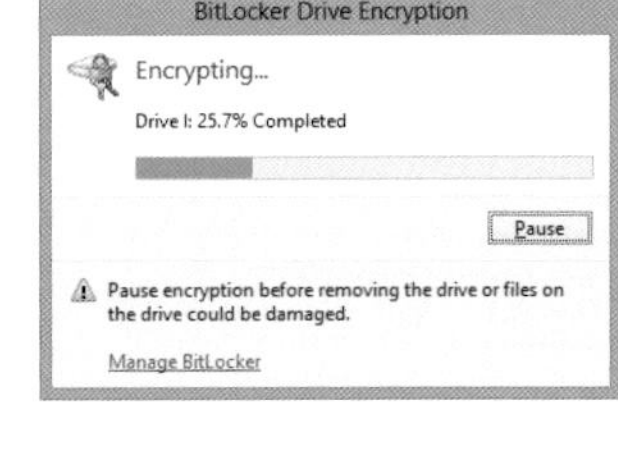

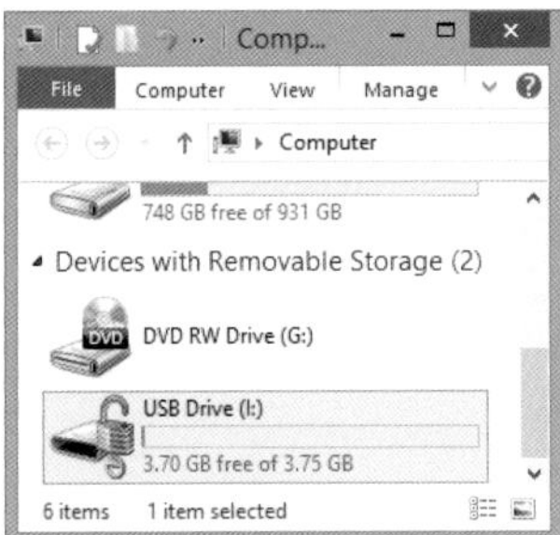

10. Open Computer, and you'll see the Lock symbol on the drive icon which indicates it is protected by encryption

Access the encrypted drive

To access the drive:

1. Insert the removable device and BitLocker will tell you the device is protected

2. Click on the message to open the password screen

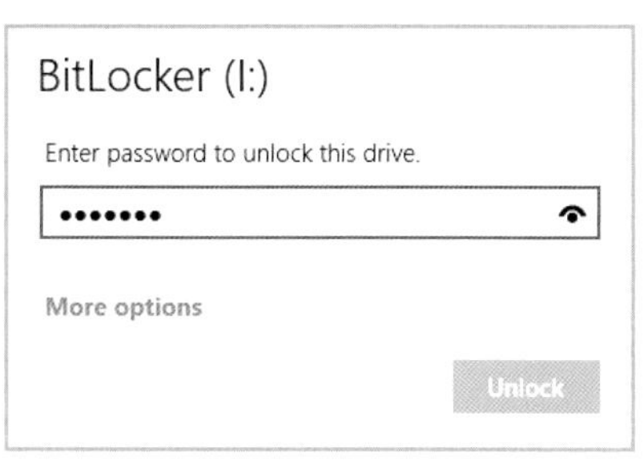

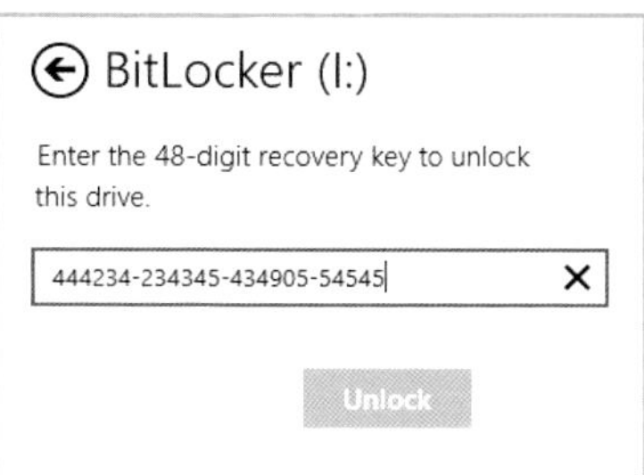

3. Unlock the drive by entering the password and clicking the Unlock button

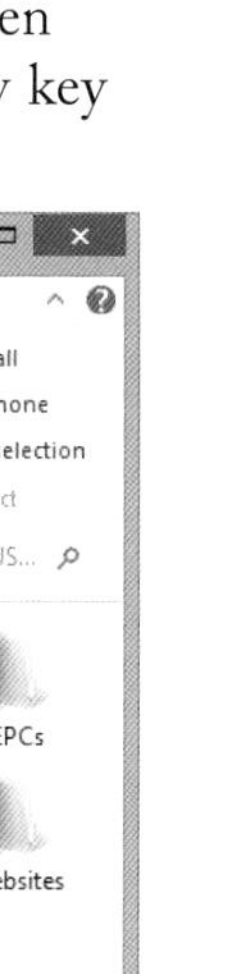

4. If you cannot remember the password, click More options. Then enter the recovery key

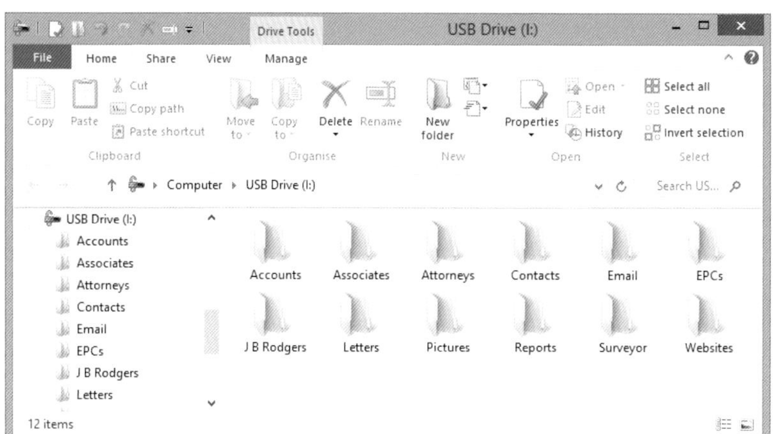

5. The drive opens. You can open, edit and save files or create new files on this drive, and they will be encrypted

6. Use Safely remove hardware when you've finished

Click More options (see step 3) and you will be able to select Automatically unlock on this computer from now on. Windows will remember the password for you.

Whole system encryption

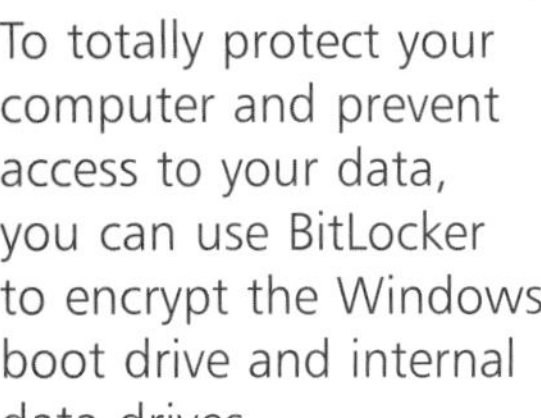

Hot tip

To totally protect your computer and prevent access to your data, you can use BitLocker to encrypt the Windows boot drive and internal data drives.

1. Go to the Control Panel, System and Security, and open BitLocker Drive Encryption

2. Select Turn BitLocker on for the system or data drive and then follow the prompts to encrypt the drive

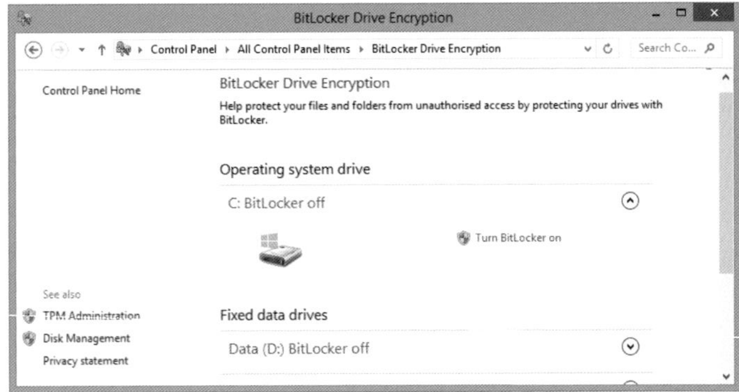

Hot tip

Open TPM Admin by typing tpm.msc in the Run box.

3. Any problems with the computer setup will be detected

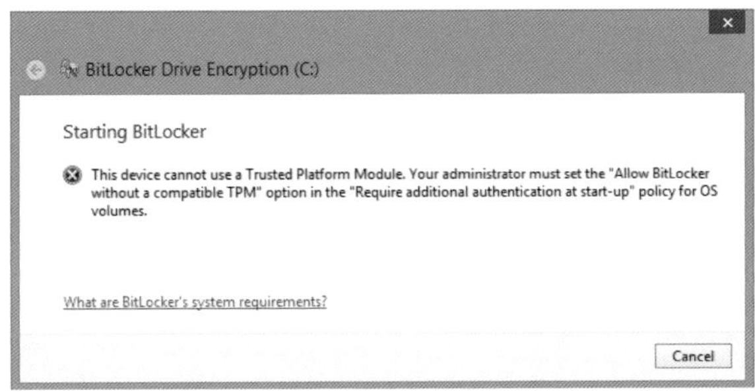

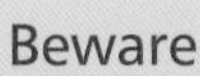

Beware

You can enable TPM in the BIOS, or you can configure BitLocker to use a USB drive instead. However, problems with BitLocker could make your system inaccessible, so only proceed with this if you have adequate technical support.

4. Select TPM (Trusted Platform Module) Administration to check the level of support, and you may find the TPM module cannot be found

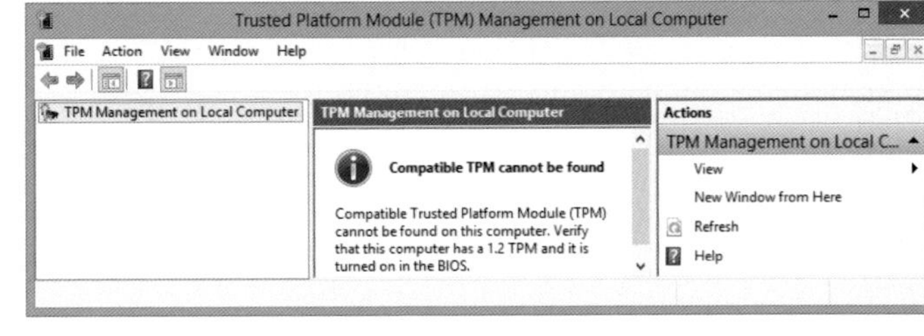

23 Command Prompt

Most users won't need it but Command Prompt in Windows can be very useful in certain situations. There's an administrator mode when necessary for the tasks being run.

Open Command Prompt

All editions of Windows 8 include the Command Prompt environment, where you can run commands, batch files and applications by typing statements at the command line.

There are a number of ways to start a Command Prompt session:

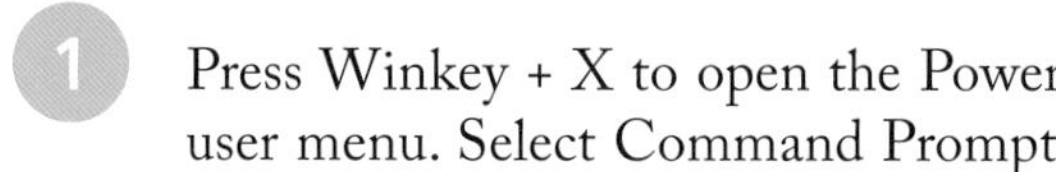

1. Press Winkey + X to open the Power user menu. Select Command Prompt

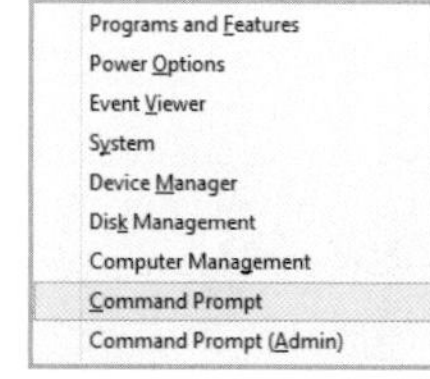

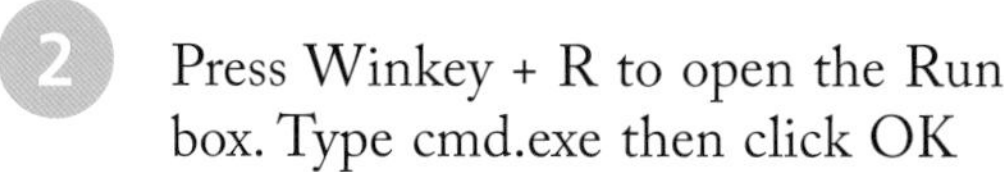

2. Press Winkey + R to open the Run box. Type cmd.exe then click OK

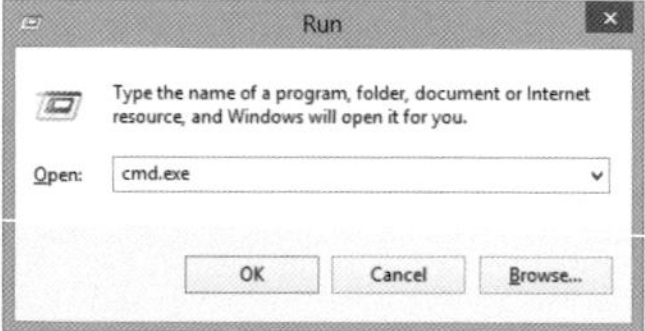

3. Open the Search charm and enter cmd. On the results pane, click Command Prompt

4. Double-click a shortcut to the program – with or without the Shortcut suffix and the arrow overlay

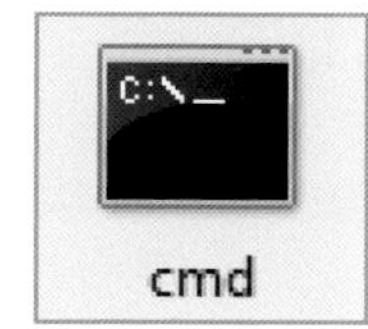

All of these methods will start a Command Prompt session, with title cmd.exe, open at C:\Users\user name and ready to accept commands.

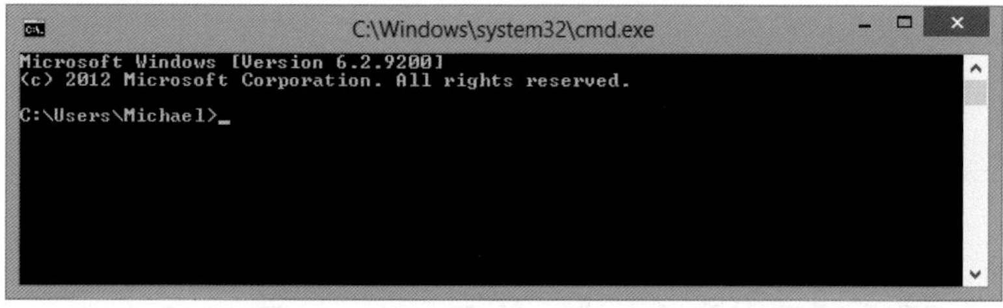

Don't forget

The Run box will display the last run program, and you can click the down-arrow and select from the list of previously run programs.

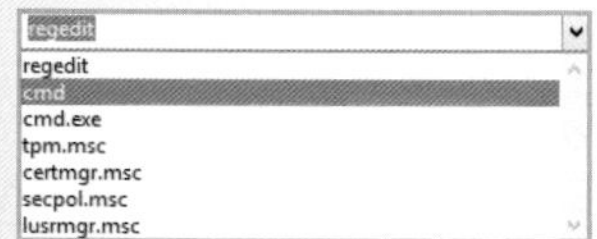

Hot tip

To create a shortcut, you right-click the program icon and select Create Shortcut. The shortcut icon will be placed on the Desktop.

5. You can open additional, independent Command Prompt sessions, using the same methods

6. Alternatively, from an existing session, type start cmd on the command line and press Enter

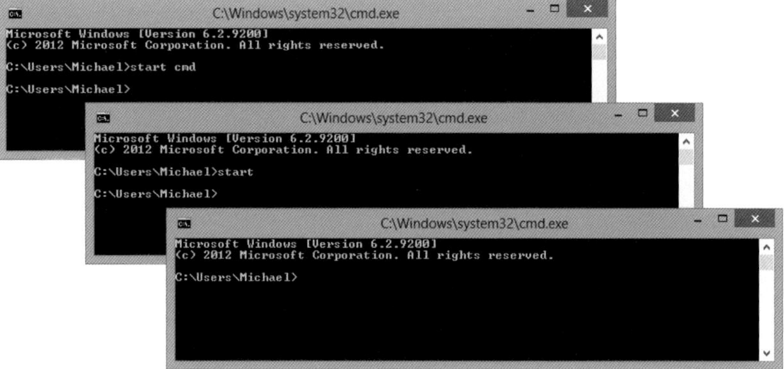

7. The new sessions are given the program path and name as title, and they open in the user's user folder

You can also open a Command Prompt at C:\Windows\System32 folder.

1. Open the folder C:\Windows\System32 and click the cmd.exe program icon

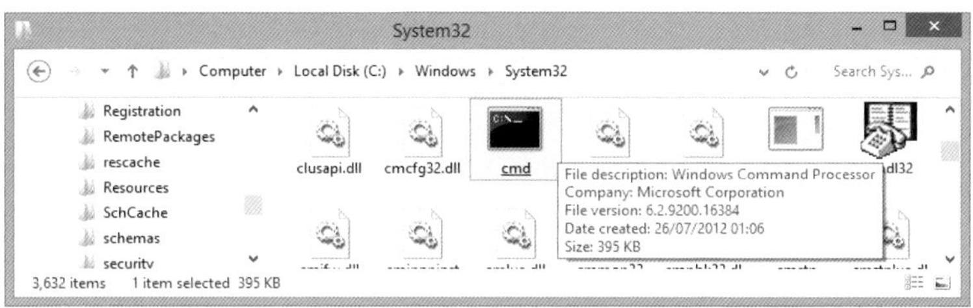

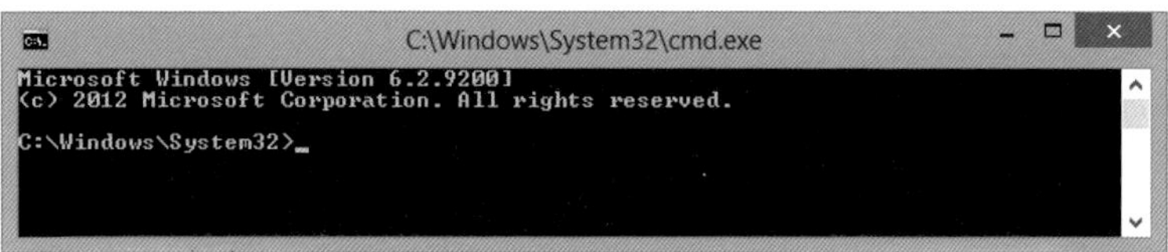

Don't forget

You might use multiple sessions to compare the contents of two or more folders.

Hot tip

If you just type Start, with no program name, it will be assumed that you want to start cmd.exe, so this also gives you a Command Prompt session.

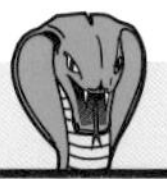

Beware

If you have a different folder or drive specified for your Windows system, folder paths will be adjusted accordingly.

Select a folder

You can switch folders in the Command Prompt session using the CD (Change Directory) command. For example, to open the current user's Pictures folder, starting from System32:

1. On the Command Line, type these four CD commands, pressing Enter after each command:
cd \   cd users   cd "john smith"   cd pictures

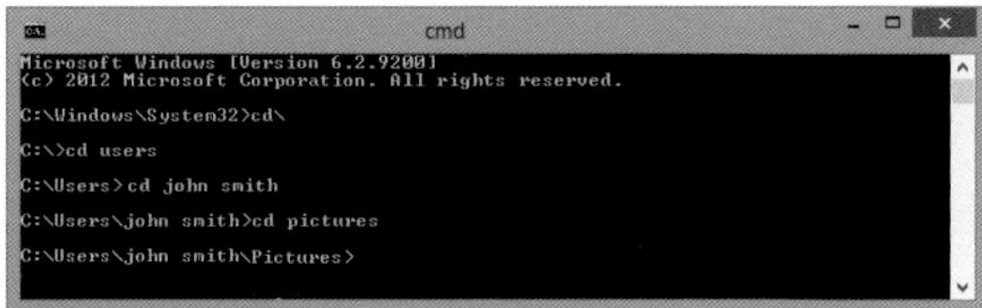

To avoid problems with long or complex filenames, you can open a Command Session directly at the required folder.

You can use the normal Windows methods for locating folders, and select the required folder from either the contents pane or the navigation pane.

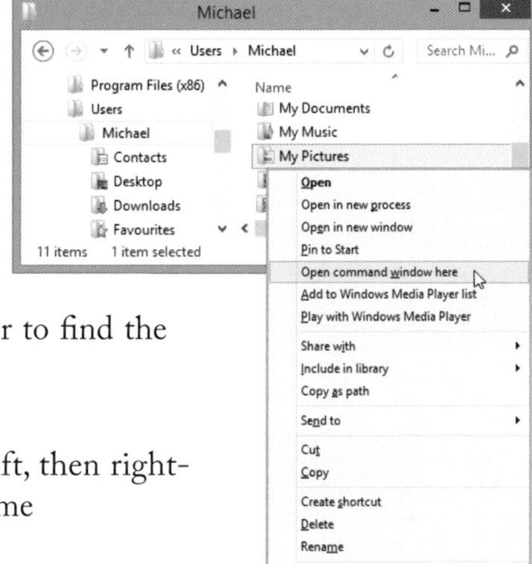

1. Open File Explorer to find the desired folder
2. Press and hold Shift, then right-click the folder name
3. From the extended right-click menu displayed, select the entry to Open Command window here

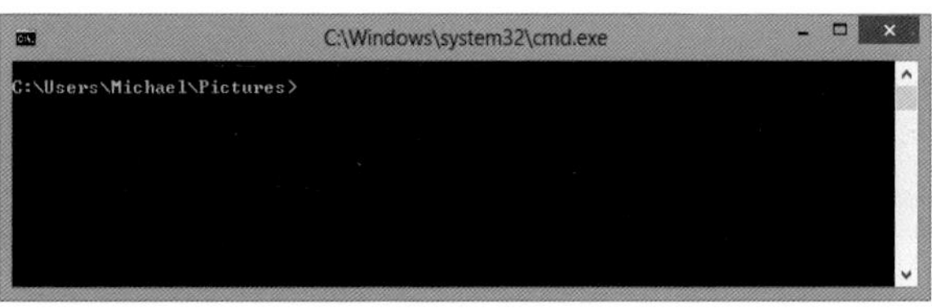

Don't forget

Note that case does not matter. When there are spaces in the file or folder names, you may need to specify quotation marks.

Hot tip

The Command Prompt session is opened and switched to the required folder.

Open as administrator

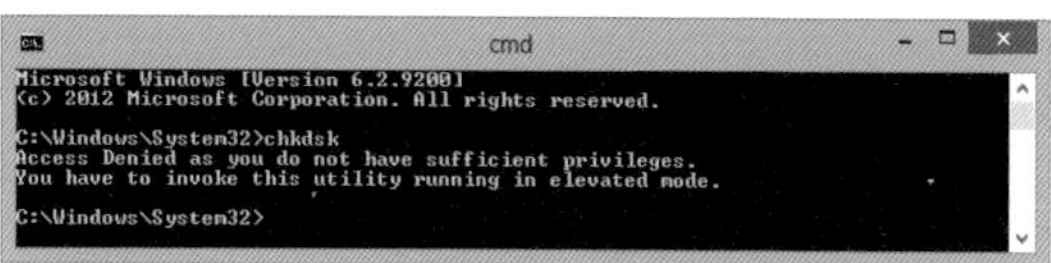

The Command Prompt session opened has the standard user level of privilege. If some commands that you want to run require administrator privilege, you can open an elevated session using the following methods:

1. Open C:\Windows\System32, right-click Cmd.exe and select Run as administrator

2. Open the Charms bar and type cmd in the Search charm. Right-click on Command Prompt and select Run as administrator from the app bar

Both methods will require you to reply to a UAC prompt to start a Command Prompt session with the title Administrator: cmd.exe, which opens at the System32 folder.

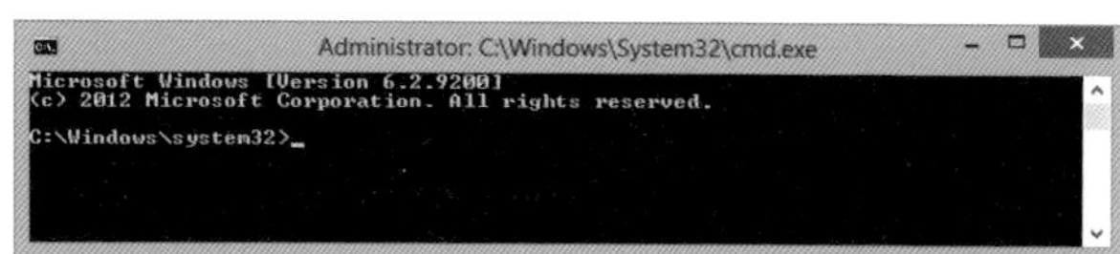

If you click the Command Prompt (Admin) entry from the Power users menu (Winkey + X), you get a Command Prompt session, entitled Administrator: Command Prompt. This also opens at the System32 folder, not the user's folder.

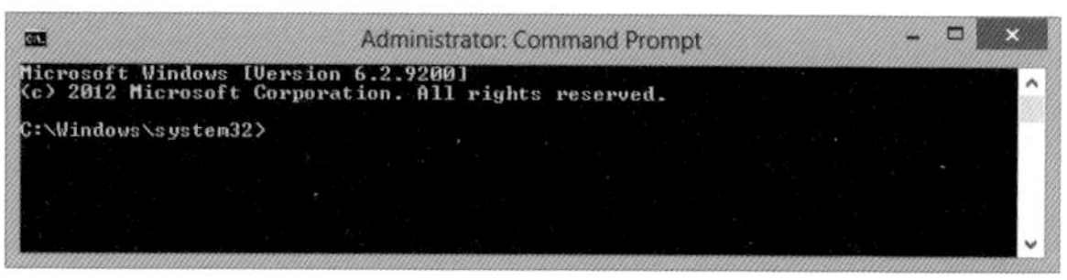

Don't forget

Commands that have system wide effect are restricted to run only in the elevated administrator mode.

Hot tip

You can also type Start or Start cmd on the command line of an existing administrator session to get another administrator session – no UAC required.

Administrator shortcut

You can configure a shortcut to Cmd.exe to always start in administrator mode.

The modified shortcut can be saved to the Desktop or the taskbar.

1. Create a shortcut to Cmd.exe (at C:\Windows\System32\cmd.exe)

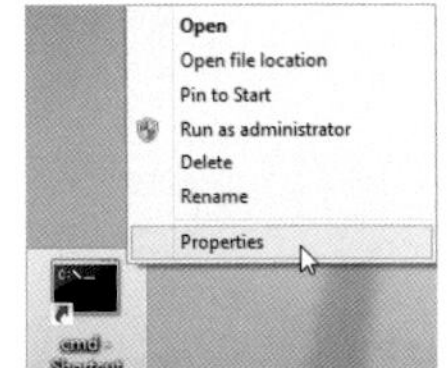

2. Right-click the shortcut and select Properties from the menu

3. Select the Shortcut tab and click the Advanced button

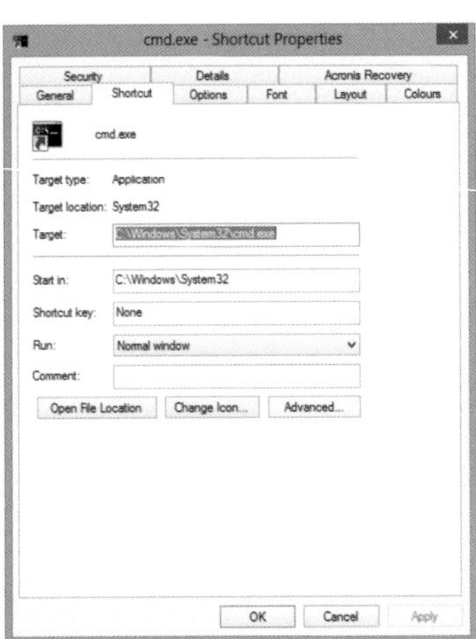

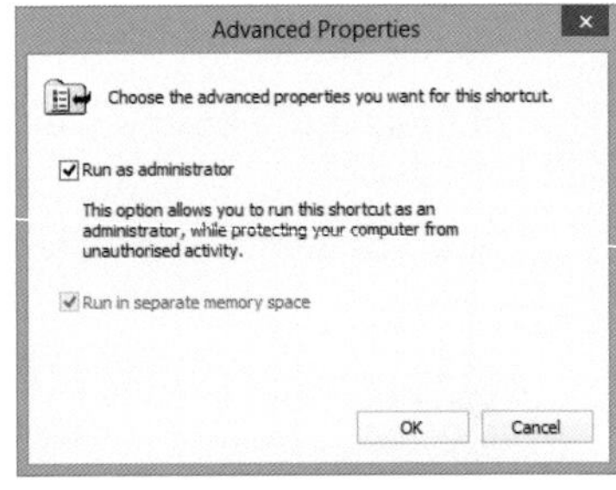

4. Click the box Run as administrator and click OK, then OK again

5. Right-click the shortcut icon, select Rename and give it a meaningful name

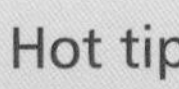

The name that you give the shortcut appears as part of the title for the session, along with the word Administrator for elevated sessions.

6. For example, you could have Standard Commands and Elevated Commands

7. Double-click the appropriate shortcut to start the administrator session

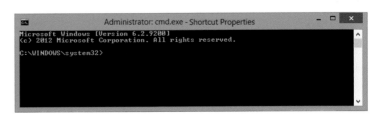

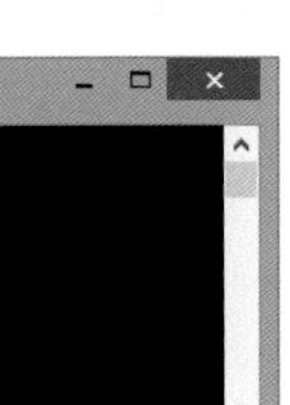


```
Administrator: cmd.exe - Shortcut Properties
Microsoft Windows [Version 6.2.9200]
(c) 2012 Microsoft Corporation. All rights reserved.

C:\WINDOWS\system32>
```

Adjust appearance

You can adjust shortcut Properties to control the appearance of the Command Prompt window that is launched by that shortcut.

1. Right-click the shortcut icon and click Properties

2. Select the Options tab

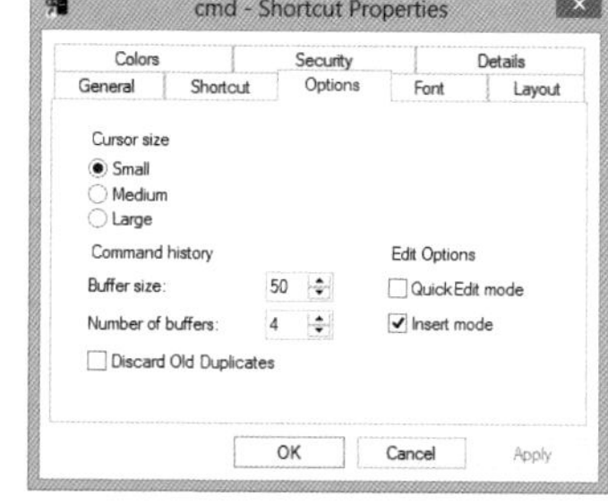

From here, you can adjust the size of the flashing cursor, change how the command history is managed, and change edit options.

3. Select the Font tab to choose a different font

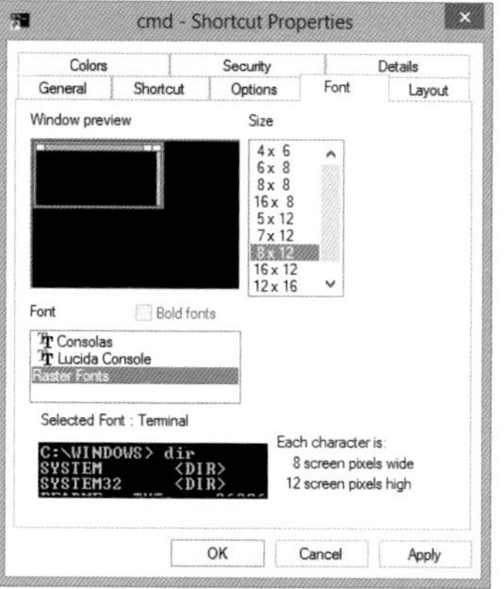

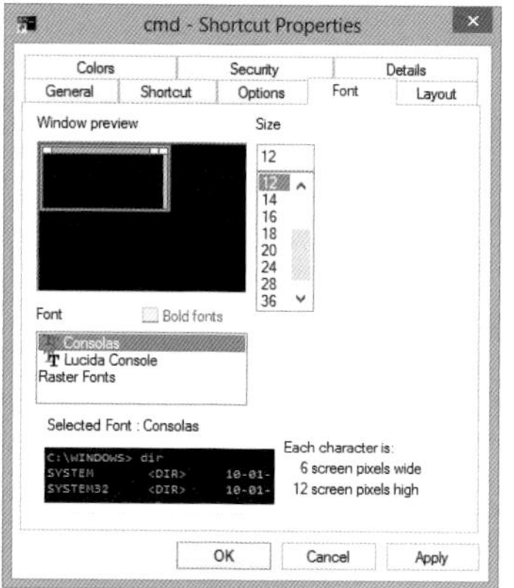

4. The recommended font is Consolas since this is a ClearType font that will be more readable in the window

5. Select Layout to change the buffer size and screen size

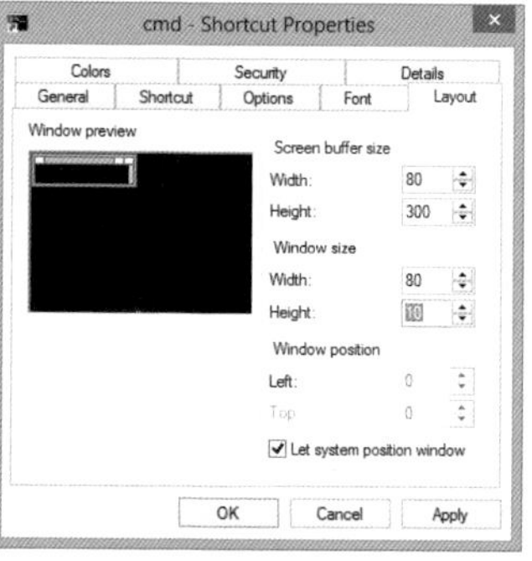

Adjust the width if the default 80 characters is not enough, and change the height (in this case from the default 25 lines to 10 rows). A vertical scrollbar allows you to view the whole buffer of information.

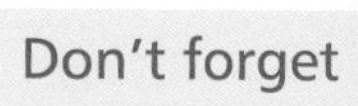

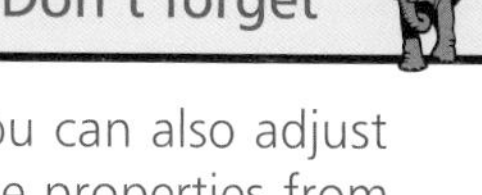

You can also adjust the properties from the Command Prompt window.

The fonts for the Command Prompt window must be fixed-pitch.

...cont'd

6 Select the Colors tab, to change the colors used for the screen text and pop-up text and their backgrounds

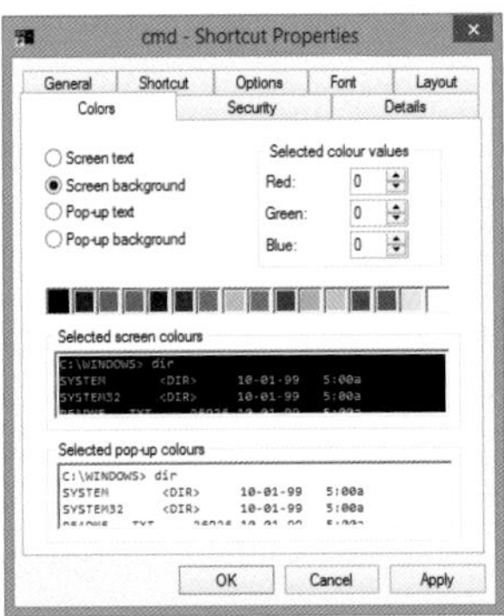

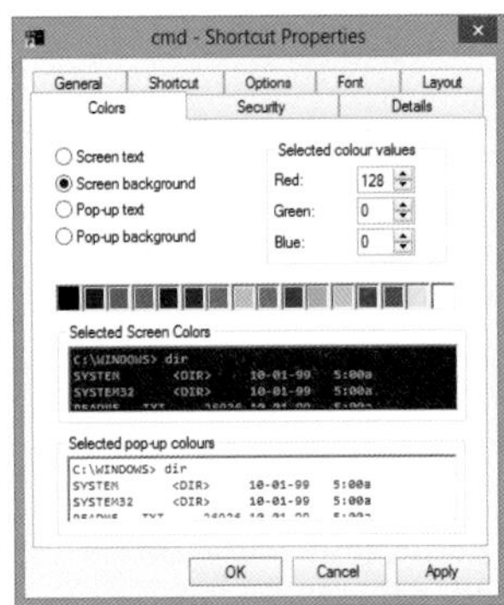

Don't forget

You choose color values between 0 and 255, for the Red, Green and Blue components.

7 For example, select Screen Background and choose a color from the selection, or enter the required color values

8 Select Apply to apply any changes immediately, and OK to complete any further changes and close the Properties

9 Double-click the shortcut icon to display the Command Prompt session and see all the changes in effect

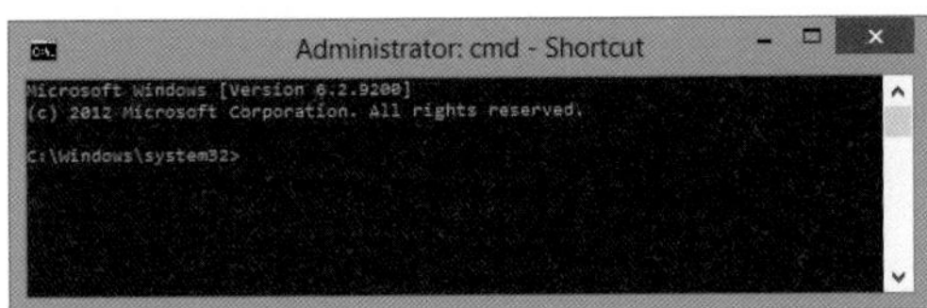

Hot tip

When you make such changes to the shortcut Properties, your new settings will be retained and applied whenever you start a Command Prompt using that shortcut.

Repeat the process to adjust the Properties for a shortcut used for a standard level Command Prompt. You might decide to choose a different screen background such as Blue, to distinguish the standard sessions from the Red administrator sessions. Double-click the Standard Commands shortcut to view the effect.

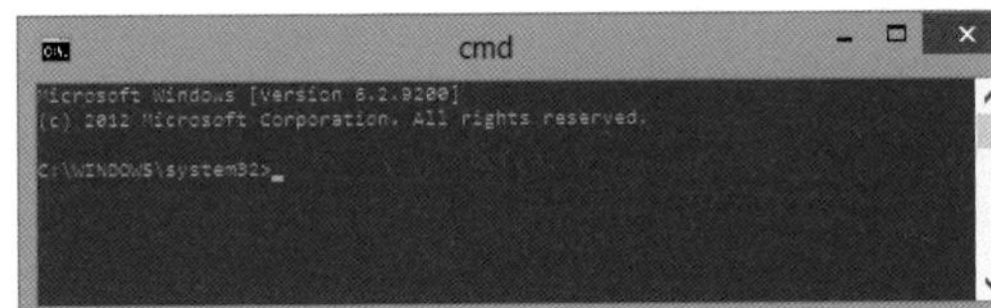

Changing window properties

1. Select Command Prompt using any of the methods

2. Right-click the titlebar and select Properties

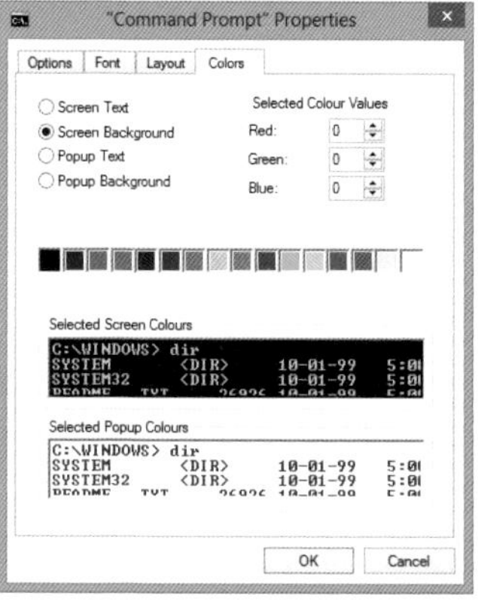

This displays the tabs Options, Font, Layout and Colors for the shortcut Properties. Any changes you make here are for the current session and any future settings started using the same method.

Similarly, if you start a session via a shortcut, the changes apply for that shortcut only.

3. To make changes that will apply to future sessions, right-click the titlebar and select Defaults from the menu

4. This opens the Console Windows Properties

The changes you make will not affect the current session but will be applied for all future sessions (except for those launched from a shortcut whose properties have been customized).

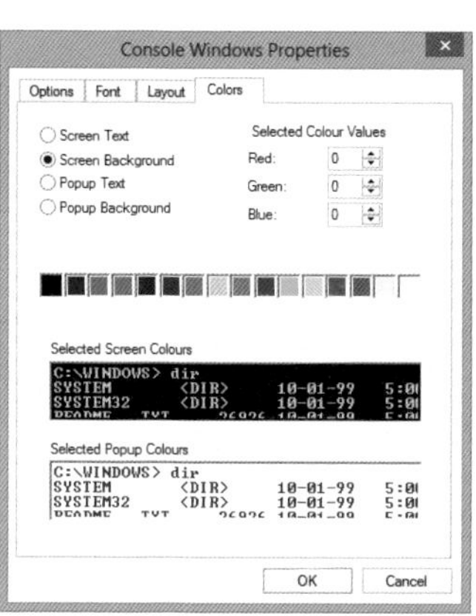

These changes also affect future sessions in character-mode, MS-DOS-based applications that do not have a program-information file (PIF) or store their own settings.

Don't forget

You can also make changes to the properties when you have a Command Prompt session already started.

Using the Command Prompt

You'll use the Command Prompt to carry out tasks that are not easily achieved using the normal Windows functions. A typical example is to create a text file containing the names of all the files of a particular type in a folder:

Hot tip

To list a different type of file, just change .jpg to the required file type, e.g. .doc. You can also list more than one file type, for example:

dir *.jpg *.tif > filelist.txt

1. Open a prompt at the required folder, using the right-click menu option Open command window here

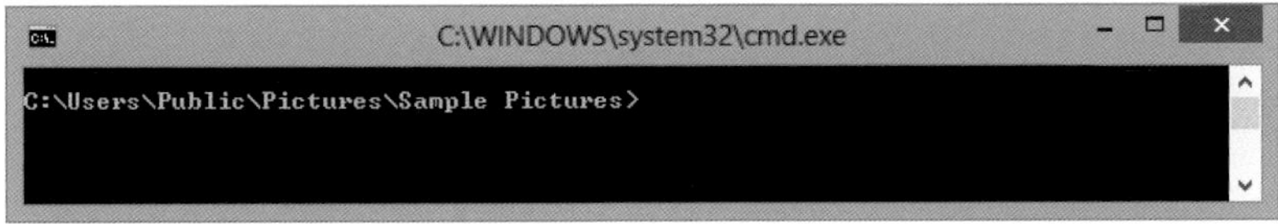

2. Put the following on the command line and press Enter:
   dir *.jpg > filelist.txt

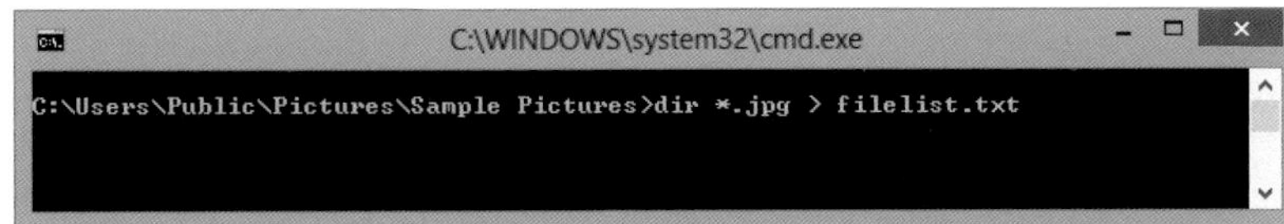

3. Now open the folder and you will see a file called filelist

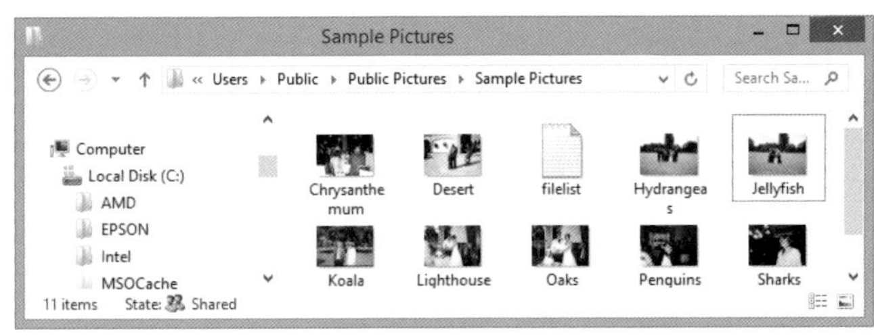

Hot tip

To see a list of files but no attributes, you'd enter dir *.jpg /b >filelist.txt

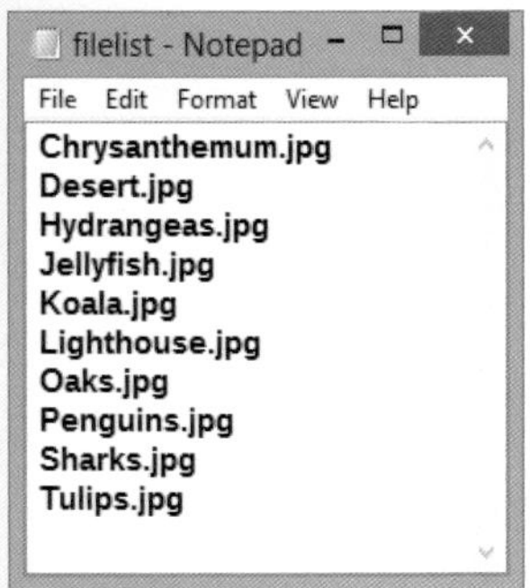

filelist - Notepad

File Edit Format View Help

Chrysanthemum.jpg
Desert.jpg
Hydrangeas.jpg
Jellyfish.jpg
Koala.jpg
Lighthouse.jpg
Oaks.jpg
Penguins.jpg
Sharks.jpg
Tulips.jpg

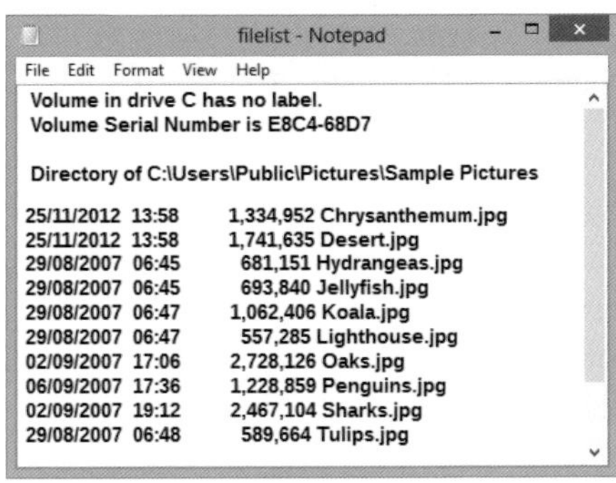

filelist - Notepad

File Edit Format View Help

Volume in drive C has no label.
Volume Serial Number is E8C4-68D7

Directory of C:\Users\Public\Pictures\Sample Pictures

25/11/2012 13:58 1,334,952 Chrysanthemum.jpg
25/11/2012 13:58 1,741,635 Desert.jpg
29/08/2007 06:45 681,151 Hydrangeas.jpg
29/08/2007 06:45 693,840 Jellyfish.jpg
29/08/2007 06:47 1,062,406 Koala.jpg
29/08/2007 06:47 557,285 Lighthouse.jpg
02/09/2007 17:06 2,728,126 Oaks.jpg
06/09/2007 17:36 1,228,859 Penguins.jpg
02/09/2007 19:12 2,467,104 Sharks.jpg
29/08/2007 06:48 589,664 Tulips.jpg

4. Open the file and you'll see a list of all the jpg files in the folder, plus the date and time they were created, and the size of each file

If your Command Prompt session is already open, you need to switch directories to get to the required folder. Here you can use Windows features to assist the Command Prompt operation.

1. Open the required folder in File Explorer

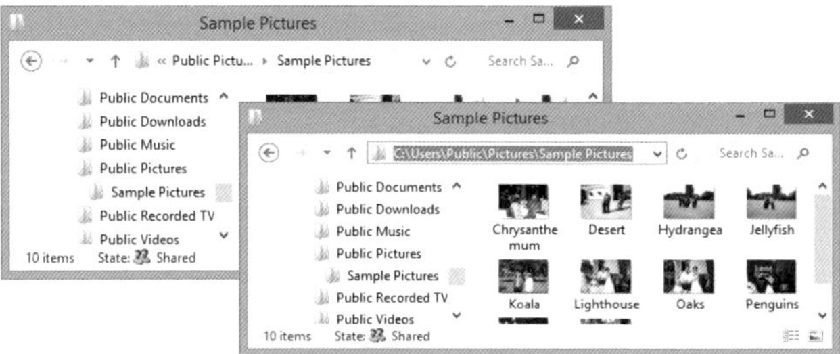

2. Click the Address bar to show the path and press Ctrl + C

3. Switch to the Command Prompt and type the command cd (followed by a single space)

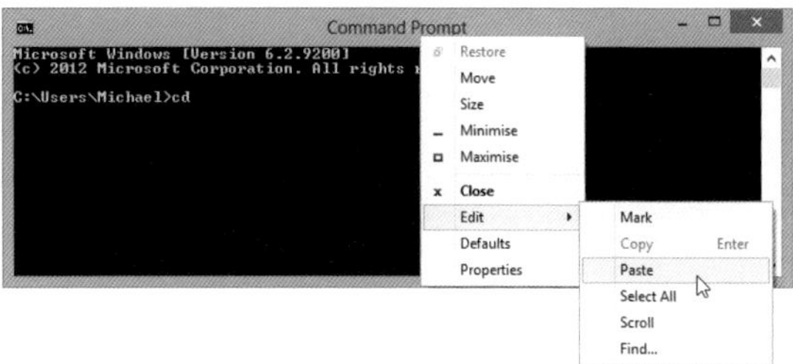

4. Right-click the titlebar and select Edit, Paste

5. Press Enter to run the command and switch directories

Hot tip

When you select Paste, the contents of the Clipboard are copied to the command line, thus completing the CD command already started.

Command line changes

There are lots of aids you can take advantage of when working on the Command line. This example session illustrates some of these.

1. To switch to a parent directory, enter the command cd ..

2. Click the Up-arrow and press Enter to repeat the command

```
C:\Windows\system32\cmd.exe
C:\Users\Public\Pictures\Sample Pictures>cd..
C:\Users\Public\Pictures>cd..
C:\Users\Public>cd..
C:\Users>cd Michael
```

3. At C:\Users, type cd then press Tab until the required user name appears, then press Enter

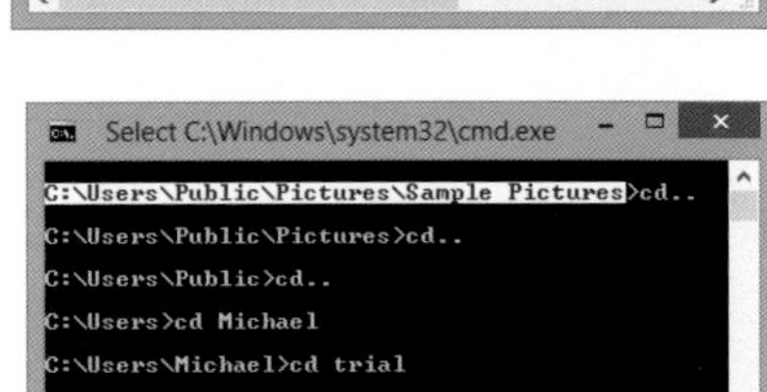

4. Change to trial and type copy (followed by space)

5. Right-click the titlebar, select Mark and highlight the path for Sample Pictures, then Copy and Paste

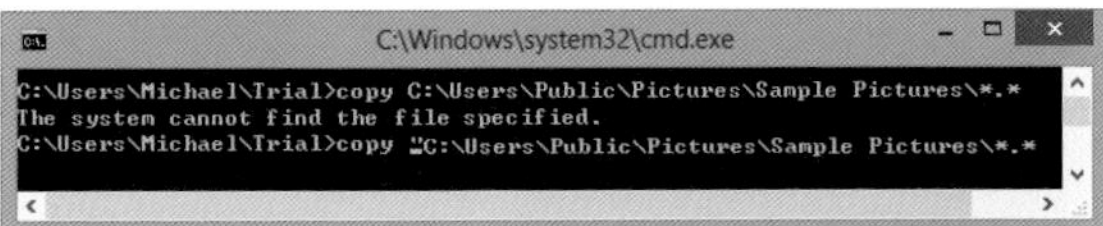

6. A Quote is needed, since there are blanks in the path, so just press Up then edit the command as needed

7. Type a Rename command, using Tab to insert the first of the file names in the directory

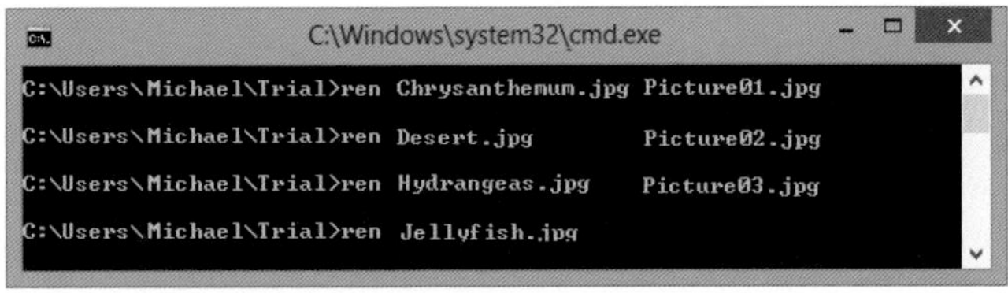

8. Use right-arrow and Tab to copy/amend the command

Don't forget 

The Tab key displays the files and directories in the current directory in alphabetic sequence, displaying the next one each time it is pressed.

Hot tip 

When you make an error in a command, the Up-arrow lets you redisplay it and you can insert or delete characters as needed to correct the command.

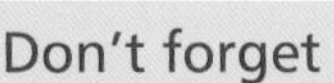

The Right-arrow copies the command, letter by letter. Tab inserts the next file name, and then you copy the new name, amending where necessary.

24 Update and maintain

You need to regularly update Windows and other applications on your PC, to ensure the system keeps working effectively and to incorporate the latest security and performance features. Windows Update automates this process.

Windows Update

The Windows operating system requires frequent updates to keep it secure and fully operational. Updates are provided on an almost weekly basis, and periodically Microsoft issues service packs that consolidate sets of updates.

To see what the update situation is for your computer:

1. Go to Control Panel, System and Security. Click System

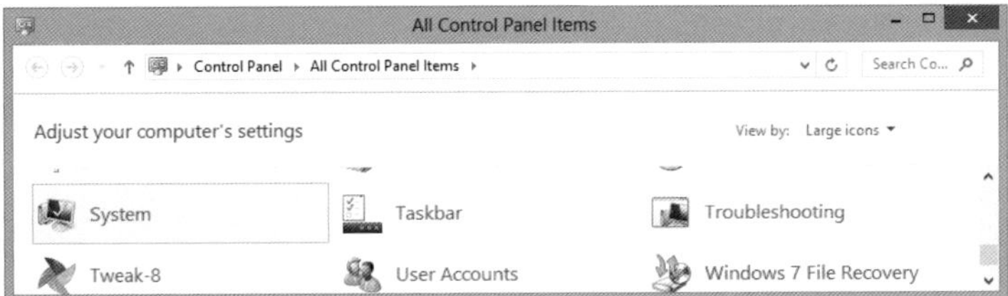

2. This shows the Windows edition, and the latest service pack that has been applied (if any)

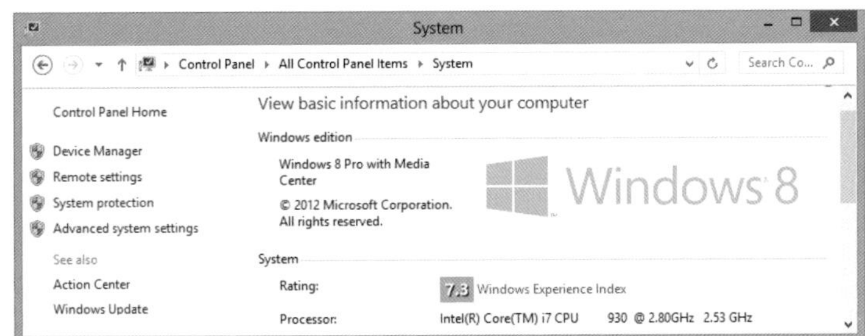

3. To see the status of your system, click Windows Update

Don't forget

This is one of a number of different ways to ask for the System Properties for your computer to be displayed.

4. Click Check for updates, then select important updates

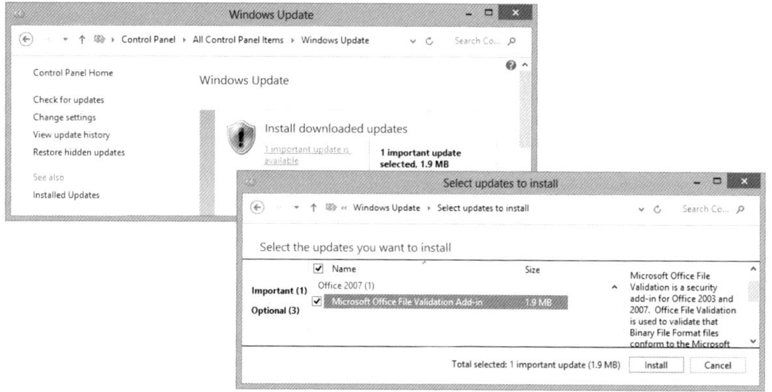

Hot tip

If Automatic Updating has been set, the indication of updates waiting appears immediately when you open Windows Update.

5. If there are updates waiting, you can click Install updates and they will be downloaded and installed

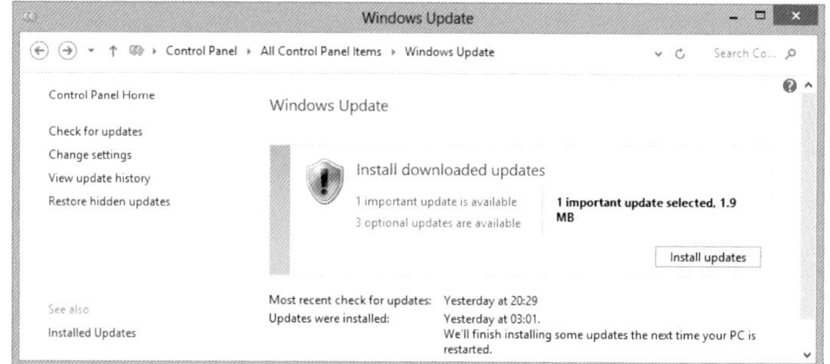

6. When installation completes you may be asked to restart the system, so that appropriate files can be updated

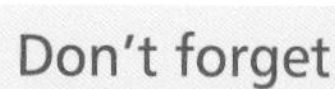

Don't forget

You can selectively apply updates in this manner, but it is much easier to let Windows Update do the job automatically.

Update settings

Hot tip

Use Change Settings to turn on Automatic Update and to specify what types of update are selected, and when updates takes place.

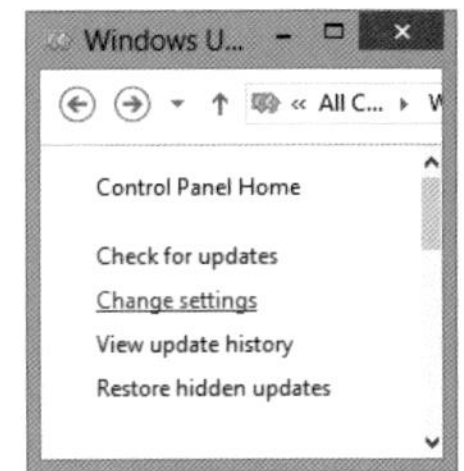

1. Open Windows Update and select Change Settings

2. Choose how you want Windows to install updates on your system

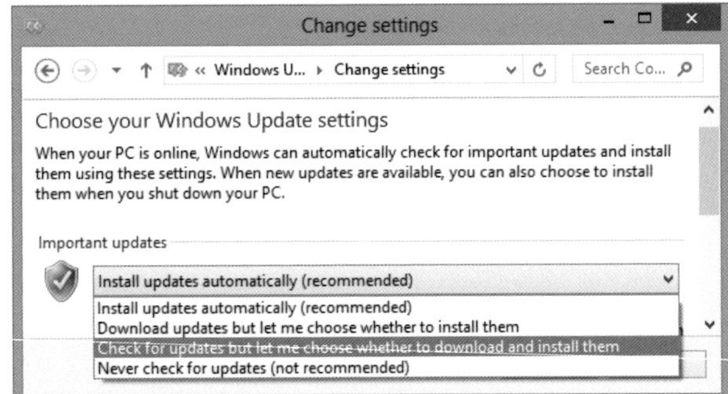

3. Install updates automatically is recommended, and you can choose how often and at what time to run the installs

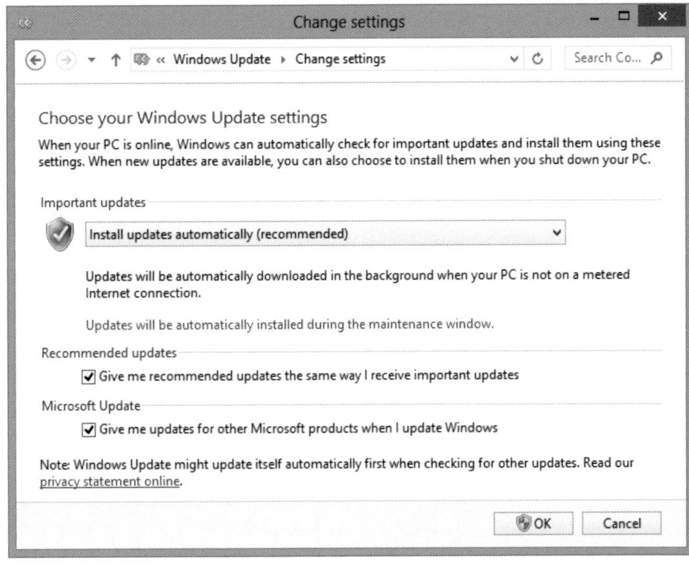

4. Click OK to apply any changes, and leave your computer running to apply the updates at the specified time

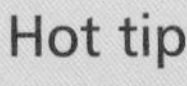

Hot tip

Updates will happen in the background, and you will get an occasional message letting you know of actions taken, such as restarts.

Microsoft Update

1. Open Windows Update and select Find out more

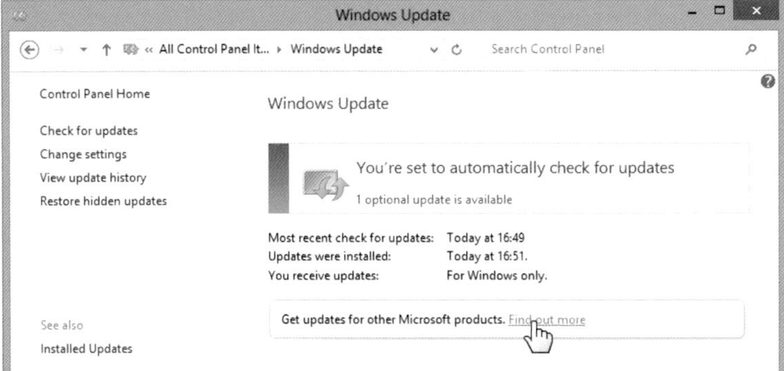

Hot tip

From Windows Update you can find out about getting updates automatically for other Microsoft products as well as the Windows operating system.

2. Agree to the terms of use, and click the Install button

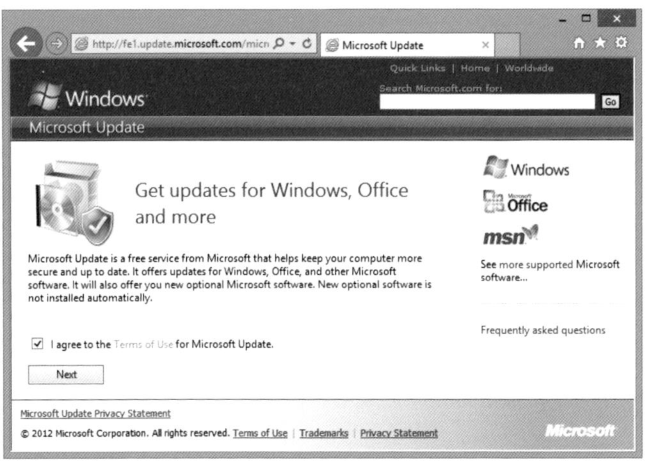

Don't forget

Microsoft Update will provide updates for Windows, Office, MSN, Windows Defender, and various Windows Server – related products.

3. Updates are detected for supported Microsoft products

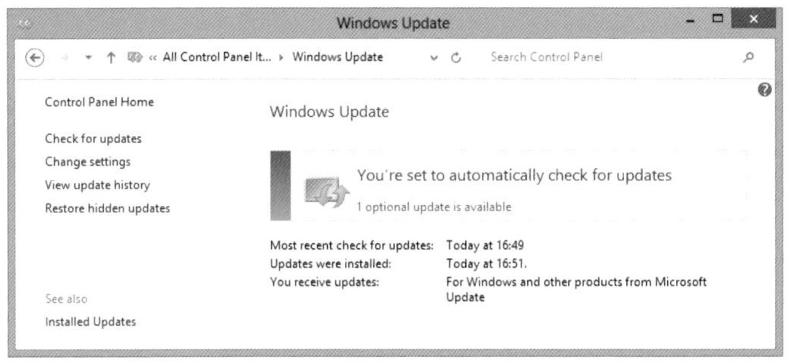

Hot tip

When you select the Windows Update option, it will show updates for all the products, to be applied at the specified time (or immediately, if you click Install Updates).

Update categories

The updates managed by Windows Update are classified as:

- **Important updates** – these updates include security and critical updates, as well as reliability improvements, and are automatically downloaded when you enable Windows Update
- **Recommended updates** – these include software updates and new or improved features, and may be treated as Important updates or Optional updates, depending on your Windows Update settings
- **Optional updates** – these include updates and software that you install manually, such as new or trial Microsoft software or optional device drivers from Microsoft partners

You must visit Windows Update to check for updates that need to be installed manually. They could include Important updates that require you to accept new terms of use. There are also updates that have an impact on the way your system operates so Microsoft chooses to require confirmation before installation. An example of this is Internet Explorer 10.

These categories apply to Windows updates, and also to updates for other products, if you have enabled Microsoft Update on your system.

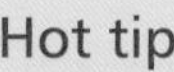

If you selected Give me recommended updates in the settings (see page 408), they are treated as Important updates. Otherwise, they are treated as Optional updates.

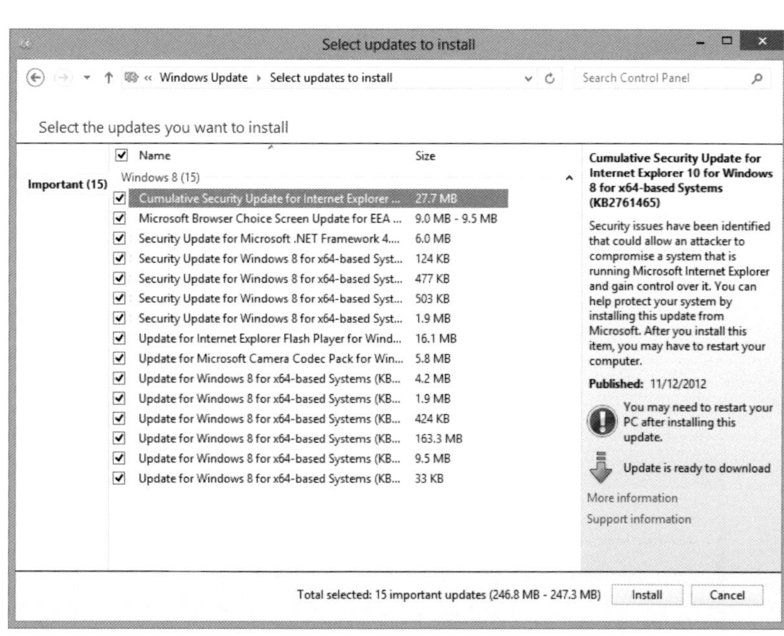

1. Select the required updates and click Install

Update history

Updates may be applied automatically, in the background, but you can review the activities:

1. Open Windows Update and select View update history

2. The updates are displayed, latest first

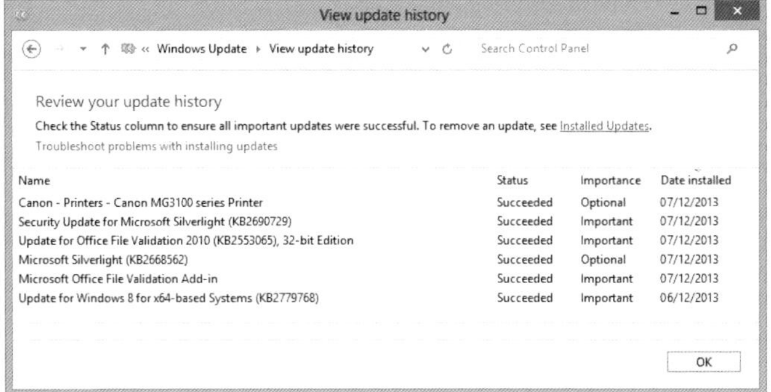

3. Click the Status heading, to review the Failed updates

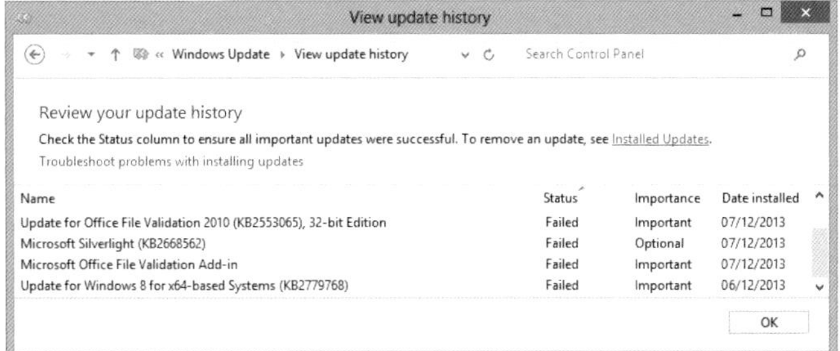

4. Sort in name order to see if the updates ever succeeded

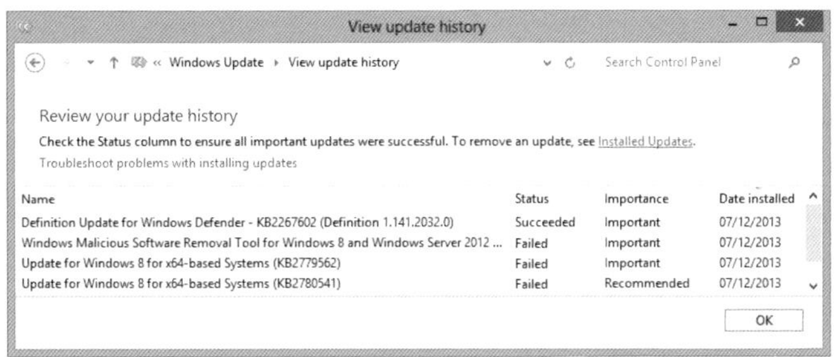

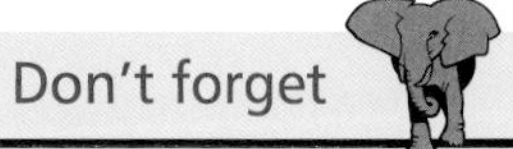

There's an entry for every attempt to apply an update, which are flagged by importance, and results are marked as Succeeded or Failed.

Hot tip

Identify Important updates that have failed, and check to ensure that a subsequent update attempt succeeded.

...cont'd

Don't forget

You'll also find the Installed updates link at the top of the Update history list.

You can review the Windows and other updates that have been installed on your computer, and remove any that may be causing problems.

1. Open Windows Update and select Installed updates at the bottom of the left-hand pane

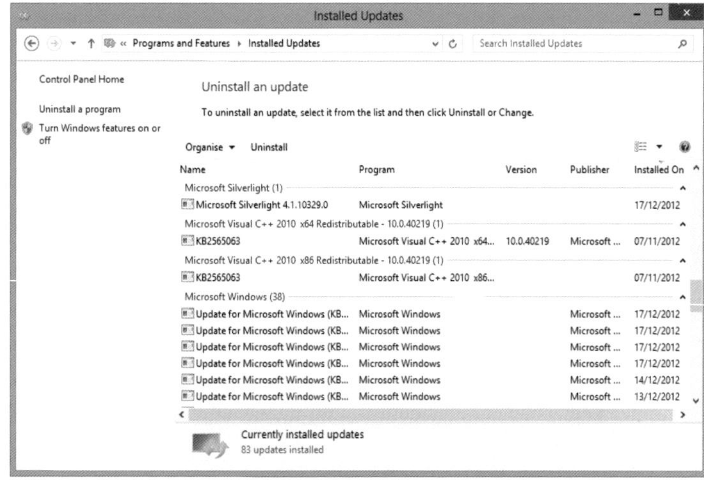

Hot tip

There are some updates that cannot be removed this way. If that is the case, there will be no Uninstall button shown when you select the update.

2. Select an update and click Uninstall on the toolbar to remove that update

3. You can also go to the Control Panel and open Programs and Features. Click Uninstall or change a program. You can also View installed updates here

Hot tip

You can switch back and forth between the Updates and the Programs list, using the links in the left hand pane.

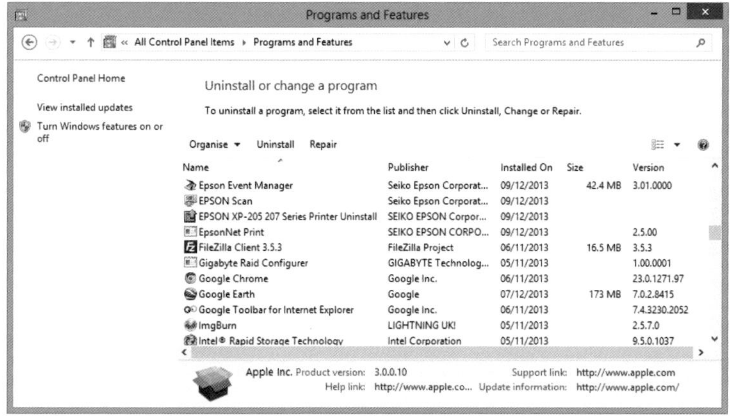

PC settings – Windows Update

Windows updates can be managed from the new Windows 8 interface as well:

1. Open the Charms bar and select Settings, Change PC Settings, and then Windows Update

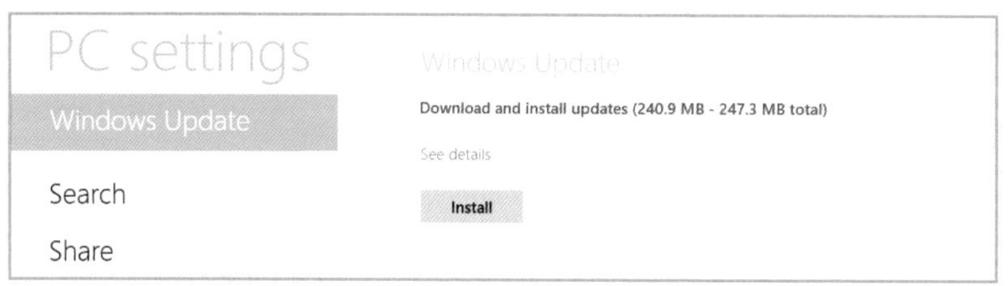

2. On the right-hand pane, you will see in red lettering that updates are available. To install all of them, click Install

3. To see details of the updates, click See details. This opens a list

15 important updates (240.9 MB - 24...
Windows 8
Cumulative Security Update for Internet Explorer 10 for Windows 8...
Microsoft Browser Choice Screen Update for EEA Users of Windows...
Security Update for Microsoft .NET Framework 4.5 on Windows 8 a...
Security Update for Windows 8 for x64-based Systems (KB2727528)
Security Update for Windows 8 for x64-based Systems (KB2753842)
Security Update for Windows 8 for x64-based Systems (KB2770660)
Security Update for Windows 8 for x64-based Systems (KB2779030)
Update for Internet Explorer Flash Player for Windows 8 for x64-bas...
Update for Microsoft Camera Codec Pack for Windows 8 for x64-b...
Update for Windows 8 for x64-based Systems (KB2751352)
Update for Windows 8 for x64-based Systems (KB2768703)
Update for Windows 8 for x64-based Systems (KB2769034)
Update for Windows 8 for x64-based Systems (KB2769165)
Update for Windows 8 for x64-based Systems (KB2771431)
Update for Windows 8 for x64-based Systems (KB2772501)
Choose which important updates you want to install.

4. If you just want to see or install the important updates, click “Choose which important...”

5. You will now be switched to Windows Update in the Control Panel where you can view or install the updates

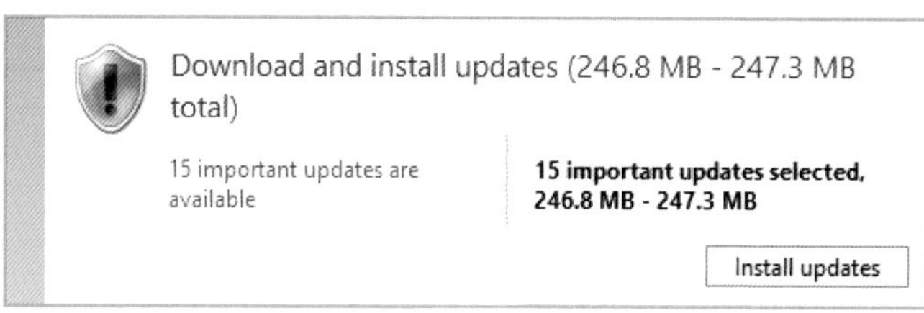

If you prefer to work in the Windows 8 interface, you can manage updates from here.

Upgrading Windows

Sometimes adding updates isn't enough - you need to upgrade your edition of Windows to an edition that has the extra functions that you need. Alternatively, you may want to upgrade from 32-bit Windows to 64-bit Windows, so that your computer can take advantage of the much larger amounts of memory that 64-bit systems can utilize.

Don't forget

You can backup your data files and folders before you make the change, and restore the backup to your revised system. However, you will have to install 64-bit versions of drivers for devices (unless Windows includes a suitable driver), and also reinstall all your application programs.

32-bit to 64-bit

This isn't an upgrade in the usual sense - you cannot install the new operating system and retain existing folders and data files. Instead, you create a complete new system, which replaces the existing setup, then install your applications (and apply Windows updates).

You can install any edition of 64-bit Windows on your computer, assuming of course that your computer is 64-bit capable and that you have enough memory to make the transition worthwhile. You will need 4GBs or more.

Upgrading editions

Changing editions can be carried out as a true upgrade. You update the operating system files, but leave your data files and folders unaffected. The application programs that you have installed will continue to operate.

Upgrade paths

With Windows 7 there were a number of upgrade paths possible between the various versions. Windows 8, however, provides only one – if you currently have the entry version, Windows 8, you can upgrade it to Windows 8 Pro.

Don't forget

The add Windows Media Center option is only available with the Pro version of Windows 8. However there is a Windows 8 Pro pack at $189.99 to upgrade Windows 8 to Windows 8 Pro and add WMC. *(Correct at the time of printing.)*

Users with Windows 8 Pro have an option available to them that allows the popular Windows Media Center to be added to Windows. This was available free of charge until January 31st 2013 but it now costs $9.99 to add WMC to Windows 8 Pro. (*Correct at the time of printing.*)

Whichever edition of Windows 8 you currently have installed, its installation DVD/ISO and the installed operating system files actually contain all the components of all the editions.

It is the product key that unlocks the functions for a particular edition. This is the basis for the upgrading feature incorporated into Windows 8 – Add Features to Windows 8.

Apply the upgrade

With Windows 7, Microsoft provided a Anytime Upgrade feature, which enabled users to upgrade to a more advanced version of Windows 7 while at the same time retaining their programs, files and settings.

In Windows 8, the Anytime Upgrade has been replaced with Add Features to Windows 8, which works in much the same way. Before it can be used, however, it is necessary to purchase a product key – these can be bought at stores and also online in most countries.

Make sure that the key you buy is specifically for Add features to Windows 8. If you need to add features to more than one computer, you will have to buy a product key for each one.

You should also be aware that Add features to Windows 8 can't be used to upgrade previous versions of Windows to Windows 8. You can only use it if you already have Windows 8 and want to get a different edition that has more features.

The upgrade procedure is as follows:

1. Open the Charms bar and type add features into the Search charm

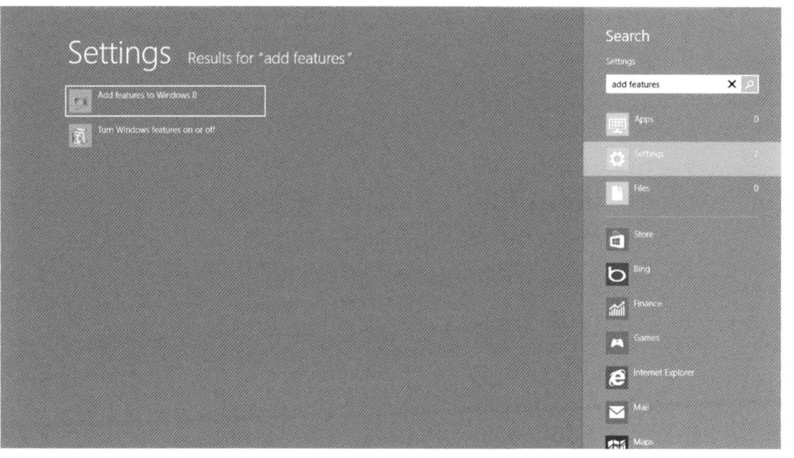

2. Click Settings and then on the results pane, click Add features to Windows 8

Hot tip

Add Features to Windows 8 is a very easy way of upgrading your edition of Windows 8 to a more advanced version. Simply buy a key, enter it when requested and the upgrade will be downloaded and installed.

Don't forget

Add Features to Windows 8 can only be used to upgrade Windows 8 – it doesn't work with previous versions of Windows.

...cont'd

3. If you haven't yet purchased a product key, click I want to buy a product key online

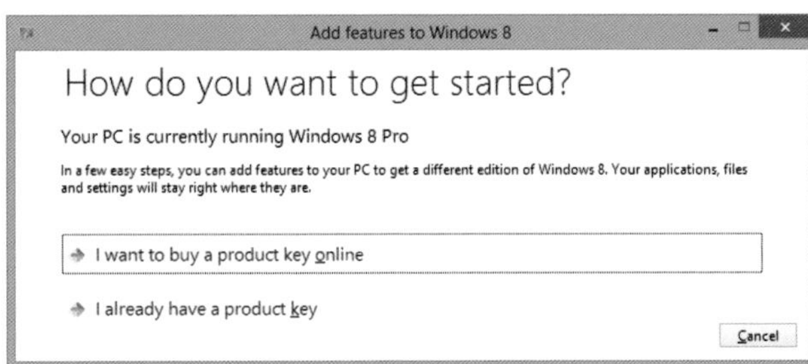

4. The available upgrades are displayed together with the prices charged. Click the Choose button next to the upgrade you want to buy

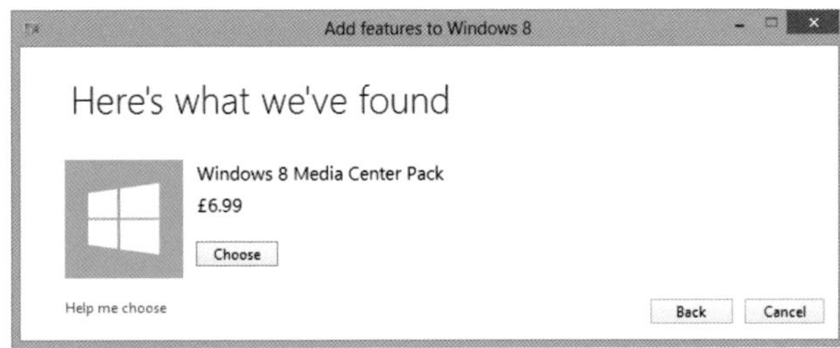

5. In the next screen enter your billing details and then follow the prompts to initiate the upgrade

6. If you already have a product key, enter it when requested. Click Next, OK the licence agreement and then click Add features. The upgrade procedure will now commence

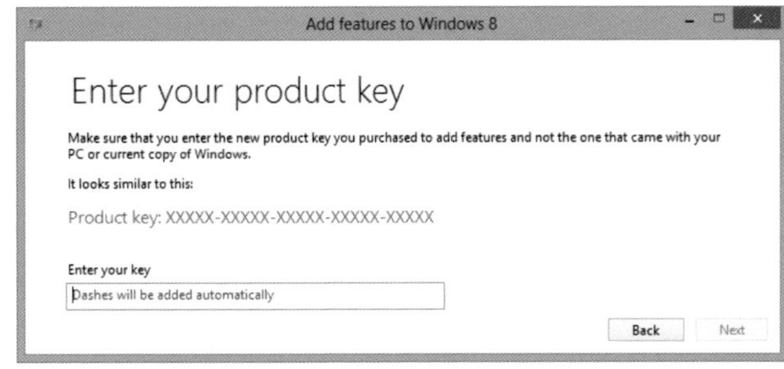

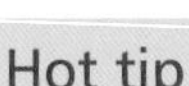

Hot tip

Our example shows just a Windows 8 Media Center Pack to be available. This is because the author's PC is running Windows 8 Pro. If it was running Windows 8, then Windows 8 Pro would be available as an upgrade.

Disk cleanup

For everyday tasks you can use the tools found in drive properties.

1. Press Winkey + X, select File Explorer, right-click on a drive and click Properties

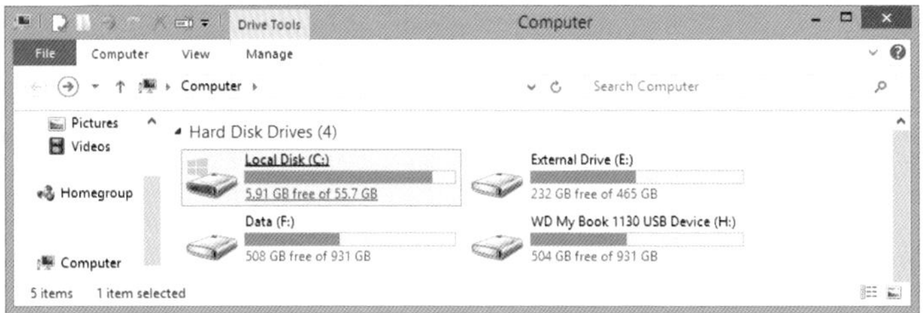

2. In Drive Properties, select the General tab and click the Disk Cleanup button

3. Disk Cleanup calculates the space to be released

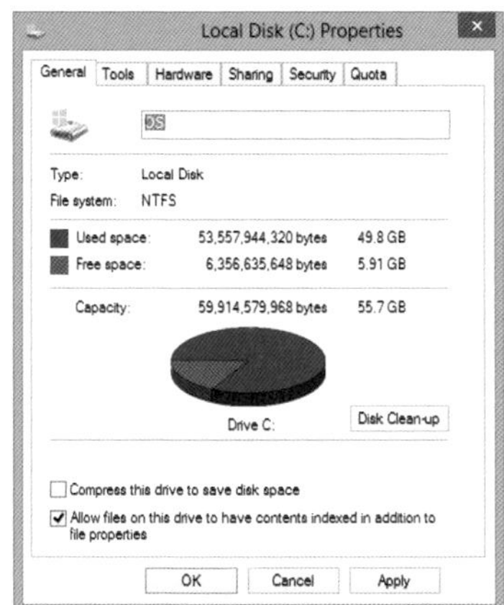

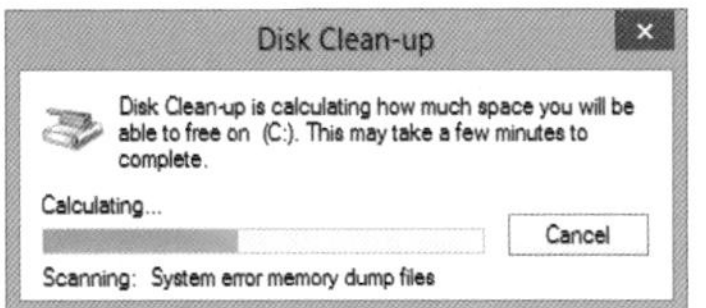

4. Select or clear file categories and click OK to proceed

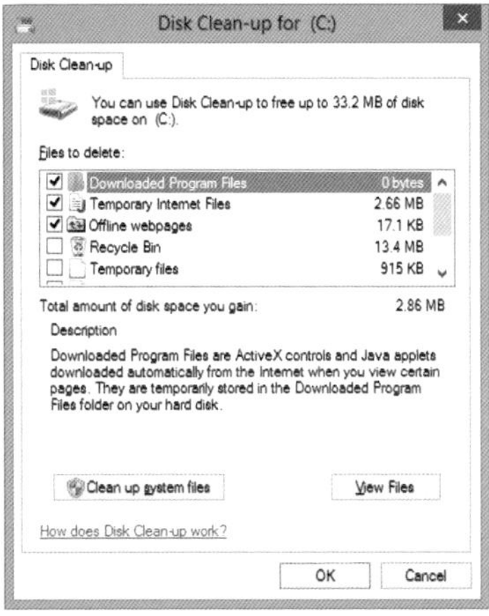

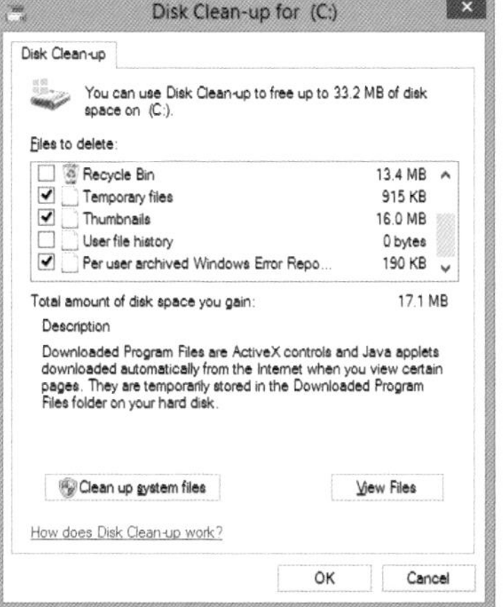

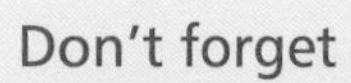

You could select Free up disk space, from the Administrative Tools in Control Panel and then specify which drive to clean up.

Hot tip

Some categories of file are suggested, but you can select others, e.g. Recycle Bin or Temporary Files, to increase the amount of space that will be made available. Select a category and click View Files to see what would be deleted.

...cont'd

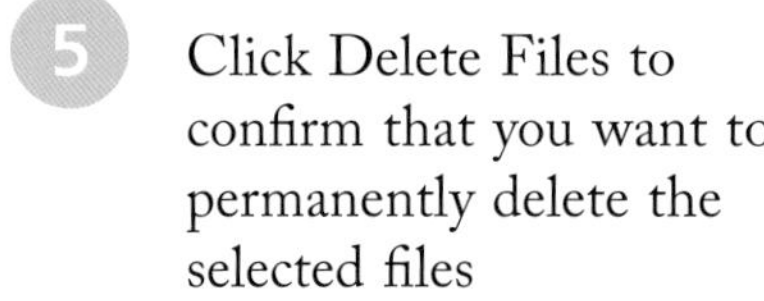

5 Click Delete Files to confirm that you want to permanently delete the selected files

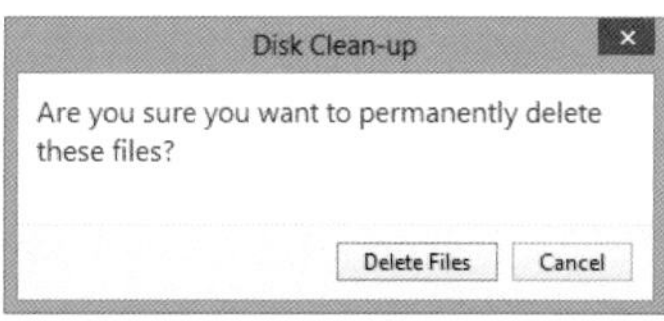

Click Cancel if you change your mind and want to look again at the categories and files selected.

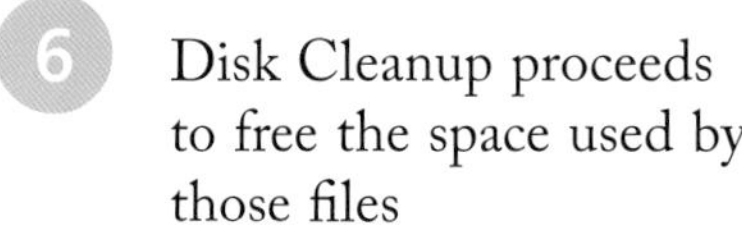

6 Disk Cleanup proceeds to free the space used by those files

Note that you may be prompted for administrator permission to remove certain types of file. If so, you'll see a box that lets you extend the permission to all the files of that type. Make sure this box is checked and then click Continue.

Clean up system files

If you need more free space, there will almost certainly be some system files that are not really necessary and can be removed safely. Old system restore files are a typical example (these can occupy GBs of disk space).

1 Select Disk Cleanup then click Clean up system files

2 Temporary files can also use a lot of disk space. System error memory dump files are also good candidates for deletion

When you choose Clean up system files, you'll get the More Options panel, where you can, additionally, remove programs that you do not use, or remove older restore points, shadow copies and backups.

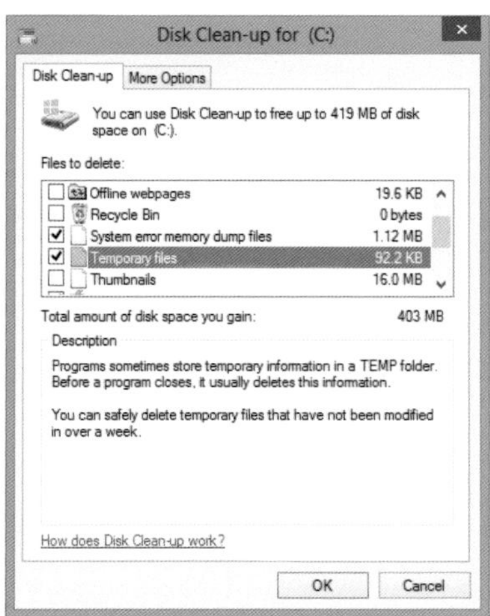

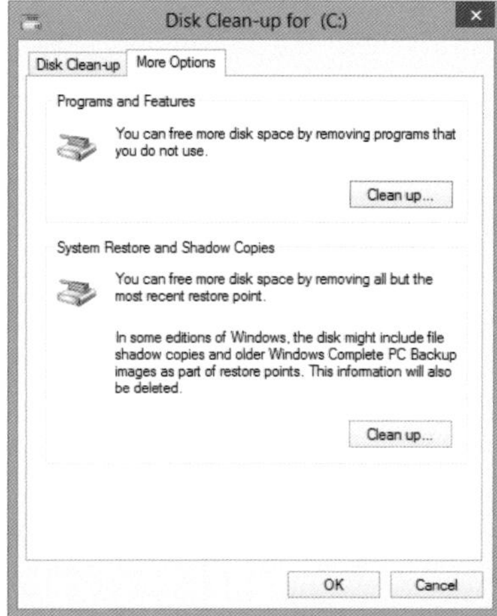

Defragmentation

1. From the Properties > Tools tab for any drive, select Optimize and defragment drive

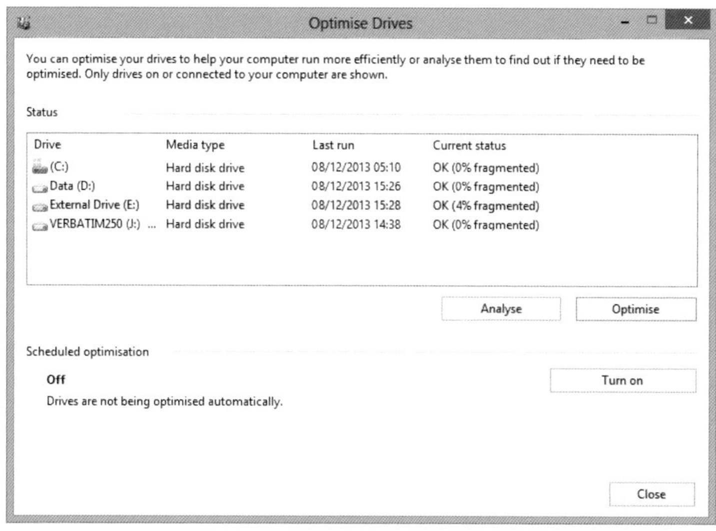

2. All drives that can be defragmented are listed, with the latest information about their fragmentation status

3. Select a drive and select Analyze, to see the current state of the drive

Drive	Media type	Last run	Current status
(C:)	Hard disk drive	08/12/2013 05:10	OK (0% fragmented)
Data (D:)	Hard disk drive	08/12/2013 15:26	OK (0% fragmented)
External Drive (E:)	Hard disk drive	08/12/2013 15:28	OK (4% fragmented)
VERBATIM250 (J:) ...	Hard disk drive	08/12/2013 14:38	OK (0% fragmented)

4. Select the drive and click Optimize, to analyze then defragment the drive

Drive	Media type	Last run	Current status
(C:)	Hard disk drive	08/12/2013 05:10	OK (0% fragmented)
Data (D:)	Hard disk drive	08/12/2013 15:26	OK (0% fragmented)
External Drive (E:)	Hard disk drive	08/12/2013 15:28	OK (0% fragmented)
VERBATIM250 (J:) ...	Hard disk drive	08/12/2013 14:38	OK (0% fragmented)

Don't forget

The larger the drive, the longer the optimization process takes.

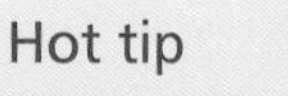

Hot tip

With schedule turned on, you can still run an immediate defragment. Click Configure schedule to change the date or time or to turn off.

...cont'd

Don't forget

You could also select Defragment your hard drive, from the Administrative Tools in the Control Panel.

Windows automates the defragmentation process so that it happens in the background on a regular basis. However, you may wish to change the default settings:

1. If it is not already done, click the Turn on button

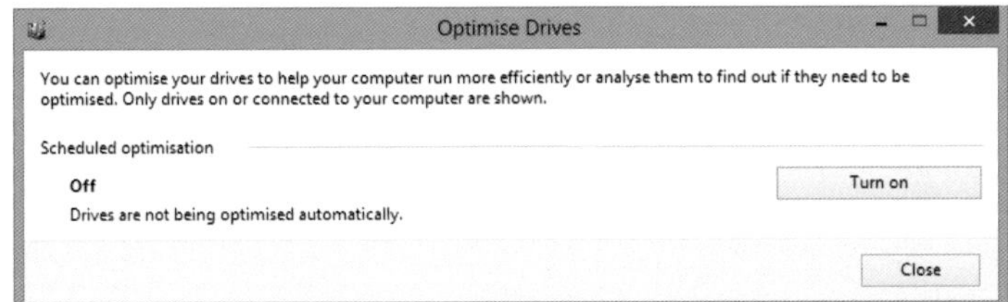

Hot tip

You can choose any drive to defragment, even if you start from Properties for a different drive.

2. Check Run on a schedule. Then set the desired schedule from the drop-down boxes

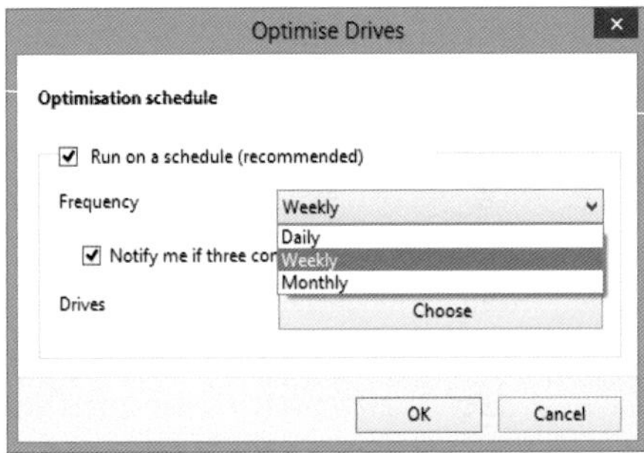

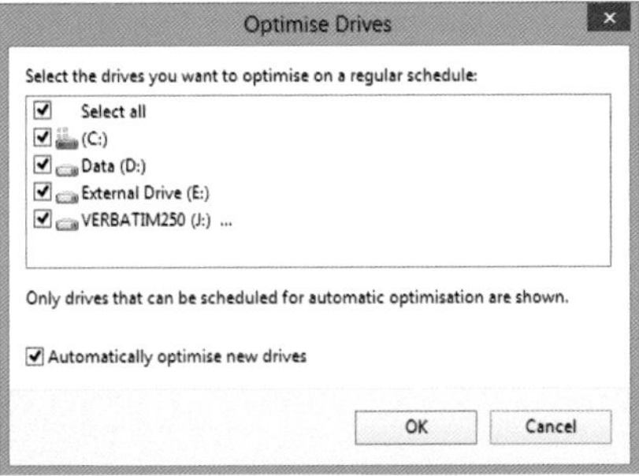

3. Select the drives to be optimized

4. Click OK. Your drives will now be defragmented according to the settings specified. Click the Close button

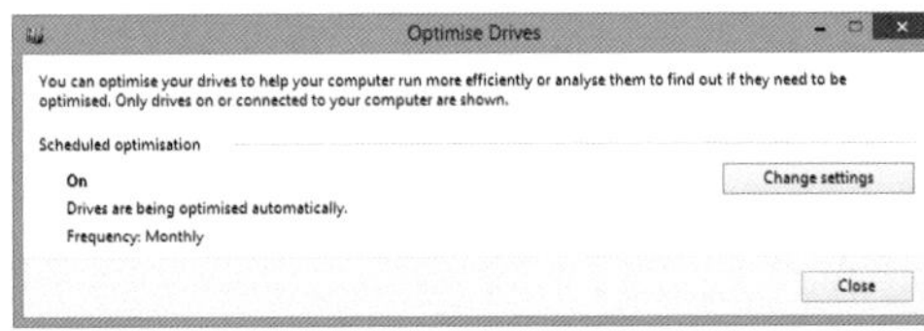

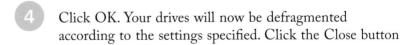

25 Windows performance

Windows provides tools that measure the performance of your PC, and identify issues affecting its performance. You can use monitoring tools and review detailed information about the PC. Windows will even help you speed up the system by using USB flash drives to act as a cache for system files.

System properties

System Properties is an important location for reviewing and adjusting the performance of your computer, so Windows provides a number of ways for displaying this panel, so that it is accessible from various areas within the system.

To display System Properties, use any of the following options:

1. Open the Power users menu by pressing Winkey + X and selecting System

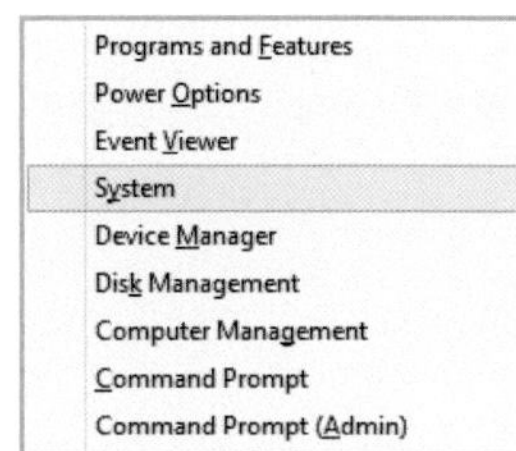

2. Press Winkey + X and select File Explorer. On the ribbon toolbar click System properties

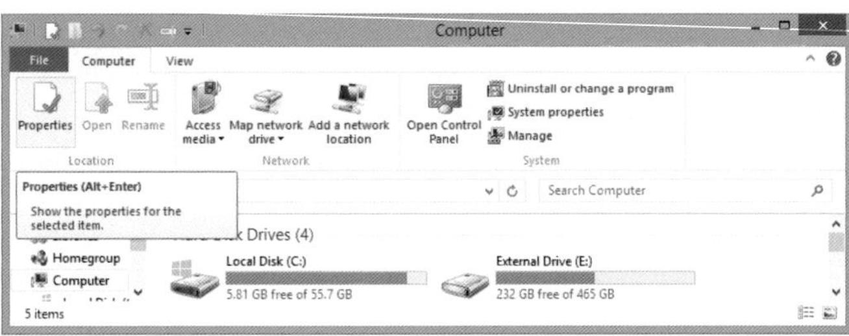

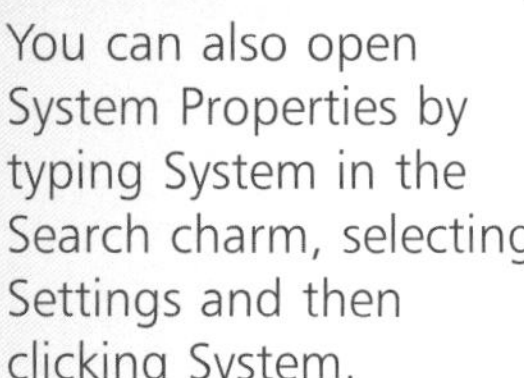

You can also open System Properties by typing System in the Search charm, selecting Settings and then clicking System.

3. Go to the Control Panel, select System and Security, and click System

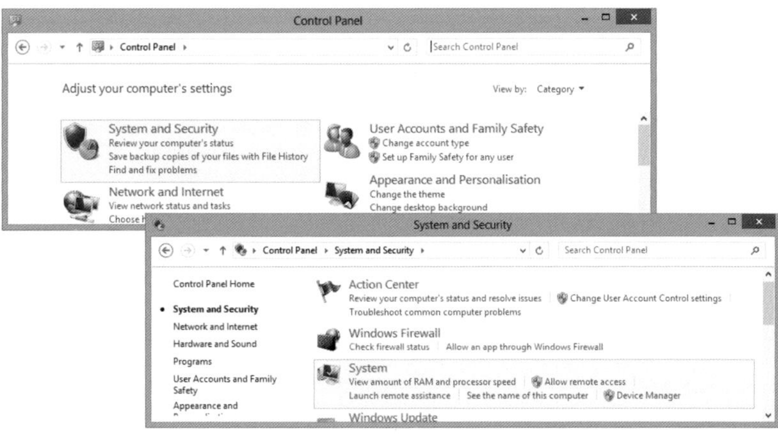

You'll also display System Properties if you click either View amount of RAM and processor speed, or See the name of this computer.

4. Press Winkey + Pause/Break

5. Whichever method you use, System Properties displays with basic information about your computer

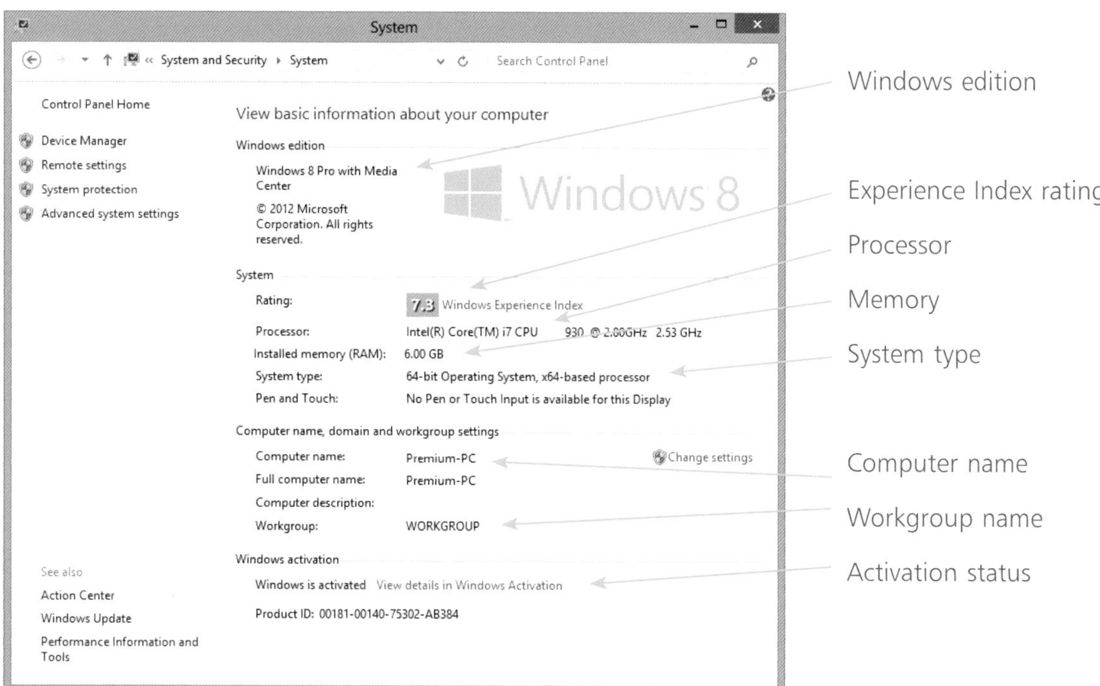

The pane on the left provides various links including:

- Device Manager
- Remote settings
- System protection
- Advanced system settings

In the center of the panel, you'll find your System Rating. This is a measure of the capability of the hardware and software in your computer, known as the Windows Experience Index. The higher your score, the better and faster your computer performs, especially with advanced or resource-intensive tasks. To see the details:

1. Select Windows Experience Index, or click Performance Information and Tools, which displays the same panel

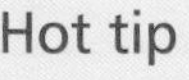

Device Manager provides details of the system components. Advanced system settings provide the full System properties.

Windows Experience Index

The Performance Information and Tools panel shows how the computer hardware has been assessed and the Windows Experience Index established.

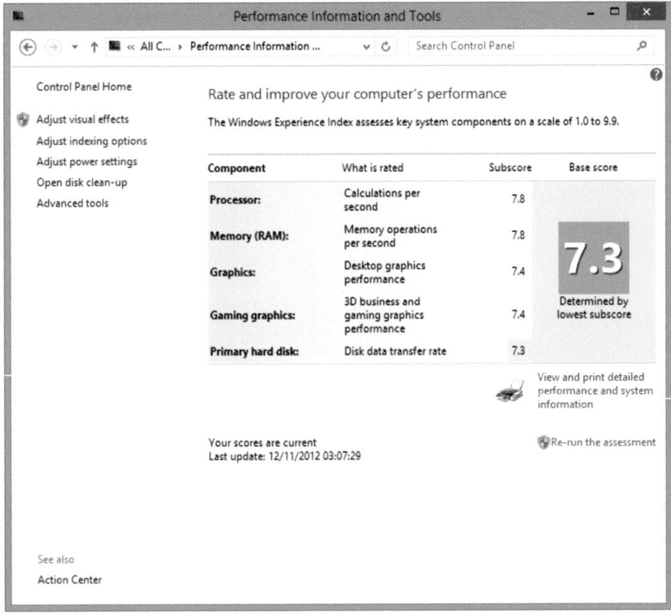

Hardware components (processor, memory, graphics, gaming graphics and primary hard disk) are each individually assessed and assigned subscores. The computer's base score is the lowest of these subscores. In the above example, subscores range up to 7.8, but it is the primary hard disk that sets the Windows Experience Index of 7.3.

In another case, a business machine running Windows 8 Enterprise, the base score is only 2.0. This is the subscore for the graphics hardware components, but subscores for the other components are between 4.0 and 5.9.

Component	Subscore	Base score
Processor:	5.5	2.0 Determined by lowest subscore
Memory (RAM):	5.5	
Graphics:	2.0	
Gaming graphics:	4.0	
Primary hard disk:	5.9	

Reviewing the details in this way makes it clear which machines are suitable for particular tasks. You'd avoid using the second machine for any tasks with graphics requirements, for example, but it should cope well with word processing or spreadsheets.

Beware

The Windows Experience Index is only applicable when your laptop or netbook computer is on mains supply. You cannot rate the machine while on battery power.

Hot tip

In Windows Vista, subscores were in the range 1.0 to 5.9. For Windows 7 and 8, the range is 1.0 to 7.9. As hardware speed and performance improves in the future, the range may extend.

1. For a detailed report, select the link View and print detailed performance and system information

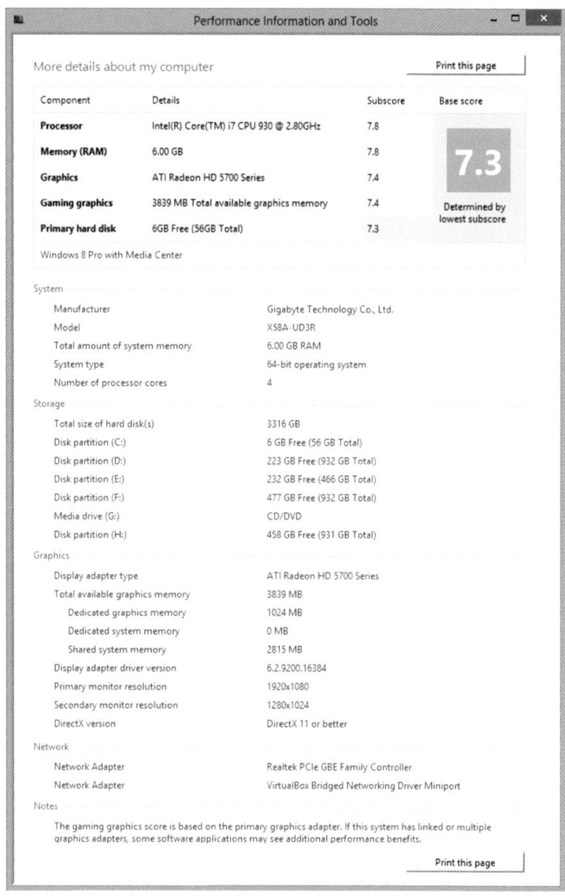

2. Click Print this page to save a copy of the report

The equivalent report for the second machine, in particular the Graphics section, illustrates why the Graphics subscores are so low, since the adapter is DirectX 8, where Windows 8 recommends DirectX 11 capability.

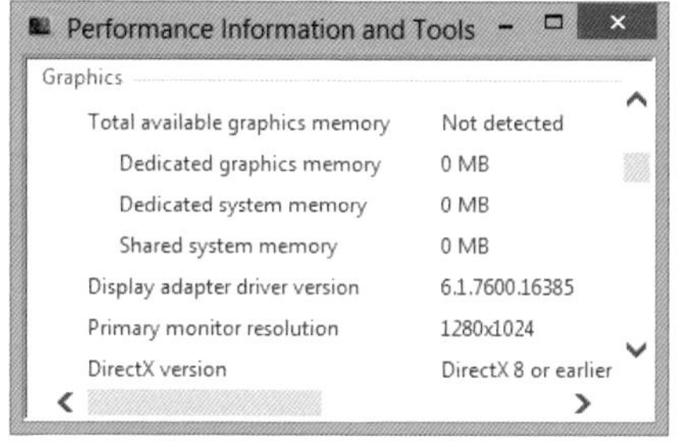

Don't forget

The report spells out in more detail the characteristics of the system, memory, storage, graphics and network components, showing, for example, how much of the system memory is shared with the graphics adapter.

Hot tip

Note that these reports only evaluate the primary hard drive and graphics adapter. There may be greater performance benefits than indicated, if you have secondary devices for either.

Beware

If any of these reports do encourage you to upgrade hardware components, you'll need to rerun the assessment to get the new rating.

Improving performance

You don't need to change hardware, you can use Performance Options to make changes to the settings to get more efficient operation.

1. From Performance Information and Tools, select Adjust visual effects

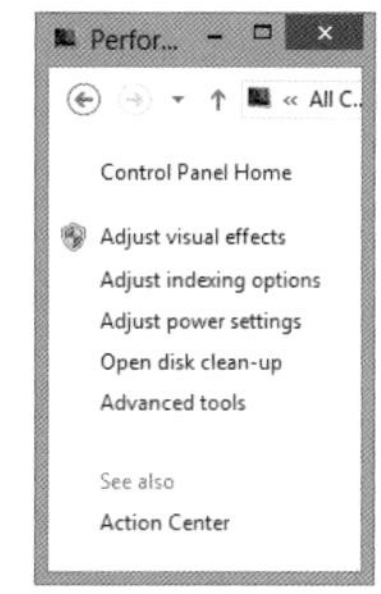

2. The default Let Windows choose will have most of the effects selected

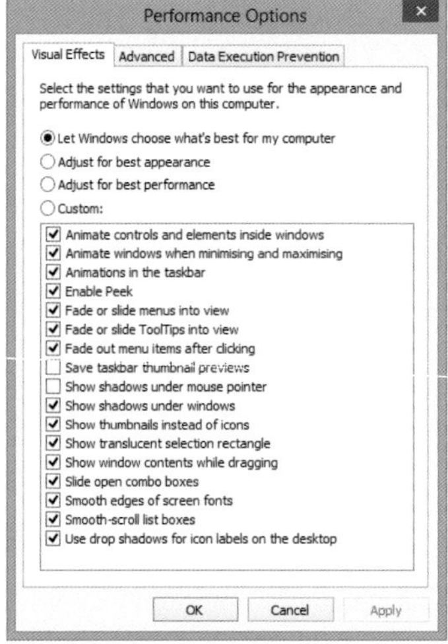

3. Choosing Adjust for best appearance means **all** the effects would be selected

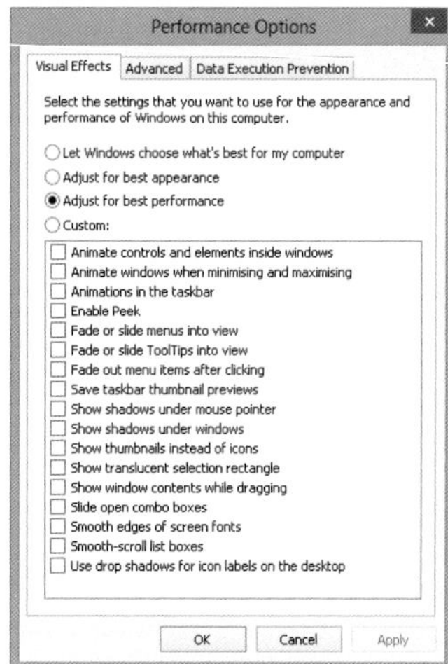

4. You get **no** effects if you Adjust for best performance

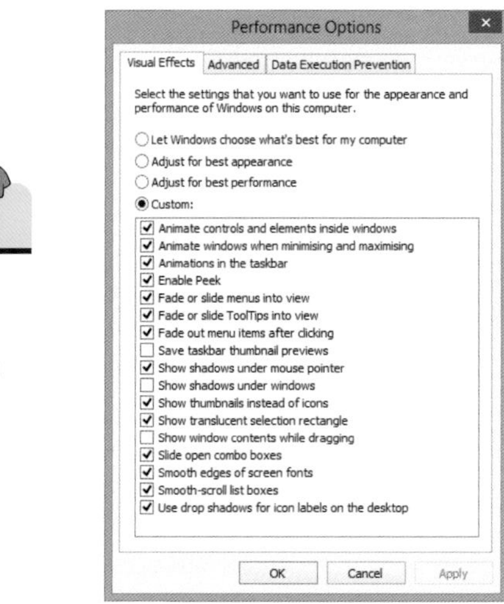

5. The best balance is to select Let Windows choose, click Apply, then deselect effects you can manage without

6. Click Apply, and your choices of effects become the Custom setting

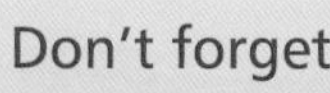

You can also display Performance Options using Advanced system settings.

Processor scheduling

1. Click the Advanced tab, and you can choose to prioritize Programs or Background services

The usual choice is Programs, but you might choose Background for a computer that acts as a print server or provides backups.

Virtual memory

Windows creates a Page file to supplement system memory. To review or change the settings:

1. From the Advanced tab, click the Virtual memory Change button

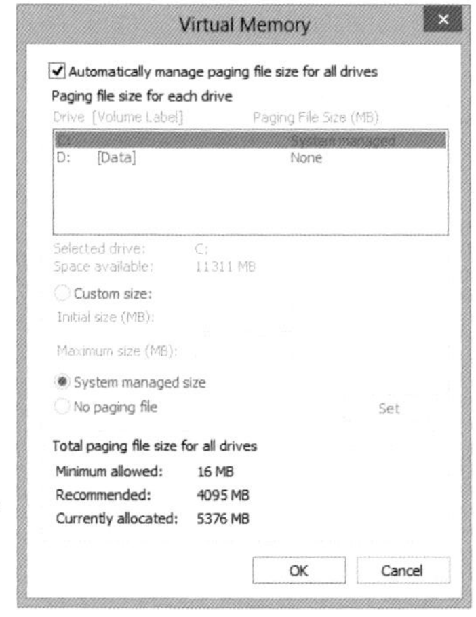

By default, Windows will automatically manage the paging file for your drive or drives. To choose the values yourself:

1. Clear Automatically manage paging file size for all drives
2. Choose an initial size, and a maximum size then click the Set button to apply

Setting the initial size the same as the maximum will avoid the need for Windows to adjust the size of the paging file, though this may not necessarily improve performance.

With multiple drives, choose the one with most space available.

Don't forget

You should only consider changing the processor scheduling on computers that are mainly used for background tasks.

Hot tip

Make sure you always have at least one drive with a paging file, even on a large memory PC, since some programs rely on the paging file.

Data execution prevention

The third tab in the Performance Options is for Data execution prevention or DEP. This is a security feature intended to prevent damage to your computer from viruses and other security threats, by monitoring programs to make sure they use system memory safely. If a program tries executing code from memory in an incorrect way, DEP closes the program.

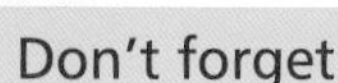

If you add a program to the exception list, but decide that you do want it to be monitored by DEP, you can clear the box next to the program.

1. By default, Windows will Turn on DEP for essential programs and services only
2. You can choose to Turn on DEP for all programs and services
3. Click Add to select programs for which you want to turn DEP off

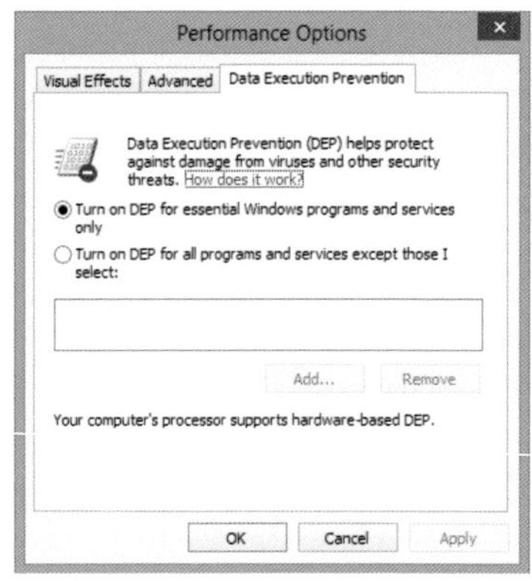

If DEP keeps closing a particular program that you trust, and your antivirus software does not detect a threat, the program might not run correctly when DEP is turned on. You should check for a DEP-compatible version of the program or an update from the software publisher before you choose to turn off DEP for that program.

Hardware-based DEP

Some processors use hardware technology to prevent programs from running code in protected memory locations. In this case, you will be told that your processor supports hardware-based DEP.

If your processor does not support hardware-based DEP, your computer will still be protected because Windows will use software-based DEP.

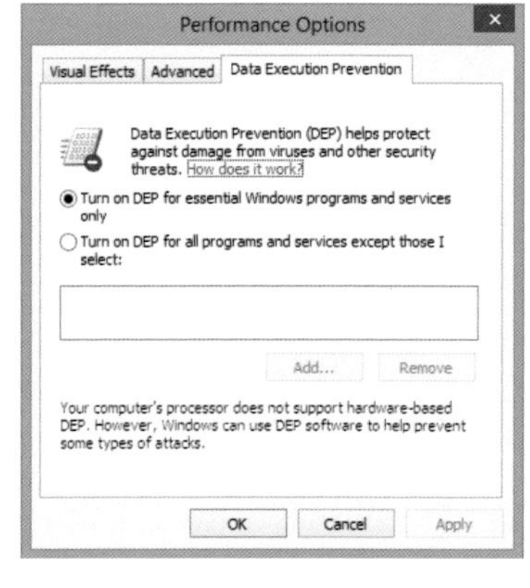

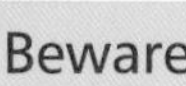

If DEP closes a program that is part of Windows, the cause could be a program you have recently installed that operates inside Windows. Check for a DEP-compatible version.

Advanced system settings

Windows provides another way to display the Performance Options:

1. Open System Properties and select Advanced system settings

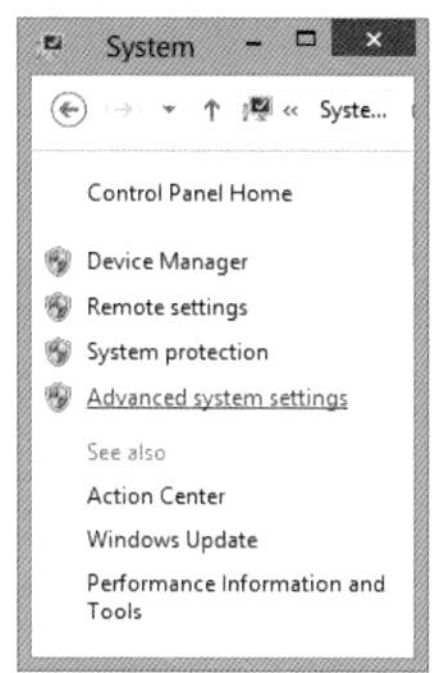

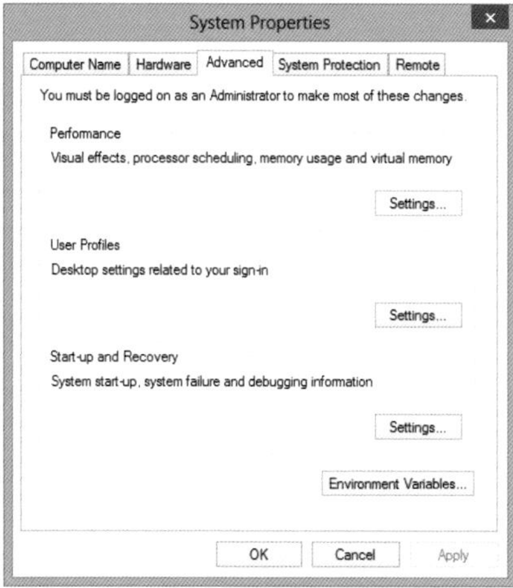

2. In the Performance section click the Settings button

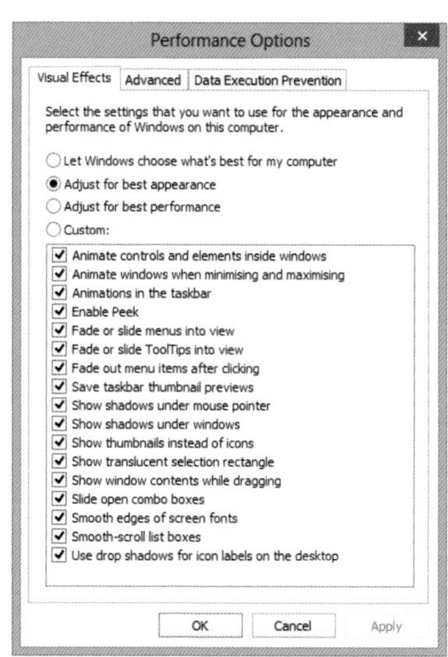

3. Performance Options display, with Visual Effects selected

4. Select a tab and adjust settings

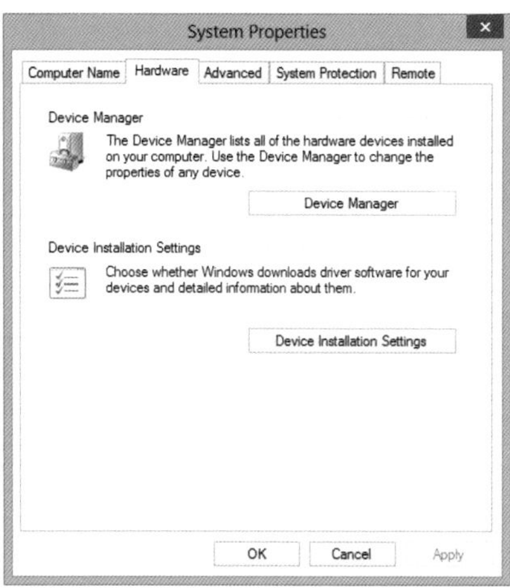

System Properties also gives access to Device Manager.

5. Click the Hardware tab, then click the Device Manager button (or click the Device Manager link in the System panel)

The Device Manager lists all the hardware devices installed on your computer, and allows you to change their properties.

Advanced tools

1. From Performance Information and Tools, select Advanced tools

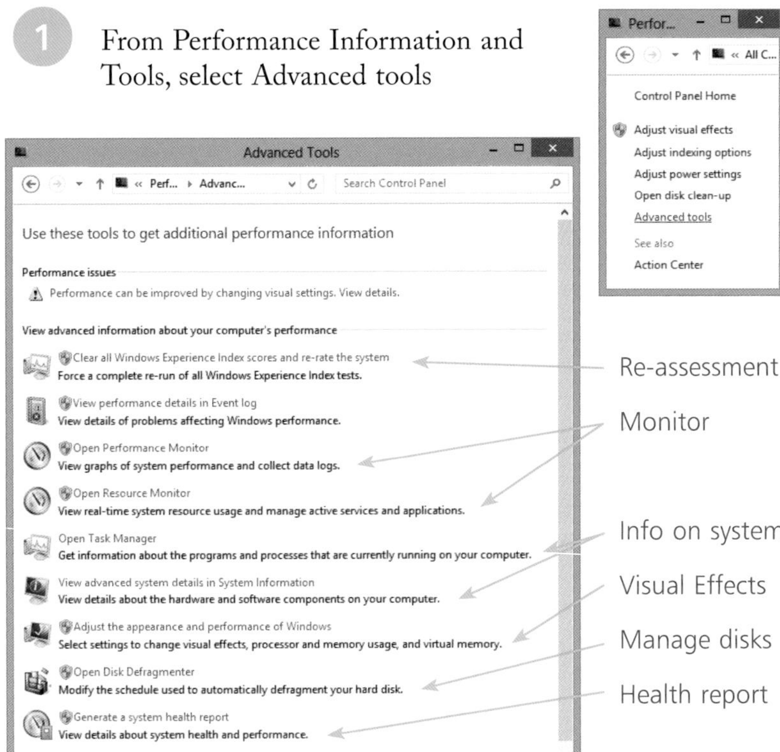

Don't forget

The Advanced tools can be used to monitor aspects of the system performance, and to carry out performance-related tasks.

The Performance issues section will list any problems that have been identified that might impact performance. For example, on a laptop computer, Advanced Tools indicates two issues:

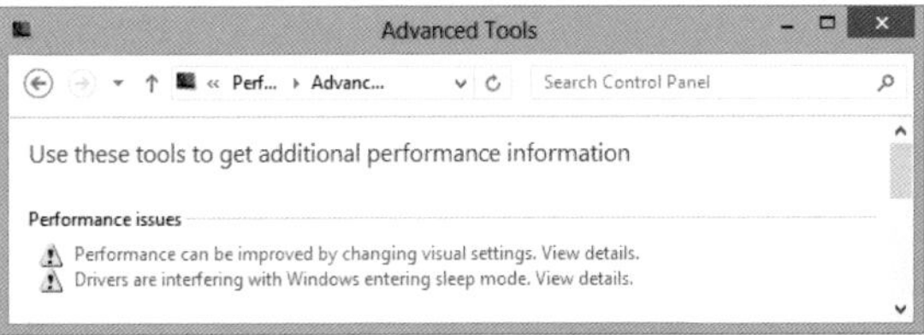

The first issue warns that the graphics adapter may not be fast enough for full operation of the visual effects. The second indicates that device drivers may interfere with Windows, and recommends updating those drivers.

1. Select an issue to display the details
2. Click help for more guidance, click Remove from list, or click OK

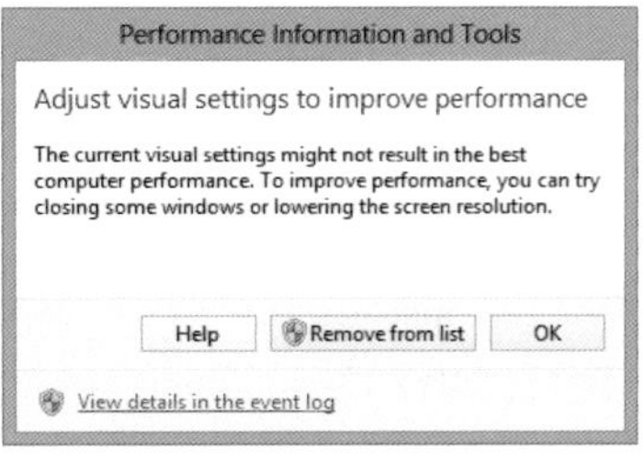

WinSAT and Event Viewer

1 Clear all Windows Experience Index scores

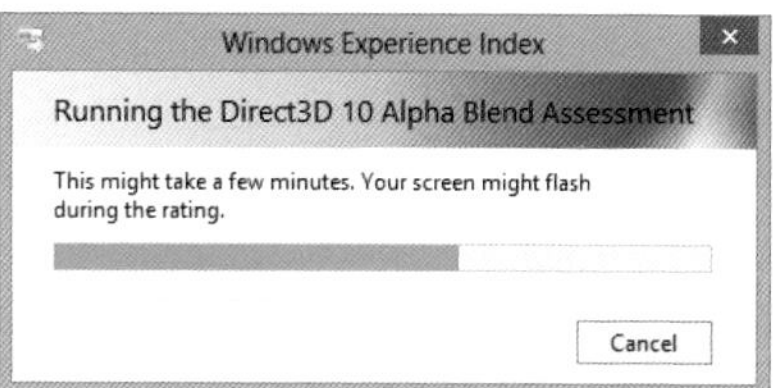

This runs WinSAT, the Windows System Assessment Tool, to repeat the assessment of the computer and generate new subscores and base score based on the latest system status.

2 View performance details in Event Log

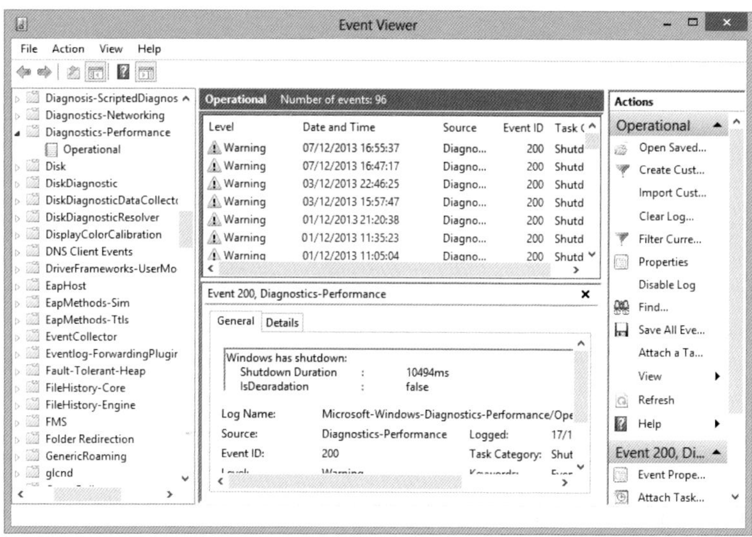

Windows identifies significant events on your computer, for example when a program encounters an error or a user logs on. The details are recorded in event logs that you can read using the Event Viewer. The Advanced Tools link opens the viewer with the Windows Diagnostics – Performance, Operational event log, but there are many other logs available.

You can also open Event Viewer from Administrative Tools, in the Control Panel, Systems and Security.

Don't forget

This re-run will take into account any hardware changes or adjustments to settings such as the virtual memory page file.

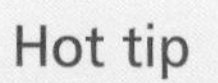

Advanced users might find the information helpful when troubleshooting problems with Windows or other programs. For most users, the Event Viewer will only be used when directed by technical support staff.

Windows monitors

Don't forget

Use Performance Monitor and Resource Monitor to view performance data either in real time or from a log file.

1. Open Performance Monitor

The program starts with an overview and a system summary, plus links to learn more about using the program. There's also a link to open the Resource Monitor program.

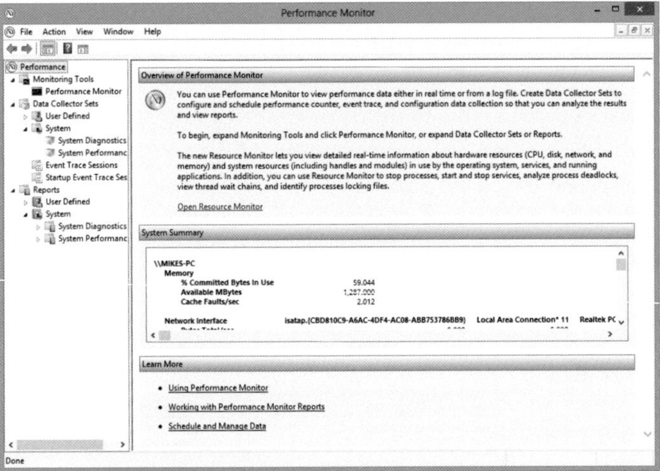

2. Expand Data Collector Sets or Reports to view log details

3. Expand Monitoring Tools and click Performance Monitor to display the graph of processor activity

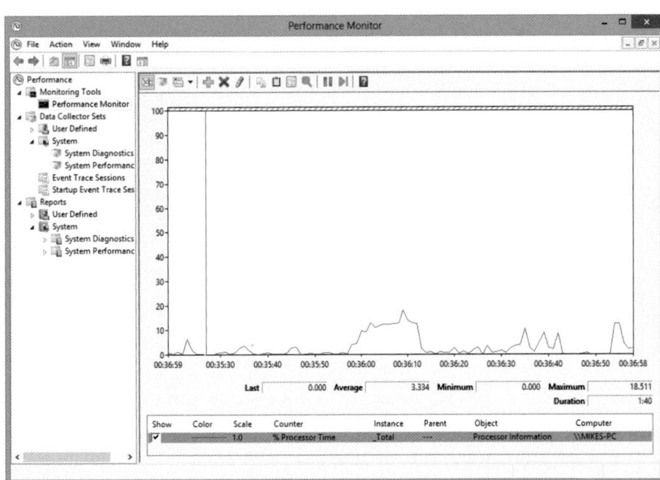

4. Open Resource Monitor

With this you can view systems resource usage in real-time, and manage the active applications and services.

5. Click Overview for a summary of computer activity

6. Click CPU for processor details

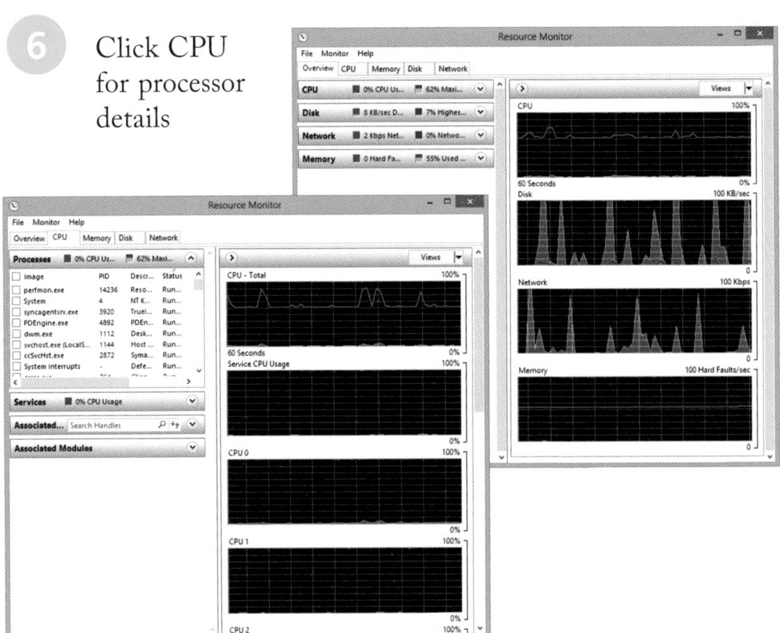

7. Click Memory for the allocation of physical memory

8. Click Disk for disk activity by process

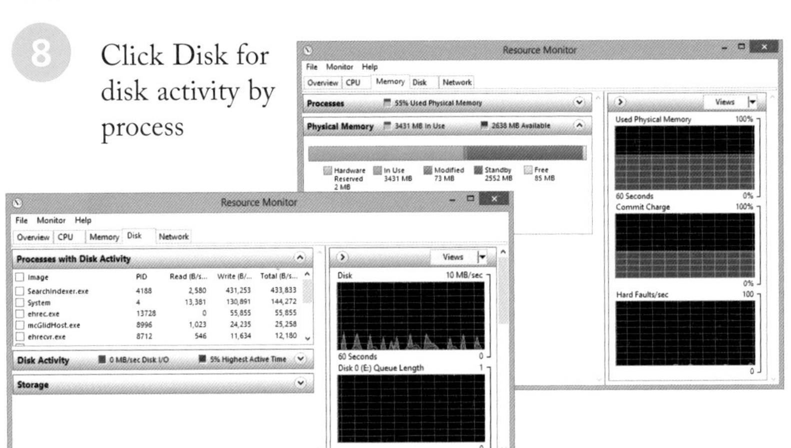

Don't forget

You can open the Resource Monitor utility from Advanced Tools, Performance Monitor or Task Manager.

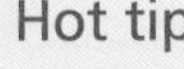

Hot tip

Resource Monitor also includes graphs for network data transfer activity.

Information on the system

1. Open Task Manager

This allows you to get information about the programs and process that are currently running on the computer.

2. Click Processes for a list of all open applications, and background processes for the current user

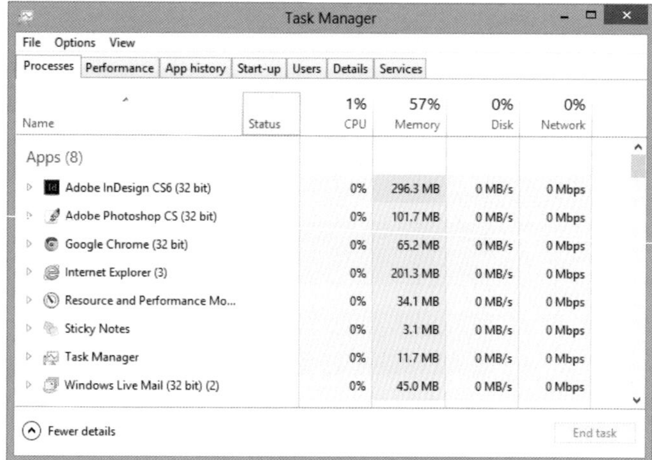

3. Click the button to Show processes from all users

4. Click Performance for graphs of CPU, memory, disk and network usage

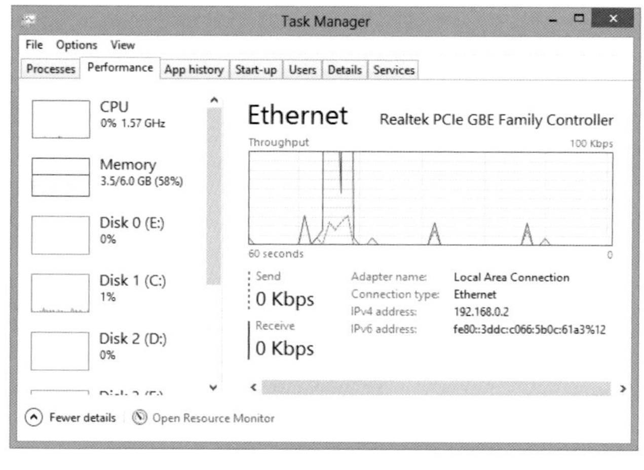

Don't forget

You can also open Task Manager by pressing the keyboard shortcut Ctrl + Shift + Esc, or by right-clicking an empty area on the taskbar and then selecting Task Manager.

Hot tip

Note that Task Manager provides a button to press that will open Resource Monitor (on the Performance tab).

Press Winkey + R and type msinfo32 in the Run box

This opens the System Information program, which shows details about the computer hardware configuration, components, software and drivers.

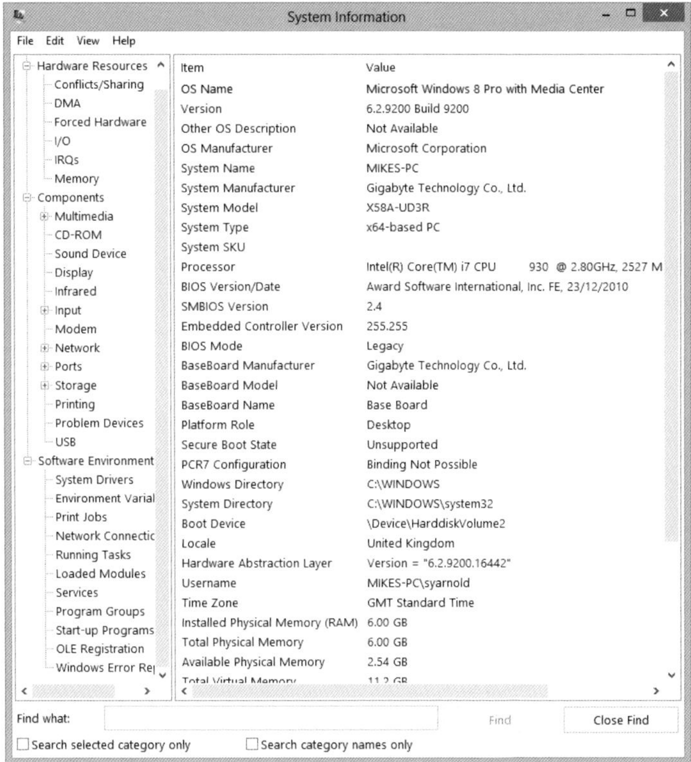

System Information lists the details in four categories:

- **System Summary** – operating system, computer name, type of BIOS, boot device, user name, amount of memory, etc.
- **Hardware Resources** – technical details of the computer's hardware, intended for IT professionals
- **Components** – details of disk drives, sound devices, modems and other devices
- **Software Environment** – shows information about drivers, network connections, and other program-related details

Don't forget

You could also enter msinfo32 in the Search charm to open System Information.

Hot tip

To find a specific detail, type keywords in the Find what box, choose Search selected category only (if appropriate) and then click Find.

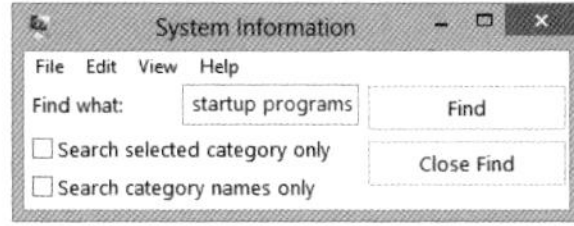

Other advanced tools

1. Adjust the appearance and performance of Windows

This will display Performance Options to adjust visual effects, processor scheduling, virtual memory and DEP.

2. Open Disk Defragmenter

This will allow you to modify the schedule for automatically defragmenting your hard disk.

3. Generate a health report

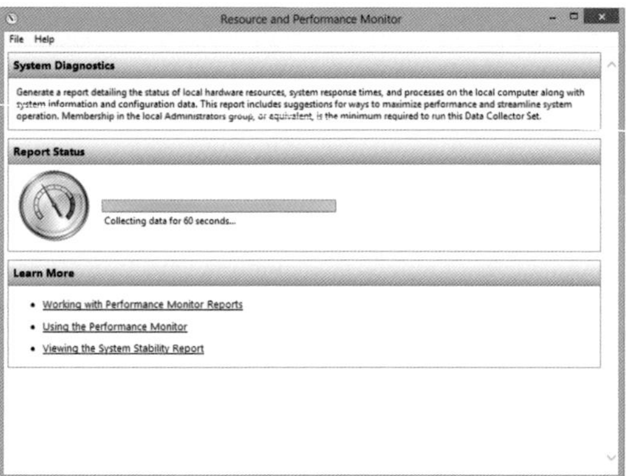

This will collect data for 60 seconds then provide a report detailing the status of the hardware resources, response times and processes, with suggestions for ways to maximize performance and system operation.

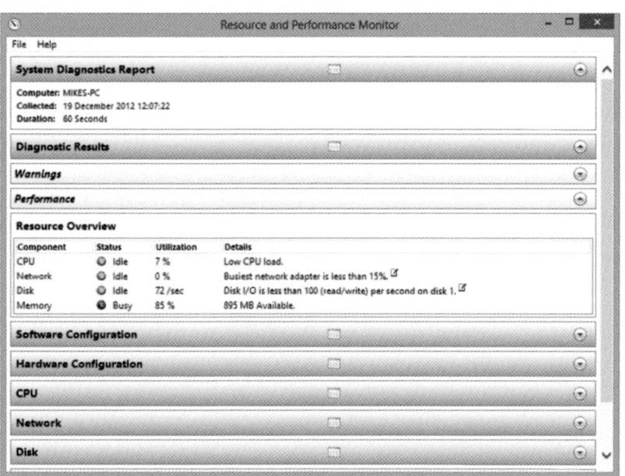

Hot tip

To get useful results and meaningful statistics, you should use the system as normal while the reports are being generated.

Boosting performance

There's another way to boost the performance of your computer, without having to make major upgrades to the hardware. You can add USB components such as an external drive or a flash drive. These won't be included in the Windows Experience Index, but they can still enhance the computer's capability.

Don't forget

Connect the drive to the mains supply via its power adapter (if required), then connect the USB cable to one of the USB ports on the computer.

1. Connect a second hard disk, for example the Western Digital My Book external drive shown here

2. The first time you do this, Windows installs the device driver software automatically

3. Windows assigns a drive letter to the drive

The USB drive is listed in the Computer as a hard disk drive, even though it is removable.

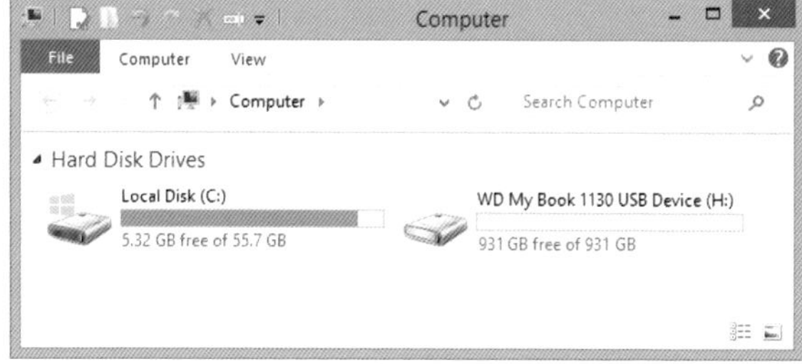

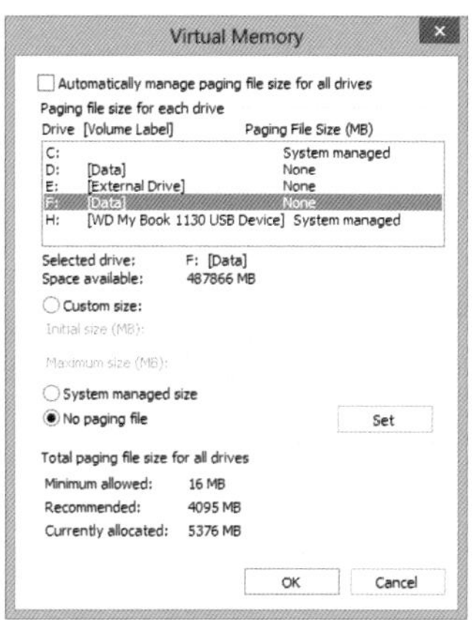

4. Open Advanced settings (see page 427) to assign a page file

5. Restart the system to apply

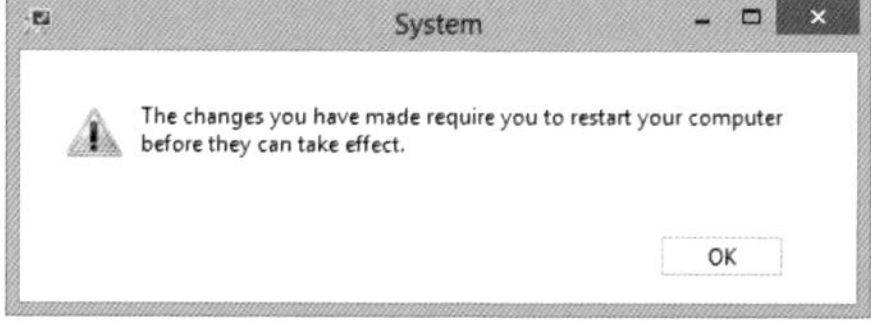

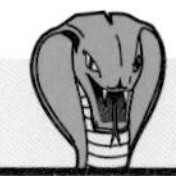

Beware

Avoid removing the drive while the system is active, if you have created a page file on it.

...cont'd

If you add a USB flash drive to your computer, you may be able to use ReadyBoost to improve the overall performance.

1. Connect the USB drive. Assuming AutoPlay is enabled, you'll be asked what to do with the drive

USB DRIVE (F:)
Tap to choose what happens with removable drives.

2. In the new windows, click Speed up my system

USB DRIVE (F:)
Choose what to do with removable drives.
Speed up my system
Windows ReadyBoost
Configure this drive for backup
File History
Open folder to view files
File Explorer
Take no action

3. The drive's properties opens at the ReadyBoost tab

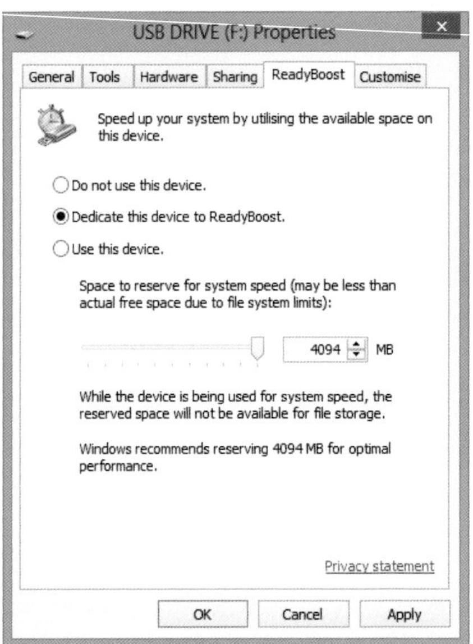

4. Select Dedicate this device to ReadyBoost

5. ReadyBoost will reserve part of the drive's space

6. Click OK

Sometimes, you may be told that a particular drive is not suitable for ReadyBoost. Typically, this is because is insufficient space, or that the device is too slow to support the use of ReadyBoost.

Users with less than 1GB of system memory (RAM) will benefit most from using ReadyBoost.

Don't forget

ReadyBoost is disk caching that uses flash memory to boost your system performance. It can use any form of flash memory such as a USB flash drive, SD card or CompactFlash.

Beware

ReadyBoost will not work with just any flash drive – it must be a good quality model.

32-bit versus 64-bit

Windows 8 editions are available as either 32-bit or 64-bit. This refers to the addressing structure used by the processor. Desktop computers generally have a 64-bit processor that can run either version of Windows. Some laptop and netbook computers have 32-bit processors, and so can only run the 32-bit Windows.

To check the processor level and the current operating system:

1. Open System and select Windows Experience Index, or click Performance Information and Tools

2. Select the link View and print detailed performance and system information

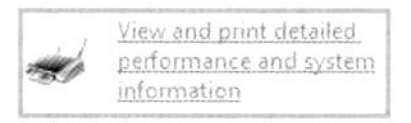

- ASUS Netbook – 32-bit Windows, 1GB, not 64-bit capable

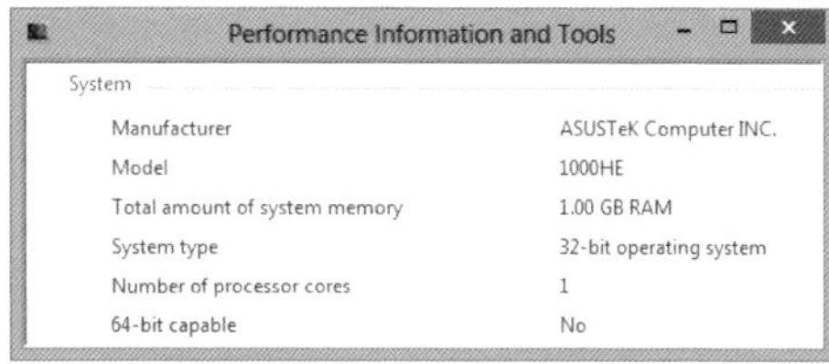

Performance Information and Tools

System

Manufacturer	ASUSTeK Computer INC.
Model	1000HE
Total amount of system memory	1.00 GB RAM
System type	32-bit operating system
Number of processor cores	1
64-bit capable	No

- Dell Laptop – 32-bit Windows, 2GB, 64-bit capable

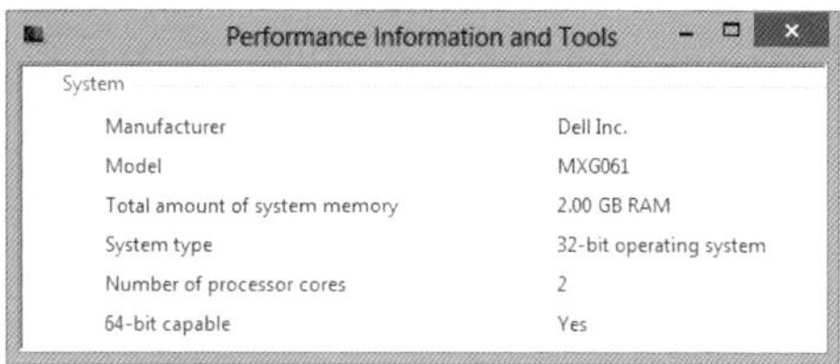

Performance Information and Tools

System

Manufacturer	Dell Inc.
Model	MXG061
Total amount of system memory	2.00 GB RAM
System type	32-bit operating system
Number of processor cores	2
64-bit capable	Yes

- Dell Desktop – 64-bit Windows, 6GB, 64-bit capable

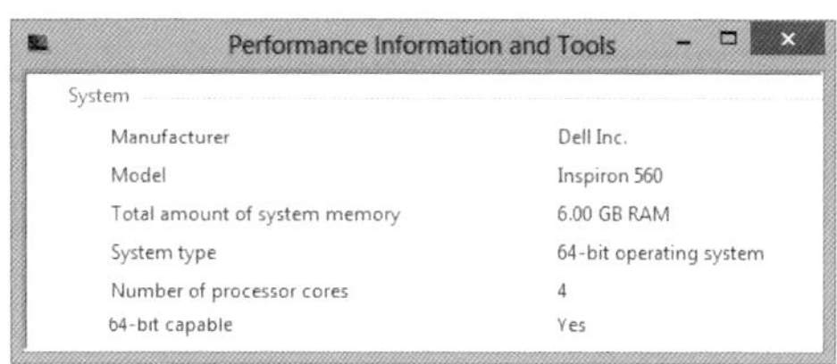

Performance Information and Tools

System

Manufacturer	Dell Inc.
Model	Inspiron 560
Total amount of system memory	6.00 GB RAM
System type	64-bit operating system
Number of processor cores	4
64-bit capable	Yes

Don't forget

You should note the amount of memory as well as 64-bit capability. You need at least 4GB memory to benefit from the 64-bit version of Windows.

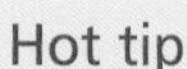

Hot tip

When the computer already has a Windows 64-bit operating system installed, the report doesn't specify the 64-bit status, because it is implicitly capable.

...cont'd

Beware

You can't upgrade from 32-bit to 64-bit – you must install a fresh system, completely replacing the existing system. So make sure you backup your data first. You also need 64-bit versions of drivers for all of your devices.

It may improve the performance of your 64-bit capable computer if you install the 64-bit operating system, but only if there is sufficient memory to make this worthwhile. You'll need at least 4GB and more if possible.

There's no information report to tell you how much memory you can add to your computer, but you can visit **www.crucial.com**, and download the Scanner tool to check your system.

1. Go to **www.crucial.com** and click Scan my computer

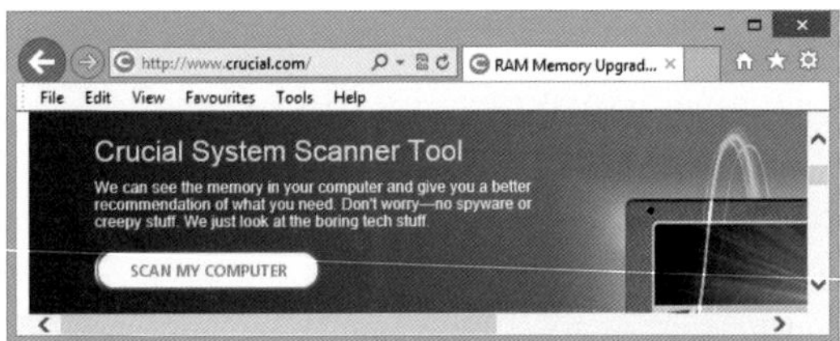

2. Follow the prompts to download the Scanner tool, and it will check your system

In the first system, current memory is 2GB, and maximum memory is 4GB. Switching to 64-bit Windows is possible, but will be of marginal benefit only.

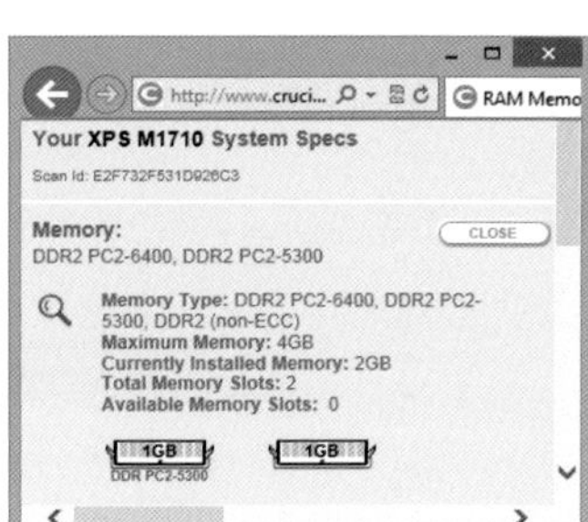

The second system already has 6GB, but can take a maximum of 8GB.

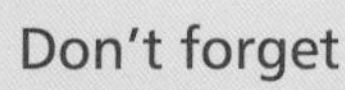

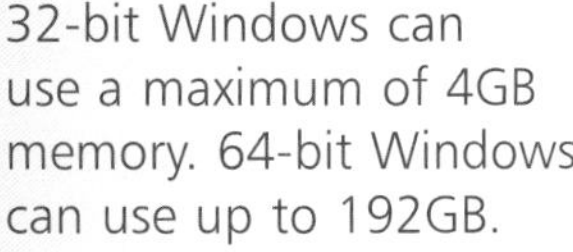

Don't forget

32-bit Windows can use a maximum of 4GB memory. 64-bit Windows can use up to 192GB.

With 64-bit Windows installed, you will find two Program File folders, one for 32-bit (often called x86) and one for 64-bit applications.

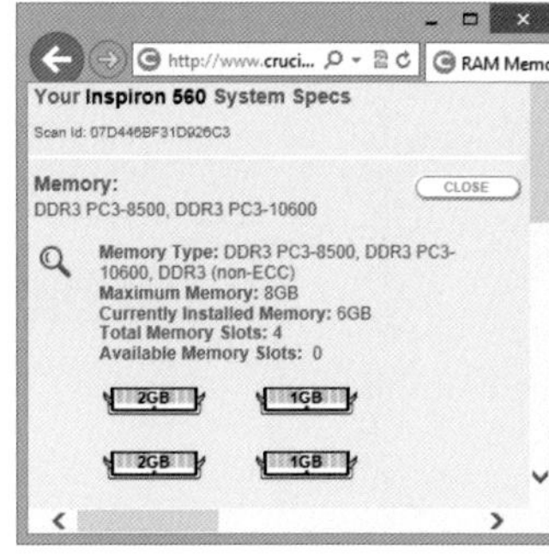

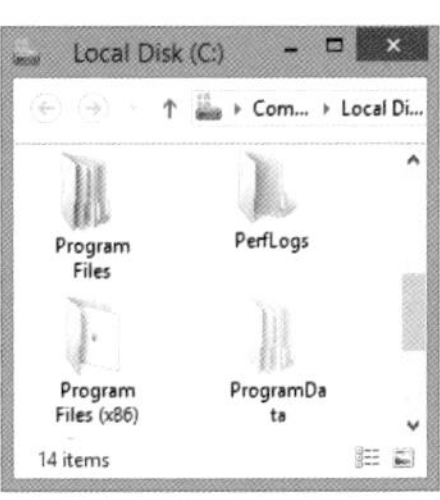

26 Windows Registry

The heart of the Windows system is the Windows Registry. Windows provides a Registry Editor for working with the Registry, and this may let you carry out tasks that are not otherwise supported. However, do be aware that errors in making such changes could leave your system unusable.

The Windows Registry

Don't forget

The Windows Registry was introduced in the early versions of Windows as a way of organizing and centralizing information that was originally stored in separate INI (initialization) files.

Hot tip

From time to time, you will encounter Windows tips that are designed to make your system better, faster or easier to use, and such tips often rely on making changes to the Registry.

Beware

Change the Registry with care. Only use trusted sources when you do make changes. And make sure you have a Registry Backup before you make any change.

Arguably the most important component in the Windows system, since it records everything about your hardware and software, the Windows Registry is something that in normal circumstances you never need to deal with directly.

The Registry is a structured database that stores the configuration settings and options for applications, device drivers, user interface, services, and all kinds of operating system components. It also stores all the counters that are used to provide the performance reports and charts.

Installation programs, applications and device software all deal directly with the Registry, so all the updates happen in the background. However, the Registry stores user-based settings in a user-specific location, thus allowing multiple users to share the same machine, yet have their own personal details and preferences. The Registry also makes it possible to establish levels of privilege, to control what actions a particular user is permitted to carry out.

Changes to the Registry Editor

When you make changes to the setup for your user account, Windows writes the necessary updates to the Registry for you. Similarly, when you install new programs or hardware devices, many Registry modifications will be applied. Normally, you won't need to know the details.

Registry Editor

However, there will be times when the developers have failed to provide a necessary change, and the only way (or the quickest way) to make the adjustment is by working directly with the Registry. Windows includes a Registry Editor that you can use, with caution since the Registry is a crucial part of your system, to browse and edit the Registry.

The Registry is made of a number of separate files, but you never need to be concerned with the physical structure, since the Registry Editor gives you access to the full Registry, displaying the logical structure and taking care of the specifics of updates.

Before you browse or edit the Registry, you should have an understanding of the structure and how changes get applied, and especially how the original values can be saved – just in case changes get applied that have unwelcome effects.

The structure of the Registry

The data in the Windows Registry is organized in a hierarchical or tree format. The nodes in the tree are called keys. Each key can contain subkeys and entries. An entry consists of a name, a data type and a value, and it is referenced by the sequence of subkeys that lead to that particular entry.

There are five top level keys:

- HKEY_LOCAL_MACHINE HKLM
  Information about the computer system, including hardware and operating system data such as bus type, system memory, device drivers, and startup control data
- HKEY_CLASSES_ROOT HKCR
  Information about file types, shortcuts and interface items (alias for parts of HKLM and HKCU)
- HKEY_CURRENT_USER HKCU
  Contains the user profile for the currently logged on user, with desktop, network, printers, and program preferences (alias for part of HKU)
- HKEY_USERS HKU
  Contains information about actively loaded user profiles and the default profile
- HKEY_CURRENT_CONFIG HKCC
  The hardware profile used at startup, for example to configure device drivers and display resolution
  (alias for part of HKLM)

Sections of the Registry are stored in the System32 and User folders, each subtree having a single file plus a log file, for example Sam and Sam.log, or System and Sytem.log. Subtrees associated with files are known as Registry hives. They include:

HKEY_LOCAL_MACHINE\SAM	Sam
HKEY_LOCAL_MACHINE\SECURITY	Security
HKEY_LOCAL_MACHINE\SOFTWARE	Software
HKEY_LOCAL_MACHINE\SYSTEM	System
HKEY_CURRENT_CONFIG	System
HKEY_CURRENT_USER	Ntuser.dat
HKEY_USERS\.DEFAULT	Default

Beware

Some products available on the Internet suggest the Registry needs regular maintenance or cleaning. Although problems can arise, in general the Registry is self-sufficient and such products are not necessary.

Hot tip

Applications read the Registry to check that a specific key exists, or to open a key and select entry values that are included.

Don't forget

The tree, subtree, alias, hive and file structure can be very complex, but the view taken via the Registry Editor is fortunately more straightforward.

Registry backup

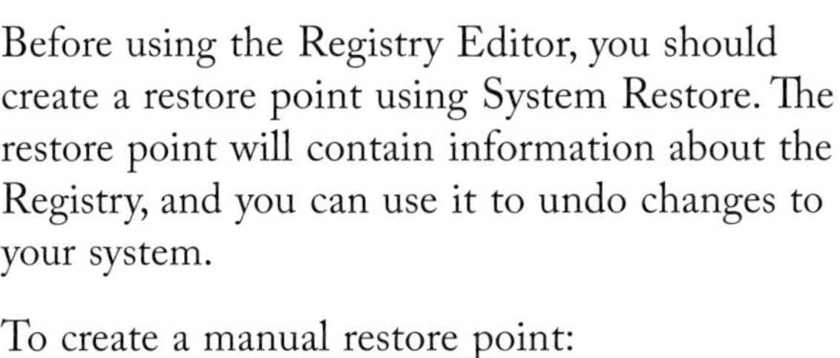

Before using the Registry Editor, you should create a restore point using System Restore. The restore point will contain information about the Registry, and you can use it to undo changes to your system.

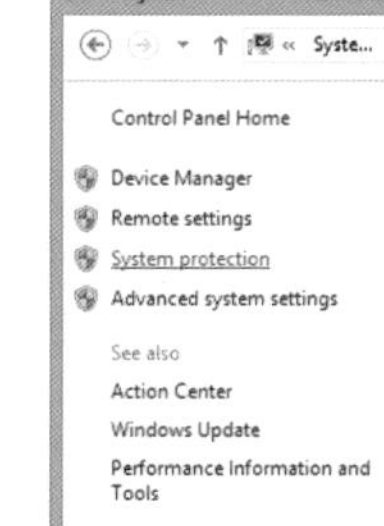

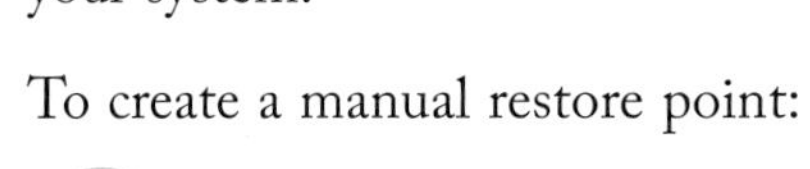

To create a manual restore point:

1. Open System Properties and select System protection

2. Select the System Protection tab and click Create to create a restore point immediately

3. Type a description, to remind you of the reason for the restore point

4. When the restore point completes, click Close – no restart is required

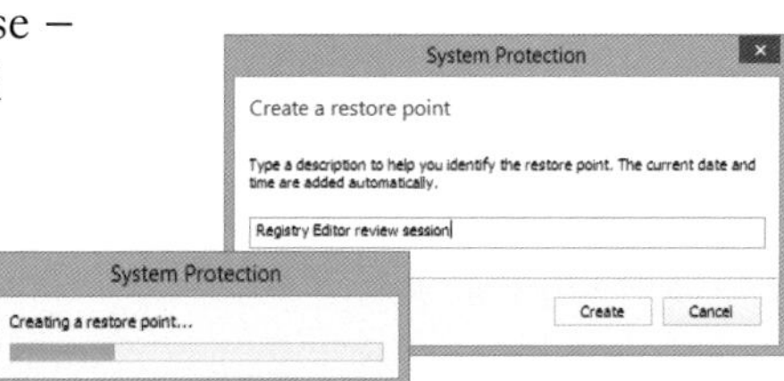

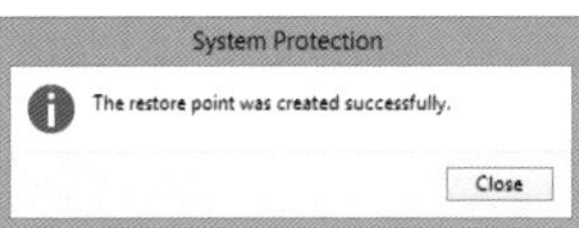

5. Just to check, open System Properties and click the System Restore button

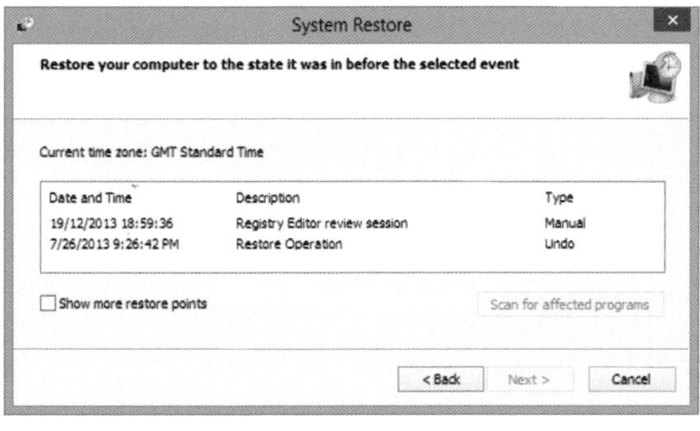

Don't forget

You can also backup individual parts of the Registry, just before you make changes to them (see page 449).

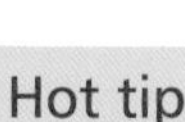

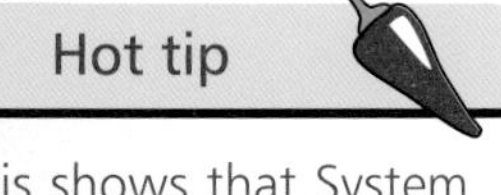

Hot tip

This shows that System Restore had made its daily restore point, so this could be used instead of a manual restore point, unless you've already made some changes during the current session.

Open Registry Editor

Registry Editor is not accessible via the Control panel, Administrative tools or through any shortcuts. You must run program Regedit.exe by name.

1. Press Winkey + R to open the Run box. Enter regedit and click OK

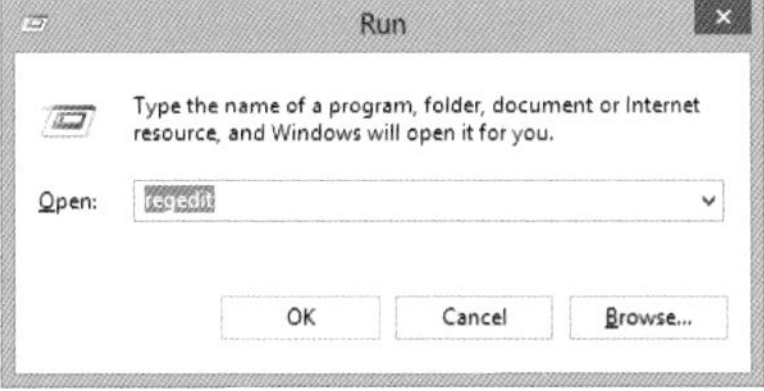

2. Assuming you have an administrator account, click Yes, to allow Registry Editor to start with full administrator privilege

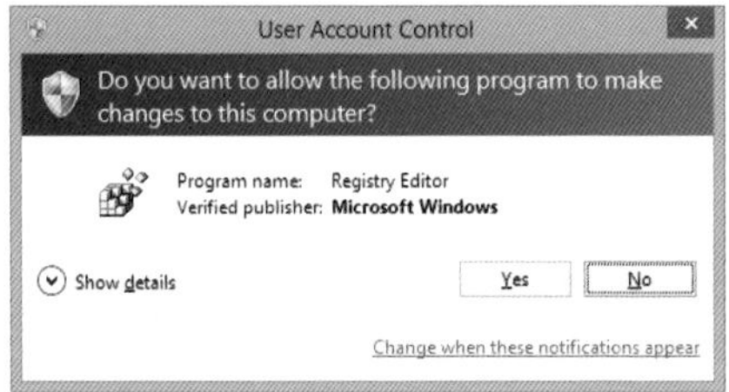

3. Registry Editor starts, and the first time it runs, you'll see the five main subtrees, with all their branches collapsed

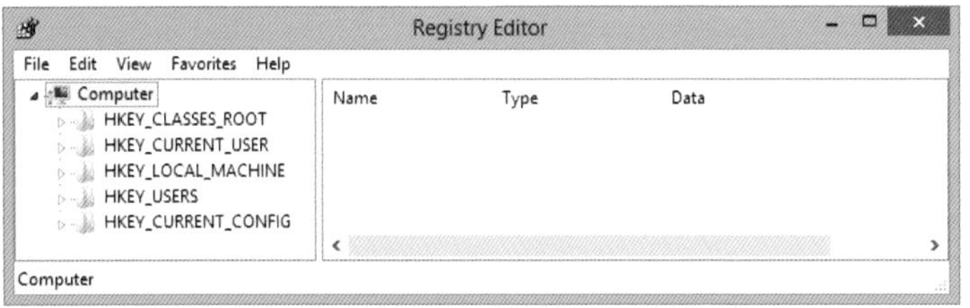

4. Select a key, e.g. HKEY_LOCAL_MACHINE (HKLM), and double-click to expand to the next level

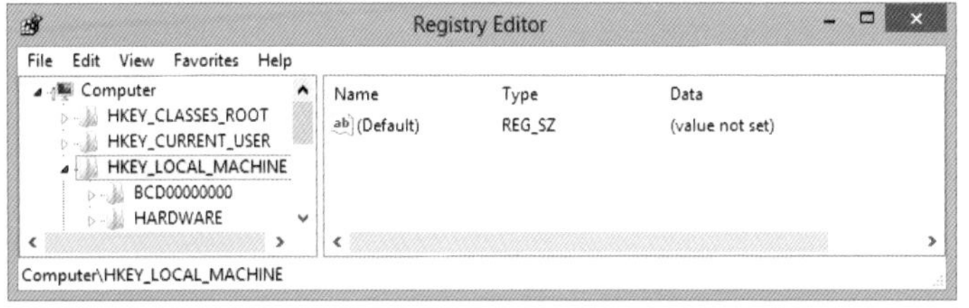

Don't forget

This is an advanced program, which will usually be run via an administrator account, though it can be run using a standard account.

Hot tip

Registry Editor will save the last key referenced in the session, and open at that point the next time you run the program.

Hot tip

The right-hand pane displays the entries and data values for the selected key. You can also click the white and black triangles to open or collapse the branches of the subtrees.

Example Registry change

Don't forget

You'll find many such suggested changes on the Internet, usually in lists of Windows hints and tips, and often referred to as Registry hacks.

Before exploring the Registry further, it will be useful to look at a typical Registry update, used to make changes for which Windows has no formal method included.

One such requirement is to change the registered organization and registered owner for the computer. These names will have been set up when Windows was installed. The names chosen may no longer be appropriate, perhaps because you've changed companies, or because the computer was passed on or purchased from another user.

To see the registration details:

1. Press Winkey + R and type winver

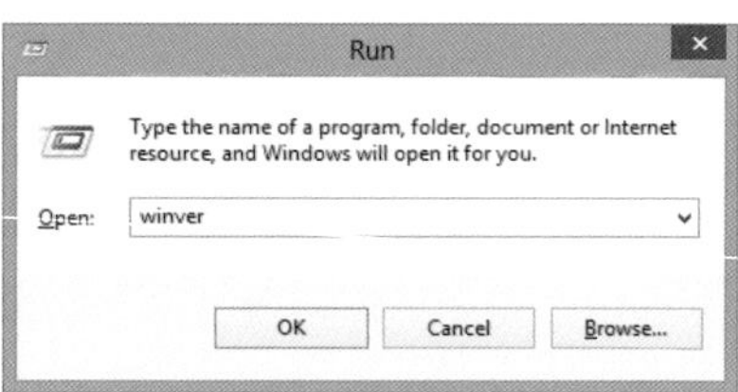

2. The details of the installed version of Windows are shown, along with the registered owner and organization

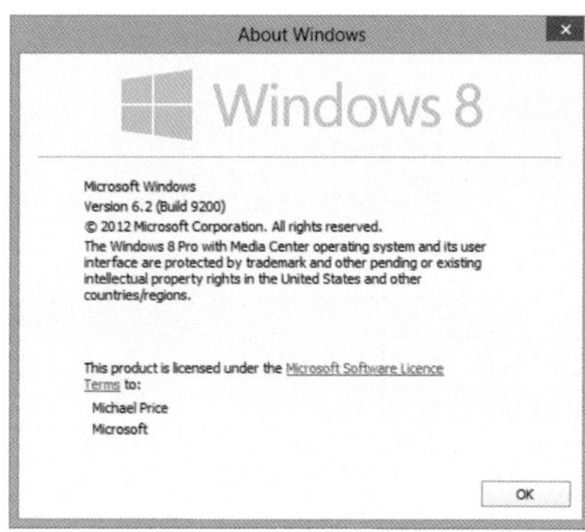

3. Assume that these details need to be revised to Sue Price and In Easy Steps

4. Search the Internet for advice on changing registered owner

Beware

Do make sure that the sites you use as sources for Registry changes are reliable, and check the details carefully to ensure the change does exactly what it claims.

You will find that this particular change is included in a number of Windows hints and tips lists. You'll even find a solution at the Microsoft website **www.microsoft.com**
All the suggestions follow a similar pattern. They advise you to run Regedit.exe and find the Registry key named HKEY_LOCAL_MACHINE\SOFTWARE\Microsoft\Windows NT\CurrentVersion, where you can change the owner and organization. Some of the websites also discuss the need for administrator authority, and they usually warn about taking backups before making changes.

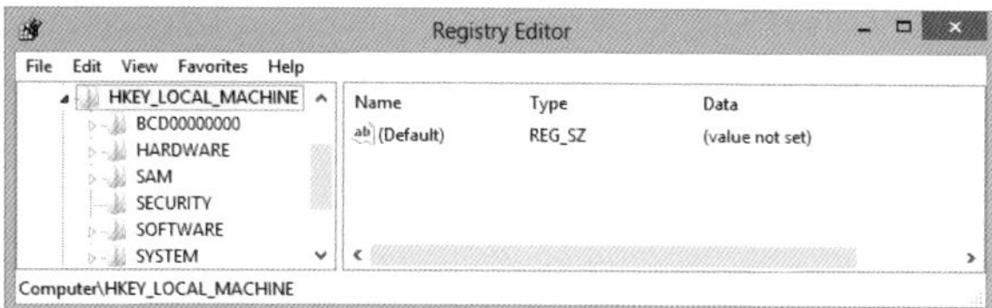

1 Locate the subkey SOFTWARE and double-click

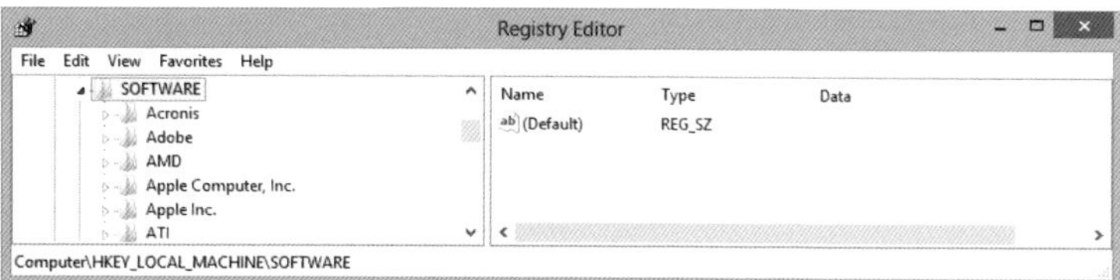

2 Scroll down to subkey Microsoft and double-click

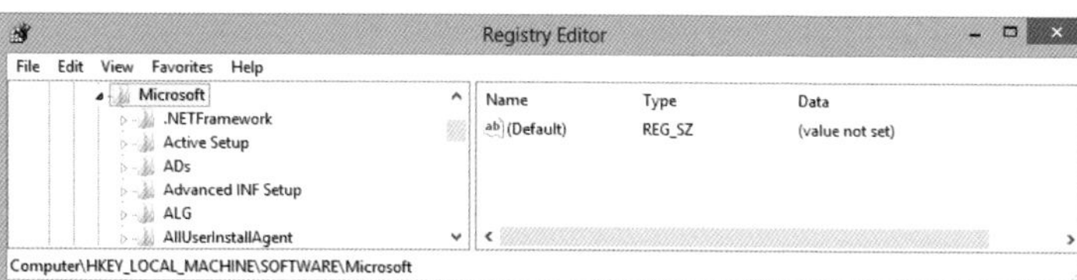

3 Scroll down to subkey Windows NT and double-click

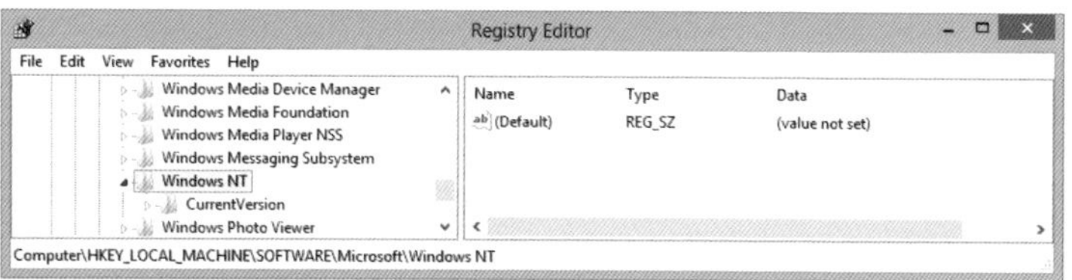

4 Select subkey CurrentVersion and scroll through the list of entries to select RegisteredOrganization

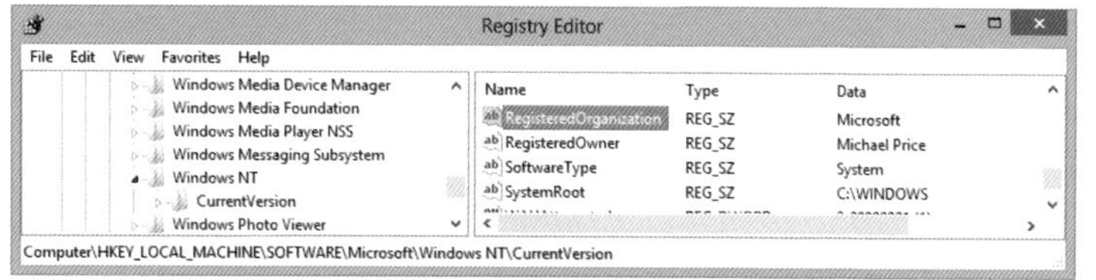

Don't forget

To locate the key, you can step through the path, subkey by subkey, double-clicking each one in turn.

Hot tip

You can double-click a subkey, or select it and press enter, to expand it to the next level.

Hot tip

Although the subkeys are shown in capitals or mixed case, as displayed in the Registry, they are in fact not case sensitive.

Finding a key

Don't forget

Rather than stepping through the path, you could use the Find command in Regedit.

Hot tip

Pressing F3 carries out the Find Next operation, to locate the next match.

Beware

You'll soon discover that subkey names are not unique, and also the same text could appear in the data content of Registry entries.

Don't forget

Find is more effective if you restrict the search, for example putting a Value entry name, and clearing the Key and Data boxes. You could also search for known text in the data content.

1. Select the highest level key Computer, and then click Edit > Find (or press Ctrl + F)

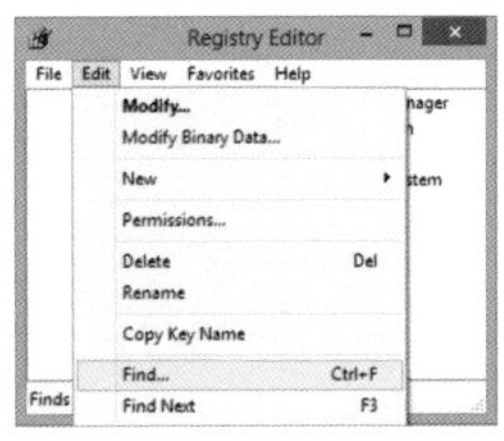

2. Type the required subkey CurrentVersion and click Find Next

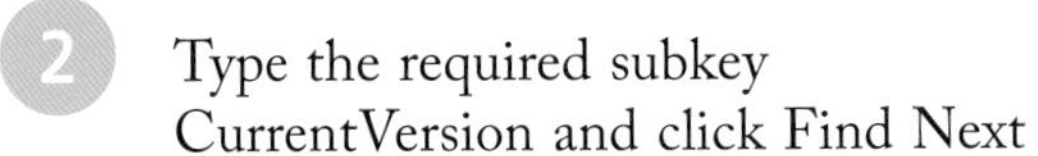

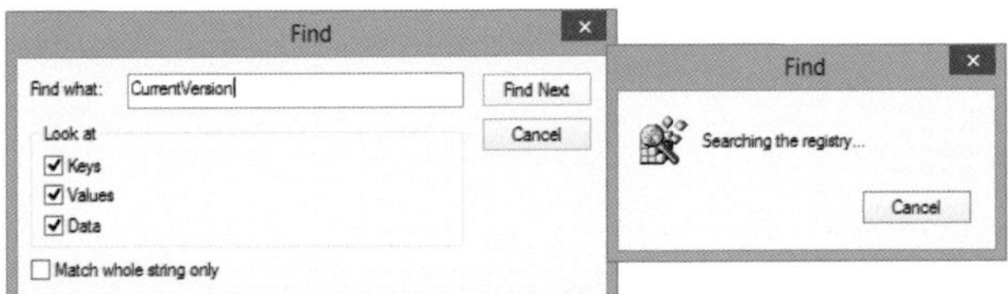

3. The subkey is in the wrong branch, so keep pressing F3

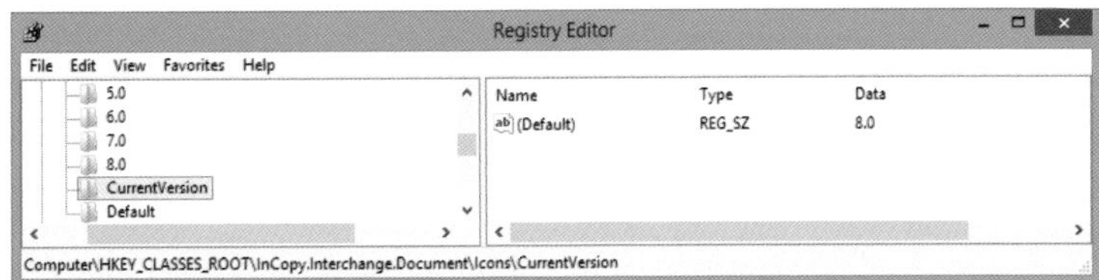

4. This is the wrong section, and matches data content

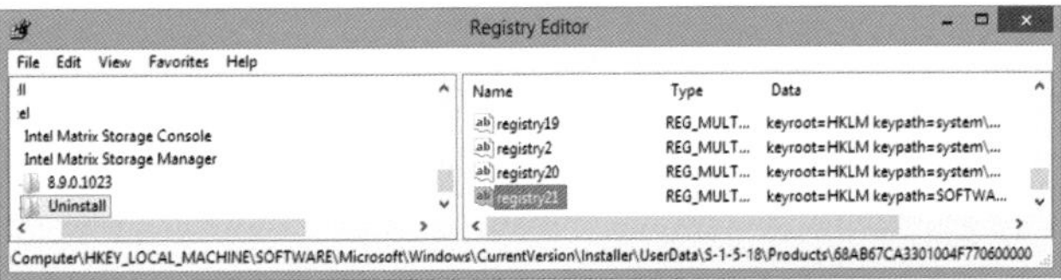

5. Search instead for the Value entry name RegisteredOrganization

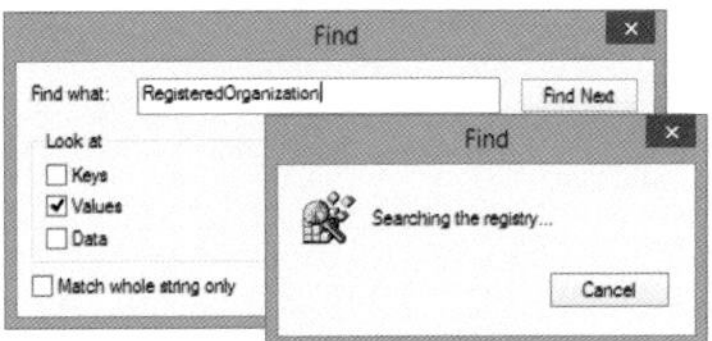

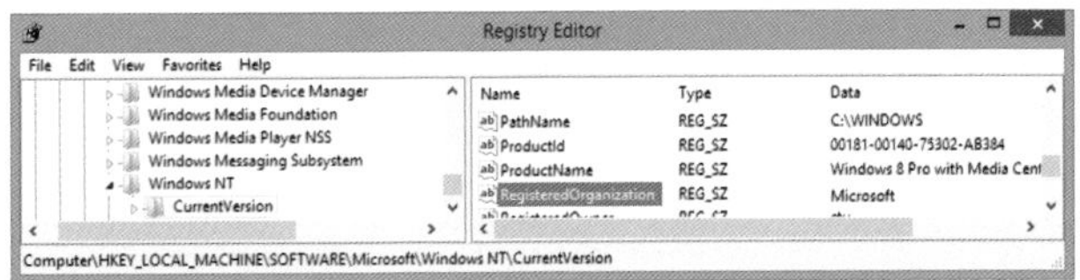

Backup before changes

1. Select the subkey, or a value entry within the subkey, and then click File > Export

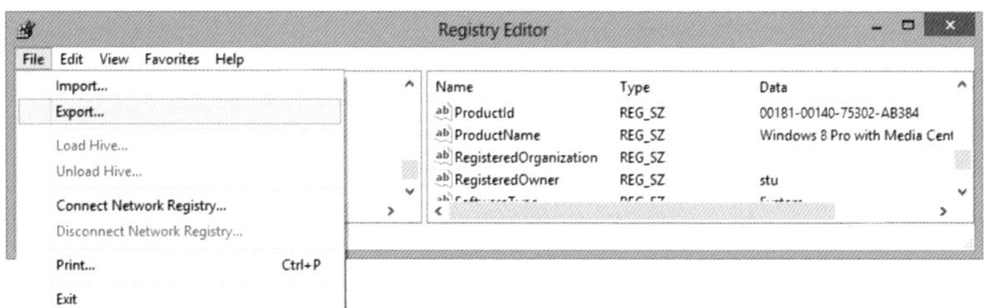

2. By default, your Documents folder will be selected, but you can choose a different folder if desired

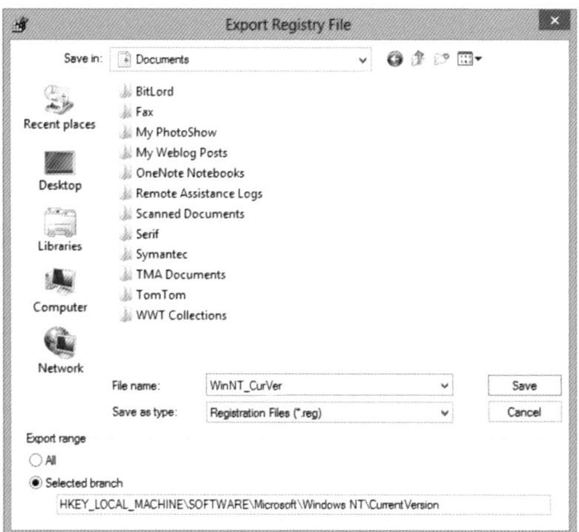

3. Provide a file name for the Registration File (.reg) that is being created and choose Selected branch

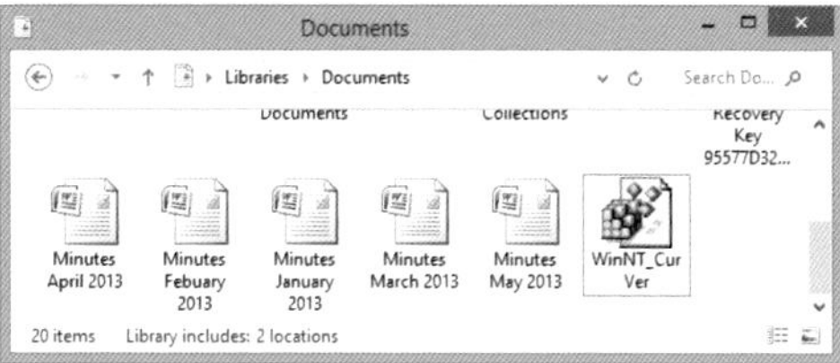

4. The Registration file is written to the selected folder

You should make a backup of the branch at the subkey within which changes are required.

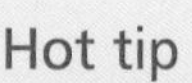

You can create a backup of the whole registry, but it is sufficient to backup just the branches being changed.

The .reg file will have all the subkeys, value entries and data contents for everything within the subkey selected for Export.

Change a Value entry

1. Select the Value entry to be changed and double-click

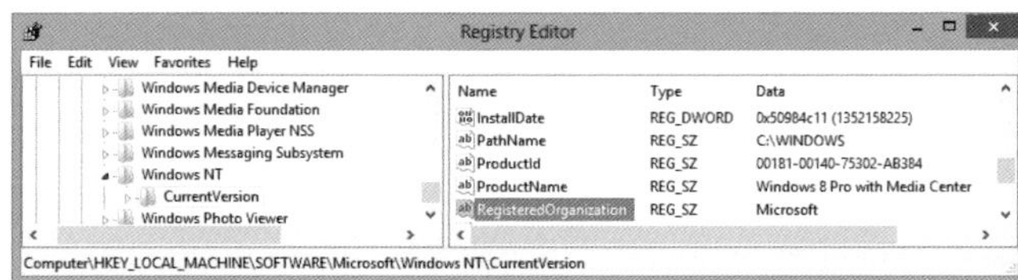

Don't forget

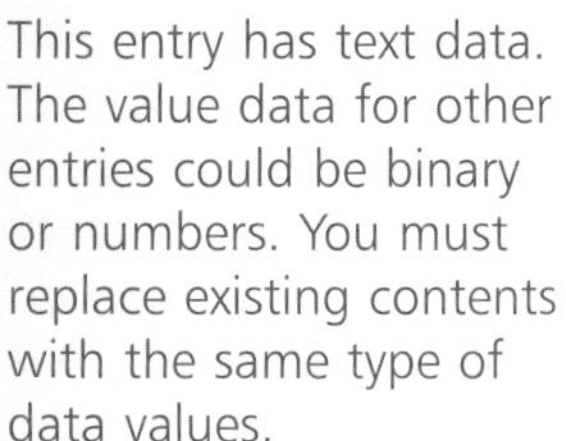

This entry has text data. The value data for other entries could be binary or numbers. You must replace existing contents with the same type of data values.

2. The Value entry is opened with Value data displayed ready for Edit

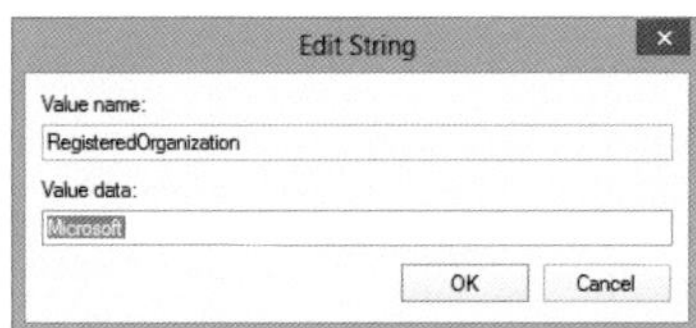

3. Replace the existing contents with the required information

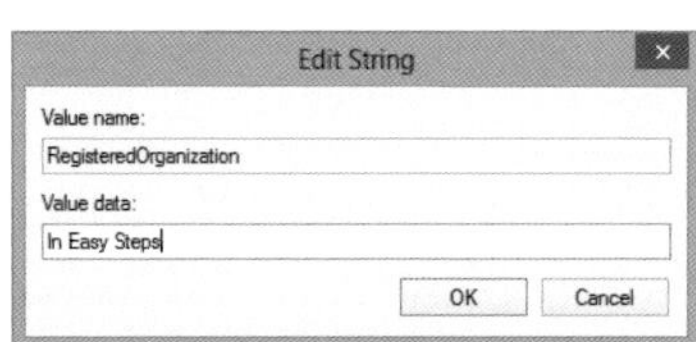

4. Click OK to apply and save the change. It is immediately in effect

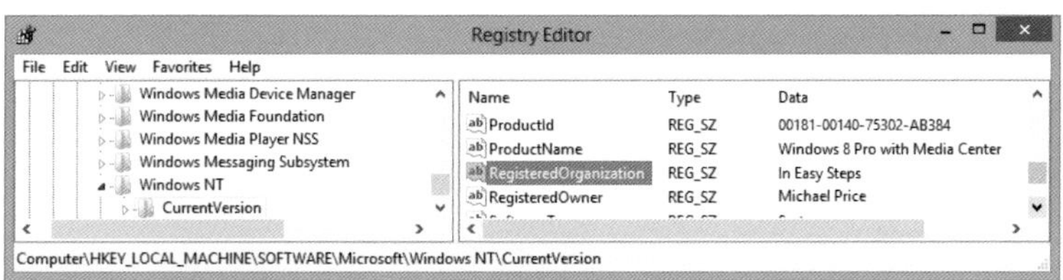

Beware

If you change your mind part way through, you cannot just close Registry Editor – you must restore the original values using the branch backup, or else reverse the changes individually.

5. Repeat for any other values to be changed

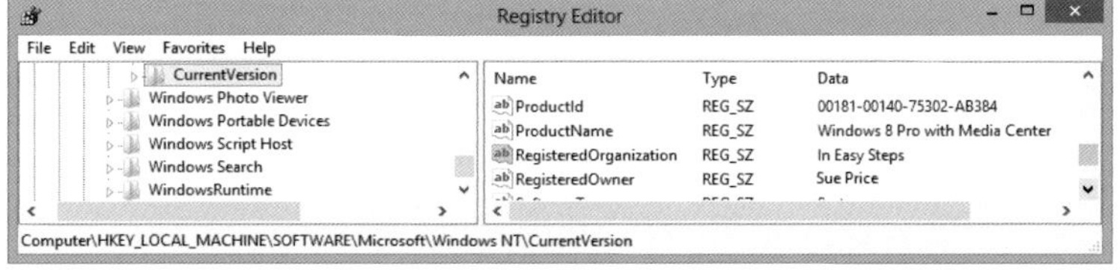

6. Close Registry Editor when you have finished – no Save is required, since changes are dynamically applied

Using a standard account

Log off and switch to a Standard user account, making sure no other accounts are active.

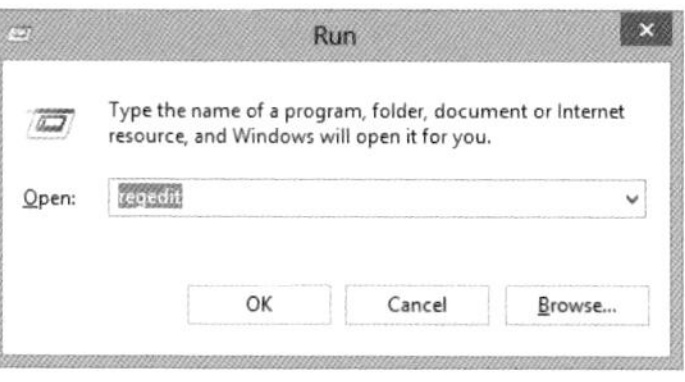

1. Press Winkey + R to open the Run box. Enter regedit and click OK

2. There's no UAC interception, Registry Editor starts up at Computer (or at the last key referenced by this account)

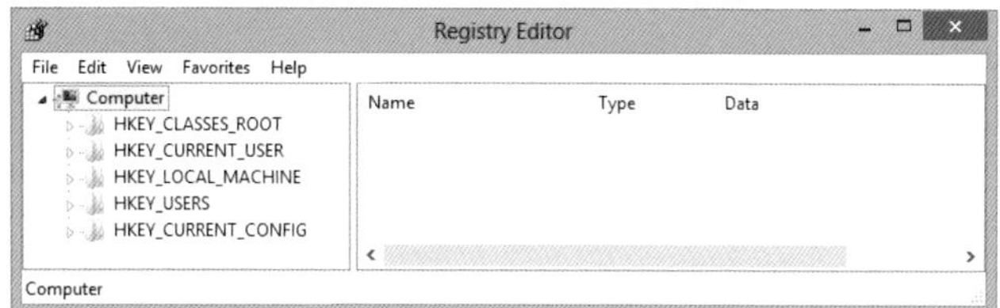

3. Locate the Value entry RegisteredOrganization in the Windows NT subkey, and double-click the name

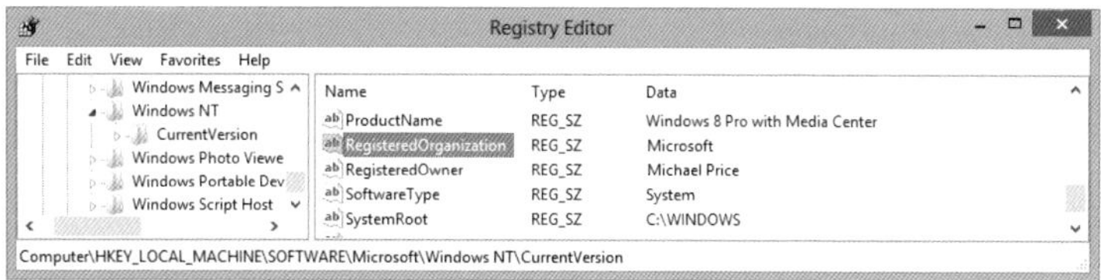

4. The current value is shown

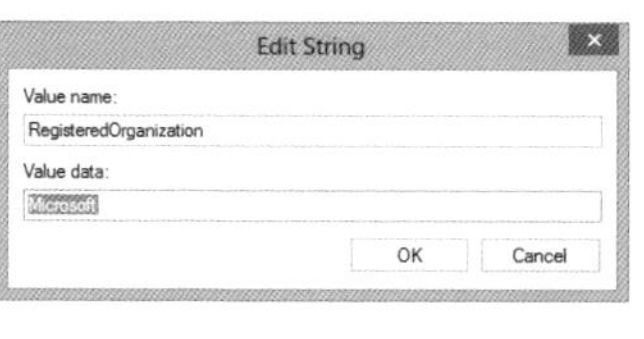

5. Change the value to the required text and click OK

6. Registry Editor displays an error message to say it is unable to edit the entry

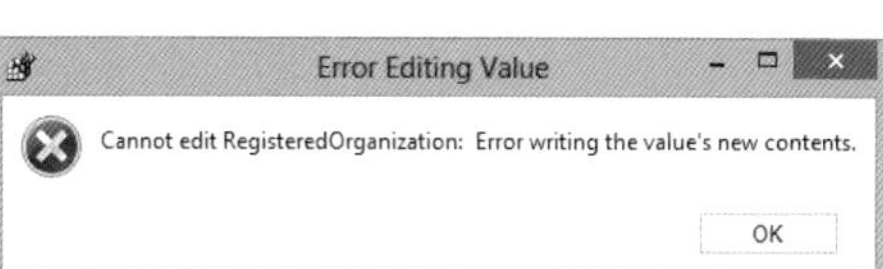

When you run Regedit from a Standard user account, it operates at a lower privilege level.

The standard account can edit and create Registry keys under HKEY_CURRENT_USER, but not entries under HKEY_LOCAL_MACHINE. Some registry entries are even blocked for reading.

...cont'd

If you are signed in with a standard user account but you need full Registry Editor access, you must run Regedit as an administrator.

1. Type regedit in the Search charm and press Enter

2. On the results pane, right-click Regedit and select Run as Administrator on the app bar at the bottom

3. Provide the password for the administrator account displayed and click Yes, to allow Registry Editor to start with full administrator privilege

Don't forget

If there are several administrator accounts, they'll be listed and you can choose the appropriate account.

Hot tip

There's no obvious visual difference between the full Regedit session and the previous limited session, but you can now make the changes.

As an alternative, you can open the Command Prompt as an administrator, and start Regedit.exe from there.

1. Press Winkey + X and click Command Prompt (Admin)

2. Respond to the UAC prompt, then type regedit.exe and press Enter. The full Registry Editor will start

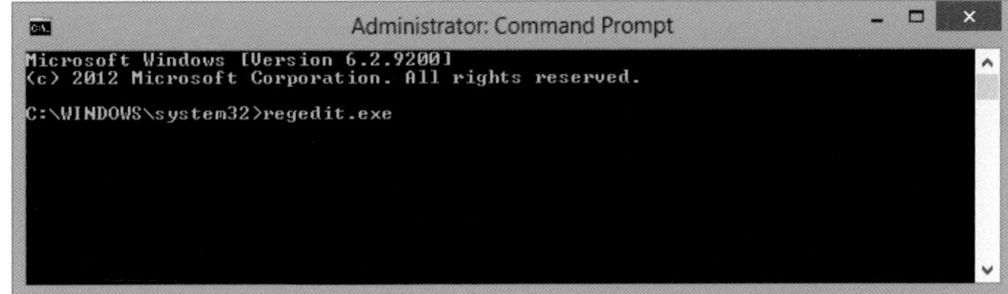

Don't forget

The Command Prompt is flagged as Administrator, and running Regedit.exe from here starts the full session, without further UAC prompts.

Scripted updates

You'll find that some websites offer scripted versions of Registry updates that you can download and run. These are similar to the Registration files that you create when you backup a branch of the Registry. To illustrate this method, you can create your own script to update the Registered owner details.

1. Open Notepad and type the Registry Editor header, the subkey path and the Value entries required

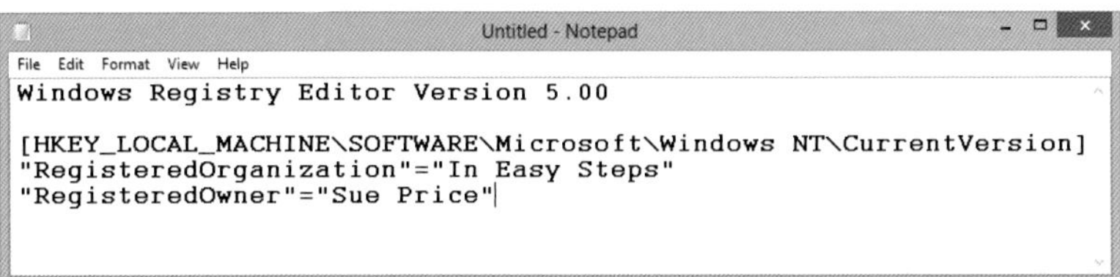

2. Select File, Save and choose a folder if required, or accept the default, normally Documents

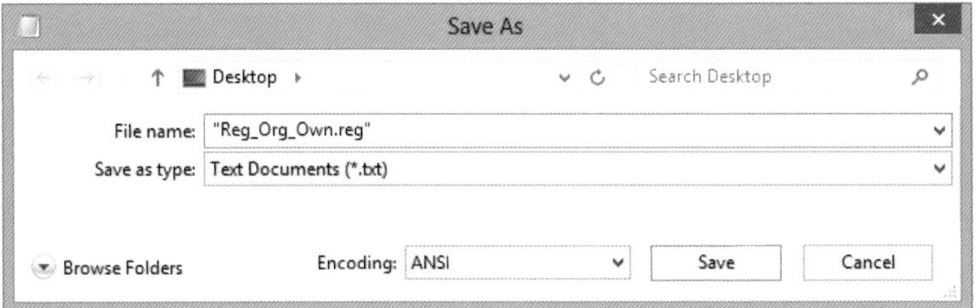

3. Type the file name and file type, e.g. "Reg_Org_Own.reg"

The quote marks ensure that the file type .reg will be used, rather than Notebook's default file type .txt.

4. Click Save, and the Registration file will be added to the specified folder

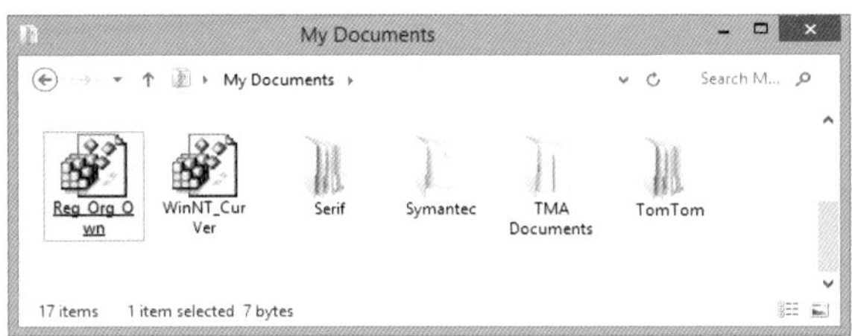

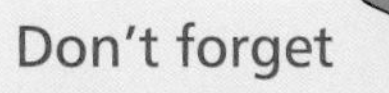

Using scripts that are provided can make it easier to apply updates, as long as you trust the source websites.

Hot tip

This .reg file automates the process followed to find the subkey and amend the Value entries for Organization and Owner.

Applying an update

Don't forget

You use this same process to apply the backup Registration file, if you decide to reverse the changes you have made.

1. To apply an update, double-click the Registration file

2. There will be a UAC prompt, and then you will be warned of the potential dangers of updates

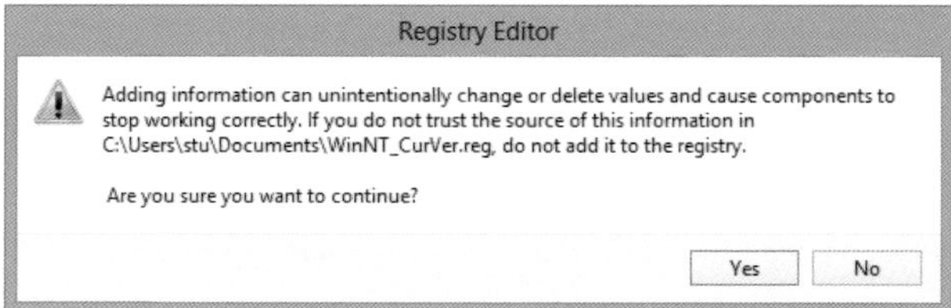

3. If you are happy with the update, click Yes

Hot tip

The update is applied without any requirement to run Regedit or open the Registry.

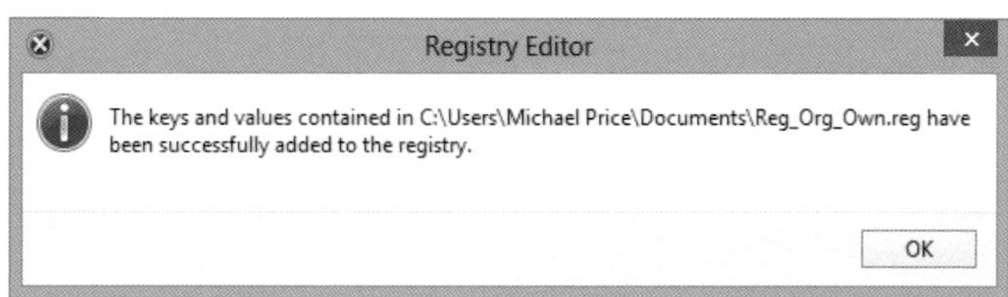

4. The keys and values included are added to the Registry

5. Confirm the update by running Winver

About Windows

Windows 8

Microsoft Windows
Version 6.2 (Build 9200)
© 2012 Microsoft Corporation. All rights reserved.
The Windows 8 Pro with Media Center operating system and its user interface are protected by trademark and other pending or existing intellectual property rights in the United States and other countries/regions.

This product is licensed under the Microsoft Software Licence Terms to:
Sue Price
In Easy Steps

OK

6. You can also open the Registry and check the subkey and its Value entries

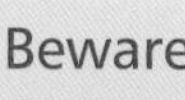

Beware

It is well worth repeating that you must change the Registry with care. Only use trusted sources when you do make changes. And make sure you have a Registry Backup before you make any change.

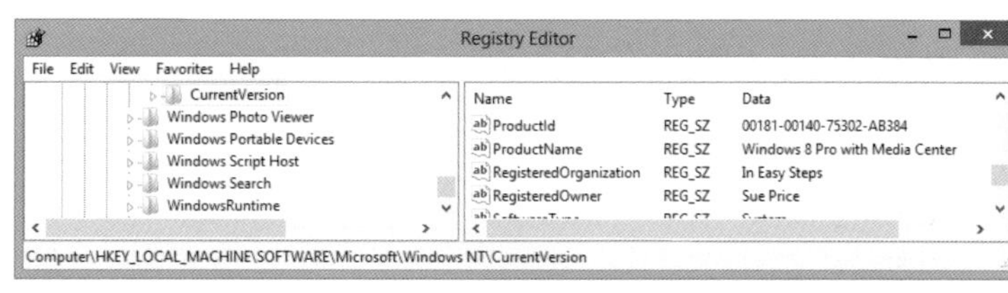

Resize taskbar thumbnails

When you move the mouse cursor over a Windows 8 taskbar button, you'll see a small version of the application window.

To make this larger in size:

1. Open Regedit.exe, and locate the subkey HKEY_CURRENT_USER\Software\Microsoft\Windows\CurrentVersion\Explorer\Taskband

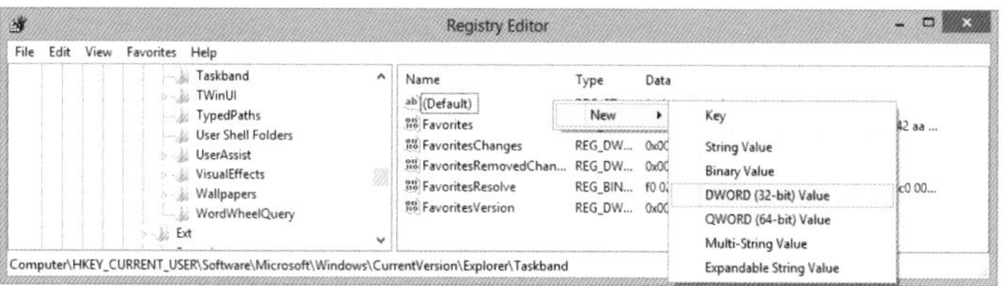

2. Right-click the right hand pane and select New, DWORD Value, then name the value MinThumbSizePx.

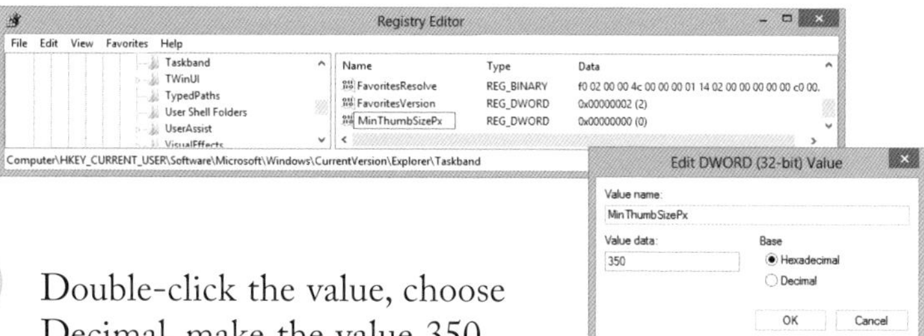

3. Double-click the value, choose Decimal, make the value 350

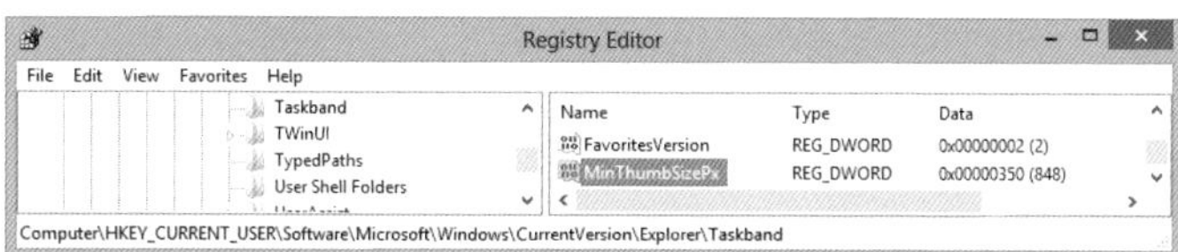

4. Log off and log on again to put the change into effect

5. View a taskbar thumbnail to see the results

Don't forget

Registry updates require you to change binary or number values, or ask you to create keys or value entries. Here are some additional updates to illustrate some of the techniques needed.

Hot tip

Adjust the value again to fine-tune the results, or delete the value entry to return to the default thumbnail.

Remove shortcut suffix

When you create a shortcut on the desktop, Windows insists on adding the word Shortcut to the name.

For example:

1. Locate the Notepad.exe program file, which is usually found in C:\windows\system32

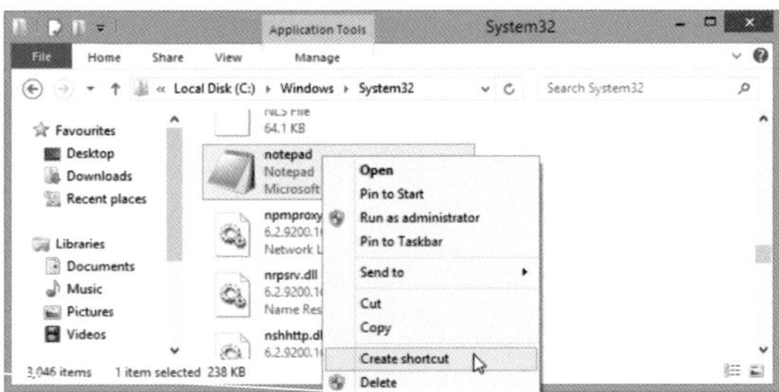

2. Right-click the program icon and select Create shortcut

3. The shortcut cannot be added to the program folder, so Click Yes to place it on the desktop

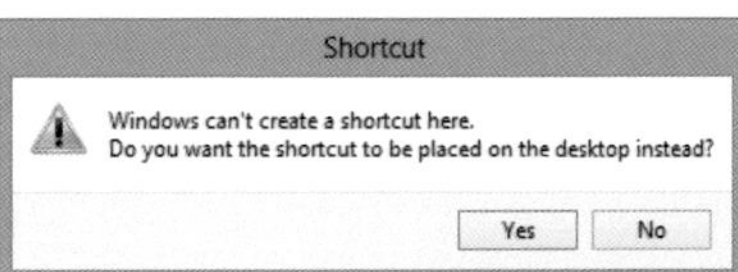

4. The shortcut is created and given the program name followed by - Shortcut

If you find yourself editing the name to remove this addition, you might like to edit the Registry to avoid the suffix for all future shortcuts you create (this change won't affect existing shortcuts).

1. Open Regedit.exe, and locate the subkey HKEY_CURRENT_USER\Software\Microsoft\Windows\CurrentVersion\Explorer

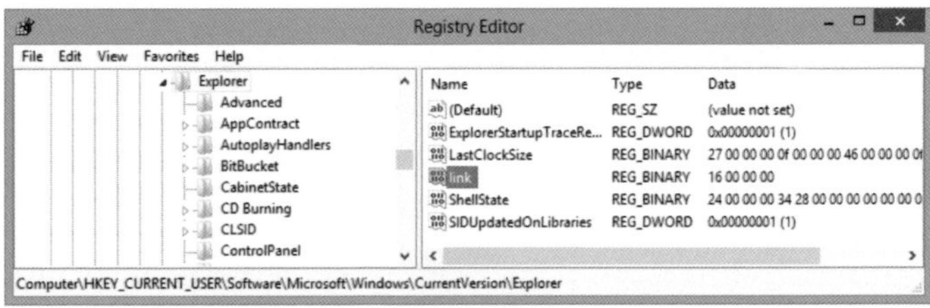

2. Select Value entry Link, then click File, Modify (or double-click Link)

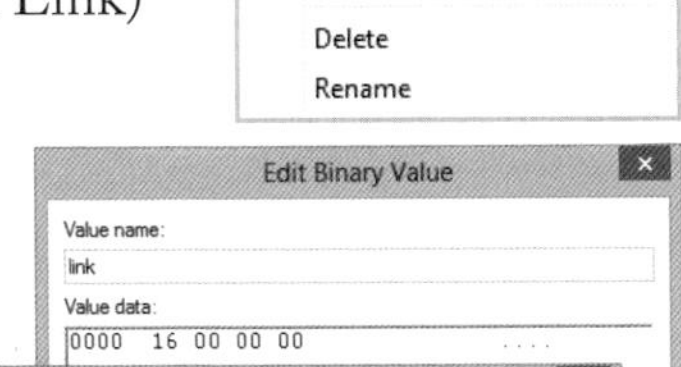

3. Change the first part of the number (16) to 00 to give a value of 00 00 00 00

4. Click OK to update the value, then close Regedit.exe

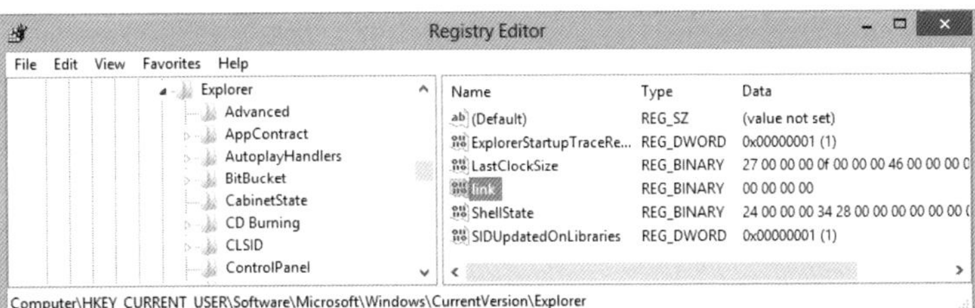

You must log off and log on again for the change to take effect. Now when you create a shortcut, it will just receive the program name with no suffix.

Remove shortcut arrows

You can also use Registry updates to change the shortcut icons, avoiding the shortcut arrow overlay, or using a different, perhaps smaller, arrow to overlay the shortcut icons.

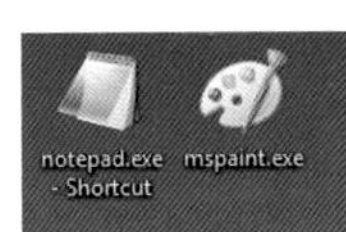

There are a number of different methods suggested for this. They involve adding a reference to an alternative icon file in a value entry in subkey [HKEY_LOCAL_MACHINE\SOFTWARE\Microsoft\Windows\CurrentVersion\explorer\Shell Icons].

You can search the Internet for articles using a search term such as "Windows 8 remove shortcut arrow" and choose your preferred website. Note that the instructions provided may differ for Windows 32-bit versus Windows 64-bit systems.

As with all Registry updates, make sure that you back up first, before making any changes.

Hot tip

Sometimes changes such as this have unexpected side effects, so a backup or restore point will be particularly important.

Adjust Aero Peek

You can change the time delay before Aero Peek reduces the screen to the Desktop.

Don't forget

When the mouse moves over the box at the bottom right of the screen, all open windows are replaced by empty frames. This can be distracting when you are just moving the mouse to a corner to help locate the pointer.

1. Open Regedit.exe and find the subkey HKEY_CURRENT_USER\Software\Microsoft\Windows\CurrentVersion\Explorer\Advanced

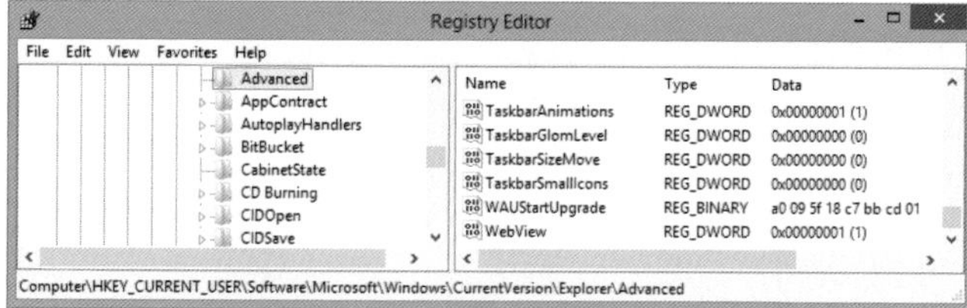

2. Right-click the right-hand pane and select New, DWORD Value (see page 455) and name the value DesktopLivePreviewHoverTime

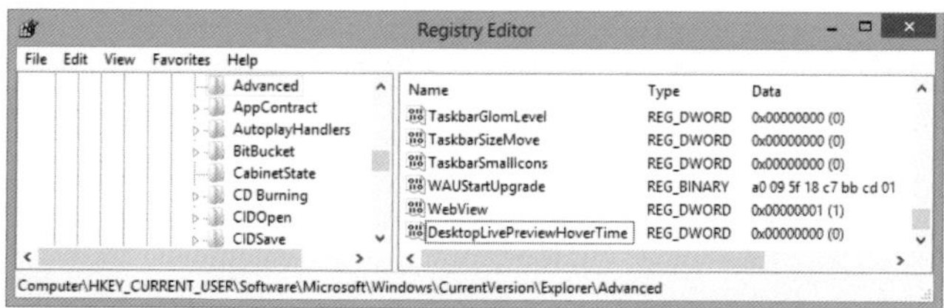

Hot tip

The default is 500 (half a second), 1000 is one second, and 0 is instant. To return to the default, set the value to 500 or delete the Value entry.

3. Double-click to edit, select Decimal and enter a value in milliseconds, for example 2000 (two seconds) then click OK

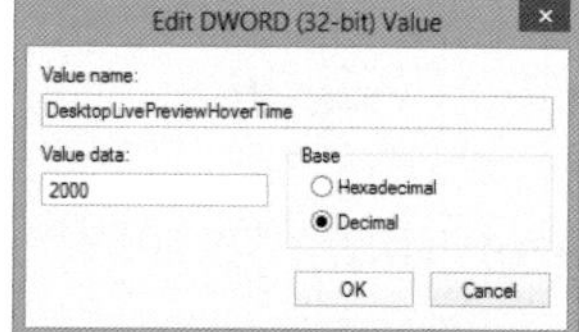

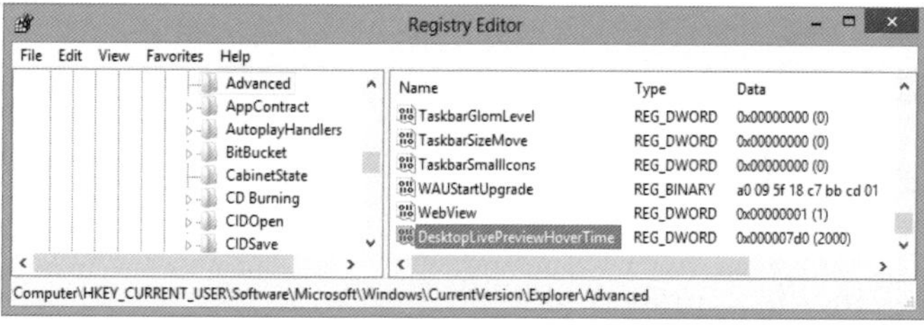

Log off, and then log on again to effect the Registry update.

27 Extending Windows

A great advantage of Windows operating systems, in general, is that their functionality can be extended. Virtual computers are a good example of this as we see in this chapter.

Remote Desktop connection

Remote Desktop is used to access one computer from another remotely, e.g. connecting to your work computer from home. You will have access to all of your programs, files, and network resources, as if you were sitting in front of your computer at work.

Hot tip 

The difference between Remote Desktop and Remote Assistance is that with the latter, both users can control the mouse. With the former, the remote PC is not physically accessible.

On the Remote Computer

Before Remote Desktop can be used, the computer to be remotely accessed needs to be configured.

1. Go to the Control Panel, System and Security. Click System. On the left, click Remote Settings

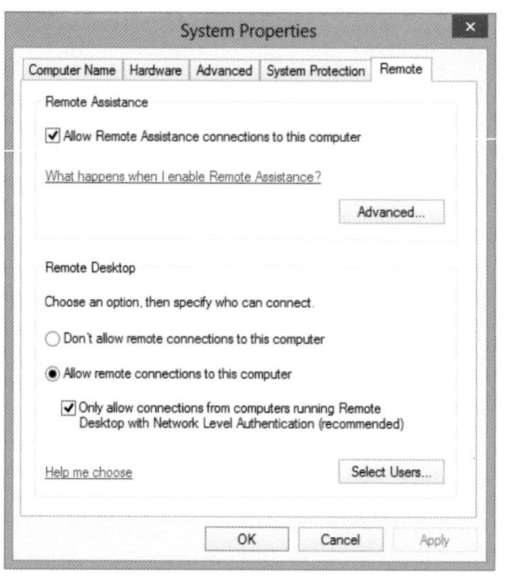

2. Click the Remote tab

3. Check Allow remote connections to this computer

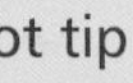 

Hot tip

For a secure connection, make sure "Only allow connections from computers running Remote Desktop with Network Level Authentication (recommended)" is checked.

4. Go back to System and make a note of the computer's name – Mikes-PC in the example below

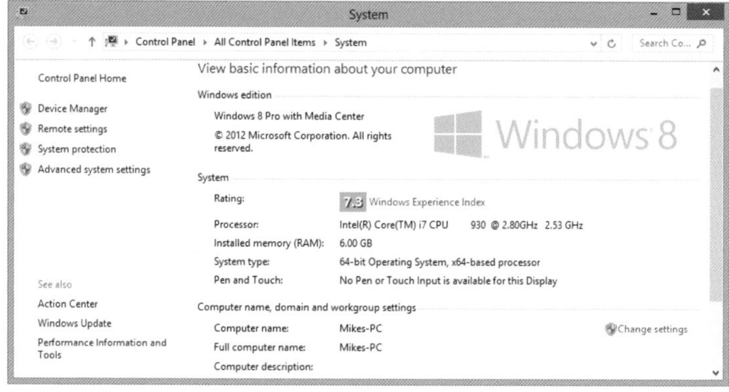

On the Access Computer

You now have to open the Remote Desktop Connection. How you access this depends on which version of Windows the PC is using.

1. If it is Windows 7, click the Start button, go to All Programs, Accessories and click Remote Desktop Connection

2. If it is Windows 8, open the Charms bar and enter remote in the Search charm. Then press Enter

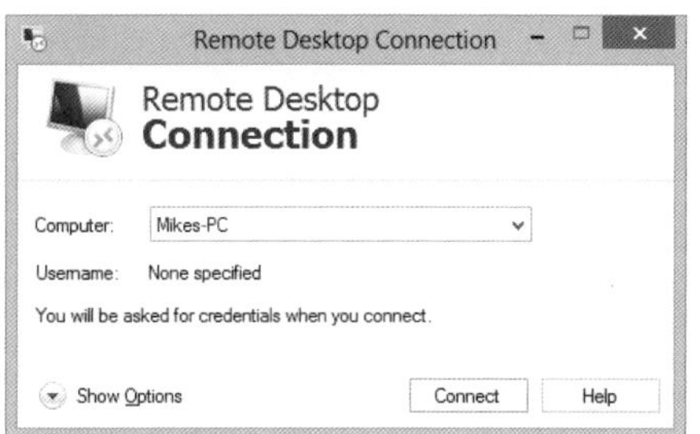

3. Enter the name of the computer to be accessed – using our example, Mikes-PC

Click Show Options to reveal a range of settings with which to enhance the remote connection.

4. Enter the password for the account being logged into at the remote PC

Once the connection is made and authenticated, everything on the remote PC is open to, and can be controlled by, the access computer.

Windows To Go

Hot tip

Windows To Go is only available on Windows 8 Enterprise.

Windows To Go is a feature found in Windows 8 Enterprise that enables a fully functional copy of Windows 8 to be created on a USB drive. The procedure makes the drive bootable in the same way that Windows installation discs are.

Not just any USB drive can be used with Windows To Go. Microsoft has specified certain requirements that manufacturers must meet in order for their USB drives to qualify as a supported Windows To Go device. One such is the Kingston DataTraveler shown below:

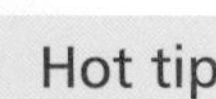

Hot tip

External USB drives can be used as well as flash drives.

The minimum storage space required by Windows To Go is 32GB. This is enough for Windows 8 itself, but if you also need to transport applications such as Microsoft Office, plus files; a larger USB drive will be required. Currently, flash drives up to 128GB are available.

A Windows To Go drive can be plugged into a USB socket on any computer and, because it is bootable, a Windows 8 session can be loaded on that computer. Once booted, it functions, and is controlled by standard enterprise management tools such as System Center Configuration Manager (SCCM) and Active Directory group policies.

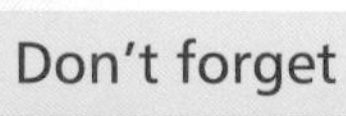

Don't forget

Windows To Go will only work on USB drives built specifically for it.

Windows To Go provides an ideal solution for anyone who needs mobile computer access. For example, business representatives out in the field will be able to work from any computer. Also, it's more cost-effective for IT departments to replace a faulty USB drive than it is to deal with the downtime and expense of returning a laptop to the office, repairing it, and returning it to the field.

Windows To Go is also ideal for trying out Windows 8 (or other software) on a machine without affecting that machine.

Virtual machine

A virtual computer is one that is created by, and run within, a computer virtualization program. It is a fully functional replica of a physical computer and can run programs, access the Internet, etc.

Popular programs of this type include VMware and VirtualBox; the latter being a free download from **www.virtualbox.org** However, with Windows 8 there is no need for third-party virtualization software – one, called Hyper-V, is supplied with the operating system. It does need to be installed first, though, as explained below:

1. Open the Charms bar and type Turn Windows features on or off into the Search charm. Click Settings and then press Enter

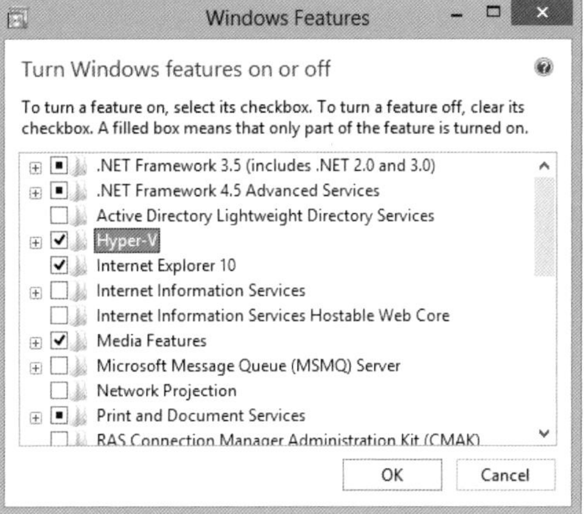

2. Check the box next to Hyper-V and click OK

3. Open the Search charm again, type hyper and press Enter. The Hyper-V Manager opens as shown below

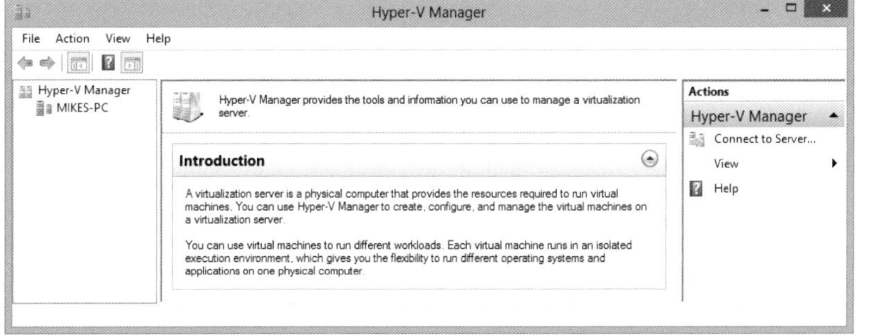

Beware

Client Hyper-V has very stringent hardware requirements. Not every PC will be able to run it.

Hot tip

Hyper-V replaces Virtual PC, the virtualization program provided in Windows 7.

Install guest system

To demonstrate Hyper-V, we are going to create a Windows XP virtual PC.

Hot tip

We show how to create a Windows XP guest system. However, you can create guest systems for other operating systems.

1. At the top-left of the Hyper-V Manager, click the computer name. Then, in the new screen click New, Virtual Machine at the right. This opens a wizard

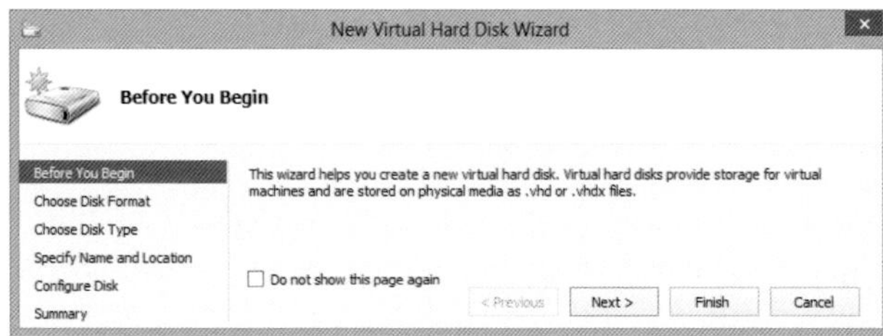

2. To instantly create a virtual PC with default settings, just click the Finish button

3. Under Virtual Machines, you'll now see your new virtual PC. Right-click on it and name it Windows XP

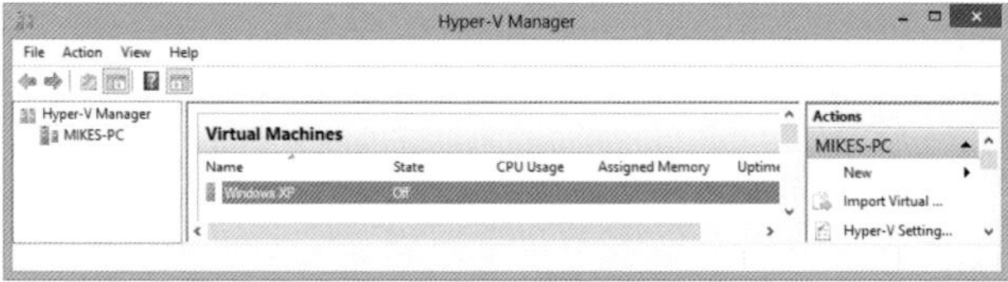

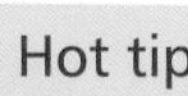

Hot tip

Hyper-V's Hardware options provide a range of settings for all the hardware components found in a computer.

4. On the right under Windows XP, click Settings... This opens the Hardware and Management options screen

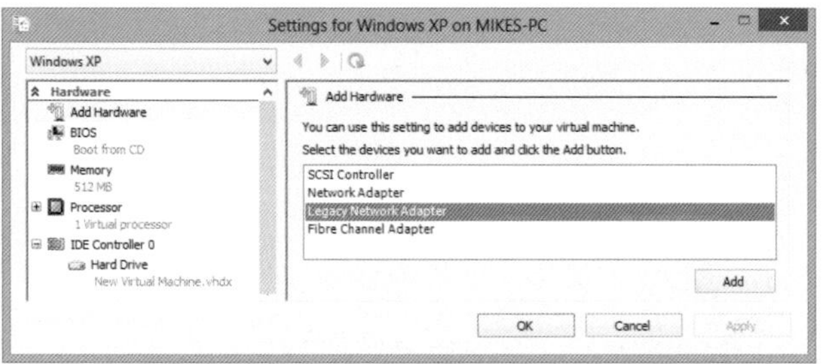

5. Select Legacy Network Adapter and click Add

6 Select Memory and change the default setting to 1024. Click Apply

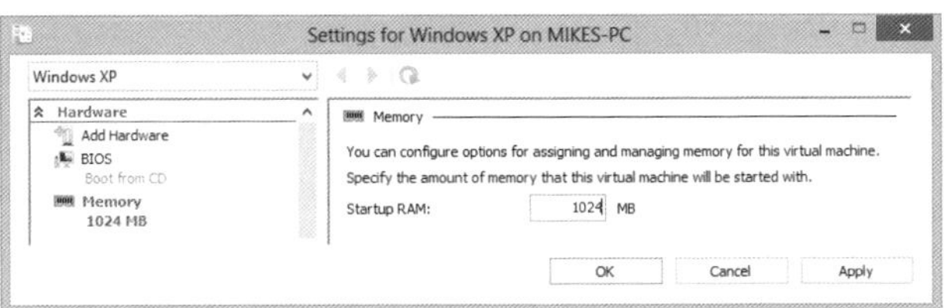

7 Click Hard Drive under IDE Controller 0. By default this is set at 127GB. Change it by clicking Edit, Expand, and Configure Disk. Enter a higher figure, e.g. 500

8 Select DVD drive under IDE Controller 1. Here you can specify an image file (ISO) or the physical DVD drive for installation of the operating system. Click Apply

9 Insert the XP installation disk in the drive, go back to the Actions pane in the Hyper-V Manager, scroll down to the virtual machine section and click the Connect command

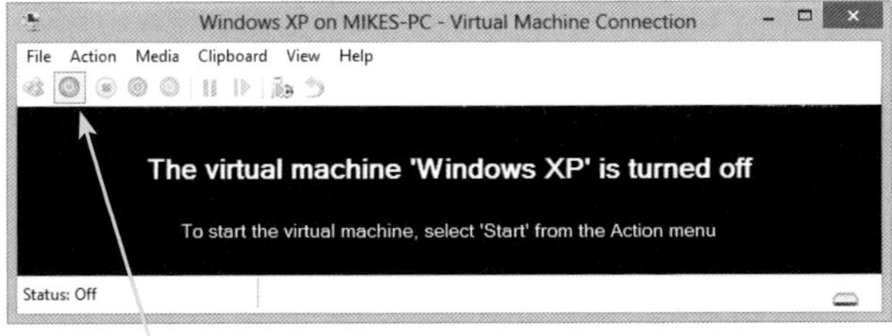

10 Click Start to begin building the virtual PC

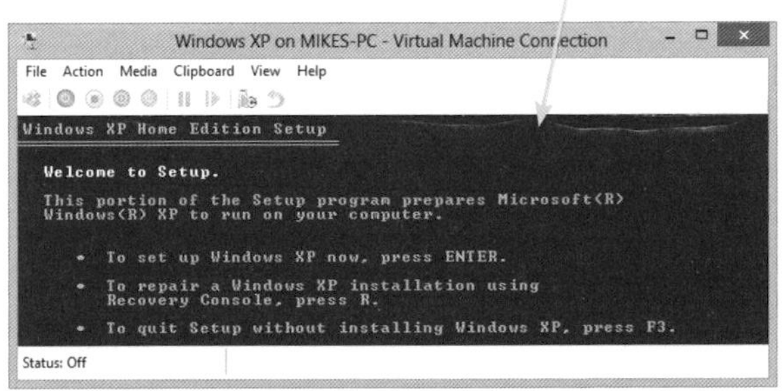

Hot tip

Potential uses for virtual PCs include sandboxed software evaluation, running other operating systems, and safe web browsing.

Hot tip

Step 9 assumes you are using an installation disk rather than a ISO file.

Hot tip

Hyper-V has a feature called Snapshots. These let you save the state of a virtual PC, so you can revert back in much the same way as a system backup lets you roll back to the point when the backup was made.

Windows Phone 8

Windows Phone 8 is a second generation proprietary smartphone operating system that replaces its predecessor, Windows Phone 7.

Hardware

One of the main changes is to the underlying architecture. Windows Phone 8 replaces the Windows CE-based architecture used in its predecessor with one based on the Windows NT kernel. This adds improved file system, drivers, network stack, security components, media and graphics support. Also, as many components are shared with Windows 8, this enables applications to be easily ported between the two platforms.

Other hardware improvements include:

- Support for larger screens, i.e. 800 x 480, 1280 x 768 and 1280 x 720
- Support for multi-core processors up to 64 cores
- Near Field Communication (NFC) for applications such as sharing content, and payments
- Support for MicroSD cards, which provides extra storage options

Software

The same system of live tiles as seen in Windows 8 is used in Windows Phone 8. These are a cross between an icon (providing a link to an app) and a widgit (showing live information from the app).

Web browsing is provided by Internet Explorer 10, which includes the key improvements found in the Desktop version.

Other new software features include:

- **Improved multi-tasking**
- **Kids Corner**, which provides a sandboxed area for games, thus protecting the owner's data
- **Rooms**, which lets users group various shared services together, e.g. lists, calendars, and photos
- **Wallet**, an app that stores boarding passes, loyalty cards, movie tickets, etc. Works in conjunction with NFC

Beware

The number of apps available for Windows Phone 8 is considerably less than for iOS and Android phones.

Sync with smartphone

With Windows Phone 7, data synchronization with a computer can only be done with the Zune PC software. With Windows Phone 8, however, users have several ways of synchronizing their data. These include:

Windows Phone App

Available from the Windows Store, this app is free. When the phone is connected to the PC, it automatically syncs the user's data. It offers a full-screen view with various content sections that include On your phone, In the Store, and On the web.

The first, On your phone, provides different areas for the pictures, music, and videos on your phone, plus tiles that let the user add pictures, video, or music to the phone.

The app only runs on the new Windows 8 interface and offers few options.

Don't forget

The Windows Phone Desktop application is the Desktop version of the Windows Phone app.

Windows Phone Desktop Application

Very similar to the Windows Phone app, this runs on the Desktop interface and provides more options. These include:

- Syncing music, photos, movies, TV shows, and podcasts from an existing Apple iTunes library or Windows Libraries to Windows Phone 8
- Automatically importing pictures and videos taken with the phone to the PC

Windows Photo Gallery

A feature new in Windows Phone 8 is support for USB media transfer. This means that pictures can be synced to a PC with any program that supports the importing of pictures. One of these is the Windows Phone app discussed above; however, a much better option is to download Windows Photo Gallery, which is part of the Windows Essentials 2012 suite.

Don't forget

Download Windows Photo Gallery from the Essentials website at http://windows.microsoft.com/en-US/windows-live/essentials-home

File Explorer

Windows Phone 8 supports direct access to a computer via the new File Explorer. This lets users drag and drop content to and from their phones just as they can with any USB hard drive or flash drive.

Windows blogs

The computing world moves at a fast pace. Windows 8 is only just out of the starting blocks and Microsoft is already working on its successor. New developments in Cloud computing are being announced on a regular basis, and the hardware that supports it all continues to develop at an almost frightening pace.

Beware

Official Microsoft blogs tend to view Microsoft products in a somewhat kinder light than they may warrant.

Keeping track of it all, and staying abreast of the latest developments, is no easy matter. Fortunately, we have the Internet and this medium provides an avenue for all interested parties to inform and stay informed. This has given rise to the phenomenon of blogging websites, which most companies in the computer and allied industries now use to keep their customers up-to-date.

As this is a book about Windows, we are going to take a look here at some blogs that concern the world's most popular operating system.

The Windows blog

For a general update on what's happening in the Windows world, head to the Windows blog at **http://blogs.windows.com**

Hot tip

There are many Windows-related blogs that offer more critical product appraisals than the Microsoft blogs do.If you are looking for information to help make a decision on buying a Microsoft product, these may offer more worthwhile advice.

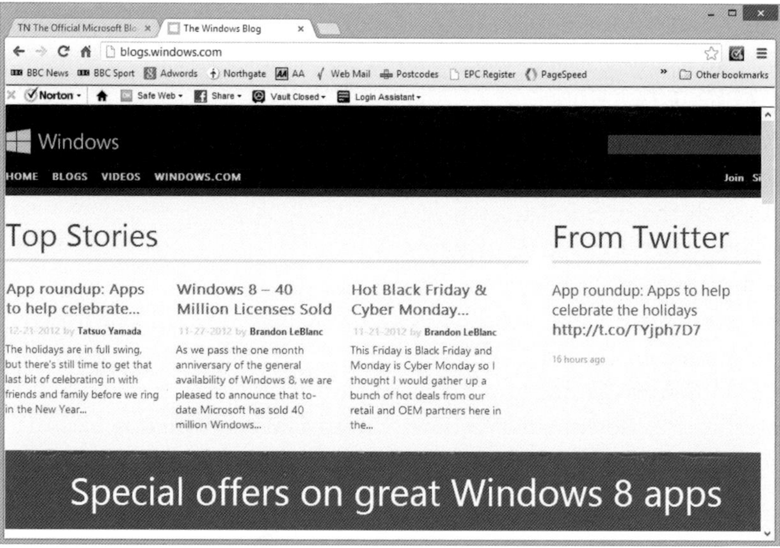

All the top stories are here. These include the latest news, how-to articles, and app reviews. You'll also find details of current Microsoft software and hardware offers that can help to save you some dollars.

Windows Phone blog

For devotees of Windows Phone 7 and 8, there is the Windows Phone Blog at **http://blogs.windows.com/windows_phone/b/windowsphone**

Blogs include details of the latest apps, updates and articles on Windows Phone, and challenges/competitions. You can also buy a Windows phone, plus find games and apps.

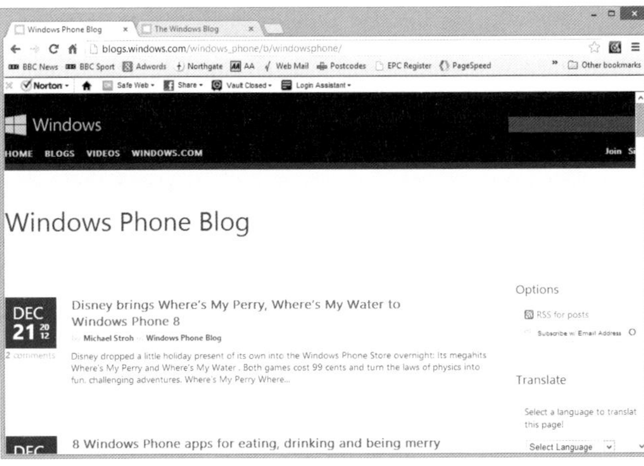

Office blogs

Keep up-to-speed with Office applications at **http://blogs.office.com**

As with the other blogs, you'll find tips, news, how-tos, and videos. For the millions who use Microsoft Office programs, this is a really useful blog site.

Hot tip

There are quite a few blogs authored by Microsoft insiders and ex-Microsoft employees. These can be well worth a read.

Where next for Windows?

As we mentioned on page 468, Microsoft is already looking beyond the just-released Windows 8 to its successor. Currently, this goes under the codename Blue.

Hot tip

Informed opinion has it that Blue will be free to encourage people to upgrade.

In a break with its traditional routine of releasing a new edition of Windows every few years, with a series of stability and security service packs in the intervening periods, word has it that Blue will actually be both, i.e the next edition of Windows and an update to Windows 8 rolled into one.

It is thought that Blue will be released in late 2013 with subsequent major updates on an annual basis (rather than a new edition every few years), just as already happens with Apple's OS X. As a result, Microsoft will be able to add new features and support for the latest technology much more frequently than it does currently.

As these annual releases will effectively be the Windows service pack of yesteryear and not a full-blown new edition, the price charged for them by Microsoft will be much less than customers are used to seeing – probably in the region of $25.00 or so. This will encourage more people to upgrade.

An anticipated change in Blue is that the Windows 8 and Windows Phone 8 SDKs (Software Development Kits) will be standardized. The result of this is that app developers will have to create a single version of their apps that work on both Windows 8 and Windows Phone 8.

Hot tip

It could well be that Windows 8 is the name given to future incarnations of Windows.

There is speculation that the standardization of the two SDKs may be intended to eventually do away with Windows Phone 8 completely so that we end up with a situation whereby Windows 8 is the only available Microsoft operating system for all computer form factors.

Such a strategy would leave Microsoft with only one operating system to keep updated, and a huge library of apps.

While none of this is confirmed, the direction Microsoft has taken with Windows 8 – the initial low pricing, the move to force users to use the new interface by removing the Start button and menu, and the tile-based interface, does indicate that this is indeed what it has in mind.

Index

Symbols

A

B

C

D

E

F

G

H

I

J

K

L

M

N

O

P

R

S

T

U

V

W

X

Y

Z